The Art of Multiprocessor Programming

T0198134

The Art of Multiprocessor Programming

Second Edition

Maurice Herlihy

Nir Shavit

Victor Luchangco

Michael Spear

MORGAN KAUFMANN PUBLISHERS

ELSEVIER AN IMPRINT OF ELSEVIER

Morgan Kaufmann is an imprint of Elsevier
50 Hampshire Street, 5th Floor, Cambridge, MA 02139, United States

Library of Congress Cataloging-in-Publication Data
A catalog record for this book is available from the Library of Congress

British Library Cataloguing-in-Publication Data
A catalogue record for this book is available from the British Library

ISBN: 978-0-12-415950-1

For information on all Morgan Kaufmann publications
visit our website at https://www.elsevier.com/books-and-journals

Publisher: Katey Birtcher
Acquisitions Editor: Stephen R. Merken
Editorial Project Manager: Beth LoGiudice
Production Project Manager: Beula Christopher
Designer: Renee Duenow

Typeset by VTeX

For my parents, David and Patricia Herlihy, and for Liuba, David, and Anna.

– M.H.

For Noun and Aliza, Shafi, Yonadav, and Lior, and for Luisa.

– N.S.

For my family, especially my parents, Guilly and Maloy Luchangco, and for God, who makes all things possible.

– V.L.

For Emily, Theodore, Bernadette, Adelaide, Teresa, Veronica, Phoebe, Leo, and Rosemary.

– M.S.

Contents

PART 2 Practice

Preface

In the decade since the first edition, this book has become a staple of undergraduate and graduate courses at universities around the world. It has also found a home on the bookshelves of practitioners at companies large and small. The audience for the book has, in turn, advanced the state of the art in multiprocessor programming. In this second edition, we aim to continue this "virtuous cycle" by providing new and updated content. Our goal is the same as with the first edition: to provide a textbook for a senior-level undergraduate course and a reference for practitioners.

Organization

The first part of this book covers the *principles* of concurrent programming, showing how to *think* as a concurrent programmer, developing fundamental skills such as understanding when operations "happen," considering all possible interleavings, and identifying impediments to progress. Like many skills—driving a car, cooking a meal, or appreciating caviar—thinking concurrently must be cultivated, and it can be learned with moderate effort. Readers who want to start programming right away may skip most of this section but should still read Chapters 2 and 3, which cover the basic ideas necessary to understand the rest of the book.

We first look at the classic *mutual exclusion* problem (Chapter 2). This chapter is essential for understanding why concurrent programming is a challenge. It covers basic concepts such as fairness and deadlock. We then ask what it means for a concurrent program to be correct (Chapter 3). We consider several alternative conditions and the circumstances under which one might want to use each one. We examine the properties of *shared memory* essential to concurrent computation (Chapter 4), and we look at the kinds of synchronization primitives needed to implement highly concurrent data structures (Chapters 5 and 6).

We think it is essential that anyone who wants to become truly skilled in the art of multiprocessor programming spend time solving the problems presented in the first part of this book. Although these problems are idealized, they distill the kind of thinking necessary to write effective multiprocessor programs. Most importantly, they distill the style of thinking necessary to avoid the common mistakes committed by nearly all novice programmers when they first encounter concurrency.

The second part of the book describes the *practice* of concurrent programming. For most of this part, we give examples in Java to avoid getting mired in low-level details. However, we have expanded this edition to include discussion of some low-level issues that are essential to understanding multiprocessor systems and how to program them effectively. We use examples in C++ to illustrate these issues.

Each chapter has a secondary theme, illustrating either a particular programming pattern or an algorithmic technique. Chapter 7 covers spin locks and contention, and introduces the importance of the underlying architecture: spin lock performance cannot be understood without understanding the multiprocessor memory hierarchy. Chapter 8 covers monitor locks and waiting, a common synchronization idiom.

Several chapters cover concurrent data structures. Linked lists, which illustrate different kinds of synchronization patterns, from coarse-grained locking to fine-grained locking to lock-free structures, are covered in Chapter 9. This chapter should be read before the remaining chapters, which depend on it. First-in-first-out (FIFO) queues illustrate the "ABA problem" that arises when using atomic synchronization primitives (Chapter 10); stacks illustrate an important synchronization pattern called *elimination* (Chapter 11); hash maps show how an algorithm can exploit natural parallelism (Chapter 13); skip lists illustrate efficient parallel search (Chapter 14); priority queues illustrate how one can sometimes relax correctness guarantees to enhance performance (Chapter 15).

We also consider other fundamental problems in concurrent computing. Chapter 12 describes counting and sorting, two classic problems with nuanced concurrent solutions. Breaking a program into parallelizable tasks and organizing their execution is an essential skill for concurrent programming, and we consider several ways to do this, including work stealing and distribution (Chapter 16), data parallelism (Chapter 17), barriers (Chapter 18), and transactional programming (Chapter 20). Memory management is another fundamental challenge for concurrent programs, and we discuss how to manually reclaim memory in Chapter 19. Because Java provides automatic memory management, we use C++ to illustrate these issues.

Much of these latter chapters are new to this edition: Chapters 17 and 19 are completely new, and Chapters 16 and 20 have been substantially updated from the first edition. In particular, Chapter 20 now covers hardware primitives for transactional programming as well as software strategies, and the examples have been recast in C++ to allow us to focus on lower-level mechanisms.

In theory, there is no difference between theory and practice. In practice, there is.

Although the origin of this quote is uncertain, it is relevant to the subject of this book. For the greatest benefit, a reader must supplement learning the conceptual material presented in this book with actual experience programming real multiprocessor systems.

Prerequisites

The prerequisites for the second edition are largely the same as for the first. To understand the algorithms and their properties, readers will need some knowledge of discrete mathematics, especially "big-O" notation and what it means for a problem to be NP-complete, and data structures such as stacks, queues, lists, balanced trees, and hash tables. It is also helpful to be familiar with elementary computer architecture and system constructs such as processors, threads, and caches. While a course on operating systems or computer organization would suffice, neither is necessary; dozens of universities have used this book successfully without either prerequisite.

A basic understanding of Java or C++ is needed to follow the examples. When we require advanced language features or advanced understanding of hardware, we provide an explanation first. More details about programming language constructs and multiprocessor hardware architectures are covered in Appendix A and Appendix B, respectively.

Acknowledgments

We would like to thank our colleagues, students, and friends, who provided guidance, comments, and suggestions during the writing of this book: Yehuda Afek, Shai Ber, Hans Boehm, Martin Buchholz, Vladimir Budovsky, Christian Cachin, Cliff Click, Yoav Cohen, Tom Cormen, Michael Coulombe, Dave Dice, Alexandra Fedorova, Pascal Felber, Christof Fetzer, Rati Gelasvili, Mohsen Ghaffari, Brian Goetz, Shafi Goldwasser, Rachid Guerraoui, Tim Harris, Will Hasenplaugh, Steve Heller, Danny Hendler, Maor Hizkiev, Alex Kogan, Justin Kopinsky, Hank Korth, Eric Koskinen, Christos Kozyrakis, Edya Ladan, Doug Lea, Oren Lederman, Will Leiserson, Pierre Leone, Yossi Lev, Wei Lu, Virendra Marathe, Kevin Marth, Alex Matveev, John Mellor-Crummey, Mark Moir, Adam Morrison, Dan Nussbaum, Roberto Palmieri, Kiran Pamnany, Ben Pere, Radia Perlman, Torvald Riegel, Ron Rivest, Vijay Saraswat, Bill Scherer, Warren Schudy, Michael Scott, Ori Shalev, Marc Shapiro, Michael Sipser, Yotam Soen, Ralf Suckow, Seth Syberg, Joseph Tassarotti, John Tristan, George Varghese, Alex Weiss, Kelly Zhang, and Zhenyuan Zhao. We apologize for any names inadvertently omitted.

We also extend our appreciation to the many people who have sent us errata to improve the book, including: Matthew Allen, Rajeev Alur, Karolos Antoniadis, Liran Barsisa, Cristina Basescu, Igor Berman, Konstantin Boudnik, Bjoern Brandenburg, Kyle Cackett, Mario Calha, Michael Champigny, Neill Clift, Eran Cohen, Daniel B. Curtis, Gil Danziger, Venkat Dhinakaran, Wan Fokkink, David Fort, Robert P. Goddard, Enes Goktas, Bart Golsteijn, K. Gopinath, Jason T. Greene, Dan Grossman, Tim Halloran, Muhammad Amber Hassaan, Matt Hayes, Francis Hools, Ben Horowitz, Barak Itkin, Paulo Janotti, Kyungho Jeon, Irena Karlinsky, Ahmed Khademzadeh, Habib Khan, Omar Khan, Namhyung Kim, Guy Korland, Sergey Kotov, Jonathan Lawrence, Adam MacBeth, Mike Maloney, Tim McIver, Sergejs Melderis, Bartosz Milewski, Jose Pedro Oliveira, Dale Parson, Jonathan Perry, Amir Pnueli, Pat Quillen, Sudarshan Raghunathan, Binoy Ravindran, Roei Raviv, Jean-Paul Rigault, Michael Rueppel, Mohamed M. Saad, Assaf Schuster, Konrad Schwarz, Nathar Shah, Huang-Ti Shih, Joseph P. Skudlarek, James Stout, Mark Summerfield, Deqing Sun, Fuad Tabba, Binil Thomas, John A Trono, Menno Vermeulen, Thomas Weibel, Adam Weinstock, Chong Xing, Jaeheon Yi, and Ruiwen Zuo.

We are also grateful to Beula Christopher, Beth LoGiudice, Steve Merken, and the staff at Morgan Kaufmann for their patience and assistance throughout the process of bringing this book to print.

Suggested ways to teach the art of multiprocessor programming

Here are three alternative tracks for teaching a multiprocessor programming course using the material in the book.

The first track is a short course for *practitioners*, focusing on techniques that can be applied directly to problems at hand.

The second track is a longer course for students who are *not Computer Science majors* but who want to learn the basics of multiprocessor programming as well as techniques likely to be useful in their own areas.

The third track is a semester-long course for *Computer Science majors*, either upper-level undergraduates or graduate students.

Practitioner track

Cover Chapter 1, emphasizing Amdahl's law and its implications. In Chapter 2, cover Sections 2.1 to 2.4 and Section 2.7. Mention the *implications* of the impossibility proofs in Section 2.9. In Chapter 3, skip Sections 3.5 and 3.6.

Cover Chapter 7, except for Sections 7.7, 7.8, and 7.9. Chapter 8, which deals with monitors and reentrant locks, may be familiar to some practitioners. Skip Section 8.5 on semaphores.

Cover Chapters 9 and 10, except for Section 10.7, and cover Sections 11.1 and 11.2. Skip the material in Chapter 11 from Section 11.3 and onwards. Skip Chapter 12.

Cover Chapters 13 and 14. Skip Chapter 15. Cover Chapter 16, except for Section 16.5. Chapter 17 is optional. In Chapter 18, teach Sections 18.1 to 18.3. For practitioners who focus on C++, Chapter 19 is essential and can be covered at any point after Chapter 9 and Section 10.6. Chapter 20 is optional.

Non-CS Major track

Cover Chapter 1, emphasizing Amdahl's law and its implications. In Chapter 2, cover Sections 2.1 to 2.4, 2.6, and 2.7. Mention the *implications* of the impossibility proofs in Section 2.9. In Chapter 3, skip Section 3.6.

Cover the material in Sections 4.1 and 4.2 and Chapter 5. Mention the universality of consensus, but skip Chapter 6.

Cover Chapter 7, except for Sections 7.7, 7.8, and 7.9. Cover Chapter 8.

Cover Chapters 9 and 10, except for Section 10.7, and cover Chapter 11. Skip Chapter 12.

Cover Chapters 13 and 14. Skip Chapter 15. Cover Chapters 16 and 17. In Chapter 18, teach Sections 18.1 to 18.3. For practitioners who focus on C++, Chapter 19 is essential and can be covered at any point after Chapter 9 and Section 10.6. Chapter 20 is optional. In Chapter 20, cover up to Section 20.3.

CS Major track

The slides on the companion website were developed for a semester-long course.

Cover Chapters 1 and 2 (Section 2.8 is optional) and Chapter 3 (Section 3.6 is optional). Cover Chapters 4, 5, and 6. Before starting Chapter 7, it may be useful to review basic multiprocessor architecture (Appendix B).

Cover Chapter 7 (Sections 7.7, 7.8, and 7.9 are optional). Cover Chapter 8 if your students are unfamiliar with Java monitors and have not taken a course on operating systems. Cover Chapters 9 and 10 (Section 10.7 is optional). Cover Chapters 11, 12 (Sections 12.7, 12.8, and 12.9 are optional), 13, and 14.

The remainder of the book should be covered as needed for degree requirements. For Math or Computer Science majors, Chapter 15 should come next, followed by Chapters 16 and 17. For Data Science majors, Chapter 15 can be skipped so that more emphasis can be placed on Chapters 16, 17, and 18. For Computer Engineering majors, emphasis should be placed on Chapters 18, 19, and 20. In the end, the instructor should of course take into account students' interests and backgrounds.

Introduction

At the dawn of the twenty-first century, the computer industry underwent yet another revolution. The major chip manufacturers had increasingly been unable to make processor chips both smaller and faster. As Moore's law approached the end of its 50-year reign, manufacturers turned to "multicore" architectures, in which multiple processors (cores) on a single chip communicate directly through shared hardware caches. Multicore chips make computing more effective by exploiting *parallelism*: harnessing multiple circuits to work on a single task.

The spread of multiprocessor architectures has had a pervasive effect on how we develop software. During the twentieth century, advances in technology brought regular increases in clock speed, so software would effectively "speed up" by itself over time. In this century, however, that "free ride" has come to an end. Today, advances in technology bring regular increases in parallelism, but only minor increases in clock speed. Exploiting that parallelism is one of the outstanding challenges of modern computer science.

This book focuses on how to program multiprocessors that communicate via a shared memory. Such systems are often called *shared-memory multiprocessors* or, more recently, *multicores*. Programming challenges arise at all scales of multiprocessor systems—at a very small scale, processors within a single chip need to coordinate access to a shared memory location, and on a large scale, processors in a supercomputer need to coordinate the routing of data. Multiprocessor programming is challenging because modern computer systems are inherently *asynchronous*: activities can be halted or delayed without warning by interrupts, preemption, cache misses, failures, and other events. These delays are inherently unpredictable, and can vary enormously in scale: a cache miss might delay a processor for fewer than ten instructions, a page fault for a few million instructions, and operating system preemption for hundreds of millions of instructions.

We approach multiprocessor programming from two complementary directions: principles and practice. In the *principles* part of this book, we focus on *computability*: figuring out what can be computed in an asynchronous concurrent environment. We use an idealized model of computation in which multiple concurrent *threads* manipulate a set of shared *objects*. The sequence of the thread operations on the objects is called the *concurrent program* or *concurrent algorithm*. This model is essentially the model presented by threads in Java, C#, and C++.

Surprisingly, there are easy-to-specify shared objects that cannot be implemented by any concurrent algorithm. It is therefore important to understand what not to try,

The Art of Multiprocessor Programming. https://doi.org/10.1016/B978-0-12-415950-1.00009-4

before proceeding to write multiprocessor programs. Many of the issues that will land multiprocessor programmers in trouble are consequences of fundamental limitations of the computational model, so we view the acquisition of a basic understanding of concurrent shared-memory computability as a necessary step. The chapters dealing with principles take the reader through a quick tour of asynchronous computability, attempting to expose various computability issues, and how they are addressed through the use of hardware and software mechanisms.

An important step in the understanding of computability is the specification and verification of what a given program actually does. This is perhaps best described as *program correctness*. The correctness of multiprocessor programs, by their very nature, is more complex than that of their sequential counterparts, and requires a different set of tools, even for the purpose of "informal reasoning" (which, of course, is what most programmers actually do).

Sequential correctness is mostly concerned with safety properties. A *safety* property states that some "bad thing" never happens. For example, a traffic light never displays green in all directions, even if the power fails. Naturally, concurrent correctness is also concerned with safety, but the problem is much, much harder, because safety must be ensured despite the vast number of ways that the steps of concurrent threads can be interleaved. Equally important, concurrent correctness encompasses a variety of *liveness* properties that have no counterparts in the sequential world. A *liveness* property states that a particular good thing will happen. For example, a red traffic light will eventually turn green.

A final goal of the part of the book dealing with principles is to introduce a variety of metrics and approaches for reasoning about concurrent programs, which will later serve us when discussing the correctness of real-world objects and programs.

The second part of the book deals with the *practice* of multiprocessor programming, and focuses on performance. Analyzing the performance of multiprocessor algorithms is also different in flavor from analyzing the performance of sequential programs. Sequential programming is based on a collection of well-established and well-understood abstractions. When we write a sequential program, we can often ignore that underneath it all, pages are being swapped from disk to memory, and smaller units of memory are being moved in and out of a hierarchy of processor caches. This complex memory hierarchy is essentially invisible, hiding behind a simple programming abstraction.

In the multiprocessor context, this abstraction breaks down, at least from a performance perspective. To achieve adequate performance, programmers must sometimes "outwit" the underlying memory system, writing programs that would seem bizarre to someone unfamiliar with multiprocessor architectures. Someday, perhaps, concurrent architectures will provide the same degree of efficient abstraction as sequential architectures, but in the meantime, programmers should beware.

The practice part of the book presents a progressive collection of shared objects and programming tools. Every object and tool is interesting in its own right, and we use each one to expose the reader to higher-level issues: spin locks illustrate contention, linked lists illustrate the role of locking in data structure design, and so on.

Each of these issues has important consequences for program performance. We hope that readers will understand the issue in a way that will later allow them to apply the lessons learned to specific multiprocessor systems. We culminate with a discussion of state-of-the-art technologies such as *transactional memory*.

For most of this book, we present code in the Java programming language, which provides automatic memory management. However, memory management is an important aspect of programming, especially concurrent programming. So, in the last two chapters, we switch to C++. In some cases, the code presented is simplified by omitting nonessential details. Complete code for all the examples is available on the book's companion website at *https://textbooks.elsevier.com/web/product_details.aspx?isbn=978124159501*.

There are, of course, other languages which would have worked as well. In the appendix, we explain how the concepts expressed here in Java or C++ can be expressed in some other popular languages or libraries. We also provide a primer on multiprocessor hardware.

Throughout the book, we avoid presenting specific performance numbers for programs and algorithms, instead focusing on general trends. There is a good reason why: multiprocessors vary greatly, and what works well on one machine may work significantly less well on another. We focus on general trends to ensure that observations are not tied to specific platforms at specific times.

Each chapter has suggestions for further reading, along with exercises suitable for Sunday morning entertainment.

1.1 Shared objects and synchronization

On the first day of your new job, your boss asks you to find all primes between 1 and 10^{10} (never mind why) using a parallel machine that supports ten concurrent threads. This machine is rented by the minute, so the longer your program takes, the more it costs. You want to make a good impression. What do you do?

As a first attempt, you might consider giving each thread an equal share of the input domain. Each thread might check 10^9 numbers, as shown in Fig. 1.1. This

```
1  void primePrint {
2    int i = ThreadID.get();    // thread IDs are in {0..9}
3    long block = power(10, 9);
4    for (long j = (i * block) + 1; j <= (i + 1) * block; j++) {
5      if (isPrime(j))
6        print(j);
7    }
8  }
```

FIGURE 1.1

Balancing the work load by dividing up the input domain. Each thread in {0..9} gets an equal subset of the range.

```
1   Counter counter = new Counter(1);    // shared by all threads
2   void primePrint {
3     long i = 0;
4     long limit = power(10, 10);
5     while (i < limit) {                 // loop until all numbers taken
6       i = counter.getAndIncrement();    // take next untaken number
7       if (isPrime(i))
8         print(i);
9     }
10  }
```

FIGURE 1.2

Balancing the work load using a shared counter. Each thread is given a dynamically determined number of numbers to test.

```
1   public class Counter {
2     private long value;                 // initialized by constructor
3     public Counter(long i) {
4       value = i;
5     }
6     public long getAndIncrement() { // increment, returning prior value
7       return value++;
8     }
9   }
```

FIGURE 1.3

An implementation of the shared counter.

approach fails to distribute the work evenly for an elementary but important reason: Equal ranges of inputs do not produce equal amounts of work. Primes do not occur uniformly; there are more primes between 1 and 10^9 than between $9 \cdot 10^9$ and 10^{10}. To make matters worse, the computation time per prime is not the same in all ranges: it usually takes longer to test whether a large number is prime than a small number. In short, there is no reason to believe that the work will be divided equally among the threads, and it is not clear even which threads will have the most work.

A more promising way to split the work among the threads is to assign each thread one integer at a time (Fig. 1.2). When a thread is finished testing an integer, it asks for another. To this end, we introduce a *shared counter*, an object that encapsulates an integer value, and that provides a getAndIncrement() method, which increments the counter's value and returns the counter's prior value.

Fig. 1.3 shows a naïve implementation of Counter in Java. This counter implementation works well when used by a single thread, but it fails when shared by multiple threads. The problem is that the expression

```
return value++;
```

is in effect an abbreviation of the following, more complex code:

```
long temp = value;
value = temp + 1;
return temp;
```

In this code fragment, value is a field of the Counter object, and is shared among all the threads. Each thread, however, has its own copy of temp, which is a local variable to each thread.

Now imagine that two threads call the counter's getAndIncrement() method at about the same time, so that they both read 1 from value. In this case, each thread would set its local temp variables to 1, set value to 2, and return 1. This behavior is not what we intended: we expect concurrent calls to the counter's getAndIncrement() to return distinct values. It could be worse: after one thread reads 1 from value, but before it sets value to 2, another thread could go through the increment loop several times, reading 1 and writing 2, then reading 2 and writing 3. When the first thread finally completes its operation and sets value to 2, it will actually be setting the counter back from 3 to 2.

The heart of the problem is that incrementing the counter's value requires two distinct operations on the shared variable: reading the value field into a temporary variable and writing it back to the Counter object.

Something similar happens when you try to pass someone approaching you head-on in a corridor. You may find yourself veering right and then left several times to avoid the other person doing exactly the same thing. Sometimes you manage to avoid bumping into them and sometimes you do not. In fact, as we will see in the later chapters, such collisions are provably unavoidable.[1] On an intuitive level, what is going on is that each of you is performing two distinct steps: looking at ("reading") the other's current position, and moving ("writing") to one side or the other. The problem is, when you read the other's position, you have no way of knowing whether they have decided to stay or move. In the same way that you and the annoying stranger must decide on which side to pass each other, threads accessing a shared Counter must decide who goes first and who goes second.

As we discuss in Chapter 5, modern multiprocessor hardware provides special *read–modify–write* instructions that allow threads to read, modify, and write a value to memory in one *atomic* (that is, indivisible) hardware step. For the Counter object, we can use such hardware to increment the counter atomically.

We can also ensure atomic behavior by guaranteeing in software (using only read and write instructions) that only one thread executes the read-and-write sequence at a time. The problem of ensuring that only one thread can execute a particular block of code at a time, called the *mutual exclusion* problem, is one of the classic coordination problems in multiprocessor programming.

---

[1] A preventive approach such as "always sidestep to the right" does not work because the approaching person may be British.

As a practical matter, you are unlikely ever to find yourself having to design your own mutual exclusion algorithm (you would probably call on a library). Nevertheless, understanding how to implement mutual exclusion from the basics is an essential condition for understanding concurrent computation in general. There is no more effective way to learn how to reason about essential and ubiquitous issues such as mutual exclusion, deadlock, bounded fairness, and blocking versus nonblocking synchronization.

1.2 A fable

Instead of treating coordination problems (such as mutual exclusion) as programming exercises, we prefer to frame concurrent coordination problems as interpersonal problems. In the next few sections, we present a sequence of fables, illustrating some of the basic problems. Like most authors of fables, we retell stories mostly invented by others (see the chapter notes at the end of this chapter).

Alice and Bob are neighbors, and they share a yard. Alice owns a cat and Bob owns a dog. Both pets like to run around in the yard, but (naturally) they do not get along. After some unfortunate experiences, Alice and Bob agree that they should coordinate to make sure that both pets are never in the yard at the same time. Of course, they rule out trivial solutions that do not allow either pet into an empty yard, or that reserve the yard exclusively to one pet or the other.

How should they do it? Alice and Bob need to agree on mutually compatible procedures for deciding what to do. We call such an agreement a *coordination protocol* (or just a *protocol*, for short).

The yard is large, so Alice cannot simply look out of the window to check whether Bob's dog is present. She could perhaps walk over to Bob's house and knock on the door, but that takes a long time, and what if it rains? Alice might lean out the window and shout "Hey Bob! Can I let the cat out?" The problem is that Bob might not hear her. He could be watching TV, visiting his girlfriend, or out shopping for dog food. They could try to coordinate by cell phone, but the same difficulties arise if Bob is in the shower, driving through a tunnel, or recharging his phone's batteries.

Alice has a clever idea. She sets up one or more empty beer cans on Bob's windowsill (Fig. 1.4), ties a string around each one, and runs the string back to her house. Bob does the same. When she wants to send a signal to Bob, she yanks the string to knock over one of the cans. When Bob notices a can has been knocked over, he resets the can.

Up-ending beer cans by remote control may seem like a creative idea, but it does not solve this problem. The problem is that Alice can place only a limited number of cans on Bob's windowsill, and sooner or later, she is going to run out of cans to knock over. Granted, Bob resets a can as soon as he notices it has been knocked over, but what if he goes to Cancún for spring break? As long as Alice relies on Bob to reset the beer cans, sooner or later, she might run out.

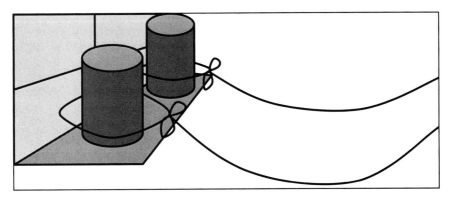

FIGURE 1.4

Communicating with cans.

So Alice and Bob try a different approach. Each one sets up a flagpole, easily visible to the other. When Alice wants to release her cat, she does the following:

1. She raises her flag.
2. When Bob's flag is lowered, she releases her cat.
3. When her cat comes back, she lowers her flag.

When Bob wants to release his dog, his behavior is a little more complicated:

1. He raises his flag.
2. While Alice's flag is raised
   a. Bob lowers his flag,
   b. Bob waits until Alice's flag is lowered,
   c. Bob raises his flag.
3. As soon as his flag is raised and hers is down, he releases his dog.
4. When his dog comes back, he lowers his flag.

This protocol rewards further study as a solution to Alice and Bob's problem. On an intuitive level, it works because of the following *flag principle*: If Alice and Bob each

1. raises his or her own flag, and then
2. looks at the other's flag,

then at least one will see the other's flag raised (clearly, the last one to look will see the other's flag raised) and will not let his or her pet enter the yard. However, this observation does not *prove* that the pets will never be in the yard together. What if, for example, Alice lets her cat in and out of the yard several times while Bob is looking?

To prove that the pets will never be in the yard together, assume by way of contradiction that there is a way the pets could end up in the yard together. Consider the last time Alice and Bob each raised their flag and looked at the other's flag before sending the pet into the yard. When Alice last looked, her flag was already fully raised. She must have not seen Bob's flag, or she would not have released the cat, so Bob must have not completed raising his flag before Alice started looking. It follows that when Bob looked for the last time, after raising his flag for the last time, it must have been after Alice started looking, so he must have seen Alice's flag raised and would not have released his dog, a contradiction.

This kind of argument by contradiction shows up over and over again, and it is worth spending some time understanding why this claim is true. It is important to note that we never assumed that "raising my flag" or "looking at your flag" happens instantaneously, nor did we make any assumptions about how long such activities take. All we care about is when these activities start or end.

1.2.1 Properties of a mutual exclusion protocol

To show that the flag protocol is a correct solution to Alice and Bob's problem, we must understand what properties a solution requires, and then show that the protocol meets them.

We already proved that the pets are excluded from being in the yard at the same time, a property we call *mutual exclusion*.

Mutual exclusion is only one of several properties of interest. After all, a protocol in which Alice and Bob never release a pet satisfies the mutual exclusion property, but it is unlikely to satisfy their pets.

Here is another property of central importance: If only one pet wants to enter the yard, then it eventually succeeds. In addition, if both pets want to enter the yard, then eventually at least one of them succeeds. We consider this *deadlock-freedom* property to be essential. Note that whereas mutual exclusion is a safety property, deadlock-freedom is a liveness property.

We claim that Alice and Bob's protocol is deadlock-free. Suppose both pets want to use the yard. Alice and Bob both raise their flags. Bob eventually notices that Alice's flag is raised, and defers to her by lowering his flag, allowing Alice's cat into the yard.

Another property of interest is *starvation-freedom* (sometimes called *lockout-freedom*): If a pet wants to enter the yard, will it eventually succeed? Here, Alice and Bob's protocol performs poorly. Whenever Alice and Bob are in conflict, Bob defers to Alice, so it is possible that Alice's cat can use the yard over and over again, while Bob's dog becomes increasingly uncomfortable. Later on, we consider protocols that prevent starvation.

The last property of interest concerns *waiting*. Imagine that Alice raises her flag, and is then suddenly stricken with appendicitis. She (and the cat) are taken to the hospital, and after a successful operation, she spends the next week under observation at the hospital. Although Bob is relieved that Alice is well, his dog cannot use the yard for an entire week until Alice returns. The problem is that the protocol states that Bob (and his dog) must *wait* for Alice to lower her flag. If Alice is delayed (even for a good reason), then Bob is also delayed (for no apparently good reason).

The question of waiting is important as an example of *fault-tolerance*. Normally, we expect Alice and Bob to respond to each other in a reasonable amount of time, but what if they do not do so? The mutual exclusion problem, by its very essence, requires waiting: No mutual exclusion protocol, no matter how clever, can avoid it. Nevertheless, we will see that many other coordination problems can be solved without waiting, sometimes in unexpected ways.

1.2.2 The moral

Having reviewed the strengths and weaknesses of Alice and Bob's protocol, we now turn our attention back to computer science.

First, we examine why shouting across the yard and placing cell phone calls does not work. Two kinds of communication occur naturally in concurrent systems:

- *Transient* communication requires both parties to participate at the same time. Shouting, gestures, or cell phone calls are examples of transient communication.
- *Persistent* communication allows the sender and receiver to participate at different times. Posting letters, sending email, or leaving notes under rocks are all examples of persistent communication.

Mutual exclusion requires persistent communication. The problem with shouting across the yard or placing cell phone calls is that it may or may not be okay for Bob to release his dog, but if Alice does not respond to messages, he will never know.

The can-and-string protocol might seem somewhat contrived, but it corresponds accurately to a common communication protocol in concurrent systems: *interrupts*. In modern operating systems, one common way for one thread to get the attention of another is to send it an interrupt. More precisely, thread A interrupts thread B by setting a bit at a location periodically checked by B. Sooner or later, B notices the bit has been set and reacts. After reacting, B typically resets the bit (A cannot reset the bit). Even though interrupts cannot solve the mutual exclusion problem, they can still be very useful. For example, interrupt communication is the basis of the Java language's `wait()` and `notifyAll()` calls.

On a more positive note, the fable shows that mutual exclusion between two threads can be solved (however imperfectly) using only two one-bit variables, each of which can be written by one thread and read by the other.

1.3 The producer–consumer problem

Mutual exclusion is not the only problem worth investigating. Eventually, Alice and Bob fall in love and marry. Eventually, they divorce. (What were they thinking?) The judge gives Alice custody of the pets, and tells Bob to feed them. The pets now get along with one another, but they side with Alice, and attack Bob whenever they see him. As a result, Alice and Bob need to devise a protocol for Bob to deliver food to the pets without Bob and the pets being in the yard together. Moreover, the protocol should not waste anyone's time: Alice does not want to release her pets into the yard unless there is food there, and Bob does not want to enter the yard unless the pets have consumed all the food. This problem is known as the *producer–consumer* problem.

Surprisingly perhaps, the can-and-string protocol we rejected for mutual exclusion does exactly what we need for the producer–consumer problem. Bob places a can *standing up* on Alice's windowsill, ties one end of his string around the can, and puts the other end of the string in his living room. He then puts food in the yard and knocks the can down. When Alice wants to release the pets, she does the following:

1. She waits until the can is down.
2. She releases the pets.
3. When the pets return, Alice checks whether they finished the food. If so, she resets the can.

Bob does the following:

1. He waits until the can is up.
2. He puts food in the yard.
3. He pulls the string and knocks the can down.

The state of the can thus reflects the state of the yard. If the can is down, it means there is food and the pets can eat, and if the can is up, it means the food is gone and Bob can put some more out. We check the following three properties:

- *Mutual exclusion*: Bob and the pets are never in the yard together.
- *Starvation-freedom*: If Bob is always willing to feed, and the pets are hungry, then the pets will eventually eat.
- *Producer–consumer*: The pets will not enter the yard unless there is food, and Bob will never provide more food if there is unconsumed food.

Both this producer–consumer protocol and the earlier mutual exclusion protocol ensure that Alice and Bob are never in the yard at the same time. However, Alice and Bob cannot use this producer–consumer protocol for mutual exclusion, and it is important to understand why: The mutual exclusion problem requires deadlock-freedom: Each person must be able to enter the yard if it is empty (and the other is not trying to enter). By contrast, the producer–consumer protocol's starvation-freedom property assumes continuous cooperation from both parties.

Here is how we reason about this protocol:

- *Mutual exclusion*: Instead of a proof by contradiction, as we used earlier, we use an inductive "state machine"-based proof. Think of the stringed can as a machine that repeatedly transitions between two states, *up* and *down*. To show that mutual exclusion always holds, we must check that it holds initially, and continues to hold when transitioning from one state to the other.

  Initially, the yard is empty, so mutual exclusion holds whether the can is up or down. Next, we check that mutual exclusion, once established, continues to hold when the state changes. Suppose the can is down. Bob is not in the yard, and from the protocol we can see that he does not enter the yard while the can is down, so only the pets may be present. The can is not raised until the pets have left the yard, so when the can is raised, the pets are not present. While the can is up, from the protocol we can see that the pets do not enter the yard, so only Bob may be present. The can is not knocked down until Bob has left the yard. These are all the possible transitions, so our protocol satisfies mutual exclusion.

- *Starvation-freedom*: Suppose the protocol is not starvation-free: it happens that the pets are hungry, there is no food, and Bob is trying to provide food, but he does not succeed. If the can is up, then Bob will provide food and knock over the can, allowing the pets to eat. If the can is down, then since the pets are hungry, Alice will eventually raise the can, bringing us back to the previous case.
- *Producer–consumer*: The mutual exclusion property implies that the pets and Bob will never be in the yard together. Bob will not enter the yard until Alice raises the can, which she will do only when there is no more food. Similarly, the pets will not enter the yard until Bob lowers the can, which he will do only after placing the food.

Like the earlier mutual exclusion protocol, this protocol exhibits *waiting*: If Bob deposits food in the yard and then goes on vacation without resetting the can, then the pets may starve despite the presence of food.

Turning our attention back to computer science, the producer–consumer problem appears in almost all parallel and distributed systems. It is the way in which threads place data in communication buffers to be read or transmitted across a network interconnect or shared bus.

1.4 The readers–writers problem

Bob and Alice decide they love their pets so much they need to communicate simple messages about them. Bob puts up a billboard in front of his house. The billboard holds a sequence of large tiles, each tile holding a single letter. Bob, at his leisure, posts a message on the bulletin board by lifting one tile at a time. Alice, whose eyesight is poor, reads the message at her leisure by looking at the billboard through a telescope, one tile at a time.

This may sound like a workable system, but it is not. Imagine that Bob posts the message

```
sell the cat
```

Alice, looking through her telescope, transcribes the message

```
sell the
```

At this point Bob takes down the tiles and writes out a new message

```
wash the dog
```

Alice, continuing to scan across the billboard, transcribes the message

`sell the dog`

You can imagine the rest.

This *readers–writers problem* has some straightforward solutions:

- Alice and Bob can use the mutual exclusion protocol to make sure that Alice reads only complete sentences. She might still miss a sentence, however.
- They can use the can-and-string protocol, with Bob producing sentences and Alice consuming them.

If this problem is so easy to solve, then why do we bring it up? Both the mutual exclusion and producer–consumer protocols require *waiting*: If one participant is subjected to an unexpected delay, then so is the other. In the context of shared-memory multiprocessors, a solution to the readers–writers problem is a way of allowing a thread to capture an instantaneous view of several memory locations. Capturing such a view without waiting, that is, without preventing other threads from modifying these locations while they are being read, is a powerful tool that can be used for backups, debugging, and in many other situations. Surprisingly, the readers–writers problem does have solutions that do *not* require waiting. We examine several such solutions in later chapters.

1.5 The harsh realities of parallelization

Here is why multiprocessor programming is so much fun. In an ideal world, upgrading from a uniprocessor to an *n*-way multiprocessor should provide about an *n*-fold increase in computational power. In practice, sadly, this (almost) never happens. The primary reason is that most real-world computational problems cannot be effectively parallelized without incurring the costs of interprocessor communication and coordination.

Consider five friends who decide to paint a five-room house. If all the rooms are the same size, then it makes sense to assign each friend to paint one room. As long as everyone paints at about the same rate, we would get a five-fold speedup over the single-painter case. The task becomes more complicated if the rooms are of different sizes. For example, if one room is twice the size of the others, then the five painters will not achieve a five-fold speedup because the overall completion time is dominated by the one room that takes the longest to paint.

This kind of analysis is very important for concurrent computation. The formula we need is called *Amdahl's law*. It captures the notion that the extent to which we can speed up any complex job (not just painting) is limited by how much of the job must be executed sequentially.

Define the *speedup S* of a job to be the ratio between the time it takes one processor to complete the job (as measured by a wall clock) versus the time it takes

n concurrent processors to complete the same job. *Amdahl's law* characterizes the maximum speedup S that can be achieved by n processors collaborating on an application, where p is the fraction of the job that can be executed in parallel. Assume, for simplicity, that it takes (normalized) time 1 for a single processor to complete the job. With n concurrent processors, the parallel part takes time p/n and the sequential part takes time $1 - p$. Overall, the parallelized computation takes time

$$1 - p + \frac{p}{n}.$$

Amdahl's law says that the maximum speedup, that is, the ratio between the sequential (single-processor) time and the parallel time, is

$$S = \frac{1}{1 - p + \dfrac{p}{n}}.$$

To illustrate the implications of Amdahl's law, consider our room painting example. Assume that each small room is one unit, and the single large room is two units. Assigning one painter (processor) per room means that five of six units can be painted in parallel, implying that $p = 5/6$, and $1 - p = 1/6$. Amdahl's law states that the resulting speedup is

$$S = \frac{1}{1 - p + \dfrac{p}{n}} = \frac{1}{1/6 + 1/6} = 3.$$

Alarmingly, five painters working on five rooms where one room is twice the size of the others yields only a three-fold speedup.

It can get worse. Imagine we have 10 rooms and 10 painters, where each painter is assigned to a room, but one room (out of 10) is twice the size of the others. Here is the resulting speedup:

$$S = \frac{1}{1/11 + 1/11} = 5.5.$$

With even a small imbalance, applying ten painters to a job yields only a five-fold speedup, roughly half of what one might naïvely expect.

The solution, therefore, as with our earlier prime printing problem, seems to be that as soon as one painter's work on a room is done, he/she helps others to paint the remaining room. The issue, of course, is that this shared painting of the room will require coordination among painters. But can we afford to avoid it?

Here is what Amdahl's law tells us about the utilization of multiprocessor machines. Some computational problems are "embarrassingly parallel": they can easily be divided into components that can be executed concurrently. Such problems sometimes arise in scientific computing or in graphics, but rarely in systems. In general, however, for a given problem and a 10-processor machine, Amdahl's law says that even if we manage to parallelize 90% of the solution, but not the remaining 10%, then we end up with a five-fold speedup, not a 10-fold speedup. In other words, the remaining 10% that we did not parallelize cut our utilization of the machine in half. It seems worthwhile to invest effort to derive as much parallelism from the remaining 10% as possible, even if it is difficult. Typically, it is hard because these additional parallel parts involve substantial communication and coordination. A major focus of this book is understanding the tools and techniques that allow programmers to effectively program the parts of the code that require coordination and synchronization, because the gains made on these parts may have a profound impact on performance.

Returning to the prime number printing program of Fig. 1.2, let us revisit the three main lines of code:

```
i = counter.getAndIncrement(); // take next untaken number
if (isPrime(i))
    print(i);
```

It would have been simpler to have threads perform these three lines atomically, that is, in a single mutually exclusive block. Instead, only the call to getAndIncrement() is atomic. This approach makes sense when we consider the implications of Amdahl's law: It is important to minimize the granularity of sequential code, in this case, the code accessed using mutual exclusion. Moreover, it is important to implement mutual exclusion in an effective way, since the communication and coordination around the mutually exclusive shared counter can substantially affect the performance of our program as a whole.

1.6 Parallel programming

For many of the applications we wish to parallelize, significant parts can easily be determined as executable in parallel because they do not require any form of coordination or communication. However, at the time this book is being written, there is no cookbook recipe for identifying these parts. This is where the application designer must use his or her accumulated understanding of the algorithm being parallelized. Luckily, in many cases it is obvious how to identify such parts. The more substantial problem, the one which this book addresses, is how to deal with the remaining parts of the program. As noted earlier, these are the parts that cannot be parallelized easily because the program must access shared data and requires interprocess coordination and communication in an essential way.

The goal of this text is to expose the reader to core ideas behind modern coordination paradigms and concurrent data structures. We present the reader with a unified, comprehensive picture of the elements that are key to effective multiprocessor programming, ranging from basic principles to best-practice engineering techniques.

Multiprocessor programming poses many challenges, ranging from grand intellectual issues to subtle engineering tricks. We tackle these challenges using successive refinement, starting with an idealized model in which mathematical concerns are paramount, and gradually moving on to more pragmatic models, where we increasingly focus on basic engineering principles.

For example, the first problem we consider is mutual exclusion, the oldest and still one of the fundamental problems in the field. We begin with a mathematical perspective, analyzing the computability and correctness properties of various algorithms on an idealized architecture. The algorithms themselves, while classical, are not practical for modern multicore architectures. Nevertheless, learning how to reason about such idealized algorithms is an important step toward learning how to reason about more realistic (and more complex) algorithms. It is particularly important to learn how to reason about subtle liveness issues such as starvation and deadlock.

Once we understand how to reason about such algorithms in general, we turn our attention to more realistic contexts. We explore a variety of algorithms and data structures using different multiprocessor architectures with the goal of understanding which are effective, and why.

1.7 Chapter notes

Most of the parable of Alice and Bob is adapted from Leslie Lamport's invited lecture at the 1984 ACM Symposium on Principles of Distributed Computing [104]. The readers–writers problem is a classical synchronization problem that has received attention in numerous papers over the past 20 years. Amdahl's law is due to Gene Amdahl, a parallel processing pioneer [9].

1.8 Exercises

Exercise 1.1. The *dining philosophers problem* was invented by E.W. Dijkstra, a concurrency pioneer, to clarify the notions of deadlock- and starvation-freedom. Imagine five philosophers who spend their lives just thinking and feasting on rice. They sit around a circular table, illustrated in Fig. 1.5. However, there are only five chopsticks

FIGURE 1.5

Traditional dining table arrangement according to Dijkstra.

(forks, in the original formulation). Each philosopher thinks. When he gets hungry, he picks up the two chopsticks closest to him. If he can pick up both chopsticks, he can eat for a while. After a philosopher finishes eating, he puts down the chopsticks and again starts to think.

1. Write a program to simulate the behavior of the philosophers, where each philosopher is a thread and the chopsticks are shared objects. Note that you must prevent a situation where two philosophers hold the same chopstick at the same time.
2. Amend your program so that it never reaches a state where philosophers are deadlocked, that is, it is never the case that every philosopher holds one chopstick and is stuck waiting for another to get the second chopstick.
3. Amend your program so that no philosopher ever starves.
4. Write a program to provide a starvation-free solution for n philosophers for any natural number n.

Exercise 1.2. For each of the following, state whether it is a safety or liveness property. Identify the bad or good thing of interest.

1. Patrons are served in the order they arrive.
2. Anything that can go wrong, will go wrong.
3. No one wants to die.
4. Two things are certain: death and taxes.
5. As soon as one is born, one starts dying.
6. If an interrupt occurs, then a message is printed within one second.
7. If an interrupt occurs, then a message is printed.
8. I will finish what Darth Vader has started.
9. The cost of living never decreases.
10. You can always tell a Harvard man.

Exercise 1.3. In the producer–consumer fable, we assumed that Bob can see whether the can on Alice's windowsill is up or down. Design a producer–consumer protocol using cans and strings that works even if Bob cannot see the state of Alice's can (this is how real-world interrupt bits work).

Exercise 1.4. You are one of P recently arrested prisoners. The warden, a deranged computer scientist, makes the following announcement:

You may meet together today and plan a strategy, but after today you will be in isolated cells and have no communication with one another.

I have set up a "switch room" which contains a light switch, which is either on or off. The switch is not connected to anything.

Every now and then, I will select one prisoner at random to enter the "switch room." This prisoner may throw the switch (from on to off, or vice versa), or may leave the switch unchanged. Nobody else will ever enter this room.

Each prisoner will visit the switch room arbitrarily often. More precisely, for any N, eventually each of you will visit the switch room at least N times.

At any time, any of you may declare: "We have all visited the switch room at least once." If the claim is correct, I will set you free. If the claim is incorrect, I will feed all of you to the crocodiles. Choose wisely!

- Devise a winning strategy when you know that the initial state of the switch is *off*.
- Devise a winning strategy when you do not know whether the initial state of the switch is *on* or *off*.

Hint: The prisoners need not all do the same thing.

Exercise 1.5. The same warden has a different idea. He orders the prisoners to stand in line, and places red and blue hats on each of their heads. No prisoner knows the color of his own hat, or the color of any hat behind him, but he can see the hats of the prisoners in front. The warden starts at the back of the line and asks each prisoner to guess the color of his own hat. The prisoner can answer only "red" or "blue." If he gives the wrong answer, he is fed to the crocodiles. If he answers correctly, he is freed. Each prisoner can hear the answer of the prisoners behind him, but cannot tell whether that prisoner was correct.

The prisoners are allowed to consult and agree on a strategy beforehand (while the warden listens in) but after being lined up, they cannot communicate any other way besides their answer of "red" or "blue."

Devise a strategy that allows at least $P - 1$ of P prisoners to be freed.

Exercise 1.6. A financial risk management program is sped up by making 85% of the application concurrent, while 15% remains sequential. However, it turns out that during a concurrent execution the number of cache misses grows in a way dependent on N, the number of cores used. The dependency is $CacheMiss = \frac{N}{N+10}$. Profiling the program reveals that 20% of the operations performed are memory accesses for both the sequential and parallel parts. The cost of other operations, including cache accesses, is 1 unit, and accessing memory has a cost of $3N + 11$ units for the parallel part and a cost of 14 for the sequential part. Compute the optimal number of processors on which the program should run.

Exercise 1.7. You are given a program that includes a method M that executes sequentially. Use Amdahl's law to resolve the following questions.

- Suppose M accounts for 30% of the program's execution time. What is the limit for the overall speedup that can be achieved on an n-processor machine?
- Suppose M accounts for 40% of the program's execution time. You hire a programmer to replace M with M', which has a k-fold speedup over M. What value of k yields an overall speedup of 2 for the whole program?
- Suppose M', the parallel replacement for M, has a four-fold speedup. What fraction of the overall execution time must M account for if replacing it with M' doubles the program's speedup?

You may assume that the program, when executed sequentially, takes unit time.

Exercise 1.8. Running your application on two processors yields a speedup of S_2. Use Amdahl's law to derive a formula for S_n, the speedup on n processors, in terms of n and S_2.

Exercise 1.9. You have a choice between buying one uniprocessor that executes five zillion instructions per second or a 10-processor multiprocessor where each processor executes one zillion instructions per second. Using Amdahl's law, explain how you would decide which to buy for a particular application.

Principles

Mutual exclusion

2

Mutual exclusion is perhaps the most prevalent form of coordination in multiprocessor programming. This chapter covers classical mutual exclusion algorithms that work by reading and writing shared memory. Although these algorithms are not used in practice, we study them because they provide an ideal introduction to the kinds of algorithmic and correctness issues that arise in every area of synchronization. The chapter also provides an impossibility proof. This proof teaches us the limitations of solutions to mutual exclusion that work by reading and writing shared memory, which helps to motivate the real-world mutual exclusion algorithms that appear in later chapters. This chapter is one of the few that contains proofs of algorithms. Though the reader should feel free to skip these proofs, it is helpful to understand the kind of reasoning they present, because we can use the same approach to reason about the practical algorithms considered in later chapters.

2.1 Time and events

Reasoning about concurrent computation is mostly reasoning about time. Sometimes we want things to happen simultaneously, and sometimes we want them to happen at different times. To reason about complicated conditions involving how multiple time intervals can overlap, or how they cannot, we need a simple but unambiguous language to talk about events and durations in time. Everyday English is too ambiguous and imprecise. Instead, we introduce a simple vocabulary and notation to describe how concurrent threads behave in time.

In 1687, Isaac Newton wrote, "Absolute, True, and Mathematical Time, of itself, and from its own nature flows equably without relation to any thing external." We endorse his notion of time, if not his prose style. Threads share a common time (though not necessarily a common clock). A thread is a *state machine*, and its state transitions are called *events*.

Events are *instantaneous*: they occur at a single instant of time. It is convenient to require that events are never simultaneous: Distinct events occur at distinct times. (As a practical matter, if we are unsure about the order of two events that happen very close in time, then either order will do.) A thread A produces a sequence of events $a_0, a_1, \ldots$. Programs typically contain loops, so a single program statement can produce many events. One event a *precedes* another event b, written $a \rightarrow b$, if a occurs at an earlier time. The *precedence* relation $\rightarrow$ is a total order on events.

The Art of Multiprocessor Programming. https://doi.org/10.1016/B978-0-12-415950-1.00011-2

Let a_0 and a_1 be events such that $a_0 \to a_1$. An *interval* (a_0, a_1) is the duration between a_0 and a_1. Interval $I_A = (a_0, a_1)$ *precedes* $I_B = (b_0, b_1)$, written $I_A \to I_B$, if $a_1 \to b_0$ (that is, if the final event of I_A precedes the starting event of I_B). The $\to$ relation is a partial order on intervals. Intervals that are unrelated by $\to$ are said to be *concurrent*. We also say that an event a *precedes* an interval $I = (b_0, b_1)$, written $a \to I$, if $a \to b_0$, and that I *precedes* a, written $I \to a$, if $b_1 \to a$.

2.2 Critical sections

In Chapter 1, we discussed the Counter class implementation shown in Fig. 2.1. We observed that this implementation is correct in a single-thread system, but misbehaves when used by two or more threads. The problem occurs if both threads read the value field at the line marked "start of danger zone," and then both update that field at the line marked "end of danger zone."

We can avoid this problem by making these two lines into a *critical section*: a block of code that can be executed by only one thread at a time. We call this property *mutual exclusion*. The standard way to achieve mutual exclusion is through a Lock object satisfying the interface shown in Fig. 2.2.

```
1   class Counter {
2     private long value;
3     public Counter(long c) {       // constructor
4       value = c;
5     }
6     // increment and return prior value
7     public long getAndIncrement() {
8       long temp = value;           // start of danger zone
9       value = temp + 1;            // end of danger zone
10      return temp;
11    }
12  }
```

FIGURE 2.1

The Counter class.

```
1   public interface Lock {
2     public void lock();       // before entering critical section
3     public void unlock();     // before leaving critical section
4   }
```

FIGURE 2.2

The Lock interface.

```
 1  public class Counter {
 2    private long value;
 3    private Lock lock;              // to protect critical section
 4
 5    public long getAndIncrement() {
 6      lock.lock();                 // enter critical section
 7      try {
 8        long temp = value;         // in critical section
 9        value = temp + 1;          // in critical section
10        return temp;
11      } finally {
12        lock.unlock();             // leave critical section
13      }
14    }
15  }
```

FIGURE 2.3

Using a lock object.

Fig. 2.3 shows how to use a Lock object to add mutual exclusion to a shared counter implementation. Threads using the lock() and unlock() methods must follow a specific format. A thread is *well formed* if:

1. each critical section is associated with a Lock object,
2. the thread calls that object's lock() method when it wants to enter the critical section, and
3. the thread calls the unlock() method when it leaves the critical section.

PRAGMA 2.2.1

In Java, the lock() and unlock() methods should be used in the following structured way:

```
1  mutex.lock();
2  try {
3    ...              // body
4  } finally {
5    ... // restore invariant if needed
6    mutex.unlock();
7  }
```

This idiom ensures that the lock is acquired before entering the **try** block, and that the lock is released when control leaves the block. If a statement in the block throws an unexpected exception, it may be necessary to restore the object to a consistent state before returning.

We say that a thread *acquires* (alternatively, *locks*) a lock when it returns from a lock() method call, and *releases* (alternatively, *unlocks*) the lock when it invokes the unlock() method. If a thread has acquired and not subsequently released a lock, we say that the thread *holds* the lock. No thread may acquire the lock while any other thread holds it, so at most one thread holds the lock at any time. We say the lock is *busy* if a thread holds it; otherwise, we say the lock is *free*.

Multiple critical sections may be associated with the same Lock, in which case no thread may execute a critical section while any other thread is executing a critical section associated with the same Lock. From the perspective of a Lock algorithm, a thread starts a critical section when its call to the lock() method returns, and it ends the critical section by invoking the unlock() method; that is, a thread executes the critical section while it holds the lock.

We now state more precisely the properties that a good Lock algorithm should satisfy, assuming that every thread that acquires the lock eventually releases it.

Mutual exclusion   At most one thread holds the lock at any time.

Freedom from deadlock   If a thread is attempting to acquire or release the lock (i.e., it invoked lock() or unlock() and has not returned), then eventually some thread acquires or releases the lock (i.e., it returns from invoking lock() or unlock()). If a thread calls lock() and never returns, then other threads must complete an infinite number of critical sections.

Freedom from starvation   Every thread that attempts to acquire or release the lock eventually succeeds (i.e., every call to lock() or unlock() eventually returns).

Note that starvation-freedom implies deadlock-freedom.

The mutual exclusion property is clearly essential. It guarantees that the critical section, that is, the code executed between the acquisition and release of the lock, is executed by at most one thread at a time. In other words, executions of the critical section cannot overlap. Without this property, we cannot guarantee that a computation's results are correct.

Let CS_A^j be the interval during which thread A executes the critical section for the jth time. Thus, $CS_A^j = (a_0, a_1)$, where a_0 is the response event for A's jth call to lock() and a_1 is the invocation event for A's jth call to unlock(). For two distinct threads A and B and integers j and k, either $CS_A^j \rightarrow CS_B^k$ or $CS_B^k \rightarrow CS_A^j$.

The deadlock-freedom property is important. It implies that the system never "freezes." If some thread calls lock() and never acquires the lock, then either some other thread acquires and never releases the lock or other threads must be completing an infinite number of critical sections. Individual threads may be stuck forever (called *starvation*), but some thread makes progress.

The starvation-freedom property, while clearly desirable, is the least compelling of the three. This property is sometimes called *lockout-freedom*. In later chapters, we discuss practical mutual exclusion algorithms that are not starvation-free. These algorithms are typically deployed in circumstances where starvation is a theoretical possibility, but is unlikely to occur in practice. Nevertheless, the ability to reason about starvation is essential for understanding whether it is a realistic threat.

The starvation-freedom property is also weak in the sense that there is no guarantee for how long a thread waits before it enters the critical section. In later chapters, we look at algorithms that place bounds on how long a thread can wait.

In the terminology of Chapter 1, mutual exclusion is a safety property, and deadlock-freedom and starvation-freedom are liveness properties.

2.3 Two-thread solutions

We now consider algorithms that solve the mutual exclusion problem for two threads. Our two-thread lock algorithms follow the following conventions: The threads have IDs 0 and 1, and a thread can acquire its ID by calling ThreadID.get(). We store the calling thread's ID in i and the other thread's ID in $j = 1 - i$.

We begin with two inadequate but interesting algorithms.

2.3.1 The LockOne class

Fig. 2.4 shows the LockOne algorithm, which maintains a Boolean flag variable for each thread. To acquire the lock, a thread sets its flag to *true* and waits until the other thread's flag is *false*. The thread releases the flag by setting its flag back to *false*.

We use write$_A(x = v)$ to denote the event in which thread A assigns value v to field x, and read$_A(x == v)$ to denote the event in which A reads v from field x. For example, in Fig. 2.4, the event write$_A(flag[i] = true)$ is caused by line 7 of the lock() method. We sometimes omit the value when it is unimportant.

Lemma 2.3.1. The LockOne algorithm satisfies mutual exclusion.

```
1   class LockOne implements Lock {
2     private boolean[] flag = new boolean[2];
3     // thread-local index, 0 or 1
4     public void lock() {
5       int i = ThreadID.get();
6       int j = 1 - i;
7       flag[i] = true;
8       while (flag[j]) {}        // wait until flag[j] == false
9     }
10    public void unlock() {
11      int i = ThreadID.get();
12      flag[i] = false;
13    }
14  }
```

FIGURE 2.4

Pseudocode for the LockOne algorithm.

> **PRAGMA 2.3.1**
>
> In practice, the Boolean flag variables in Fig. 2.4, as well as the victim and label variables in later algorithms, must all be declared **volatile** to work properly. We explain the reasons in Chapter 3 and Appendix B. For readability, we omit the **volatile** declarations for now. We begin declaring the appropriate variables as volatile in Chapter 7.

Proof. Suppose not. Then there are overlapping critical sections CS_A and CS_B of threads A and B, respectively ($A \neq B$). Consider each thread's last execution of the lock() method before entering its critical section. Inspecting the code, we see that

$$\text{write}_A(\text{flag}[A] = true) \rightarrow \text{read}_A(\text{flag}[B] == false) \rightarrow CS_A,$$
$$\text{write}_B(\text{flag}[B] = true) \rightarrow \text{read}_B(\text{flag}[A] == false) \rightarrow CS_B.$$

Note that once flag[B] is set to *true* it remains *true* until B exits its critical section. Since the critical sections overlap, A must read flag[B] before B sets it to *true*. Similarly, B must read flag[A] before A sets it to *true*. Combining these, we get

$$\text{write}_A(\text{flag}[A] = true) \rightarrow \text{read}_A(\text{flag}[B] == false)$$
$$\rightarrow \text{write}_B(\text{flag}[B] = true) \rightarrow \text{read}_B(\text{flag}[A] == false)$$
$$\rightarrow \text{write}_A(\text{flag}[A] = true).$$

There is a cycle in $\rightarrow$, which is a contradiction, because $\rightarrow$ is a partial order (an event cannot precede itself). $\qquad\square$

The LockOne algorithm is inadequate because it can deadlock if thread executions are interleaved: If $\text{write}_A(\text{flag}[A] = true)$ and $\text{write}_B(\text{flag}[B] = true)$ events occur before $\text{read}_A(\text{flag}[B])$ and $\text{read}_B(\text{flag}[A])$ events, then both threads wait forever. Nevertheless, LockOne has an interesting property: If one thread runs before the other, no deadlock occurs, and all is well.

2.3.2 The LockTwo class

Fig. 2.5 shows an alternative lock algorithm, the LockTwo class, which uses a single victim field that indicates which thread should yield. To acquire the lock, a thread sets the victim field to its own ID and then waits until the other thread changes it.

Lemma 2.3.2. The LockTwo algorithm satisfies mutual exclusion.

Proof. Suppose not. Then there are overlapping critical sections CS_A and CS_B of threads A and B, respectively ($A \neq B$). As before, consider each thread's last execution of the lock() method before entering its critical section. Inspecting the code, we see that

```
1  class LockTwo implements Lock {
2    private int victim;
3    public void lock() {
4      int i = ThreadID.get();
5      victim = i;              // let the other go first
6      while (victim == i) {}   // wait
7    }
8    public void unlock() {}
9  }
```

FIGURE 2.5

Pseudocode for the LockTwo algorithm.

$$\text{write}_A(\text{victim} = A) \to \text{read}_A(\text{victim} == B) \to CS_A,$$
$$\text{write}_B(\text{victim} = B) \to \text{read}_B(\text{victim} == A) \to CS_B.$$

Thread B must assign B to the victim field between events $\text{write}_A(\text{victim} = A)$ and $\text{read}_A(\text{victim} = B)$, so in particular, B must write victim after A. However, by the same reasoning, A must write victim after B, which is a contradiction. □

The LockTwo algorithm is inadequate because it gets stuck *unless* the threads run concurrently. Nevertheless, LockTwo has an interesting property: If the threads run concurrently, the lock() method succeeds. The LockOne and LockTwo classes complement one another: Each succeeds under conditions that cause the other to get stuck.

2.3.3 The Peterson lock

We combine the LockOne and LockTwo algorithms to construct a starvation-free lock algorithm, shown in Fig. 2.6. This algorithm—known as *Peterson's algorithm*, after its inventor—is arguably the most succinct and elegant two-thread mutual exclusion algorithm.

Lemma 2.3.3. The Peterson lock algorithm satisfies mutual exclusion.

Proof. Suppose not. As before, consider the last executions of the lock() method by threads A and B before overlapping critical sections CS_A and CS_B. Inspecting the code, we see that

$$\text{write}_A(\text{flag}[A] = true) \to \text{write}_A(\text{victim} = A) \tag{2.3.1}$$
$$\to \text{read}_A(\text{flag}[B]) \to \text{read}_A(\text{victim}) \to CS_A,$$
$$\text{write}_B(\text{flag}[B] = true) \to \text{write}_B(\text{victim} = B) \tag{2.3.2}$$
$$\to \text{read}_B(\text{flag}[A]) \to \text{read}_B(\text{victim}) \to CS_B.$$

```
1   class Peterson implements Lock {
2     // thread-local index, 0 or 1
3     private boolean[] flag = new boolean[2];
4     private int victim;
5     public void lock() {
6       int i = ThreadID.get();
7       int j = 1 - i;
8       flag[i] = true;          // I'm interested
9       victim = i;              // you go first
10      while (flag[j] && victim == i) {} // wait
11    }
12    public void unlock() {
13      int i = ThreadID.get();
14      flag[i] = false;         // I'm not interested
15    }
16  }
```

FIGURE 2.6

Pseudocode for the Peterson lock algorithm.

Assume, without loss of generality, that A was the last thread to write to the victim field, i.e.,

$$\text{write}_B(\text{victim} = B) \rightarrow \text{write}_A(\text{victim} = A). \qquad (2.3.3)$$

Eq. (2.3.3) implies that A observed victim to be A in Eq. (2.3.1). Since A nevertheless entered its critical section, it must have observed flag[B] to be *false*, so we have

$$\text{write}_A(\text{victim} = A) \rightarrow \text{read}_A(\text{flag}[B] == false). \qquad (2.3.4)$$

Putting Eqs. (2.3.2) to (2.3.4) together yields:

$$\text{write}_B(\text{flag}[B] = true) \rightarrow \text{write}_B(\text{victim} = B) \qquad (2.3.5)$$
$$\rightarrow \text{write}_A(\text{victim} = A) \rightarrow \text{read}_A(\text{flag}[B] == false).$$

By the transitivity of $\rightarrow$, $\text{write}_B(\text{flag}[B] = true) \rightarrow \text{read}_A(\text{flag}[B] == false)$. This observation yields a contradiction because no other write to flag[B] was performed before the critical section executions. □

Lemma 2.3.4. The Peterson lock algorithm is starvation-free.

Proof. Suppose not, so some thread runs forever in the lock() method. Suppose (without loss of generality) that it is A. It must be executing the **while** statement, waiting until either flag[B] becomes *false* or victim is set to B.

What is B doing while A fails to make progress? Perhaps B is repeatedly entering and leaving its critical section. If so, however, then B sets victim to B before it reenters the critical section. Once victim is set to B, it does not change, and A must eventually return from the lock() method, a contradiction.

So it must be that B is also stuck in its lock() method call, waiting until either flag[A] becomes *false* or victim is set to A. But victim cannot be both A and B, a contradiction. □

Corollary 2.3.5. The Peterson lock algorithm is deadlock-free.

2.4 Notes on deadlock

Although the Peterson lock algorithm is deadlock-free (and even starvation-free), another kind of deadlock can arise in programs that use multiple Peterson locks (or any other lock implementation). For example, suppose that threads A and B share locks ℓ_0 and ℓ_1, and that A acquires ℓ_0 and B acquires ℓ_1. If A then tries to acquire ℓ_1 and B tries to acquire ℓ_0, the threads deadlock because each one waits for the other to release its lock.

In the literature, the term *deadlock* is sometimes used more narrowly to refer to the case in which the system enters a state from which there is no way for threads to make progress. The LockOne and LockTwo algorithms are susceptible to this kind of deadlock: In both algorithms, both threads can get stuck waiting in their respective while loops.

This narrower notion of deadlock is distinguished from *livelock*, in which two or more threads actively prevent each other from making progress by taking steps that subvert steps taken by other threads. When the system is livelocked rather than deadlocked, there is some way to schedule the threads so that the system can make progress (but also some way to schedule them so that there is no progress). Our definition of deadlock-freedom proscribes livelock as well as this narrower notion of deadlock.

Consider, for example, the Livelock algorithm in Fig. 2.7. (This is a variant of the flag protocol described in Section 1.2 in which both threads follow Bob's part of the protocol.) If both threads execute the lock() method, they may indefinitely repeat the following steps:

- Set their respective flag variables to *true*.
- See that the other thread's flag is *true*.
- Set their respective flag variables to *false*.
- See that the other thread's flag is *false*.

Because of this possible livelock, Livelock is not deadlock-free by our definition.

However, Livelock does not deadlock by the narrower definition because there is always some way to schedule the threads so that one of them makes progress: If one thread's flag is *false*, then execute the other thread until it exits the loop and returns. If both threads' flag variables are *true*, then execute one thread until it sets its flag to *false*, and then execute the other as described above (i.e., until it returns).

```
1   class Livelock implements Lock {
2     // thread-local index, 0 or 1
3     private boolean[] flag = new boolean[2];
4     public void lock() {
5       int i = ThreadID.get();
6       int j = 1 - i;
7       flag[i] = true;
8       while (flag[j]) {
9         flag[i] = false;
10        while (flag[j]) {}          // wait
11        flag[i] = true;
12      }
13    }
14    public void unlock() {
15      int i = ThreadID.get();
16      flag[i] = false;
17    }
18  }
```

FIGURE 2.7

Pseudocode for a lock algorithm that may livelock.

2.5 The filter lock

The Filter lock, shown in Fig. 2.8, generalizes the Peterson lock to work for $n > 2$ threads. It creates $n - 1$ "waiting rooms," called *levels*, that a thread must traverse before acquiring the lock. The levels are depicted in Fig. 2.9. Levels satisfy two important properties:

- At least one thread trying to enter level ℓ succeeds.
- If more than one thread is trying to enter level ℓ, then at least one is blocked (i.e., continues to wait without entering that level).

The Peterson lock uses a two-element Boolean flag array to indicate whether a thread is trying to enter the critical section. The Filter lock generalizes this notion with an n-element integer level[] array, where the value of level[A] indicates the highest level that thread A is trying to enter. Each thread must pass through $n - 1$ levels of "exclusion" to enter its critical section. Each level ℓ has a distinct victim[ℓ] field used to "filter out" one thread, excluding it from that level unless no thread is at that level or higher.

Initially, a thread A is at level 0. A *enters* level ℓ for $\ell > 0$ when it completes the waiting loop on line 17 with level[A] $= \ell$ (i.e., when it stops waiting at that loop). A enters its critical section when it enters level $n - 1$. When A leaves the critical section, it sets level[A] to 0.

```
1   class Filter implements Lock {
2     int[] level;
3     int[] victim;
4     public Filter(int n) {
5       level = new int[n];
6       victim = new int[n]; // use 1..n-1
7       for (int i = 0; i < n; i++) {
8         level[i] = 0;
9       }
10    }
11    public void lock() {
12      int me = ThreadID.get();
13      for (int i = 1; i < n; i++) { // attempt to enter level i
14        level[me] = i;
15        victim[i] = me;
16        // spin while conflicts exist
17        while ((∃k != me) (level[k] >= i && victim[i] == me)) {};
18      }
19    }
20    public void unlock() {
21      int me = ThreadID.get();
22      level[me] = 0;
23    }
24  }
```

FIGURE 2.8

Pseudocode for the Filter lock algorithm.

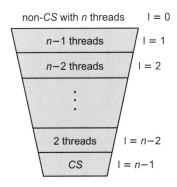

FIGURE 2.9

Threads pass through $n-1$ levels, the last of which is the critical section. Initially, all n threads are at level 0. At most $n-1$ enter level 1, at most $n-2$ enter level 2, and so on, so that only one thread enters the critical section at level $n-1$.

Lemma 2.5.1. For j between 0 and $n-1$, at most $n-j$ threads have entered level j (and not subsequently exited the critical section).

Proof. We prove this by induction on j. The base case, where $j = 0$, is trivial. For the induction step, the induction hypothesis implies that at most $n-j+1$ threads have entered level $j-1$. To show that at least one thread does not enter level j, we argue by contradiction. Assume that $n-j+1$ threads have entered level j. Because $j \leq n-1$, there must be at least two such threads.

Let A be the last thread to write victim[j]. A must have entered level j since victim[j] is written only by threads that have entered level $j-1$, and, by the induction hypothesis, every thread that has entered level $j-1$ has also entered level j. Let B be any thread other than A that has entered level j. Inspecting the code, we see that before B enters level j, it first writes j to level[B] and then writes B to victim[j]. Since A is the last to write victim[j], we have

$$\text{write}_B(\text{level}[B]=j) \rightarrow \text{write}_B(\text{victim}[j]) \rightarrow \text{write}_A(\text{victim}[j]).$$

We also see that A reads level[B] (line 17) after it writes to victim[j], so

$$\text{write}_B(\text{level}[B]=j) \rightarrow \text{write}_B(\text{victim}[j])$$
$$\rightarrow \text{write}_A(\text{victim}[j]) \rightarrow \text{read}_A(\text{level}[B]).$$

Because B has entered level j, every time A reads level[B], it observes a value greater than or equal to j, and since victim[j] $= A$ (because A was the last to write it), A could not have completed its waiting loop on line 17, a contradiction.   □

Corollary 2.5.2. The Filter lock algorithm satisfies mutual exclusion.

Proof. Entering the critical section is equivalent to entering level $n-1$, so at most one thread enters the critical section.   □

Lemma 2.5.3. The Filter lock algorithm is starvation-free.

Proof. We prove by induction on j that every thread that enters level $n-j$ eventually enters and leaves the critical section (assuming that it keeps taking steps and that every thread that enters the critical section eventually leaves it). The base case, with $j = 1$, is trivial because level $n-1$ is the critical section.

For the induction step, we suppose that every thread that enters level $n-j$ or higher eventually enters and leaves the critical section, and show that every thread that enters level $n-j-1$ does too.

Suppose, for contradiction, that a thread A has entered level $n-j-1$ and is stuck. By the induction hypothesis, it never enters level $n-j$, so it must be stuck at line 17 with level[A] $= n-j$ and victim[$n-j$] $= A$. After A writes victim[$n-j$], no thread enters level $n-j-1$ because any thread that did would overwrite victim[$n-j$], allowing A to enter level $n-j$. Furthermore, any other thread B trying to enter level $n-j$ will eventually succeed because victim[$n-j$] $= A \neq B$, so eventually no threads other than A are trying to enter level $n - j$. Moreover, any thread that enters level $n - j$ will, by the induction hypothesis, enter and leave the critical section, setting its level to 0. At some point, A is the only thread that has entered level $n - j - 1$ and not entered and left the critical section. In particular, after this point, $\text{level}[B] < n - j$ for every thread B other than A, so A can enter level $n - j$, a contradiction. $\square$

Corollary 2.5.4. The Filter lock algorithm is deadlock-free.

2.6 Fairness

The starvation-freedom property guarantees that every thread that calls lock() eventually enters the critical section, but it makes no guarantees about how long this may take, nor does it guarantee that the lock will be "fair" to the threads attempting to acquire it. For example, although the Filter lock algorithm is starvation-free, a thread attempting to acquire the lock may be overtaken arbitrarily many times by another thread.

Ideally (and very informally), if A calls lock() before B, then A should enter the critical section before B. That is, the lock should be "first-come-first-served." However, with the tools we have introduced so far, we cannot determine which thread called lock() first.

To define fairness, we split the lock() method into a *doorway* section and a *waiting* section, where the doorway section always completes in a bounded number of steps (the waiting section may take an unbounded number of steps). That is, there is a fixed limit on the number of steps a thread may take after invoking lock() before it completes the doorway section.

A section of code that is guaranteed to complete in a bounded number of steps is said to be *bounded wait-free*. The bounded wait-free property is a strong progress requirement. It is satisfied by code that has no loops. In later chapters, we discuss ways to provide this property in code that has loops. With this definition, we define the following fairness property.

Definition 2.6.1. A lock is *first-come-first-served* if its lock() method can be split into a bounded wait-free doorway section followed by a waiting section so that whenever thread A finishes its doorway before thread B starts its doorway, A cannot be overtaken by B. That is,

$$\text{if } D_A^j \rightarrow D_B^k \text{ then } CS_A^j \rightarrow CS_B^k$$

for any threads A and B and integers j and k, where D_A^j and CS_A^j are the intervals during which A executes the doorway section of its jth call to the lock() method and its jth critical section, respectively.

Note that any algorithm that is both deadlock-free and first-come-first-served is also starvation-free.

```
1   class Bakery implements Lock {
2     boolean[] flag;
3     Label[] label;
4     public Bakery (int n) {
5       flag = new boolean[n];
6       label = new Label[n];
7       for (int i = 0; i < n; i++) {
8         flag[i] = false; label[i] = 0;
9       }
10    }
11    public void lock() {
12      int i = ThreadID.get();
13      flag[i] = true;
14      label[i] = max(label[0], ...,label[n-1]) + 1;
15      while ((∃k != i)(flag[k] && (label[k],k) << (label[i],i))) {};
16    }
17    public void unlock() {
18      flag[ThreadID.get()] = false;
19    }
20  }
```

FIGURE 2.10

Pseudocode for the Bakery lock algorithm.

2.7 Lamport's Bakery algorithm

Perhaps the most elegant solution to the mutual exclusion problem for n threads is the Bakery lock algorithm, which appears in Fig. 2.10. It guarantees the *first-come-first-served* property by using a distributed version of the number-dispensing machines often found in bakeries: Each thread takes a number in the doorway, and then waits until no thread with an earlier number is trying to enter the critical section.

In the Bakery lock, flag[A] is a Boolean flag that indicates whether A wants to enter the critical section, and label[A] is an integer that indicates the thread's relative order when entering the bakery, for each thread A. To acquire the lock, a thread first raises its flag, and then picks a new label by reading the labels of all the threads (in any order) and generating a label greater than all the labels it read. The code from the invocation of the lock() method to the writing of the new label (line 14) is the *doorway*: it establishes that thread's order with respect to other threads trying to acquire the lock. Threads that execute their doorways concurrently may read the same labels and pick the same new label. To break this symmetry, the algorithm uses a lexicographical ordering $\ll$ on pairs of labels and thread IDs:

$$(\text{label}[i], i) \ll (\text{label}[j], j))$$

$$\text{if and only if} \tag{2.7.1}$$

$$\text{label}[i] < \text{label}[j] \quad \text{or} \quad \text{label}[i] = \text{label}[j] \quad \text{and} \quad i < j.$$

In the waiting section of the Bakery algorithm (line 15), a thread repeatedly reads the flags and labels of the other threads in any order until it determines that no thread with a raised flag has a lexicographically smaller label/ID pair.

Since releasing a lock does not reset the label[], it is easy to see that each thread's labels are strictly increasing. Interestingly, in both the doorway and waiting sections, threads read the labels asynchronously and in an arbitrary order. For example, the set of labels seen prior to picking a new one may have never existed in memory at the same time. Nevertheless, the algorithm works.

Lemma 2.7.1. The Bakery lock algorithm is deadlock-free.

Proof. Some waiting thread A has the unique least (label[A], A) pair, and that thread never waits for another thread. □

Lemma 2.7.2. The Bakery lock algorithm is first-come-first-served.

Proof. If A's doorway precedes B's, then A's label is smaller since

$$\text{write}_A(\text{label}[A]) \rightarrow \text{read}_B(\text{label}[A]) \rightarrow \text{write}_B(\text{label}[B]) \rightarrow \text{read}_B(\text{flag}[A]),$$

so B is locked out while flag[A] is *true*. □

Corollary 2.7.3. The Bakery lock algorithm is starvation-free.

Proof. This follows immediately from Lemmas 2.7.1 and 2.7.2 because any deadlock-free first-come-first-served lock algorithm is also starvation-free. □

Lemma 2.7.4. The Bakery lock algorithm satisfies mutual exclusion.

Proof. Suppose not. Let A and B be two threads concurrently in the critical section with (label[A], A) $\ll$ (label[B], B). Let labeling$_A$ and labeling$_B$ be the last respective sequences of acquiring new labels (line 14) prior to entering the critical section. To complete its waiting section, B must have read either that flag[A] was *false* or that (label[B], B) $\ll$ (label[A], A). However, for a given thread, its ID is fixed and its label[] values are strictly increasing, so B must have seen that flag[A] was *false*. It follows that

$$\text{labeling}_B \rightarrow \text{read}_B(\text{flag}[A] == false) \rightarrow \text{write}_A(\text{flag}[A] = true) \rightarrow \text{labeling}_A,$$

which contradicts the assumption that (label[A], A) $\ll$ (label[B], B). □

2.8 Bounded timestamps

Note that the labels of the Bakery lock grow without bound, so in a long-lived system we may have to worry about overflow. If a thread's label field silently rolls over from a large number to zero, then the first-come-first-served property no longer holds.

In later chapters, we discuss constructions in which counters are used to order threads, or even to produce unique IDs. How important is the overflow problem in the real world? It is difficult to generalize. Sometimes it matters a great deal. The celebrated "Y2K" bug that captivated the media in the last years of the 20th century is an example of a genuine overflow problem, even if the consequences were not as dire as predicted. On January 19, 2038, the Unix `time_t` data structure will overflow when the number of seconds since January 1, 1970 exceeds 2^{31}. No one knows whether it will matter. Sometimes, of course, counter overflow is a nonissue. Most applications that use, say, a 64-bit counter are unlikely to last long enough for roll-over to occur. (Let the grandchildren worry!)

In the `Bakery` lock, labels act as *timestamps*: They establish an order among the contending threads. Informally, we need to ensure that if one thread takes a label after another, then the latter has the larger label. Inspecting the code for the `Bakery` lock, we see that a thread needs two abilities:

- to read the other threads' timestamps (*scan*), and
- to assign itself a later timestamp (*label*).

A Java interface to such a timestamping system appears in Fig. 2.11. Since our principal application for a bounded timestamping system is to implement the doorway section of the `Lock` class, the timestamping system must be wait-free. It is possible to construct such a wait-free *concurrent* timestamping system (see the chapter notes), but the construction is long and technical. Instead, we focus on a simpler problem, interesting in its own right: constructing a *sequential* timestamping system, in which threads perform *scan*-and-*label* operations one completely after the other, that is, as if each were performed using mutual exclusion. In other words, we consider only executions in which a thread can perform a scan of the other threads' labels, or a scan and then an assignment of a new label, where each such sequence is a single atomic step. Although the details of concurrent and sequential timestamping systems differ substantially, the principles underlying them are essentially the same.

Think of the range of possible timestamps as nodes of a directed graph (called a *precedence graph*). An edge from node a to node b means that a is a later timestamp than b. The timestamp order is *irreflexive*: There is no edge from any node a to itself. The order is also *antisymmetric*: If there is an edge from a to b, then there is no edge

```
1   public interface Timestamp {
2     boolean compare(Timestamp);
3   }
4   public interface TimestampSystem {
5     public Timestamp[] scan();
6     public void label(Timestamp timestamp, int i);
7   }
```

FIGURE 2.11

A timestamping system interface.

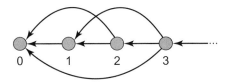

FIGURE 2.12

The precedence graph for an unbounded timestamping system. The nodes represent the set of all natural numbers and the edges represent the total order among them.

from b to a. We do *not* require that the order be *transitive*: There can be an edge from a to b and from b to c, without necessarily implying there is an edge from a to c.

Think of assigning a timestamp to a thread as placing that thread's token on that timestamp's node. A thread performs a scan by locating the other threads' tokens, and it assigns itself a new timestamp by moving its own token to a node a such that there is an edge from a to every other thread's node.

Pragmatically, we can implement such a system as an array of single-writer multi-reader fields, with an element for each thread A that indicates the node that A most recently assigned its token. The scan() method takes a "snapshot" of the array, and the label() method for thread A updates the array element for A.

Fig. 2.12 illustrates the precedence graph for the unbounded timestamp system used in the Bakery lock. Not surprisingly, the graph is infinite: There is one node for each natural number, with a directed edge from node a to node b whenever $a > b$.

Consider the precedence graph T^2 shown in Fig. 2.13. This graph has three nodes, labeled 0, 1, and 2, and its edges define an ordering relation on the nodes in which 0 is less than 1, 1 is less than 2, and 2 is less than 0. If there are only two threads, then we can use this graph to define a bounded (sequential) timestamping system. The system satisfies the following invariant: The two threads always have tokens on adjacent nodes, with the direction of the edge indicating their relative order. Suppose A's token is on node 0, and B's token on node 1 (so B has the later timestamp). For B, the label() method is trivial: It already has the latest timestamp, so it does nothing. For A, the label() method "leapfrogs" B's node by jumping from 0 to 2.

Recall that a *cycle* in a directed graph is a set of nodes $n_0, n_1, \ldots, n_k$ such that there is an edge from n_0 to n_1, from n_1 to n_2, and eventually from n_{k-1} to n_k, and back from n_k to n_0.

The only cycle in the graph T^2 has length three, and there are only two threads, so the order among the threads is never ambiguous. To go beyond two threads, we need additional conceptual tools. Let G be a precedence graph, and A and B subgraphs of G (possibly single nodes). We say that A *dominates* B in G if every node of A has edges directed to every node of B. Let *graph multiplication* be the following noncommutative composition operation for graphs (denoted $G \circ H$):

Replace every node v of G by a copy of H (denoted H_v), and let H_v dominate H_u in $G \circ H$ if v dominates u in G.

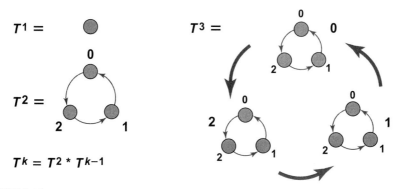

$T^1 =$

$T^2 =$

$T^k = T^2 * T^{k-1}$

$T^3 =$

FIGURE 2.13

The precedence graph for a bounded timestamping system. Consider an initial situation in which there is a token A on node 12 (node 2 in subgraph 1) and tokens B and C on nodes 21 and 22 (nodes 1 and 2 in subgraph 2). Token B will move to node 20 to dominate the others. Token C will then move to node 21 to dominate the others, and B and C can continue to cycle in the T^2 subgraph 2 forever. If A is to move to dominate B and C, it cannot pick a node in subgraph 2 since it is full (any T^k subgraph can accommodate at most k tokens). Instead, token A moves to node 00. If B now moves, it will choose node 01, C will choose node 10, and so on.

Define the graph T^k inductively as follows:

1. T^1 is a single node.
2. T^2 is the three-node graph defined earlier.
3. For $k > 2$, $T^k = T^2 \circ T^{k-1}$.

For example, the graph T^3 is illustrated in Fig. 2.13.

The precedence graph T^n is the basis for an n-thread bounded sequential time-stamping system. We can "address" any node in the T^n graph with $n - 1$ digits, using ternary notation. For example, the nodes in graph T^2 are addressed by 0, 1, and 2. The nodes in graph T^3 are denoted by $00, 01, \ldots, 22$, where the high-order digit indicates one of the three subgraphs, and the low-order digit indicates one node within that subgraph.

The key to understanding the n-thread labeling algorithm is that the nodes covered by tokens can never form a cycle. As mentioned, two threads can never form a cycle on T^2, because the shortest cycle in T^2 requires three nodes.

How does the label() method work for three threads? When A calls label(), if both the other threads have tokens on the same T^2 subgraph, then move to a node on the next highest T^2 subgraph, the one whose nodes dominate that T^2 subgraph. For example, consider the graph T^3 as illustrated in Fig. 2.13. We assume an initial acyclic situation in which there is a token A on node 12 (node 2 in subgraph 1) and tokens B and C on nodes 21 and 22 (nodes 1 and 2 in subgraph 2). Token B will move to node 20 to dominate all others. Token C will then move to node 21 to dominate all others, and B and C can continue to cycle in the T^2 subgraph 2 forever. If A is to move to dominate B and C, it cannot pick a node in subgraph 2 since it is full (any T^k subgraph can accommodate at most k tokens). Token A thus moves to node 00. If B now moves, it will choose node 01, C will choose node 10, and so on.

2.9 Lower bounds on the number of locations

The Bakery lock is succinct, elegant, and fair. So why is it not considered practical? The principal drawback is the need to read and write n distinct locations, where n is the maximum number of concurrent threads (which may be very large).

Is there a clever Lock algorithm based on reading and writing memory that avoids this overhead? We now demonstrate that the answer is *no*. Any deadlock-free mutual exclusion algorithm requires allocating and then reading or writing at least n distinct locations in the worst case. This result is crucial: it motivates us to augment our multiprocessor machines with synchronization operations stronger than reads and writes, and use them as the basis of our mutual exclusion algorithms. We discuss practical mutual exclusion algorithms in later chapters.

In this section, we examine why this linear bound is inherent. We observe the following limitation of memory accessed solely by *read* or *write* instructions (typically called *loads* and *stores*): Information written by a thread to a given location may be *overwritten* (i.e., stored to) without any other thread ever seeing it.

Our proof requires us to argue about the state of all memory used by a given multithreaded program. An object's *state* is just the state of its fields. A thread's *local state* is the state of its program counters and local variables. A *global state* or *system state* is the state of all objects, plus the local states of the threads.

Definition 2.9.1. A Lock object state s is *inconsistent* in any global state where some thread is in the critical section, but the lock state is compatible with a global state in which no thread is in the critical section or is trying to enter the critical section.

Lemma 2.9.2. No deadlock-free Lock algorithm can enter an inconsistent state.

Proof. Suppose the Lock object is in an inconsistent state s, where some thread A is in the critical section. If thread B tries to enter the critical section, it must eventually succeed because the algorithm is deadlock-free and B cannot determine that A is in the critical section, a contradiction.   □

Any Lock algorithm that solves deadlock-free mutual exclusion must have n distinct locations. Here, we consider only the three-thread case, showing that a deadlock-free Lock algorithm accessed by three threads must use three distinct locations.

Definition 2.9.3. A *covering state* for a Lock object is one in which there is at least one thread about to write to each shared location, but the Lock object's locations "look" like the critical section is empty (i.e., the locations' states appear as if there is no thread either in the critical section or trying to enter the critical section).

In a covering state, we say that each thread *covers* the location it is about to write.

Theorem 2.9.4. Any Lock algorithm that, by reading and writing memory, solves deadlock-free mutual exclusion for three threads must use at least three distinct memory locations.

Proof. Assume by way of contradiction that we have a deadlock-free Lock algorithm for three threads with only two locations. Initially, in state s, no thread is in the critical section or trying to enter. If we run any thread by itself, then it must write to at least one location before entering the critical section, as otherwise it creates an inconsistent state. It follows that every thread must write at least one location before entering. If the shared locations are single-writer locations as in the Bakery lock, then it is immediate that three distinct locations are needed.

Now consider multiwriter locations such as elements of the victim array in Peterson's algorithm (Fig. 2.6). Assume that we can bring the system to a covering Lock state s where A and B cover distinct locations. Consider the following possible execution starting from state s as depicted in Fig. 2.14:

Let C run alone. Because the Lock algorithm satisfies the deadlock-free property, C enters the critical section eventually. Then let A and B respectively update their covered locations, leaving the Lock object in state s'.

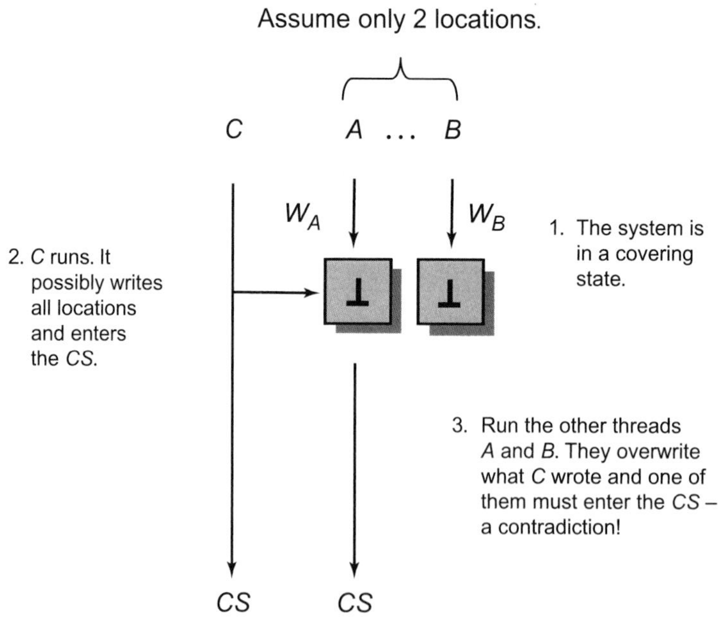

FIGURE 2.14

Contradiction using a covering state for two locations. Initially both locations have the empty value $\perp$.

The state s' is inconsistent because no thread can tell whether C is in the critical section. Thus, a lock with two locations is impossible.

It remains to show how to maneuver threads A and B into a covering state. Consider an execution in which B runs through the critical section three times. Each time around, it must write to some location, so consider the first location to which it writes when trying to enter the critical section. Since there are only two locations, B must "write first" to the same location twice. Call that location L_B.

Let B run until it is poised to write to location L_B for the first time. If A runs now, it would enter the critical section, since B has not written anything. A must write to L_A before entering the critical section. Otherwise, if A writes only to L_B, then let A enter the critical section, and let B write to L_B (obliterating A's last write). The result is an inconsistent state: B cannot tell whether A is in the critical section.

Let A run until it is poised to write to L_A. This state might not be a covering state because A could have written something to L_B indicating to thread C that it is trying to enter the critical section. Let B run, obliterating any value A might have written to L_B, entering and leaving the critical section at most three times, and halting just before its second write to L_B. Note that every time B enters and leaves the critical section, whatever it wrote to the locations is no longer relevant.

In this state, A is about to write to L_A, B is about to write to L_B, and the locations are consistent with no thread trying to enter or in the critical section, as required in a covering state. Fig. 2.15 illustrates this scenario. □

This line of argument can be extended to show that n-thread deadlock-free mutual exclusion requires n distinct locations. The Peterson and Bakery locks are thus optimal (within a constant factor). However, the need to allocate n locations per Lock makes them impractical.

This proof shows the inherent limitation of read and write operations: Information written by a thread may be overwritten without any other thread ever reading it. We will recall this limitation when we discuss other algorithms.

As discussed in later chapters, modern machine architectures provide specialized instructions that overcome the "overwriting" limitation of read and write instructions, allowing n-thread Lock implementations that use only a constant number of memory locations. However, making effective use of these instructions to solve mutual exclusion is far from trivial.

2.10 Chapter notes

Isaac Newton's ideas about the flow of time appear in his famous *Principia* [135]. The "→" formalism is due to Leslie Lamport [101]. The first three algorithms in this chapter are due to Gary Peterson, who published them in a two-page paper in 1981 [138]. The Bakery lock presented here is a simplification of the original Bakery algorithm due to Leslie Lamport [100]. The sequential timestamp algorithm is due to Amos Israeli and Ming Li [85], who invented the notion of a bounded timestamping system. Danny Dolev and Nir Shavit [39] invented the first bounded concurrent

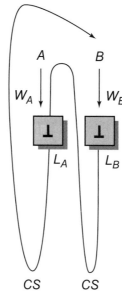

2. Run system until *A* is about to write L_A. There must be such a case; otherwise let *A* enter the *CS* and then *B* can overwrite its value. But there could be traces left by *A* in L_B. ...

1. Start in a covering state for L_B.

3. Run *B* again. It erases traces in L_B. Then let it enter the *CS* and return again. If one repeats this pattern twice more, *B* must return to a covering state for the exact same location (in the figure it is L_B).

FIGURE 2.15

Reaching a covering state. In the initial covering state for L_B both locations have the empty value $\perp$.

timestamping system. Other bounded timestamping schemes include ones by Sibsankar Haldar and Paul Vitányi [56] and Cynthia Dwork and Orli Waarts [42]. The lower bound on the number of lock fields is due to Jim Burns and Nancy Lynch [24]. Their proof technique, called a *covering argument*, has since been widely used to prove lower bounds in distributed computing. Readers interested in further reading can find a historical survey of mutual exclusion algorithms in a classic book by Michel Raynal [147].

2.11 Exercises

Exercise 2.1. A mutual exclusion algorithm provides *r-bounded waiting* if there is a way to define a doorway such that if $D_A^j \rightarrow D_B^k$, then $CS_A^j \rightarrow CS_B^{k+r}$. Does the Peterson algorithm provide *r*-bounded waiting for some value of *r*?

Exercise 2.2. Why must we define a *doorway* section, rather than defining first-come-first-served in a mutual exclusion algorithm based on the order in which the first instruction in the lock() method was executed? Argue your answer in a case-by-case manner based on the nature of the first instruction executed by the lock(): a read or a write, to separate locations or the same location.

```
1   class Flaky implements Lock {
2     private int turn;
3     private boolean busy = false;
4     public void lock() {
5       int me = ThreadID.get();
6       do {
7         do {
8           turn = me;
9         } while (busy);
10        busy = true;
11      } while (turn != me);
12    }
13    public void unlock() {
14      busy = false;
15    }
16  }
```

FIGURE 2.16

The Flaky lock used in Exercise 2.3.

```
1   public void unlock() {
2     int i = ThreadID.get();
3     flag[i] = false;
4     int j = 1 - i;
5     while (flag[j] == true) {}
6   }
```

FIGURE 2.17

The revised unlock method for Peterson's algorithm used in Exercise 2.5.

Exercise 2.3. Programmers at the Flaky Computer Corporation designed the protocol shown in Fig. 2.16 to achieve n-thread mutual exclusion. For each question, either sketch a proof, or display an execution where it fails.

- Does this protocol satisfy mutual exclusion?
- Is this protocol starvation-free?
- Is this protocol deadlock-free?
- Is this protocol livelock-free?

Exercise 2.4. Show that the Filter lock allows some threads to overtake others an arbitrary number of times.

Exercise 2.5. Consider a variant of Peterson's algorithm, where we change the unlock method to be as shown in Fig. 2.17. Does the modified algorithm satisfy deadlock-freedom? What about starvation-freedom? Sketch a proof showing why it satisfies both properties, or display an execution where it fails.

Exercise 2.6. Another way to generalize the two-thread Peterson lock is to arrange a number of two-thread Peterson locks in a binary tree. Suppose n is a power of two. Each thread is assigned a leaf lock which it shares with one other thread. Each lock treats one thread as thread 0 and the other as thread 1.

In the tree-lock's acquire method, the thread acquires every two-thread Peterson lock from that thread's leaf to the root. The tree-lock's release method for the tree-lock unlocks each of the two-thread Peterson locks that thread has acquired, from the root back to its leaf. At any time, a thread can be delayed for a finite duration. (In other words, threads can take naps, or even vacations, but they do not drop dead.) For each of the following properties, either sketch a proof that it holds, or describe a (possibly infinite) execution where it is violated:

1. mutual exclusion,
2. freedom from deadlock,
3. freedom from starvation.

Is there an upper bound on the number of times the tree-lock can be acquired and released between the time a thread starts acquiring the tree-lock and when it succeeds?

Exercise 2.7. The ℓ-exclusion problem is a variant of the starvation-free mutual exclusion problem with two changes: Up to ℓ threads may be in the critical section at the same time, and fewer than ℓ threads might fail (by halting) in the critical section.

An implementation must satisfy the following conditions:

ℓ-Exclusion: At any time, at most ℓ threads are in the critical section.

ℓ-Starvation-freedom: As long as fewer than ℓ threads are in the critical section, some thread that wants to enter the critical section will eventually succeed (even if some threads in the critical section have halted).

Modify the n-thread `Filter` mutual exclusion algorithm to solve ℓ-exclusion.

Exercise 2.8. In practice, almost all lock acquisitions are uncontended, so the most practical measure of a lock's performance is the number of steps needed for a thread to acquire a lock when no other thread is concurrently trying to acquire the lock.

Scientists at Cantaloupe-Melon University have devised the following "wrapper" for an arbitrary lock, shown in Fig. 2.18. They claim that if the base `Lock` class provides mutual exclusion and is starvation-free, so does the `FastPath` lock, but it can be acquired in a constant number of steps in the absence of contention. Sketch an argument why they are right, or give a counterexample.

Exercise 2.9. Suppose n threads call the `visit()` method of the `Bouncer` class shown in Fig. 2.19. Prove the following:

- At most one thread gets the value STOP.
- At most $n - 1$ threads get the value DOWN.
- At most $n - 1$ threads get the value RIGHT. (This is *not* symmetric with the proof for the previous item.)

```
1   class FastPath implements Lock {
2     private Lock lock;
3     private int x, y = -1;
4     public void lock() {
5       int i = ThreadID.get();
6       x = i;                    // I'm here
7       while (y != -1) {}        // is the lock free?
8       y = i;                    // me again?
9       if (x != i)               // Am I still here?
10        lock.lock();            // slow path
11    }
12    public void unlock() {
13      y = -1;
14      lock.unlock();
15    }
16  }
```

FIGURE 2.18

Fast-path mutual exclusion algorithm used in Exercise 2.8.

```
1   class Bouncer {
2     public static final int DOWN = 0;
3     public static final int RIGHT = 1;
4     public static final int STOP = 2;
5     private boolean goRight = false;
6     private int last = -1;
7     int visit() {
8       int i = ThreadID.get();
9       last = i;
10      if (goRight)
11        return RIGHT;
12      goRight = true;
13      if (last == i)
14        return STOP;
15      else
16        return DOWN;
17    }
18  }
```

FIGURE 2.19

The Bouncer class implementation for Exercise 2.9.

Exercise 2.10. So far, we have assumed that all n threads have small unique IDs. Here is one way to assign small unique IDs to threads. Arrange Bouncer objects in a triangular matrix, where each Bouncer is given an ID as shown in Fig. 2.20. Each

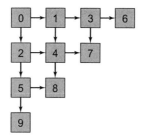

FIGURE 2.20

Array layout for Bouncer objects for Exercise 2.10.

thread starts by visiting Bouncer 0. If it gets STOP, it stops. If it gets RIGHT, it visits 1, and if it gets DOWN, it visits 2. In general, if a thread gets STOP, it stops. If it gets RIGHT, it visits the next Bouncer on that row, and if it gets DOWN, it visits the next Bouncer in that column. Each thread takes the ID of the Bouncer object where it stops.

- Prove that each thread eventually stops at some Bouncer object.
- How many Bouncer objects do you need in the array if you know in advance the total number n of threads?

Exercise 2.11. Prove, by way of a counterexample, that the sequential timestamp system T^3, starting in a valid state (with no cycles among the labels), does not work for three threads in the concurrent case. Note that it is not a problem to have two identical labels since one can break such ties using thread IDs. The counterexample should display a state of the execution where three labels are not totally ordered.

Exercise 2.12. The sequential timestamp system T^n had a range of $O(3^n)$ different possible label values. Design a sequential timestamp system that requires only $O(n2^n)$ labels. Note that in a timestamp system, one may look at all the labels to choose a new label, yet once a label is chosen, it should be comparable to any other label without knowing what the other labels in the system are. Hint: Think of the labels in terms of their bit representation.

Exercise 2.13. Give Java code to implement the Timestamp interface of Fig. 2.11 using unbounded labels. Then, show how to replace the pseudocode of the Bakery lock of Fig. 2.10 using your Timestamp Java code.

Exercise 2.14. We saw earlier the following theorem on the bounds of shared memory for mutual exclusion: Any deadlock-free mutual exclusion algorithm for n threads must use at least n shared registers. For this exercise, we examine a new algorithm that shows that the space lower bound of the above theorem is tight. Specifically, we will show the following:

> **Theorem**: There is a deadlock-free mutual exclusion algorithm for n threads that uses exactly n shared bits.

```
1   class OneBit implements Lock {
2     private boolean[] flag;
3     public OneBit (int n) {
4       flag = new boolean[n]; // all initially false
5     }
6     public void lock() {
7       int i = ThreadID.get();
8       do {
9         flag[i] = true;
10        for (int j = 0; j < i; j++) {
11          if (flag[j] == true) {
12            flag[i] = false;
13            while (flag[j] == true) {} // wait until flag[j] == false
14            break;
15          }
16        }
17      } while (flag[i] == false);
18      for (int j = i+1; j < n; j++) {
19        while (flag[j] == true) {} // wait until flag[j] == false
20      }
21    }
22    public void unlock() {
23      flag[ThreadID.get()] = false;
24    }
25  }
```

FIGURE 2.21

Pseudocode for the OneBit algorithm.

To prove this new theorem, we study the OneBit algorithm shown in Fig. 2.21. This algorithm, developed independently by J. E. Burns and L. Lamport, uses exactly n bits to achieve mutual exclusion; that is, it uses the minimum possible shared space.

The OneBit algorithm works as follows: First, a thread indicates that it wants to acquire the lock by setting its bit to *true*. Then, it loops and reads the bits of all threads with smaller IDs than its own. If all of these bits are *false* (while its own bit is *true*), then the thread exits the loop. Otherwise, the thread sets its bit to *false*, waits until the bit it found to be *true* becomes *false*, and starts all over again. Afterwards, the thread reads the bits of all threads that have IDs greater than its own, and waits until they are all *false*. Once this check passes, the thread can safely enter the critical section.

- Prove that the OneBit algorithm satisfies mutual exclusion.
- Prove that the OneBit algorithm is deadlock-free.

Concurrent objects

3

The behavior of concurrent objects is best described through their safety and liveness properties, often called *correctness* and *progress*. In this chapter, we examine various ways of specifying correctness and progress.

All notions of correctness for concurrent objects are based on some notion of equivalence with sequential behavior, but different notions are appropriate for different systems. We examine three correctness conditions. *Sequential consistency* is a strong condition, often useful for describing standalone systems such as hardware memory interfaces. *Linearizability* is an even stronger condition that supports *composition*: It is useful for describing systems composed from *linearizable* components. *Quiescent consistency* is appropriate for applications that require high performance at the cost of placing relatively weak constraints on object behavior.

Along a different dimension, different method implementations provide different progress guarantees. Some are *blocking*, where the delay of one thread can prevent other threads from making progress; some are *nonblocking*, where the delay of a thread cannot delay other threads indefinitely.

3.1 Concurrency and correctness

What does it mean for a concurrent object to be correct? Fig. 3.1 shows a simple lock-based concurrent "first-in-first-out" (FIFO) queue. The enq() and deq() methods synchronize using a mutual exclusion lock of the kind studied in Chapter 2. We immediately intuit that this implementation should be correct: Because each method holds an exclusive lock the entire time it accesses and updates fields, the method calls take effect sequentially.

This idea is illustrated in Fig. 3.2, which shows an execution in which thread A enqueues a, B enqueues b, and C dequeues twice, first throwing EmptyException, and second returning b. Overlapping intervals indicate concurrent method calls. All the method calls overlap in time. In this figure, as in others, time moves from left to right, and dark lines indicate intervals. The intervals for a single thread are displayed along a single horizontal line. When convenient, the thread name appears on the left. A bar represents an interval with a fixed start and stop time. A bar with dotted lines on the right represents an interval with a fixed start-time and an unknown stop-time. The label "q.enq(x)" means that a thread enqueues item x at object q, while "q.deq(x)" means that the thread dequeues item x from object q.

The Art of Multiprocessor Programming. https://doi.org/10.1016/B978-0-12-415950-1.00012-4

```
1   class LockBasedQueue<T> {
2     int head, tail;
3     T[] items;
4     Lock lock;
5     public LockBasedQueue(int capacity) {
6       head = 0; tail = 0;
7       lock = new ReentrantLock();
8       items = (T[])new Object[capacity];
9     }
10    public void enq(T x) throws FullException {
11      lock.lock();
12      try {
13        if (tail - head == items.length)
14          throw new FullException();
15        items[tail % items.length] = x;
16        tail++;
17      } finally {
18        lock.unlock();
19      }
20    }
21    public T deq() throws EmptyException {
22      lock.lock();
23      try {
24        if (tail == head)
25          throw new EmptyException();
26        T x = items[head % items.length];
27        head++;
28        return x;
29      } finally {
30        lock.unlock();
31      }
32    }
33  }
```

FIGURE 3.1

A lock-based FIFO queue. The queue's items are kept in an array items, where head is the index of the next item (if any) to dequeue, and tail is the index of the first open array slot (modulo the capacity). The lock field contains a lock that ensures that methods are mutually exclusive. Initially head and tail are zero, and the queue is empty. If enq() finds the queue is full (i.e., head and tail differ by the queue capacity), then it throws an exception. Otherwise, there is room, so enq() stores the item at array entry for tail, and then increments tail. The deq() method works in a symmetric way.

The timeline shows which thread holds the lock. Here, C acquires the lock, observes the queue to be empty, releases the lock, and throws an exception. It does not modify the queue. B acquires the lock, inserts b, and releases the lock. A acquires the lock, inserts a, and releases the lock. C reacquires the lock, dequeues b, releases the

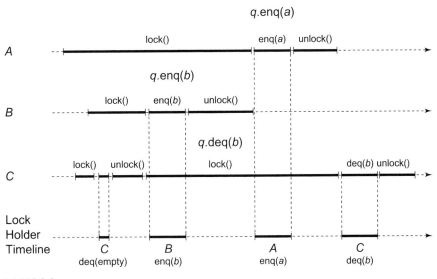

FIGURE 3.2

Lock-based queue execution. Here, C acquires the lock, observes the queue to be empty, releases the lock, and throws an exception. B acquires the lock, inserts b, and releases the lock. A acquires the lock, inserts a, and releases the lock. C reacquires the lock, dequeues b, releases the lock, and returns b.

lock, and returns b. Each of these calls takes effect sequentially, and we can easily verify that dequeuing b before a is consistent with our understanding of sequential FIFO queue behavior.

Unfortunately, it follows from Amdahl's law (Chapter 1) that concurrent objects whose methods hold exclusive locks, and therefore effectively execute one after the other, are less desirable than ones with finer-grained locking or no locks at all. We therefore need a way to specify the behavior required of concurrent objects, and to reason about their implementations, without relying on method-level locking.

Consider the alternative concurrent queue implementation in Fig. 3.3. It has almost the same internal representation as the lock-based queue of Fig. 3.1; the only difference is the absence of a lock. We claim that this implementation is correct provided there is only a single enqueuer and a single dequeuer. But it is no longer easy to explain why. If the queue supported concurrent enqueues or concurrent dequeues, it would not even be clear what it means for a queue *to be FIFO*.

The lock-based queue example illustrates a useful principle: It is easier to reason about the behavior of concurrent objects if we can somehow map their concurrent executions to sequential ones, and otherwise limit our reasoning to these sequential executions. This principle is the key to the correctness properties introduced in this chapter. Therefore, we begin by considering specifications of sequential objects.

```
1   class WaitFreeQueue<T> {
2     int head = 0, tail = 0;
3     T[] items;
4     public WaitFreeQueue(int capacity) {
5       items = (T[]) new Object[capacity];
6     }
7     public void enq(T x) throws FullException {
8       if (tail - head == items.length)
9         throw new FullException();
10      items[tail % items.length] = x;
11      tail++;
12    }
13    public T deq() throws EmptyException {
14      if (tail - head == 0)
15        throw new EmptyException();
16      T x = items[head % items.length];
17      head++;
18      return x;
19    }
20  }
```

FIGURE 3.3

A single-enqueuer/single-dequeuer FIFO queue. The structure is identical to that of the lock-based FIFO queue, except that there is no need for the lock to coordinate access.

3.2 Sequential objects

An *object* in languages such as Java and C++ is a container for data and a set of *methods*, which are the only way to manipulate those data. Each object has a *class*, which defines the object's methods and how they behave. An object has a well-defined *state* (for example, the FIFO queue's current sequence of items). There are many ways to describe how an object's methods behave, ranging from formal specifications to plain English. The application program interface (API) documentation that we use every day lies somewhere in between.

The API documentation typically says something like the following: If the object is in such-and-such a state before you call the method, then the object will be in some other state when the method returns, and the call will return a particular value, or throw a particular exception. This kind of description divides naturally into a *precondition*, which describes the object's state before invoking the method, and a *postcondition*, which describes the object's state and return value when the method returns. A change to an object's state is sometimes called a *side effect*.

For example, a FIFO queue might be described as follows: The class provides two methods, enq() and deq(). The queue state is a sequence of items, possibly empty. If the queue state is a sequence q (precondition), then a call to enq(z) leaves the queue in state $q \cdot z$ (postcondition with side effect), where "$\cdot$" denotes concatenation. If the queue object is nonempty, say, $a \cdot q$ (precondition), then the deq() method removes the sequence's first element a, leaving the queue in state q, and returns this element (postcondition). If, instead, the queue object is empty (precondition), the method throws EmptyException and leaves the queue state unchanged (postcondition, no side effect).

This style of documentation, called a *sequential specification*, is so familiar that it is easy to overlook how elegant and powerful it is. The length of the object's documentation is linear in the number of methods, because each method can be described in isolation. There are a vast number of potential interactions among methods, and all such interactions are characterized succinctly by the methods' side effects on the object state. The object's documentation describes the object state before and after each call, and we can safely ignore any intermediate states that the object may assume while the method call is in progress.

Defining objects in terms of preconditions and postconditions makes sense in a *sequential* model of computation, where a single thread manipulates a collection of objects. But this familiar style of documentation fails for objects shared by multiple threads. If an object's methods can be invoked concurrently by multiple threads, then method calls can overlap in time, and it no longer makes sense to talk about their order. What does it mean, for example, if x and y are enqueued onto a FIFO queue during overlapping intervals? Which will be dequeued first? Can we continue to describe methods in isolation, via preconditions and postconditions, or must we provide explicit descriptions of every possible interaction among every possible collection of concurrent method calls?

Even the notion of an object's state becomes confusing. In a single-threaded program, an object must assume a meaningful state only between method calls.[1] In a multithreaded program, however, overlapping method calls may be in progress at every instant, so a concurrent object might *never* be between method calls. Every method call must be prepared to encounter an object state that reflects the incomplete effects of concurrent method calls, a problem that does not arise in single-threaded programs.

3.3 Sequential consistency

One way to develop an intuition about how concurrent objects should behave is to review examples of concurrent computations involving simple objects, and decide, in each case, whether the behavior agrees with our intuition about how the objects should behave.

Method calls take time. A *method call* is the interval that starts with an *invocation* event and continues until the corresponding *response* event, if any. Method calls by

---

[1] There is an exception: Care must be taken if one method partially changes an object's state and then calls another method of that same object.

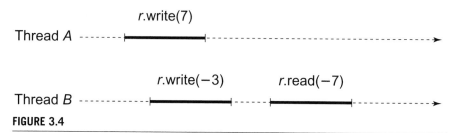

FIGURE 3.4

Why each method call should appear to take effect in one-at-a-time order. Two threads concurrently write −3 and 7 to a shared register r. Later, one thread reads r and returns the value −7. We expect to find either 7 or −3 in the register, not a mixture of both.

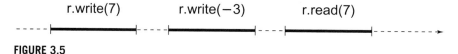

FIGURE 3.5

Why method calls should appear to take effect in program order. This behavior is not acceptable because the value the thread read is not the last value it wrote (and no other thread writes to the register).

concurrent threads may overlap, while method calls by a single thread are always sequential (nonoverlapping, one-after-the-other). We say a method call is *pending* if its invocation event has occurred, but its response event has not.

For historical reasons, the object version of a read–write memory location is called a *register* (see Chapter 4). In Fig. 3.4, two threads concurrently write −3 and 7 to a shared register r (as before, "r.read(x)" means that a thread reads value x from register object r, and similarly for "r.write(x)"). Later, one thread reads r and returns the value −7. This behavior is surprising. We expect to find either 7 or −3 in the register, not a mixture of both. This example suggests the following principle:

Principle 3.3.1. Method calls should appear to happen in a one-at-a-time, sequential order.

By itself, this principle is too weak to be useful. For example, it permits reads to always return the object's initial state, even in sequential executions (i.e., executions in which method calls do not overlap). Or consider the execution in Fig. 3.5, in which a single thread writes 7 and then −3 to a shared register r. Later, it reads r and returns 7. For some applications, this behavior might not be acceptable because the value the thread read is not the value it wrote most recently. The order in which a single thread issues method calls is called its *program order*. (Method calls by different threads are unrelated by program order.) In this example, we were surprised that operation calls did not take effect in program order. This example suggests the following principle:

Principle 3.3.2. Method calls should appear to take effect in program order.

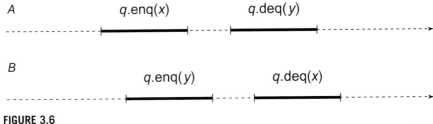

FIGURE 3.6

There are two possible sequential orders that can justify this execution. Both orders are consistent with the method calls' program order, and either one is enough to show that the execution is sequentially consistent.

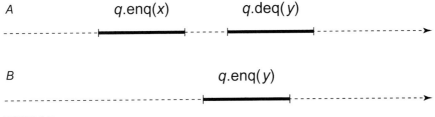

FIGURE 3.7

Sequential consistency versus real-time order. Thread A enqueues x, and later thread B enqueues y, and finally A dequeues y. This execution may violate our intuitive notion of how a FIFO queue should behave because the method call enqueuing x finishes before the method call enqueuing y starts, so y is enqueued after x. But it is dequeued before x. Nevertheless, this execution is sequentially consistent.

This principle ensures that purely sequential computations behave the way we expect. Together, Principles 3.3.1 and 3.3.2 define *sequential consistency*, a correctness condition that is widely used in the literature on multiprocessor synchronization.

Sequential consistency requires that method calls act as if they occurred in a sequential order consistent with program order. That is, there is a way to order all the method calls in any concurrent execution so that they (1) are consistent with program order and (2) meet the object's sequential specification. Multiple sequential orders may satisfy these conditions. For example, in Fig. 3.6, thread A enqueues x while thread B enqueues y, and then A dequeues y while B dequeues x. Two sequential orders explain these results: (1) A enqueues x, B enqueues y, B dequeues x, and then A dequeues y, or (2) B enqueues y, A enqueues x, A dequeues y, and then B dequeues x. Both orders are consistent with the program order; either suffices to show that the execution is sequentially consistent.

3.3.1 Sequential consistency versus real-time order

In Fig. 3.7, thread A enqueues x, and later B enqueues y, and finally A dequeues y. This execution may violate our intuitive notion of how a FIFO queue should behave:

The call enqueuing x finishes before the call enqueuing y starts, so y is enqueued after x. But it is dequeued before x. Nevertheless, this execution is sequentially consistent. Even though the call that enqueues x happens before the call that enqueues y, these calls are unrelated by program order, so sequential consistency is free to reorder them. When one operation completes before another begins, we say that the first operation precedes the second in the *real-time order*. This example shows that sequential consistency need not preserve the real-time order.

One could argue whether it is acceptable to reorder method calls whose intervals do not overlap, even if they occur in different threads. For example, we might be unhappy if we deposit our paycheck on Monday, but the bank bounces our rent check the following Friday because it reordered our deposit after your withdrawal.

3.3.2 Sequential consistency is nonblocking

How much does sequential consistency limit concurrency? Specifically, under what circumstances does sequential consistency require one method call to block waiting for another to complete? Perhaps surprisingly, the answer is (essentially) *never*. More precisely, for any pending method call in a sequentially consistent concurrent execution, there is some sequentially consistent response, that is, a response to the invocation that could be given immediately without violating sequential consistency. We say that a correctness condition with this property is *nonblocking*. Sequential consistency is a *nonblocking* correctness condition.

Note that this observation does not mean that it is easy to figure out a sequentially consistent response for a pending method call, only that the correctness condition itself does not stand in the way. The observation holds only for *total methods*, which

---

REMARK 3.3.1

The term *nonblocking* is used to denote several different notions. In this context, referring to correctness conditions, it means that for any pending call of a total method, there is a response that satisfies the correctness condition. In Section 3.8, referring to progress conditions, it means that a progress condition guarantees that the delay of one or more threads cannot prevent other threads from making progress. When referring to an object implementation, it means that the implementation meets a nonblocking progress condition. (It may even be used with finer granularity, referring to an individual method of an object implementation that cannot be prevented from making progress by the delay of other threads.) In the systems literature, a *nonblocking* operation returns immediately without waiting for the operation to take effect, whereas a *blocking* operation does not return until the operation is complete. (*Blocking* is also used to describe a lock implementation that suspends a thread that tries to acquire a lock that is held by another thread, as opposed to *spinning* implementations, which we discuss in Chapter 7). Unfortunately, these various uses are all too well established to change, but it should be clear from the context which meaning is intended.

are defined for every object state (i.e., for any state on which a total method is invoked, there is some response allowed by the sequential specification). There is, of course, no sequentially consistent response to a method call if there is no response that satisfies the sequential specification. Our informal description of sequential consistency thus far is not sufficient to capture this and other important details, such as what it exactly means for an execution with pending method calls to be sequentially consistent. We make this notion more precise in Section 3.6.

3.3.3 Compositionality

Any sufficiently complex system must be designed and implemented in a *modular* fashion. Components are designed, implemented, and proved correct independently. Each component makes a clear distinction between its *implementation*, which is hidden, and its *interface*, which characterizes the guarantees it makes to the other components. For example, if a concurrent object's interface states that it is a sequentially consistent FIFO queue, then users of the queue need not know anything about how the queue is implemented. The result of composing individually correct components that rely only on one another's interfaces should itself be a correct system.

A correctness property P is *compositional* if, whenever each object in the system satisfies P, the system as a whole satisfies P. Compositionality is important because it enables a system to be assembled easily from independently derived components. A system based on a noncompositional correctness property cannot rely solely on its components' interfaces: Some kind of additional constraints are needed to ensure that the components are actually compatible.

Is sequential consistency compositional? That is, is the result of composing multiple sequentially consistent objects itself sequentially consistent? The answer, unfortunately, is *no*. In Fig. 3.8, two threads, A and B, call enqueue and dequeue methods for two queue objects, p and q. It is not hard to see that p and q are each sequentially consistent: The sequence of method calls for p is the same as in the sequentially consistent execution shown in Fig. 3.7, and the behavior of q is symmetric. Nevertheless, the execution as a whole is *not* sequentially consistent.

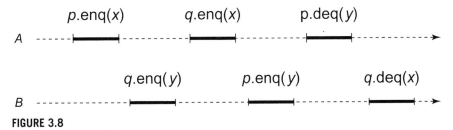

FIGURE 3.8

Sequential consistency is not compositional. Two threads, *A* and *B*, call enqueue and dequeue methods on two queue objects, *p* and *q*. It is not hard to see that *p* and *q* are each sequentially consistent, yet the execution as a whole is *not* sequentially consistent.

To see that there is no correct sequential execution of these methods calls that is consistent with their program order, assume, by way of contradiction, that there is such an execution. We use the following shorthand: $\langle p.\text{enq}(x)\ A \rangle \to \langle p.\text{deq}()x\ B \rangle$ means that any sequential execution must order A's enqueue of x at p before B's dequeue of x at p, and so on. Because p is FIFO and A dequeues y from p, y must have been enqueued at p before x:

$$\langle p.\text{enq}(y)\ B \rangle \to \langle p.\text{enq}(x)\ A \rangle.$$

Similarly, x must have been enqueued onto q before y:

$$\langle q.\text{enq}(x)\ A \rangle \to \langle q.\text{enq}(y)\ B \rangle.$$

But program order implies that

$$\langle p.\text{enq}(x)\ A \rangle \to \langle q.\text{enq}(x)\ A \rangle \quad \text{and} \quad \langle q.\text{enq}(y)\ B \rangle \to \langle p.\text{enq}(y)\ B \rangle.$$

Together, these orderings form a cycle.

3.4 Linearizability

Sequential consistency has a serious drawback: it is not compositional. That is, the result of composing sequentially consistent components is not itself necessarily sequentially consistent. To fix this shortcoming, we replace the requirement that method calls appear to happen in program order with the following stronger constraint:

Principle 3.4.1. Each method call should appear to take effect instantaneously at some moment between its invocation and response.

This principle states that the real-time order of method calls must be preserved. We call this correctness property *linearizability*. Every linearizable execution is sequentially consistent, but not vice versa.

3.4.1 Linearization points

The usual way to show that a concurrent object implementation is linearizable is to identify for each method a *linearization point*, an instant when the method takes effect. We say that a method *is linearized at* its linearization point. For lock-based implementations, any point within each method's critical section can serve as its linearization point. For implementations that do not use locks, the linearization point is typically a single step where the effects of the method call become visible to other method calls.

For example, recall the single-enqueuer/single-dequeuer queue of Fig. 3.3. This implementation has no critical sections, and yet we can identify linearization points for its methods. For example, if a deq() method returns an item, its linearization point is when the head field is updated (line 17). If the queue is empty, the deq() method is linearized when it reads the tail field (line 14). The enq() method is similar.

3.4.2 Linearizability versus sequential consistency

Like sequential consistency, linearizability is nonblocking: There is a linearizable response to any pending call of a total method. In this way, linearizability does not limit concurrency.

Threads that communicate only through a single shared object (e.g., the memory of a shared-memory multiprocessor) cannot distinguish between sequential consistency and linearizability. Only an external observer, who can see that one operation precedes another in the real-time order, can tell that a sequentially consistent object is not linearizable. For this reason, the difference between sequential consistency and linearizability is sometimes called *external consistency*. Sequential consistency is a good way to describe standalone systems, where composition is not an issue. However, if the threads share multiple objects, these objects may be external observers for each other, as we saw in Fig. 3.8.

Unlike sequential consistency, linearizability is compositional: The result of composing linearizable objects is linearizable. For this reason, linearizability is a good way to describe components of large systems, where components must be implemented and verified independently. Because we are interested in systems that compose, most (but not all) data structures considered in this book are linearizable.

3.5 Quiescent consistency

For some systems, implementors may be willing to trade consistency for performance. That is, we may relax the consistency condition to allow cheaper, faster, and/or more efficient implementations. One way to relax consistency is to enforce ordering only when an object is *quiescent*, that is, when it has no pending method calls. Instead of Principles 3.3.2 and 3.4.1, we would adopt the following principle:

Principle 3.5.1. Method calls separated by a period of quiescence should appear to take effect in their real-time order.

For example, suppose A and B concurrently enqueue x and y in a FIFO queue. The queue becomes quiescent, and then C enqueues z. We are not able to predict the relative order of x and y in the queue, but we do know they are ahead of z.

Together, Principles 3.3.1 and 3.5.1 define a correctness property called *quiescent consistency*. Informally, it says that any time an object becomes quiescent, the execution so far is equivalent to some sequential execution of the completed calls.

As an example of quiescent consistency, consider the shared counter from Chapter 1. A quiescently consistent shared counter would return numbers, not necessarily in the order of the getAndIncrement() requests, but always without duplicating or omitting a number. The execution of a quiescently consistent object is somewhat like a game of musical chairs: At any point, the music might stop, that is, the state could become quiescent. At that point, each pending method call must return an index so that all the indices together meet the specification of a sequential counter, implying no duplicated or omitted numbers. In other words, a quiescently consistent counter is an *index distribution* mechanism, useful as a "loop counter" in programs that do not care about the order in which indices are issued.

3.5.1 Properties of quiescent consistency

Note that sequential consistency and quiescent consistency are *incomparable*: There exist sequentially consistent executions that are not quiescently consistent, and vice versa. Quiescent consistency does not necessarily preserve program order, and sequential consistency is unaffected by quiescent periods. On the other hand, linearizability is stronger than both quiescent consistency and sequential consistency. That is, a linearizable object is both quiescently consistent and sequentially consistent.

Like sequential consistency and linearizability, quiescent consistency is nonblocking: Any pending call to a total method in a quiescently consistent execution can be completed.

Quiescent consistency is compositional: A system composed of quiescently consistent objects is itself quiescently consistent. It follows that quiescently consistent objects can be composed to construct more complex quiescently consistent objects. It is interesting to consider whether we could build useful systems using quiescent consistency rather than linearizability as the fundamental correctness property, and how the design of such systems would differ from existing system designs.

3.6 Formal definitions

We now consider more precise definitions. We focus on linearizability, since it is the property most often used in this book. We leave it as an exercise to provide analogous definitions for quiescent consistency and sequential consistency.

Informally, a concurrent object is linearizable if each method call appears to take effect instantaneously at some moment between that method's invocation and return events. This statement suffices for most informal reasoning, but a more precise formulation is needed to cover some tricky cases (such as method calls that have not returned), and for more rigorous styles of argument.

3.6.1 Histories

We model the observable behavior of an execution of a concurrent system by a sequence of *events* called a *history*, where an event is an *invocation* or *response* of a method. We write a method invocation as $\langle x.m(a^*) \, A \rangle$, where x is an object, m is a method name, a^* is a sequence of arguments, and A is a thread. We write a method response as $\langle x : t(r^*) \, A \rangle$, where t is either OK or an exception name, and r^* is a sequence of result values.

An invocation and a response *match* if they name the same object and thread. An invocation in H is *pending* if no matching response follows the invocation. A *method call* in a history H is a pair consisting of an invocation and either the next matching response in H or a special $\perp$ value (pronounced "bottom") if the invocation is pending (i.e., if there is no subsequent matching response). We say that a method call is *pending* if its invocation is pending, and that it is *complete* otherwise. A history is complete if all its method calls are complete. For a history H, we denote the subsequence of H consisting of all events of complete method calls (i.e., eliding all the pending invocations of H) by *complete(H)*.

The *interval* of a method call in a history H is the history's sequence of events starting from its invocation and ending with its response, or the suffix of H starting from its invocation if the method call is pending. Two method calls *overlap* if their intervals overlap.

A history is *sequential* if its first event is an invocation, and each invocation, except possibly the last, is followed immediately by a matching response, and each response is immediately preceded by an invocation. No method calls overlap in a sequential history, and a sequential history has at most one pending invocation.

A *subhistory* of a history H is a subsequence of H. Sometimes we focus on a single thread or object: A *thread subhistory*, $H|A$ ("H at A"), of a history H is the subsequence of all events in H whose thread names are A. An *object subhistory* $H|x$ is similarly defined for an object x. We require each thread to complete each method call before calling another method: A history H is *well formed* if each thread subhistory is sequential. Henceforth, we consider only well-formed histories. Although thread subhistories of a well-formed history are always sequential, object subhistories need not be; method calls to the same object may overlap in a well-formed history. Finally, because what matters in the end is how each thread views the history, we say that two histories are *equivalent* if every thread has the same thread subhistory in both histories; that is, H and H' are equivalent if $H|A = H'|A$ for every thread A.

How can we tell whether a concurrent object is correct? Or, said differently, how do we define correctness for a concurrent object? The basic idea is to require a concurrent execution to be equivalent, in some sense, to some sequential history; the exact sense of equivalence is different for different correctness properties. We assume that we can tell whether a sequential object is correct, that is, whether a sequential object history is a legal history for the object's class. A *sequential specification* for an object is just a set of legal sequential histories for the object. A sequential history H is *legal* if each object subhistory is legal for that object.

A method m of an object x is *total* if for every finite complete history H in the sequential specification of x and every invocation $\langle x.m(a^*)\ A \rangle$ of m, there is a response $\langle x : t(r^*)\ A \rangle$ such that $H \cdot \langle x.m(a^*)\ A \rangle \cdot \langle x : t(r^*)\ A \rangle$ is in the sequential specification of x. A method is *partial* if it is not total.

3.6.2 Linearizability

A key concept in defining linearizability is the *real-time order* of a history. Recall that a *(strict) partial order* $\to$ on a set X is a relation that is irreflexive and transitive. That is, it is never true that $x \to x$, and whenever $x \to y$ and $y \to z$, then $x \to z$.

Note that there may be distinct x and y such that neither $x \to y$ nor $y \to x$. A *total order* $<$ on X is a partial order such that for all distinct x and y in X, either $x < y$ or $y < x$.

Any partial order can be extended to a total order.

Fact 3.6.1. If $\to$ is a partial order on X, then there exists a total order $<$ on X such that if $x \to y$ then $x < y$.

We say that a method call m_0 *precedes* a method call m_1 in history H if m_0 finishes before m_1 starts, that is, if m_0's response event occurs before m_1's invocation event in H. This notion is important enough to introduce some shorthand notation: Given a history H containing method calls m_0 and m_1, we write $m_0 \to_H m_1$ if m_0 precedes m_1 in H. We leave it as an exercise to show that $\to_H$ is a partial order. Note that if H is sequential, then $\to_H$ is a total order. Given a history H and an object x such that $H|x$ contains method calls m_0 and m_1, when H is clear from the context, we write $m_0 \to_x m_1$ if m_0 precedes m_1 in $H|x$.

For linearizability, the basic rule is that if one method call precedes another, then the earlier call must take effect before the later call (each call must linearize within its interval, and the interval of the earlier interval is entirely in front of the interval of the later call). By contrast, if two method calls overlap, then their order is ambiguous, and we are free to order them in any convenient way.

Definition 3.6.2. A legal sequential history S is a *linearization* of a history H if H can be extended to a history H' by appending zero or more responses such that:

L1 *complete*(H') is equivalent to S, and
L2 if method call m_0 precedes method call m_1 in H, then the same is true in S (i.e., $m_0 \to_H m_q$ implies $m_0 \to_S m_1$).

H is *linearizable* if there is a linearization of H.

Informally, extending H to H' captures the idea that some pending invocations may have taken effect, even though their responses have not yet been returned to the caller. Fig. 3.9 illustrates the notion: We must complete the pending enq(x) method call to justify the deq() call that returns x. The second condition says that if one method call precedes another in the original history, then that ordering must be preserved in the linearization.

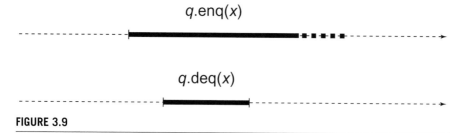

FIGURE 3.9

The pending enq(x) method call must take effect early to justify the deq() call that returns x.

3.6.3 **Linearizability is compositional**

Linearizability is compositional.

Theorem 3.6.3. H is linearizable if, and only if, for each object x, $H|x$ is linearizable.

Proof. The "only if" part is left as an exercise.

For each object x, pick a linearization of $H|x$. Let R_x be the set of responses appended to $H|x$ to construct that linearization, and let $\to_x$ be the corresponding linearization order. Let H' be the history constructed by appending to H each response in R_x (the order in which they are appended does not matter).

We argue by induction on the number of method calls in H'. For the base case, if H' contains no method calls, we are done. Otherwise, assume the claim for every H' containing fewer than $k \geq 1$ method calls. For each object x, consider the last method call in $H'|x$. One of these calls m must be maximal with respect to $\to_H$; that is, there is no m' such that $m \to_H m'$. Let G' be the history defined by removing m from H'. Because m is maximal, H' is equivalent to $G' \cdot m$. By the induction hypothesis, G' is linearizable to a sequential history S', and both H' and H are linearizable to $S' \cdot m$. $\qquad\square$

3.6.4 **Linearizability is nonblocking**

Linearizability is a *nonblocking* property: A pending invocation of a total method is never required to wait for another pending invocation to complete.

Theorem 3.6.4. If m is a total method of an object x and $\langle x.m(a^*)\ P\rangle$ is a pending invocation in a linearizable history H, then there exists a response $\langle x : t(r^*)\ P\rangle$ such that $H \cdot \langle x : t(r^*)\ P\rangle$ is linearizable.

Proof. Let S be any linearization of H. If S includes a response $\langle x : t(r^*)\ P\rangle$ to $\langle x.m(a^*)\ P\rangle$, we are done, since S is also a linearization of $H \cdot \langle x : t(r^*)\ P\rangle$. Otherwise, $\langle x.m(a^*)\ P\rangle$ does not appear in S either, since a linearization, by definition, has no pending invocations. Because the method is total, there exists a response $\langle x : t(r^*)\ P\rangle$ such that

$$S' = S \cdot \langle x.m(a^*)\ P\rangle \cdot \langle x : t(r^*)\ P\rangle$$

is a legal sequential history. S' is a linearization of $H \cdot \langle x : t(r^*)\ P\rangle$, and hence is also a linearization of H. $\qquad\square$

This theorem implies that linearizability by itself never forces a thread with a pending invocation of a total method to block. Of course, blocking (or even deadlock) may occur as artifacts of particular implementations of linearizability, but it is not inherent to the correctness property itself. This theorem suggests that linearizability is an appropriate correctness property for systems where concurrency and real-time response are important.

The nonblocking property does not rule out blocking in situations where it is explicitly intended. For example, it may be sensible for a thread attempting to dequeue from an empty queue to block, waiting until another thread enqueues an item. A queue specification would capture this intention by making the deq() method's specification partial, leaving its effect undefined when applied to an empty queue. The most natural concurrent interpretation of a partial sequential specification is simply to wait until the object reaches a state in which that method call's response is defined.

3.7 Memory consistency models

We can consider the memory read and written by a program as a single object—the composition of many registers—shared by all threads of the program. This shared memory is often the only means of communication among threads (i.e., the only way that threads can observe the effects of other threads). Its correctness property is called the *memory consistency model*, or *memory model* for short.

Early concurrent programs assumed sequentially consistent memory. Indeed, the notion of sequential consistency was introduced to capture the assumptions implicit in those programs. However, the memory of most modern multiprocessor systems is *not* sequentially consistent: Compilers and hardware may reorder memory reads and writes in complex ways. Most of the time no one can tell, because the vast majority of reads and writes are not used for synchronization. These systems also provide synchronization primitives that inhibit reordering.

We follow this approach in the first part of this book, where we focus on the principles of multiprocessor programming. For example, the pseudocode for the various lock algorithms in Chapter 2 assumes that if a thread writes two locations, one after the other, then the two writes are made visible to other threads in the same order, so that any thread that sees the later write will also see the earlier write. However, Java does not guarantee this ordering for ordinary reads and writes. As mentioned in Pragma 2.3.1, these locations would need to be declared **volatile** to work in real systems. We omit these declarations because these algorithms are not practical in any case, and the declarations would clutter the code and obscure the ideas embodied in those algorithms. In the second part of the book, where we discuss practical algorithms, we include these declarations. (We describe the Java memory model in Appendix A.3.)

3.8 Progress conditions

The nonblocking property of linearizability (and sequential consistency and quiescent consistency) ensures that any pending invocation has a correct response. But linearizability does not tell us how to compute such a response, nor even require an implementation to produce a response at all. Consider, for example, the lock-based queue shown in Fig. 3.1. Suppose the queue is initially empty, and thread A halts halfway through enqueuing x, while holding the lock, and B then invokes deq(). The nonblocking property guarantees that there is a correct response to B's call to deq(); indeed, there are two: It could throw an exception or return x. In this implementation, however, B is unable to acquire the lock, and will be delayed as long as A is delayed.

Such an implementation is called *blocking*, because delaying one thread can prevent others from making progress. Unexpected thread delays are common in multiprocessors. A cache miss might delay a processor for a hundred cycles, a page fault for a few million cycles, preemption by the operating system for hundreds of millions of cycles. These delays depend on the specifics of the machine and the operating system. The part of the system that determines when threads take steps is called the *scheduler*, and the order in which threads take steps is the *schedule*.

In this section, we consider *progress conditions*, which require implementations to produce responses to pending invocations. Ideally, we would like to say simply that every pending invocation gets a response. Of course, this is not possible if the threads with pending invocations stop taking steps. So we require progress only for those threads that keep taking steps.

3.8.1 Wait-freedom

A method of an object implementation is *wait-free* if every call finishes its execution in a finite number of steps; that is, if a thread with a pending invocation to a wait-free method keeps taking steps, it completes in a finite number of steps. We say that an object implementation is *wait-free* if all its methods are wait-free, and that a class is *wait-free* if every object of that class is wait-free.

The queue shown in Fig. 3.3 is wait-free. For example, if B invokes deq() while A is halted halfway through enqueuing x, then B will either throw EmptyException (if A halted before incrementing tail) or it will return x (if A halted afterward). In contrast, the lock-based queue is not wait-free because B may take an unbounded number of steps unsuccessfully trying to acquire the lock.

We say that wait-freedom is a *nonblocking* progress condition[2] because a wait-free implementation cannot be blocking: An arbitrary delay by one thread (say, one holding a lock) cannot prevent other threads from making progress.

3.8.2 Lock-freedom

Wait-freedom is attractive because it guarantees that every thread that takes steps makes progress. However, wait-free algorithms can be inefficient, and sometimes we are willing to settle for a weaker progress guarantee.

One way to relax the progress condition is to guarantee progress only to *some* thread, rather than *every* thread. A method of an object implementation is *lock-free* if executing the method guarantees that *some* method call finishes in a finite number of

---

[2] See Remark 3.3.1 for various ways in which the term *nonblocking* is used.

steps; that is, if a thread with a pending invocation to a lock-free method keeps taking steps, then within a finite number of its steps, some pending call to a method of that object (not necessarily the lock-free method) completes. An object implementation is *lock-free* if all its methods are lock-free. We say that lock-freedom guarantees *minimal progress* because executing a lock-free method guarantees that the system as a whole makes progress, but not that any thread in particular makes progress. In contrast, wait-freedom guarantees *maximal progress*: Every thread that keeps taking steps makes progress.

Clearly, any wait-free method implementation is also lock-free, but not vice versa. Although lock-freedom is weaker than wait-freedom, if a program executes only a finite number of method calls, then lock-freedom is equivalent to wait-freedom for that program.

Lock-free algorithms admit the possibility that some threads could starve. As a practical matter, there are many situations in which starvation, while possible, is extremely unlikely, so a fast lock-free algorithm may be preferable to a slower wait-free algorithm. We consider several lock-free concurrent objects in later chapters.

Lock-freedom is also a nonblocking progress condition: A delayed thread does not prevent other threads from making progress as long as the system as a whole keeps taking steps.

3.8.3 Obstruction-freedom

Another way to relax the progress condition is to guarantee progress only under certain assumptions about how threads are scheduled, that is, about the order in which threads take steps. For example, an implementation may guarantee progress only if no other threads actively interfere with it. We say that a thread executes *in isolation* in an interval if no other threads take steps in that interval. A method of an object implementation is *obstruction-free* if, from any point after which it executes in isolation, it finishes in a finite number of steps; that is, if a thread with a pending invocation to an obstruction-free method executes in isolation from any point (not necessarily from its invocation), it completes in a finite number of steps.

Like other nonblocking progress conditions, obstruction-freedom ensures that a thread cannot be blocked by the delay of other threads. Obstruction-freedom guarantees progress to every thread that executes in isolation, so like wait-freedom, it guarantees maximal progress.

By guaranteeing progress only when one thread is scheduled to execute in isolation (i.e., preventing other threads from taking steps concurrently), obstruction-freedom seems to defy most operating system schedulers, which try to ensure a schedule in which every thread keeps taking steps (such a schedule is called *fair*). In practice, however, there is no problem. Ensuring progress for an obstruction-free method does not require pausing all other threads, only those threads that *conflict*, meaning those that are executing method calls on the same object. In later chapters, we consider a variety of *contention management techniques* to reduce or eliminate conflicting concurrent method calls. The simplest such technique is to introduce a *back-off* mechanism: a thread that detects a conflict pauses to give an earlier thread time to finish. Choosing when to back off, and for how long, is discussed in detail in Chapter 7.

3.8.4 **Blocking progress conditions**

In Chapter 2, we defined two progress conditions for lock implementations: *deadlock-freedom* and *starvation-freedom*. Analogous to lock-freedom and wait-freedom, respectively, deadlock-freedom guarantees that some thread makes progress and starvation-freedom guarantees that every thread makes progress *provided the lock is not held by some other thread*. The caveat that the lock is not held is necessary because, while one thread holds the lock, no other thread can acquire it without violating mutual exclusion, the correctness property for locks. To guarantee progress, we must also assume that a thread holding a lock will eventually release it. This assumption has two parts: (a) Each thread that acquires the lock must release it after a finite number of steps, and (b) the scheduler must allow a thread holding the lock to keep taking steps.

We can generalize deadlock-freedom and starvation-freedom to concurrent objects by making a similar assumption for threads executing method calls. Specifically, we assume that the scheduler is fair; that is, it allows every thread with a pending method call to take steps. (The first part of the assumption must be guaranteed by the concurrent object implementation.) We say that a method of an object implementation is *starvation-free* if it completes in a finite number of steps provided that every thread with a pending method call keeps taking steps. We say that a method of an object implementation is *deadlock-free* if, whenever there is a pending call to that method and every thread with a pending method call keeps taking steps, some method call completes in a finite number of steps.

Deadlock-freedom and starvation-freedom are useful progress conditions when the operating system guarantees that every thread keeps taking steps, and particularly that each thread takes a step *in a timely manner*. We say these properties are *blocking progress conditions* because they admit blocking implementations where the delay of a single thread can prevent all other threads from making progress.

A class whose methods rely on lock-based synchronization can guarantee, at best, a blocking progress condition. Does this observation mean that lock-based algorithms should be avoided? Not necessarily. If preemption in the middle of a critical section is sufficiently rare, then blocking progress conditions may be effectively indistinguishable from their nonblocking counterparts. If preemption is common enough to cause concern, or if the cost of preemption-based delay is sufficiently high, then it is sensible to consider nonblocking progress conditions.

3.8.5 **Characterizing progress conditions**

We now consider the various progress conditions and how they relate to one another. For example, wait-freedom and lock-freedom guarantee progress no matter how threads are scheduled. We say that they are *independent* progress conditions.

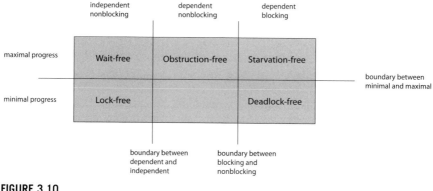

FIGURE 3.10

Progress conditions and their properties.

By contrast, obstruction-freedom, starvation-freedom, and deadlock-freedom are all *dependent* progress conditions, where progress is guaranteed only if the underlying operating system satisfies certain properties: fair scheduling for starvation-freedom and deadlock-freedom, isolated execution for obstruction-freedom. Also, as we already discussed, wait-freedom, lock-freedom, and obstruction-freedom are all nonblocking progress conditions, whereas starvation-freedom and deadlock-freedom are blocking.

We can also characterize these progress conditions by whether they guarantee maximal or minimal progress under their respective system assumptions: Wait-freedom, starvation-freedom, and obstruction-freedom guarantee maximal progress, whereas lock-freedom and deadlock-freedom guarantee only minimal progress.

Fig. 3.10 summarizes this discussion with a table that shows the various progress conditions and their properties. There is a "hole" in this table because any condition that guarantees minimal progress to threads that execute in isolation also guarantees maximal progress to these threads.

Picking a progress condition for a concurrent object implementation depends on both the needs of the application and the characteristics of the underlying platform. Wait-freedom and lock-freedom have strong theoretical properties, they work on just about any platform, and they provide guarantees useful to real-time applications such as music, electronic games, and other interactive applications. The dependent obstruction-free, deadlock-free, and starvation-free properties rely on guarantees provided by the underlying platform. Given those guarantees, however, the dependent properties often admit simpler and more efficient implementations.

3.9 Remarks

Which correctness condition is right for your application? It depends on your application's needs. A lightly loaded printer server might be satisfied with a quiescently consistent queue of jobs, since the order in which documents are printed is of little importance. A banking server that must execute customer requests in program order (e.g., transfer $100 from savings to checking, then write a check for $50), might require a sequentially consistent queue. A stock trading server that is required to be fair, ensuring that orders from different customers must be executed in the order they arrive, would require a linearizable queue.

Which progress condition is right for your application? Again, it depends on the application's needs. In a way, this is a trick question. Different methods, even ones for the same object, might have different progress conditions. For example, the table lookup method of a firewall program, which checks whether a packet source is suspect, is called frequently and is time-critical, so we might want it to be wait-free. By contrast, the method that updates table entries, which is rarely called, might be implemented using mutual exclusion. As we shall see, it is quite natural to write applications whose methods differ in their progress guarantees.

So what progress condition is right for a particular operation? Programmers typically intend any operation they execute to eventually complete. That is, they want maximal progress. However, ensuring progress requires assumptions about the underlying platform. For example, how does the operating system schedule threads for execution? The choice of progress condition reflects what the programmer is willing to assume to guarantee that an operation will complete. For any progress guarantee, the programmer must assume that the thread executing the operation is eventually scheduled. For certain critical operations, the programmer may be unwilling to assume more than that, incurring extra overhead to ensure progress. For other operations, stronger assumptions, such as fairness or a particular priority scheme for scheduling, may be acceptable, enabling less expensive solutions.

The following joke circulated in Italy in the 1920s: According to Mussolini, the ideal citizen is intelligent, honest, and fascist. Unfortunately, no one is perfect, which explains why everyone you meet is either intelligent and fascist but not honest, honest and fascist but not intelligent, or honest and intelligent but not fascist.

As programmers, it would be ideal to have linearizable hardware, linearizable data structures, and good performance. Unfortunately, technology is imperfect, and for the time being, hardware that performs well is usually not even sequentially consistent. As the joke goes, that leaves open the possibility that data structures might still be linearizable while performing well. Nevertheless, there are many challenges to make this vision work, and the remainder of this book presents a road map toward attaining this goal.

3.10 **Chapter notes**

Leslie Lamport [102] introduced the notion of *sequential consistency*, while Christos Papadimitriou [137] formulated the canonical formal characterization of *serializability*. William Weihl [166] was the first to point out the importance of *compositionality* (which he called *locality*). Maurice Herlihy and Jeannette Wing [75] introduced the notion of *linearizability*. *Quiescent consistency* was introduced implicitly by James Aspnes, Maurice Herlihy, and Nir Shavit [14], and more explicitly by Nir Shavit and Asaph Zemach [158]. Leslie Lamport [99,105] introduced the notion of an *atomic register*.

The two-thread queue is considered folklore; as far as we are aware, it first appeared in print in a paper by Leslie Lamport [103].

To the best of our knowledge, the notion of *wait-freedom* first appeared implicitly in Leslie Lamport's Bakery algorithm [100]. *Lock-freedom* has had several historical meanings and only in recent years has it converged to its current definition. The notions of *dependent progress* and of *minimal* and *maximal progress* and the table of progress conditions were introduced by Maurice Herlihy and Nir Shavit [72]. *Obstruction-freedom* was introduced by Maurice Herlihy, Victor Luchangco, and Mark Moir [68].

3.11 Exercises

Exercise 3.1. Explain why quiescent consistency is compositional.

Exercise 3.2. Consider a *memory object* that encompasses two register components. We know that if both registers are quiescently consistent, then so is the memory. Does the converse hold? That is, if the memory is quiescently consistent, are the individual registers quiescently consistent? Outline a proof, or give a counterexample.

Exercise 3.3. Give an example of an execution that is quiescently consistent but not sequentially consistent, and another that is sequentially consistent but not quiescently consistent.

Exercise 3.4. For each of the histories shown in Figs. 3.11 and 3.12, are they quiescently consistent? Sequentially consistent? Linearizable? Justify your answer.

Exercise 3.5. If we drop condition L2 from the linearizability definition, is the resulting property the same as sequential consistency? Explain.

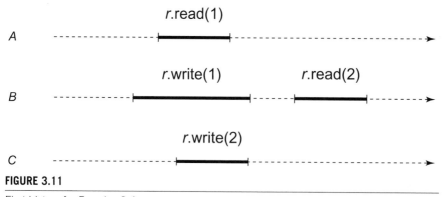

FIGURE 3.11

First history for Exercise 3.4.

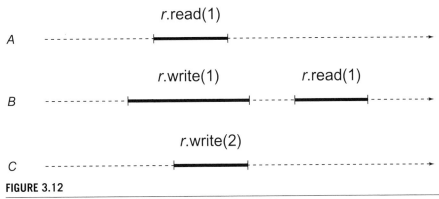

FIGURE 3.12

Second history for Exercise 3.4.

Exercise 3.6. Prove the "only if" part of Theorem 3.6.3.

Exercise 3.7. The AtomicInteger class (in the java.util.concurrent.atomic package) is a container for an integer value. One of its methods is

```
boolean compareAndSet(int expect, int update).
```

This method compares the object's current value with expect. If the values are equal, then it atomically replaces the object's value with update and returns *true*. Otherwise, it leaves the object's value unchanged, and returns *false*. This class also provides

```
int get()
```

which returns the object's value.

Consider the FIFO queue implementation shown in Fig. 3.13. It stores its items in an array items, which, for simplicity, we assume has unbounded size. It has two AtomicInteger fields: head is the index of the next slot from which to remove an item, and tail is the index of the next slot in which to place an item. Give an example showing that this implementation is *not* linearizable.

Exercise 3.8. Consider the following rather unusual implementation of a method m: In every history, the i-th time a thread calls m, the call returns after 2^i steps. Is this method wait-free?

Exercise 3.9. Consider a system with an object x and n threads. Determine if each of the following properties are equivalent to saying x is deadlock-free, starvation-free, obstruction-free, lock-free, wait-free, or none of these. Briefly justify your answers.

1. For every infinite history H of x, an infinite number of method calls complete.
2. For every finite history H of x, there is an infinite history $H' = H \cdot G$.
3. For every infinite history H of x, every thread takes an infinite number of steps.
4. For every infinite history H of x, every thread that takes an infinite number of steps in H completes an infinite number of method calls.

```
1   class IQueue<T> {
2     AtomicInteger head = new AtomicInteger(0);
3     AtomicInteger tail = new AtomicInteger(0);
4     T[] items = (T[]) new Object[Integer.MAX_VALUE];
5     public void enq(T x) {
6       int slot;
7       do {
8         slot = tail.get();
9       } while (!tail.compareAndSet(slot, slot+1));
10      items[slot] = x;
11    }
12    public T deq() throws EmptyException {
13      T value;
14      int slot;
15      do {
16        slot = head.get();
17        value = items[slot];
18        if (value == null)
19          throw new EmptyException();
20      } while (!head.compareAndSet(slot, slot+1));
21      return value;
22    }
23  }
```

FIGURE 3.13

IQueue implementation for Exercise 3.7.

5. For every finite history H of x, there are n infinite histories $H'_i = H \cdot G_i$ where only thread i takes steps in G_i, where it completes an infinite number of method calls.

6. For every finite history H of x, there is an infinite history $H' = H \cdot G$ where every thread completes an infinite number of method calls in G.

Exercise 3.10. This exercise examines the queue implementation in Fig. 3.14, whose enq() method does not have a single fixed linearization point in the code.

The queue stores its items in an items array, which, for simplicity, we assume is unbounded. The tail field is an AtomicInteger, initially zero.

The enq() method reserves a slot by incrementing tail, and then stores the item at that location. Note that these two steps are not atomic: There is an interval after tail has been incremented but before the item has been stored in the array.

The deq() method reads the value of tail, and then traverses the array in ascending order from slot zero to the tail. For each slot, it swaps *null* with the current contents, returning the first non-*null* item it finds. If all slots are *null*, the procedure is restarted.

```
1   public class HWQueue<T> {
2     AtomicReference<T>[] items;
3     AtomicInteger tail;
4     static final int CAPACITY = Integer.MAX_VALUE;
5
6     public HWQueue() {
7       items =(AtomicReference<T>[])Array.newInstance(AtomicReference.class,
8         CAPACITY);
9       for (int i = 0; i < items.length; i++) {
10        items[i] = new AtomicReference<T>(null);
11      }
12      tail = new AtomicInteger(0);
13    }
14    public void enq(T x) {
15      int i = tail.getAndIncrement();
16      items[i].set(x);
17    }
18    public T deq() {
19      while (true) {
20        int range = tail.get();
21        for (int i = 0; i < range; i++) {
22          T value = items[i].getAndSet(null);
23          if (value != null) {
24            return value;
25          }
26        }
27      }
28    }
29  }
```

FIGURE 3.14

Herlihy–Wing queue for Exercise 3.10.

- Give an execution showing that the linearization point for enq() cannot occur at line 15. (Hint: Give an execution in which two enq() calls are not linearized in the order they execute line 15.)
- Give another execution showing that the linearization point for enq() cannot occur at line 16.
- Since these are the only two memory accesses in enq(), we must conclude that enq() has no single linearization point. Does this mean enq() is not linearizable?

Exercise 3.11. This exercise examines a stack implementation (Fig. 3.15) whose push() method does not have a single fixed linearization point in the code.

The stack stores its items in an items array, which, for simplicity, we assume is unbounded. The top field is an AtomicInteger, initially zero.

```
 1  public class AGMStack<T> {
 2    AtomicReferenceArray<T> items;
 3    AtomicInteger top;
 4    static final int CAPACITY = Integer.MAX_VALUE;
 5
 6    public AGMStack() {
 7      items = new AtomicReferenceArray<T>(CAPACITY);
 8      top = new AtomicInteger(0);
 9    }
10    public void push(T x) {
11      int i = top.getAndIncrement();
12      items.set(i,x);
13    }
14    public T pop() {
15      int range = top.get();
16      for (int i = range - 1; i > -1; i--) {
17        T value = items.getAndSet(i, null);
18        if (value != null) {
19          return value;
20        }
21      }
22      // Return Empty.
23      return null;
24    }
25  }
```

FIGURE 3.15

Afek–Gafni–Morrison stack for Exercise 3.11.

The push() method reserves a slot by incrementing top, and then stores the item at that location. Note that these two steps are not atomic: There is an interval after top has been incremented but before the item has been stored in the array.

The pop() method reads the value of top and then traverses the array in descending order from the top to slot zero. For each slot, it swaps *null* with the current contents, returning the first *nonnull* item it finds. If all slots are *null*, the method returns *null*, indicating an empty stack.

- Give an execution showing that the linearization point for push() cannot occur at line 11. (Hint: Give an execution in which two push() calls are not linearized in the order they execute line 11.)
- Give another execution showing that the linearization point for push() cannot occur at line 12.
- Since these are the only two memory accesses in push(), we conclude that push() has no single fixed linearization point. Does this mean push() is not linearizable?

Exercise 3.12. Prove that sequential consistency is nonblocking.

Foundations of shared memory

4

For millennia, chicken farmers around the world were forced to wait 5 to 6 weeks before they could tell male and female chickens apart. This delay meant weeks of wasted time and money, because unlike females, which grow to maturity, lay eggs, and can ultimately be fried Kentucky style, the young males have no value, and are discarded. Then, in the 1920s, Japanese scientists discovered an invaluable trick: Male chicks have a small bump in their vent (anus) that females lack. If you press on a chick's behind and examine it, you can tell immediately which chicks should be discarded (no need to wait 5 weeks). The trouble was that a sizable fraction of males and females had bumps that were not clearcut, and could be either male or female. Thus began the profession of "chicken sexing." Japan opened schools for training specialists who could sex on the order of 1000 chicks an hour with almost perfect accuracy. After proper training, expert chicken sexers could reliably determine the sex of day-old chicks at a glance using a collection of subtle perceptual cues. This profession continues to this day. In interviews, chicken sexers claim that in many cases they have no idea how they make their decisions. There is a technical name for this ability: *intuition*. Our unsettling example suggests that training and practice can enhance your intuition.

In this chapter, we begin our study of the foundations of *concurrent shared-memory computation*. As you read through the algorithms, you might question their "real-world value." If you do, remember that their value is in training you, the reader, to tell which types of algorithmic approaches work in a concurrent shared-memory setting, and which do not, even when it is hard to tell. This will help you discard bad ideas earlier, saving time and money.

The foundations of sequential computing were established in the 1930s by Alan Turing and Alonzo Church, who independently formulated what has come to be known as the *Church–Turing thesis*: Anything that *can* be computed, can be computed by a Turing machine (or, equivalently, by Church's lambda calculus). Any problem that cannot be solved by a Turing machine (such as deciding whether a program halts on any input) is universally considered to be unsolvable by any kind of practical computing device. The Church–Turing thesis is a *thesis*, not a theorem, because the notion of "what is computable" is not defined in a precise, mathematically rigorous way. Nevertheless, just about everyone believes this thesis.

To study concurrent shared-memory computation, we begin with a computational model. A shared-memory computation consists of multiple *threads*, each of which is a sequential program in its own right. These threads communicate by calling methods of objects that reside in a shared memory. Threads are *asynchronous*, meaning that they may run at different speeds, and any thread can halt for an unpredictable duration at any time. This notion of asynchrony reflects the realities of modern multiprocessor architectures, where thread delays are unpredictable, ranging from microseconds (cache misses) to milliseconds (page faults) to seconds (scheduling interruptions).

The classical theory of sequential computability proceeds in stages. It starts with finite-state automata, moves on to push-down automata, and culminates in Turing machines. We, too, consider a progression of models for concurrent computing. We start with the simplest form of shared-memory computation: Concurrent threads read and write shared memory locations, which are called *registers* for historical reasons. We start with very simple registers, and we show how to use them to construct a series of more complex registers.

The classical theory of sequential computability is, for the most part, not concerned with efficiency: To show that a problem is computable, it is enough to show that it can be solved by a Turing machine. There is little incentive to make such a Turing machine efficient, because a Turing machine is not a practical model of computation. In the same way, we make little attempt to make our register constructions efficient. We are interested in understanding whether such constructions exist and how they work. They are not intended to be practical. We prefer inefficient but easy-to-understand constructions over efficient but complicated ones.

In particular, some of our constructions use *timestamps* (i.e., counter values) to distinguish older values from newer values. The problem with timestamps is that they grow without bound, and eventually overflow any fixed-size variable. Bounded solutions (such as the one in Section 2.8) are (arguably) more intellectually satisfying, and we encourage readers to investigate them further through the references provided in the chapter notes. Here, however, we focus on simpler, unbounded constructions, because they illustrate the fundamental principles of concurrent programming with less danger of becoming distracted by technicalities.

4.1 The space of registers

At the hardware level, threads communicate by reading and writing shared memory. A good way to understand interthread communication is to abstract away from hardware primitives, and to think about communication as happening through *shared concurrent objects*. Chapter 3 provides a detailed description of shared objects. For now, it suffices to recall the two key properties of their design: *safety*, defined by consistency conditions, and *liveness*, defined by progress conditions.

A *read–write register* (or just a *register*) is an object that encapsulates a value that can be observed by a read() method and modified by a write() method (these methods are often called *load* and *store*). Fig. 4.1 shows the Register<T> interface implemented by all registers. The type T of the value is typically Boolean, Integer, or a reference to an object. A register that implements the Register<Boolean> interface is called a *Boolean* register (sometimes 1 and 0 are used as synonyms for *true* and

```
1  public interface Register<T> {
2    T read();
3    void write(T v);
4  }
```

FIGURE 4.1

The Register<T> interface.

```
1  public class SequentialRegister<T> implements Register<T> {
2    private T value;
3    public T read() {
4      return value;
5    }
6    public void write(T v) {
7      value = v;
8    }
9  }
```

FIGURE 4.2

The SequentialRegister class.

false). A register that implements the Register<Integer> for a range of *M* integer values is called an *M-valued register*. We do not explicitly discuss any other kind of register, except to note that any algorithm that implements integer registers can be adapted to implement registers that hold references to other objects by representing the references as integers.

If method calls do not overlap, a register implementation should behave as shown in Fig. 4.2. On a multiprocessor, however, we expect method calls to overlap all the time, so we need to specify what the concurrent method calls mean.

An *atomic register* is a linearizable implementation of the sequential register class shown in Fig. 4.2. Informally, an atomic register behaves exactly as we would expect: Each read returns the "last" value written. A model in which threads communicate by reading and writing to atomic registers is intuitively appealing, and for a long time was the standard model of concurrent computation.

One approach to implementing atomic registers is to rely on mutual exclusion: protect each register with a mutual exclusion lock acquired by each call to read() or write(). Unfortunately, we cannot use the lock algorithms of Chapter 2 here; those algorithms accomplish mutual exclusion using registers, so it makes little sense to implement registers using mutual exclusion. Moreover, as we saw in Chapter 3, using mutual exclusion, even if it is deadlock- or starvation-free, would mean that the computation's progress would depend on the operating system scheduler to guarantee that threads never get stuck in critical sections. Since we wish to examine the basic building blocks of concurrent computation using shared objects, it makes little sense to assume the existence of a separate entity to provide the key progress property.

Here is a different approach: Recall that an object implementation is *wait-free* if each method call finishes in a finite number of steps, independently of how its execution is interleaved with steps of other concurrent method calls. The wait-free condition may seem simple and natural, but it has far-reaching consequences. In particular, it rules out any kind of mutual exclusion, and guarantees independent progress, that is, without making assumptions about the operating system scheduler. We therefore require our register implementations to be wait-free.

It is also important to specify how many readers and writers are expected. Not surprisingly, it is easier to implement a register that supports only a single reader and a single writer than one that supports multiple readers and writers. For brevity, we use SRSW for "single-reader, single-writer," MRSW for "multi-reader, single-writer," and MRMW for "multi-reader, multi-writer."

In this chapter, we address the following fundamental question:

Can any data structure implemented using the most powerful registers also be implemented using the weakest?

Recall from Chapter 1 that any useful form of interthread communication must be persistent: The message sent must outlive the active participation of the sender. The weakest form of persistent synchronization is (arguably) the ability to set a single persistent bit in shared memory, and the weakest form of synchronization is (unarguably) none at all: If the act of setting a bit does not overlap the act of reading that bit, then the value read is the same as the value written. Otherwise, a read overlapping a write could return any value.

Different kinds of registers come with different guarantees that make them more or less powerful. For example, we have seen that registers may differ in the range of values they may encapsulate (e.g., Boolean versus M-valued), and in the number of readers and writers they support. They may also differ in the degree of consistency they provide.

An SRSW or MRSW register implementation is *safe* if:

- A read() call that does not overlap a write() call returns the value written by the most recent write() call. (The "most recent write() call" is well defined because there is a single writer.)
- A read() call that overlaps a write() call may return any value within the register's allowed range of values (e.g., 0 to $M - 1$ for an M-valued register).

Be aware that the term "safe" is a historical accident. Because they provide such weak guarantees, "safe" registers are actually quite unsafe.

Consider the history shown in Fig. 4.3. If the register is *safe*, then the three read calls might behave as follows:

- R^1 returns 0, the most recently written value.
- R^2 and R^3 are concurrent with $W(1)$, so they may return any value in the range of the register.

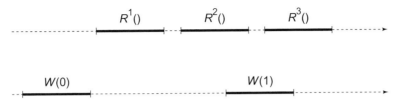

FIGURE 4.3

An SRSW register execution: R^i is the i-th read and $W(v)$ is a write of value v. Time flows from left to right. No matter whether the register is *safe*, *regular*, or *atomic*, R^1 must return 0, the most recently written value. If the register is *safe*, then because R^2 and R^3 are concurrent with $W(1)$, they may return any value in the range of the register. If the register is *regular*, R^2 and R^3 may each return either 0 or 1. If the register is *atomic*, then if R^2 returns 1, then R^3 must also return 1, and if R^2 returns 0, then R^3 may return 0 or 1.

It is convenient to define an intermediate level of consistency between safe and atomic. A *regular* register is an SRSW or MRSW register where writes do not happen atomically. Instead, while the write() call is in progress, the value being read may "flicker" between the old and new value before finally replacing the older value. More precisely:

- A regular register is safe, so any read() call that does not overlap a write() call returns the most recently written value.
- Suppose a read() call overlaps one or more write() calls. Let v^0 be the value written by the latest preceding write() call, and let $v^1, \ldots, v^k$ be the sequence of values written by write() calls that overlap the read() call. The read() call may return v^i for any i in the range $0 \ldots k$.

For the execution in Fig. 4.3, a regular register might behave as follows:

- R^1 returns the old value, 0.
- R^2 and R^3 each return either the old value 0 or the new value 1.

Regular registers are quiescently consistent (Chapter 3), but not vice versa. Both safe and regular registers permit only a single writer. Note that a regular register is actually a quiescently consistent single-writer sequential register.

For an atomic register, the execution in Fig. 4.3 might produce the following results:

- R^1 returns the old value, 0.
- If R^2 returns 1, then R^3 also returns 1.
- If R^2 returns 0, then R^3 returns either 0 or 1.

Fig. 4.4 shows a schematic view of the range of possible registers as a three-dimensional space: The register size defines one dimension, the numbers of readers and writers define another, and the register's consistency property defines the third.

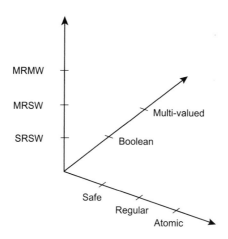

FIGURE 4.4

The three-dimensional space of possible read–write register-based implementations.

This view should not be taken literally: There are several combinations, such as multi-writer safe registers, that are not well defined.

To reason about algorithms for implementing regular and atomic registers, it is convenient to rephrase our definitions directly in terms of object histories. From now on, we consider only histories in which each read() call returns a value written by some write() call (regular and atomic registers do not allow reads to make up return values). For simplicity, we assume values read or written are unique.[1]

Recall that an object history is a sequence of *invocation* and *response* events, where an invocation event occurs when a thread calls a method, and a matching response event occurs when that call returns. A *method call* (or just a *call*) is the interval between matching invocation and response events (including the invocation and response events). Any history induces a partial order $\rightarrow$ on method calls, defined as follows: If m_0 and m_1 are method calls, $m_0 \rightarrow m_1$ if m_0's response event precedes m_1's call event. (See Chapter 3 for complete definitions.)

Any register implementation (whether safe, regular, or atomic) defines a total order on the write() calls called the *write order*, the order in which writes "take effect" in the register. For safe and regular registers, the write order is trivial because they allow only one writer at a time. For atomic registers, method calls have a linearization order. We use this order to index the write calls: Write call W^0 is ordered first, W^1 second, and so on. We use v^i to denote the unique value written by W^i. Note that for SRSW or MRSW safe or regular registers, the write order is exactly the same as the precedence order on writes.

---

[1] If values are not inherently unique, we can use the standard technique of appending to them auxiliary values invisible to the algorithm itself, used only in our reasoning to distinguish one value from another.

We use R^i to denote any read call that returns v^i. Note that although a history contains at most one W^i call, it might contain multiple R^i calls.

One can show that the following conditions provide a precise statement of what it means for a register to be regular. First, no read call returns a value from the future:

$$\text{It is never the case that} \quad R^i \to W^i. \tag{4.1.1}$$

Second, no read call returns a value from the distant past, that is, one that precedes the most recently written nonoverlapping value:

$$\text{It is never the case that for some } j, \quad W^i \to W^j \to R^i. \tag{4.1.2}$$

To prove that a register implementation is regular, we must show that its histories satisfy Conditions (4.1.1) and (4.1.2).

An atomic register satisfies one additional condition:

$$\text{if} \quad R^i \to R^j, \quad \text{then} \quad i \le j. \tag{4.1.3}$$

This condition states that an earlier read cannot return a value later than that returned by a later read. Regular registers are *not* required to satisfy Condition (4.1.3). To show that a register implementation is atomic, we need first to define a write order, and then to show that its histories satisfy Conditions (4.1.1)–(4.1.3).

4.2 Register constructions

We now show how to implement a range of surprisingly powerful registers from simple safe Boolean SRSW registers. We consider a series of constructions, shown in Fig. 4.5, that implement stronger from weaker registers. These constructions imply that all read–write register types are equivalent, at least in terms of computability.

Base class	Implemented class	Section
safe SRSW	safe MRSW	4.2.1
safe Boolean MRSW	regular Boolean MRSW	4.2.2
regular Boolean MRSW	regular MRSW	4.2.3
regular SRSW	atomic SRSW	4.2.4
atomic SRSW	atomic MRSW	4.2.5
atomic MRSW	atomic MRMW	4.2.6
atomic MRSW	atomic snapshot	4.3

FIGURE 4.5

The sequence of register constructions.

In the last step, we show how atomic registers (and therefore safe registers) can implement an atomic snapshot: an array of MRSW registers written by different threads that can be read atomically by any thread.

Some of these constructions are more powerful than necessary to complete the sequence of derivations (for example, we do not need to provide the multi-reader property for regular and safe registers to complete the derivation of an atomic SRSW register). We present them anyway because they provide valuable insights.

Our code samples follow these conventions. When we display an algorithm to implement a particular kind of register, say, a safe Boolean MRSW register, we present the algorithm using a form somewhat like this:

```
class SafeBooleanMRSWRegister implements Register<Boolean>
  {
  ...
  }
```

While this notation makes clear the properties of the Register<> class being implemented, it becomes cumbersome when we want to use this class to implement other classes. Instead, when describing a class implementation, we use the following conventions to indicate whether a particular field is safe, regular, or atomic: A field otherwise named mumble is called s_mumble if it is safe, r_mumble if it is regular, and a_mumble if it is atomic. Other important aspects of the field, such as its type and whether it supports multiple readers or writers, are noted as comments within the code, and should also be clear from the context.

4.2.1 Safe MRSW registers

Fig. 4.6 shows how to construct a safe MRSW register from safe SRSW registers.

Lemma 4.2.1. The construction in Fig. 4.6 is a *safe MRSW register.*

Proof. If A's read() call does not overlap any write() call, then it does not overlap any write() call of the component register s_table[A], so the read() call returns

```
1   public class SafeBooleanMRSWRegister implements Register<Boolean> {
2     boolean[] s_table; // array of safe SRSW registers
3     public SafeBooleanMRSWRegister(int capacity) {
4       s_table = new boolean[capacity];
5     }
6     public Boolean read() {
7       return s_table[ThreadID.get()];
8     }
9     public void write(Boolean x) {
10      for (int i = 0; i < s_table.length; i++)
11        s_table[i] = x;
12    }
13  }
```

FIGURE 4.6

The SafeBooleanMRSWRegister class: a safe Boolean MRSW register.

the value of s_table[A], which is the most recently written value. If A's read() call overlaps a write() call, it is allowed to return any value. □

4.2.2 A regular Boolean MRSW register

The next construction, shown in Fig. 4.7, builds a regular Boolean MRSW register from a safe Boolean MRSW register. For Boolean registers, the only difference between safe and regular registers arises when the newly written value x is the same as the old. A regular register can only return x, while a safe register may return either Boolean value. We circumvent this problem simply by ensuring that a value is written only if it is distinct from the previously written value.

Lemma 4.2.2. The construction in Fig. 4.7 is a regular Boolean MRSW register.

Proof. A read() call that does not overlap any write() call returns the most recently written value. If the calls do overlap, there are two cases to consider:

- If the value being written is the same as the last value written, then the writer avoids writing to the safe register, ensuring that the reader reads the correct value.
- If the value written now is distinct from the last value written, then those values must be *true* and *false* because the register is Boolean. A concurrent read returns some value in the range of the register, namely, either *true* or *false*, either of which is correct. □

```
1  public class RegularBooleanMRSWRegister implements Register<Boolean> {
2    ThreadLocal<Boolean> last;
3    boolean s_value; // safe MRSW register
4    RegularBooleanMRSWRegister(int capacity) {
5      last = new ThreadLocal<Boolean>() {
6        protected Boolean initialValue() { return false; };
7      };
8    }
9    public void write(Boolean x) {
10     if (x != last.get()) {
11       last.set(x);
12       s_value = x;
13     }
14   }
15   public Boolean read() {
16     return s_value;
17   }
18 }
```

FIGURE 4.7

The RegularBooleanMRSWRegister class: a regular Boolean MRSW register constructed from a safe Boolean MRSW register.

```
1   public class RegularMRSWRegister implements Register<Byte> {
2     private static int RANGE = Byte.MAX_VALUE - Byte.MIN_VALUE + 1;
3     boolean[] r_bit = new boolean[RANGE]; // regular Boolean MRSW
4     public RegularMRSWRegister(int capacity) {
5       for (int i = 1; i < r_bit.length; i++)
6         r_bit[i] = false;
7       r_bit[0] = true;
8     }
9     public void write(Byte x) {
10      r_bit[x] = true;
11      for (int i = x - 1; i >= 0; i--)
12        r_bit[i] = false;
13    }
14    public Byte read() {
15      for (int i = 0; i < RANGE; i++)
16        if (r_bit[i]) {
17          return i;
18        }
19      return -1; // impossible
20    }
21  }
```

FIGURE 4.8

The `RegularMRSWRegister` class: a regular M-valued MRSW register.

4.2.3 A regular *M*-valued MRSW register

The jump from Boolean to M-valued registers is simple, if astonishingly inefficient: We represent the value in unary notation. In Fig. 4.8, we implement an M-valued register as an array of M Boolean registers. Initially the register is set to value zero, indicated by the 0th bit being set to *true*. A write method of value x writes *true* in location x and then in descending array-index order sets all lower locations to *false*. A reading method reads the locations in ascending index order until the first time it reads the value *true* in some index i. It then returns i. The example in Fig. 4.9 illustrates an *8-valued* register.

Lemma 4.2.3. The read() call in the construction in Fig. 4.8 always returns a value corresponding to a bit in $0..M - 1$ set by some write() call.

Proof. The following property is invariant: If a reading thread is reading r_bit[j], then some bit at index j or higher, written by a write() call, is set to *true*.

When the register is initialized, there are no readers; the constructor sets r_bit[0] to *true*. Assume a reader is reading r_bit[j], and that r_bit[k] is *true* for $k \geq j$.

- If the reader advances from j to $j + 1$, then r_bit[j] is *false*, so $k > j$ (i.e., a bit greater than or equal to $j + 1$ is *true*).
- The writer clears r_bit[k] only if it has set a higher r_bit[ℓ] to *true* for $\ell > k$. ☐

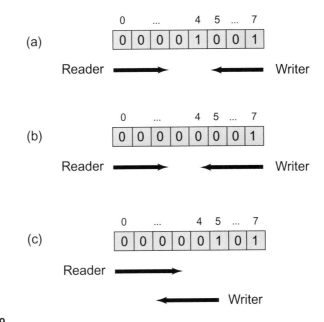

FIGURE 4.9

The `RegularMRSWRegister` class: an execution of a regular *8-valued* MRSW register. The values *false* and *true* are represented by 0 and 1 respectively. In part (a), the value prior to the write was 4, and thread *W*'s write of 7 is not read by thread *R* because *R* reaches array entry 4 before *W* overwrites *false* at that location. In part (b), entry 4 is overwritten by *W* before it is read, so the read returns 7. In part (c), *W* starts to write 5. Since it wrote array entry 5 before it was read, the reader returns 5 even though entry 7 is also set to *true*.

Lemma 4.2.4. The construction in Fig. 4.8 is a regular M-valued MRSW register.

Proof. For any read, let x be the value written by the most recent nonoverlapping write(). At the time the write() completed, a_bit[x] was set to *true*, and a_bit[i] is *false* for $i < x$. By Lemma 4.2.3, if the reader returns a value that is not x, then it observed some a_bit[j], $j \neq x$, to be *true*, and that bit must have been set by a concurrent write, proving Conditions (4.1.1) and (4.1.2). □

4.2.4 An atomic SRSW register

We show how to construct an atomic SRSW register from a regular SRSW register. (Note that our construction uses unbounded timestamps.)

A regular register satisfies Conditions (4.1.1) and (4.1.2), while an atomic register must also satisfy Condition (4.1.3). Since a regular SRSW register has no concurrent reads, the only way Condition (4.1.3) can be violated is if two reads that overlap the same write read values out-of-order, the first returning v^i and the latter returning v^j, where $j < i$.

Fig. 4.10 describes a class of values that each have an added tag that contains a timestamp. Our implementation of an `AtomicSRSWRegister`, shown in Fig. 4.11, uses

```
1   public class StampedValue<T> {
2     public long stamp;
3     public T value;
4     // initial value with zero timestamp
5     public StampedValue(T init) {
6       stamp = 0;
7       value = init;
8     }
9     // later values with timestamp provided
10    public StampedValue(long ts, T v) {
11      stamp = ts;
12      value = v;
13    }
14    public static StampedValue max(StampedValue x, StampedValue y) {
15      if (x.stamp > y.stamp) {
16        return x;
17      } else {
18        return y;
19      }
20    }
21    public static StampedValue MIN_VALUE = new StampedValue(null);
22  }
```

FIGURE 4.10

The `StampedValue<T>` class: allows a timestamp and a value to be read or written together.

these tags to order write calls so that they can be ordered properly by concurrent read calls. Each read remembers the latest (highest timestamp) timestamp/value pair ever read, so that it is available to future reads. If a later read then reads an earlier value (one having a lower timestamp), it ignores that value and simply uses the remembered latest value. Similarly, the writer remembers the latest timestamp it wrote, and tags each newly written value with a later timestamp (i.e., a timestamp greater by 1).

This algorithm requires the ability to read or write a value and a timestamp as a single unit. In a language such as C, we would treat both the value and the timestamp as uninterpreted bits ("raw seething bits"), and use bit shifting and logical masking to pack and unpack both values in and out of one or more words. In Java, it is easier to create a `StampedValue<T>` structure that holds a timestamp/value pair, and to store a *reference* to that structure in the register.

Lemma 4.2.5. The construction in Fig. 4.11 is an atomic SRSW register.

Proof. The register is regular, so Conditions (4.1.1) and (4.1.2) are met. The algorithm satisfies Condition (4.1.3) because writes are totally ordered by their timestamps, and if a read returns a given value, a later read cannot read an earlier written value, since it would have a lower timestamp.   □

```
1   public class AtomicSRSWRegister<T> implements Register<T> {
2     ThreadLocal<Long> lastStamp;
3     ThreadLocal<StampedValue<T>> lastRead;
4     StampedValue<T> r_value;              // regular SRSW timestamp-value pair
5     public AtomicSRSWRegister(T init) {
6       r_value = new StampedValue<T>(init);
7       lastStamp = new ThreadLocal<Long>() {
8         protected Long initialValue() { return 0; };
9       };
10      lastRead = new ThreadLocal<StampedValue<T>>() {
11        protected StampedValue<T> initialValue() { return r_value; };
12      };
13    }
14    public T read() {
15      StampedValue<T> value = r_value;
16      StampedValue<T> last = lastRead.get();
17      StampedValue<T> result = StampedValue.max(value, last);
18      lastRead.set(result);
19      return result.value;
20    }
21    public void write(T v) {
22      long stamp = lastStamp.get() + 1;
23      r_value = new StampedValue(stamp, v);
24      lastStamp.set(stamp);
25    }
26  }
```

FIGURE 4.11

The AtomicSRSWRegister class: an atomic SRSW register constructed from a regular SRSW register.

4.2.5 An atomic MRSW register

To understand how to construct an atomic MRSW register from atomic SRSW registers, we first consider a simple algorithm based on direct use of the construction in Section 4.2.1, which took us from safe SRSW to safe MRSW registers. Let the SRSW registers composing the table array a_table[0..n − 1] be atomic instead of safe, with all other calls remaining the same: The writer writes the array locations in increasing index order and then each reader reads and returns its associated array entry. The result is not an atomic multi-reader register. Condition (4.1.3) holds for any single reader because each reader reads from an atomic register, yet it does not hold for distinct readers. Consider, for example, a write that starts by setting the first SRSW register a_table[0], and is delayed before writing the remaining locations a_table[1..n − 1]. A subsequent read by thread 0 returns the correct new value, but a subsequent read by thread 1 that completely follows the read by thread 0 reads and returns the earlier value because the writer has yet to update a_table[1..n − 1]. We

```
1   public class AtomicMRSWRegister<T> implements Register<T> {
2     ThreadLocal<Long> lastStamp;
3     private StampedValue<T>[][] a_table; // each entry is an atomic SRSW register
4     public AtomicMRSWRegister(T init, int readers) {
5       lastStamp = new ThreadLocal<Long>() {
6         protected Long initialValue() { return 0; };
7       };
8       a_table = (StampedValue<T>[][]) new StampedValue[readers][readers];
9       StampedValue<T> value = new StampedValue<T>(init);
10      for (int i = 0; i < readers; i++) {
11        for (int j = 0; j < readers; j++) {
12          a_table[i][j] = value;
13        }
14      }
15    }
16    public T read() {
17      int me = ThreadID.get();
18      StampedValue<T> value = a_table[me][me];
19      for (int i = 0; i < a_table.length; i++) {
20        value = StampedValue.max(value, a_table[i][me]);
21      }
22      for (int i = 0; i < a_table.length; i++) {
23        if (i == me) continue;
24        a_table[me][i] = value;
25      }
26      return value;
27    }
28    public void write(T v) {
29      long stamp = lastStamp.get() + 1;
30      lastStamp.set(stamp);
31      StampedValue<T> value = new StampedValue<T>(stamp, v);
32      for (int i = 0; i < a_table.length; i++) {
33        a_table[i][i] = value;
34      }
35    }
36  }
```

FIGURE 4.12

The AtomicMRSWRegister class: an atomic MRSW register constructed from atomic SRSW registers.

address this problem by having earlier reader threads *help out* later threads by telling them which value they read.

This implementation appears in Fig. 4.12. The n threads share an n-by-n array a_table[0..n − 1][0..n − 1] of stamped values. As in Section 4.2.4, we use time-stamped values to allow early reads to tell later reads which of the values read is

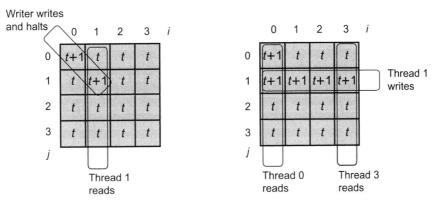

Writer writes and halts

Thread 1 writes

Thread 1 reads

Thread 0 reads

Thread 3 reads

FIGURE 4.13

An execution of the atomic MRSW register. Each reader thread has an index between 0 and 3, and we refer to each thread by its index. Here, the writer writes a new value with timestamp $t+1$ to locations a_table[0][0] and a_table[1][1] and then halts. Then, thread 1 reads its corresponding column a_table[i][1] for all i, and writes its corresponding row a_table[1][i] for all i, returning the new value with timestamp $t+1$. Threads 0 and 3 both read completely after thread 1's read. Thread 0 reads a_table[0][0] with value $t+1$. Thread 3 cannot read the new value with timestamp $t+1$ because the writer has yet to write a_table[3][3]. Nevertheless, it reads a_table[1][3] and returns the correct value with timestamp $t+1$ that was read by the earlier thread 1.

the latest. The locations along the diagonal, a_table[i][i] for all i, correspond to the registers in the failed simple construction mentioned earlier. The writer simply writes the diagonal locations one after the other with a new value and a timestamp that increases from one write() call to the next. Each reader A first reads a_table[A][A] as in the earlier algorithm. It then uses the remaining SRSW locations a_table[A][B], $A \neq B$, for communication between readers A and B. Each reader A, after reading a_table[A][A], checks to see if some other reader has read a later value by traversing its corresponding column (a_table[B][A] for all B), and checking if it contains a later value (one with a higher timestamp). The reader then lets all later readers know the latest value it read by writing this value to all locations in its corresponding row (a_table[A][B] for all B). It thus follows that after a read by A is completed, every later read by B sees the last value A read (since it reads a_table[A][B]). Fig. 4.13 shows an example execution of the algorithm.

Lemma 4.2.6. The construction in Fig. 4.12 is an atomic MRSW register.

Proof. First, no reader returns a value from the future, so Condition (4.1.1) is clearly satisfied. By construction, write() calls write strictly increasing timestamps. The key to understanding this algorithm is the simple observation that the maximum timestamp along any row or column is also strictly increasing. If A writes v with timestamp t, then any subsequent read() call by B (where A's call completely precedes B's) reads (from the diagonal of a_table) a maximum timestamp greater than or equal to t, satisfying Condition (4.1.2). Finally, as noted earlier, if a read call by A completely precedes a read call by B, then A writes a stamped value with timestamp t to B's row, so B chooses a value with a timestamp greater than or equal to t, satisfying Condition (4.1.3). □

On an intuitive, "chicken sexing" level, note that our counterexample that violates atomicity is caused by two read events that do not overlap, the earlier read reading an older value than the latter read. If the reads overlapped, we could have reordered their linearization points however we wanted. However, because the two reads do not overlap, the order of their linearization points is fixed, so we cannot satisfy the atomicity requirement. This is the type of counterexample we should look for when designing algorithms. (We used this same counterexample, by the way, in the single-reader atomic register construction.)

Our solution used two algorithmic tools: timestamping, which appears later in many practical algorithms, and indirect helping, where one thread tells the others what it read. In this way, if a writer pauses after communicating information to only a subset of readers, then those readers collaborate by passing on that information.

4.2.6 An atomic MRMW register

Here is how to construct an atomic MRMW register from an array of atomic MRSW registers, one per thread.

To write to the register, A reads all the array elements, chooses a timestamp higher than any it has observed, and writes a stamped value to array element A. To read the register, a thread reads all the array elements, and returns the one with the highest timestamp. This is exactly the timestamp algorithm used by the Bakery algorithm of Section 2.7. As in the Bakery algorithm, we resolve ties in favor of the thread with the lesser index, in other words, using a lexicographic order on pairs of timestamp and thread IDs.

Lemma 4.2.7. The construction in Fig. 4.14 is an atomic MRMW register.

Proof. Define the write order among write() calls based on the lexicographic order of their timestamps and thread IDs so that the write() call by A with timestamp t_A precedes the write() call by B with timestamp t_B if $t_A < t_B$ or if $t_A = t_B$ and $A < B$. We leave as an exercise to the reader to show that this lexicographic order is consistent with $\rightarrow$. As usual, index write() calls in write order: $W^0, W^1, \ldots$.

Clearly a read() call cannot read a value written in a_table[] after it is completed, and any write() call completely preceded by the read has a timestamp higher than all those written before the read is completed, implying Condition (4.1.1).

Consider Condition (4.1.2), which prohibits skipping over the most recent preceding write(). Suppose a write() call by A preceded a write call by B, which in turn preceded a read() by C. If $A = B$, then the later write overwrites a_table[A] and the read() does not return the value of the earlier write. If $A \neq B$, then since A's timestamp is smaller than B's timestamp, any C that sees both returns B's value (or one with higher timestamp), meeting Condition (4.1.2).

```
1   public class AtomicMRMWRegister<T> implements Register<T>{
2     private StampedValue<T>[] a_table; // array of atomic MRSW registers
3     public AtomicMRMWRegister(int capacity, T init) {
4       a_table = (StampedValue<T>[]) new StampedValue[capacity];
5       StampedValue<T> value = new StampedValue<T>(init);
6       for (int j = 0; j < a_table.length; j++) {
7         a_table[j] = value;
8       }
9     }
10    public void write(T value) {
11      int me = ThreadID.get();
12      StampedValue<T> max = StampedValue.MIN_VALUE;
13      for (int i = 0; i < a_table.length; i++) {
14        max = StampedValue.max(max, a_table[i]);
15      }
16      a_table[me] = new StampedValue(max.stamp + 1, value);
17    }
18    public T read() {
19      StampedValue<T> max = StampedValue.MIN_VALUE;
20      for (int i = 0; i < a_table.length; i++) {
21        max = StampedValue.max(max, a_table[i]);
22      }
23      return max.value;
24    }
25  }
```

FIGURE 4.14

Atomic MRMW register.

Finally, we consider Condition (4.1.3), which prohibits values from being read out of write order. Consider any read() call by A completely preceding a read() call by B, and any write() call by C which is ordered before the write() by D in the write order. We must show that if A returns D's value, then B does not return C's value. If $t_C < t_D$, then if A reads timestamp t_D from a_table[D], B reads t_D or a higher timestamp from a_table[D], and does not return the value associated with t_C. If $t_C = t_D$, that is, the writes were concurrent, then from the write order, $C < D$, so if A reads timestamp t_D from a_table[D], B also reads t_D from a_table[D], and returns the value associated with t_D (or higher), even if it reads t_C in a_table[C]. □

Our series of constructions shows that one can construct a wait-free atomic multi-valued MRMW register from safe Boolean SRSW registers. Naturally, no one wants to write a concurrent algorithm using safe registers, but these constructions show that any algorithm using atomic registers can be implemented on an architecture that supports only safe registers. Later on, when we consider more realistic architectures, we return to the theme of implementing algorithms that assume strong synchronization properties on architectures that directly provide only weaker properties.

```
1  public interface Snapshot<T> {
2    public void update(T v);
3    public T[] scan();
4  }
```

FIGURE 4.15

The Snapshot interface.

4.3 Atomic snapshots

We have seen how a register value can be read and written atomically. What if we want to read multiple register values atomically? We call such an operation an *atomic snapshot*.

An atomic snapshot constructs an instantaneous view of an array of MRSW registers. We construct a wait-free snapshot, meaning that a thread can take a snapshot of the array without delaying any other thread. Atomic snapshots can be useful for backups or checkpoints.

The Snapshot interface (Fig. 4.15) is just an array of atomic MRSW registers, one for each thread. The update() method writes a value v to the calling thread's register in that array; the scan() method returns an atomic snapshot of that array.

Our goal is to construct a wait-free implementation that is equivalent (that is, linearizable) to the sequential specification shown in Fig. 4.16. The key property of this sequential implementation is that scan() returns a collection of values, each corresponding to the latest preceding update(); that is, it returns a collection of register values that existed together in the same instant.

4.3.1 An obstruction-free snapshot

We begin with a SimpleSnapshot class for which update() is wait-free but scan() is obstruction-free. We then extend this algorithm to make scan() wait-free.

As in the atomic MRSW register construction, each value is a StampedValue<T> object with stamp and value fields. Each update() call increments the timestamp.

A *collect* is the nonatomic act of copying the register values one-by-one into an array. If we perform two collects one after the other, and both collects read the same set of timestamps, then we know that there was an interval during which no thread updated its register, so the result of the collect is a snapshot of the array immediately after the end of the first collect. We call such a pair of collects a *clean double collect*.

In the construction shown in the SimpleSnapshot<T> class (Fig. 4.17), each thread repeatedly calls collect() (line 25), and returns as soon as it detects a clean double collect (one in which both sets of timestamps were identical).

This construction always returns correct values. The update() calls are wait-free, but scan() is not because any call can be repeatedly interrupted by update(), and may run forever without completing. It is, however, obstruction-free: a scan() completes if it runs by itself for long enough.

```
1   public class SeqSnapshot<T> implements Snapshot<T> {
2     T[] a_value;
3     public SeqSnapshot(int capacity, T init) {
4       a_value = (T[]) new Object[capacity];
5       for (int i = 0; i < a_value.length; i++) {
6         a_value[i] = init;
7       }
8     }
9     public synchronized void update(T v) {
10      a_value[ThreadID.get()] = v;
11    }
12    public synchronized T[] scan() {
13      T[] result = (T[]) new Object[a_value.length];
14      for (int i = 0; i < a_value.length; i++)
15        result[i] = a_value[i];
16      return result;
17    }
18  }
```

FIGURE 4.16

A sequential snapshot.

Note that we use timestamps to verify the double collect, and not the values in the registers. Why? We encourage the reader to come up with a counterexample in which the repeated appearance of the same value is interleaved with others so that reading the same value creates the illusion that "nothing has changed." This is a common mistake that concurrent programmers make, trying to save the space needed for timestamps by using the values being written as indicators of a property. We advise against it: More often than not, this will lead to a bug, as in the case of the clean double collect: It must be detected by checking timestamps, not the equality of the sets of values collected.

4.3.2 A wait-free snapshot

To make the scan() method wait-free, each update() call *helps* a potentially interfering scan() by taking a snapshot before writing to its register. A scan() that repeatedly fails to take a clean double collect can use the snapshot from one of the interfering update() calls as its own. The tricky part is that we must make sure that the snapshot taken from the helping update is one that can be linearized within the scan() call's execution interval.

We say that a thread *moves* if it completes an update(). If thread *A* fails to make a clean collect because thread *B* moved, then can *A* simply take *B*'s most recent snapshot as its own? Unfortunately, no. As illustrated in Fig. 4.18, it is possible for *A* to see *B* move when *B*'s snapshot was taken before *A* started its scan() call, so the snapshot did not occur within the interval of *A*'s scan.

```
1    public class SimpleSnapshot<T> implements Snapshot<T> {
2      private StampedValue<T>[] a_table; // array of atomic MRSW registers
3      public SimpleSnapshot(int capacity, T init) {
4        a_table = (StampedValue<T>[]) new StampedValue[capacity];
5        for (int i = 0; i < capacity; i++) {
6          a_table[i] = new StampedValue<T>(init);
7        }
8      }
9      public void update(T value) {
10       int me = ThreadID.get();
11       StampedValue<T> oldValue = a_table[me];
12       StampedValue<T> newValue = new StampedValue<T>((oldValue.stamp)+1, value);
13       a_table[me] = newValue;
14     }
15     private StampedValue<T>[] collect() {
16       StampedValue<T>[] copy = (StampedValue<T>[]) new StampedValue[a_table.length];
17       for (int j = 0; j < a_table.length; j++)
18         copy[j] = a_table[j];
19       return copy;
20     }
21     public T[] scan() {
22       StampedValue<T>[] oldCopy, newCopy;
23       oldCopy = collect();
24       collect: while (true) {
25         newCopy = collect();
26         if (! Arrays.equals(oldCopy, newCopy)) {
27           oldCopy = newCopy;
28           continue collect;
29         }
30         T[] result = (T[]) new Object[a_table.length];
31         for (int j = 0; j < a_table.length; j++)
32           result[j] = newCopy[j].value;
33         return result;
34       }
35     }
36   }
```

FIGURE 4.17

Simple snapshot object.

The wait-free construction is based on the following observation: If a scanning thread A sees a thread B move *twice* while it is performing repeated collects, then B executed a complete update() call within the interval of A's scan(), so it is correct for A to use B's snapshot.

Figs. 4.19 and 4.20 show the wait-free snapshot algorithm. Each update() calls scan(), and appends the result of the scan to the value (in addition to the timestamp).

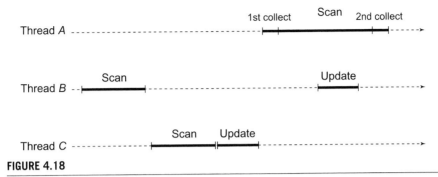

FIGURE 4.18

Here is why a thread *A* that fails to complete a clean double collect cannot simply take the latest snapshot of a thread *B* that performed an update() during *A*'s second collect. *B*'s snapshot was taken before *A* started its scan(), i.e., *B*'s snapshot did not overlap *A*'s scan. The danger, illustrated here, is that a thread *C* could have called update() after *B*'s scan() and before *A*'s scan(), making it incorrect for *A* to use the results of *B*'s scan().

```
1   public class StampedSnap<T> {
2     public long stamp;
3     public T value;
4     public T[] snap;
5     public StampedSnap(T value) {
6       stamp = 0;
7       value = value;
8       snap = null;
9     }
10    public StampedSnap(long ts, T v, T[] s) {
11      stamp = ts;
12      value = v;
13      snap = s;
14    }
15  }
```

FIGURE 4.19

The stamped snapshot class.

More precisely, each value written to a register has the structure shown in Fig. 4.19: a stamp field incremented each time the thread updates its value, a value field containing the register's actual value, and a snap field containing that thread's most recent scan. The snapshot algorithm is described in Fig. 4.20. A scanning thread creates a Boolean array called moved[] (line 24), which records which threads have been observed to move in the course of the scan. As before, each thread performs two collects (lines 25 and 27) and tests whether any thread's timestamp has changed. If no thread's timestamp has changed, then the collect is clean, and the scan returns the result of the collect. If any thread's timestamp has changed (line 29), the scanning thread tests the

```
1   public class WFSnapshot<T> implements Snapshot<T> {
2     private StampedSnap<T>[] a_table; // array of atomic MRSW registers
3     public WFSnapshot(int capacity, T init) {
4       a_table = (StampedSnap<T>[]) new StampedSnap[capacity];
5       for (int i = 0; i < a_table.length; i++) {
6         a_table[i] = new StampedSnap<T>(init);
7       }
8     }
9     private StampedSnap<T>[] collect() {
10      StampedSnap<T>[] copy = (StampedSnap<T>[]) new StampedSnap[a_table.length];
11      for (int j = 0; j < a_table.length; j++)
12        copy[j] = a_table[j];
13      return copy;
14    }
15    public void update(T value) {
16      int me = ThreadID.get();
17      T[] snap = scan();
18      StampedSnap<T> oldValue = a_table[me];
19      StampedSnap<T> newValue = new StampedSnap<T>(oldValue.stamp+1, value, snap);
20      a_table[me] = newValue;
21    }
22    public T[] scan() {
23      StampedSnap<T>[] oldCopy, newCopy;
24      boolean[] moved = new boolean[a_table.length]; // initially all false
25      oldCopy = collect();
26      collect: while (true) {
27        newCopy = collect();
28        for (int j = 0; j < a_table.length; j++) {
29          if (oldCopy[j].stamp != newCopy[j].stamp) {
30            if (moved[j]) {
31              return newCopy[j].snap;
32            } else {
33              moved[j] = true;
34              oldCopy = newCopy;
35              continue collect;
36            }
37          }
38        }
39        T[] result = (T[]) new Object[a_table.length];
40        for (int j = 0; j < a_table.length; j++)
41          result[j] = newCopy[j].value;
42        return result;
43      }
44    }
45  }
```

FIGURE 4.20

Single-writer atomic snapshot class.

moved[] array to detect whether this is the second time this thread has moved (line 30). If so, it returns that thread's scan (line 31); otherwise, it updates moved[] and resumes the outer loop (line 32).

4.3.3 Correctness arguments

In this section, we review the correctness arguments for the wait-free snapshot algorithm a little more carefully.

Lemma 4.3.1. If a scanning thread makes a clean double collect, then the values it returns were the values that existed in the registers in some state of the execution.

Proof. Consider the interval between the last read of the first collect and the first read of the second collect. If any register were updated in that interval, the timestamps would not match, and the double collect would not be clean.   □

Lemma 4.3.2. If a scanning thread A observes changes in another thread B's timestamp during two different double collects, then the value of B's register read during the last collect was written by an update() call that began after the first collect started.

Proof. If during a scan(), two successive reads by A of B's register return different timestamps, then at least one write by B occurs between this pair of reads. Thread B writes to its register as the final step of an update() call, so some update() call by B ended sometime after the first read by A, and the write step of another update() call occurs between the last pair of reads by A. The claim follows because only B writes to its register.   □

Lemma 4.3.3. The values returned by a scan() were in the registers at some state between the call's invocation and response.

Proof. If the scan() call made a clean double collect, then the claim follows from Lemma 4.3.1. If the call took the scan value from another thread B's register, then by Lemma 4.3.2, the scan value found in B's register was obtained by a scan() call by B whose interval lies between A's first and last reads of B's register. Either B's scan() call had a clean double collect, in which case the result follows from Lemma 4.3.1, or there is an embedded scan() call by a thread C occurring within the interval of B's scan() call. This argument can be applied inductively, noting that there can be at most $n - 1$ nested calls before we run out of threads, where n is the maximum number of threads (see Fig. 4.21). Eventually, some nested scan() call must have had a clean double collect.   □

Lemma 4.3.4. Every scan() or update() returns after at most $O(n^2)$ reads or writes.

Proof. Consider a particular scan(). There are only $n - 1$ other threads, so after n double collects, either one double collect is clean, or some thread is observed to move twice. The claim follows because each double collect does $O(n)$ reads.   □

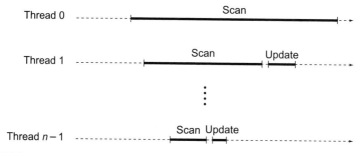

FIGURE 4.21

There can be at most $n-1$ nested calls of scan() before we run out of threads, where n is the maximum number of threads. The scan() by thread $n-1$, contained in the intervals of all other scan() calls, must have a clean double collect.

By Lemma 4.3.3, the values returned by a scan() form a snapshot as they are all in the registers in some state during the call: linearize the call at that point. Similarly, linearize update() calls at the point the register is written.

Theorem 4.3.5. The code in Fig. 4.20 is a wait-free snapshot implementation.

Our wait-free atomic snapshot construction is another, somewhat different example of the dissemination approach we discussed in our atomic register constructions. In this example, threads tell other threads about their snapshots, and those snapshots are reused. Another useful trick is that even if one thread interrupts another and prevents it from completing, we can still guarantee wait-freedom if the interrupting thread completes the interrupted thread's operation. This helping paradigm is extremely useful in designing multiprocessor algorithms.

4.4 Chapter notes

Alonzo Church introduced lambda calculus around 1935 [30]. Alan Turing defined the Turing machine in a classic paper in 1937 [163]. Leslie Lamport defined the notions of *safe*, *regular*, and *atomic* registers and the register hierarchy, and was the first to show that one could implement nontrivial shared memory from safe bits [99, 105]. Gary Peterson suggested the problem of constructing atomic registers [139]. Jaydev Misra gave an axiomatic treatment of atomic registers [128]. The notion of *linearizability*, which generalizes Lamport's and Misra's notions of atomic registers, is due to Herlihy and Wing [75]. Susmita Haldar and Krishnamurthy Vidyasankar gave a bounded atomic MRSW register construction from regular registers [55]. The problem of constructing an atomic multi-reader register from atomic single-reader registers was mentioned as an open problem by Leslie Lamport [99,105] and by Paul Vitányi and Baruch Awerbuch [165], who were the first to propose an approach for atomic MRMW register design. The first solution is due to Jim Anderson, Mohamed

Gouda, and Ambuj Singh [87,160]. Other atomic register constructions, to name only a few, were proposed by Jim Burns and Gary Peterson [25], Richard Newman-Wolfe [134], Lefteris Kirousis, Paul Spirakis, and Philippas Tsigas [92], Amos Israeli and Amnon Shaham [86], and Ming Li, John Tromp and Paul Vitányi [113]. The simple timestamp-based atomic MRMW construction we present here is due to Danny Dolev and Nir Shavit [39].

Collect operations were first formalized by Mike Saks, Nir Shavit, and Heather Woll [152]. The first atomic snapshot constructions were discovered concurrently and independently by Jim Anderson [10] and Yehuda Afek, Hagit Attiya, Danny Dolev, Eli Gafni, Michael Merritt, and Nir Shavit [2]. The latter algorithm is the one presented here. Later snapshot algorithms are due to Elizabeth Borowsky and Eli Gafni [21] and Yehuda Afek, Gideon Stupp, and Dan Touitou [4].

The timestamps in all the algorithms mentioned in this chapter can be bounded so that the constructions themselves use registers of bounded size. Bounded timestamp systems were introduced by Amos Israeli and Ming Li [85], and bounded concurrent timestamp systems by Danny Dolev and Nir Shavit [39].

Horsey [78] has a beautiful article on chicken sexing and its relation to intuition.

4.5 Exercises

Exercise 4.1. Consider the safe Boolean MRSW construction shown in Fig. 4.6. True or false: If we replace the safe Boolean SRSW register array with an array of safe M-valued SRSW registers, then the construction yields a safe M-valued MRSW register. Justify your answer.

Exercise 4.2. Consider the safe Boolean MRSW construction shown in Fig. 4.6. True or false: If we replace the safe Boolean SRSW register array with an array of regular Boolean SRSW registers, then the construction yields a regular Boolean MRSW register. Justify your answer.

Exercise 4.3. Consider the safe Boolean MRSW construction shown in Fig. 4.6. True or false: If we replace the safe Boolean SRSW register array with an array of regular M-valued SRSW registers, then the construction yields a regular M-valued MRSW register. Justify your answer.

Exercise 4.4. Consider the regular Boolean MRSW construction shown in Fig. 4.7. True or false: If we replace the safe Boolean MRSW register with a safe M-valued MRSW register, then the construction yields a regular M-valued MRSW register. Justify your answer.

Exercise 4.5. Consider the atomic MRSW construction shown in Fig. 4.12. True or false: If we replace the atomic SRSW registers with regular SRSW registers, then the construction still yields an atomic MRSW register. Justify your answer.

Exercise 4.6. Give an example of a quiescently consistent register execution that is not regular.

```
1    public class AtomicSRSWRegister implements Register<int> {
2      private static int RANGE = M;
3      boolean[] r_bit = new boolean[RANGE]; // atomic boolean SRSW
4      public AtomicSRSWRegister(int capacity) {
5        for (int i = 1; i <= RANGE; i++)
6          r_bit[i] = false;
7        r_bit[0] = true;
8      }
9      public void write(int x) {
10       r_bit[x] = true;
11       for (int i = x - 1; i >= 0; i--)
12         r_bit[i] = false;
13     }
14     public int read() {
15       for (int i = 0; i <= RANGE; i++)
16         if (r_bit[i]) {
17           return i;
18         }
19       return -1; // impossible
20     }
21   }
```

FIGURE 4.22

Boolean to *M*-valued atomic SRSW register algorithm.

Exercise 4.7. You are given the algorithm in Fig. 4.22 for constructing an atomic *M*-valued SRSW register using atomic Boolean SRSW registers. Does this proposal work? Either prove the correctness or present a counterexample.

Exercise 4.8. Imagine running a 64-bit system on a 32-bit system, where each 64-bit memory location (register) is implemented using two atomic 32-bit memory locations (registers). A write operation is implemented by simply writing the first 32 bits in the first register and then the second 32 bits in the second register. A read, similarly, reads the first half from the first register, then reads the second half from the second register, and returns the concatenation. What is the strongest property that this 64-bit register satisfies?

- safe register,
- regular register,
- atomic register,
- it does not satisfy any of these properties.

Exercise 4.9. Does Peterson's two-thread mutual exclusion algorithm work if the shared atomic flag registers are replaced by regular registers?

Exercise 4.10. Consider the following implementation of a register in a distributed, message passing system. There are n processors $P_0, \ldots, P_{n-1}$ arranged in a ring, where P_i can send messages only to $P_{i+1 \bmod n}$. Messages are delivered in FIFO order along each link. Each processor keeps a copy of the shared register.

- To read the register, the processor reads the copy in its local memory.
- A processor P_i starts a write() call of value v to register x, by sending the message "P_i: write v to x" to $P_{i+1 \bmod n}$.
- If P_i receives a message "P_j: write v to x," for $i \neq j$, then it writes v to its local copy of x, and forwards the message to $P_{i+1 \bmod n}$.
- If P_i receives a message "P_i: write v to x," then it writes v to its local copy of x, and discards the message. The write() call is now complete.

Give a short justification or counterexample.
If write() calls never overlap,

- is this register implementation regular?
- is it atomic?

If multiple processors call write(),

- is this register implementation safe?

Exercise 4.11. Fig. 4.23 shows an implementation of a multivalued *write-once*, MRSW register from an array of multivalued safe, MRSW registers. Remember, there is one writer, who can overwrite the register's initial value with a new value, but it can only write once. You do not know the register's initial value.
Is this implementation regular? Atomic?

```
1   class WriteOnceRegister implements Register{
2     private SafeMRSWRegister[] s = new SafeMRSWRegister[3];
3
4     public void write(int x) {
5       s[0].write(x);
6       s[1].write(x);
7       s[2].write(x);
8     }
9     public int read() {
10      v2 = s[2].read()
11      v1 = s[1].read()
12      v0 = s[0].read()
13      if (v0 == v1) return v0;
14      else if (v1 == v2) return v1;
15      else return v0;
16    }
17  }
```

FIGURE 4.23

Write-once register.

Exercise 4.12. A (single-writer) register is *1-regular* if the following conditions hold:

- If a read() operation does not overlap with any write() operations, then it returns the value written by the last write() operation.
- If a read() operation overlaps with exactly one write() operation, then it returns a value written either by the last write() operation or the concurrent write() operation.
- Otherwise, a read() operation may return an arbitrary value.

Construct an SRSW M-valued 1-regular register using $O(\log M)$ SRSW Boolean regular registers. Explain why your construction works.

Exercise 4.13. Prove that the safe Boolean MRSW register construction from safe Boolean SRSW registers illustrated in Fig. 4.6 is a correct implementation of a regular MRSW register if the component registers are regular SRSW registers.

Exercise 4.14. Define a *wraparound* register that has the property that there is a value k such that writing the value v sets the value of the register to $v \bmod k$.

If we replace the Bakery algorithm's shared variables with either (a) regular, (b) safe, or (c) atomic wraparound registers, then does it still satisfy (1) mutual exclusion and (2) FIFO ordering?

You should provide six answers (some may imply others). Justify each claim.

The relative power of primitive synchronization operations

5

Imagine you are in charge of designing a new multiprocessor. What kinds of atomic instructions should you include? The literature includes a bewildering array of different choices: read() and write(), getAndIncrement(), getAndComplement(), swap(), compareAndSet(), and many, many others. Supporting them all would be complicated and inefficient, but supporting the wrong ones could make it difficult or even impossible to solve important synchronization problems.

Our goal is to identify a set of primitive synchronization operations powerful enough to solve synchronization problems likely to arise in practice. (We might also support other, nonessential synchronization operations, for convenience.) To this end, we need some way to evaluate the *power* of various synchronization primitives: what synchronization problems they can solve, and how efficiently they can solve them.

A concurrent object implementation is *wait-free* if each method call finishes in a finite number of steps. A method is *lock-free* if it guarantees that infinitely often, *some* method call finishes in a finite number of steps. We have already seen wait-free (and therefore also lock-free) register implementations in Chapter 4. One way to evaluate the power of synchronization instructions is to see how well they support implementations of shared objects such as queues, stacks, trees, and so on. As we explain in Section 4.1, we evaluate solutions that are wait-free or lock-free, that is, that guarantee progress without relying on the underlying platform.[1]

Not all synchronization instructions are created equal. If one thinks of primitive synchronization instructions as objects whose exported methods are the instructions themselves (these objects are often called *synchronization primitives*), one can show that there is an infinite hierarchy of synchronization primitives, such that no primitive at one level can be used for a wait-free or lock-free implementation of any primitives at higher levels. The basic idea is simple: Each class in the hierarchy has an associated *consensus number*, which is the maximum number of threads for which objects of the class can solve an elementary synchronization problem called *consensus*. In a system of n or more concurrent threads, it is impossible to implement a wait-free or lock-free object with consensus number n from objects with a lower consensus number.

---

[1] It makes no sense to evaluate solutions that only meet dependent progress conditions such as obstruction-freedom or deadlock-freedom because the real power of such solutions is masked by the contribution of the operating system they depend on.

The Art of Multiprocessor Programming. https://doi.org/10.1016/B978-0-12-415950-1.00014-8

```
1  public interface Consensus<T> {
2    T decide(T value);
3  }
```

FIGURE 5.1

Consensus object interface.

5.1 Consensus numbers

Consensus is an innocuous-looking, somewhat abstract problem that has enormous consequences for everything from algorithm design to hardware architecture. A *consensus object* provides a single method decide(), as shown in Fig. 5.1. Each thread calls the decide() method with its input v *at most once*. The object's decide() method returns a value meeting the following conditions:

- *consistent*: all threads decide the same value,
- *valid*: the common decision value is some thread's input.

In other words, a concurrent consensus object is linearizable to a sequential consensus object in which the thread whose value was chosen completes its decide() first. To simplify the presentation, we focus on *binary consensus*, in which all inputs are either 0 or 1 but our claims apply to consensus in general.

We are interested in wait-free solutions to the consensus problem, that is, wait-free concurrent implementations of consensus objects. The reader will notice that since the decide() method of a given consensus object is executed only once by each thread, and there are a finite number of threads, a lock-free implementation would also be wait-free and vice versa. Henceforth, we mention only wait-free implementations, and for historical reasons, call any class that implements *consensus* in a wait-free manner a *consensus protocol*.

We want to understand whether a particular class of objects is powerful enough to solve the consensus problem.[2] How can we make this notion more precise? If we think of such objects as supported by a lower level of the system, perhaps the operating system or even the hardware, then we care about the properties of the class, not about the number of objects. (If the system can provide one object of this class, it can probably provide more.) Second, it is reasonable to suppose that any modern system can provide a generous amount of read–write memory for bookkeeping. These two observations suggest the following definitions.

Definition 5.1.1. A class C *solves* n-thread consensus if there exists a consensus protocol for n threads using any number of objects of class C and any number of atomic registers.

---

[2] We restrict ourselves to object classes with deterministic sequential specifications (i.e., ones in which each sequential method call has a single outcome). We avoid nondeterministic objects since their structure is significantly more complex. See the discussion in the notes at the end of this chapter.

Definition 5.1.2. The *consensus number* of a class C is the largest n for which that class solves n-thread consensus. If no largest n exists, we say the consensus number of the class is *infinite*.

Corollary 5.1.3. Suppose one can implement an object of class C from one or more objects of class D, together with some number of atomic registers. If class C solves n-consensus, then so does class D.

5.1.1 States and valence

A good place to start is to think about the simplest interesting case: binary consensus (i.e., inputs 0 or 1) for two threads (call them A and B). Each thread makes moves until it decides on a value. Here, a *move* is a method call to a shared object. A *protocol state* consists of the states of the threads and the shared objects. An *initial state* is a protocol state before any thread has moved, and a *final state* is a protocol state after all threads have finished. The *decision value* of any final state is the value decided by all threads in that state.

A wait-free protocol's set of possible states forms a tree, where each node represents a possible protocol state and each edge represents a possible move by some thread. Fig. 5.2 shows the tree for a two-thread protocol in which each thread moves twice. An edge for A from node s to node s' means that if A moves in protocol state s, then the new protocol state is s'. We refer to s' as a *successor state* to s. Because the protocol is wait-free, every (simple) path starting from the root is finite (i.e., eventually ends at a leaf node). Leaf nodes represent final protocol states, and are labeled with their decision values, either 0 or 1.

A protocol state is *bivalent* if the decision value is not yet fixed: There is some execution starting from that state in which the threads decide 0, and one in which they decide 1. By contrast, a protocol state is *univalent* if the outcome is fixed: Every execution starting from that state decides the same value. A protocol state is *1-valent* if it is univalent, and the decision value will be 1, and similarly for *0-valent*. As illustrated in Fig. 5.2, a bivalent state is a node whose descendants in the tree include both leaves labeled with 0 and leaves labeled with 1, while a univalent state is a node whose descendants include only leaves labeled with a single decision value.

Our next lemma says that an initial bivalent state exists. This observation means that the outcome of the protocol cannot be fixed in advance, but must depend on how `reads` and `writes` are interleaved.

Lemma 5.1.4. Every two-thread consensus protocol has a bivalent initial state.

Proof. Consider the initial state where A has input 0 and B has input 1. If A finishes the protocol before B takes a step, then A must decide 0, because it must decide some thread's input, and 0 is the only input it has seen (it cannot decide 1 because it has no way of distinguishing this state from the one in which B has input 0). Symmetrically, if B finishes the protocol before A takes a step, then B must decide 1. It follows that the initial state where A has input 0 and B has input 1 is bivalent. □

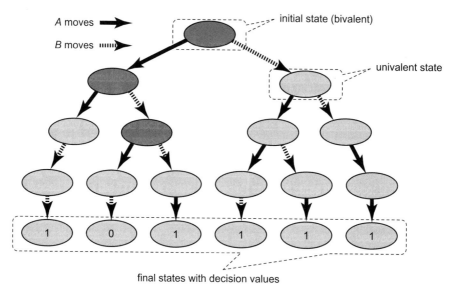

A moves ➡
B moves ⇒

initial state (bivalent)

univalent state

final states with decision values

FIGURE 5.2

An execution tree for two threads A and B. The dark shaded nodes denote bivalent states, and the lighter ones denote univalent states.

Lemma 5.1.5. Every n-thread consensus protocol has a bivalent initial state.

Proof. Left as an exercise.   □

A protocol state is *critical* if:

- it is bivalent, and
- if any thread moves, the protocol state becomes univalent.

Lemma 5.1.6. Every wait-free consensus protocol has a critical state.

Proof. By Lemma 5.1.5, the protocol has a bivalent initial state. Start the protocol in this state. As long as some thread can move without making the protocol state univalent, let that thread move. The protocol cannot run forever because it is wait-free. Therefore, the protocol eventually enters a state where no such move is possible, which is, by definition, a critical state.   □

Everything we have proved so far applies to any consensus protocol, no matter what class(es) of shared objects it uses. Now we consider specific classes of objects.

5.2 Atomic registers

The obvious place to begin is to ask whether we can solve consensus using atomic registers. Surprisingly, perhaps, the answer is *no*. We show that there is no binary consensus protocol for two threads. We leave it as an exercise to show that if two threads cannot reach consensus on two values, then n threads cannot reach consensus on k values, for $n \geq 2$ and $k \geq 2$.

Often, when we argue about whether or not there exists a protocol that solves a particular problem, we construct a scenario of the form: "If we had such a protocol, it would behave like this under these circumstances." One particularly useful scenario is to have one thread, say, A, run completely by itself until it finishes the protocol. This particular scenario is common enough that we give it its own name: A runs *solo*.

Theorem 5.2.1. Atomic registers have consensus number 1.

Proof. Suppose there exists a binary consensus protocol for two threads A and B. We reason about the properties of such a protocol and derive a contradiction.

By Lemma 5.1.6, we can run the protocol until it reaches a critical state s. Suppose A's next move carries the protocol to a 0-valent state, and B's next move carries the protocol to a 1-valent state. (If not, then swap thread names.) What methods could A and B be about to call? We now consider an exhaustive list of the possibilities: one of them reads from a register, they both write to separate registers, or they both write to the same register.

Suppose A is about to read a given register (B may be about to either read or write the same register or a different register), as depicted in Fig. 5.3. Consider two possible execution scenarios. In the first scenario, B moves first, driving the protocol to a 1-valent state s', and then B runs solo and eventually decides 1. In the second execution scenario, A moves first, driving the protocol to a 0-valent state, and then

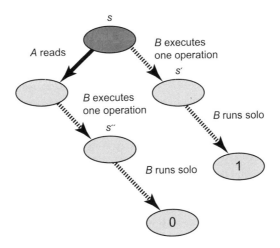

FIGURE 5.3

Case: A reads first. In the first execution scenario, B moves first, driving the protocol to a 1-valent state s', and then B runs solo and eventually decides 1. In the second execution scenario, A moves first, driving the protocol to a 0-valent state, and then B takes a step to reach state s''. B then runs solo starting in s'' and eventually decides 0.

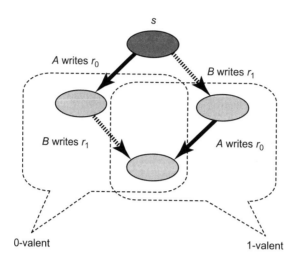

FIGURE 5.4

Case: *A* and *B* write to different registers.

B takes a step to reach state s''. *B* then runs solo starting in s'' and eventually decides 0. The problem is that the states s' and s'' are indistinguishable to *B* (the read *A* performed could only change its thread-local state, which is not visible to *B*), which means that *B* must decide the same value in both scenarios, a contradiction.

Suppose, instead of this scenario, both threads are about to write to different registers, as depicted in Fig. 5.4. *A* is about to write to r_0 and *B* to r_1. Consider two possible execution scenarios. In the first, *A* writes to r_0 and then *B* writes to r_1; the resulting protocol state is 0-valent because *A* went first. In the second, *B* writes to r_1 and then *A* writes to r_0; the resulting protocol state is 1-valent because *B* went first.

The problem is that both scenarios lead to the same protocol state. Neither *A* nor *B* can tell which move was first. The resulting state is therefore both 0-valent and 1-valent, a contradiction.

Finally, suppose both threads write to the same register r, as depicted in Fig. 5.5. Again, consider two possible execution scenarios. In one scenario *A* writes first, and then *B* writes; the resulting protocol state s' is 0-valent, and *B* then runs solo and decides 0. In the other scenario, *B* writes first, the resulting protocol state s'' is 1-valent, and *B* then runs solo and decides 1. The problem is that *B* cannot tell the difference between s' and s'' (because in both s' and s'', *B* overwrote the register r and obliterated any trace of *A*'s write) so *B* must decide the same value starting from either state, a contradiction.   □

Corollary 5.2.2. It is impossible to construct a wait-free implementation of any object with consensus number greater than 1 using atomic registers.

This corollary is one of the most striking impossibility results in computer science. It explains why, if we want to implement lock-free concurrent data structures

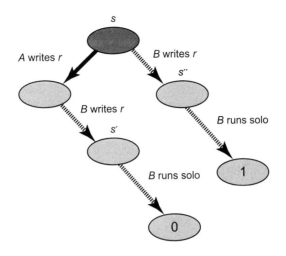

FIGURE 5.5

Case: *A* and *B* write to the same register.

on modern multiprocessors, our hardware must provide primitive synchronization operations other than loads and stores (i.e., reads and writes).

5.3 Consensus protocols

We now consider a variety of interesting object classes, asking how well each can solve the consensus problem. These protocols have a generic form, shown in Fig. 5.6. The object has an array of atomic registers in which each decide() method proposes its input value and then goes on to execute a sequence of steps in order to decide on one of the proposed values. We devise different implementations of the decide() method using various synchronization objects.

```
1  public abstract class ConsensusProtocol<T> implements Consensus<T> {
2    protected T[] proposed = (T[]) new Object[N]; // N is the number of threads
3    // announce my input value to the other threads
4    void propose(T value) {
5      proposed[ThreadID.get()] = value;
6    }
7    // figure out which thread was first
8    abstract public T decide(T value);
9  }
```

FIGURE 5.6

The generic consensus protocol.

```
1   public class QueueConsensus<T> extends ConsensusProtocol<T> {
2     private static final int WIN = 0; // first thread
3     private static final int LOSE = 1; // second thread
4     Queue queue;
5     // initialize queue with two items
6     public QueueConsensus() {
7       queue = new Queue();
8       queue.enq(WIN);
9       queue.enq(LOSE);
10    }
11    // figure out which thread was first
12    public T decide(T value) {
13      propose(value);
14      int status = queue.deq();
15      int i = ThreadID.get();
16      if (status == WIN)
17        return proposed[i];
18      else
19        return proposed[1-i];
20    }
21  }
```

FIGURE 5.7

Two-thread consensus using a FIFO queue.

5.4 FIFO queues

In Chapter 3, we saw a wait-free FIFO queue implementation using only atomic registers, subject to the limitation that only one thread could enqueue to the queue, and
only one thread could dequeue from the queue. It is natural to ask whether one can
provide a wait-free implementation of a FIFO queue that supports multiple enqueuers
and dequeuers. For now, let us focus on a more specific problem: Can we provide a
wait-free implementation of a two-dequeuer FIFO queue using atomic registers?

Lemma 5.4.1. The two-dequeuer FIFO queue class has consensus number at least 2.

Proof. Fig. 5.7 shows a two-thread consensus protocol using a single FIFO queue.
Here, the queue stores integers. The queue is initialized by enqueuing the value
WIN followed by the value LOSE. As in all the consensus protocols considered here,
decide() first calls propose(v), which stores v in proposed[], a shared array of proposed input values. It then proceeds to dequeue the next item from the queue. If that
item is the value WIN, then the calling thread was first, and it decides on its own value.
If that item is the value LOSE, then the other thread was first, so the calling thread
returns the other thread's input, as declared in the proposed[] array.

  The protocol is wait-free, since it contains no loops. If each thread returns its own
input, then they must both have dequeued WIN, violating the FIFO queue specifica-

tion. If each returns the other's input, then they must both have dequeued LOSE, also violating the queue specification.

The validity condition follows from the observation that the thread that dequeued WIN stored its input in the proposed[] array before any value was dequeued.   □

Trivial variations of this program yield protocols for stacks, priority queues, lists, sets, or any object with methods that return different results if applied in different orders.

Corollary 5.4.2. It is impossible to construct a wait-free implementation of a queue, stack, priority queue, list, or set from a set of atomic registers.

Although FIFO queues solve two-thread consensus, they do not solve three-thread consensus.

Theorem 5.4.3. FIFO queues have consensus number 2.

Proof. By contradiction, assume we have a consensus protocol for a thread A, B, and C. By Lemma 5.1.6, the protocol has a critical state s. Without loss of generality, we can assume that A's next move takes the protocol to a 0-valent state, and B's next move takes the protocol to a 1-valent state. The rest, as before, is a case analysis.

We know that A and B's pending moves cannot commute. Thus, they are both about to call methods of the same object. We also know that A and B cannot be about to read or write shared registers by the proof of Theorem 5.2.1. It follows that they are about to call methods of a single queue object.

First, suppose A and B both call deq(), as depicted in Fig. 5.8. Let s' be the protocol state if A dequeues and then B dequeues, and let s'' be the state if the dequeues

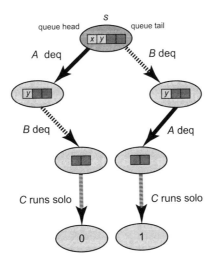

FIGURE 5.8

Case: A and B both call deq().

occur in the opposite order. Since s' is 0-valent, if C runs uninterrupted from s', then it decides 0. Since s'' is 1-valent, if C runs uninterrupted from s'', then it decides 1. But s' and s'' are indistinguishable to C (the same two items were removed from the queue), so C must decide the same value in both states, a contradiction.

Second, suppose A calls enq(a) and B calls deq(). If the queue is nonempty, the contradiction is immediate because the two methods commute (each operates on a different end of the queue): C cannot observe the order in which they occurred. If the queue is empty, then the 1-valent state reached if B executes a dequeue on the empty queue and then A enqueues is indistinguishable to C from the 0-valent state reached if A alone enqueues. Note that it does not matter what a deq() on an empty queue does, that is, aborts or waits, since this does not affect the state visible to C.

Finally, suppose A calls enq(a) and B calls enq(b), as depicted in Fig. 5.9. Let s' be the state at the end of the following execution:

1. Let A and B enqueue items a and b in that order.

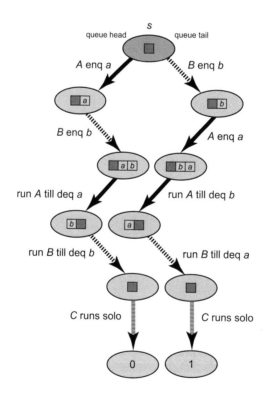

FIGURE 5.9

Case: A calls enq(a) and B calls enq(b). Note that a new item is enqueued by A after A and B enqueued their respective items and before it dequeued (and B could have also enqueued items before dequeuing), but that this item is the same in both of the execution scenarios.

2. Run A until it dequeues a. (Since the only way to observe the queue's state is via the deq() method, A cannot decide before it observes one of a or b.)
3. Before A takes any further steps, run B until it dequeues b.

Let s'' be the state after the following alternative execution:

1. Let B and A enqueue items b and a in that order.
2. Run A until it dequeues b.
3. Before A takes any further steps, run B until it dequeues a.

Clearly, s' is 0-valent and s'' is 1-valent. Both of A's executions are identical until A dequeues a or b. Since A is halted before it can modify any other objects, B's executions are also identical until it dequeues a or b. By a now familiar argument, a contradiction arises because s' and s'' are indistinguishable to C. □

Variations of this argument can be applied to show that many similar data types, such as sets, stacks, double-ended queues, and priority queues, all have consensus number exactly 2.

5.5 **Multiple assignment objects**

In the (m, n)-*assignment* problem for $n \geq m > 1$ (sometimes called *multiple assignment*), we are given an object with n fields (sometimes an n-element array). The assign() method takes as arguments m values v_j and m indices $i_j \in 0, \ldots, n - 1$ for $j \in 0, \ldots, m - 1$. It atomically assigns v_j to array element i_j. The read() method takes an index argument i, and returns the ith array element.

Fig. 5.10 shows a lock-based implementation of a $(2, 3)$-assignment object. Here, threads can assign atomically to any two out of three array entries.

Multiple assignment is the dual of the *atomic snapshot* (Section 4.3), where we assign to one field and read multiple fields atomically. Because snapshots can be implemented from read–write registers, Theorem 5.2.1 implies snapshot objects have consensus number 1. However, the same is not true for multiple assignment objects.

Theorem 5.5.1. There is no wait-free implementation of an (m, n)-assignment object by atomic registers for any $n > m > 1$.

Proof. It is enough to show that we can solve 2-consensus given two threads and a $(2, 3)$-assignment object. (Exercise 5.26 asks you to justify this claim.) As usual, the decide() method must figure out which thread went first. All array entries are initialized with *null* values. Fig. 5.11 shows the protocol. Thread A, with ID 0, writes (atomically) to fields 0 and 1, while thread B, with ID 1, writes (atomically) to fields 1 and 2. Then they try to determine who went first. From A's point of view, there are three cases, as shown in Fig. 5.12:

- If A's assignment was ordered first, and B's assignment has not (yet) happened, then fields 0 and 1 have A's value, and field 2 is *null*. A decides its own input.

```
1   public class Assign23 {
2     int[] r = new int[3];
3     public Assign23(int init) {
4       for (int i = 0; i < r.length; i++)
5         r[i] = init;
6     }
7     public synchronized void assign(int v0, int v1, int i0, int i1) {
8       r[i0] = v0;
9       r[i1] = v1;
10    }
11    public synchronized int read(int i) {
12      return r[i];
13    }
14  }
```

FIGURE 5.10

A lock-based implementation of a (2,3)-assignment object.

```
1   public class MultiConsensus<T> extends ConsensusProtocol<T> {
2     private final int NULL = -1;
3     Assign23 assign23 = new Assign23(NULL);
4     public T decide(T value) {
5       propose(value);
6       int i = ThreadID.get();
7       int j = 1-i;
8       // double assignment
9       assign23.assign(i, i, i, i+1);
10      int other = assign23.read((i+2) % 3);
11      if (other == NULL || other == assign23.read(1))
12        return proposed[i];      // I win
13      else
14        return proposed[j];      // I lose
15    }
16  }
```

FIGURE 5.11

Two-thread consensus using (2,3)-multiple assignment.

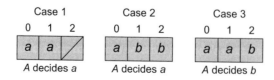

FIGURE 5.12

Consensus using multiple assignment: possible views.

- If A's assignment was ordered first, and B's second, then field 0 has A's value, and fields 1 and 2 have B's. A decides its own input.
- If B's assignment was ordered first, and A's second, then fields 0 and 1 have A's value, and 2 has B's. A decides B's input.

A similar analysis holds for B. □

Theorem 5.5.2. $(n, \frac{n(n+1)}{2})$-assignment for $n > 1$ has consensus number at least n.

Proof. We design a consensus protocol for n threads with IDs $0, \ldots, n - 1$ that uses an $(n, \frac{n(n+1)}{2})$-assignment object. For convenience, we name the object fields as follows. There are n fields $r_0, \ldots, r_{n-1}$ where thread i writes to register r_i, and $n(n - 1)/2$ fields r_{ij}, for $i > j$, where threads i and j both write to field r_{ij}. All fields are initialized to *null*. Each thread i atomically assigns its input value to n fields: its single-writer field r_i and its $n - 1$ multi-writer fields r_{ij} and r_{ji}. The protocol decides the first value to be assigned.

After assigning to its fields, a thread determines the relative ordering of the assignments for every two threads i and j as follows:

- Read r_{ij} or r_{ji}. If the value is *null*, then neither assignment has occurred.
- Otherwise, read r_i and r_j. If r_i's value is *null*, then j precedes i, and similarly for r_j.
- If neither r_i nor r_j is *null*, reread r_{ij}. If its value is equal to the value read from r_i, then j precedes i, else vice versa.

Repeating this procedure, a thread can determine which value was written by the earliest assignment. Two example orderings appear in Fig. 5.13. □

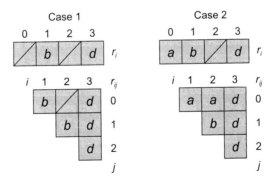

FIGURE 5.13

Two possible cases of (4,10)-assignment solving consensus for four threads. In Case 1, only threads B and D show up. B is the first to assign and wins the consensus. In Case 2, there are three threads, A, B, and D, and as before, B wins by assigning first and D assigns last. The order among the threads can be determined by looking at the pairwise order among any two. Because the assignments are atomic, these individual orders are always consistent and define the total order among the calls.

Note that $(n, \frac{n(n+1)}{2})$-assignment solves consensus for $n > 1$ threads, while its dual structures, atomic snapshots, have consensus number 1. Although these two problems may appear similar, we have just shown that writing atomically to multiple memory locations requires more computational power than reading atomically.

5.6 Read–modify–write operations

Many, if not all, synchronization operations commonly provided by multiprocessors in hardware can be expressed as *read–modify–write* (RMW) operations, or, as they are called in their object form, *read–modify–write registers*. Consider an RMW register that encapsulates integer values, and let $\mathcal{F}$ be a set of functions from integers to integers.[3] (Sometimes $\mathcal{F}$ is a singleton set.)

A method is an RMW for the function set $\mathcal{F}$ if it atomically replaces the current register value v with $f(v)$, for some $f \in \mathcal{F}$, and returns the original value v. We (mostly) follow the Java convention that an RMW method that applies the function mumble is called getAndMumble().

For example, the java.util.concurrent.atomic package provides AtomicInteger, a class with a rich set of RMW methods.

- The getAndSet(v) method atomically replaces the register's current value with v and returns the prior value. This method (also called swap()) is an RMW method for the set of constant functions of the type $f_v(x) = v$.
- The getAndIncrement() method atomically adds 1 to the register's current value and returns the prior value. This method (also called *fetch-and-increment*) is an RMW method for the function $f(x) = x + 1$.
- The getAndAdd(k) method atomically adds k to the register's current value and returns the prior value. This method (also called *fetch-and-add*) is an RMW method for the set of functions $f_k(x) = x + k$.
- The compareAndSet() method takes two values, an *expected* value e and an *update* value u. If the register value is equal to e, it is atomically replaced with u; otherwise it is unchanged. Either way, the method returns a Boolean value indicating whether the value was changed. Informally, $f_{e,u}(x) = x$ if $x \neq e$ and u otherwise. (Strictly speaking, compareAndSet() is not an RMW method for $f_{e,u}$, because an RMW method would return the register's prior value instead of a Boolean value, but this distinction is a technicality.)
- The get() method returns the register's value. This method is an RMW method for the identity function $f(v) = v$.

The RMW methods are interesting precisely because they are potential hardware primitives, engraved not in stone, but in silicon. Here, we define RMW registers

---

[3] For simplicity, we consider only registers that hold integer values, but they could equally well hold other values (e.g., references to other objects).

```
1   class RMWConsensus extends ConsensusProtocol {
2     // initialize to v such that f(v) != v
3     private RMWRegister r = new RMWRegister(v);
4     public Object decide(Object value) {
5       propose(value);
6       int i = ThreadID.get();      // my index
7       int j = 1-i;                 // other's index
8       if (r.rmw() == v)            // I'm first, I win
9         return proposed[i];
10      else                         // I'm second, I lose
11        return proposed[j];
12    }
13  }
```

FIGURE 5.14

Two-thread consensus using RMW.

and their methods in terms of **synchronized** Java methods, but, pragmatically, they correspond (exactly or nearly) to many real or proposed hardware synchronization primitives.

A set of functions is *nontrivial* if it includes at least one function that is not the identity function. An RMW method is *nontrivial* if its set of functions is nontrivial, and a RMW register is *nontrivial* if it has a nontrivial RMW method.

Theorem 5.6.1. Any nontrivial RMW register has consensus number at least 2.

Proof. Fig. 5.14 shows a two-thread consensus protocol. Since there exists f in $\mathcal{F}$ that is not the identity, there exists a value v such that $f(v) \neq v$. In the decide() method, as usual, the propose(v) method writes the thread's input v to the proposed[] array. Then each thread applies the RMW method to a shared register. If a thread's call returns v, it is linearized first, and it decides its own value. Otherwise, it is linearized second, and it decides the other thread's proposed value. □

Corollary 5.6.2. It is impossible to construct a wait-free implementation of any nontrivial RMW method from atomic registers for two or more threads.

5.7 Common2 RMW operations

We now identify a class of RMW registers, called *Common2*, that correspond to many of the common synchronization primitives provided by processors in the late 20th century. Although *Common2* registers, like all nontrivial RMW registers, are more powerful than atomic registers, we show that they have consensus number exactly 2, implying that they have limited synchronization power. Fortunately, these synchronization primitives have by-and-large fallen from favor in contemporary processor architectures.

Definition 5.7.1. A nontrivial set of functions $\mathcal{F}$ belongs to *Common2* if for all values v and all f_i and f_j in $\mathcal{F}$, either:

- f_i and f_j *commute*: $f_i(f_j(v)) = f_j(f_i(v))$, or
- one function *overwrites* the other: $f_i(f_j(v)) = f_i(v)$ or $f_j(f_i(v)) = f_j(v)$.

Definition 5.7.2. An RMW register belongs to *Common2* if its set of functions $\mathcal{F}$ belongs to *Common2*.

Many RMW registers in the literature belong to *Common2*. For example, the getAndSet() method uses a constant function, which overwrites any prior value. The getAndIncrement() and getAndAdd() methods use functions that commute with one another.

Very informally, here is why RMW registers in *Common2* cannot solve three-thread consensus: The first thread (the *winner*) can always tell it was first, and each of the second and third threads (the *losers*) can tell that it was not. However, because the functions defining the state following operations in *Common2* commute or overwrite, a loser cannot tell which of the others was the winner (i.e., went first), and because the protocol is wait-free, it cannot wait to find out. Let us make this argument more precise.

Theorem 5.7.3. Any RMW register in *Common2* has consensus number (exactly) 2.

Proof. Theorem 5.6.1 states that any such register has consensus number at least 2. We show that no *Common2* register solves consensus for three threads.

Assume by contradiction that a three-thread protocol exists using only *Common2* registers and read–write registers. Suppose threads A, B, and C reach consensus through *Common2* registers. By Lemma 5.1.6, any such protocol has a critical state s in which the protocol is bivalent, but any method call by any thread will cause the protocol to enter a univalent state.

We now do a case analysis, examining each possible method call. The kind of reasoning used in the proof of Theorem 5.2.1 shows that the pending methods cannot be reads or writes, nor can the threads be about to call methods of different objects. It follows that the threads are about to call RMW methods of a single register r.

Suppose A is about to call a method for function f_A, sending the protocol to a 0-valent state, and B is about to call a method for f_B, sending the protocol to a 1-valent state. There are two possible cases:

1. As depicted in Fig. 5.15, one function overwrites the other: $f_B(f_A(v)) = f_B(v)$. Let s' be the state that results if A applies f_A and then B applies f_B. Because s' is 0-valent, C will decide 0 if it runs alone from s' until it finishes the protocol. Let s'' be the state that results if B alone calls f_B. Because s'' is 1-valent, C will decide 1 if it runs alone from s'' until it finishes the protocol. The problem is that the two possible register states $f_B(f_A(v))$ and $f_B(v)$ are the same, so s' and s'' differ only in the internal states of A and B. If we now let thread C execute, since C completes the protocol without communicating with A or B, these two states look identical to C, so it cannot decide different values from the two states.

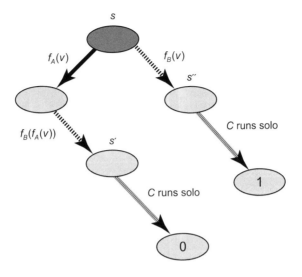

FIGURE 5.15

Case: two functions that overwrite.

2. The functions commute: $f_A(f_B(v)) = f_B(f_A(v))$. Let s' be the state that results if A applies f_A and then B applies f_B. Because s' is 0-valent, C will decide 0 if it runs alone from s' until it finishes the protocol. Let s'' be the state that results if A and B perform their calls in reverse order. Because s'' is 1-valent, C will decide 1 if it runs alone from s'' until it finishes the protocol. The problem is that the two possible register states $f_A(f_B(v))$ and $f_B(f_A(v))$ are the same, so s' and s'' differ only in the internal states of A and B. Now let thread C execute. Since C completes the protocol without communicating with A or B, these two states look identical to C, so it cannot decide different values from the two states. □

5.8 The compareAndSet operation

We now consider the compareAndSet() operation (also called *compare-and-swap*), a synchronization operation supported by several contemporary architectures (e.g., CMPXCHG on the Intel Pentium). It takes two arguments: an *expected* value and an *update* value. If the current register value is equal to the expected value, then it is replaced by the update value; otherwise the value is left unchanged. The method call returns a Boolean indicating whether the value changed.

Theorem 5.8.1. A register providing compareAndSet() and get() methods has an infinite consensus number.

Proof. Fig. 5.16 shows a consensus protocol for n threads using the AtomicInteger class's compareAndSet() method. The threads share an AtomicInteger object, initialized to a constant FIRST, distinct from any thread index. Each thread calls

```
 1  class CASConsensus extends ConsensusProtocol {
 2    private final int FIRST = -1;
 3    private AtomicInteger r = new AtomicInteger(FIRST);
 4    public Object decide(Object value) {
 5      propose(value);
 6      int i = ThreadID.get();
 7      if (r.compareAndSet(FIRST, i)) // I won
 8        return proposed[i];
 9      else                          // I lost
10        return proposed[r.get()];
11    }
12  }
```

FIGURE 5.16

Consensus using `compareAndSet()`.

`compareAndSet()` with FIRST as the expected value, and its own index as the new value. If thread A's call returns *true*, then that method call was first in the linearization order, so A decides its own value. Otherwise, A reads the current AtomicInteger value, and takes that thread's input from the proposed[] array. □

We remark that the get() method provided by compareAndSet() register in Fig. 5.16 is only a convenience, and not necessary for the protocol.

Corollary 5.8.2. A register providing only compareAndSet() has an infinite consensus number.

As we will see in Chapter 6, machines that provide primitive operations like compareAndSet()[4] are asynchronous computation's equivalents of the Turing machines of sequential computation: Any concurrent object that can be implemented in a wait-free manner on such machines. Thus, in the words of Maurice Sendak, compareAndSet() is the "king of all wild things."

5.9 Chapter notes

Michael Fischer, Nancy Lynch, and Michael Paterson [46] were the first to prove that consensus is impossible in a message-passing system where a single thread can halt. Their seminal paper introduced the "bivalence" style of impossibility argument now widely used in distributed computing. M. Loui and H. Abu-Amara [116] and Herlihy [69] were the first to extend this result to shared memory.

---

[4] Some architectures provide a pair of operations similar to get()/compareAndSet() called *load-linked/store-conditional*. In general, the *load-linked* method marks a location as loaded, and the *store-conditional* method fails if another thread modified that location since it was loaded. See Appendix B.

Clyde Kruskal, Larry Rudolph, and Marc Snir [96] coined the term read–modify–write operation as part of the NYU Ultracomputer project.

Maurice Herlihy [69] introduced the notion of a consensus number as a measure of computational power, and was the first to prove most of the impossibility and universality results presented in this and the next chapter.

The class *Common2*, which includes several common primitive synchronization operations, was defined by Yehuda Afek, Eytan Weisberger, and Hanan Weisman [5]. The "sticky-bit" object used in the exercises is due to Serge Plotkin [140].

The n-bounded `compareAndSet()` object with arbitrary consensus number n in Exercise 5.24 is based on a construction by Prasad Jayanti and Sam Toueg [90]. In the hierarchy used here, we say that X solves consensus if one can construct a wait-free consensus protocol from any number of instances of X and any amount of read–write memory. Prasad Jayanti [88] observed that one could also define resource-bounded hierarchies where one is restricted to using only a fixed number of instances of X, or a fixed amount of memory. The unbounded hierarchy used here seems to be the most natural one, since any other hierarchy is a coarsening of the unbounded one.

Jayanti also raised the question whether the hierarchy is *robust*, that is, whether an object X at level m can be "boosted" to a higher consensus level by combining it with another object Y at the same or a lower level. Wai-Kau Lo and Vassos Hadzilacos [114] and Eric Schenk [159] showed that the consensus hierarchy is not robust: Certain objects can be boosted. Informally, their constructions went like this: Let X be an object with the following curious properties. X solves n-thread consensus but "refuses" to reveal the results unless the caller can prove he or she can solve an intermediate task weaker than n-thread consensus, but stronger than any task solvable by atomic read–write registers. If Y is an object that can be used to solve the intermediate task, Y can boost X by convincing X to reveal the outcome of an n-thread consensus. The objects used in these proofs are nondeterministic.

The Maurice Sendak quote is from *Where the Wild Things Are* [155].

5.10 Exercises

Exercise 5.1. Prove Lemma 5.1.5, that is, that every n-thread consensus protocol has a bivalent initial state.

Exercise 5.2. Prove that in a critical state, one successor state must be 0-valent, and the other 1-valent.

Exercise 5.3. Show that if binary consensus using atomic registers is impossible for two threads, then it is also impossible for n threads, where $n > 2$. (Hint: Argue by *reduction*: If we have a protocol to solve binary consensus for n threads, then we can transform it into a two-thread protocol.)

Exercise 5.4. Show that if binary consensus using atomic registers is impossible for n threads, then so is consensus over k values, where $k > 2$.

```
1   public class ConsensusProposal {
2         boolean proposed = new boolean[2];
3         int speed = new Integer[2];
4         int position = new Integer[2];
5         public ConsensusProposal(){
6              position[0] = 0;
7              position[1] = 0;
8              speed[0] = 3;
9              speed[1] = 1;
10        }
11        public decide(Boolean value) {
12             int i = myIndex.get();
13             int j = 1 - i;
14             proposed[i] = value;
15             while (true) {
16                  position[i] = position[i] + speed[i];
17                  if (position[i] > position[j] + speed[j]) // I am far ahead of you
18                       return proposed[i];
19                  else if (position[i] < position[j]) // I am behind you
20                       return proposed[j];
21             }
22        }
23  }
```

FIGURE 5.17

Proposed consensus code for thread $i \in \{0, 1\}$.

Exercise 5.5. Show that with sufficiently many n-thread binary consensus objects and atomic registers, one can implement n-thread consensus over n values.

Exercise 5.6. Consider the algorithm in Fig. 5.17 for two-thread binary consensus.

- Show that the algorithm is consistent and valid (that is, an output value must be an input of one of the threads, and the output values cannot differ).
- Since the algorithm is consistent and valid and only uses read–write registers, it cannot be wait-free. Give an execution history that is a counterexample to wait-freedom.

Exercise 5.7. The Stack class provides two methods: push(x) pushes a value onto the top of the stack, and pop() removes and returns the most recently pushed value. Prove that the Stack class has consensus number *exactly* 2.

Exercise 5.8. Suppose we augment the FIFO Queue class with a peek() method that returns but does not remove the first element in the queue. Show that the augmented queue has infinite consensus number.

Exercise 5.9. Consider three threads, A, B, and C, each of which has an MRSW register, X_A, X_B, and X_C, that it alone can write and the others can read. Each pair also shares a RMWRegister register that provides a compareAndSet() method: A and B

share R_{AB}, B and C share R_{BC}, and A and C share R_{AC}. Only the threads that share a register can call that register's compareAndSet() method or read its value.

Either give a three-thread consensus protocol and explain why it works, or sketch an impossibility proof.

Exercise 5.10. Consider the situation described in Exercise 5.9 except that A, B, and C can apply a *double* compareAndSet() to both registers at once.

Exercise 5.11. In the consensus protocol shown in Fig. 5.7, what would happen if we announced the thread's value after dequeuing from the queue?

Exercise 5.12. Objects of the StickyBit class have three possible states, $\bot, 0, 1$, initially $\bot$. A call to write(v), where v is 0 or 1, has the following effects:

- If the object's state is $\bot$, then it becomes v.
- If the object's state is 0 or 1, then it is unchanged.

  A call to read() returns the object's current state.

1. Show that such an object can solve wait-free *binary* consensus (that is, all inputs are 0 or 1) for any number of threads.
2. Show that an array of $\log_2 m$ StickyBit objects with atomic registers can solve wait-free consensus for any number of threads when there are m possible inputs. (Hint: Give each thread one atomic multi-reader single-writer register.)

Exercise 5.13. The SetAgree class, like the Consensus class, provides a decide() method whose call returns a value that was the input of some thread's decide() call. However, unlike the Consensus class, the values returned by decide() calls are not required to agree. Instead, these calls may return no more than k distinct values. (When k is 1, SetAgree is the same as consensus.)

What is the consensus number of the SetAgree class when $k > 1$?

Exercise 5.14. The two-thread *approximate agreement* class for a given $\epsilon > 0$ is defined as follows: Threads A and B each call decide(x_a) and decide(x_b) methods, where x_a and x_b are real numbers. These method calls respectively return values y_a and y_b such that y_a and y_b both lie in the closed interval $[\min(x_a, x_b), \max(x_a, x_b)]$, and $|y_a - y_b| \le \epsilon$. Note that this object is nondeterministic.

What is the consensus number of the *approximate agreement* object?

Exercise 5.15. An A2Cas object represents two locations for values that can be read individually and be modified by a2cas(). If both locations have the corresponding expected values $e0$ and $e1$, then a call to a2cas($e0, e1, v$) will write v to *exactly one* of the two locations, chosen nondeterministically.

What is the consensus number of the a2cas() object? Prove your claim.

Exercise 5.16. Consider a distributed system where threads communicate by message passing. A *type A* broadcast guarantees:

1. every nonfaulty thread eventually gets each message,

2. if P broadcasts M_1 and then M_2, then every thread receives M_1 before M_2, but
3. messages broadcast by different threads may be received in different orders at different threads.

A *type B* broadcast guarantees:

1. every nonfaulty thread eventually gets each message,
2. if P broadcasts M_1 and Q broadcasts M_2, then every thread receives M_1 and M_2 in the same order.

For each kind of broadcast,

• give a consensus protocol if possible;
• otherwise, sketch an impossibility proof.

Exercise 5.17. Consider the following two-thread QuasiConsensus problem.
Two threads, A and B, are each given a binary input. If both have input v, then both must decide v. If they have mixed inputs, then either they must agree, or B may decide 0 and A may decide 1 (but not vice versa).
Here are three possible exercises (only one of which works):

1. Give a two-thread consensus protocol using QuasiConsensus showing it has consensus number (at least) 2.
2. Give a critical-state proof that this object's consensus number is 1.
3. Give a read–write implementation of QuasiConsensus, thereby showing it has consensus number 1.

Exercise 5.18. Explain why the critical-state proof of the impossibility of consensus fails if the shared object is, in fact, a Consensus object.

Exercise 5.19. A *team consensus* object provides the same decide() method as consensus. A team consensus object solves consensus as long as at most *two* distinct values are ever proposed. (If more than two are proposed, any result is allowed.)
Show how to solve n-thread consensus, with up to n distinct input values, from a supply of team consensus objects.

Exercise 5.20. A *trinary* register holds values $\perp, 0, 1$, and provides compareAndSet() and get() methods with the usual meaning. Each such register is initially $\perp$. Give a protocol that uses one such register to solve n-thread consensus if the inputs of the threads are *binary*, that is, either 0 or 1.
Can you use multiple such registers (perhaps with atomic read–write registers) to solve n-thread consensus even if the threads' inputs are in the range $0 \ldots 2^K - 1$ for $K > 1$? (You may assume an input fits in an atomic register.) *Important:* Remember that a consensus protocol must be wait-free.

• Devise a solution that uses at most $O(n)$ trinary registers.
• Devise a solution that uses $O(K)$ trinary registers.

Feel free to use all the atomic registers you want (they are cheap).

```
1   class Queue {
2     AtomicInteger head = new AtomicInteger(0);
3     AtomicReference items[] = new AtomicReference[Integer.MAX_VALUE];
4     void enq(Object x){
5       int slot = head.getAndIncrement();
6       items[slot] = x;
7     }
8     Object deq() {
9       while (true) {
10        int limit = head.get();
11        for (int i = 0; i < limit; i++) {
12          Object y = items[i].getAndSet(); // swap
13          if (y != null)
14            return y;
15        }
16      }
17    }
18  }
```

FIGURE 5.18

Queue implementation.

Exercise 5.21. Earlier we defined lock-freedom. Prove that there is no lock-free implementation of consensus using read–write registers for two or more threads.

Exercise 5.22. Fig. 5.18 shows a FIFO queue implemented with read(), write(), getAndSet() (that is, swap), and getAndIncrement() methods. You may assume this queue is linearizable, and wait-free as long as deq() is never applied to an empty queue. Consider the following sequence of statements:

- Both getAndSet() and getAndIncrement() methods have consensus number 2.
- We can add a peek() simply by taking a snapshot of the queue (using the methods studied earlier) and returning the item at the head of the queue.
- Using the protocol devised for Exercise 5.8, we can use the resulting queue to solve n-consensus for any n.

We have just constructed an n-thread consensus protocol using only objects with consensus number 2.

Identify the faulty step in this chain of reasoning, and explain what went wrong.

Exercise 5.23. Recall that in our definition of compareAndSet(), we noted that strictly speaking, compareAndSet() is not an RMW method for $f_{e,u}$, because an RMW method would return the register's prior value instead of a Boolean value. Use an object that supports compareAndSet() and get() to provide a new object with a linearizable NewCompareAndSet() method that returns the register's current value instead of a Boolean.

Exercise 5.24. Define an *n-bounded* `compareAndSet()` object as follows: It provides a `compareAndSet()` method that takes two values, an *expected* value e and an *update* value u. For the first n times `compareAndSet()` is called, it behaves like a conventional `compareAndSet()` register: If the object value is equal to e, it is atomically replaced with u, and the method call returns *true*. If the object value v is not equal to e, then it is left unchanged, and the method call returns *false*, along with the value v. After `compareAndSet()` has been called n times, however, the object enters a faulty state, and all subsequent method calls return $\perp$.

Show that an n-bounded `compareAndSet()` object for $n \geq 2$ has consensus number exactly n.

Exercise 5.25. Provide a wait-free implementation of a two-thread (2, 3)-assignment object from three `compareAndSet()` objects (that is, objects supporting the operations `compareAndSet()` and `get()`).

Exercise 5.26. In the proof of Theorem 5.5.1, we claimed that it is enough to show that we can solve 2-consensus given two threads and a (2, 3)-assignment object. Justify this claim.

Exercise 5.27. We can treat the scheduler as an *adversary* who uses the knowledge of our protocols and input values to frustrate our attempts at reaching consensus. One way to outwit an adversary is through randomization. Assume that there are two threads that want to reach consensus, each of which can flip an unbiased coin, and that the adversary cannot control future coin flips but can observe the result of each coin flip and each value read or written. The adversary scheduler can stop a thread before or after a coin flip or a read or write to a shared register. A *randomized consensus protocol* terminates with probability arbitrarily close to 1 (given sufficiently long time) against an adversary scheduler.

Fig. 5.19 shows a plausible-looking randomized binary consensus protocol. Give an example showing that this protocol is incorrect.

- Does the algorithm satisfy the safety properties of consensus (i.e., validity and consistency)? That is, is it true that each thread can only output a value that is the input of one of the two threads, and also that the outputs cannot be different?
- Does it terminate with a probability arbitrarily close to 1?

Exercise 5.28. One can implement a consensus object using read–write registers by implementing a deadlock- or starvation-free mutual exclusion lock. However, this implementation provides only dependent progress, and the operating system must make sure that threads do not get stuck in the critical section so that the computation as a whole progresses.

- Is the same true for obstruction-freedom, the nonblocking dependent progress condition? Show an obstruction-free implementation of a consensus object using only atomic registers.
- What is the role of the operating system in the obstruction-free solution to consensus? Explain where the critical state-based proof of the impossibility of consensus

```
1   Object prefer[2] = {null, null};
2
3   Object decide(Object input) {
4     int i = Thread.getID();
5     int j = 1-i;
6     prefer[i] = input;
7     while (true) {
8       if (prefer[j] == null) {
9         return prefer[i];
10      } else if (prefer[i] == prefer[j]) {
11        return prefer[i];
12      } else {
13        if (flip()) {
14          prefer[i] = prefer[j];
15        }
16      }
17    }
18  }
```

FIGURE 5.19

Is this a randomized consensus protocol?

breaks down if we repeatedly allow an oracle to halt threads so as to allow others to make progress.

(Hint: Think of how you could restrict the set of allowed executions.)

Universality of consensus

6

6.1 Introduction

In Chapter 5, we considered a simple technique for proving statements of the form "there is no wait-free implementation of X by Y." We considered object classes with deterministic sequential specifications.[1] We derived a hierarchy in which no object from one level can implement an object at a higher level (see Fig. 6.1). Recall that each object has an associated *consensus number*, which is the maximum number of threads for which the object can solve the consensus problem. In a system of n or more concurrent threads, it is impossible to construct a wait-free implementation of an object with consensus number n from objects with lower consensus numbers. The same result holds for lock-free implementations, and henceforth unless we explicitly state otherwise, it is implied that a result that holds for wait-free implementations holds for lock-free ones as well.

The impossibility results of Chapter 5 do not by any means imply that wait-free synchronization is impossible or infeasible. In this chapter, we show that there are classes of objects that are *universal*: Given sufficiently many of them, one can construct a wait-free linearizable implementation of *any* concurrent object.

A class is universal in a system of n threads if and only if it has a consensus number greater than or equal to n. In Fig. 6.1, each class at level n is universal for a system of n threads. A machine architecture or programming language is computationally powerful enough to support arbitrary wait-free synchronization if and only if it provides objects of a universal class as primitives. For example, modern multiprocessor machines that provide a `compareAndSet()` operation are universal for any number of threads: They can implement any concurrent object in a wait-free manner.

This chapter describes a *universal construction* that implements any concurrent object from consensus objects. The chapter does *not* describe practical techniques for implementing wait-free objects. Like classical computability theory, understanding the universal construction and its implications allows us to avoid the naïve mistake of trying to solve unsolvable problems. Once we understand *why* consensus is powerful enough to implement any kind of object, we will be better prepared to undertake the engineering effort needed to make such constructions efficient.

---

[1] The situation with nondeterministic objects is significantly more complicated.

The Art of Multiprocessor Programming. https://doi.org/10.1016/B978-0-12-415950-1.00015-X

129

Consensus	
Number	**Object**
1	*atomic registers*
2	getAndSet(), getAndAdd(), Queue, Stack
$\vdots$	$\vdots$
m	$(m, m(m+1)/2)$-*assignment*
$\vdots$	$\vdots$
∞	*memory-to-memory move*, compareAndSet(), *load-linked/store-conditional*[a]

[a] *See Appendix B for details.*

FIGURE 6.1

Concurrent computability and the universality hierarchy of synchronization operations.

6.2 Universality

A class *C* is *universal* if one can construct a wait-free implementation of any object from some number of objects of *C* and some number of read–write registers. Our construction uses multiple objects of class *C* because we are ultimately interested in understanding the synchronization power of machine instructions, and most machines allow their instructions to be applied to multiple memory locations. We allow an implementation to use multiple read–write registers because it is convenient for bookkeeping, and memory is usually in plentiful supply on modern architectures. To avoid distraction, we use an unlimited number of read–write registers and consensus objects, leaving the question of recycling memory as an exercise. We begin by presenting a lock-free implementation, later extending it to a slightly more complex wait-free one.

6.3 A lock-free universal construction

Fig. 6.2 shows a *generic* definition for a sequential object, based on the invocation–response formulation of Chapter 3. Each object is created in a fixed initial state. The apply() method takes as argument an *invocation* which describes the method being called and its arguments, and returns a *response* containing the call's termination

```
1  public interface SeqObject {
2    public abstract Response apply(Invoc invoc);
3  }
```

FIGURE 6.2

A generic sequential object: The apply() method applies the invocation and returns a response.

```
1   public class Node {
2     public Invoc invoc;                 // method name and args
3     public Consensus<Node> decideNext;  // decide next Node in list
4     public Node next;                   // the next node
5     public int seq;                     // sequence number
6     public Node(Invoc invoc) {
7       invoc = invoc;
8       decideNext = new Consensus<Node>()
9       seq = 0;
10    }
11    public static Node max(Node[] array) {
12      Node max = array[0];
13      for (int i = 1; i < array.length; i++)
14        if (max.seq < array[i].seq)
15          max = array[i];
16      return max;
17    }
18  }
```

FIGURE 6.3

The Node class.

condition (normal or exceptional) and the return value, if any. For example, a stack invocation might be push() with an argument, and the corresponding response would be normal and **void**.

Figs. 6.3 and 6.4 show a universal construction that transforms any sequential object into a lock-free linearizable concurrent object. This construction assumes that sequential objects are *deterministic*: If we apply a method to an object in a particular state, then there is only one possible response and one possible new object state. We can represent any object as a combination of a sequential object in its initial state and a *log*: a linked list of nodes representing the sequence of method calls applied to the object (and hence the object's sequence of state transitions). A thread executes a method call by adding the new call to the head of the list. It then traverses the list, from tail to head, applying the method calls to a private copy of the object. The thread finally returns the result of applying its own operation. It is important to understand that only the head of the log is mutable: The initial state and nodes preceding the head never change.

How do we make this log-based construction concurrent, that is, allow threads to make concurrent calls to apply()? A thread attempting to call apply() creates a node to hold its invocation. The threads then compete to append their respective nodes to the head of the log by running an n-thread consensus protocol to agree which node was appended to the log. The inputs to this consensus are references to the threads' nodes, and the result is the unique winning node.

The winner can then proceed to compute its response. It does so by creating a local copy of the sequential object and traversing the log, following next references

```
1   public class LFUniversal {
2     private Node[] head;
3     private Node tail;
4     public LFUniversal() {
5       tail = new Node();
6       tail.seq = 1;
7       for (int i = 0; i < n; i++)
8         head[i] = tail
9     }
10    public Response apply(Invoc invoc) {
11      int i = ThreadID.get();
12      Node prefer = new Node(invoc);
13      while (prefer.seq == 0) {
14        Node before = Node.max(head);
15        Node after = before.decideNext.decide(prefer);
16        before.next = after;
17        after.seq = before.seq + 1;
18        head[i] = after;
19      }
20      SeqObject myObject = new SeqObject();
21      Node current = tail.next;
22      while (current != prefer){
23        myObject.apply(current.invoc);
24        current = current.next;
25      }
26      return myObject.apply(current.invoc);
27    }
28  }
```

FIGURE 6.4

The lock-free universal construction.

from tail to head, applying the operations in the log to its copy, finally returning the response associated with its own invocation. This algorithm works even when apply() calls are concurrent because the prefix of the log up to the thread's own node never changes. The losing threads, which were not chosen by the consensus object, must try again to set the node currently at the head of the log (which changes between attempts) to point to them.

We now consider this construction in detail. The code for the lock-free universal construction appears in Fig. 6.4. A sample execution appears in Fig. 6.5. The object state is defined by a linked list of nodes, each one containing an invocation. The code for a node appears in Fig. 6.3. The node's decideNext field is a consensus object used to decide which node is appended next in the list, and next is the field in which the outcome of that consensus, the reference to the next node, is recorded. The seq field is the node's sequence number in the list. This field is 0 while the node is not

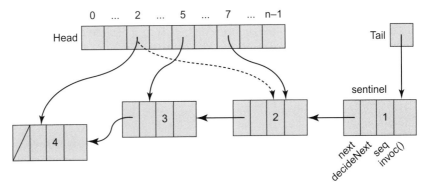

FIGURE 6.5

Execution of the lock-free universal construction. Thread 2 appends the second node in the log winning consensus on decideNext in the sentinel node. It then sets the node's sequence number from 0 to 2, and refers to it from its entry in the head[] array. Thread 7 loses the decideNext consensus at the sentinel node, sets the next reference and sequence number of the decided successor node to 2 (they were already set to the same values by thread 2), and refers to the node from its entry in the head[] array. Thread 5 appends the third node, updates its sequence number to 3, and updates its entry in the head[] array to this node. Finally, thread 2 appends the fourth node, sets its sequence number to 4, and refers to it from its entry in the head[] array. The maximal value in the head array keeps track of the head of the log.

yet threaded onto the list, and positive otherwise. Sequence numbers for successive nodes in the list increase by 1. Initially, the log consists of a unique sentinel node with sequence number 1.

The hard part about designing the concurrent lock-free universal construction is that consensus objects can be used only once.[2]

In our lock-free algorithm in Fig. 6.4, each thread allocates a node holding its invocation, and repeatedly tries to append that node to the head of the log. Each node has a decideNext field, which is a consensus object. A thread tries to append its node by proposing it as input to a consensus protocol on the head's decideNext field. Because threads that do not participate in this consensus may need to traverse the list, the result of this consensus is stored in the node's next field. Multiple threads may update this field simultaneously, but they all write the same value. When a thread appends a node, it sets the node's sequence number.

Once a thread's node is part of the log, the thread computes the response to its invocation by traversing the log from the tail to the newly added node. It applies each of the invocations to a private copy of the object, and returns the response from its

---

[2] Creating a reusable consensus object, or even one whose decision is readable, is not a simple task. It is essentially the same problem as the universal construction we are about to design. For example, consider the queue-based consensus protocol in Section 5.4. It is not obvious how to use a Queue to allow repeated reading of the consensus object state after it is decided.

own invocation. Note that when a thread computes its response, all its predecessors' next references must already be set, because these nodes have already been added to the head of the list. Any thread that added a node to the list has updated the next reference of its predecessor with the result of the decideNext consensus.

How do we locate the head of the log? We cannot track the head with a consensus object because the head must be updated repeatedly, and consensus objects can only be accessed once by each thread. Instead, we create a per-thread structure of the kind used in the bakery algorithm (Section 2.7). We use an n-entry array head[], where head[i] is the last node in the list that thread i has observed. Initially all entries refer to the tail sentinel node. The head is the node with the maximum sequence number among the nodes referenced in the head[] array. The max() method in Fig. 6.3 performs a collect, reading head[] and returning the node with the highest sequence number.

The construction is a linearizable implementation of the sequential object. Each apply() call can be linearized to the decide() call adding the node to the log.

Why is this construction lock-free? The head of the log, the latest node appended, is added to the head[] array within a finite number of steps. The node's predecessor must appear in the head array, so any node repeatedly attempting to add a new node will repeatedly run the max() function on the head array. It detects this predecessor, applies consensus on its decideNext field, and then updates the winning node's fields, including its sequence number. Finally, it stores the decided node in that thread's head array entry. The new head node always eventually appears in head[]. It follows that the only way a thread can repeatedly fail to add its own node to the log is if other threads repeatedly succeed in appending their own nodes to the log. Thus, a node can starve only if other nodes are continually completing their invocations, implying that the construction is lock-free.

6.4 A wait-free universal construction

How do we make a lock-free algorithm wait-free? The full wait-free algorithm appears in Fig. 6.6. We must guarantee that every thread completes an apply() call within a finite number of steps; that is, no thread starves. To guarantee this property, threads making progress help less fortunate threads complete their calls. This *helping* pattern shows up later in a specialized form in other wait-free algorithms.

To enable helping, each thread shares with other threads the apply() call that it is trying to complete. We add an n-element announce[] array, where announce[i] is the node that thread i is currently trying to append to the list. Initially, all entries refer to the sentinel node, which has a sequence number 1. Thread i *announces* a node when it stores the node in announce[i].

To execute apply(), a thread first announces its new node. This step ensures that if the thread itself does not succeed in appending its node onto the list, some other thread can append that node on its behalf. It then proceeds as before, attempting to append the node into the log. To do so, it reads the head[] array only once (line 15), and then enters the main loop of the algorithm, which it executes until its own node

```
1   public class Universal {
2     private Node[] announce; // array added to coordinate helping
3     private Node[] head;
4     private Node tail = new Node();
5     public Universal() {
6       tail.seq = 1;
7       for (int j = 0; j < n; j++) {
8         head[j] = tail;
9         announce[j] = tail;
10      }
11    }
12    public Response apply(Invoc invoc) {
13      int i = ThreadID.get();
14      announce[i] = new Node(invoc);
15      head[i] = Node.max(head);
16      while (announce[i].seq == 0) {
17        Node before = head[i];
18        Node help = announce[(before.seq + 1) % n];
19        if (help.seq == 0)
20          prefer = help;
21        else
22          prefer = announce[i];
23        Node after = before.decideNext.decide(prefer);
24        before.next = after;
25        after.seq = before.seq + 1;
26        head[i] = after;
27      }
28      head[i] = announce[i];
29      SeqObject myObject = new SeqObject();
30      Node current = tail.next;
31      while (current != announce[i]){
32        myObject.apply(current.invoc);
33        current = current.next;
34      }
35      return myObject.apply(current.invoc);
36    }
37  }
```

FIGURE 6.6

The wait-free universal construction.

has been appended to the list (detected on line 16 after its sequence number becomes nonzero). Here is a change from the lock-free algorithm. A thread first checks to see if there is a node that needs help ahead of it in the announce[] array (line 18). The node to be helped must be determined dynamically because nodes are continually added to the log. A thread attempts to help nodes in the announce[] array in increasing order, determined by the sequence number modulo the width n of the announce[] array. We prove that this approach guarantees that any node that does not make progress on its own will eventually be helped by others once its owner thread's index matches the maximal sequence number modulo n. If this helping step were omitted, then an individual thread could be overtaken an arbitrary number of times. If the node selected for help does not require help (i.e., its sequence number is nonzero in line 19), then each thread attempts to append its own node (line 22). (All announce[] array entries are initialized to the sentinel node, with sequence number 1.) The rest of the algorithm is almost the same as in the lock-free algorithm. A node is appended when its sequence number becomes nonzero. In this case, the thread proceeds as before to compute its result based on the immutable segment of the log from the tail to its own node.

Fig. 6.7 shows an execution of the wait-free universal construction in which, starting from the initial state, thread 5 announces its new node and appends it to the

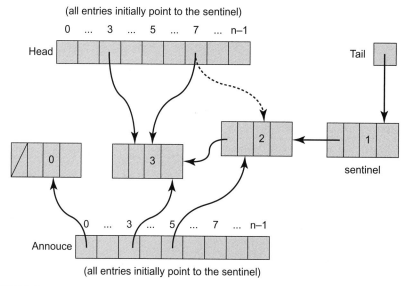

FIGURE 6.7

Execution of the wait-free universal construction. Thread 5 announces its new node and appends it to the log, but halts before adding it to the head[] array. Thread 7 does not see thread 5's node in the head[] array. Since thread 2 (whose ID is (before.seq + 1) mod n) is not trying to add a node, thread 7 tries to add its own node. However, it loses the consensus on the sentinel node's decideNext object since thread 5 already won. Thread 7 therefore completes updating the fields of thread 5's node, setting the node's sequence number to 2, and adding the node to the head[] array. Note that thread 5's own entry in the head[] array is not yet set to its announced node. Next, thread 3 announces its node and then pauses before entering the main loop. Thread 7 now successfully helps thread 3, appending its node and setting its sequence number to 3. Now thread 3 wakes up. It does not enter the main loop because its node's sequence number is nonzero, but will update the head[] array and compute its output value using a copy of the sequential object.

log, and pauses before adding the node to head[]. Thread 7 then takes steps. The value of (before.seq + 1) mod n is 2, but thread 2 is not trying to add a node, so thread 7 tries to add its own node. It loses the consensus on the sentinel node's decideNext object since thread 5 already won, and thus completes the operation of thread 5, setting the node's sequence number to 2 and adding the node to the head[] array. Next, thread 3 announces its node and pauses before entering the main loop. Then thread 7 helps thread 3: it appends thread 3's node, but pauses after setting its sequence number to 3 but before adding the node to head[]. Now thread 3 wakes up. It does not enter the main loop because its node's sequence number is nonzero, but updates head[] on line 28 and computes its output value using a copy of the sequential object.

There is a delicate point to understand about these modifications to the lock-free algorithm. Since more than one thread can attempt to append a particular node to the log, we must make sure that no node is appended twice. One thread might append the node and set the node's sequence number at the same time that another thread appends the same node and sets its sequence number. The algorithm avoids this error because of the order in which threads read the maximum head[] array value and the sequence number of a node in the announce[] array. Let a be a node created by thread A and appended by threads A and B. It must be added at least once to head[] before the second append. Note, however, that the before node read from head[A] by B (line 17) must be a itself, or a successor of a in the log. Moreover, before any node is added to head[] (either on line 26 or on line 28), its sequence number is made nonzero (line 25). The order of operations ensures that B sets its head[B] entry (the entry based on which B's before variable will be set, resulting in an erroneous append) in line 15 or line 26, and only then validates that the sequence number of a is nonzero in line 16 or line 19 (depending on whether A or another thread performs the operation). It follows that the validation of the erroneous second append will fail because the sequence number of node a will already be nonzero, and it will not be added to the log a second time.

Linearizability follows because no node is ever added twice, and the order in which nodes are appended to the log is clearly compatible with the natural partial order of the corresponding method calls.

To prove that the algorithm is wait-free, we must show that the helping mechanism guarantees that any node that is announced is eventually added to the head[] array (implying that it is in the log) and the announcing thread can complete computation of its outcome. To assist in the proof, it is convenient to define some notation. Let max(head[]) be the node with the largest sequence number in the head[] array, and let "$c \in$ head[]" denote the assertion that head[i] is set to node c, for some i.

An *auxiliary* variable (sometimes called a *ghost* variable) is one that does not appear explicitly in the code, does not alter the program's behavior in any way, and yet helps us reason about the behavior of the algorithm. We use the following auxiliary variables:

- *concur*(A) is the set of nodes that have been stored in the head[] array since thread A's last announcement.
- *start*(A) is the sequence number of max(head[]) when thread A last announced.

```
12   public Response apply(Invoc invoc) {
13     int i = ThreadID.get();
14     < announce[i] = new Node(invoc); start(i) = max(head); concur(i) = {}; >
15     head[i] = Node.max(head);
16     while (announce[i].seq == 0) {
17       Node before = head[i];
18       Node help = announce[(before.seq + 1) % n];
19       if (help.seq == 0)
20         prefer = help;
21       else
22         prefer = announce[i];
23       Node after = before.decideNext.decide(prefer);
24       before.next = after;
25       after.seq = before.seq + 1;
26       < head[i] = after; (∀j) (concur(j) = concur(j) ∪ {after}); >
27     }
28     < head[i] = announce[i]; (∀j) (concur(j) = concur(j) ∪ {after}); >
29     SeqObject MyObject = new SeqObject();
30     Node current = tail.next;
31     while (current != announce[i]){
32       MyObject.apply(current.invoc);
33       current = current.next;
34     }
35     return MyObject.apply(current.invoc);
36   }
```

FIGURE 6.8

The apply() method of the wait-free universal construction with auxiliary variables. Operations in angled brackets are assumed to happen atomically.

The code reflecting the auxiliary variables and how they are updated appears in Fig. 6.8. For example, the statement

$$(\forall j) \ (concur(j) = concur(j) \cup \{after\});$$

means that the node *after* is added to *concur(j)* for all threads j. The code statements within the angled brackets are considered to be executed atomically. This atomicity can be assumed because auxiliary variables do not affect the computation in any way. For brevity, we slightly abuse the notation by letting the function max() applied to a node or array of nodes return the maximal among their sequence numbers.

Note the following property is invariant throughout the execution of the universal construction:

$$|concur(A)| + start(A) = \max(head[]). \tag{6.4.1}$$

Lemma 6.4.1. For all threads A, the following claim is always true:

$$|concur(A)| > n \Rightarrow announce[A] \in head[].$$

Proof. Let $a = $ announce$[A]$. If $|concur(A)| > n$, then $concur(A)$ includes successive nodes b and c (appended to the log by threads B and C) whose respective sequence numbers plus 1 are equal to $A - 1$ and A modulo n (note that B and C are the threads that add b and c to the log, not necessarily the ones that announced them). Thread C appends to the log the node located in announce$[A]$ at the time it executes lines 18–22, unless it had already been added to the log. We need to show that when C reads announce$[A]$, A has already announced a, so c adds a to the log, or a was already added. Later, when c is added to head$[]$ and $|concur(A)| > n$, a will be in head$[]$ as the lemma requires.

To see why a must have already been announced when C reached lines 18–22, note that (1) because C appended its node c to b, it must have read b as the *before* node on line 17, implying that B added b to the log before it was read from head$[]$ by C on line 17, and (2) because b is in $concur(A)$, A announced a before b was added to head$[]$. From (1) and (2), it follows that A announced before C executed lines 18–22, and the claim follows.   □

Lemma 6.4.1 places a bound on the number of nodes that can be appended while a method call is in progress. We now give a sequence of lemmas showing that when A finishes scanning the head$[]$ array, either announce$[A]$ is appended or head$[A]$ lies within $n + 1$ nodes of the end of the list.

Lemma 6.4.2. The following property always holds:

$$\max(\text{head}[]) \geq start(A).$$

Proof. The sequence number for each head$[i]$ is nondecreasing.   □

Lemma 6.4.3. The following is a loop invariant for line 13 of Fig. 6.3 (i.e., it holds during each iteration of the loop):

$$\max(\text{max}, \text{head}[i], \ldots, \text{head}[n - 1]) \geq start(A),$$

where i is the loop index, max is the node with the maximum sequence number found so far, and A is the thread executing the loop.

In other words, the maximum sequence number of max and all head$[]$ entries from the current value of i to the end of the loop never become smaller than the maximum value in the array when A announced.

Proof. When i is 1, the assertion is implied by Lemma 6.4.2 (since max = head$[0]$). The truth of the assertion is preserved at each iteration, when max is replaced by the node with the sequence number $\max(\text{max}, \text{head}[i])$.   □

Lemma 6.4.4. The following assertion holds just before line 16 (of Fig. 6.8):

$$\text{head}[A].\text{seq} \geq start(A).$$

Proof. After the call to Node.max() at line 15, the result follows from Lemma 6.4.3. Otherwise, head[A] is set to point to A's last appended node on line 26, which increases head[A].seq by 1.   □

Lemma 6.4.5. The following property always holds:

$$|concur(A)| \geq head[A].seq - start(A) \geq 0.$$

Proof. The lower bound follows from Lemma 6.4.4, and the upper bound follows from Eq. (6.4.1).   □

Theorem 6.4.6. The algorithm in Fig. 6.6 is correct and wait-free.

Proof. To see that the algorithm is wait-free, note that A can execute the main loop no more than $n + 1$ times. At each successful iteration, head[A].seq increases by 1. After $n + 1$ iterations, Lemma 6.4.5 implies that

$$|concur(A)| \geq head[A].seq - start(A) \geq n.$$

Lemma 6.4.1 implies that announce[A] must have been added to head[].   □

6.5 Chapter notes

The universal construction described here is adapted from Maurice Herlihy's 1991 paper [69]. An alternative lock-free universal construction using *load-linked/store-conditional* appears in [65]. The complexity of this construction can be improved in several ways. Yehuda Afek, Dalia Dauber, and Dan Touitou [3] showed how to improve the time complexity to depend on the number of concurrent threads, not the maximum possible number of threads. Mark Moir [130] showed how to design lock-free and wait-free constructions that do not require copying the entire object. James Anderson and Mark Moir [11] extended the construction to allow multiple objects to be updated. Prasad Jayanti [89] showed that any universal construction has worst-case $\Omega(n)$ complexity, where n is the maximal number of threads. Tushar Chandra, Prasad Jayanti, and King Tan [27] identified a large class of objects for which a more efficient universal construction exists.

Our classification of dependent progress conditions has implications for the foundations of shared-memory computability. Lamport's register-based approach to read–write memory computability [99,105] is based on wait-free implementations of one register type from another. Similarly, Herlihy's consensus hierarchy [69] applies to wait-free or lock-free object implementations. Combined, these structures form the basis of a theory of concurrent shared-memory computability that explains what objects can be used to implement other objects in an asynchronous shared-memory multiprocessor environment. One might ask why such a theory should rest on non-blocking progress conditions (that is, wait-free or lock-free) and not on locks. After all, locking implementations are common in practice. Moreover, the obstruction-free condition is a nonblocking progress condition where read–write registers are universal [68], effectively leveling the consensus hierarchy. We are now in a position to address this question. Perhaps surprisingly, Fig. 3.10 suggests that the lock-free and wait-free conditions provide a sound basis for a concurrent computability theory because they are independent progress conditions (i.e., they do not rely on the good behavior of the operating system scheduler). A theory based on a dependent condition would require strong, perhaps arbitrary assumptions about the environment in which programs are executed. When studying the computational power of synchronization primitives, it is unsatisfactory to rely on the operating system to ensure progress, both because it obscures the inherent synchronization power of the primitives, and because we might want to use such primitives in the construction of the operating system itself. For these reasons, a satisfactory theory of shared-memory computability should rely on independent progress conditions such as wait-freedom or lock-freedom, not on dependent properties.

6.6 Exercises

Exercise 6.1. Consider a concurrent atomic PeekableStack(k) object: an atomic Stack with an added look operation. It allows each of n threads to execute push() and pop() operations atomically with the usual LIFO semantics. In addition, it offers a look operation, the first k calls of which return the value at the bottom of the stack (the least recently pushed value that is currently in the stack) without popping it. All subsequent calls to look after the first k return *null*. Also, look returns *null* when the Stack is empty.

- Is it possible to construct a wait-free Queue (accessed by at most two threads) from an arbitrary number of PeekableStack(1) (i.e., with $k = 1$) objects and atomic read–write registers? Prove your claim.
- Is it possible to construct a wait-free n-thread PeekableStack(2) object from an arbitrary number of atomic Stack objects and atomic read–write registers? Prove your claim.

Exercise 6.2. Give an example showing how the universal construction can fail for objects with nondeterministic sequential specifications.

Exercise 6.3. Propose a way to fix the universal construction of Fig. 6.8 to work for objects with nondeterministic sequential specifications.

Exercise 6.4. In both the lock-free and wait-free universal constructions, the sequence number of the sentinel node at the tail of the list is initially set to 1. Which of these algorithms, if any, would cease to work correctly if the sentinel node's sequence number were initially set to 0?

Exercise 6.5. In the lock-free universal construction, every thread has its own view of the head pointer. To append a new method invocation, at line 14 of Fig. 6.4, a thread selects the furthest among these head pointers:

```
Node before = Node.max(head);
```

Consider changing this line to:

```
Node before = head[i];
```

Does the construction still work?

Exercise 6.6. Suppose, instead of a universal construction, you simply want to use consensus to implement a wait-free linearizable register with read() and compareAndSet() methods. Show how you would adapt this algorithm to do so.

Exercise 6.7. In the wait-free universal construction shown in Section 6.4, each thread first looks for another thread to help, and then tries to append its own node.

Suppose that instead, each thread first tries to append its own node, and then tries to help the other thread. Explain whether this alternative approach works. Justify your answer.

Exercise 6.8. In the construction in Fig. 6.4, we use a "distributed" implementation of a "head" reference (to the node whose decideNext field it will try to modify) to avoid having to create an object that allows repeated consensus. Replace this implementation with one that has no head reference at all, and finds the next "head" by traversing down the log from the start until it reaches a node with a sequence number of 0 or with the highest nonzero sequence number.

Exercise 6.9. In the wait-free protocol, a thread adds its newly appended node to the head[] array on line 28 even though it may have already added it on line 26. This is done because, unlike in the lock-free protocol, it could be that the thread's node was added by another thread on line 26, and that "helping" thread stopped at line 26 right after updating the node's sequence number but before updating the head[] array.

1. Explain how removing line 28 would violate Lemma 6.4.4.
2. Would the algorithm still work correctly?

Exercise 6.10. Propose a way to fix the universal construction to work with a bounded amount of memory, that is, a bounded number of consensus objects and a bounded number of read–write registers.
Hint: Add a before field to the nodes and build a memory recycling scheme into the code.

Exercise 6.11. Implement a consensus object that is accessed more than once by each thread using read() and compareAndSet() methods, creating a "multiple access" consensus object. Do not use the universal construction.

Exercise 6.12. Your mission is to transform a sequential stack implementation into a wait-free, linearizable stack implementation, without regard for questions of efficiency or memory use.

You are given a "black-box" Sequence type with the following methods: You can atomically *append* an item to the end of the sequence. For example, if the sequence is $\langle 1, 2, 3 \rangle$, and you append 4, the sequence becomes $\langle 1, 2, 3, 4 \rangle$. This operation is wait-free and linearizable: if a concurrent thread tries to append 5, the sequence becomes either $\langle 1, 2, 3, 4, 5 \rangle$. or $\langle 1, 2, 3, 5, 4 \rangle$. Note that Sequence items *do not* have to be integers: they can be any kind of object you like.

You can also iterate through the elements of a sequence. Here, we iterate through a sequence printing each value until we see the string "stop".

```
1  foreach x in s {
2    if (x == "stop") break;
3    System.out.println(x)
4  }
```

(Note that if another thread is appending new values while you are iterating through a sequence, you might keep going forever.)

Implement a wait-free linearizable stack using an atomic sequence object, and as much atomic read–write memory and sequential stack objects as you like. Your stack should support both push() and pop() operations with the usual meanings. Again, do not worry about efficiency or memory use.

Explain briefly why your construction is wait-free and linearizable (in particular, identify the linearization points).

Practice

Spin locks and contention

7

When writing programs for uniprocessors, it is usually safe to ignore the underlying system's architectural details. Unfortunately, multiprocessor programming has yet to reach that state; for now, it is crucial to understand the underlying machine architecture. The goal of this chapter is to explain how architecture affects performance, and how to exploit this knowledge to write efficient concurrent programs. We revisit the familiar mutual exclusion problem, this time with the aim of devising mutual exclusion protocols that work well with today's multiprocessors.

Any mutual exclusion protocol poses the question: "What do you do if you cannot acquire the lock?" There are two alternatives. If you keep trying, the lock is called a *spin lock*, and repeatedly testing the lock is called *spinning*, or *busy-waiting*. The Filter and Bakery algorithms are spin locks. Spinning makes sense when you expect the lock delay to be short (and only on multiprocessors, of course). The alternative is to suspend yourself and ask the operating system to schedule another thread on your processor, which is sometimes called *blocking*. Because switching from one thread to another is expensive, blocking makes sense only if you expect the lock delay to be long. Many operating systems mix both strategies, spinning for a short time and then blocking. Both spinning and blocking are important techniques. In this chapter, we turn our attention to locks that use spinning.

7.1 Welcome to the real world

We approach real-world mutual exclusion via the Lock interface from the java.util. concurrent.locks package. For now, we consider only the two principal methods, lock() and unlock(). As mentioned in Pragma 2.2.1, these methods are often used in the following structured way:

```
1  Lock mutex = new LockImpl(...); // lock implementation
2  ...
3  mutex.lock();
4  try {
5    ...          // body
6  } finally {
7    ... // restore object invariant if needed
8    mutex.unlock();
9  }
```

We create a new Lock object called mutex (line 1). Because Lock is an interface and not a class, we cannot create Lock objects directly. Instead, we create an object that *implements* the Lock interface. (The java.util.concurrent.locks package includes several classes that implement Lock, and we provide others in this chapter.) Next, we acquire the lock (line 3), and enter the critical section in a **try** block (line 4). The **finally** block (line 6) ensures that no matter what, the lock is released when control leaves the critical section. We do not put the lock() call inside the **try** block, because the lock() call might throw an exception before acquiring the lock, causing the **finally** block to call unlock() when the lock has not actually been acquired. (Java does not permit instructions to be executed between program lines, so once line 3 is completed and the lock is taken, the thread is in the **try** block.)

Why not use one of the Lock algorithms studied in Chapter 2, such as Filter or Bakery? One reason is the space lower bound proved in Chapter 2: No matter what we do, mutual exclusion using reads and writes requires space linear in n, the number of threads that potentially access the location. It gets worse.

Consider, for example, the two-thread Peterson lock algorithm of Chapter 2, presented again in Fig. 7.1. There are two threads, with IDs 0 and 1. When thread A wants to acquire the lock, it sets flag[A] to *true*, sets victim to A, and tests victim and flag[$1 - A$]. As long as victim is A and flag[$1 - A$] is *true*, the thread spins, repeating the test. Once either victim is not A or flag[$1 - A$] is *false*, the thread enters the critical section, setting flag[A] to *false* as it leaves. We know from Chapter 2 that the Peterson lock provides starvation-free mutual exclusion.

Suppose we write a simple concurrent program in which each of the threads repeatedly acquires the Peterson lock, increments a shared counter, and then releases the lock. We run it on a multiprocessor, where each thread executes this acquire–increment–release cycle, say, half a million times. On most modern architectures, the threads finish quickly. Alarmingly, however, we may discover that the counter's final value may be slightly off from the expected million mark. Proportionally, the error

```
1   class Peterson implements Lock {
2     private boolean[] flag = new boolean[2];
3     private int victim;
4     public void lock() {
5       int i = ThreadID.get(); // either 0 or 1
6       int j = 1-i;
7       flag[i] = true;
8       victim = i;
9       while (flag[j] && victim == i) {}; // spin
10    }
11  }
```

FIGURE 7.1

The Peterson class (Chapter 2): the order of reads and writes in lines 7–9 is crucial to providing mutual exclusion.

may be tiny, but why is there any error at all? Somehow, it must be that both threads are occasionally in the critical section at the same time, even though we have proved that this cannot happen. To quote Sherlock Holmes:

> *How often have I said to you that when you have eliminated the impossible, whatever remains, however improbable, must be the truth?*

Our proof fails, not because there is anything wrong with our logic, but because our assumptions about the real world are mistaken.

When programming our multiprocessor, we implicitly assumed that read–write operations are atomic, that is, they are linearizable to some sequential execution, or at the very least, that they are sequentially consistent. (Recall that linearizability implies sequential consistency.) As we saw in Chapter 3, sequential consistency implies that there is some global order on all operations in which each thread's operations take effect as ordered by its program. When we proved the Peterson lock correct, we relied, without calling attention to it, on the assumption that memory is sequentially consistent. In particular, mutual exclusion depends on the order of the steps in lines 7–9 of Fig. 7.1. Our proof that the Peterson lock provides mutual exclusion implicitly relied on the assumption that any two memory accesses by the same thread, even to separate variables, take effect in program order. Specifically, B's write to flag[B] must take effect before its write to victim (Eq. (2.3.2)) and A's write to victim must take effect before its read of flag[B] (Eq. (2.3.4)).

Unfortunately, modern multiprocessors, and programming languages for modern multiprocessors, typically do not provide sequentially consistent memory, nor do they necessarily guarantee program order among reads and writes by a given thread.

Why not? The first culprits are compilers that reorder instructions to enhance performance. It is possible that the order of writes by thread B of flag[B] and victim will be reversed by the compiler, invalidating Eq. (2.3.2). In addition, if a thread reads a variable repeatedly without writing it, a compiler may eliminate all but the first read of the variable, using the value read the first time for all subsequent reads. For example, the loop on line 9 of Fig. 7.1 may be replaced with a conditional statement that spins forever if the thread may not immediately enter the critical section.

A second culprit is the multiprocessor hardware itself. (Appendix B has a more extensive discussion of the multiprocessor architecture issues raised in this chapter.) Hardware vendors make no secret of the fact that writes to multiprocessor memory do not necessarily take effect when they are issued, because in most programs the vast majority of writes do not *need* to take effect in shared memory right away. On many multiprocessor architectures, writes to shared memory are buffered in a special *write buffer* (sometimes called a *store buffer*), to be written to memory only when needed. If thread A's write to victim is delayed in a write buffer, it may arrive in memory only after A reads flag[B], invalidating Eq. (2.3.4).

How then does one program multiprocessors, given such weak memory consistency guarantees? To prevent the reordering of operations resulting from write buffering, modern architectures provide a special *memory barrier* instruction (sometimes called a *memory fence*) that forces outstanding operations to take effect. Synchronization methods such as getAndSet() and compareAndSet() of AtomicInteger, include a memory barrier on many architectures, as do reads and writes to **volatile** fields. It is the programmer's responsibility to know where memory barriers are needed (e.g., the Peterson lock can be fixed by placing a barrier immediately before each read, and how to insert them. We discuss how to do this for Java in the next section.

Not surprisingly, memory barriers are expensive, so we want to minimize their use. Because operations such as getAndSet() and compareAndSet() have higher consensus numbers than reads and writes, and can be used in a straightforward way to reach a kind of consensus on who can and cannot enter the critical section, it may be sensible to design mutual exclusion algorithms that use these operations directly.

7.2 Volatile fields and atomic objects

As a rule of thumb, any object field, accessed by concurrent threads, that is not protected by a critical section should be declared **volatile**. Without such a declaration, that field will not act like an atomic register: Reads may return stale values, and writes may be delayed.

A **volatile** declaration does not make compound operations atomic: If x is a volatile variable, then the expression $x++$ will not necessarily increment x if concurrent threads can modify x. For tasks such as these, the java.util.concurrent.atomic package provides classes such as AtomicReference<T> or AtomicInteger that provide many useful atomic operations.

In earlier chapters, we did not put **volatile** declarations in our pseudocode because we assumed memory was linearizable. From now on, however, we assume the Java memory model, and so we put **volatile** declarations where they are needed. The Java memory model is described in more detail in Appendix A.3.

7.3 Test-and-set locks

The principal synchronization instruction on many early multiprocessor architectures was the *test-and-set* instruction. It operates on a single memory word (or byte) that may be either *true* or *false*. The test-and-set instruction, which has consensus number two, atomically stores *true* in the word and returns that word's previous value; that is, it *swaps* the value *true* for the word's current value. At first glance, test-and-set seems ideal for implementing a spin lock: The lock is free when the word's value is *false*, and busy when it is *true*. The lock() method repeatedly applies test-and-set to the word until it returns *false* (i.e., until the lock is free). The unlock() method simply writes the value *false* to it.

The TASLock class in Fig. 7.2 implements this lock in Java using the AtomicBoolean class in the java.util.concurrent package. This class stores a Boolean value, and it provides a set(b) method to replace the stored value with value b, and a

```
1  public class TASLock implements Lock {
2    AtomicBoolean state = new AtomicBoolean(false);
3    public void lock() {
4      while (state.getAndSet(true)) {}
5    }
6    public void unlock() {
7      state.set(false);
8    }
9  }
```

FIGURE 7.2

The TASLock class.

```
1   public class TTASLock implements Lock {
2     AtomicBoolean state = new AtomicBoolean(false);
3     public void lock() {
4       while (true) {
5         while (state.get()) {};
6         if (!state.getAndSet(true))
7           return;
8       }
9     }
10    public void unlock() {
11      state.set(false);
12    }
13  }
```

FIGURE 7.3

The TTASLock class.

getAndSet(b) that atomically replaces the current value with b and returns the previous value. The test-and-set instruction is equivalent to getAndSet($true$). (We follow common practice by using test-and-set in prose, but we use getAndSet($true$) in our code examples to be compatible with Java.)

Now consider TTASLock (Fig. 7.3), a variant of the TASLock algorithm called a *test-and-test-and-set* lock. In this algorithm, a thread reads the lock to check that it is free *before* performing the test-and-set. If the lock is not free, the thread repeatedly reads the lock until it is (i.e., until get() returns *false*), and only after that does the thread apply test-and-set. From the point of view of correctness, TASLock and TTASLock are equivalent: Each guarantees deadlock-free mutual exclusion. Under the simple model we have been using so far, there should be no difference between these two algorithms.

How do they compare on a real multiprocessor? Experiments that measure the elapsed time for n threads to execute a short critical section a fixed total number of times invariably yield results that look like Fig. 7.4. Each data point represents the

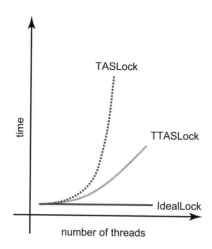

FIGURE 7.4

Schematic performance of a TASLock, a TTASLock, and an ideal lock with no overhead.

same amount of work, so in the absence of contention effects, all curves would be flat. The top curve is the TASLock, the middle curve is the TTASLock, and the bottom curve shows the time that would be needed if the threads did not interfere at all. The difference is dramatic: The TASLock performs very poorly; the TTASLock performance, while substantially better, still falls far short of the ideal.

To understand these results, we must study the architecture of modern multiprocessors. First, a word of caution: Modern multiprocessors have a variety of architectures, so we must be careful about overgeneralizing. Nevertheless, (almost) all modern architectures have similar issues concerning caching and locality. The details differ, but the principles remain the same.

For simplicity, we consider a typical multiprocessor architecture in which processors communicate by a shared broadcast medium called a *bus*. The memory typically also resides in nodes connected to the bus, each with its own *memory controller*. The processors and memory controllers can broadcast on the bus, but only one at a time. All processors and memory controllers can listen at the same time. Bus-based architectures are common today because they are easy to build, but they do not scale well to many processors; the bus becomes a point of contention.

Each processor has a *cache*, a small high-speed memory in which it keeps data likely to be of interest. Memory access typically takes orders of magnitude longer than access to the cache. Technology trends are not helping: Memory access time is unlikely to catch up with processor cycle time in the near future, so cache performance is critical to the overall performance of a multiprocessor.

A processor's cache contains copies of memory locations, along with their addresses. These copies are maintained by a *cache coherence protocol*, and may be *shared* or *exclusive*. As the name suggests, if any processor has an exclusive copy of a memory location, then no other processor has a copy of that location, shared or exclusive.

When accessing a memory location, a processor first checks whether its cache has a copy of that location. If it is writing the location, the copy must be exclusive. If the cache has the location's current data, then we say that the processor *hits* in its cache. In this case, the processor may read or write the copy in its cache immediately. Otherwise, the processor has a *cache miss*, and it requests a copy by broadcasting the address of the location on the bus. The other processors (and the memory controllers) *snoop* on the bus. If some processor has an exclusive copy of the location in its cache, it responds by broadcasting the address and value (making its copy shared). Otherwise, the memory controller responsible for that location responds. If the request was to write the location, then all previous copies are *invalidated*, so that the requester has an exclusive copy of that location.

We now consider how the simple TASLock algorithm performs on this architecture: Because getAndSet() may write the location, a thread must request an exclusive copy of the lock whenever it calls getAndSet(), unless its processor's cache already has such a copy. This request forces other processors to invalidate their cached copies of the lock. If multiple threads are spinning on the lock, almost every call to getAndSet() will result in a cache miss and a request on the bus to fetch the (unchanged) value. Compounding the injury, when the thread holding the lock tries to release it, it may be delayed because the bus is monopolized by the spinners. Indeed, because all threads use the bus to communicate with memory, even threads not waiting for the lock may be delayed. We now understand why the TASLock performs so poorly.

Now consider the behavior of the TTASLock algorithm while the lock is held by a thread *A*. The first time thread *B* reads the lock, it has a cache miss, forcing *B* to block while the value is loaded into *B*'s cache. However, because *B* is only reading the lock, it only requests a shared copy, which is stored in its processor's cache. As long as *A* holds the lock, *B* repeatedly rereads the value, but hits in its cache every time. *B* produces no bus traffic after its first request, and does not slow down other threads' memory accesses.

The situation deteriorates, however, when the lock holder *A* releases the lock by writing *false* to the lock's state variable. Because the lock is now shared with all the threads spinning on it, this write causes a cache miss, resulting in a request on the bus for an exclusive copy of the lock. This request invalidates the cached copies of the spinning threads. Each one has a cache miss and rereads the new value, and they all (more or less simultaneously) call getAndSet() to acquire the lock. The first to succeed invalidates the others, which must then reread the value, causing a storm of bus traffic. Eventually, the threads settle down once again to local spinning.

This notion of *local spinning*, where threads repeatedly reread cached values instead of repeatedly using the bus, is an important principle critical to the design of efficient spin locks.

7.4 Exponential back-off

We now consider how to improve the TTASLock algorithm by reducing the bus traffic induced when a thread releases the lock and many threads are waiting to acquire it. First, some terminology: *Contention* on a lock occurs when multiple threads try to acquire the lock at the same time. *High contention* means there are many such threads; *low contention* means there are few. As discussed above, attempting to acquire a highly contended lock is a bad idea: Such an attempt contributes to bus traffic (making the traffic jam worse) at a time when the thread's chances of acquiring the lock are slim. Instead, it is more effective for the thread to *back off* for some duration, giving the competing threads a chance to finish.

Recall that in the TTASLock class, the lock() method takes two steps: It repeatedly reads the lock until the lock is free, and then it attempts to acquire the lock by calling getAndSet(*true*). Here is a key observation: If a thread fails to acquire the lock in the second step, then some other thread must have acquired the lock between the first and second step, so most likely there is high contention for that lock. Here is a simple approach: Whenever a thread sees the lock has become free but fails to acquire it, it backs off before retrying. To ensure that competing threads do not fall into lockstep, each backing off and then trying again to acquire the lock at the same time, the thread backs off for a random duration.

For how long should the thread back off before retrying? A good rule of thumb is that the larger the number of unsuccessful tries, the higher the likely contention, so the longer the thread should back off. To incorporate this rule, each time a thread tries and fails to get the lock, it doubles the expected back-off time, up to a fixed maximum.

Because backing off is common to several locking algorithms, we encapsulate this logic in a simple Backoff class, shown in Fig. 7.5. The constructor takes two arguments: minDelay is the initial minimum delay (it makes no sense for the thread to back off for too short a duration), and maxDelay is the final maximum delay (a final limit is necessary to prevent unlucky threads from backing off for much too long). The limit field controls the current delay limit. The backoff() method computes a random delay between zero and the current limit, and blocks the thread for that duration before returning. It doubles the limit for the next back-off, up to maxDelay.

Fig. 7.6 shows the BackoffLock class. It uses a Backoff object whose minimum and maximum back-off durations are governed by the constants chosen for MIN_DELAY and MAX_DELAY. Note that the thread backs off only when it fails to acquire a lock that it had immediately before observed to be free. Observing that the lock is held by another thread says nothing about the level of contention.

The BackoffLock is easy to implement, and typically performs significantly better than TASLock and TTASLock on many architectures. Unfortunately, its performance is sensitive to the choice of MIN_DELAY and MAX_DELAY values. To deploy this lock on a particular architecture, it is easy to experiment with different values, and to choose the ones that work best. Experience shows, however, that these optimal values are sensitive to the number of processors and their speed, so it is not easy to tune BackoffLock to be portable across a range of different machines.

```
1   public class Backoff {
2     final int minDelay, maxDelay;
3     int limit;
4     public Backoff(int min, int max) {
5       minDelay = min;
6       maxDelay = max;
7       limit = minDelay;
8     }
9     public void backoff() throws InterruptedException {
10      int delay = ThreadLocalRandom.current().nextInt(limit);
11      limit = Math.min(maxDelay, 2 * limit);
12      Thread.sleep(delay);
13    }
14  }
```

FIGURE 7.5

The Backoff class: adaptive back-off logic. To ensure that concurrently contending threads do not repeatedly try to acquire the lock at the same time, threads back off for a random duration. Each time the thread tries and fails to get the lock, it doubles the expected time to back off, up to a fixed maximum.

```
1   public class BackoffLock implements Lock {
2     private AtomicBoolean state = new AtomicBoolean(false);
3     private static final int MIN_DELAY = ...;
4     private static final int MAX_DELAY = ...;
5     public void lock() {
6       Backoff backoff = new Backoff(MIN_DELAY, MAX_DELAY);
7       while (true) {
8         while (state.get()) {};
9         if (!state.getAndSet(true)) {
10          return;
11        } else {
12          backoff.backoff();
13        }
14      }
15    }
16    public void unlock() {
17      state.set(false);
18    }
19    ...
20  }
```

FIGURE 7.6

The exponential back-off lock. Whenever the thread fails to acquire a lock that became free, it backs off before retrying.

One drawback of BackoffLock is that it underutilizes the critical section when the lock is contended: Because threads back off when they notice contention, when a thread releases the lock, there may be some delay before another thread attempts to acquire it, even though many threads are waiting to acquire the lock. Indeed, because threads back off for longer at higher contention, this effect is more pronounced at higher levels of contention.

Finally, the BackoffLock can be unfair, allowing one thread to acquire the lock many times while other threads are waiting. TASLock and TTASLock may also be unfair, but BackoffLock exacerbates this problem because the thread that just released the lock might never notice that the lock is contended, and so not back off at all.

Although this unfairness has obvious negative consequences, including the possibility of starving other threads, it also has some positive consequences: Because a lock often protects accesses to some shared data structure, which is also cached, granting repeated access to the same thread without intervening accesses by threads at different processors reduces cache misses due to accesses to this data structure, and so reduces bus traffic and avoids the latency of communication. For longer critical sections, this effect can be more significant than the effect of reduced contention on the lock itself. So there is a tension between fairness and performance.

7.5 Queue locks

We now explore a different approach to implementing scalable spin locks, one that is slightly more complicated than back-off locks, but inherently more portable, and avoids or ameliorates many of the problems of back-off locks. The idea is to have threads waiting to acquire the lock form a *queue*. In a queue, each thread can discover when its turn has arrived by checking whether its predecessor has finished. Cache-coherence traffic is reduced by having each thread spin on a different location. A queue also allows better utilization of the critical section, since there is no need to guess when to attempt to access it: Each thread is notified directly by its predecessor in the queue. Finally, a queue provides first-come-first-served fairness, the same high degree of fairness achieved by the Bakery algorithm. We now explore different ways to implement *queue locks*, a family of locking algorithms that exploit these insights.

7.5.1 Array-based locks

Fig. 7.7 shows the ALock,[1] a simple array-based queue lock. The threads share an AtomicInteger tail field, initially zero. To acquire the lock, each thread atomically increments tail (line 17). Call the resulting value the thread's *slot*. The slot is used as an index into a Boolean flag array.

If flag[j] is *true*, then the thread with slot j has permission to acquire the lock. Initially, flag[0] is *true*. To acquire the lock, a thread spins until the flag at its slot

---

[1] Most of our lock classes use the initials of their inventors, as explained in Section 7.11.

```
1   public class ALock implements Lock {
2     ThreadLocal<Integer> mySlotIndex = new ThreadLocal<Integer> (){
3       protected Integer initialValue() {
4         return 0;
5       }
6     };
7     AtomicInteger tail;
8     volatile boolean[] flag;
9     int size;
10    public ALock(int capacity) {
11      size = capacity;
12      tail = new AtomicInteger(0);
13      flag = new boolean[capacity];
14      flag[0] = true;
15    }
16    public void lock() {
17      int slot = tail.getAndIncrement() % size;
18      mySlotIndex.set(slot);
19      while (!flag[slot]) {};
20    }
21    public void unlock() {
22      int slot = mySlotIndex.get();
23      flag[slot] = false;
24      flag[(slot + 1) % size] = true;
25    }
26  }
```

FIGURE 7.7

Array-based queue lock.

becomes *true* (line 19). To release the lock, the thread sets the flag at its slot to *false* (line 23), and sets the flag at the next slot to *true* (line 24). All arithmetic is modulo *n*, where *n* is at least as large as the maximum number of concurrent threads.

In the ALock algorithm, mySlotIndex is a *thread-local* variable (see Appendix A). Thread-local variables differ from their regular counterparts in that each thread has its own, independently initialized copy of each variable. Thread-local variables need not be stored in shared memory, do not require synchronization, and do not generate any coherence traffic since they are accessed by only one thread. The value of a thread-local variable is accessed by get() and set() methods.

The flag[] array, on the other hand, is shared.[2] However, contention on the array locations is minimized since each thread, at any given time, spins on its locally cached copy of a single array location, greatly reducing invalidation traffic.

---

[2] The role of the **volatile** declaration here is not to introduce a memory barrier but rather to prevent the compiler from applying any optimizations to the loop in line 19.

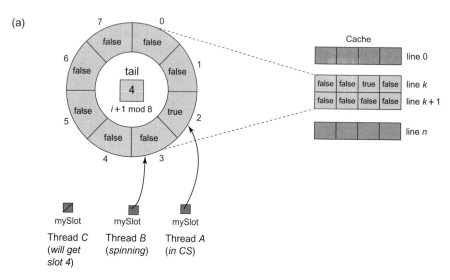

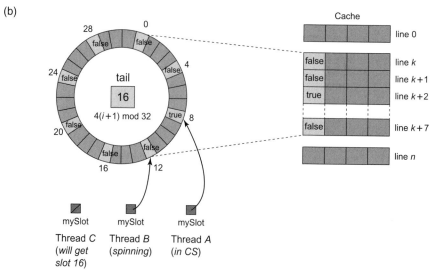

FIGURE 7.8

The ALock with padding to avoid false sharing. In part (a), the ALock has eight slots which are accessed via a modulo 8 counter. Array entries are typically mapped into cache lines consecutively. As illustrated, when thread A changes the status of its entry, thread B, whose entry is mapped to the same cache line k, incurs a false invalidation. In part (b), each location is padded so it is 4 apart from the others with a modulo 32 counter. Even if array entries are mapped consecutively, the entry for B is mapped to a different cache line from that of A, so B's entry is not invalidated when A invalidates its entry.

Contention may still occur because of a phenomenon called *false sharing*, which occurs when adjacent data items (such as array elements) share a single cache line. A write to one item invalidates that item's cache line, which causes invalidation traffic to processors that are spinning on nearby unchanged items that happen to fall in the same cache line. In the example in part (a) of Fig. 7.8, threads accessing the eight ALock locations may suffer unnecessary invalidations because the locations were all cached in the same two four-word lines.

One way to avoid false sharing is to *pad* array elements so that distinct elements are mapped to distinct cache lines. Padding is easier in low-level languages like C or C++, where the programmer has direct control over the layout of objects in memory. In the example in part (b) of Fig. 7.8, we pad the eight original ALock locations by increasing the lock array size four-fold, and placing the locations four words apart so that no two locations can fall in the same cache line. (We increment from one location i to the next by computing $4(i + 1) \bmod 32$ instead of $i + 1 \bmod 8$.)

The ALock improves on BackoffLock: it reduces invalidations to a minimum and minimizes the interval between when a lock is freed by one thread and when it is acquired by another. Unlike the TASLock and BackoffLock, this algorithm guarantees that no starvation occurs, and provides first-come-first-served fairness.

Unfortunately, the ALock lock is not space-efficient. It requires a known bound n on the maximum number of concurrent threads, and it allocates an array of that size per lock. Synchronizing L distinct objects requires $O(Ln)$ space, even if a thread accesses only one lock at a time.

7.5.2 The CLH queue lock

We now turn our attention to a different style of queue lock, the CLHLock (Fig. 7.9). This class records each thread's status in a QNode object, which has a Boolean locked field. If that field is *true*, then the corresponding thread has either acquired the lock or is waiting for the lock. If that field is *false*, then the thread has released the lock. The lock itself is represented as a virtual linked list of QNode objects. We use the term "virtual" because the list is implicit: Each thread refers to its predecessor through a thread-local pred variable. The public tail field is an AtomicReference<QNode> to the node most recently added to the queue.

To acquire the lock, a thread sets the locked field of its QNode to *true*, indicating that the thread is not ready to release the lock. The thread applies getAndSet() to the tail field to make its own node the tail of the queue, simultaneously acquiring a reference to its predecessor's QNode. The thread then spins on the predecessor's locked field until the predecessor releases the lock. To release the lock, the thread sets its node's locked field to *false*. It then reuses its predecessor's QNode as its new node for future lock accesses. It can do so because at this point the thread's predecessor's QNode is no longer used by the predecessor. It cannot use its old QNode because that node could be referenced both by the thread's successor and by the tail. Although we do not do so in our implementation, it is possible to recycle nodes so that if there are L locks and each thread accesses at most one lock at a time, then the CLHLock class

```
1   public class CLHLock implements Lock {
2     AtomicReference<QNode> tail;
3     ThreadLocal<QNode> myPred;
4     ThreadLocal<QNode> myNode;
5     public CLHLock() {
6       tail = new AtomicReference<QNode>(new QNode());
7       myNode = new ThreadLocal<QNode>() {
8         protected QNode initialValue() {
9           return new QNode();
10        }
11      };
12      myPred = new ThreadLocal<QNode>() {
13        protected QNode initialValue() {
14          return null;
15        }
16      };
17    }
18    public void lock() {
19      QNode qnode = myNode.get();
20      qnode.locked = true;
21      QNode pred = tail.getAndSet(qnode);
22      myPred.set(pred);
23      while (pred.locked) {}
24    }
25    public void unlock() {
26      QNode qnode = myNode.get();
27      qnode.locked = false;
28      myNode.set(myPred.get());
29    }
30    class QNode {
31      volatile boolean locked = false;
32    }
33  }
```

FIGURE 7.9

The CLHLock class.

needs only $O(L + n)$ space, as compared with $O(Ln)$ for the ALock class.[3] Fig. 7.10 shows a typical CLHLock execution.

Like the ALock, this algorithm has each thread spin on a distinct location, so when one thread releases its lock, it invalidates only its successor's cache. This algorithm requires much less space than the ALock class, and does not require knowledge of

---

[3] There is no need to reuse nodes in garbage-collected languages such as Java or C#, but reuse would be needed in languages such as C++ or C.

(a)

Initially

tail

false

(b)

A:lock()

tail

tail.getAndSet()

true   false

myNode   myPred

Thread A

(c)

A:unlock()
B:lock()

tail

true   false   false

myNode myPred myNode myPred

myNode = myPred

Thread B   Thread A

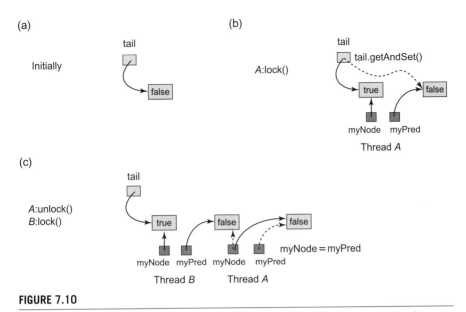

FIGURE 7.10

CLHLock class: lock acquisition and release. Initially the tail field refers to a QNode whose locked field is *false*. Thread *A* then applies getAndSet() to the tail field to insert its QNode at the tail of the queue, simultaneously acquiring a reference to its predecessor's QNode. Next, *B* does the same to insert its QNode at the tail of the queue. *A* then releases the lock by setting its node's locked field to *false*. It then recycles the QNode referenced by pred for future lock accesses.

the number of threads that might access the lock. Like the ALock class, it provides first-come-first-served fairness.

Perhaps the only disadvantage of this lock algorithm is that it performs poorly on cacheless NUMA architectures. Each thread spins waiting for its predecessor's node's locked field to become *false*. If this memory location is remote, then performance suffers. On cache-coherent architectures, however, this approach should work well.

7.5.3 The MCS queue lock

The MCSLock (Fig. 7.11) is another lock represented as a linked list of QNode objects, where each QNode represents either a lock holder or a thread waiting to acquire the lock. Unlike the CLHLock class, the list is explicit, not virtual: Instead of embodying the list in thread-local variables, it is embodied in the (globally accessible) QNode objects, via their next fields.

To acquire the lock, a thread appends its own QNode at the tail of the list (line 14). If the queue was not previously empty, it sets the predecessor's QNode's next field to refer to its own QNode. The thread then spins on a (local) locked field in its own QNode waiting until its predecessor sets this field to *false* (lines 15–20).

```
1   public class MCSLock implements Lock {
2     AtomicReference<QNode> tail;
3     ThreadLocal<QNode> myNode;
4     public MCSLock() {
5       tail = new AtomicReference<QNode>(null);
6       myNode = new ThreadLocal<QNode>() {
7         protected QNode initialValue() {
8           return new QNode();
9         }
10      };
11    }
12    public void lock() {
13      QNode qnode = myNode.get();
14      QNode pred = tail.getAndSet(qnode);
15      if (pred != null) {
16        qnode.locked = true;
17        pred.next = qnode;
18        // wait until predecessor gives up the lock
19        while (qnode.locked) {}
20      }
21    }
22    public void unlock() {
23      QNode qnode = myNode.get();
24      if (qnode.next == null) {
25        if (tail.compareAndSet(qnode, null))
26          return;
27        // wait until successor fills in its next field
28        while (qnode.next == null) {}
29      }
30      qnode.next.locked = false;
31      qnode.next = null;
32    }
33    class QNode {
34      volatile boolean locked = false;
35      volatile QNode next = null;
36    }
37  }
```

FIGURE 7.11

The MCSLock class.

To release the lock, a thread checks whether its node's next field is *null* (line 24). If so, then either no other thread is contending for the lock, or there is another thread, but it is slow. To distinguish these cases, it applies compareAndSet(*q*, *null*) to the tail field, where *q* is the thread's node. If the call succeeds, then no other thread is trying to acquire the lock, so the thread just returns. Otherwise, another (slow) thread is

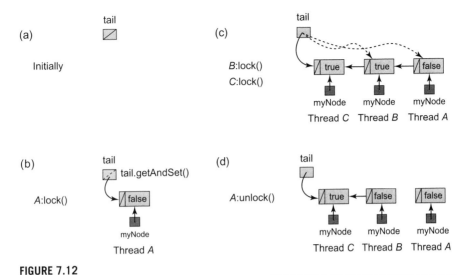

FIGURE 7.12

A lock acquisition and release in an MCSLock. (a) Initially the tail is *null*. (b) To acquire the lock, thread A places its own QNode at the tail of the list and since it has no predecessor, it enters the critical section. (c) Thread B enqueues its own QNode at the tail of the list and modifies its predecessor's QNode to refer back to its own. Thread B then spins on its locked field waiting until A, its predecessor, sets this field from *true* to *false*. Thread C repeats this sequence. (d) To release the lock, A follows its next field to its successor B and sets B's locked field to *false*. It can now reuse its QNode.

trying to acquire the lock, so the thread spins waiting for the other thread to finish adding its node to the queue (line 28). Once the successor appears (or if it was there at the beginning), the thread sets its successor's locked field to *false*, indicating that the lock is now free. At this point, no other thread can access this QNode, and so it can be reused. Fig. 7.12 shows an example execution of the MCSLock.

This lock shares the advantages of the CLHLock, in particular, the property that each lock release invalidates only the successor's cache entry. It is better suited to cacheless NUMA architectures because each thread controls the location on which it spins. Like the CLHLock, nodes can be recycled so that this lock has space complexity $O(L + n)$. One drawback of the MCSLock algorithm is that releasing a lock requires spinning. Another is that it requires more reads, writes, and compareAndSet() calls than the CLHLock algorithm.

7.6 A queue lock with timeouts

The Java Lock interface includes a tryLock() method that allows the caller to specify a *timeout*, that is, a maximum duration the caller is willing to wait to acquire the lock. If the timeout expires before the caller acquires the lock, the attempt is aban-

```
1   public class TOLock implements Lock{
2     static QNode AVAILABLE = new QNode();
3     AtomicReference<QNode> tail;
4     ThreadLocal<QNode> myNode;
5     public TOLock() {
6       tail = new AtomicReference<QNode>(null);
7       myNode = new ThreadLocal<QNode>() {
8         protected QNode initialValue() {
9           return new QNode();
10        }
11      };
12    }
13    ...
14    static class QNode {
15      public volatile QNode pred = null;
16    }
17  }
```

FIGURE 7.13

TOLock class: fields, constructor, and QNode class.

doned. A Boolean return value indicates whether the lock attempt succeeded. (For an explanation why these methods throw InterruptedException, see Pragma 8.2.1.)

Abandoning a BackoffLock request is trivial: a thread can simply return from the tryLock() call. Responding to a timeout is wait-free, requiring only a constant number of steps. By contrast, timing out any of the queue lock algorithms is far from trivial: if a thread simply returns, the threads queued up behind it will starve.

Here is a bird's-eye view of a queue lock with timeouts. As in the CLHLock, the lock is a virtual queue of nodes, and each thread spins on its predecessor's node waiting for the lock to be released. As noted, when a thread times out, it cannot simply abandon its queue node, because its successor will never notice when the lock is released. On the other hand, it seems extremely difficult to unlink a queue node without disrupting concurrent lock releases. Instead, we take a *lazy* approach: When a thread times out, it marks its node as abandoned. Its successor in the queue, if there is one, notices that the node on which it is spinning has been abandoned, and starts spinning on the abandoned node's predecessor. This approach has the added advantage that the successor can recycle the abandoned node.

Fig. 7.13 shows the fields, constructor, and QNode class for the TOLock (timeout lock) class, a queue lock based on the CLHLock class that supports wait-free timeout even for threads in the middle of the list of nodes waiting for the lock.

When a QNode's pred field is *null*, the associated thread has either not acquired the lock or has released it. When a QNode's pred field refers to the distinguished static QNode AVAILABLE, the associated thread has released the lock. Finally, if the pred field refers to some other QNode, the associated thread has abandoned the lock request, so

```
18    public boolean tryLock(long time, TimeUnit unit) throws InterruptedException {
19      long startTime = System.currentTimeMillis();
20      long patience = TimeUnit.MILLISECONDS.convert(time, unit);
21      QNode qnode = new QNode();
22      myNode.set(qnode);
23      qnode.pred = null;
24      QNode myPred = tail.getAndSet(qnode);
25      if (myPred == null || myPred.pred == AVAILABLE) {
26        return true;
27      }
28      while (System.currentTimeMillis() - startTime < patience) {
29        QNode predPred = myPred.pred;
30        if (predPred == AVAILABLE) {
31          return true;
32        } else if (predPred != null) {
33          myPred = predPred;
34        }
35      }
36      if (!tail.compareAndSet(qnode, myPred))
37        qnode.pred = myPred;
38      return false;
39    }
40    public void unlock() {
41      QNode qnode = myNode.get();
42      if (!tail.compareAndSet(qnode, null))
43        qnode.pred = AVAILABLE;
44    }
```

FIGURE 7.14

TOLock class: tryLock() and unlock() methods.

the thread owning the successor node should wait on the abandoned node's predecessor.

Fig. 7.14 shows the TOLock class's tryLock() and unlock() methods. The tryLock() method creates a new QNode with a *null* pred field and appends it to the list as in the CLHLock class (lines 21–24). If the lock was free (line 25), the thread enters the critical section. Otherwise, it spins waiting for its predecessor's QNode's pred field to change (lines 28–35). If the predecessor thread times out, it sets the pred field to its own predecessor, and the thread spins instead on the new predecessor. An example of such a sequence appears in Fig. 7.15. Finally, if the thread itself times out (line 36), it attempts to remove its QNode from the list by applying compareAndSet() to the tail field. If the compareAndSet() call fails, indicating that the thread has a successor, the thread sets its QNode's pred field, previously *null*, to its predecessor's QNode, indicating that it has abandoned the queue.

In the unlock() method, a thread uses compareAndSet() to check whether it has a successor (line 42), and if so, sets its pred field to AVAILABLE. Note that it is not safe

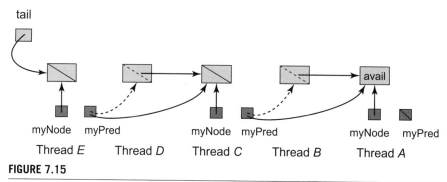

FIGURE 7.15

Timed-out nodes that must be skipped to acquire the TOLock. Threads *B* and *D* have timed out, redirecting their pred fields to their predecessors in the list. Thread *C* notices that *B*'s field is directed at *A* and so it starts spinning on *A*. Similarly, thread *E* spins waiting for *C*. When *A* completes and sets its pred to AVAILABLE, *C* will access the critical section and upon leaving it will set its pred to AVAILABLE, releasing *E*.

to recycle a thread's old node at this point, since the node may be referenced by its immediate successor, or by a chain of such references. The nodes in such a chain can be recycled as soon as a thread skips over the timed-out nodes and enters the critical section.

The TOLock has many of the advantages of the original CLHLock: local spinning on a cached location and quick detection that the lock is free. It also has the wait-free timeout property of the BackoffLock. However, it has some drawbacks, among them the need to allocate a new node per lock access and the fact that a thread spinning on the lock may have to traverse a chain of timed-out nodes before it can access the critical section.

7.7 Hierarchical locks

Many of today's cache-coherent architectures organize processors into *clusters*, where communication within a cluster is significantly faster than communication between clusters. For example, a cluster might correspond to a group of processors that share memory through a fast interconnect, or to the threads running on a single core in a multicore architecture. Such systems are called *nonuniform memory access* (NUMA) systems. On a NUMA system, passing a lock between threads in different clusters (i.e., *remote* threads) incurs significantly more overhead than passing it between threads in the same cluster (i.e., *local* threads). This increased overhead is due not only to the increased cost of synchronization on the lock, but also to the cost of transferring the data protected by the lock. We can reduce this overhead by preferentially passing the lock to a local thread rather than a remote one (i.e., to a thread in the same cluster as the thread releasing the lock, rather than to one in a different cluster). Such a lock is called a *hierarchical lock*.

```
1  public class ClusterLocal<T> {
2    protected T initialValue();
3    T get();
4    void set(T value);
5  }
```

FIGURE 7.16

The ClusterLocal class.

We consider an architecture with a two-level memory hierarchy, consisting of clusters of processors, where processors in the same cluster communicate efficiently through a shared cache, and intercluster communication is much more expensive than intracluster communication. For architectures whose memory hierarchy has more than two levels, we can apply the techniques in this section at each boundary between levels in the hierarchy.

We assume that each cluster has a unique *cluster ID* known to each thread in the cluster, available via ThreadID.getCluster(), and that threads do not migrate between clusters. We also assume there is a class ClusterLocal<T> (Fig. 7.16), analogous to ThreadLocal<T>, which manages one variable for each cluster, and provides get(), set(), and initialValue() for reading, writing, and initializing these variables.

7.7.1 A hierarchical back-off lock

Simple back-off locks, such as test-and-set and test-and-test-and-set locks, can easily be adapted to exploit clustering: By increasing the back-off times of threads in different clusters from the thread holding the lock (relative to those of threads in the same cluster), local threads are more likely to acquire the lock than remote threads. To do this, we must record the cluster of the thread that holds the lock. Fig. 7.17 shows the HBOLock class, a hierarchical back-off lock based on this principle.

HBOLock suffers from some of the same problems as BackoffLock, as described in Section 7.4. These problems may be even worse on NUMA systems because of the greater disparity in communication costs and the longer back-off times for remote threads. For example, longer back-off times increase delays between the release of a lock and its subsequent acquisition, resulting in greater underutilization of the critical section. As before, choosing back-off durations can be difficult, and acquiring or releasing the lock can generate a "storm" of cache-coherence traffic. And as with BackoffLock, the HBOLock may be *too* successful at passing the lock among threads in a single cluster, starving remote threads attempting to acquire the lock. In short, the problems with back-off locks that led us to explore queue locks still exist and are more severe on NUMA systems.

7.7.2 Cohort locks

We can address these problems by *lock cohorting*, a simple but effective technique that enables threads in a cluster to pass the lock among themselves without inter-

```
1   public class HBOLock implements Lock {
2     private static final int LOCAL_MIN_DELAY = ...;
3     private static final int LOCAL_MAX_DELAY = ...;
4     private static final int REMOTE_MIN_DELAY = ...;
5     private static final int REMOTE_MAX_DELAY = ...;
6     private static final int FREE = -1;
7     AtomicInteger state;
8     public HBOLock() {
9       state = new AtomicInteger(FREE);
10    }
11    public void lock() {
12      int myCluster = ThreadID.getCluster();
13      Backoff localBackoff =
14          new Backoff(LOCAL_MIN_DELAY, LOCAL_MAX_DELAY);
15      Backoff remoteBackoff =
16          new Backoff(REMOTE_MIN_DELAY, REMOTE_MAX_DELAY);
17      while (true) {
18        if (state.compareAndSet(FREE, myCluster)) {
19          return;
20        }
21        int lockState = state.get();
22        if (lockState == myCluster) {
23          localBackoff.backoff();
24        } else {
25          remoteBackoff.backoff();
26        }
27      }
28    }
29    public void unlock() {
30      state.set(FREE);
31    }
32  }
```

FIGURE 7.17

The HBOLock class: a hierarchical back-off lock.

cluster communication. The set of threads in a single cluster waiting to acquire the lock is called a *cohort*, and a lock based on this technique is called a *cohort lock*.

The key idea of lock cohorting is to use multiple locks to provide exclusion at different levels of the memory hierarchy. In a cohort lock, each cluster has a *cluster lock*, held by a thread, and the clusters share a *global lock*, held by a cluster. A thread holds the cohort lock if it holds its cluster lock and its cluster holds the global lock. To acquire the cohort lock, a thread first acquires the lock of its cluster, and then ensures that its cluster holds the global lock. When releasing the cohort lock, the thread checks whether there is any thread in its cohort (i.e., a thread in its cluster is waiting to acquire the lock). If so, the thread releases its cluster lock without releasing

```
1  public interface CohortDetectionLock extends Lock {
2    public boolean alone();
3  }
```

FIGURE 7.18

Interface for locks that support cohort detection.

the global lock. In this way, the thread in its cluster that next acquires the cluster lock also acquires the cohort lock (since its cluster already holds the global lock) without intercluster communication. If the cohort is empty when a thread releases the lock, it releases both the cluster lock and the global lock. To prevent remote threads from starving, a cohort lock must also have some policy that restricts local threads from passing the lock among themselves indefinitely without releasing the global lock.

A cohort lock algorithm requires certain properties of its component locks. A thread releasing the lock must be able to detect whether another thread is attempting to acquire its cluster lock, and it must be able to pass ownership of the global lock directly to another thread without releasing it.

A lock *supports cohort detection* if it provides a predicate method alone() with the following meaning: If alone() returns *false* when called by the thread holding a lock, then another thread is attempting to acquire that lock. The converse need not hold: If alone() returns *true*, there may be another thread attempting to acquire the lock, but such false positives should be rare. Fig. 7.18 shows an interface for a lock that supports cohort detection.

A lock is *thread-oblivious* if the thread releasing a thread-oblivious lock need not be the thread that most recently acquired it. The pattern of lock accesses must still be well formed (for example, unlock() may not be invoked when the lock is free).

Fig. 7.19 shows code for the CohortLock class, which must be instantiated with a thread-oblivious global lock and a lock that supports cohort detection for each cluster. The global lock must be thread-oblivious because its ownership may be passed implicitly among threads in a cluster, and eventually released by a different thread than the one that acquired the lock.

The lock() function acquires the thread's cluster lock, and then checks whether the lock was passed locally, meaning that its cluster already owns the global lock. If so, it returns immediately. Otherwise, it acquires the global lock before returning.

The unlock() function first determines whether a local thread is trying to acquire the lock, and if so, whether it should pass the lock locally. The latter decision is made by a "turn arbiter." We adopt a simple policy of bounding the number of times a thread may be passed locally without releasing the global lock. To emphasize that other policies are possible, we encapsulate the policy in a TurnArbiter class, shown in Fig. 7.20. The passedLocally field and the arbiter are updated to reflect the decision of whether to pass the lock locally. If the lock is not to be passed locally, both the global lock and the cluster lock are released. Otherwise, only the cluster lock is released.

```
 1  public class CohortLock implements Lock {
 2    final Lock globalLock;
 3    final ClusterLocal<CohortDetectionLock> clusterLock;
 4    final TurnArbiter localPassArbiter;
 5    ClusterLocal<Boolean> passedLocally;
 6    public CohortLock(Lock gl, ClusterLocal<CohortDetectonLock> cl, int passLimit) {
 7      globalLock = gl;
 8      clusterLock = cl;
 9      localPassArbiter = new TurnArbiter(passLimit);
10    }
11    public void lock() {
12      clusterLock.get().lock();
13      if (passedLocally.get()) return;
14      globalLock.lock();
15    }
16    public void unlock() {
17      CohortDetectionLock cl = clusterLock.get();
18      if (cl.alone() || !localPassArbiter.goAgain()) {
19        localPassArbiter.passed();
20        passedLocally.set(false);
21        globalLock.unlock();
22      } else {
23        localPassArbiter.wentAgain();
24        passedLocally.set(true);
25      }
26      cl.unlock();
27    }
28  }
```

FIGURE 7.19

The CohortLock class.

7.7.3 A cohort lock implementation

We now describe a cohort lock implementation that uses BackoffLock, which is
thread-oblivious, for the global lock, and a version of MCSLock modified to provide an
alone() method for the cluster locks. The modified MCSLock is shown in Fig. 7.21. The
alone() method simply checks whether the next field of the invoking thread's QNode is
null. This test provides cohort detection, because whenever the next field of a QNode is
not *null*, it points to the QNode of a thread waiting to acquire the lock. Fig. 7.22 shows
how to extend CohortLock to use BackoffLock and the modified MCSLock. Fig. 7.23
illustrates an execution of this cohort lock.

CohortBackoffMCSLock can be improved slightly by recording in the QNode whether
the lock has been passed locally. Instead of a locked field, the QNode maintains a field
that indicates whether its thread must wait, or whether it has acquired the lock, and
if so, whether the lock was passed locally or globally. There is no need for a separate
cluster-local field to record whether the lock was passed locally, and the cache miss
that would be incurred by accessing that field after the lock is acquired. We leave the
details as an exercise.

```
1  public class TurnArbiter {
2    private final int TURN_LIMIT;
3    private int turns = 0;
4    public LocalPassingArbiter(int limit) {
5      TURN_LIMIT = limit;
6    }
7    public boolean goAgain() {
8      return (turns < TURN_LIMIT);
9    }
10   public void wentAgain() {
11     turns++;
12   }
13   public void passed() {
14     turns = 0;
15   }
16 }
```

FIGURE 7.20

TurnArbiter class.

```
1  public class CohortDetectionMCSLock extends MCSLock
2                    implements CohortDetectionLock {
3    public boolean alone() {
4      return (myNode.get().next == null);
5    }
6  }
```

FIGURE 7.21

Adding support for cohort detection to MCSLock.

```
1  public class CohortBackoffMCSLock extends CohortLock {
2    public CohortBackoffMCSLock(int passLimit) {
3      ClusterLocal<CohortDetectionMCSLock> cl = new ClusterLocal<CohortDetectionMCSLock> {
4        protected CohortDetectionMCSLock initialValue() {
5          return new CohortDetectionMCSLock();
6        }
7      }
8      super(new BackoffLock(), cl, passLimit);
9    }
10 }
```

FIGURE 7.22

CohortBackoffMCSLock class.

7.8 A composite lock

Spin lock algorithms impose trade-offs. Queue locks provide first-come-first-served fairness, fast lock release, and low contention, but require nontrivial protocols for

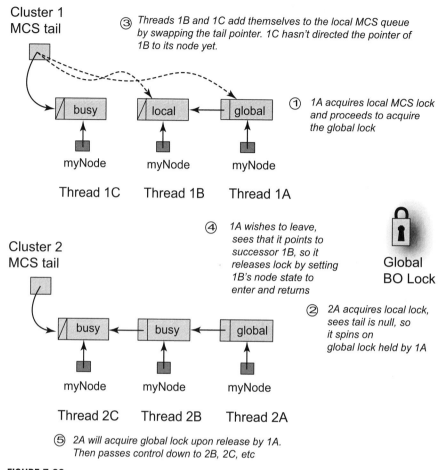

Cluster 1 MCS tail

③ *Threads 1B and 1C add themselves to the local MCS queue by swapping the tail pointer. 1C hasn't directed the pointer of 1B to its node yet.*

① *1A acquires local MCS lock and proceeds to acquire the global lock*

busy   local   global

myNode   myNode   myNode

Thread 1C   Thread 1B   Thread 1A

Cluster 2 MCS tail

④ *1A wishes to leave, sees that it points to successor 1B, so it releases lock by setting 1B's node state to enter and returns*

Global BO Lock

② *2A acquires local lock, sees tail is null, so it spins on global lock held by 1A*

busy   busy   global

myNode   myNode   myNode

Thread 2C   Thread 2B   Thread 2A

⑤ *2A will acquire global lock upon release by 1A. Then passes control down to 2B, 2C, etc*

FIGURE 7.23

An example execution of `CohortBackoffMCSLock`.

recycling abandoned nodes. By contrast, back-off locks support trivial timeout protocols, but are inherently not scalable, and may have slow lock release if timeout parameters are not well tuned. In this section, we consider an advanced lock algorithm that combines the best of both approaches.

Consider the following simple observation: In a queue lock, only the threads at the front of the queue need to perform lock hand-offs. One way to balance the merits of queue locks versus back-off locks is to keep a small number of waiting threads in a queue on the way to the critical section, and have the rest use exponential back-off while attempting to enter this short queue. It is trivial for the threads employing back-off to quit.

```
1   public class CompositeLock implements Lock{
2     private static final int SIZE = ...;
3     private static final int MIN_BACKOFF = ...;
4     private static final int MAX_BACKOFF = ...;
5     AtomicStampedReference<QNode> tail;
6     QNode[] waiting;
7     ThreadLocal<QNode> myNode = new ThreadLocal<QNode>() {
8       protected QNode initialValue() { return null; };
9     };
10    public CompositeLock() {
11      tail = new AtomicStampedReference<QNode>(null,0);
12      waiting = new QNode[SIZE];
13      for (int i = 0; i < waiting.length; i++) {
14        waiting[i] = new QNode();
15      }
16    }
17    public void unlock() {
18      QNode acqNode = myNode.get();
19      acqNode.state.set(State.RELEASED);
20      myNode.set(null);
21    }
22    ...
23  }
```

FIGURE 7.24

The CompositeLock class: fields, constructor, and unlock() method.

The CompositeLock class keeps a short, fixed-size array of lock nodes. Each thread that tries to acquire the lock selects a node in the array at random. If that node is in use, the thread backs off (adaptively) and tries again. Once the thread acquires a node, it enqueues that node in a TOLock-style queue. The thread spins on the preceding node; when that node's owner signals it is done, the thread enters the critical section. When the thread leaves (after it completes or times out), it releases its node, and another thread may acquire it. The tricky part is recycling the freed nodes of the array while multiple threads attempt to acquire control over them.

The CompositeLock's fields, constructor, and unlock() method appears in Fig. 7.24. The tail field is an AtomicStampedReference<QNode> that combines a reference to a node with a version number (see Pragma 10.6.1 for a more detailed explanation of the AtomicStampedReference<T> class); the version number is needed to avoid the *ABA* problem.[4] The tail field either is *null* or refers to the last node inserted in the queue.

---

[4] The ABA problem typically arises when using dynamically allocated memory in non-garbage-collected languages. See Section 10.6 for a more complete discussion of this problem in that context. We encounter it here because we are manually managing memory by using an array to implement a dynamic linked list.

```
24    enum State {FREE, WAITING, RELEASED, ABORTED};
25    class QNode {
26      AtomicReference<State> state;
27      QNode pred;
28      public QNode() {
29        state = new AtomicReference<State>(State.FREE);
30      }
31    }
```

FIGURE 7.25

The CompositeLock class: the QNode class.

```
32    public boolean tryLock(long time, TimeUnit unit) throws InterruptedException {
33      long patience = TimeUnit.MILLISECONDS.convert(time, unit);
34      long startTime = System.currentTimeMillis();
35      Backoff backoff = new Backoff(MIN_BACKOFF, MAX_BACKOFF);
36      try {
37        QNode node = acquireQNode(backoff, startTime, patience);
38        QNode pred = spliceQNode(node, startTime, patience);
39        waitForPredecessor(pred, node, startTime, patience);
40        return true;
41      } catch (TimeoutException e) {
42        return false;
43      }
44    }
```

FIGURE 7.26

The CompositeLock class: the tryLock() method.

Fig. 7.25 shows the QNode class. Each QNode includes a State field and a reference to the predecessor node in the queue. The waiting field is a constant-size QNode array.

A QNode has four possible states: WAITING, RELEASED, ABORTED, and FREE. A WAITING node is linked into the queue, and the owning thread is either in the critical section or waiting to enter. A node becomes RELEASED when its owner leaves the critical section and releases the lock. The other two states occur when a thread abandons its attempt to acquire the lock. If the quitting thread has acquired a node but not enqueued it, then it marks the thread as FREE. If the node is enqueued, then it is marked as ABORTED.

Fig. 7.26 shows the tryLock() method. A thread acquires the lock in three steps. It first *acquires* a node in the waiting array (line 37), then enqueues that node in the queue (line 38), and finally waits until that node is at the head of the queue (line 39).

The algorithm for acquiring a node in the waiting array appears in Fig. 7.27. The thread selects a node at random and tries to acquire the node by changing that node's state from FREE to WAITING (line 51). If it fails, it examines the node's status. If the node is ABORTED or RELEASED (line 56), the thread may "clean up" the node. To avoid synchronization conflicts with other threads, a node can be cleaned up only if it is

```
45   private QNode acquireQNode(Backoff backoff, long startTime, long patience)
46      throws TimeoutException, InterruptedException {
47   QNode node = waiting[ThreadLocalRandom.current().nextInt(SIZE)];
48   QNode currTail;
49   int[] currStamp = {0};
50   while (true) {
51     if (node.state.compareAndSet(State.FREE, State.WAITING)) {
52       return node;
53     }
54     currTail = tail.get(currStamp);
55     State state = node.state.get();
56     if (state == State.ABORTED || state == State.RELEASED) {
57       if (node == currTail) {
58         QNode myPred = null;
59         if (state == State.ABORTED) {
60           myPred = node.pred;
61         }
62         if (tail.compareAndSet(currTail, myPred, currStamp[0], currStamp[0]+1)) {
63           node.state.set(State.WAITING);
64           return node;
65         }
66       }
67     }
68     backoff.backoff();
69     if (timeout(patience, startTime)) {
70       throw new TimeoutException();
71     }
72   }
73   }
```

FIGURE 7.27

The `CompositeLock` class: the `acquireQNode()` method.

the last queue node (that is, the value of `tail`). If the tail node is `ABORTED`, `tail` is redirected to that node's predecessor; otherwise `tail` is set to *null*. If, instead, the allocated node is `WAITING`, then the thread backs off and retries. If the thread times out before acquiring its node, it throws `TimeoutException` (line 70).

Once the thread acquires a node, the `spliceQNode()` method (Fig. 7.28) splices that node into the queue by repeatedly trying to set `tail` to the allocated node. If it times out, it marks the allocated node as `FREE` and throws `TimeoutException`. If it succeeds, it returns the prior value of `tail`, acquired by the node's predecessor in the queue.

Finally, once the node has been enqueued, the thread must wait its turn by calling `waitForPredecessor()` (Fig. 7.29). If the predecessor is *null*, then the thread's node is first in the queue, so the thread saves the node in the thread-local myNode field (for later use by `unlock()`), and enters the critical section. If the predecessor node is not

```
74      private QNode spliceQNode(QNode node, long startTime, long patience)
75         throws TimeoutException {
76       QNode currTail;
77       int[] currStamp = {0};
78       do {
79         currTail = tail.get(currStamp);
80         if (timeout(startTime, patience)) {
81           node.state.set(State.FREE);
82           throw new TimeoutException();
83         }
84       } while (!tail.compareAndSet(currTail, node, currStamp[0], currStamp[0]+1));
85       return currTail;
86     }
```

FIGURE 7.28

The CompositeLock class: the spliceQNode() method.

```
87      private void waitForPredecessor(QNode pred, QNode node,
88                                      long startTime, long patience)
89         throws TimeoutException {
90       int[] stamp = {0};
91       if (pred == null) {
92         myNode.set(node);
93         return;
94       }
95       State predState = pred.state.get();
96       while (predState != State.RELEASED) {
97         if (predState == State.ABORTED) {
98           QNode temp = pred;
99           pred = pred.pred;
100          temp.state.set(State.FREE);
101        }
102        if (timeout(patience, startTime)) {
103          node.pred = pred;
104          node.state.set(State.ABORTED);
105          throw new TimeoutException();
106        }
107        predState = pred.state.get();
108      }
109      pred.state.set(State.FREE);
110      myNode.set(node);
111      return;
112    }
```

FIGURE 7.29

The CompositeLock class: the waitForPredecessor() method.

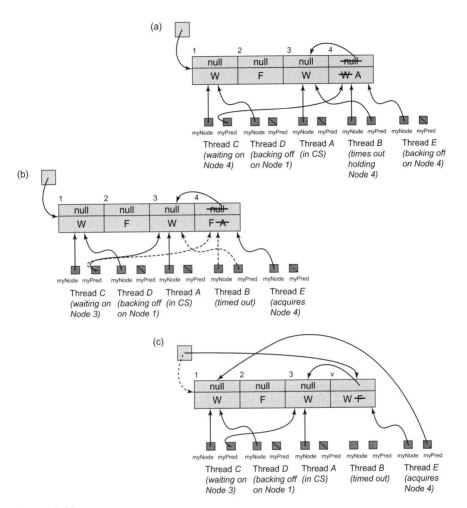

FIGURE 7.30

The `CompositeLock` class: an execution. In part (a), thread A (which acquired Node 3) is in the critical section. Thread B (Node 4) is waiting for A to release the critical section, and thread C (Node 1) is in turn waiting for B. Threads D and E are backing off, waiting to acquire a node. Node 2 is free. The `tail` field refers to Node 1, the last node to be inserted into the queue. At this point, B times out, inserting an explicit reference to its predecessor, and changing Node 4's state from `WAITING` (denoted by W) to `ABORTED` (denoted by A). In part (b), thread C cleans up the `ABORTED` Node 4, setting its state to `FREE` and following the explicit reference from 4 to 3 (by redirecting its local `myPred` field). It then starts waiting for A (Node 3) to leave the critical section. In part (c), E acquires the `FREE` Node 4, using `compareAndSet()` to set its state to `WAITING`. Thread E then inserts Node 4 into the queue, using `compareAndSet()` to swap Node 4 into the tail, then waiting on Node 1, which was previously referred to by `tail`.

RELEASED, the thread checks whether it is ABORTED (line 97). If so, the thread marks the node FREE and waits on the aborted node's predecessor. If the thread times out, then it marks its own node as ABORTED and throws TimeoutException. Otherwise, when the predecessor node becomes RELEASED the thread marks it FREE, records its own node in the thread-local myPred field, and enters the critical section.

The unlock() method (Fig. 7.24) simply retrieves its node from myNode and marks it RELEASED.

Fig. 7.30 illustrates an example execution of CompositeLock.

CompositeLock has a number of attractive properties. Lock hand-off is fast, just as in the CLHLock and TOLock algorithms. When threads back off, they access different locations, reducing contention. Abandoning a lock request is trivial for threads in the back-off stage, and relatively straightforward for threads that have acquired queue nodes. For L locks and n threads, the CompositeLock class requires only $O(L)$ space in the worst case, as compared to the TOLock class's $O(L \cdot n)$.

There are some drawbacks: CompositeLock does not guarantee first-come-first-served access. Also, a thread running alone must redirect the tail field away from a released node, claim the node, and then splice it into the queue.

7.9 A fast path for threads running alone

Although performance under contention is important, so is performance in the absence of concurrency. Ideally, for a thread running alone, acquiring a lock should be as simple as acquiring an uncontended TASLock. Unfortunately, as mentioned above, this is not true for the CompositeLock. We can address this shortcoming by adding a "fast path" to CompositeLock.

A *fast path* for a complex, expensive algorithm is a simpler, cheaper alternative that works (or is efficient) only under certain (typically, common) conditions. In this case, we want a fast path for CompositeLock for a thread that is running alone. We can accomplish this by extending the CompositeLock algorithm so that a solitary thread acquires an idle lock without acquiring a node and splicing it into the queue.

Here is a bird's-eye view. We add an extra state, distinguishing between a lock held by an ordinary thread and a lock held by a fast-path thread. If a thread discovers the lock is free, it tries a fast-path acquire. If it succeeds, then it has acquired the lock in a single atomic step. If it fails, then it enqueues itself just as before.

We now examine the algorithm in detail. To reduce code duplication, we define the CompositeFastPathLock class to be a subclass of CompositeLock. The code appears in Figs. 7.31 and 7.32.

We use a *fast-path flag* to indicate that a thread has acquired the lock through the fast path. Because we need to manipulate this flag together with the tail field's reference, we "steal" a high-order bit from the tail field's integer stamp using a FASTPATH bitmask (line 2). The private fastPathLock() method checks whether the tail field's stamp has a clear fast-path flag and a *null* reference. If so, it tries to acquire the lock simply by applying compareAndSet() to set the fast-path flag to *true*, ensuring that

```
1   public class CompositeFastPathLock extends CompositeLock {
2     private static final int FASTPATH = 1 << 30;
3     private boolean fastPathLock() {
4       int oldStamp, newStamp;
5       int stamp[] = {0};
6       QNode qnode;
7       qnode = tail.get(stamp);
8       oldStamp = stamp[0];
9       if (qnode != null) {
10        return false;
11      }
12      if ((oldStamp & FASTPATH) != 0) {
13        return false;
14      }
15      newStamp = (oldStamp + 1) | FASTPATH;
16      return tail.compareAndSet(qnode, null, oldStamp, newStamp);
17    }
18    public boolean tryLock(long time, TimeUnit unit) throws InterruptedException {
19      if (fastPathLock()) {
20        return true;
21      }
22      if (super.tryLock(time, unit)) {
23        while ((tail.getStamp() & FASTPATH ) != 0){};
24        return true;
25      }
26      return false;
27    }
```

FIGURE 7.31

CompositeFastPathLock class: The private fastPathLock() method returns true if it succeeds in acquiring the lock through the fast path.

the reference remains *null*. An uncontended lock acquisition thus requires a single atomic operation. The fastPathLock() method returns *true* if it succeeds, and *false* otherwise.

The tryLock() method (lines 18–27) first tries the fast path by calling fastPathLock(). If it fails, then it pursues the slow path by calling the CompositeLock class's tryLock() method. Before it can return from the slow path, however, it must ensure that no other thread holds the fast-path lock by waiting until the fast-path flag is clear (line 23).

The unlock() method first calls fastPathUnlock() (line 44). If that call fails to release the lock, it then calls the CompositeLock's unlock() method (line 45). The fastPathUnlock() method returns *false* if the fast-path flag is not set (line 31). Otherwise, it repeatedly tries to clear the flag, leaving the reference component unchanged (lines 36–40), returning *true* when it succeeds.

```
28    private boolean fastPathUnlock() {
29      int oldStamp, newStamp;
30      oldStamp = tail.getStamp();
31      if ((oldStamp & FASTPATH) == 0) {
32        return false;
33      }
34      int[] stamp = {0};
35      QNode qnode;
36      do {
37        qnode = tail.get(stamp);
38        oldStamp = stamp[0];
39        newStamp = oldStamp & (~FASTPATH);
40      } while (!tail.compareAndSet(qnode, qnode, oldStamp, newStamp));
41      return true;
42    }
43    public void unlock() {
44      if (!fastPathUnlock()) {
45        super.unlock();
46      };
47    }
```

FIGURE 7.32

CompositeFastPathLock class: fastPathUnlock() and unlock() methods.

7.10 One lock to rule them all

In this chapter, we have seen a variety of spin locks that vary in characteristics and performance. Such a variety is useful, because no single algorithm is ideal for all applications. For some applications, complex algorithms work best; for others, simple algorithms are preferable. The best choice usually depends on specific aspects of the application and the target architecture.

7.11 Chapter notes

The TTASLock is due to Larry Rudolph and Zary Segall [150]. Exponential back-off is a well-known technique used in ethernet routing, presented in the context of multiprocessor mutual exclusion by Anant Agarwal and Mathews Cherian [6]. Tom Anderson [12] invented the ALock algorithm and was one of the first to empirically study the performance of spin locks in shared-memory multiprocessors. The MCSLock, due to John Mellor-Crummey and Michael Scott [124], is perhaps the best-known queue lock algorithm. Today's Java virtual machines use object synchronization based on simplified monitor algorithms such as the *Thinlock* of David Bacon, Ravi Konuru, Chet Murthy, and Mauricio Serrano [15], the *Metalock* of Ole Agesen, Dave Detlefs,

Alex Garthwaite, Ross Knippel, Y. S. Ramakrishna, and Derek White [7], or the *RelaxedLock* of Dave Dice [36]. All these algorithms are variations of the MCSLock lock.

The CLHLock lock is due to Travis Craig, Erik Hagersten, and Anders Landin [32, 118]. The TOLock with nonblocking timeout is due to Bill Scherer and Michael Scott [153,154]. The CompositeLock and its variations are due to Virendra Marathe, Mark Moir, and Nir Shavit [121]. The notion of using a fast path in a mutual exclusion algorithm is due to Leslie Lamport [106]. Hierarchical locks were invented by Zoran Radović and Erik Hagersten. The HBOLock is a variant of their original algorithm [144]. Cohort locks are due to Dave Dice, Virendra Marathe, and Nir Shavit [37].

Faith Fich, Danny Hendler, and Nir Shavit [45] have extended the work of Jim Burns and Nancy Lynch to show that any starvation-free mutual exclusion algorithm requires $\Omega(n)$ space, even if strong operations such as getAndSet() or compareAndSet() are used, implying that the queue-lock algorithms considered here are space-optimal.

The schematic performance graph in this chapter is loosely based on empirical studies by Tom Anderson [12], as well as on data collected by the authors on various modern machines. We present schematic rather than actual data because of the great variation in machine architectures and their significant effect on lock performance.

Programming languages such as C or C++ were not defined with concurrency in mind, so they did not define a memory model. The actual behavior of a concurrent C or C++ program is the result of a complex combination of the underlying hardware, the compiler, and the concurrency library. See Hans Boehm [19] for a more detailed discussion of these issues. The Java memory model proposed here is the *second* memory model proposed for Java. Jeremy Manson, Bill Pugh, and Sarita Adve [119] give a more complete description of this model.

The Sherlock Holmes quote is from *The Sign of Four* [41].

7.12 Exercises

Exercise 7.1. Fig. 7.33 shows an alternative implementation of CLHLock in which a thread reuses its own node instead of its predecessor node. Explain how this implementation can go wrong, and how the MCS lock avoids the problem even though it reuses thread-local nodes.

Exercise 7.2. Imagine n threads, each of which executes method foo() followed by method bar(). Suppose we want to make sure that no thread starts bar() until all threads have finished foo(). For this kind of synchronization, we place a *barrier* between foo() and bar().

First barrier implementation: We have a counter protected by a test-and-test-and-set lock. Each thread locks the counter, increments it, releases the lock, and spins, rereading the counter until it reaches n.

Second barrier implementation: We have an n-element Boolean array b[0..n − 1], all initially *false*. Thread 0 sets b[0] to *true*. Every thread i, for $0 < i < n$, spins until

```
1   public class BadCLHLock implements Lock {
2     AtomicReference<Qnode> tail = new AtomicReference<QNode>(new QNode());
3     ThreadLocal<Qnode> myNode = new ThreadLocal<QNode> {
4       protected QNode initialValue() {
5         return new QNode();
6       }
7     };
8     public void lock() {
9       Qnode qnode = myNode.get();
10      qnode.locked = true;      // I'm not done
11      // Make me the new tail, and find my predecessor
12      Qnode pred = tail.getAndSet(qnode);
13      while (pred.locked) {}
14    }
15    public void unlock() {
16      // reuse my node next time
17      myNode.get().locked = false;
18    }
19    static class Qnode { // Queue node inner class
20      volatile boolean locked = false;
21    }
22  }
```

FIGURE 7.33

An incorrect attempt to implement a CLHLock.

$b[i-1]$ is *true*, sets $b[i]$ to *true*, and then waits until $b[n-1]$ is *true*, after which it proceeds to leave the barrier.

Compare (in 10 lines) the behavior of these two implementations on a bus-based cache-coherent architecture. Explain which approach you expect will perform better under low load and high load.

Exercise 7.3. Show how to eliminate the separate cluster-local field that records whether the lock is passed locally by recording this information directly in each QNode, as described in Section 7.7.3.

Exercise 7.4. Prove that the CompositeFastPathLock implementation guarantees mutual exclusion, but is not starvation-free.

Exercise 7.5. Design an isLocked() method that tests whether any thread is holding a lock (but does not acquire the lock). Give implementations for

- a test-and-set spin lock,
- the CLH queue lock, and
- the MCS queue lock.

Exercise 7.6. (Hard) Where does the $\Omega(n)$ space complexity lower bound proof for deadlock-free mutual exclusion of Chapter 2 break when locks are allowed to use read–modify–write operations?

Monitors and blocking synchronization

8

8.1 Introduction

A *monitor* is a structured way of combining synchronization and data, encapsulating data, methods, and synchronization in a single modular package in the same way that a class encapsulates data and methods.

Here is why modular synchronization is important: Imagine an application with two threads, a producer and a consumer, that communicate through a shared FIFO queue. The threads might share two objects: an unsynchronized queue and a lock to protect the queue. The producer might look something like this:

```
mutex.lock();
try {
  queue.enq(x)
} finally {
  mutex.unlock();
}
```

This is no way to run a railroad! Suppose the queue is bounded, meaning that an attempt to add an item to a full queue cannot proceed until the queue has room. Here, the decision whether to block the call or to let it proceed depends on the queue's internal state, which is (and should be) inaccessible to the caller. Moreover, suppose the application grows to have multiple producers, consumers, or both. Each such thread must keep track of both the lock and the queue objects, and the application will be correct only if every thread follows the same locking conventions.

A more sensible approach is to allow each queue to manage its own synchronization. The queue itself has its own internal lock, acquired by each method when it is called and released when it returns. There is no need to ensure that every thread that uses the queue follows a cumbersome synchronization protocol. If a thread tries to enqueue an item to a queue that is already full, then the enq() method itself can detect the problem, suspend the caller, and resume the caller when the queue has room.

8.2 Monitor locks and conditions

As in Chapters 2 and 7, a lock is the basic mechanism for ensuring mutual exclusion. Only one thread at a time can *hold* a lock. A thread *acquires* a lock when it first starts to hold the lock. A thread *releases* a lock when it stops holding the lock. A monitor exports a collection of methods, each of which acquires the lock when it is called, and releases it when it returns.

If a thread must wait for some condition to hold, it can either *spin*, repeatedly testing for the desired condition, or *block*, giving up the processor for a while to allow another thread to run.[1] Spinning makes sense on a multiprocessor if we expect to wait for a short time, because blocking a thread requires an expensive call to the operating system. On the other hand, blocking makes sense if we expect to wait for a long time, because a spinning thread keeps a processor busy without doing any work.

For example, a thread waiting for another thread to release a lock should spin if that particular lock is held briefly, while a consumer thread waiting to dequeue an item from an empty buffer should block, since there is usually no way to predict how long it may have to wait. Often, it makes sense to combine spinning and blocking: A thread waiting to dequeue an item might spin for a brief duration, and then switch to blocking if the delay appears to be long. Blocking works on both multiprocessors and uniprocessors, while spinning works only on multiprocessors.

Most of the locks in this book follow the interface shown in Fig. 8.1. Here is a description of the Lock interface's methods:

- The lock() method blocks the caller until it acquires the lock.
- The lockInterruptibly() method acts like lock(), but throws an exception if the thread is interrupted while it is waiting (see Pragma 8.2.1).
- The unlock() method releases the lock.
- The newCondition() method is a *factory* that creates and returns a Condition object associated with the lock (explained in Section 8.2.1).
- The tryLock() method acquires the lock if it is free, and immediately returns a Boolean indicating whether it acquired the lock. This method can also be called with a timeout.

```
1   public interface Lock {
2     void lock();
3     void lockInterruptibly() throws InterruptedException;
4     boolean tryLock();
5     boolean tryLock(long time, TimeUnit unit);
6     Condition newCondition();
7     void unlock();
8   }
```

FIGURE 8.1

The Lock interface.

---

[1] In Chapter 3, we make a distinction between blocking and nonblocking synchronization algorithms. There, we mean something entirely different: A blocking algorithm is one where a delay by one thread can cause a delay in another. Remark 3.3.1 discusses various ways in which the term *blocking* is used.

8.2.1 Conditions

While a thread is waiting for something to happen, say, for another thread to place an item in a queue, it must release the lock on the queue; otherwise, the other thread will never be able to enqueue the anticipated item. After the waiting thread has released the lock, we need a way to be notify it when to reacquire the lock and try again.

In the java.util.concurrent package (and in similar packages such as Pthreads), the ability to release a lock temporarily is provided by a Condition object associated with a lock. (Conditions are often called *condition variables* in the literature.) Fig. 8.2 shows how to use the Condition interface provided in the java.util.concurrent.locks library. A condition is associated with a lock, and is created by calling that lock's newCondition() method. If the thread holding that lock calls the associated condition's await() method, it releases that lock and suspends itself, giving another thread the opportunity to acquire the lock. When the calling thread awakens, it reacquires the lock, perhaps competing with other threads.

Like locks, Condition objects must be used in a stylized way. Suppose a thread wants to wait until a certain property holds. The thread tests the property while holding the lock. If the property does not hold, then the thread calls await() to release the lock and sleep until it is awakened by another thread. Here is the key point: There is no guarantee that the property will hold when the thread awakens. The await() method can return spuriously (i.e., for no reason), or the thread that signaled the condition may have awakened too many sleeping threads. Whatever the reason, the thread must retest the property, and if it finds the property does not hold at that time, it must call await() again.

The Condition interface in Fig. 8.3 provides several variations of this call, some of which provide the ability to specify a maximum time the caller can be suspended, or whether the thread can be interrupted while it is waiting. When the queue changes, the thread that made the change can notify other threads waiting on a condition. Calling signal() wakes up one thread waiting on a condition (if there is one), while calling signalAll() wakes up all waiting threads.

```
1  Condition condition = mutex.newCondition();
2  ...
3  mutex.lock()
4  try {
5    while (!property) { // not happy
6      condition.await(); // wait for property
7    } catch (InterruptedException e) {
8      ... // application-dependent response
9    }
10   ... // happy: property must hold
11 }
```

FIGURE 8.2

How to use Condition objects.

```
1  public interface Condition {
2    void await() throws InterruptedException;
3    boolean await(long time, TimeUnit unit) throws InterruptedException;
4    boolean awaitUntil(Date deadline) throws InterruptedException;
5    long awaitNanos(long nanosTimeout) throws InterruptedException;
6    void awaitUninterruptibly();
7    void signal();      // wake up one waiting thread
8    void signalAll();   // wake up all waiting threads
9  }
```

FIGURE 8.3

The `Condition` interface: `await()` and its variants release the lock, and give up the processor, and then later awaken and reacquire the lock. The `signal()` and `signalAll()` methods awaken one or more waiting threads.

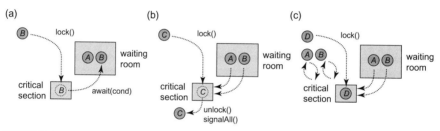

FIGURE 8.4

A schematic representation of a monitor execution. In part (a), thread A has acquired the monitor lock, called `await()` on a condition, released the lock, and is now in the waiting room. Thread B then goes through the same sequence of steps, entering the critical section, calling `await()` on the condition, relinquishing the lock, and entering the waiting room. In part (b), both A and B leave the waiting room after thread C exits the critical section and calls `signalAll()`. A and B then attempt to reacquire the monitor lock. However, thread D manages to acquire the critical section lock first, and so both A and B spin until D leaves the critical section. Note that if C had issued a `signal()` instead of a `signalAll()`, only A or B would have left the waiting room, and the other would have continued to wait.

PRAGMA 8.2.1

Threads in Java can be *interrupted* by other threads. If a thread is interrupted during a call to a `Condition`'s `await()` method, the call throws `InterruptedException`. The proper response to an interrupt is application-dependent. Fig. 8.2 shows a schematic example.

To avoid clutter, we usually omit `InterruptedException` handlers from example code, even though they would be required in actual code. (It is bad programming practice to ignore interrupts.)

This combination of methods, mutual exclusion locks, and condition objects is called a *monitor*. It is common to talk of threads that have called await() (and have not yet returned) as being in a "waiting room". We use this imagery to illustrate an execution of a monitor in Fig. 8.4.

Fig. 8.5 shows how to implement a bounded FIFO queue using explicit locks and conditions. The lock field is a lock that must be acquired by all methods. We must initialize it to hold an instance of a class that implements the Lock interface. Here, we choose ReentrantLock, a useful lock type provided by the java.util.concurrent.locks package. This lock is *reentrant*: A thread that is holding the lock can acquire it again without blocking. (See Section 8.4 for more discussion on reentrant locks.)

There are two condition objects: notEmpty notifies waiting dequeuers when the queue goes from being empty to nonempty, and notFull for the opposite direction. Although using two conditions instead of one is more complex, it is more efficient, since fewer threads are woken up unnecessarily.

8.2.2 The lost-wakeup problem

Just as locks are inherently vulnerable to deadlock, Condition objects are inherently vulnerable to *lost wakeups*, in which one or more threads wait forever without realizing that the condition for which they are waiting has become true.

Lost wakeups can occur in subtle ways. Fig. 8.6 shows an ill-considered optimization of the Queue<T> class. Instead of signaling the notEmpty condition each time enq() enqueues an item, would it not be more efficient to signal the condition only when the queue actually transitions from empty to nonempty? This optimization works as intended if there is only one producer and one consumer, but it is incorrect if there are multiple producers or consumers. Consider the following scenario: Consumers A and B both try to dequeue an item from an empty queue, both detect the queue is empty, and both block on the notEmpty condition. Producer C enqueues an item in the buffer, and signals notEmpty, waking A. Before A can acquire the lock, however, another producer D puts a second item in the queue, and because the queue is not empty, it does not signal notEmpty. Then A acquires the lock and removes the first item, but B, victim of a lost wakeup, waits forever, even though there is an item in the queue to be consumed.

Although there is no substitute for reasoning carefully about our program, there are simple programming practices that minimize vulnerability to lost wakeups.

- Always signal *all* processes waiting on a condition, not just one.
- Specify a timeout when waiting.

Either of these two practices would fix the bounded queue error we just described. Each has a small performance penalty, but negligible compared to the cost of a lost wakeup.

Java provides support for monitors in the form of **synchronized** blocks and methods, and built-in wait(), notify(), and notifyAll() methods (see Appendix A).

```
1   class LockedQueue<T> {
2     final Lock lock = new ReentrantLock();
3     final Condition notFull = lock.newCondition();
4     final Condition notEmpty = lock.newCondition();
5     final T[] items;
6     int tail, head, count;
7     public LockedQueue(int capacity) {
8       items = (T[])new Object[capacity];
9     }
10    public void enq(T x) {
11      lock.lock();
12      try {
13        while (count == items.length)
14          notFull.await();
15        items[tail] = x;
16        if (++tail == items.length)
17          tail = 0;
18        ++count;
19        notEmpty.signal();
20      } finally {
21        lock.unlock();
22      }
23    }
24    public T deq() {
25      lock.lock();
26      try {
27        while (count == 0)
28          notEmpty.await();
29        T x = items[head];
30        if (++head == items.length)
31          head = 0;
32        --count;
33        notFull.signal();
34        return x;
35      } finally {
36        lock.unlock();
37      }
38    }
39  }
```

FIGURE 8.5

The LockedQueue class: a FIFO queue using locks and conditions. There are two condition fields, one to detect when the queue becomes nonempty, and one to detect when it becomes nonfull.

```
1    public void enq(T x) {
2      lock.lock();
3      try {
4        while (count == items.length)
5          notFull.await();
6        items[tail] = x;
7        if (++tail == items.length)
8          tail = 0;
9        ++count;
10       if (count == 1) {  // Wrong!
11         notEmpty.signal();
12       }
13     } finally {
14       lock.unlock();
15     }
16   }
```

FIGURE 8.6

This example is *incorrect.* It suffers from lost wakeups. The enq() method signals notEmpty only if it is the first to place an item in an empty buffer. A lost wakeup occurs if multiple consumers are waiting, but only the first is awakened to consume an item.

8.3 Readers–writers locks

Many shared objects have the property that most method calls return information about the object's state without modifying the object, and relatively few calls actually modify the object. We call method calls of the first kind *readers*, and method calls of the latter kind *writers*.

Readers need not synchronize with one another; it is perfectly safe for them to access the object concurrently. Writers, on the other hand, must lock out readers as well as other writers. A *readers–writers lock* allows multiple readers or a single writer to enter the critical section concurrently. We use the following interface:

```
public interface ReadWriteLock {
  Lock readLock();
  Lock writeLock();
}
```

This interface exports two lock objects: the *read lock* and the *write lock*. They satisfy the following safety properties:

- No thread can acquire the write lock while any thread holds either the write lock or the read lock.
- No thread can acquire the read lock while any thread holds the write lock.

Naturally, multiple threads may hold the read lock at the same time.

We now consider two readers–writers lock implementations.

```
1   public class SimpleReadWriteLock implements ReadWriteLock {
2     int readers;
3     boolean writer;
4     Lock lock;
5     Condition condition;
6     Lock readLock, writeLock;
7     public SimpleReadWriteLock() {
8       writer = false;
9       readers = 0;
10      lock = new ReentrantLock();
11      readLock = new ReadLock();
12      writeLock = new WriteLock();
13      condition = lock.newCondition();
14    }
15    public Lock readLock() {
16      return readLock;
17    }
18    public Lock writeLock() {
19      return writeLock;
20    }
21    ...
22  }
```

FIGURE 8.7

The SimpleReadWriteLock class: fields and public methods.

8.3.1 Simple readers–writers lock

The SimpleReadWriteLock class appears in Figs. 8.7 and 8.8. To define the associated read and write locks, this code uses *inner classes*, a Java feature that allows an object to create other objects that can access the first object's private fields. The SimpleReadWriteLock object has fields that keep track of the number of readers that hold the lock and whether a writer holds the lock; the read lock and write lock use these fields to guarantee the readers–writers lock properties. To allow the methods of the read lock and the write lock to synchronize access to these fields, the class also maintains a private lock and a condition associated with that lock.

How are waiting writers notified when the last reader releases its lock? When a writer tries to acquire the write lock, it acquires lock (i.e., the SimpleReadWriteLock object's private lock), and if any readers (or another writer) hold the lock, it waits on condition. A reader releasing the read lock also acquires lock, and signals condition if all readers have released their locks. Similarly, readers that try to acquire the lock while a writer holds it wait on condition, and writers releasing the lock signal condition to notify waiting readers and writers.

Although the SimpleReadWriteLock algorithm is correct, it is not quite satisfactory. If readers are much more frequent than writers, as is usually the case, then writers could be locked out indefinitely by a continual stream of readers.

```
23    class ReadLock implements Lock {
24      public void lock() {
25        lock.lock();
26        try {
27          while (writer)
28            condition.await();
29          readers++;
30        } finally {
31          lock.unlock();
32        }
33      }
34      public void unlock() {
35        lock.lock();
36        try {
37          readers--;
38          if (readers == 0)
39            condition.signalAll();
40        } finally {
41          lock.unlock();
42        }
43      }
44    }
45    protected class WriteLock implements Lock {
46      public void lock() {
47        lock.lock();
48        try {
49          while (readers > 0 || writer)
50            condition.await();
51          writer = true;
52        } finally {
53          lock.unlock();
54        }
55      }
56      public void unlock() {
57        lock.lock();
58        try {
59          writer = false;
60          condition.signalAll();
61        } finally {
62          lock.unlock();
63        }
64      }
65    }
```

FIGURE 8.8

The SimpleReadWriteLock class: the inner read and write locks classes.

```
1   public class FifoReadWriteLock implements ReadWriteLock {
2     int readAcquires, readReleases;
3     boolean writer;
4     Lock lock;
5     Condition condition;
6     Lock readLock, writeLock;
7     public FifoReadWriteLock() {
8       readAcquires = readReleases = 0;
9       writer = false;
10      lock = new ReentrantLock();
11      condition = lock.newCondition();
12      readLock = new ReadLock();
13      writeLock = new WriteLock();
14    }
15    public Lock readLock() {
16      return readLock;
17    }
18    public Lock writeLock() {
19      return writeLock;
20    }
21    ...
22  }
```

FIGURE 8.9

The FifoReadWriteLock class: fields and public methods.

8.3.2 Fair readers–writers lock

The FifoReadWriteLock class (Figs. 8.9 and 8.10) shows one way to prevent writers from being starved by a continual stream of readers. This class ensures that once a writer calls the write lock's lock() method, no more readers will acquire the read lock until the writer has acquired and released the write lock. Eventually, the readers holding the read lock will drain out without letting any more readers in, and the writer can acquire the write lock.

The readAcquires field counts the total number of read-lock acquisitions, and the readReleases field counts the total number of read-lock releases. When these quantities match, no thread is holding the read lock. (For simplicity, we are ignoring potential integer overflow and wraparound problems.) As in the SimpleReadWriteLock class, the FifoReadWriteLock class has private lock and condition fields that the methods of the read lock and write lock use to synchronize accesses to the other fields of FifoReadWriteLock. The difference is that in FifoReadWriteLock, a thread attempting to acquire the writer lock sets the writer flag even if readers hold the lock. If a writer holds the lock, however, it waits for the writer to release the lock, and unset the writer flag, before proceeding. That is, the thread first waits until no writer holds the lock, then sets writer, and then waits until no reader holds the lock (lines 49–53).

```
23    private class ReadLock implements Lock {
24      public void lock() {
25        lock.lock();
26        try {
27          while (writer)
28            condition.await();
29          readAcquires++;
30        } finally {
31          lock.unlock();
32        }
33      }
34      public void unlock() {
35        lock.lock();
36        try {
37          readReleases++;
38          if (readAcquires == readReleases)
39            condition.signalAll();
40        } finally {
41          lock.unlock();
42        }
43      }
44    }
45    private class WriteLock implements Lock {
46      public void lock() {
47        lock.lock();
48        try {
49          while (writer)
50            condition.await();
51          writer = true;
52          while (readAcquires != readReleases)
53            condition.await();
54        } finally {
55          lock.unlock();
56        }
57      }
58      public void unlock() {
59        lock.lock();
60        try {
61          writer = false;
62          condition.signalAll();
63        } finally {
64          lock.unlock();
65        }
66      }
67    }
```

FIGURE 8.10

The FifoReadWriteLock class: inner read and write lock classes.

8.4 Our own reentrant lock

Using the locks described in Chapters 2 and 7, a thread that attempts to reacquire a lock it already holds will deadlock with itself. This situation can arise if a method that acquires a lock makes a nested call to another method that acquires the same lock.

A lock is *reentrant* if it can be acquired multiple times by the same thread. We now examine how to create a reentrant lock from a nonreentrant lock. This exercise is intended to illustrate how to use locks and conditions. The java.util.concurrent.locks package provides reentrant lock classes, so in practice there is no need to write our own.

Fig. 8.11 shows the SimpleReentrantLock class. The owner field holds the ID of the last thread to acquire the lock, and the holdCount field is incremented each time the lock is acquired, and decremented each time it is released. The lock is free when the holdCount value is zero. Because these two fields are manipulated atomically, we need an internal, short-term lock. The lock field is a lock used by lock() and unlock() to manipulate the fields, and the condition field is used by threads waiting for the lock to become free. We initialize the internal lock field to an object of a (fictitious) SimpleLock class, which is presumably not reentrant (line 6).

The lock() method acquires the internal lock (line 13). If the current thread is already the owner, it increments the hold count and returns (line 15). Otherwise, if the hold count is not zero, the lock is held by another thread, and the caller releases the internal lock and waits until the condition is signaled (line 20). When the caller awakens, it must still check whether the hold count is zero. If it is, the calling thread makes itself the owner and sets the hold count to 1.

The unlock() method acquires the internal lock (line 29). It throws an exception if either the lock is free, or the caller is not the owner (line 31). Otherwise, it decrements the hold count. If the hold count is zero, then the lock is free, so the caller signals the condition to wake up a waiting thread (line 35).

8.5 Semaphores

As we have seen, a mutual exclusion lock guarantees that only one thread at a time can enter a critical section. If another thread wants to enter the critical section while it is occupied, then it blocks, suspending itself until another thread notifies it to try again. One of the earliest forms of synchronization, a *semaphore* is a generalization of the mutual exclusion lock. Each semaphore has a *capacity* that is determined when the semaphore is initialized. Instead of allowing only one thread at a time into the critical section, a semaphore allows at most c threads, where c is its capacity.

The Semaphore class of Fig. 8.12 provides two methods: A thread calls acquire() to request permission to enter the critical section, and release() to announce that it is leaving the critical section. The Semaphore itself is just a counter: It keeps track of the number of threads that have been granted permission to enter. If a new acquire() call is about to exceed the capacity, the calling thread is suspended until there is room.

```
1   public class SimpleReentrantLock implements Lock{
2     Lock lock;
3     Condition condition;
4     int owner, holdCount;
5     public SimpleReentrantLock() {
6       lock = new SimpleLock();
7       condition = lock.newCondition();
8       owner = 0;
9       holdCount = 0;
10    }
11    public void lock() {
12      int me = ThreadID.get();
13      lock.lock();
14      try {
15        if (owner == me) {
16          holdCount++;
17          return;
18        }
19        while (holdCount != 0) {
20          condition.await();
21        }
22        owner = me;
23        holdCount = 1;
24      } finally {
25        lock.unlock();
26      }
27    }
28    public void unlock() {
29      lock.lock();
30      try {
31        if (holdCount == 0 || owner != ThreadID.get())
32          throw new IllegalMonitorStateException();
33        holdCount--;
34        if (holdCount == 0) {
35          condition.signal();
36        }
37      } finally {
38        lock.unlock();
39      }
40    }
41    ...
42  }
```

FIGURE 8.11

The SimpleReentrantLock class: lock() and unlock() methods.

```
1   public class Semaphore {
2     final int capacity;
3     int state;
4     Lock lock;
5     Condition condition;
6     public Semaphore(int c) {
7       capacity = c;
8       state = 0;
9       lock = new ReentrantLock();
10      condition = lock.newCondition();
11    }
12    public void acquire() {
13      lock.lock();
14      try {
15        while (state == capacity) {
16          condition.await();
17        }
18        state++;
19      } finally {
20        lock.unlock();
21      }
22    }
23    public void release() {
24      lock.lock();
25      try {
26        state--;
27        condition.signalAll();
28      } finally {
29        lock.unlock();
30      }
31    }
32  }
```

FIGURE 8.12

Semaphore implementation.

When a thread calls release() after leaving the critical section, it signals to notify any waiting thread that there is now room.

8.6 Chapter notes

Monitors were invented by Per Brinch-Hansen [57] and Tony Hoare [77]. Semaphores were invented by Edsger Dijkstra [38]. McKenney [122] surveys different kinds of locking protocols.

8.7 Exercises

Exercise 8.1. Reimplement the SimpleReadWriteLock class using Java **synchronized**, wait(), notify(), and notifyAll() constructs in place of explicit locks and conditions.

Hint: You must figure out how methods of the inner read and write lock classes can lock the outer SimpleReadWriteLock object.

Exercise 8.2. Design a "nested" readers–writers lock in which a thread must first grab the read lock in order to grab the write lock, and releasing the write lock does not release the read lock. In order for a reader to become a writer with exclusive write access, every other reader must either unlock the read lock or also attempt to lock the write lock. Show that your implementation is correct and has a reasonable fairness guarantee between readers and writers.

Exercise 8.3. Read–write locks are fundamentally asymmetric in that many readers can enter at once but only one writer can enter. Design a symmetric locking protocol for two types of threads: RED and BLUE. For correctness, never allow a RED and BLUE thread to enter simultaneously. For progress, allow for multiple RED threads or multiple BLUE threads to enter at once, and have a symmetric fairness mechanism for draining RED threads to allow waiting BLUE threads to enter, and vice versa. Show that your implementation is correct, and describe the exact fairness property it guarantees and why you chose to use it.

Exercise 8.4. The ReentrantReadWriteLock class provided by the java.util.concurrent.locks package does not allow a thread holding the lock in read mode to then access that lock in write mode (the thread will block). Justify this design decision by sketching what it would take to permit such lock upgrades.

Exercise 8.5. A *savings account* object holds a nonnegative balance, and provides deposit(k) and withdraw(k) methods, where deposit(k) adds k to the balance, and withdraw(k) subtracts k, if the balance is at least k, and otherwise blocks until the balance becomes k or greater.

1. Implement this savings account using locks and conditions.
2. Now suppose there are two kinds of withdrawals: *ordinary* and *preferred*. Devise an implementation that ensures that no ordinary withdrawal occurs if there is a preferred withdrawal waiting to occur.
3. Now add a transfer() method that transfers a sum from one account to another:

```
void transfer(int k, Account reserve) {
  lock.lock();
  try {
    reserve.withdraw(k);
    deposit(k);
  } finally {
    lock.unlock();
  }
}
```

We are given a set of 10 accounts, whose balances are unknown. At 1:00pm, each of n threads tries to transfer $100 from another account into its own account. At 2:00pm, a boss thread deposits $1000 to each account. Is every transfer method called at 1:00pm certain to return?

Exercise 8.6. In the *shared-bathroom problem*, there are two classes of threads, called MALE and FEMALE. There is a single Bathroom resource that must be used in the following way:

1. Mutual exclusion: persons of opposite sex may not occupy the bathroom simultaneously.
2. Weak starvation-freedom: Assuming that eventually there will be both a male and a female who want to use the bathroom, then everyone who needs to use the bathroom eventually enters.

The protocol specifies the following four procedures: enterMale() delays the caller until a male can enter the bathroom, and leaveMale() is called when a male leaves the bathroom, while enterFemale() and leaveFemale() do the same for females. For example,

```
enterMale();
teeth.brush(toothpaste);
leaveMale();
```

Implement this class using locks and condition variables. Explain why your implementation satisfies mutual exclusion and weak starvation-freedom.

Exercise 8.7. The Rooms class manages a collection of *rooms*, indexed from 0 to $m - 1$ (m is an argument to the constructor). Threads can enter or exit any room in that range. Each room can hold an arbitrary number of threads simultaneously, but only one room can be occupied at a time. For example, if there are two rooms, indexed 0 and 1, then any number of threads might enter room 0, but no thread can enter room 1 while room 0 is occupied. Fig. 8.13 shows an outline of the Rooms class.

Each room can be assigned an *exit handler*: Calling setExitHandler(i, h) sets the exit handler for room i to handler h. The exit handler is called by the last thread to

```
1   public class Rooms {
2     public interface Handler {
3       void onEmpty();
4     }
5     public Rooms(int m) { ... };
6     public void enter(int i) { ... };
7     public boolean exit() { ... };
8     public void setExitHandler(int i, Rooms.Handler h) { ... };
9   }
```

FIGURE 8.13

The Rooms class.

leave a room, but before any threads subsequently enter any room. This method is called once per room and while it is running, no threads are in any rooms.

Implement the Rooms class. Make sure that:

- If some thread is in room i, then no thread is in room $j \neq i$.
- The last thread to leave a room calls the room's exit handler, and no threads are in any room while that handler is running.
- Your implementation is *fair*: Any thread that tries to enter a room eventually succeeds. (You may assume that every thread that enters a room eventually leaves.)

Exercise 8.8. Consider an application with distinct sets of *active* and *passive* threads, where we want to block the passive threads until every active thread has given permission for the passive threads to proceed.

A CountDownLatch encapsulates a counter, initialized to the number n of active threads. An active thread gives permission for the passive threads to run by calling countDown(), which decrements the counter. Each passive thread calls await(), which blocks the thread until the counter reaches zero (Fig. 8.14).

Provide a CountDownLatch implementation. Do not worry about reusing the CountDownLatch object.

```
1  class Driver {
2    void main() {
3      CountDownLatch startSignal = new CountDownLatch(1);
4      CountDownLatch doneSignal = new CountDownLatch(n);
5      for (int i = 0; i < n; ++i) // start threads
6        new Thread(new Worker(startSignal, doneSignal)).start();
7      doSomethingElse();          // get ready for threads
8      startSignal.countDown();    // unleash threads
9      doSomethingElse();          // biding my time ...
10     doneSignal.await();         // wait for threads to finish
11   }
12   class Worker implements Runnable {
13     private final CountDownLatch startSignal, doneSignal;
14     Worker(CountDownLatch myStartSignal, CountDownLatch myDoneSignal) {
15       startSignal = myStartSignal;
16       doneSignal = myDoneSignal;
17     }
18     public void run() {
19       startSignal.await();       // wait for driver's OK to start
20       doWork();
21       doneSignal.countDown();    // notify driver we're done
22     }
23     ...
24   }
25 }
```

FIGURE 8.14

The CountDownLatch class: an example usage.

Exercise 8.9. This exercise is a followup to Exercise 8.8. Provide a CountDownLatch implementation where the CountDownLatch object can be reused.

Exercise 8.10. Fig. 8.15 shows a proposed implementation of a RateLimiter class, which runs jobs but limits the "weight" of the jobs started per minute using a quota, which is increased to LIMIT every minute by a separate thread. We want to guarantee that jobs will run promptly if there is enough quota. You may assume a fast processor and fair scheduler, so that the RateLimiter reaches a quiescent state (all jobs are sleeping in await() or running), if possible, before each call to increaseQuota().

a. Describe the distributions of weight values ($0 \leq$ weight $\leq$ LIMIT) under which this implementation works or fails and explain why.

b. Fix this implementation so it allows jobs to have any weight value from 0 to LIMIT, and describe how it may impact performance.

```
1   public class RateLimiter {
2       static final int LIMIT = 100; // example value
3       public int quota = LIMIT;
4       private Lock lock = new ReentrantLock();
5       private Condition needQuota = lock.newCondition();
6       public void increaseQuota() { // called once per minute
7           synchronized(lock) {        // grab the lock
8               if (quota < LIMIT) {    // if some of the quote has been used up:
9                   quota = LIMIT;      // increase quota to LIMIT
10                  needQuota.signal(); // wake up a sleeper
11              }
12          }                           // unlock
13      }
14      private void throttle(int weight) {
15          synchronized(lock) {        // grab the lock
16              while (quota < weight) { // while not enough quota:
17                  needQuota.await(); // sleep until increased
18              }
19              quota -= weight;        // claim my job's part of the quota
20              if (quota > 0) {        // if still quota left over:
21                  needQuota.signal(); // wake up another sleeper
22              }
23          }                           // unlock
24      }
25      public void run(Runnable job, int weight) {
26          throttle(weight);           // sleep if under quota
27          job.run();                  // run my job
28      }
29  }
```

FIGURE 8.15

A proposed RateLimiter class implementation.

Linked lists: The role of locking

9

9.1 Introduction

In Chapter 7, we saw how to build scalable spin locks that provide mutual exclusion efficiently, even when they are heavily used. We might think that it is now a simple matter to construct scalable concurrent data structures: Take a sequential implementation of the class, add a scalable lock field, and ensure that each method call acquires and releases that lock. We call this approach *coarse-grained synchronization*.

Coarse-grained synchronization often works well, but there are important cases where it does not. The problem is that a class that uses a single lock to mediate all its method calls is not always scalable, even if the lock itself is scalable. Coarse-grained synchronization works well when levels of concurrency are low, but if too many threads try to access the object at the same time, then the object becomes a sequential bottleneck, forcing threads to wait in line for access.

This chapter introduces several useful techniques that go beyond coarse-grained locking to allow multiple threads to access a single object at the same time.

- *Fine-grained synchronization:* Instead of using a single lock to synchronize every access to an object, we partition the object into independently synchronized components, allowing method calls that access disjoint components to execute concurrently.
- *Optimistic synchronization:* Many objects, such as trees or lists, consist of multiple components linked together by references. Some methods search for a particular component (e.g., a list or tree node containing a particular key). One way to reduce the cost of fine-grained locking is to search without acquiring any locks at all. If the method finds the sought-after component, it locks that component, and then checks that the component has not changed in the interval between when it was inspected and when it was locked. This technique is worthwhile only if it succeeds more often than not, which is why we call it optimistic.
- *Lazy synchronization:* Sometimes it makes sense to postpone hard work. For example, the task of removing a component from a data structure can be split into two phases: The component is *logically removed* simply by setting a tag bit, and later, the component can be *physically removed* by unlinking it from the rest of the data structure.
- *Nonblocking synchronization:* Sometimes we can eliminate locks entirely, relying on built-in atomic operations such as compareAndSet() for synchronization.

The Art of Multiprocessor Programming. https://doi.org/10.1016/B978-0-12-415950-1.00019-7
Copyright © 2021 Elsevier Inc. All rights reserved.

```
1  public interface Set<T> {
2    boolean add(T x);
3    boolean remove(T x);
4    boolean contains(T x);
5  }
```

FIGURE 9.1

The Set<T> interface: add() adds an item to the set (no effect if that item is already present), remove() removes it (if present), and contains() returns a Boolean indicating whether the item is present.

Each of these techniques can be applied (with appropriate customization) to a variety of common data structures. In this chapter, we consider how to use linked lists to implement a *set*, a collection of *items* that contains no duplicate elements.

For our purposes, as shown in Fig. 9.1, a *set* provides the following three methods:

- The add(x) method adds x to the set, returning *true* if and only if x was not already in the est.
- The remove(x) method removes x from the set, returning *true* if and only if x was in the set.
- The contains(x) returns *true* if and only if the set contains x.

For each method, we say that a call is *successful* if it returns *true*, and *unsuccessful* otherwise. In typical applications using sets, there are significantly more contains() calls than add() or remove() calls.

9.2 List-based sets

This chapter presents a range of concurrent set algorithms, all based on the same basic idea. A set is implemented as a linked list of nodes. The Node<T> class, shown in Fig. 9.2, has three fields. The item field is the actual item of interest. The key field is the item's hash code. Nodes are sorted in key order, providing an efficient way to detect when an item is absent. The next field is a reference to the next node in the

```
1  private class Node {
2    T item;
3    int key;
4    Node next;
5  }
```

FIGURE 9.2

The Node<T> class: This internal class keeps track of the item, the item's key, and the next node in the list. Some algorithms require changes to this class.

(a)

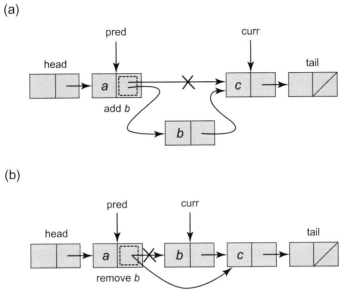

(b)

FIGURE 9.3

A sequential Set<> implementation: adding and removing nodes. In part (a), a thread adding a node *b* uses two variables: curr is the current node, and pred is its predecessor. The thread moves down the list comparing the keys for curr and *b*. If a match is found, the item is already present, so it returns *false*. If curr reaches a node with a higher key, the item is not in the set, so it sets *b*'s next field to curr, and pred's next field to *b*. In part (b), to delete curr, the thread sets pred's next field to curr's next field.

list. (Some of the algorithms we consider require changes to this class, such as adding new fields, changing the types of existing fields, or making some fields volatile.) For simplicity, we assume that each item's hash code is unique. (Relaxing this assumption is left as an exercise.) We associate an item with the same node and key throughout any given example, which allows us to abuse notation and use the same symbol to refer to a node, its key, and its item. That is, node *a* may have key *a* and item *a*, and so on.

In addition to nodes that hold items in the set, the list contains two *sentinel* nodes, head and tail, as the first and last nodes in the list. Sentinel nodes are never added, removed, or searched for, and their keys are the minimum and maximum integer values.[1] Ignoring synchronization for the moment, the top part of Fig. 9.3 schematically describes how an item is added to the set. A thread uses two local variables to traverse the list: curr is the current node and pred is its predecessor. To add an item to

---

[1] The algorithms presented here work for any ordered set of keys that has maximum and minimum values and is well founded, that is, there are only finitely many keys smaller than any given key. For simplicity, we assume here that keys are integers, and that no item's key is the maximum or minimum integer value.

the set, a thread sets pred to head and curr to its successor, and moves down the list, comparing curr's key to the key of the item being added until it finds a node whose key is greater than or equal to the new item's key. If the keys match, the item is already present in the set, so the call returns *false*. Otherwise, pred's key is less than that of the new item, and curr's key is greater, so the item is not present in the list. The method creates a new node *b* to hold the item, sets *b*'s next field to curr, and then sets pred's to *b*. Removing an item from the set works in a similar way.

9.3 Concurrent reasoning

Reasoning about concurrent data structures may seem impossibly difficult, but it is a skill that can be learned. Often, the key to understanding a concurrent data structure is to understand its *invariants*: properties that always hold. We can show that a property is invariant by showing that:

1. the property holds when the object is created, and
2. once the property holds, no thread can take a step that makes it *false*.

Most interesting invariants hold trivially when the list is created, so it makes sense to focus on how invariants, once established, are preserved.

Specifically, we can check that each invariant is preserved by each invocation of insert(), remove(), and contains() methods. This approach works only if we can assume that these methods are the *only* ones that modify nodes, a property sometimes called *freedom from interference*. In the list algorithms considered here, nodes are internal to the list implementation, so freedom from interference is guaranteed because users of the list have no opportunity to modify its internal nodes.

We require freedom from interference even for nodes that have been removed from the list, since some of our algorithms permit a thread to unlink a node while it is being traversed by others. Fortunately, we do not attempt to reuse list nodes that have been removed from the list, relying instead on a garbage collector to recycle that memory. The algorithms described here work in languages without garbage collection, but sometimes require nontrivial modifications that are beyond the scope of this chapter. We discuss issues that arise in the absence of garbage collection and how to deal with them in Chapter 19.

When reasoning about concurrent object implementations, it is important to understand the distinction between an object's *abstract value* (here, a set of items) and its *concrete representation* (here, a list of nodes).

Not every list of nodes is a meaningful representation for a set. An algorithm's *representation invariant* characterizes which representations make sense as abstract values. If *a* and *b* are nodes, we say that *a points to b* if *a*'s next field is a reference to *b*. We say that *b* is *reachable* if there is a sequence of nodes starting at head and ending at *b*, where each node in the sequence points to its successor.

The set algorithms in this chapter require the following invariants (some require more, as explained later):

1. The key of any node in the list is less than the key of its successor (if it has one). This implies that nodes in the list are sorted by key, and that keys are unique.
2. The key of any item added, removed, or searched for is greater than the key of head and less than the key of tail. (Hence, the sentinel nodes are neither added nor removed.)

Think of the representation invariant as a contract among the object's methods. Each method call preserves the invariant, and relies on the other methods to preserve the invariant. In this way, we can reason about each method in isolation, without having to consider all the possible ways they might interact.

Given a list satisfying the representation invariant, which set does it represent? The meaning of such a list is given by an *abstraction map* carrying lists that satisfy the representation invariant to sets. Here, the abstraction map is simple: An item is in the set if and only if it is (in a node) reachable from head.

What safety and liveness properties do we need? For safety, we want *linearizability*. As we saw in Chapter 3, to show that a concurrent data structure is a linearizable implementation of a sequential object, it suffices to identify a *linearization point*, an atomic step where the method call "takes effect"; we say it is *linearized* at this point. This step can be a read, a write, or a more complex atomic operation. Looking at any execution history of a list-based set, it must be the case that if the abstraction map is applied to the representation at the linearization points, the resulting sequence of states and method calls defines a valid sequential set execution. Here, add(a) adds a to the abstract set, remove(a) removes a from the abstract set, and contains(a) returns *true* or *false*, depending on whether a was already in the set.

Different list algorithms make different progress guarantees. Some use locks, and care is required to ensure they are deadlock- and starvation-free. Some *nonblocking* list algorithms do not use locks at all, while others restrict locking to certain methods. Here is a brief summary, from Chapter 3, of the nonblocking properties we use:[2]

- A method is *wait-free* if every call finishes in a finite number of steps.
- A method is *lock-free* if *some* call always finishes in a finite number of steps.

We are now ready to consider a variety of list-based set algorithms. We start with algorithms that use coarse-grained synchronization, and successively refine them to reduce the granularity of locking, culminating in a nonblocking algorithm. Formal proofs of correctness lie beyond the scope of this book. Instead, we focus on informal reasoning useful in everyday problem solving.

As mentioned, in each of these algorithms, methods traverse the list using two local variables: curr is the current node and pred is its predecessor. Because these variables are local, each thread has its own instances of them; we use $pred_A$ and $curr_A$ to denote the instances used by thread A.

---

[2] Chapter 3 introduces an even weaker nonblocking property called *obstruction-freedom*.

```
1   public class CoarseList<T> {
2     private Node head;
3     private Lock lock = new ReentrantLock();
4     public CoarseList() {
5       head = new Node(Integer.MIN_VALUE);
6       head.next = new Node(Integer.MAX_VALUE);
7     }
8     public boolean add(T item) {
9       Node pred, curr;
10      int key = item.hashCode();
11      lock.lock();
12      try {
13        pred = head;
14        curr = pred.next;
15        while (curr.key < key) {
16          pred = curr;
17          curr = curr.next;
18        }
19        if (key == curr.key) {
20          return false;
21        } else {
22          Node node = new Node(item);
23          node.next = curr;
24          pred.next = node;
25          return true;
26        }
27      } finally {
28        lock.unlock();
29      }
30    }
```

FIGURE 9.4

The CoarseList class: the add() method.

9.4 Coarse-grained synchronization

We start with a simple algorithm using coarse-grained synchronization. Figs. 9.4 and 9.5 show the add() and remove() methods for this coarse-grained algorithm. (The contains() method works in much the same way, and is left as an exercise.) The list itself has a single lock which every method call must acquire. The principal advantage of this algorithm, which should not be discounted, is that it is obviously correct. All methods act on the list only while holding the lock, so the execution is essentially sequential.

The linearization point for an add(a) or remove(a) call depends on whether the call was successful (i.e., whether a was already present). A successful add(a) call (a absent) is linearized at the point that it updates the next field of the predecessor of

```
31   public boolean remove(T item) {
32     Node pred, curr;
33     int key = item.hashCode();
34     lock.lock();
35     try {
36       pred = head;
37       curr = pred.next;
38       while (curr.key < key) {
39         pred = curr;
40         curr = curr.next;
41       }
42       if (key == curr.key) {
43         pred.next = curr.next;
44         return true;
45       } else {
46         return false;
47       }
48     } finally {
49       lock.unlock();
50     }
51   }
```

FIGURE 9.5

The CoarseList class: the remove() method. All methods acquire a single lock, which is released on exit by the **finally** block.

the node added (line 24). Similarly, a successful remove(a) call (i.e., if a is present before the call) is linearized when it updates the next field of the predecessor of the node removed (line 43). An unsuccessful add(a) or remove(a) method call, or any contains(a) call, can be linearized when the lock is acquired (or any time while the lock is held).[3]

The CoarseList class satisfies the same progress condition as its lock: If the Lock is starvation-free, so is our implementation. If contention is very low, this algorithm is an excellent way to implement a list. If, however, there is contention, then even if the lock itself performs well, threads will still be delayed waiting for one another.

9.5 Fine-grained synchronization

We can improve concurrency by locking individual nodes, rather than locking the list as a whole. Instead of placing a lock on the entire list, we add a Lock to each node,

---

[3] We can linearize every method call at the instant it acquires the lock, but doing so requires a different abstraction map than the one described in Section 9.3.

along with lock() and unlock() methods. As a thread traverses the list, it locks each node when it first visits, and sometime later releases it. Such *fine-grained* locking permits concurrent threads to traverse the list together in a pipelined fashion.

Consider two nodes a and b, where a points to b. It is not safe to unlock a before locking b because another thread could remove b from the list in the interval between unlocking a and locking b. Instead, a thread acquires locks using a "hand-over-hand" protocol: it acquires the lock for a node (except the head node) while holding (i.e., before releasing) the lock for its predecessor. This locking protocol is sometimes called *lock coupling*. (Note that there is no obvious way to implement lock coupling using Java's **synchronized** methods.)

Figs. 9.6 and 9.7 show the FineList algorithm's add() and remove() methods. As in the coarse-grained list, remove() makes $curr_A$ unreachable by setting $pred_A$'s next

```
1   public boolean add(T item) {
2     int key = item.hashCode();
3     head.lock();
4     Node pred = head;
5     try {
6       Node curr = pred.next;
7       curr.lock();
8       try {
9         while (curr.key < key) {
10          pred.unlock();
11          pred = curr;
12          curr = curr.next;
13          curr.lock();
14        }
15        if (curr.key == key) {
16          return false;
17        }
18        Node node = new Node(item);
19        node.next = curr;
20        pred.next = node;
21        return true;
22      } finally {
23        curr.unlock();
24      }
25    } finally {
26      pred.unlock();
27    }
28  }
```

FIGURE 9.6

The FineList class: The add() method uses hand-over-hand locking to traverse the list. The **finally** blocks release locks before returning.

```
29  public boolean remove(T item) {
30    int key = item.hashCode();
31    head.lock();
32    Node pred = head;
33    try {
34      Node curr = pred.next;
35      curr.lock();
36      try {
37        while (curr.key < key) {
38          pred.unlock();
39          pred = curr;
40          curr = curr.next;
41          curr.lock();
42        }
43        if (curr.key == key) {
44          pred.next = curr.next;
45          return true;
46        }
47        return false;
48      } finally {
49        curr.unlock();
50      }
51    } finally {
52      pred.unlock();
53    }
54  }
```

FIGURE 9.7

The FineList class: The remove() method locks both the node to be removed and its predecessor before removing that node.

field to $curr_A$'s successor. To be safe, remove() must lock both $pred_A$ and $curr_A$. To see why, consider the scenario illustrated in Fig. 9.8. Thread A is about to remove node a, the first node in the list, while thread B is about to remove node b, where a points to b. Suppose A locks head, and B locks a. A then sets head.next to b, while B sets a.next to c. The net effect is the removal of a, but not b. The problem is that there is no overlap between the locks held by the two remove() calls. Fig. 9.9 illustrates how hand-over-hand locking avoids this problem.

To guarantee progress, it is important that all methods acquire locks in the same order, starting at head and following next references toward tail. As Fig. 9.10 shows, a deadlock could occur if different method calls were to acquire locks in different orders. In this example, thread A, trying to add a, has locked b and is attempting to lock head, while B, trying to remove b, has locked head and is trying to lock b. Clearly, these method calls will never finish. Avoiding deadlocks is one of the principal challenges of programming with locks.

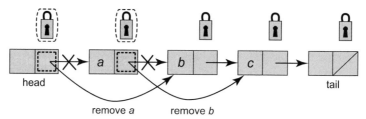

FIGURE 9.8

The `FineList` class: why `remove()` must acquire two locks. Thread *A* is about to remove *a*, the first node in the list, while thread *B* is about to remove *b*, where *a* points to *b*. Suppose *A* locks `head`, and *B* locks *a*. Thread *A* then sets `head.next` to *b*, while *B* sets *a*'s `next` field to *c*. The net effect is to remove *a*, but not *b*.

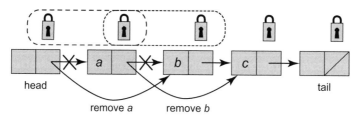

FIGURE 9.9

The `FineList` class: Hand-over-hand locking ensures that if concurrent `remove()` calls try to remove adjacent nodes, then they acquire conflicting locks. Thread *A* is about to remove node *a*, the first node in the list, while thread *B* is about to remove node *b*, where *a* points to *b*. Because *A* must lock both `head` and *a* and *B* must lock both *a* and *b*, they are guaranteed to conflict on *a*, forcing one call to wait for the other.

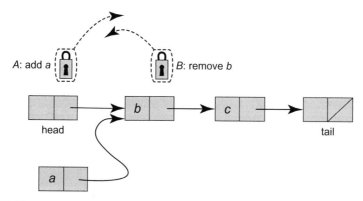

FIGURE 9.10

The `FineList` class: A deadlock could occur if, for example, `remove()` and `add()` calls acquired locks in opposite order. Then we could have the scenario depicted, in which thread *A* is about to insert *a* by locking first *b* and then `head`, and thread *B* is about to remove node *b* by locking first `head` and then *b*. Each thread holds the lock the other is waiting to acquire, so neither makes progress.

The representation invariant and abstraction map for FineList are the same as for CoarseList: Sentinels are never added or removed, nodes are sorted by key value without duplicates, and an item is in the set if and only if its node is reachable.

As in CoarseList, a successful add(a) or remove(a) call of FineList is linearized when it updates the next field of the predecessor of the node added or removed (line 20 or 44). An unsuccessful add(a) or remove(a) call, or any contains(a) call, can be linearized when it acquires the lock to a node whose key is greater than or equal to a (line 7 or 13 for add(a); line 35 or 41 for remove(a)).

The FineList algorithm is starvation-free if all the node locks are starvation-free, but arguing this property is harder than in the coarse-grained case: Because all methods acquire locks in the same down-the-list order, deadlock is impossible. If thread A attempts to lock head, it eventually succeeds. From that point on, because there are no deadlocks, eventually all locks held by threads ahead of A in the list will be released, and A will succeed in locking $pred_A$ and $curr_A$.

Although fine-grained locking reduces contention compared to coarse-grained locking, it imposes a potentially long sequence of lock acquisitions and releases. Moreover, threads accessing disjoint parts of the list may still block one another. For example, a thread removing the second item in the list blocks all concurrent threads searching for later nodes.

9.6 Optimistic synchronization

One way to reduce synchronization costs is to take a chance: Search without acquiring locks, lock the nodes found, and then confirm that the locked nodes are correct. If a synchronization conflict causes the wrong nodes to be locked, then release the locks and start over. When this kind of conflict is rare, this technique works well, which is why we call it *optimistic synchronization*.

Code for the optimistic add(a) method appears in Fig. 9.11. When thread A calls this method, it traverses the list without acquiring any locks (lines 6–8). In fact, it ignores the locks completely. It stops the traversal when $curr_A$'s key is greater than or equal to a. It then locks $pred_A$ and $curr_A$, and calls validate() to check that $pred_A$ is reachable and its next field still refers to $curr_A$. If validation succeeds, then thread A proceeds as before: If $curr_A$'s key is greater than a, thread A adds a new node with item a between $pred_A$ and $curr_A$, and returns *true*. Otherwise it returns *false*. The remove() and contains() methods (Figs. 9.12 and 9.13) operate similarly, traversing the list without locking, and then locking the target nodes and validating they are still in the list. To be consistent with the Java memory model, the next fields in the nodes must be declared volatile.

The code of validate() appears in Fig. 9.14. We are reminded of a story:

A tourist takes a taxi in a foreign town. The taxi driver speeds through a red light. The tourist, frightened, asks, "What are you are doing?" The driver answers, "Do not worry, I am an expert." He speeds through more red lights, and the tourist, on

```
1   public boolean add(T item) {
2     int key = item.hashCode();
3     while (true) {
4       Node pred = head;
5       Node curr = pred.next;
6       while (curr.key < key) {
7         pred = curr; curr = curr.next;
8       }
9       pred.lock();
10      try {
11        curr.lock();
12        try {
13          if (validate(pred, curr)) {
14            if (curr.key == key) {
15              return false;
16            } else {
17              Node node = new Node(item);
18              node.next = curr;
19              pred.next = node;
20              return true;
21            }
22          }
23        } finally {
24          curr.unlock();
25        }
26      } finally {
27        pred.unlock();
28      }
29    }
30  }
```

FIGURE 9.11

The `OptimisticList` class: the `add()` method traverses the list ignoring locks, acquires locks, and validates before adding the new node.

the verge of hysteria, complains again, more urgently. The driver replies, "Relax, relax, you are in the hands of an expert." Suddenly, the light turns green, the driver slams on the brakes, and the taxi skids to a halt. The tourist picks himself off the floor of the taxi and asks, "For crying out loud, why stop now that the light is finally green?" The driver answers, "Too dangerous, another expert could be crossing."

Ignoring locks while traversing a dynamically changing lock-based data structure requires careful thought (there are other expert threads out there). We must be sure to use some form of *validation* and guarantee *freedom from interference*.

Validation is necessary because the trail of references leading to $pred_A$, or the reference from $pred_A$ to $curr_A$, could have changed between when they were last

```
31   public boolean remove(T item) {
32     int key = item.hashCode();
33     while (true) {
34       Node pred = head;
35       Node curr = pred.next;
36       while (curr.key < key) {
37         pred = curr; curr = curr.next;
38       }
39       pred.lock();
40       try {
41         curr.lock();
42         try {
43           if (validate(pred, curr)) {
44             if (curr.key == key) {
45               pred.next = curr.next;
46               return true;
47             } else {
48               return false;
49             }
50           }
51         } finally {
52           curr.unlock();
53         }
54       } finally {
55         pred.unlock();
56       }
57     }
58   }
```

FIGURE 9.12

The OptimisticList class: The remove() method traverses ignoring locks, acquires locks, and validates before removing the node.

read by A and when A acquired the locks. In particular, A could be traversing parts of the list that have already been removed. For example, as shown in Fig. 9.15, the node $curr_A$ and all nodes between $curr_A$ and a (including a) may be removed while A is still traversing $curr_A$. Thread A discovers that $curr_A$ points to a; without validation, it would "successfully" remove a, even though a is no longer in the list. A validate() call detects that a is no longer in the list, and the caller restarts the method.

Because we ignore the locks that protect concurrent modifications while traversing the list, a method call may traverse nodes that have been removed from the list. Nevertheless, freedom from interference implies that once a node has been unlinked from the list, the value of its next field does not change, so following a sequence of such links eventually leads back to the list. Freedom from interference, in turn, relies on garbage collection to ensure that no node is recycled while it is being traversed.

```
59  public boolean contains(T item) {
60    int key = item.hashCode();
61    while (true) {
62      Node pred = head;
63      Node curr = pred.next;
64      while (curr.key < key) {
65        pred = curr; curr = curr.next;
66      }
67      pred.lock();
68      try {
69        curr.lock();
70        try {
71          if (validate(pred, curr)) {
72            return (curr.key == key);
73          }
74        } finally {
75          curr.unlock();
76        }
77      } finally {
78        pred.unlock();
79      }
80    }
81  }
```

FIGURE 9.13

The OptimisticList class: The contains() method searches, ignoring locks, then acquires locks, and validates to determine if the node is in the list.

```
82  private boolean validate(Node pred, Node curr) {
83    Node node = head;
84    while (node.key <= pred.key) {
85      if (node == pred)
86        return pred.next == curr;
87      node = node.next;
88    }
89    return false;
90  }
```

FIGURE 9.14

The OptimisticList: Validation checks that pred points to curr and is reachable from head.

The linearization points of the optimistic algorithm are the same as those of the fine-grained algorithm, except that we must take into account the possibility of failed validation. In particular, we only linearize a method call when it acquires a lock if the subsequent validation succeeds.

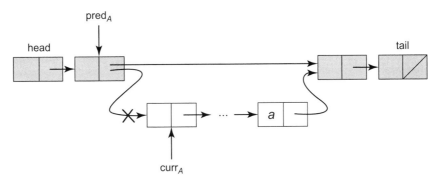

FIGURE 9.15

The OptimisticList class: why validation is needed. Thread A is attempting to remove a node a. While traversing the list, curr$_A$ and all nodes between curr$_A$ and a (including a) might be removed (denoted by a lighter node color). In such a case, thread A would proceed to the point where curr$_A$ points to a, and, without validation, would successfully remove a, even though it is no longer in the list. Validation is required to determine that a is no longer reachable from head.

The OptimisticList algorithm is not starvation-free, even if all node locks are individually starvation-free. A thread might be delayed indefinitely if new nodes are repeatedly added and removed (see Exercise 9.6). Nevertheless, we expect this algorithm to do well in practice, since starvation is rare. It works best if the cost of traversing the list twice without locking is significantly less than the cost of traversing the list once with locking.

Although optimistic synchronization can be applied to coarse-grained locking, it does not improve that algorithm because validation requires retraversing the list while holding the lock. However, we can eliminate the need to traverse the list during validation by maintaining a version number that is incremented whenever the list is modified. We explore such an approach in the exercises.

9.7 Lazy synchronization

One drawback of the OptimisticList algorithm (and the CoarseList and FineList algorithms) is that contains() acquires locks, which is unattractive since contains() calls are typically much more common than calls to other methods. We show how to refine this algorithm so that contains() is wait-free, and add() and remove() methods, while still blocking, traverse the list only once (in the absence of contention).

We add to each node a Boolean marked field indicating whether that node is in the set. Now, traversals do not need to lock the target node, and there is no need to validate that the node is reachable by retraversing the whole list. Instead, the algorithm maintains the invariant that every unmarked node is reachable. If a traversing thread does not find a node, or finds it marked, then that item is not in the set. As a result,

```
1    private boolean validate(Node pred, Node curr) {
2      return !pred.marked && !curr.marked && pred.next == curr;
3    }
```

FIGURE 9.16

The LazyList class: Validation checks that neither the pred nor the curr node has been logically deleted, and that pred points to curr.

contains() needs only one wait-free traversal. To add an element to the list, add() traverses the list, locks the target's predecessor, and inserts the node. The remove() method is lazy, taking two steps: It first marks the target node, *logically* removing it, and then redirects the next field of its predecessor, *physically* removing it.

In more detail, as in the OptimisticList algorithm, all methods traverse the list (possibly traversing logically and physically removed nodes) ignoring the locks. The add() and remove() methods lock the $pred_A$ and $curr_A$ nodes, and validates them, as before, except that the validate() method (Fig. 9.16) does not retraverse the list to determine that the nodes are still in the list. Instead, because of the new invariant, it suffices to check that they are not marked. We must check that both $pred_A$ and $curr_A$ are not marked because $pred_A$ is the node that is being modified. (See Fig. 9.19 for an illustration of why validation is necessary.)

Except for calling a different validate() method, the add() method of LazyList is exactly the same as that of OptimisticList. The remove() method (Fig. 9.17) has a small difference: it marks the node (line 18) before (physically) removing it from the list, maintaining the invariant that every unmarked node is reachable.

Logical removals require a small change to the abstraction map: An item is in the set if and only if it is referred to by an *unmarked* reachable node. Note that the path along which the node is reachable may contain marked nodes. (The diligent reader should check that any unmarked reachable node remains reachable, even if its predecessor is logically or physically deleted.) As in the OptimisticList algorithm, add() and remove() are not starvation-free, because list traversals may be arbitrarily delayed by ongoing modifications.

The contains() method (Fig. 9.18) traverses the list once ignoring locks and returns *true* if the node it was searching for is present and unmarked, and *false* otherwise. It is thus wait-free.[4] A marked node's value is ignored. Each time the traversal moves to a new node, the new node has a larger key than the previous one, even if the node is logically deleted.

The linearization points for LazyList add() and unsuccessful remove() calls are the same as for the OptimisticList. A successful remove() call is linearized when the node is marked (i.e., when the marked bit is set on line 18), and a successful contains() call is linearized when an unmarked matching node is found.

---

[4] The number of nodes a thread must traverse cannot increase without bound due to newly inserted nodes because the set of keys is well founded.

```
4   public boolean remove(T item) {
5     int key = item.hashCode();
6     while (true) {
7      Node pred = head;
8      Node curr = head.next;
9      while (curr.key < key) {
10        pred = curr; curr = curr.next;
11     }
12     pred.lock();
13     try {
14       curr.lock();
15       try {
16         if (validate(pred, curr)) {
17           if (curr.key == key) {
18             curr.marked = true;
19             pred.next = curr.next;
20             return true;
21           } else {
22             return false;
23           }
24         }
25       } finally {
26         curr.unlock();
27       }
28     } finally {
29       pred.unlock();
30     }
31    }
32  }
```

FIGURE 9.17

The LazyList class: The remove() method removes nodes in two steps, logical and physical.

```
33  public boolean contains(T item) {
34    int key = item.hashCode();
35    Node curr = head;
36    while (curr.key < key)
37      curr = curr.next;
38    return curr.key == key && !curr.marked;
39  }
```

FIGURE 9.18

The LazyList class: the contains() method.

(a)

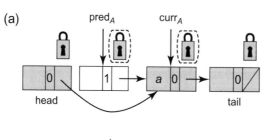

(b)

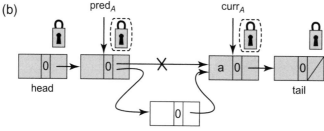

FIGURE 9.19

The LazyList class: why validation is needed. In part (a), thread A is attempting to remove node a. After it reaches the point where pred_A refers to curr_A, and before it acquires locks on these nodes, the node pred_A is logically and physically removed. After A acquires the locks, validation will detect the problem. In part (b), A is attempting to remove node a. After it reaches the point where pred_A refers to curr_A, and before it acquires locks on these nodes, a new node is added between pred_A and curr_A. After A acquires the locks, even though neither pred_A nor curr_A is marked, validation detects that pred_A is not the same as curr_A, and A's call to remove() will be restarted.

It is trickier to see how to linearize an unsuccessful contains() method call. Consider the scenario depicted in Fig. 9.20, in which thread A is executing contains(a). In part (a), while A is traversing the list, another thread removes, both logically and physically, curr_A and all subsequent nodes up to and including a. Thread A will still follow the links until curr_A points to a, and detect that a is marked, and hence no longer in the abstract set. We might be tempted to linearize it at that point (i.e., when A executes line 38). However, as depicted in part (b), this is not always a valid linearization point: while A is traversing the removed section of the list, and before it reaches the removed node a, another thread may call add(a), adding a new node with key a to the reachable part of the list. In this case, A's unsuccessful contains(a) method call cannot be linearized at the point it finds the marked node a, because this point occurs *after* the new node with key a has been inserted in the list. The unsuccessful method call must be linearized to a point before the new node is inserted.

We therefore linearize an unsuccessful contains(a) method call within its execution interval at the earlier of the following points: (1) the point where a marked node with key a, or a node with a key greater than a, is found, or (2) the point immediately before a new node with key a is added to the list. The second point is guaranteed to be within the execution interval because the insertion of the new node with the same

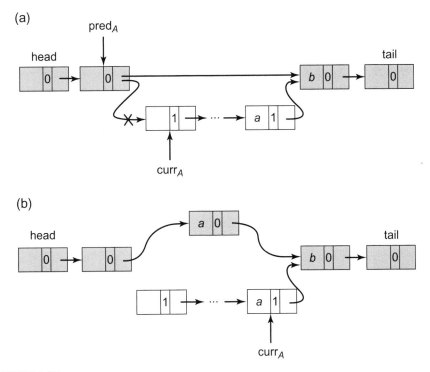

FIGURE 9.20

The LazyList class: linearizing an unsuccessful contains() call. Dark nodes are physically in the list and white nodes are physically removed. In part (a), while thread A is traversing the list, another thread disconnects the sublist referred to by curr$_A$. We can linearize A's call at the point it sees that a is marked and is no longer in the abstract set. However, in part (b), while A is traversing the removed part of the list leading to the marked node a, another thread adds a new node with key a. It would be wrong to linearize A's unsuccessful contains(a) call to when it found the marked node a, since this point occurs *after* the insertion of the new node with key a to the list.

key must have happened after the start of the contains() method, or the contains() method would have found that item. As can be seen, the linearization point of the unsuccessful contains() is determined by the ordering of events in the execution, and is not a predetermined point in the method's code, and indeed, may not even be at a point where the thread takes a step (e.g., it may be linearized when another thread takes a step).

One benefit of lazy synchronization is that we can separate unobtrusive logical steps, such as setting a flag, from disruptive physical changes to the structure, such as disconnecting a node. The example presented here is simple because we disconnect one node at a time. In general, however, delayed operations can be batched and performed lazily at a convenient time, reducing the overall disruptiveness of physical modifications to the structure.

A principal disadvantage of the LazyList algorithm is that add() and remove() calls are blocking: If one thread is delayed, then others may also be delayed.

9.8 Nonblocking synchronization

We have seen that we can avoid locking in contains() by marking nodes as logically removed before physically removing them from the list. We now show how to extend this idea to eliminate locks altogether, allowing all three methods, add(), remove(), and contains(), to be nonblocking. (The first two methods are lock-free and the last wait-free.)

A naïve approach would be to use compareAndSet() to change the next fields. For example, if thread A wants to remove $curr_A$ from the list, it might call compareAndSet() to set $pred_A$'s next field to $curr_A$'s successor. Unfortunately, this idea does not work, as shown in Fig. 9.21. Part (a) shows a thread A attempting to remove a node a while thread B is adding a node b. Suppose A applies compareAndSet() to head.next, while B applies compareAndSet() to a.next. The net effect is that a is correctly deleted but b is not added to the list. In part (b), A attempts to remove a, the first node in the list, while B is about to remove b, where a points to b. Suppose

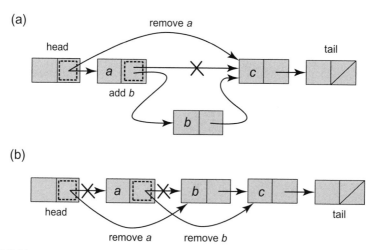

FIGURE 9.21

The LockFreeList class: why mark and reference fields must be modified atomically. In part (a), thread A is about to remove a, the first node in the list, while B is about to add b. Suppose A applies compareAndSet() to head.next, while B applies compareAndSet() to a.next. The net effect is that a is correctly deleted but b is not added to the list. In part (b), thread A is about to remove a, the first node in the list, while B is about to remove b, where a points to b. Suppose A applies compareAndSet() to head.next, while B applies compareAndSet() to a.next. The net effect is to remove a, but not b.

A applies compareAndSet() to head.next, while *B* applies compareAndSet() to a.next. The net effect is the removal of *a*, but not *b*.

We need a way to ensure that a node's fields cannot be updated after that node has been logically or physically removed from the list. Our approach is to treat the node's next and marked fields as a single atomic unit: any attempt to update the next field when the marked field is *true* will fail.

As described in detail in Pragma 9.8.1, an AtomicMarkableReference<T> object encapsulates both a reference to an object of type T and a Boolean mark. These fields can be atomically updated, either together or individually.

We make each node's next field an AtomicMarkableReference<Node>. Thread *A* logically removes $curr_A$ by setting the mark bit in the node's next field, and shares the physical removal with other threads performing add() or remove(): As each thread traverses the list, it cleans up the list by physically removing any marked nodes it encounters. In other words, threads performing add() and remove() do not traverse

---

PRAGMA 9.8.1

An AtomicMarkableReference<T> object (defined by the java.util.concurrent. atomic package) encapsulates both a reference to an object of type T and a Boolean mark, also called a *mark bit*. These fields can be updated atomically, either together or individually. The compareAndSet() method tests the expected reference and mark values, and if both tests succeed, replaces them with updated reference and mark values. The get() method has an unusual interface: It returns the object's reference value and stores the mark value in a Boolean array argument. The getReference() and isMarked() methods return the reference and mark values, respectively. The interfaces of these methods are shown in Fig. 9.22.

In C or C++, one could provide this functionality efficiently by "stealing" a bit from a pointer, using bit-wise operators to extract the mark and the pointer from a single word. In Java, one cannot manipulate pointers directly, so this functionality must be provided by a library.

```
1  public boolean compareAndSet(T expectedReference,
2                                T newReference,
3                                boolean expectedMark,
4                                boolean newMark);
5  public T get(boolean[] marked);
6  public T getReference();
7  public boolean isMarked();
```

FIGURE 9.22

Some AtomicMarkableReference<T> methods: compareAndSet() tests and updates both the mark and reference fields; get() returns the encapsulated reference and stores the mark at position 0 in the argument array; getReference() and isMarked() return the reference and mark, respectively.

marked nodes; they remove them before continuing. The contains() method remains the same as in the LazyList algorithm, traversing all nodes whether they are marked or not, and testing if an item is in the list based on its key and mark.

It is worth pondering a design decision that differentiates the LockFreeList algorithm from the LazyList algorithm. Why do threads that add or remove nodes never traverse marked nodes, and instead physically remove all marked nodes they encounter? Suppose that thread A were to traverse marked nodes without physically removing them, and after logically removing $curr_A$, were to attempt to physically remove it as well. It could do so by calling compareAndSet() to try to redirect $pred_A$'s next field, simultaneously verifying that $pred_A$ is not marked and that it refers to $curr_A$. The difficulty is that, because A is not holding locks on $pred_A$ and $curr_A$, other threads could insert new nodes or remove $pred_A$ before the compareAndSet() call.

Consider a scenario in which another thread marks $pred_A$. As illustrated in Fig. 9.21, we cannot safely redirect the next field of a marked node, so A would have to restart the physical removal by retraversing the list. This time, however, A would have to physically remove $pred_A$ before it could remove $curr_A$. Even worse, if there is a sequence of logically removed nodes leading to $pred_A$, A must remove them all, one after the other, before it can remove $curr_A$ itself.

This example illustrates why add() and remove() calls do not traverse marked nodes: When they arrive at the node to be modified, they may be forced to retraverse the list to remove previous marked nodes. Instead, we choose to have both add() and remove() physically remove any marked nodes on the path to their target node. The contains() method, by contrast, performs no modification, and therefore need not participate in the cleanup of logically removed nodes, allowing it, as in the LazyList, to traverse both marked and unmarked nodes.

In presenting the LockFreeList algorithm, we factor out functionality common to the add() and remove() methods by creating a nested Window class to help with traversal. As shown in Fig. 9.23, a Window object is a structure with pred and curr fields. The find() method takes a head node and a key a, and traverses the list, seeking to set pred to the node with the largest key less than a, and curr to the node with the least key greater than or equal to a. As thread A traverses the list, each time it advances $curr_A$, it checks whether that node is marked (line 16). If so, it calls compareAndSet() to attempt to physically remove the node by setting $pred_A$'s next field to $curr_A$'s next field. This call tests both the field's reference and Boolean mark values, and fails if either value has changed. A concurrent thread could change the mark value by logically removing $pred_A$, or it could change the reference value by physically removing $curr_A$. If the call fails, A restarts the traversal from the head of the list; otherwise the traversal continues.

The LockFreeList class uses the same abstraction map as the LazyList class: An item is in the set if and only if it is referred to by an *unmarked* reachable node. The compareAndSet() call at line 17 of the find() method is an example of a *benevolent side effect*: It changes the concrete list without changing the abstract set, because removing a marked node does not change the value of the abstraction map.

```
1    class Window {
2      public Node pred, curr;
3      Window(Node myPred, Node myCurr) {
4        pred = myPred; curr = myCurr;
5      }
6    }
7    Window find(Node head, int key) {
8      Node pred = null, curr = null, succ = null;
9      boolean[] marked = {false};
10     boolean snip;
11     retry: while (true) {
12       pred = head;
13       curr = pred.next.getReference();
14       while (true) {
15         succ = curr.next.get(marked);
16         while (marked[0]) {
17           snip = pred.next.compareAndSet(curr, succ, false, false);
18           if (!snip) continue retry;
19           curr = succ;
20           succ = curr.next.get(marked);
21         }
22         if (curr.key >= key)
23           return new Window(pred, curr);
24         pred = curr;
25         curr = succ;
26       }
27     }
28   }
```

FIGURE 9.23

The LockFreeList class: nested Window class and find() method: find() returns a Window object with nodes on either side of the key; it removes marked nodes that it encounters.

Fig. 9.24 shows the LockFreeList class's add() method. Suppose thread A calls add(a). A uses find() to locate $pred_A$ and $curr_A$. If $curr_A$'s key is equal to a's, the call returns *false*. Otherwise, add() initializes a new node a to hold a, and makes a point to $curr_A$. It then calls compareAndSet() (line 39) to make $pred_A$ point to a. Because the compareAndSet() tests both the mark and the reference, it succeeds only if $pred_A$ is unmarked and points to $curr_A$. If the compareAndSet() is successful, the method returns *true*; otherwise it starts over from head.

Fig. 9.25 shows the LockFreeList algorithm's remove() method. When A calls remove() to remove item a, it uses find() to locate $pred_A$ and $curr_A$. If $curr_A$'s key fails to match a's, the call returns *false*. Otherwise, remove() uses a compareAndSet() to attempt to mark $curr_A$ as logically removed (line 55). This call succeeds only if no other thread has set the mark first. If it succeeds, the call returns *true*. A single attempt is made to physically remove the node, but there is no need to try again

```
29  public boolean add(T item) {
30    int key = item.hashCode();
31    while (true) {
32      Window window = find(head, key);
33      Node pred = window.pred, curr = window.curr;
34      if (curr.key == key) {
35        return false;
36      } else {
37        Node node = new Node(item);
38        node.next = new AtomicMarkableReference(curr, false);
39        if (pred.next.compareAndSet(curr, node, false, false)) {
40          return true;
41        }
42      }
43    }
44  }
```

FIGURE 9.24

The LockFreeList class: The add() method calls find() to locate pred and curr. It adds a
new node only if pred is unmarked and refers to curr.

```
45  public boolean remove(T item) {
46    int key = item.hashCode();
47    boolean snip;
48    while (true) {
49      Window window = find(head, key);
50      Node pred = window.pred, curr = window.curr;
51      if (curr.key != key) {
52        return false;
53      } else {
54        Node succ = curr.next.getReference();
55        snip = curr.next.compareAndSet(succ, succ, false, true);
56        if (!snip)
57          continue;
58        pred.next.compareAndSet(curr, succ, false, false);
59        return true;
60      }
61    }
62  }
```

FIGURE 9.25

The LockFreeList class: The remove() method calls find() to locate pred and curr, and
atomically marks the node for removal.

```
63  public boolean contains(T item) {
64    int key = item.hashCode();
65    Node curr = head;
66    while (curr.key < key) {
67      curr = curr.next.getReference();
68    }
69    return (curr.key == key && !curr.next.isMarked())
70  }
```

FIGURE 9.26

The LockFreeList class: The wait-free contains() method is the same as in the LazyList class, except that it calls curr.next.getReference() to get the successor of curr and curr.next.isMarked() to test whether curr is marked.

because the node will be removed by the next thread to traverse that region of the list. If the compareAndSet() call fails, remove() starts over.

The contains() method of the LockFreeList algorithm, shown in Fig. 9.26, is the same as that of the LazyList algorithm, except that it uses curr.next.getReference() and curr.next.isMarked() to get the successor and mark bit of curr.

9.9 Discussion

We have seen a progression of list-based lock implementations in which the granularity and frequency of locking was gradually reduced, eventually reaching a fully nonblocking list. The final transition from the LazyList to the LockFreeList exposes some of the design decisions that concurrent programmers face. As we will see, approaches such as optimistic and lazy synchronization will appear time and again when designing more complex data structures.

On the one hand, the LockFreeList algorithm guarantees progress in the face of arbitrary delays. However, there is a price for this strong progress guarantee:

- The need to support atomic modification of a reference and a Boolean mark has an added performance cost.[5]
- As add() and remove() traverse the list, they engage in concurrent cleanup of removed nodes, introducing the possibility of contention among threads, sometimes forcing threads to restart traversals, even if there was no change near the node each was trying to modify.

On the other hand, the lazy lock-based list does not guarantee progress in the face of arbitrary delays: Its add() and remove() methods are blocking. However, unlike the

---

[5] In the java.util.concurrent package, this cost is somewhat reduced by using a reference to an intermediate dummy node to signify that the marked bit is set.

lock-free algorithm, it does not require each node to include an atomically markable reference. It also does not require traversals to clean up logically removed nodes; they progress down the list, ignoring marked nodes.

Which approach is preferable depends on the application. In the end, the balance of factors such as the potential for arbitrary thread delays, the relative frequency of calls to the add() and remove() methods, the overhead of implementing an atomically markable reference, and so on, determines the choice of whether to lock, and if so, at what granularity.

9.10 **Chapter notes**

Lock coupling was invented by Rudolf Bayer and Mario Schkolnick [17]. The first designs of lock-free linked list algorithms are credited to John Valois [164]. The lock-free list implementation shown here is a variation on the lists of Maged Michael [126], who based his work on earlier linked list algorithms by Tim Harris [58]. This algorithm, referred to by many as the Harris–Michael algorithm, is the one used in the java.util.concurrent package. The OptimisticList algorithm was invented for this chapter, and the lazy algorithm is credited to Steve Heller, Maurice Herlihy, Victor Luchangco, Mark Moir, Bill Scherer, and Nir Shavit [60].

9.11 **Exercises**

Exercise 9.1. Describe how to modify each of the linked list algorithms if object hash codes are not guaranteed to be unique.

Exercise 9.2. Suppose every method call of CoarseList is linearized at the instant the lock is acquired. Explain why we cannot use the abstraction map described in Section 9.3. Give an alternative abstraction map that works for these linearization points.

Exercise 9.3. Explain why the fine-grained locking algorithm is does not deadlock.

Exercise 9.4. Explain why the fine-grained list's add() method is linearizable.

Exercise 9.5. Explain why the optimistic and lazy locking algorithms are not subject to deadlock.

Exercise 9.6. Show an execution of the optimistic algorithm in which a thread is forever attempting to delete a node.

Hint: Since we assume that all the individual node locks are starvation-free, the livelock is not on any individual lock, and a bad execution must repeatedly add and remove nodes from the list.

Exercise 9.7. Provide the code for the contains() method missing from the fine-grained algorithm. Explain why your implementation is correct.

Exercise 9.8. Is the optimistic list implementation still correct if we switch the order in which add() locks the pred and curr nodes?

Exercise 9.9. Show that in the optimistic list algorithm, if $pred_A$ is not *null*, then tail is reachable from $pred_A$, even if $pred_A$ itself is not reachable.

Exercise 9.10. Show that in the optimistic algorithm, the add() method needs to lock only pred.

Exercise 9.11. Design a coarse-grained optimistic locking linked list-based set algorithm that does not traverse the list while holding the lock by augmenting the list with a version number.

Exercise 9.12. Design a fine-grained optimistic locking algorithm that uses a version number to avoid traversing the list while holding any lock if the list does not change during the first traversal of the list. What are the advantages and disadvantages of this list compared with the coarse-grained list from the previous exercise?

Exercise 9.13. For each of the following modifications of the sorted linked list algorithms, explain why the respective algorithm is still linearizable, or give a counterexample showing it is not.

a. In the optimistic algorithm, the contains() method locks two nodes before deciding whether a key is present. Suppose, instead, it locks no nodes, returning *true* if it observes the value, and *false* otherwise.
b. In the lazy algorithm, the contains() method executes without inspecting the locks, but it inspects the mark bit; it returns *false* if a node is marked for removal. Suppose, instead, the contains() does not inspect the mark bit of the nodes, and returns *true* even for nodes that may be marked.

Exercise 9.14. Would the lazy algorithm still work if we marked a node as removed simply by setting its next field to *null*? Why or why not? What about the lock-free algorithm?

Exercise 9.15. In the lazy algorithm, can $pred_A$ ever be unreachable? Justify your answer.

Exercise 9.16. Your new employee claims that the lazy list's validation method (Fig. 9.16) can be simplified by dropping the check that pred.next is equal to curr. After all, the code always sets pred to the old value of curr, and before pred.next can be changed, the new value of curr must be marked, causing the validation to fail. Explain the error in this reasoning.

Exercise 9.17. Can you modify the lazy algorithm's remove() so it locks only one node?

Exercise 9.18. In the lock-free algorithm, argue the benefits and drawbacks of having the contains() method help in the cleanup of logically removed nodes.

Exercise 9.19. In the lock-free algorithm, if an add() method call fails because pred does not point to curr, but pred is not marked, do we need to traverse the list again from head in order to attempt to complete the call?

Exercise 9.20. Would the contains() method of the lazy and lock-free algorithms still be correct if logically removed entries were not guaranteed to be sorted?

Exercise 9.21. The add() method of the lock-free algorithm never finds a marked node with the same key. Can one modify the algorithm so that it will simply insert its new added object into the existing marked node with the same key if such a node exists in the list, thus saving the need to insert a new node?

Exercise 9.22. Explain why the following cannot happen in the LockFreeList algorithm: A node with item x is logically but not yet physically removed by some thread, then the same item x is added into the list by another thread, and finally a contains() call by a third thread traverses the list, finding the logically removed node, and returning *false*, even though the linearization order of the remove() and add() implies that x is in the set.

Exercise 9.23. Consider the following two modifications for the sorted linked list algorithms:

a. In the optimistic algorithm, the contains() method locks two nodes before deciding whether a key is present. Suppose, instead, it locks no nodes, returning *true* if it observes the value, and *false* otherwise.

b. In the lazy algorithm, the contains() method executes without inspecting the locks, but it inspects the mark bit; it returns *false* if a node is marked for removal. Suppose, instead, the contains() does not inspect the mark bit of the nodes, and returns *true* even for nodes that may be marked.

For both of the modifications, explain why the respective algorithm is still linearizable, or give a counterexample showing it is not.

Exercise 9.24. In the lock-free algorithm, we attempt to logically remove the node curr by calling curr.next.compareAndSet(succ,succ,**false**,**true**) (line 55 of Fig. 9.25). For each of the following implementations in which this call is replaced with a different method call, either explain why it is correct or describe an execution in which it fails.

a. We instead call curr.next.compareAndSetMark(**false,true**), where compareAndSetMark() is a fictional method that atomically performs a normal compare-and-swap operation on just the mark bit.

b. We instead call curr.next.attemptMark(succ,**true**), where attemptMark() is a real method of the AtomicMarkableReference<T> class that atomically changes the mark bit to the specified value if the reference has the expected value, but is allowed to spuriously fail (if there are concurrent modifications).

CHAPTER

Queues, memory management, and the ABA problem

10

10.1 Introduction

In the next few chapters, we look at a broad class of objects known as *pools*. A pool is similar to the Set<> class studied in Chapter 9, with two main differences: A pool does not necessarily provide a contains() method to test membership, and it allows the same item to appear more than once. The Pool<> has put() and get() methods, as shown in Fig. 10.1. Pools show up in many places in concurrent systems. For example, in many applications, one or more *producer* threads produce items to be consumed by one or more *consumer* threads. These items may be jobs to perform, keystrokes to interpret, purchase orders to execute, or packets to decode. Sometimes producers are *bursty*, suddenly and briefly producing items faster than consumers can consume them. To allow consumers to keep up, we can place a *buffer* between the producers and the consumers. Items produced faster than they can be consumed accumulate in the buffer, from which they are consumed as quickly as possible. Often, pools act as producer–consumer buffers.

Pools come in several varieties.

- A pool may be *bounded* or *unbounded*. A bounded pool holds a limited number of items. This limit is called its *capacity*. By contrast, an unbounded pool can hold any number of items. Bounded pools are useful when we want to keep producer and consumer threads loosely synchronized, ensuring that producers do not get too far ahead of consumers. Bounded pools may also be simpler to implement than unbounded pools. On the other hand, unbounded pools are useful when it is not easy to fix a limit on how far producers can outstrip consumers.
- Pool methods may be *total* or *partial*. Some partial methods are *synchronous*.

```
public interface Pool<T> {
  void put(T item);
  T get();
}
```

FIGURE 10.1

The Pool<T> interface.

The Art of Multiprocessor Programming. https://doi.org/10.1016/B978-0-12-415950-1.00020-3

- A method is *partial* if calls may wait for certain conditions to hold. For example, a partial get() call that tries to remove an item from an empty pool blocks until an item is available to return. If the pool is bounded, a partial put() call that tries to add an item to a full pool blocks until an empty slot is available to fill. A partial interface makes sense when the producer (or consumer) has nothing better to do than to wait for the pool to become nonfull (or nonempty).
- A method is *total* if calls never need to wait for conditions to become true. For example, a get() call that tries to remove an item from an empty pool, or a put() call that tries to add an item to a full pool, may immediately return a failure code or throw an exception. A total interface makes sense when the producer (or consumer) thread has something better to do than wait for the method call to take effect.
- A partial method is *synchronous* if it waits for another method to overlap its call interval. For example, in a synchronous pool, a method call that adds an item to the pool is blocked until that item is removed by another method call. Symmetrically, a method call that removes an item from the pool is blocked until another method call makes an item available to be removed. Synchronous pools are used for communication in programming languages such as CSP and Ada, in which threads *rendezvous* to exchange information.

- Pools provide different *fairness* guarantees. They may be FIFO (i.e., a queue) or last-in-first-out (LIFO) (i.e., a stack), or have other, typically weaker, properties. The importance of fairness when buffering using a pool is clear to anyone who has ever called a bank or a technical support line, only to be placed in a pool of waiting calls. The longer you wait, the more consolation you draw from the recorded message asserting that calls are answered in the order they arrive. Perhaps.

10.2 Queues

In this chapter, we consider a kind of pool that provides *first-in-first-out* (FIFO) fairness. A sequential Queue<T> is an ordered sequence of items (of type T). It provides an enq(x) method that puts item *x* at one end of the queue, called the *tail*, and a deq() method that removes and returns the item at the other end of the queue, called the *head*. A concurrent queue is linearizable to a sequential queue. Queues are pools where enq() implements put() and deq() implements get(). We use queue implementations to illustrate a number of important principles. In later chapters we consider pools that provide other fairness guarantees.

10.3 A bounded partial queue

For simplicity, we assume it is illegal to add a *null* value to a queue. Of course, there may be circumstances where it makes sense to add and remove *null* values; we leave it as an exercise to adapt our algorithms to accommodate *null* values.

```
1   public class BoundedQueue<T> {
2     ReentrantLock enqLock, deqLock;
3     Condition notEmptyCondition, notFullCondition;
4     AtomicInteger size;
5     volatile Node head, tail;
6     final int capacity;
7     public BoundedQueue(int _capacity) {
8       capacity = _capacity;
9       head = new Node(null);
10      tail = head;
11      size = new AtomicInteger(0);
12      enqLock = new ReentrantLock();
13      notFullCondition = enqLock.newCondition();
14      deqLock = new ReentrantLock();
15      notEmptyCondition = deqLock.newCondition();
16    }
17    ...
18  }
```

FIGURE 10.2

The BoundedQueue class: fields and constructor.

```
19    protected class Node {
20      public T value;
21      public volatile Node next;
22      public Node(T x) {
23        value = x;
24        next = null;
25      }
26    }
```

FIGURE 10.3

The BoundedQueue class: list node.

How much concurrency can we expect a bounded queue implementation with multiple concurrent enqueuers and dequeuers to provide? Informally, the enq() and deq() methods operate on opposite ends of the queue; as long as the queue is neither full nor empty, an enq() call and a deq() call should be able to proceed without interference. For the same reason, concurrent enq() calls probably will interfere, and the same holds for deq() calls. This informal reasoning may sound convincing, and it is mostly correct, but realizing this level of concurrency is nontrivial.

Here, we implement a bounded queue as a linked list. (We could also have used an array.) Fig. 10.2 shows the queue's fields and constructor, and Fig. 10.3 shows a queue node. Figs. 10.4 and 10.5 show the enq() and deq() methods. Like the lists studied in Chapter 9, a queue node has value and next fields.

```
27    public void enq(T x) {
28      boolean mustWakeDequeuers = false;
29      Node e = new Node(x);
30      enqLock.lock();
31      try {
32        while (size.get() == capacity)
33          notFullCondition.await();
34        tail.next = e;
35        tail = e;
36        if (size.getAndIncrement() == 0)
37          mustWakeDequeuers = true;
38      } finally {
39        enqLock.unlock();
40      }
41      if (mustWakeDequeuers) {
42        deqLock.lock();
43        try {
44          notEmptyCondition.signalAll();
45        } finally {
46          deqLock.unlock();
47        }
48      }
49    }
```

FIGURE 10.4

The BoundedQueue class: the enq() method.

As shown in Fig. 10.6, the queue has head and tail fields that respectively refer to the first and last nodes in the list. The queue always contains at least one node, and the first node is a *sentinel*. Like the sentinel nodes in Chapter 9, it marks a position in the queue (in this case, the head of the queue), but its value is meaningless. Unlike the list algorithms in Chapter 9, in which the same nodes always act as sentinels, the queue repeatedly replaces the sentinel node. The abstraction map for this algorithm carries a list of nodes to a queue with the items referred to by the nonsentinel nodes in the list in the same order as they appear in the list. The item referred to by the first node is *not* in the abstract queue. The abstract queue is empty if there is only one node in the list (i.e., if head.next == null).

We use two locks, enqLock and deqLock, to ensure that at any time, at most one enqueuer and at most one dequeuer can manipulate the queue object's fields. Using two locks instead of one allows an enqueuer to not lock out a dequeuer unnecessarily, and vice versa. Each lock has an associated *condition*: notFullCondition for enqLock is used to notify waiting enqueuers when the queue is no longer full; notEmptyCondition for deqLock is used to notify waiting dequeuers when the queue is no longer empty.

To keep the queue bounded, we must prevent items from being enqueued when the queue is at capacity. The size field is an AtomicInteger that tracks the number

```
50    public T deq() {
51      T result;
52      boolean mustWakeEnqueuers = false;
53      deqLock.lock();
54      try {
55        while (head.next == null)
56          notEmptyCondition.await();
57        result = head.next.value;
58        head = head.next;
59        if (size.getAndDecrement() == capacity) {
60          mustWakeEnqueuers = true;
61        }
62      } finally {
63        deqLock.unlock();
64      }
65      if (mustWakeEnqueuers) {
66        enqLock.lock();
67        try {
68          notFullCondition.signalAll();
69        } finally {
70          enqLock.unlock();
71        }
72      }
73      return result;
74    }
```

FIGURE 10.5

The BoundedQueue class: the deq() method.

of objects currently in the queue. This field is decremented by deq() calls and incremented by enq() calls. We use an AtomicInteger because this field is not protected by either lock: An enqueuer and a dequeuer may access it concurrently.

To enqueue an item, a thread acquires the enqLock (line 30), and reads the size field (line 32). If that field is equal to the capacity, the queue is full, and the enqueuer must wait until a dequeuer makes room. The enqueuer waits on notFullCondition (line 33), releasing the enqLock temporarily, and blocking until that condition is signaled. Each time the thread awakens, it checks whether there is room; if not, it goes back to sleep.

Once the enqueuer determines there is room, it can proceed to completion. No other thread can fill the queue while the enqueue is in progress: All other enqueuers are locked out, and concurrent dequeuers only increase the space available.

We must carefully check that this implementation does not suffer from the kind of "lost-wakeup" bug described in Chapter 8. Care is needed because an enqueuer encounters a full queue in two steps: First, it sees that size is the queue capacity, and second, it waits on notFullCondition until there is room in the queue. When

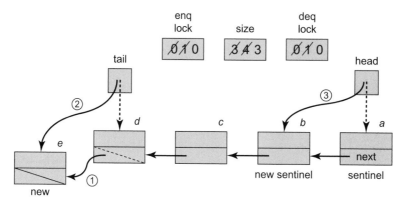

FIGURE 10.6

The enq() and deq() methods of the BoundedQueue with four slots. First a node is enqueued into the queue by acquiring the enqLock. The enq() checks that the size is 3, which is less than the bound. It then redirects the next field of the node referenced by the tail field (step 1), redirects tail to the new node (step 2), increments the size to 4, and releases the lock. Since size is now 4, any further calls to enq() will cause the threads to block until the notFullCondition is signaled by some deq(). Next, a node is dequeued from the queue by some thread. The deq() acquires the deqLock, reads the new value b from the successor of the node referenced by head (this node is the current sentinel), redirects head to this successor node (step 3), decrements the size to 3, and releases the lock. Before completing the deq(), because the size was 4 when it started, the thread acquires the enqLock and signals any enqueuers waiting on notFullCondition that they can proceed.

a dequeuer changes the queue from full to nonfull, it acquires enqLock and signals notFullCondition. Even though the size field is not protected by the enqLock, the dequeuer acquires the enqLock before it signals the condition, so the dequeuer cannot signal between the enqueuer's two steps.

To dequeue an item, a thread acquires the deqLock and checks whether the queue is empty. However, unlike in the enq() method, a dequeuer does not read the size field. Instead, it checks whether head.next == **null** (line 55); if so, the abstract queue is empty and the thread must wait until an item is enqueued. Like in the enq() method, the dequeuer waits on notEmptyCondition, which temporarily releases deqLock, and blocks until the condition is signaled. Each time the thread awakens, it checks whether the queue is empty, and if so, goes back to sleep.

Once a dequeuer establishes that the queue is nonempty, the queue will remain nonempty for the duration of the deq() call, because all other dequeuers have been locked out. Because the queue is nonempty, it has a nonsentinel node; the dequeuer accesses the first such node (i.e., the node referenced by the sentinel node's next field). It reads this node's value field, and makes the node the new sentinel node by setting the queue's head to refer to it. The dequeuer then decrements size and releases the deqLock. If the dequeuer found the former size was the queue capacity, then there may be enqueuers waiting on notEmptyCondition, so the dequeuer acquires enqLock, and signals all such threads to wake up.

Note that the abstract queue's last item is not always the one in the node referenced by tail. An item is logically added to the queue as soon as the last node's next field is redirected to the new node, even if the enqueuer has not yet updated tail (i.e., an enq() call linearizes to line 34). For example, suppose a thread is in the process of inserting a new node: It has acquired the enqLock and redirected the last node to point to the new node, but has not yet redirected the tail field. A concurrent dequeuing thread could acquire the deqLock, read and return the new node's value, redirect the head to the new node, and decrement size, all before the enqueuer redirects tail to the newly inserted node. In this example, size would be negative temporarily because the dequeuer decrements it before the enqueuer increments it. The enqueuer need not wake any waiting dequeuers in this case, because the item it enqueued has already been dequeued.

One drawback of this implementation is that concurrent enq() and deq() calls interfere with each other, but not through locks. All method calls apply getAndIncrement() or getAndDecrement() calls to the size field. These methods are more expensive than ordinary reads and writes, and they could cause a sequential bottleneck.

We can reduce such interactions by splitting this field into two: enqSideSize is an integer field incremented by enq(), and deqSideSize is an integer field decremented by deq(); the actual size of the queue is the sum of these two counters (deqSideSize is always 0 or negative). A thread calling enq() tests enqSideSize, and as long as it is less than the capacity, it proceeds. When the field reaches capacity, the thread locks deqLock, adds deqSideSize to enqSideSize, and resets deqSideSize to 0. Instead of synchronizing on every method call, this technique synchronizes sporadically when the enqueuer's size estimate becomes too large.

10.4 **An unbounded total queue**

We now describe an implementation of an unbounded queue. The enq() method always enqueues its item, and deq() throws EmptyException if there is no item to dequeue. The representation is the same as the bounded queue, except there is no need to count the number of items in the queue, or to provide conditions on which to wait. As shown in Figs. 10.7 and 10.8, this algorithm is simpler than the bounded algorithm.

This queue cannot deadlock, because each method acquires only one lock, either enqLock or deqLock. A sentinel node alone in the queue will never be deleted, so each enq() call will succeed as soon as it acquires the lock. Of course, a deq() method may fail if the queue is empty (i.e., if head.next is *null*). As in the bounded queue implementation, an item is actually enqueued when the enq() call sets the last node's next field to the new node, even before enq() resets tail to refer to the new node. After that instant, the new item is reachable along a chain of the next references. As usual, the queue's actual head and tail are not necessarily the items referenced by head and tail. Instead, the actual head is the item reference by the successor of head,

```
1    public void enq(T x) {
2      Node e = new Node(x);
3      enqLock.lock();
4      try {
5        tail.next = e;
6        tail = e;
7      } finally {
8        enqLock.unlock();
9      }
10   }
```

FIGURE 10.7

The UnboundedQueue<T> class: the enq() method.

```
11   public T deq() throws EmptyException {
12     T result;
13     deqLock.lock();
14     try {
15       if (head.next == null) {
16         throw new EmptyException();
17       }
18       result = head.next.value;
19       head = head.next;
20     } finally {
21       deqLock.unlock();
22     }
23     return result;
24   }
```

FIGURE 10.8

The UnboundedQueue<T> class: the deq() method.

and the actual tail is the last item reachable from the head. Both the enq() and deq() methods are total as they do not wait for the queue to become empty or full.

10.5 A lock-free unbounded queue

We now describe a lock-free unbounded queue implementation. Figs. 10.9–10.12 show the LockFreeQueue<T> class, a natural extension of the unbounded total queue of Section 10.4. It prevents method calls from starving by having the quicker threads help the slower threads.

As before, we represent the queue as a list of nodes, in which the first node is a sentinel whose value is meaningless. However, as shown in Figs. 10.9 and 10.10,

```
1  public class LockFreeQueue<T> {
2    AtomicReference<Node> head, tail;
3    public LockFreeQueue() {
4      Node node = new Node(null);
5      head = new AtomicReference(node);
6      tail = new AtomicReference(node);
7    }
8    ...
9  }
```

FIGURE 10.9

The LockFreeQueue<> class: fields and constructor.

```
10   public class Node {
11     public T value;
12     public AtomicReference<Node> next;
13     public Node(T value) {
14       this.value = value;
15       next = new AtomicReference<Node>(null);
16     }
17   }
```

FIGURE 10.10

The LockFreeQueue<T> class: list node.

```
18   public void enq(T value) {
19     Node node = new Node(value);
20     while (true) {
21       Node last = tail.get();
22       Node next = last.next.get();
23       if (last == tail.get()) {
24         if (next == null) {
25           if (last.next.compareAndSet(next, node)) {
26             tail.compareAndSet(last, node);
27             return;
28           }
29         } else {
30           tail.compareAndSet(last, next);
31         }
32       }
33     }
34   }
```

FIGURE 10.11

The LockFreeQueue<T> class: the enq() method.

```
35    public T deq() throws EmptyException {
36      while (true) {
37        Node first = head.get();
38        Node last = tail.get();
39        Node next = first.next.get();
40        if (first == head.get()) {
41          if (first == last) {
42            if (next == null) {
43              throw new EmptyException();
44            }
45            tail.compareAndSet(last, next);
46          } else {
47            T value = next.value;
48            if (head.compareAndSet(first, next))
49              return value;
50          }
51        }
52      }
53    }
```

FIGURE 10.12

The LockFreeQueue<T> class: the deq() method.

head and tail fields are AtomicReference<Node> fields that refer to the first node and the last node in the queue, respectively, and each node's next field is an AtomicReference<Node> that refers to the next node in the list. The queue constructor creates a new sentinel node and sets both head and tail to refer to it.

The enq() method (Fig. 10.11) creates a new node (line 19), locates the last node in the queue (lines 21–22), and then updates the list to append the new node. This method is *lazy*: It does the update in two distinct steps, illustrated in Fig. 10.13:

1. it calls compareAndSet() to append the new node (line 25), and then
2. it calls compareAndSet() to change the queue's tail field from the prior last node to the new last node (line 26).

Because these two steps are not executed atomically, every other method call must be prepared to encounter a half-finished enq() call, and to finish the job. This is a real-world example of the "helping" technique we first saw in the universal construction of Chapter 6.

We now review all the steps in detail. An enqueuer thread *A* creates a new node with the new value to be enqueued (line 19), and finds the node that appears to be last by reading tail (line 21–23). To verify that the node found is indeed last, *A* checks that it has no successor (line 24). If so, *A* attempts to append the new node by calling compareAndSet() (line 25). (A compareAndSet() is required because other threads may be trying the same thing.) If the compareAndSet() succeeds, *A* uses a sec-

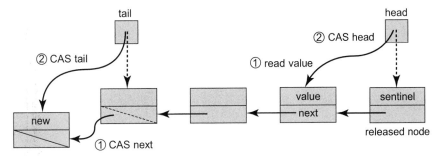

FIGURE 10.13

The enq() and deq() methods of the LockFreeQueue. The enq() method is lazy: a node is inserted into the queue in two steps. First, a compareAndSet() call changes the next field of the node referenced by the queue's tail from *null* to the new node. Then a compareAndSet() call advances tail itself to refer to the new node. An item is removed from the queue by checking that the sentinel has a successor, and then calling compareAndSet() to redirect head from the current sentinel to its successor, making the latter the new sentinel. The item removed is the one referred to by the new sentinel. Both enq() and deq() methods help complete unfinished tail updates.

ond compareAndSet() to advance tail to the new node (line 26). Even if this second compareAndSet() call fails, *A* can still return successfully because, as we will see, this compareAndSet() fails only if some other thread "helped" *A* by advancing tail.

If the tail node has a successor (line 29), then some other enqueuer must have appended its node but not updated tail before *A* read it. In this case, *A* tries to "help" that other thread by advancing tail to refer directly to the successor (line 30) before trying again to insert its own node.

This enq() is total, meaning that it never waits for a dequeuer. A successful enq() is linearized at the instant where the executing thread (or a concurrent helping thread) successfully calls compareAndSet() to redirect the tail field to the new node at line 30.

The deq() method is similar to its counterpart from the UnboundedQueue. If the queue is nonempty, the dequeuer calls compareAndSet() to change head from the sentinel node to its successor, making the successor the new sentinel node. The deq() method makes sure that the queue is not empty in the same way as before: by checking that the next field of the head node is not *null*.

There is, however, a subtle issue in the lock-free case, depicted in Fig. 10.14: Before advancing head, a dequeuer must make sure that tail is not left referring to the sentinel node that is about to be removed from the queue. To avoid this problem we add a test: If head equals tail (line 41) and the (sentinel) node they refer to has a *nonnull* next field (line 42), then the tail is deemed to be lagging behind. In this case, as in the enq() method, the dequeuer attempts to help make tail consistent by swinging it to the sentinel node's successor (line 45), and only then updates head to remove the sentinel (line 48). As in the partial queue, the value is read from the successor of the sentinel node (line 47). If this method returns a value, then its lin-

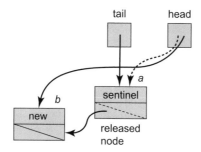

FIGURE 10.14

Why dequeuers must help advance `tail` in line 45 of Fig. 10.12. Consider the scenario in which a thread enqueuing node b has redirected a's `next` field to b, but has yet to redirect `tail` from a to b. If another thread starts dequeuing, it will read b's value and redirect `head` from a to b, effectively removing node a while `tail` still refers to it. To avoid this problem, the dequeuing thread must help advance `tail` from a to b before redirecting `head`.

earization point occurs when it successfully appends a node to the list (i.e., when the compareAndSet() at line 48 succeeds); otherwise it is linearized when it saw that the sentinel node has no successor (i.e., when it got a *null* value at line 39).

It is easy to check that the resulting queue is lock-free. Every method call first checks for an incomplete enq() call, and tries to complete it. In the worst case, all threads are trying to advance the queue's `tail` field, and one of them must succeed. A thread fails to enqueue or dequeue a node only if another thread's method call succeeds in changing the reference, so some method call always completes. As it turns out, being lock-free substantially enhances the performance of queue implementations, and lock-free algorithms often outperform the most efficient blocking ones.

10.6 Memory reclamation and the ABA problem

Our queue implementations so far rely on the Java garbage collector to recycle nodes after they have been dequeued. What happens if we choose to do our own memory management? There are several reasons why we might want to do this. Languages such as C or C++ do not provide garbage collection. Even if garbage collection is available, it is often more efficient for a class to do its own memory management, particularly if it creates and releases many small objects. Finally, if the garbage collection process is not lock-free, we might want to supply our own lock-free memory reclamation.

A natural way to recycle nodes in a lock-free manner is to have each thread maintain its own private (i.e., thread-local) *free list* of unused queue entries.

```
ThreadLocal<Node> freeList = new ThreadLocal<Node>() {
  protected Node initialValue() { return null; };
};
```

(a)

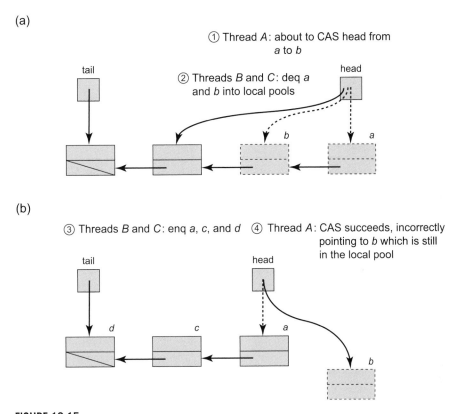

① Thread *A*: about to CAS head from
a to *b*

② Threads *B* and *C*: deq *a*
and *b* into local pools

tail

head

b

a

(b)

③ Threads *B* and *C*: enq *a*, *c*, and *d*   ④ Thread *A*: CAS succeeds, incorrectly
pointing to *b* which is still
in the local pool

tail

head

d

c

a

b

FIGURE 10.15

An ABA scenario: Assume that we use local pools of recycled nodes in our lock-free queue
algorithm. In part (a), the dequeuer thread *A* observes that the sentinel node is *a*, and next
node is *b*. (Step 1) It then prepares to update head by applying a compareAndSet() with old
value *a* and new value *b*. (Step 2) Suppose, however, that before it takes another step, other
threads dequeue *b*, then its successor, placing both *a* and *b* in the free pool. In part (b),
(Step 3) node *a* is reused, and eventually reappears as the sentinel node in the queue.
(Step 4) Thread *A* now wakes up, calls compareAndSet(), and succeeds in setting head to *b*,
since the old value of head is indeed *a*. Now, head is incorrectly set to a recycled node.

When an enqueuing thread needs a new node, it tries to remove one from its thread-
local free list. If the free list is empty, it simply allocates a node using the **new** operator.
When a dequeuing thread is ready to retire a node, it links it back onto the thread-local
list. Because the list is thread-local, there is no need for expensive synchronization.
This design works well as long as each thread performs roughly the same number of
enqueues and dequeues. If there is an imbalance, then there may be a need for more
complex techniques, such as periodically stealing nodes from other threads.

Surprisingly, perhaps, the lock-free queue will not work if nodes are recycled
in the most straightforward way. Consider the scenario depicted in Fig. 10.15. In

part (a), the dequeuing thread A observes the sentinel node is a, and the next node is b. It then prepares to update head by calling compareAndSet() with old value a and new value b. Before it takes another step, other threads dequeue b and its successor, placing both a and b in the free pool. Node a is recycled, and eventually reappears as the sentinel node in the queue, as depicted in part (b). The thread now wakes up, calls compareAndSet(), and succeeds, since the old value of the head is indeed a. Unfortunately, it has redirected head to a recycled node!

This phenomenon is called the *ABA problem*. It shows up often, especially in dynamic memory algorithms that use conditional synchronization operations such as compareAndSet(). Typically, a reference about to be modified by a compareAndSet() changes from a to b and back to a again. As a result, the compareAndSet() call succeeds even though its effect on the data structure has changed, and no longer has the desired effect.

One straightforward way to fix this problem is to tag each atomic reference with a unique *stamp*. An AtomicStampedReference<T> object, described in detail in Pragma 10.6.1, encapsulates both a reference to an object of Type T and an integer *stamp*. These fields can be atomically updated either together or individually.

PRAGMA 10.6.1

The AtomicStampedReference<T> class encapsulates both a reference to an object of Type T and an integer *stamp*. It generalizes the AtomicMarkableReference<T> class (Pragma 9.8.1), replacing the Boolean *mark* with an integer stamp.

We most commonly use this stamp as a *version number* to avoid the ABA problem, incrementing the value of the stamp each time we modify the object. Sometimes, as in the LockFreeExchanger<> class of Chapter 11, we use the stamp to hold one of a finite set of states.

The stamp and reference fields can be updated atomically, either together or individually. For example, the compareAndSet() method tests expected reference and stamp values, and if both tests succeed, replaces them with updated reference and stamp values. The get() method has an unusual interface: It returns the object's reference value and stores the stamp value in an integer array argument. Fig. 10.16 illustrates the signatures for these methods.

In a language like C or C++, one could provide this functionality efficiently in a 64-bit architecture by "stealing" bits from pointers. A 32-bit architecture would probably require a level of indirection.

Fig. 10.17 shows the deq() method using the AtomicStampedReference<Node> to avoid the ABA problem. Each time through the loop, it reads both the reference and stamp values for the first, next, and last nodes (lines 6–8). It uses compareAndSet() to compare both the reference and the stamp (line 18). It increments the stamp each time it uses compareAndSet() to update a reference (lines 15 and 18).[1]

---

[1] For simplicity, we ignore the (remote) possibility that the stamp could wrap around and cause an error.

```
1   public boolean compareAndSet(T expectedReference,
2                                T newReference,
3                                int expectedStamp,
4                                int newStamp);
5   public T get(int[] stampHolder);
6   public T getReference();
7   public int getStamp();
8   public void set(T newReference, int newStamp);
```

FIGURE 10.16

The AtomicStampedReference<T> class: the compareAndSet() and get() methods. The compareAndSet() method tests and updates both the stamp and reference fields; the get() method returns the encapsulated reference and stores the stamp at position 0 in the argument array; the getReference() and getStamp() methods return the reference and stamp, respectively; and the put() method updates the encapsulated reference and the stamp.

```
1    public T deq() throws EmptyException {
2      int[] lastStamp = new int[1];
3      int[] firstStamp = new int[1];
4      int[] nextStamp = new int[1];
5      while (true) {
6        Node first = head.get(firstStamp);
7        Node last = tail.get(lastStamp);
8        Node next = first.next.get(nextStamp);
9        if (head.getStamp() == firstStamp[0]) {
10         if (first == last) {
11           if (next == null) {
12             throw new EmptyException();
13           }
14           tail.compareAndSet(last, next,
15               lastStamp[0], lastStamp[0]+1);
16         } else {
17           T value = next.value;
18           if (head.compareAndSet(first, next, firstStamp[0],
19                     firstStamp[0]+1)) {
19             free(first);
20             return value;
21           }
22         }
23       }
24     }
25   }
```

FIGURE 10.17

The LockFreeQueueRecycle<T> class: The deq() method uses stamps to avoid ABA.

The ABA problem can occur in many synchronization scenarios, not just those involving conditional synchronization. For example, it can occur when using only loads and stores. Conditional synchronization operations such as *load-linked/store-conditional*, available on some architectures (see Appendix B), avoid the ABA problem by testing not whether a value is the same at two points in time, but whether the value has ever changed between those points.

10.6.1 A naïve synchronous queue

We now turn our attention to an even tighter kind of synchronization. One or more *producer* threads produce items to be removed, in FIFO order, by one or more *consumer* threads. Here, however, producers and consumers *rendezvous* with one another: A producer that puts an item in the queue blocks until that item is removed by a consumer, and vice versa. Such rendezvous synchronization is built into languages such as CSP and Ada.

Fig. 10.18 shows he SynchronousQueue<T> class, a straightforward monitor-based synchronous queue implementation. It has the following fields: item is the first item waiting to be dequeued, enqueuing is a Boolean value used by enqueuers to synchronize among themselves, lock is the lock used for mutual exclusion, and condition is used to block partial methods. If the enq() method finds enqueuing to be *true* (line 10), then another enqueuer has supplied an item and is waiting to rendezvous with a dequeuer, so the enqueuer repeatedly releases the lock, sleeps, and, when it awakens, checks whether enqueuing has become *false* (line 11). When this condition is satisfied, the enqueuer sets enqueuing to *true*, which locks out other enqueuers until the current rendezvous is complete, and sets item to refer to the new item (lines 12–13). It then notifies any waiting threads (line 14), and waits until item becomes *null* (lines 15–16). When the wait is over, the rendezvous has occurred, so the enqueuer sets enqueuing to *false*, notifies any waiting threads, and returns (lines 17 and 19).

The deq() method simply waits until item is not *null* (lines 26–27), records the item, sets the item field to *null*, and notifies any waiting threads before returning the item (lines 28–31).

Although the design of the queue is relatively simple, it incurs a high synchronization cost. Whenever one thread might wake up another, both enqueuers and dequeuers wake up all waiting threads, leading to a number of wakeups quadratic in the number of waiting threads. Although it is possible to use multiple condition objects to reduce the number of wakeups, it is still necessary to block on every call, which is expensive.

10.7 Dual data structures

To reduce the synchronization overheads of the synchronous queue, we consider an alternative synchronous queue implementation that treats enq() and deq() methods symmetrically, splitting a deq() method call that finds the queue empty into two steps. In the first step, the dequeuer puts a *reservation* object in the queue, indicating that

```
1   public class SynchronousQueue<T> {
2     T item = null;
3     boolean enqueuing;
4     Lock lock;
5     Condition condition;
6     ...
7     public void enq(T value) {
8       lock.lock();
9       try {
10        while (enqueuing)
11          condition.await();
12        enqueuing = true;
13        item = value;
14        condition.signalAll();
15        while (item != null)
16          condition.await();
17        enqueuing = false;
18        condition.signalAll();
19      } finally {
20        lock.unlock();
21      }
22    }
23    public T deq() {
24      lock.lock();
25      try {
26        while (item == null)
27          condition.await();
28        T t = item;
29        item = null;
30        condition.signalAll();
31        return t;
32      } finally {
33        lock.unlock();
34      }
35    }
36  }
```

FIGURE 10.18

The SynchronousQueue<T> class.

the dequeuer is waiting for an enqueuer with which to rendezvous. The reservation object contains an empty slot, on which the dequeuer spins until the slot is occupied; an enqueuer *fulfills* the reservation by depositing an item into that slot. Similarly, when an enqueuer adds an item to the queue, if there is no reservation to fulfill, it spins on the item until it is removed by a dequeuer. The queue contains either only

```
1    private enum NodeType {ITEM, RESERVATION};
2    private class Node {
3      volatile NodeType type;
4      volatile AtomicReference<T> item;
5      volatile AtomicReference<Node> next;
6      Node(T myItem, NodeType myType) {
7        item = new AtomicReference<T>(myItem);
8        next = new AtomicReference<Node>(null);
9        type = myType;
10     }
11   }
```

FIGURE 10.19

The SynchronousDualQueue<T> class: queue node.

items waiting to be dequeued or only reservations waiting to be fulfilled, or it is empty; it never contains items and reservations at the same time.

This structure is called a *dual data structure*, because it can contain both items and reservations. It has a number of nice properties. First, waiting threads can spin on a locally cached flag, which we have seen is essential for scalability. Second, it ensures fairness in a natural way. Reservations are queued in the order they arrive, ensuring that requests are fulfilled in the same order. Note that this data structure is linearizable, since each partial method call can be ordered when it is fulfilled.

The queue is implemented as a list of nodes, where a node represents either an item waiting to be dequeued, or a reservation waiting to be fulfilled (Fig. 10.19). A node's type field indicates which. At any time, all nodes in the queue have the same type: Either the queue consists entirely of items waiting to be dequeued, or entirely of reservations waiting to be fulfilled.

When an item is enqueued, the node's item field holds the item, which is reset to *null* when that item is dequeued. When a reservation is enqueued, the node's item field is *null*, and is reset to an item when fulfilled by an enqueuer.

Fig. 10.20 shows the SynchronousDualQueue's constructor and enq() method. (The deq() method is symmetric.) As in earlier queues we have considered, the head field always refers to a *sentinel* node that serves as a placeholder, and whose actual value (and type) is unimportant. The queue is empty when head and tail refer to the same node (i.e., the sentinel node). The constructor creates a sentinel node with an arbitrary value, referred to by both head and tail.

The enq() method first checks whether the queue is empty or contains enqueued items waiting to be dequeued (line 21). If so, then just as in the lock-free queue, it reads the queue's tail field (line 22), and checks that the values read are consistent (line 23). If the tail field does not refer to the last node in the queue, then the method advances the tail field and starts over (lines 24–25). Otherwise, the enq() method tries to append the new node to the end of the queue by resetting the tail node's next field to refer to the new node (line 26). If it succeeds, it tries to advance the tail to the

```
12    public SynchronousDualQueue() {
13      Node sentinel = new Node(null, NodeType.ITEM);
14      head = new AtomicReference<Node>(sentinel);
15      tail = new AtomicReference<Node>(sentinel);
16    }
17    public void enq(T e) {
18      Node offer = new Node(e, NodeType.ITEM);
19      while (true) {
20        Node t = tail.get(), h = head.get();
21        if (h == t || t.type == NodeType.ITEM) {
22          Node n = t.next.get();
23          if (t == tail.get()) {
24            if (n != null) {
25              tail.compareAndSet(t, n);
26            } else if (t.next.compareAndSet(n, offer)) {
27              tail.compareAndSet(t, offer);
28              while (offer.item.get() == e);
29              h = head.get();
30              if (offer == h.next.get())
31                head.compareAndSet(h, offer);
32              return;
33            }
34          }
35        } else {
36          Node n = h.next.get();
37          if (t != tail.get() || h != head.get() || n == null) {
38            continue;
39          }
40          boolean success = n.item.compareAndSet(null, e);
41          head.compareAndSet(h, n);
42          if (success)
43            return;
44        }
45      }
46    }
```

FIGURE 10.20

The SynchronousDualQueue<T> class: enq() method and constructor.

newly appended node (line 27), and then spins, waiting for a dequeuer to announce that it has dequeued the item by setting the node's item field to *null*. Once the item is dequeued, the method tries to clean up by making its node the new sentinel. This last step serves only to enhance performance, because the implementation remains correct, whether or not the method advances the head reference.

If, however, the enq() method discovers that the queue contains dequeuers' reservations waiting to be fulfilled, then it tries to find a reservation to fulfill. Since the queue's head node is a sentinel with no meaningful value, enq() reads the head's successor (line 36), checks that the values it has read are consistent (lines 37–39), and tries to switch that node's item field from *null* to the item being enqueued. Whether or not this step succeeds, the method tries to advance head (line 41). If the compareAndSet() call succeeds (line 40), the method returns; otherwise it retries.

10.8 Chapter notes

The partial queue employs a mixture of techniques adapted from Doug Lea [110] and from an algorithm by Maged Michael and Michael Scott [125]. The lock-free queue is a slightly simplified version of a queue algorithm by Maged Michael and Michael Scott [125]. The synchronous queue implementations are adapted from algorithms by Bill Scherer, Doug Lea, and Michael Scott [167].

10.9 Exercises

Exercise 10.1. Change the SynchronousDualQueue<T> class to work correctly with *null* items.

Exercise 10.2. Consider the queue presented in Fig. 10.21, a variant of the simple lock-free queue for a single enqueuer and a single dequeuer described in Chapter 3. This queue is blocking; that is, removing an item from an empty queue, or adding an item to a full one, causes the threads to spin. Surprisingly, this queue requires only loads and stores and not a more powerful read–modify–write synchronization operation.

Does the queue implementation, however, require the use of a memory barrier? If so, where in the code is such a barrier needed and why? If not, explain why not.

Exercise 10.3. Design a bounded lock-based queue implementation using an array instead of a linked list.

1. Allow parallelism by using two separate locks for head and tail.
2. Try to transform your algorithm to be lock-free. Where do you run into difficulty?

Exercise 10.4. In the deq() method of the unbounded lock-based queue (Fig. 10.8), is it necessary to hold the lock when checking that the queue is not empty? Explain.

Exercise 10.5. In Dante's *Inferno*, he describes a visit to Hell. In a recently discovered chapter, he encounters five people sitting at a table with a pot of stew in the middle. Although each one holds a spoon that reaches the pot, each spoon's handle is much longer than each person's arm, so no one can feed him- or herself. They are famished and desperate.

Dante then suggests: "Why do you not feed one another?"
The rest of the chapter is lost.

```
1   class TwoThreadLockFreeQueue<T> {
2     int head = 0, tail = 0;
3     T[] items;
4     public TwoThreadLockFreeQueue(int capacity) {
5       head = 0; tail = 0;
6       items = (T[]) new Object[capacity];
7     }
8     public void enq(T x) {
9       while (tail - head == items.length) {};
10      items[tail % items.length] = x;
11      tail++;
12    }
13    public Object deq() {
14      while (tail - head == 0) {};
15      Object x = items[head % items.length];
16      head++;
17      return x;
18    }
19  }
```

FIGURE 10.21

A lock-free FIFO queue with blocking semantics for a single enqueuer and single dequeuer. The queue is implemented in an array. Initially the head and tail fields are equal and the queue is empty. If the head and tail differ by capacity, then the queue is full. The enq() method reads the head field, and if the queue is full, it repeatedly checks the head until the queue is no longer full. It then stores the object in the array, and increments the tail field. The deq() method works in a symmetric way.

1. Write an algorithm to allow these unfortunates to feed one another. Two or more people may not feed the same person at the same time. Your algorithm must be, well, starvation-free.
2. Discuss the advantages and disadvantages of your algorithm. Is it centralized or decentralized, high or low in contention, and deterministic or randomized?

Exercise 10.6. Consider the linearization points of the enq() and deq() methods of the lock-free queue (Figs.10.11 and 10.12).

1. Can we choose the point at which the returned value is read from a node as the linearization point of a successful deq()? Explain.
2. Can we choose the linearization point of the enq() method to be the point at which the tail field is updated, possibly by other threads? Explain.

Exercise 10.7. Consider the unbounded queue implementation shown in Fig. 10.22. This queue is blocking, meaning that the deq() method does not return until it has found an item to dequeue.

The queue has two fields: items is a very large array, and tail is the index of the next unused element in the array.

```
1   public class HWQueue<T> {
2     AtomicReference<T>[] items;
3     AtomicInteger tail;
4     ...
5     public void enq(T x) {
6       int i = tail.getAndIncrement();
7       items[i].set(x);
8     }
9     public T deq() {
10      while (true) {
11        int range = tail.get();
12        for (int i = 0; i < range; i++) {
13          T value = items[i].getAndSet(null);
14          if (value != null) {
15            return value;
16          }
17        }
18      }
19    }
20  }
```

FIGURE 10.22

Queue used in Exercise 10.7.

1. Are the enq() and deq() methods wait-free? If not, are they lock-free? Explain.
2. Identify linearization points for the enq() and deq() methods. (Careful! They may be execution-dependent.)

Stacks and elimination

11

11.1 Introduction

The Stack<T> class is a collection of items (of type T) that provides push() and pop() methods satisfying the *last-in-first-out* (LIFO) property: The last item pushed is the first popped. This chapter considers how to implement concurrent stacks. At first glance, stacks seem to provide little opportunity for concurrency, because push() and pop() calls seem to need to synchronize at the top of the stack.

Surprisingly, perhaps, stacks are not inherently sequential. In this chapter, we show how to implement concurrent stacks that can achieve a high degree of parallelism. As a first step, we consider how to build a lock-free stack in which pushes and pops synchronize at a single location.

11.2 An unbounded lock-free stack

Fig. 11.1 shows a concurrent LockFreeStack class. The lock-free stack is a linked list, where the top field points to the first node (or *null* if the stack is empty.) For

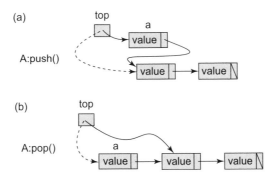

FIGURE 11.1

A lock-free stack. In part (a), a thread pushes value *a* onto the stack by applying a compareAndSet() to the top field. In part (b), a thread pops value *a* from the stack by applying a compareAndSet() to the top field.

The Art of Multiprocessor Programming. https://doi.org/10.1016/B978-0-12-415950-1.00021-5

```
1   public class LockFreeStack<T> {
2     AtomicReference<Node> top = new AtomicReference<Node>(null);
3     static final int MIN_DELAY = ...;
4     static final int MAX_DELAY = ...;
5     Backoff backoff = new Backoff(MIN_DELAY, MAX_DELAY);
6
7     protected boolean tryPush(Node node){
8       Node oldTop = top.get();
9       node.next = oldTop;
10      return(top.compareAndSet(oldTop, node));
11    }
12    public void push(T value) {
13      Node node = new Node(value);
14      while (true) {
15        if (tryPush(node)) {
16          return;
17        } else {
18          backoff.backoff();
19        }
20      }
21    }
22    ...
23  }
```

FIGURE 11.2

The LockFreeStack<T> class: In the push() method, threads alternate between trying to alter the top reference by calling tryPush(), and backing off using the Backoff class from Fig. 7.5.

```
24  public class Node {
25    public T value;
26    public Node next;
27    public Node(T value) {
28      value = value;
29      next = null;
30    }
31  }
```

FIGURE 11.3

Lock-free stack list node.

simplicity, we usually assume it is illegal to add a *null* value to a stack. Code for this class appears in Figs. 11.2–11.4.

The push() method creates a new node (line 13), and then calls tryPush() to make the new node's next field point to the current top-of-stack and then tries to swing the top reference from the current top-of-stack to the new node. If tryPush() succeeds,

```
32    protected Node tryPop() throws EmptyException {
33      Node oldTop = top.get();
34      if (oldTop == null) {
35        throw new EmptyException();
36      }
37      Node newTop = oldTop.next;
38      if (top.compareAndSet(oldTop, newTop)) {
39        return oldTop;
40      } else {
41        return null;
42      }
43    }
44    public T pop() throws EmptyException {
45      while (true) {
46        Node returnNode = tryPop();
47        if (returnNode != null) {
48          return returnNode.value;
49        } else {
50          backoff.backoff();
51        }
52      }
53    }
```

FIGURE 11.4

The LockFreeStack<T> class: The pop() method alternates between trying to change the top field and backing off.

push() returns; if not, the tryPush() attempt is repeated after backing off. The pop() method calls tryPop(), which uses compareAndSet() to try to remove the first node from the stack. If it succeeds, it returns the node; otherwise it returns *null*. (It throws an exception if the stack is empty.) The tryPop() method is called until it succeeds (or throws an exception), at which point pop() returns the value from the removed node.

As we have seen in Chapter 7, one can significantly reduce contention at the top field using exponential back-off (see Fig. 7.5). Accordingly, both the push() and pop() methods back off after an unsuccessful call to tryPush() or tryPop().

This implementation is lock-free because a thread fails to complete a push() or pop() method call only if there were infinitely many successful calls that modified the top of the stack. The linearization point of both the push() and the pop() methods is the successful compareAndSet(), or the seeing top equal to *null* (lines 33 and 34), in the case of a pop() on an empty stack. Note that the compareAndSet() call by pop() does not have an ABA problem (see Chapter 10) because the Java garbage collector ensures that a node cannot be reused by any thread, as long as that node is accessible to another thread. Designing a lock-free stack that avoids the ABA problem without a garbage collector is left as an exercise.

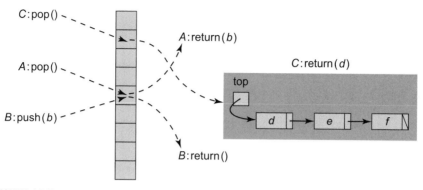

FIGURE 11.5

The EliminationBackoffStack<T> class. Each thread selects a random location in the array. If thread A's pop() and B's push() calls arrive at the same location at about the same time, then they exchange values without accessing the shared LockFreeStack. Thread C that does not meet another thread eventually pops the shared LockFreeStack.

11.3 Elimination

The LockFreeStack implementation scales poorly, not so much because the stack's top field is a source of *contention*, but primarily because it is a *sequential bottleneck*: Method calls can proceed only one after the other, ordered by compareAndSet() calls successfully applied to the stack's top field. Although exponential back-off can reduce contention, it does nothing to alleviate the sequential bottleneck.

To make the stack parallel, we exploit this simple observation: A push() immediately followed by a pop() cancel each other out, and the stack's state does not change. It is as if both operations never happened. If one could somehow cause concurrent pairs of pushes and pops to cancel, then threads calling push() could exchange values with threads calling pop(), without ever modifying the stack itself. These two calls would *eliminate* one another.

Fig. 11.5 depicts threads eliminating one another through an EliminationArray, in which threads pick random array entries to try to meet complementary calls. Pairs of complementary push() and pop() calls exchange values and return. A thread whose call cannot be eliminated, either because it has failed to find a partner, or found a partner with the wrong kind of method call (such as a push() meeting a push()), can either try again to find a partner at a new location, or access the shared LockFreeStack. The combined data structure, array and shared stack, is linearizable because the shared stack is linearizable, and the eliminated calls can be ordered as if they happened at the point at which they exchanged values.

We can use the EliminationArray as a back-off scheme on a shared LockFreeStack. Each thread first accesses the LockFreeStack, and if it fails to complete its call (that is, the compareAndSet() attempt fails), it attempts to eliminate its call using the array instead of simply backing off. If it fails to eliminate itself, it calls the LockFreeStack again, and so on. We call this structure an EliminationBackoffStack.

11.4 The elimination back-off stack

We now show how to construct an EliminationBackoffStack, a lock-free linearizable stack implementation.

We are reminded of a story about two friends discussing politics on election day, each trying, to no avail, to convince the other to switch sides. Finally, one says to the other: "Look, it's clear that we are unalterably opposed on every political issue. Our votes will surely cancel out. Why not save ourselves some time and both agree to not vote today?"

The other agrees enthusiastically and they part.

Shortly after that, a friend of the first, who had heard the conversation, says, "That was a sporting offer you made."

"Not really," came the reply. "This is the third time I've done this today."

The principle behind our construction is the same. We wish to allow threads with pushes and pops to coordinate and cancel out, but must avoid a situation in which a thread can make a sporting offer to more than one other thread. To do so, we implement the EliminationArray using coordination structures called *exchangers*, objects that allow exactly two threads (and no more) to rendezvous and exchange values.

We already saw how to exchange values using locks in the synchronous queue of Chapter 10. Here, we need a lock-free exchange, one in which threads spin rather than block, as we expect them to wait only for very short durations.

11.4.1 A lock-free exchanger

A LockFreeExchanger<T> object permits two threads to exchange values of type T. If thread *A* calls the object's exchange() method with argument *a* and *B* calls the same object's exchange() method with argument *b*, then *A*'s call will return value *b* and vice versa. On a high level, the exchanger works by having the first thread arrive to write its value, and spin until a second arrives. The second then detects that the first is waiting, reads its value, and signals the exchange. They each have now read the other's value, and can return. The first thread's call may time out if the second does not show up, allowing it to leave the exchanger if it is unable to exchange a value within a reasonable duration.

The LockFreeExchanger<T> class, shown in Fig. 11.6, has a single field slot of type AtomicStampedReference<T> (see Pragma 10.6.1). The exchanger has three possible states: EMPTY, BUSY, or WAITING. The reference's stamp records the exchanger's state (line 14). The exchanger's main loop continues until the timeout limit passes, when it throws an exception (line 10). In the meantime, a thread reads the state of the slot (line 12) and proceeds as follows:

- If the state is EMPTY, then the thread tries to place its item in the slot and set the state to WAITING using compareAndSet() (line 16). If it fails, then some other thread has succeeded, so it retries. If it was successful (line 17), then its item is in the slot and the state is WAITING, so it spins, waiting for another thread to complete the exchange. If another thread shows up, it will take the item in the slot, replace it with

```
1   public class LockFreeExchanger<T> {
2     static final int EMPTY = ..., WAITING = ..., BUSY = ...;
3     AtomicStampedReference<T> slot = new AtomicStampedReference<T>(null, 0);
4     public T exchange(T myItem, long timeout, TimeUnit unit)
5       throws TimeoutException {
6       long nanos = unit.toNanos(timeout);
7       long timeBound = System.nanoTime() + nanos;
8       int[] stampHolder = {EMPTY};
9       while (true) {
10        if (System.nanoTime() > timeBound)
11          throw new TimeoutException();
12        T yrItem = slot.get(stampHolder);
13        int stamp = stampHolder[0];
14        switch(stamp) {
15        case EMPTY:
16          if (slot.compareAndSet(yrItem, myItem, EMPTY, WAITING)) {
17            while (System.nanoTime() < timeBound) {
18              yrItem = slot.get(stampHolder);
19              if (stampHolder[0] == BUSY) {
20                slot.set(null, EMPTY);
21                return yrItem;
22              }
23            }
24            if (slot.compareAndSet(myItem, null, WAITING, EMPTY)) {
25              throw new TimeoutException();
26            } else {
27              yrItem = slot.get(stampHolder);
28              slot.set(null, EMPTY);
29              return yrItem;
30            }
31          }
32          break;
33        case WAITING:
34          if (slot.compareAndSet(yrItem, myItem, WAITING, BUSY))
35            return yrItem;
36          break;
37        case BUSY:
38          break;
39        default: // impossible
40          ...
41        }
42      }
43    }
44  }
```

FIGURE 11.6

The LockFreeExchanger<T> class.

its own, and set the state to BUSY (line 19), indicating to the waiting thread that the exchange is complete. The waiting thread will consume the item and reset the state to EMPTY. Resetting to EMPTY can be done using a simple write because the waiting thread is the only one that can change the state from BUSY to EMPTY (line 20). If no other thread shows up, the waiting thread needs to reset the state of the slot to EMPTY. This change requires a compareAndSet() because other threads might be attempting to exchange by setting the state from WAITING to BUSY (line 24). If the call is successful, it raises a timeout exception. If, however, the call fails, some exchanging thread must have shown up, so the waiting thread completes the exchange (line 26).

- If the state is WAITING, then some thread is waiting and the slot contains its item. The thread uses compareAndSet() to try to exchange the item with its own and change the state from WAITING to BUSY (line 34). If it fails, because another thread succeeds or the waiting thread resets the state to EMPTY following a timeout, the thread must retry. If it succeeds in exchanging items, it can return the item.
- If the state is BUSY then two other threads are currently using the slot for an exchange and the thread must retry (line 37).

Note that the algorithm allows the inserted item to be *null*, something used later in the elimination array construction. There is no ABA problem because the compareAndSet() call that changes the state never inspects the item. The linearization point of a successful exchange occurs when the second thread to arrive changes the state from WAITING to BUSY (line 34). At this point both exchange() calls overlap, and the exchange is committed to being successful. The linearization point of an unsuccessful exchange occurs when the timeout exception is thrown.

The algorithm is lock-free because overlapping exchange() calls with sufficient time to exchange will fail only if other exchanges are repeatedly succeeding. Clearly, too short an exchange time can cause a thread never to succeed, so care must be taken when choosing timeout durations.

11.4.2 The elimination array

An EliminationArray is implemented as an array of Exchanger objects. A thread attempting to perform an exchange picks an array entry at random, and calls that entry's exchange() method, providing its own input as a value for exchange with another thread. Code for the EliminationArray appears in Fig. 11.7. The constructor takes as an argument the capacity of the array (the number of distinct exchangers). The EliminationArray class provides a single method, visit(), which takes timeout arguments. (Following the conventions used in the java.util.concurrent package, a timeout is expressed as a number and a time unit.) The visit() call takes a value of type T and either returns the value input by its exchange partner, or throws an exception if the timeout expires without exchanging a value with another thread. At any point in time, each thread will select a random location in a subrange of the array (line 11). This subrange will be determined dynamically based on the load on the data structure, and will be passed as a parameter to the visit() method.

```
1   public class EliminationArray<T> {
2     private static final int duration = ...;
3     LockFreeExchanger<T>[] exchanger;
4     public EliminationArray(int capacity) {
5       exchanger = (LockFreeExchanger<T>[]) new LockFreeExchanger[capacity];
6       for (int i = 0; i < capacity; i++) {
7         exchanger[i] = new LockFreeExchanger<T>();
8       }
9     }
10    public T visit(T value, int range) throws TimeoutException {
11      int slot = ThreadLocalRandom.current().nextInt(range);
12      return (exchanger[slot].exchange(value, duration,
13              TimeUnit.MILLISECONDS));
14    }
15  }
```

FIGURE 11.7

The EliminationArray<T> class: In each visit, a thread can choose dynamically the subrange of the array from which it will randomly select a slot.

It is critical that each thread uses its own random number generator to select its location. As discussed in Appendix A.2.5, if threads share a random number generator, they would introduce the contention that the elimination array is designed to avoid.

The EliminationBackoffStack is a subclass of LockFreeStack that overrides the push() and pop() methods, and adds an EliminationArray field. The new push() and pop() methods appear in Figs. 11.8 and 11.9. If tryPush() or tryPop() fails, instead of simply backing off, these methods try to use the EliminationArray to exchange values (lines 15 and 33). A push() call calls visit() with its input value as argument, a pop() call with *null* as argument. Both push() and pop() have a thread-local RangePolicy object that determines the EliminationArray subrange to be used.

When push() calls visit(), it selects a random array entry within its range and attempts to exchange a value with another thread. If the exchange is successful, the pushing thread checks whether the value was exchanged with a pop() method (line 17) by testing if the value exchanged was *null*. (Recall that pop() always offers *null* to the exchanger while push() always offers a *nonnull* value.) Symmetrically, when pop() calls visit(), it attempts an exchange, and if the exchange is successful, it checks (line 35) whether the value was exchanged with a push() call by checking whether it is not *null*.

The exchange may be unsuccessful, either because no exchange took place (the call to visit() timed out) or because the exchange was with the same type of operation (e.g., a pop() with a pop()). For brevity, we choose a simple approach to deal with such cases: we retry the tryPush() or tryPop() calls (lines 13 and 30).

One important parameter is the range of the EliminationArray from which a thread selects an Exchanger location. A smaller range increases the chance of a successful exchange when there are few threads, while a larger range lowers the chance

```
1   public class EliminationBackoffStack<T> extends LockFreeStack<T> {
2     static final int capacity = ...;
3     EliminationArray<T> eliminationArray = new EliminationArray<T>(capacity);
4     static ThreadLocal<RangePolicy> policy = new ThreadLocal<RangePolicy>() {
5       protected synchronized RangePolicy initialValue() {
6         return new RangePolicy();
7       }
8
9     public void push(T value) {
10      RangePolicy rangePolicy = policy.get();
11      Node node = new Node(value);
12      while (true) {
13        if (tryPush(node)) {
14          return;
15        } else try {
16          T otherValue = eliminationArray.visit(value, rangePolicy.getRange());
17          if (otherValue == null) {
18            rangePolicy.recordEliminationSuccess();
19            return; // exchanged with pop
20          }
21        } catch (TimeoutException ex) {
22          rangePolicy.recordEliminationTimeout();
23        }
24      }
25    }
26  }
```

FIGURE 11.8

The EliminationBackoffStack<T> class: This push() method overrides the LockFreeStack push() method. Instead of using a simple Backoff class, it uses an EliminationArray and a dynamic RangePolicy to select the subrange of the array within which to eliminate.

of threads waiting on a busy Exchanger (recall that an Exchanger can only handle one exchange at a time). Thus, if few threads access the array, they should choose a small range; as the number of threads increases, so should the range. One can control the range dynamically using a RangePolicy object that records both successful exchanges (as in line 36) and timeout failures (line 39). We ignore exchanges that fail because the operations do not match (such as push() with push()), because they account for a fixed fraction of the exchanges for any given distribution of push() and pop() calls. One simple policy is to shrink the range as the number of failures increases and vice versa.

There are many other possible policies. For example, one can devise a more elaborate range selection policy, vary the delays on the exchangers dynamically, add additional back-off delays before accessing the shared stack, and control whether to access the shared stack or the array dynamically. We leave these as exercises.

```
27    public T pop() throws EmptyException {
28      RangePolicy rangePolicy = policy.get();
29      while (true) {
30        Node returnNode = tryPop();
31        if (returnNode != null) {
32          return returnNode.value;
33        } else try {
34          T otherValue = eliminationArray.visit(null, rangePolicy.getRange());
35          if (otherValue != null) {
36            rangePolicy.recordEliminationSuccess();
37            return otherValue;
38          }
39        } catch (TimeoutException ex) {
40          rangePolicy.recordEliminationTimeout();
41        }
42      }
43    }
```

FIGURE 11.9

The EliminationBackoffStack<T> class: This pop() method overrides the LockFreeStack pop() method.

The EliminationBackoffStack is a linearizable stack: Any successful push() or pop() call that completes by accessing the LockFreeStack can be linearized at the point of its LockFreeStack access. Any pair of eliminated push() and pop() calls can be linearized when they collide. As noted earlier, the method calls completed through elimination do not affect the linearizability of those completed in the LockFreeStack, because they could have taken effect in any state of the LockFreeStack, and having taken effect, the state of the LockFreeStack would not have changed.

Because the EliminationArray is effectively used as a back-off scheme, we expect it to deliver performance comparable to the LockFreeStack at low loads. Unlike the LockFreeStack, it has the potential to scale. As the load increases, the number of successful eliminations will grow, allowing many operations to complete in parallel. Moreover, contention at the LockFreeStack is reduced because eliminated operations never access the stack.

11.5 Chapter notes

The LockFreeStack is credited to Treiber [162]. Actually, it predates Treiber's report in 1986. It was probably invented in the early 1970s to motivate the CAS operation on the IBM 370. The EliminationBackoffStack is due to Danny Hendler, Nir Shavit, and Lena Yerushalmi [62]. An efficient exchanger, which quite interestingly uses an elimination array, was introduced by Doug Lea, Michael Scott, and Bill Scherer [167]. A variant of this exchanger appears in the java.util.concurrent package. The EliminationBackoffStack we present here is modular, making use of exchangers, but somewhat inefficient. Mark Moir, Daniel Nussbaum, Ori Shalev, and Nir Shavit presented a highly effective implementation of an EliminationArray [131].

11.6 **Exercises**

Exercise 11.1. Design an unbounded lock-based Stack<T> implementation based on a linked list.

Exercise 11.2. Design a bounded lock-based Stack<T> using an array.

1. Use a single lock and a bounded array.
2. Try to make your algorithm lock-free. Where do you run into difficulty?

Exercise 11.3. Modify the unbounded lock-free stack of Section 11.2 to work in the absence of a garbage collector. Create a thread-local pool of preallo-cated nodes and recycle them. To avoid the ABA problem, consider using the AtomicStampedReference<T> class from java.util.concurrent.atomic (see Pragma 10.6.1), which encapsulates both a reference and an integer *stamp*.

Exercise 11.4. Discuss the back-off policies used in our implementation. Does it make sense to use the same shared Backoff object for both pushes and pops in our LockFreeStack<T> object? How else could we structure the back-off in space and time in the EliminationBackoffStack<T>?

Exercise 11.5. Implement a stack algorithm assuming there is a known bound on the difference between the total number of successful pushes and pops to the stack in any state of the execution.

Exercise 11.6. Consider the problem of implementing a bounded stack using an array indexed by a top counter, initially zero. In the absence of concurrency, these methods are almost trivial. To push an item, increment top to reserve an array entry, and then store the item at that index. To pop an item, decrement top, and return the item at the previous top index.

Clearly, this strategy does not work for concurrent implementations, because one cannot make atomic changes to multiple memory locations. A single synchronization operation can either increment or decrement the top counter, but not both, and there is no way atomically to increment the counter and store a value.

Nevertheless, Bob D. Hacker decides to solve this problem. He decides to adapt the dual data structure approach of Chapter 10 to implement a *dual* stack. His DualStack<T> class splits push() and pop() methods into *reservation* and *fulfillment* steps. Bob's implementation appears in Fig. 11.10.

The stack's top is indexed by the top field, an AtomicInteger manipulated only by getAndIncrement() and getAndDecrement() calls. Bob's push() method's reservation step reserves a slot by applying getAndIncrement() to top. Suppose the call returns

```
1    public class DualStack<T> {
2      private class Slot {
3        boolean full = false;
4        volatile T value = null;
5      }
6      Slot[] stack;
7      int capacity;
8      private AtomicInteger top = new AtomicInteger(0); // array index
9      public DualStack(int myCapacity) {
10       capacity = myCapacity;
11       stack = (Slot[]) new Object[capacity];
12       for (int i = 0; i < capacity; i++) {
13         stack[i] = new Slot();
14       }
15     }
16     public void push(T value) throws FullException {
17       while (true) {
18         int i = top.getAndIncrement();
19         if (i > capacity - 1) { // is stack full?
20           top.getAndDecrement(); // restore index
21           throw new FullException();
22         } else if (i >= 0) { // i in range, slot reserved
23           stack[i].value = value;
24           stack[i].full = true; // push fulfilled
25           return;
26         }
27       }
28     }
29     public T pop() throws EmptyException {
30       while (true) {
31         int i = top.getAndDecrement();
32         if (i < 0) { // is stack empty?
33           top.getAndDecrement() // restore index
34           throw new EmptyException();
35         } else if (i <= capacity - 1) {
36           while (!stack[i].full){};
37           T value = stack[i].value;
38           stack[i].full = false;
39           return value; // pop fulfilled
40         }
41       }
42     }
43   }
```

FIGURE 11.10

Bob's problematic dual stack.

index i. If i is in the range $0 \ldots$ capacity $- 1$, the reservation is complete. In the fulfillment phase, push(x) stores x at index i in the array, and raises the full flag to indicate that the value is ready to be read. The value field must be **volatile** to guarantee that once flag is raised, the value has already been written to index i of the array.

If the index returned from push()'s getAndIncrement() is less than 0, the push() method repeatedly retries getAndIncrement() until it returns an index greater than or equal to 0. The index could be less than 0 due to getAndDecrement() calls of failed pop() calls to an empty stack. Each such failed getAndDecrement() decrements the top by one more past the 0 array bound. If the index returned is greater than capacity-1, push() throws an exception because the stack is full.

The situation is symmetric for pop(). It checks that the index is within the bounds and removes an item by applying getAndDecrement() to top, returning index i. If i is in the range $0 \ldots$ capacity $- 1$, the reservation is complete. For the fulfillment phase, pop() spins on the full flag of array slot i, until it detects that the flag is true, indicating that the push() call is successful.

What is wrong with Bob's algorithm? Is this problem inherent or can you think of a way to fix it?

Exercise 11.7. Exercise 8.7 asks you to implement the Rooms interface, reproduced in Fig. 11.11. The Rooms class manages a collection of *rooms*, indexed from 0 to m (where m is a known constant). Threads can enter or exit any room in that range. Each room can hold an arbitrary number of threads simultaneously, but only one room can be occupied at a time. The last thread to leave a room triggers an onEmpty() handler, which runs while all rooms are empty.

Fig. 11.12 shows an incorrect concurrent stack implementation.

1. Explain why this stack implementation does not work.
2. Fix it by adding calls to a two-room Rooms class: one room for pushing and one for popping.

Exercise 11.8. This exercise is a follow-on to Exercise 11.7. Instead of having the push() method throw FullException, exploit the push room's exit handler to resize the

```
1   public interface Rooms {
2     public interface Handler {
3       void onEmpty();
4     }
5     void enter(int i);
6     boolean exit();
7     public void setExitHandler(int i, Rooms.Handler h) ;
8   }
```

FIGURE 11.11

The Rooms interface.

```
1   public class Stack<T> {
2     private AtomicInteger top;
3     private T[] items;
4     public Stack(int capacity) {
5       top = new AtomicInteger();
6       items = (T[]) new Object[capacity];
7     }
8     public void push(T x) throws FullException {
9       int i = top.getAndIncrement();
10      if (i >= items.length) { // stack is full
11        top.getAndDecrement(); // restore state
12        throw new FullException();
13      }
14      items[i] = x;
15    }
16    public T pop() throws EmptyException {
17      int i = top.getAndDecrement() - 1;
18      if (i < 0) {              // stack is empty
19        top.getAndIncrement(); // restore state
20        throw new EmptyException();
21      }
22      return items[i];
23    }
24  }
```

FIGURE 11.12

Unsynchronized concurrent stack.

array. Remember that no thread can be in any room when an exit handler is running, so (of course) only one exit handler can run at a time.

Counting, sorting, and distributed coordination

12

12.1 Introduction

This chapter shows how some important problems that seem inherently sequential can be made highly parallel by "spreading out" coordination tasks among multiple parties. What does this spreading out buy us?

To answer this question, we need to understand how to measure the performance of a concurrent data structure. There are two measures that come to mind: *latency*, the time it takes an individual method call to complete, and *throughput*, the overall rate at which method calls complete. For example, real-time applications might care more about latency, and databases might care more about throughput.

In Chapter 11, we saw how to apply distributed coordination to the EliminationBackoffStack class. Here, we cover several useful patterns for distributed coordination: combining, counting, diffraction, and sampling. Some are deterministic, while others use randomization. We also cover two basic structures underlying these patterns: trees and combinatorial networks. Interestingly, for some data structures based on distributed coordination, high throughput does not necessarily mean low latency.

12.2 Shared counting

We recall from Chapter 10 that a *pool* is a collection of items that provides put() and get() methods to insert and remove items (Fig. 10.1). Familiar classes such as stacks and queues can be viewed as pools that provide additional fairness guarantees.

One way to implement a pool is to use coarse-grained locking, perhaps making both put() and get() **synchronized** methods. The problem, of course, is that coarse-grained locking is heavy-handed: The lock creates both a *sequential bottleneck*, forcing all method calls to synchronize, and a *hotspot*, a source of memory contention. We would prefer to have Pool method calls work in parallel, with less synchronization and lower contention.

Let us consider the following alternative: The pool's items reside in a cyclic array, where each array entry contains either an item or *null*. We route threads through two counters. Threads calling put() increment one counter to choose an array index into which the new item should be placed. (If that entry is full, the thread waits until it becomes empty.) Similarly, threads calling get() increment another counter to choose an array index from which the new item should be removed. (If that entry is empty, the thread waits until it becomes full.)

This approach replaces one bottleneck, the lock, with two, the counters. Naturally, two bottlenecks are better than one (think about that claim for a second). We now explore the idea that shared counters need not be bottlenecks, and can be effectively parallelized. We face two challenges:

1. We must avoid *memory contention*, where too many threads try to access the same memory location, stressing the underlying communication network and cache-coherence protocols.
2. We must achieve real parallelism. Is incrementing a counter an inherently sequential operation, or is it possible for n threads to increment a counter faster than it takes one thread to increment a counter n times?

We now look at several ways to build highly parallel counters through data structures that coordinate the distribution of counter indices.

12.3 Software combining

Here is a linearizable shared-counter class using a pattern called *software combining*. A CombiningTree is a binary tree of *nodes*, where each node contains bookkeeping information. The counter's value is stored at the root. Each thread is assigned a leaf, and at most two threads share a leaf, so if there are p physical processors, then there are $\lceil p/2 \rceil$ leaves; the number of leaves in a combining tree is its *width*. To increment the counter, a thread starts at its leaf, and works its way up the tree to the root. If two threads reach a node at approximately the same time, then they *combine* their increments by adding them together. One thread, the *active* thread, propagates their combined increments up the tree, while the other, the *passive* thread, waits for the active thread to complete their combined work. A thread may be active at one level and become passive at a higher level.

For example, suppose threads A and B share a leaf node. They start at the same time, and their increments are combined at their shared leaf. The first one, say, B, actively continues up to the next level, with the mission of adding 2 to the counter value, while the second, A, passively waits for B to return from the root with an acknowledgment that A's increment has occurred. At the next level in the tree, B may combine with another thread C, and advance with the renewed intention of adding 3 to the counter value.

When a thread reaches the root, it adds the sum of its combined increments to the counter's current value. The thread then moves back down the tree, notifying each waiting thread that the increments are now complete.

Combining trees have an inherent disadvantage with respect to locks: Each increment has a higher latency, that is, the time it takes an individual method call to complete. With a lock, a getAndIncrement() call takes $O(1)$ time, while with a CombiningTree, it takes $O(\log p)$ time. Nevertheless, a CombiningTree is attractive because it promises far better throughput, that is, the overall rate at which method calls complete. For example, using a queue lock, p getAndIncrement() calls complete in $O(p)$ time, at best, while using a CombiningTree, under ideal conditions where all threads move up the tree together, p getAndIncrement() calls complete in $O(\log p)$ time, an exponential improvement. Of course, the actual performance is often less than ideal, a subject examined in detail later on. Still, the CombiningTree class, like other techniques we consider later, is intended to benefit throughput, not latency.

Combining trees can be adapted to apply any associative and commutative function, not just increment, to the value maintained by the tree.

12.3.1 Overview

Although the idea behind a CombiningTree is simple, the implementation is not. To keep the overall (simple) structure from being submerged in (not-so-simple) detail, we split the data structure into two classes: the CombiningTree class manages navigation within the tree, moving up and down the tree as needed, while the Node class manages each visit to a node. As you go through the algorithm's description, it may be helpful to consult Fig. 12.3, which shows an example CombiningTree execution.

This algorithm uses two kinds of synchronization. Short-term synchronization is provided by synchronized methods of the Node class. Each method locks the node for the duration of the call to ensure that it can read and write node fields without interference from other threads. The algorithm also requires excluding threads from a node for durations longer than a single method call. Such long-term synchronization is provided by a Boolean locked field. When this field is *true*, no other thread is allowed to access the node.

The fields of the Node class are shown in Fig. 12.1. Every node has a *combining status* (field CStatus), which defines what stage of combining concurrent requests a node is in. The possible values for the combining status, and their associated meanings, are:

- IDLE: This node is not in use.
- FIRST: One active thread has visited this node, and will return to check whether another passive thread has left a value with which to combine.
- SECOND: A second thread has visited this node and stored a value in the node's value field to be combined with the active thread's value, but the combined operation is not yet complete.
- RESULT: Both threads' operations have been combined and completed, and the second thread's result has been stored in the node's result field.
- ROOT: This value is a special case to indicate that the node is the root, and must be treated specially.

The CombiningTree class has a field leaf, which is an array of w leaves, where w is the width of the combining tree. Thread i is assigned to leaf[i/2], so a combining tree for p threads has width $w = \lceil p/2 \rceil$.

```
1   public class Node {
2     enum CStatus{IDLE, FIRST, SECOND, RESULT, ROOT};
3     boolean locked;
4     CStatus cStatus;
5     int firstValue, secondValue;
6     int result;
7     Node parent;
8     public Node() {
9       cStatus = CStatus.ROOT;
10      locked = false;
11    }
12    public Node(Node myParent) {
13      parent = myParent;
14      cStatus = CStatus.IDLE;
15      locked = false;
16    }
17    ...
18  }
```

FIGURE 12.1

The Node class: the constructors and fields.

```
1    public CombiningTree(int width) {
2      Node[] nodes = new Node[2 * width - 1];
3      nodes[0] = new Node();
4      for (int i = 1; i < nodes.length; i++) {
5        nodes[i] = new Node(nodes[(i-1)/2]);
6      }
7      leaf = new Node[width];
8      for (int i = 0; i < leaf.length; i++) {
9        leaf[i] = nodes[nodes.length - i - 1];
10     }
11   }
```

FIGURE 12.2

The CombiningTree class: constructor.

Fig. 12.2 shows the CombiningTree class constructor. To construct a CombiningTree of width w, we create an array of Node objects of length $2w - 1$. The root is node[0], and for $0 < i < 2w - 1$, the parent of node[i] is node[$(i - 1)/2$]. The leaf nodes are the last w nodes in the array. The initial combining state is ROOT for the root, and IDLE for every other node.

The CombiningTree's getAndIncrement() method, shown in Fig. 12.4, has four phases. In the *precombining phase* (lines 16–20), it moves up the tree, applying precombine() to each node. The precombine() method returns a Boolean indicating

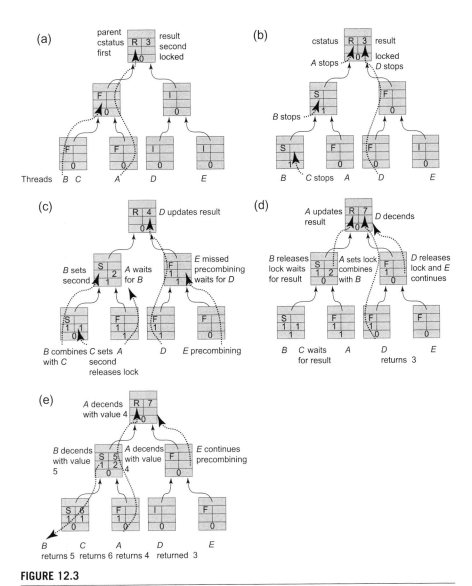

FIGURE 12.3

The concurrent traversal of a width 8 combining tree by five threads. The structure is initialized with all nodes unlocked, the root node having the CStatus ROOT and all other nodes having the CStatus IDLE.

whether the thread was the first to arrive at the node. If so, the getAndIncrement() method continues moving up the tree. The stop variable is set to the last node visited, which is either the first node at which the thread arrived second, or the root. Parts (a) and (b) of Fig. 12.3 show a precombining phase example. Thread A, which is fastest,

```
12    public int getAndIncrement() {
13      Stack<Node> stack = new Stack<Node>();
14      Node myLeaf = leaf[ThreadID.get()/2];
15      Node node = myLeaf;
16      // precombining phase
17      while (node.precombine()) {
18        node = node.parent;
19      }
20      Node stop = node;
21      // combining phase
22      int combined = 1;
23      for (node = myLeaf; node != stop; node = node.parent) {
24        combined = node.combine(combined);
25        stack.push(node);
26      }
27      // operation phase
28      int prior = stop.op(combined);
29      // distribution phase
30      while (!stack.empty()) {
31        node = stack.pop();
32        node.distribute(prior);
33      }
34      return prior;
35    }
```

FIGURE 12.4

The CombiningTree class: the getAndIncrement() method.

stops at the root, while B stops in the middle-level node where it arrived after A, and C stops at the leaf where it arrived after B.

Fig. 12.5 shows Node's precombine() method. The thread waits until the locked field is *false* (line 20), and then proceeds based on the node's combining status (line 21):

- IDLE: The thread sets the node's status to FIRST to indicate that it will return to look for a value for combining. If it finds such a value, it proceeds as the active thread, and the thread that provided that value is passive. The call then returns *true*, instructing the thread to move up the tree.
- FIRST: An earlier thread has recently visited this node, and will return to look for a value to combine. The thread stops moving up the tree (by returning *false*), and starts the next phase, computing the value to combine. Before precombine() returns, the thread places a long-term lock on the node (by setting locked to *true*) to prevent the earlier visiting thread from proceeding without combining with the thread's value.

```
19    synchronized boolean precombine() {
20      while (locked) wait();
21      switch (cStatus) {
22        case IDLE:
23          cStatus = CStatus.FIRST;
24          return true;
25        case FIRST:
26          locked = true;
27          cStatus = CStatus.SECOND;
28          return false;
29        case ROOT:
30          return false;
31        default:
32          throw new PanicException("unexpected Node state" + cStatus);
33      }
34    }
```

FIGURE 12.5

The Node class: the precombining phase.

- ROOT: If the thread has reached the root node, it instructs the thread to start the next phase.

(Line 31 is a *default* case that is executed if an unexpected status is encountered.)

PRAGMA 12.3.1

It is good programming practice always to provide an arm for every possible enumeration value, even if we know it cannot happen. If we are wrong, the program is easier to debug, and if we are right, the program may later be changed even by someone who does not know as much as we do. Always program defensively.

In the *combining phase* (Fig. 12.4, lines 21–26), the thread revisits the nodes it visited in the precombining phase, combining its value with values left by other threads. It stops when it arrives at the node stop, where the precombining phase ended. We push the nodes we visit onto a stack so that we can traverse them later in reverse order.

The Node class's combine() method, shown in Fig. 12.6, adds any values left by a recently arrived passive process to the values combined so far. As before, the thread first waits until the locked field is *false*. It then sets the long-term lock on the node, to ensure that late-arriving threads do not attempt to combine with it. If the status is SECOND, it adds the other thread's value to the accumulated value; otherwise it returns the value unchanged. In part (c) of Fig. 12.3, thread A starts ascending the tree in the combining phase. It reaches the second-level node locked by thread B and waits.

```
35    synchronized int combine(int combined) {
36      while (locked) wait();
37      locked = true;
38      firstValue = combined;
39      switch (cStatus) {
40        case FIRST:
41          return firstValue;
42        case SECOND:
43          return firstValue + secondValue;
44        default:
45          throw new PanicException("unexpected Node state " + cStatus);
46      }
47    }
```

FIGURE 12.6

The Node class: the combining phase. This method applies addition to firstValue and secondValue, but any other commutative operation would work just as well.

In part (d), B releases the lock on the second-level node, and A locks the node and, seeing that the node's combining state is SECOND, moves to the root with the combined value 3, the sum of the firstValue and secondValue fields written by A and B, respectively.

At the start of the *operation phase* (line 28), the thread has combined all method calls from lower-level nodes; it now examines the node where it stopped at the end of the precombining phase (Fig. 12.7). If the node is the root, as in part (d) of Fig. 12.3, then the thread, in this case A, carries out the combined getAndIncrement() operations: It adds its accumulated value (3 in the example) to the result and returns the prior value. Otherwise, the thread had set the long-term lock on this node at the end of its precombining phase (Fig. 12.5, line 26), so it deposits its value as the secondValue, unlocks the node, notifies any blocked thread, and waits for the other thread to return a result after propagating the combined operations toward the root. For example, this is the sequence of actions taken by thread B in parts (c) and (d) of Fig. 12.3. In this case, the other thread will have set the long-term lock, and left it set so that a thread arriving later will wait until the thread has retrieved the result. Thus, the thread must release the long-term lock and notify any blocked thread.

When the result arrives, A enters the *distribution phase*, propagating the result down the tree. In this phase (lines 29–34), the thread moves down the tree, releasing locks and informing passive partners of the values they should report to their own passive partners or to the caller (at the lowest level). The distribute method is shown in Fig. 12.8. If the state of the node is FIRST, no thread combines with the distributing thread, and it can reset the node to its initial state by releasing the lock and setting the state to IDLE. If, on the other hand, the state is SECOND, the distributing thread updates the result to be the sum of the prior value brought from higher up the tree, and the FIRST value. This reflects a situation in which the active thread at the node managed

```
48    synchronized int op(int combined) {
49      switch (cStatus) {
50        case ROOT:
51          int prior = result;
52          result += combined;
53          return prior;
54        case SECOND:
55          secondValue = combined;
56          locked = false;
57          notifyAll(); // wake up waiting threads
58          while (cStatus != CStatus.RESULT) wait();
59          locked = false;
60          notifyAll();
61          cStatus = CStatus.IDLE;
62          return result;
63        default:
64          throw new PanicException("unexpected Node state");
65      }
66    }
```

FIGURE 12.7

The Node class: applying the operation.

```
67    synchronized void distribute(int prior) {
68      switch (cStatus) {
69        case FIRST:
70          cStatus = CStatus.IDLE;
71          locked = false;
72          break;
73        case SECOND:
74          result = prior + firstValue;
75          cStatus = CStatus.RESULT;
76          break;
77        default:
78          throw new PanicException("unexpected Node state");
79      }
80      notifyAll();
81    }
```

FIGURE 12.8

The Node class: the distribution phase.

to perform its increment before the passive one. The passive thread waiting to get a value reads the result once the distributing thread sets the status to RESULT. For example, in part (e) of Fig. 12.3, the active thread A executes its distribution phase in the middle-level node, setting the `result` to 5, changing the state to RESULT, and descending down to the leaf, returning the value 4 as its output. The passive thread B awakes and sees that the middle-level node's state has changed, and reads result 5.

12.3.2 An extended example

Fig. 12.3 describes the various phases of a `CombiningTree` execution. There are five threads, labeled A through E. Each node has six fields, as shown in Fig. 12.1. Initially, all nodes are unlocked and all but the root are in an IDLE combining state. The counter value in the initial state in part (a) is 3, the result of an earlier computation.

In part (a), to perform a `getAndIncrement()`, threads A and B start the precombining phase. A ascends the tree, changing the nodes it visits from IDLE to FIRST, indicating that it will be the active thread in combining the values up the tree. Thread B is the active thread at its leaf node, but has not yet arrived at the second-level node shared with A.

In part (b), B arrives at the second-level node and stops, changing it from FIRST to SECOND, indicating that it will collect its combined values and wait here for A to proceed with them to the root. B locks the node (changing the `locked` field from *false* to *true*), preventing A from proceeding with the combining phase without B's combined value. But B has not combined the values. Before it does so, C starts precombining, arrives at the leaf node, stops, and changes its state to SECOND. It also locks the node to prevent B from ascending without its input to the combining phase. Similarly, D starts precombining and successfully reaches the root node. Neither A nor D changes the root node state, and in fact it never changes. They simply mark it as the node where they stopped precombining.

In part (c), A starts up the tree in the combining phase. It locks the leaf so that any later thread will not be able to proceed in its precombining phase, and will wait until A completes its combining and distribution phases. It reaches the second-level node, locked by B, and waits. In the meantime, C starts combining, but since it stopped at the leaf node, it executes the `op()` method on this node, setting `secondValue` to 1 and then releasing the lock. When B starts its combining phase, the leaf node is unlocked and marked SECOND, so B writes 1 to `firstValue` and ascends to the second-level node with a combined value of 2, the result of adding the `firstValue` and `secondValue` fields.

When it reaches the second-level node, the one at which it stopped in the precombining phase, it calls the `op()` method on this node, setting `secondValue` to 2. A must wait until it releases the lock. Meanwhile, in the right-hand side of the tree, D executes its combining phase, locking nodes as it ascends. Because it meets no other threads with which to combine, it reads 3 in the `result` field in the root and updates it to 4. Thread E then starts precombining, but is late in meeting D. It cannot continue precombining as long as D locks the second-level node.

In part (d), B releases the lock on the second-level node, and A, seeing that the node is in state SECOND, locks the node and moves to the root with the combined value 3, the sum of the `firstValue` and `secondValue` fields written, respectively, by A and

B. *A* is delayed while *D* completes updating the root. Once *D* is done, *A* reads 4 in the root's result field and updates it to 7. *D* descends the tree (by popping its local Stack), releasing the locks, and returning the value 3 that it originally read in the root's result field. *E* now continues its ascent in the precombining phase.

Finally, in part (e), *A* executes its distribution phase. It returns to the second-level node, setting result to 5, changing the state to RESULT, and descending to the leaf, returning the value 4 as its output. *B* awakens and sees the state of the middle-level node has changed, reads 5 as the result, and descends to its leaf where it sets the result field to 6 and the state to RESULT. *B* then returns 5 as its output. Finally, *C* awakens and observes that the leaf node state has changed, reads 6 as the result, which it returns as its output value. Threads *A* through *D* return values 3 to 6, which fit the root's result field value of 7. The linearization order of the getAndIncrement() method calls by the different threads is determined by their order in the tree during the precombining phase.

12.3.3 Performance and robustness

Like all the algorithms described in this chapter, CombiningTree's throughput depends in complex ways on the characteristics of both the application and the underlying architecture. Nevertheless, it is worthwhile to review, in qualitative terms, some experimental results from the literature. Readers interested in detailed experimental results (mostly for obsolete architectures) may consult the chapter notes.

As a thought experiment, a CombiningTree should provide high throughput under ideal circumstances when each thread can combine its increment with another's. But it may provide poor throughput under worst-case circumstances, where many threads arrive late at a locked node, missing the chance to combine, and are forced to wait for the earlier request to ascend and descend the tree.

In practice, experimental evidence supports this informal analysis. The higher the contention, the greater the observed rate of combining, and the greater the observed speedup. Worse is better. Combining trees are less attractive when concurrency is low. The combining rate decreases rapidly as the arrival rate of increment requests is reduced. Throughput is sensitive to the arrival rate of requests.

Because combining increases throughput and failure to combine does not, it makes sense for a request arriving at a node to wait for a reasonable duration for another thread to arrive with an increment with which to combine. Not surprisingly, it makes sense to wait for a short time when the contention is low, and longer when contention is high. When contention is sufficiently high, unbounded waiting works very well.

An algorithm is *robust* if it performs well in the presence of large fluctuations in request arrival times. The literature suggests that the CombiningTree algorithm with a fixed waiting time is not robust, because high variance in request arrival rates seems to reduce the combining rate.

12.4 Quiescently consistent pools and counters

First shalt thou take out the Holy Pin. Then shalt thou count to three, no more, no less. Three shall be the number thou shalt count, and the number of the counting shall be three.... Once the number three, being the third number, be reached, then lobbest thou thy Holy Hand Grenade of Antioch towards thy foe, who, being naughty in my sight, shall snuff it.

From Monty Python and the Holy Grail.

Not all applications require linearizable counting. Indeed, counter-based Pool implementations require only quiescently consistent[1] counting: All that matters is that the counters produce no duplicates and no omissions. It is enough that for every item placed by a put() in an array entry, another thread eventually executes a get() that accesses that entry, eventually matching put() and get() calls. (Wraparound may still cause multiple put() calls or get() calls to compete for the same array entry.)

12.5 Counting networks

Students of tango know that the partners must be tightly coordinated: If they do not move together, the dance does not work, no matter how skilled the dancers may be as individuals. In the same way, combining trees must be tightly coordinated: If requests do not arrive together, the algorithm does not work efficiently, no matter how fast the individual processes.

We now consider *counting networks*, which look less like tango and more like a rave: each participant moves at its own pace, but collectively the counter delivers a quiescently consistent set of indices with high throughput.

Let us imagine that we replace the combining tree's single counter with multiple counters, each of which distributes a subset of indices (see Fig. 12.9). We allocate w counters (in the figure, $w = 4$), each of which distributes a set of unique indices modulo w (in the figure, for example, the second counter distributes 2, 6, 10, ... $i \cdot w + 2$ for increasing i). The challenge is how to distribute the threads among the counters so that there are no duplications or omissions, and how to do so in a distributed and loosely coordinated way.

12.5.1 Networks that count

A *balancer* is a simple switch with two input wires and two output wires, called the *top* and *bottom* wires (or sometimes the *north* and *south* wires). Tokens arrive on the balancer's input wires at arbitrary times, and emerge on their output wires, at some later time. A balancer can be viewed as a toggle: given a stream of input tokens, it sends one token to the top output wire, and the next to the bottom, and so on,

---

[1] See Chapter 3 for a detailed definition of quiescent consistency.

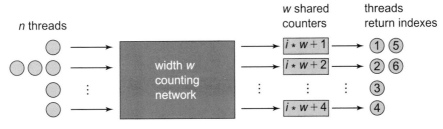

FIGURE 12.9

A quiescently consistent shared counter based on $w = 4$ counters preceded by a counting network. Threads traverse the counting network to choose which counters to access.

FIGURE 12.10

A balancer. Tokens arrive at arbitrary times on arbitrary input lines and are redirected to ensure that when all tokens have exited the balancer, there is at most one more token on the top wire than on the bottom one.

effectively balancing the number of tokens between the two wires (see Fig. 12.10). More precisely, a balancer has two states: *up* and *down*. If the state is *up*, the next token exits on the top wire; otherwise it exits on the bottom wire.

We use x_0 and x_1 to denote the number of tokens that respectively arrive on a balancer's top and bottom input wires, and y_0 and y_1 to denote the number that exit on the top and bottom output wires. For brevity, we also use x_i and y_i to denote the wires themselves. A balancer never creates tokens; at all times,

$$x_0 + x_1 \geq y_0 + y_1.$$

A balancer is said to be *quiescent* if every token that arrived on an input wire has emerged on an output wire:

$$x_0 + x_1 = y_0 + y_1.$$

A *balancing network* is constructed by connecting some balancers' output wires to other balancers' input wires. A balancing network of width w has input wires $x_0, x_1, \ldots, x_{w-1}$ (not connected to output wires of balancers), and w output wires $y_0, y_1, \ldots, y_{w-1}$ (similarly unconnected). The balancing network's *depth* is the maximum number of balancers one can traverse starting from any input wire. We consider only balancing networks of finite depth (meaning the wires do not form a loop). Like balancers, balancing networks do not create tokens:

$$\sum x_i \geq \sum y_i.$$

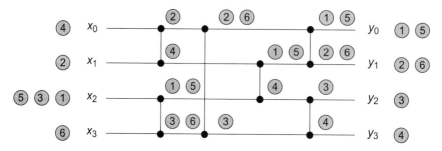

FIGURE 12.11

A sequential execution of a BITONIC [4] counting network. Each vertical line represents a balancer, and each balancer's two input and output wires are the horizontal lines it connects to at the dots. In this sequential execution, tokens pass through the network, one completely after the other in the order specified by the numbers on the tokens. We track every token as it passes through the balancers on the way to an output wire. For example, token number 3 enters on wire 2, goes down to wire 3, and ends up on wire 2. Note how the step property is maintained in every balancer, and also in the network as a whole.

(We often drop indices from summations when we sum over every element in a sequence.) A balancing network is *quiescent* if every token that arrived on an input wire has emerged on an output wire:

$$\sum x_i = \sum y_i.$$

So far, we have described balancing networks as if they were switches in a network. On a shared-memory multiprocessor, however, a balancing network can be implemented as an object in memory. Each balancer is an object, whose wires are references from one balancer to another. Each thread repeatedly traverses the object, starting on some input wire, and emerging at some output wire, effectively shepherding a token through the network.

Some balancing networks have interesting properties. The network shown in Fig. 12.11 has four input wires and four output wires. Initially, all balancers are *up*. We can check for ourselves that if any number of tokens enter the network, in any order, on any set of input wires, then they emerge in a regular pattern on the output wires. Informally, no matter how token arrivals are distributed among the input wires, the output distribution is balanced across the output wires, where the top output wires are filled first. If the number of tokens n is a multiple of four (the network width), then the same number of tokens emerges from each wire. If there is one excess token, it emerges on output wire 0; if there are two, they emerge on output wires 0 and 1, and so on. In general, if

$$n = \sum x_i,$$

then, when the network is quiescent,

$$y_i = \lceil (n - i)/w \rceil.$$

We call this property the *step property*.

A balancing network that satisfies the step property is called a *counting network* because it can easily be adapted to count the number of tokens that have traversed the network. Counting is done, as we described earlier in Fig. 12.9, by adding a local counter to each output wire i, so that tokens emerging on that wire are assigned consecutive numbers $i + 1, i + w + 1, \ldots, i + (y_i - 1)w + 1$.

The step property can be defined in a number of equivalent ways.

Lemma 12.5.1. If $y_0, \ldots, y_{w-1}$ is a sequence of nonnegative integers, the following statements are all equivalent:

1. For any $i < j$, $0 \leq y_i - y_j \leq 1$.
2. Either $y_i = y_j$ for all i, j, or there exists some c such that for any $i < c$ and $j \geq c$, $y_i - y_j = 1$.
3. If $m = \sum y_i$, then $y_i = \left\lceil \frac{m-i}{w} \right\rceil$.

12.5.2 The bitonic counting network

In this section, we describe the *bitonic counting network*, which generalizes the counting network of Fig. 12.11 to a counting network whose width is any power of 2. We give an inductive construction.

When describing counting networks, we do not care about when tokens arrive, we care only that, when the network is quiescent, the numbers of tokens exiting on the output wires satisfy the step property. Define a width-w sequence of inputs or outputs $x = x_0, \ldots, x_{w-1}$ to be a collection of tokens, partitioned into w subsets x_i. The x_i are the input tokens that arrive or leave on wire i. As before, we also use x_i to denote the size of the set x_i.

We first define the MERGER $[2k]$ network, which has two input sequences, x and x', of width k, and a single output sequence y of width $2k$. It guarantees that in any quiescent state, if x and x' both satisfy the step property, then so does y. The MERGER $[2k]$ network is defined inductively, as illustrated in Fig. 12.12 for $k = 4$. For $k = 1$, the MERGER $[2k]$ network is a single balancer. For $k > 1$, we construct the MERGER $[2k]$ network with input sequences x and x' from two MERGER $[k]$ networks and k balancers as follows: Using a MERGER $[k]$ network, we merge the even subsequence $x_0, x_2, \ldots, x_{k-2}$ of x with the odd subsequence $x'_1, x'_3, \ldots, x'_{k-1}$ of x' (that is, the sequence $x_0, \ldots, x_{k-2}, x'_1, \ldots, x'_{k-1}$ is the input to the MERGER $[k]$ network), while with a second MERGER $[k]$ network, we merge the odd subsequence of x with the even subsequence of x'. We call the outputs of these two MERGER $[k]$ networks z and z'. The final stage of the network combines z and z' by sending each pair of wires z_i and z'_i into a balancer whose outputs yield y_{2i} and y_{2i+1}.

The MERGER $[2k]$ network consists of $\log 2k$ layers of k balancers each. It provides the step property for its outputs only when its two input sequences also have the step property, which we ensure by filtering the inputs through smaller balancing networks.

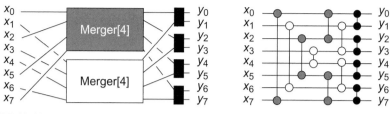

FIGURE 12.12

On the left-hand side, we see the logical structure of a MERGER [8] network, into which feed two BITONIC [4] networks, as depicted in Fig. 12.11. The gray MERGER [4] network has as inputs the even wires coming out of the top BITONIC [4] network and the odd ones from the lower BITONIC [4] network. In the lower MERGER [4] the situation is reversed. Once the wires exit the two MERGER [4] networks, each pair of identically numbered wires is combined by a balancer. On the right-hand side, we see the physical layout of a MERGER [8] network. The different balancers are color-coded to match the logical structure in the left-hand figure.

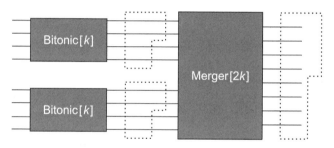

FIGURE 12.13

The recursive structure of a BITONIC [2k] counting network. Two BITONIC [k] counting networks feed into a MERGER [2k] balancing network.

The BITONIC [2k] network is constructed by passing the outputs from two BITONIC [k] networks into a MERGER [2k] network, where the induction is grounded in the BITONIC [2] network consisting of a single balancer, as depicted in Fig. 12.13. This construction gives us a network consisting of $\left(\begin{array}{c} \log 2k+1 \\ 2 \end{array} \right)$ layers, each consisting of k balancers.

12.5.2.1 A software bitonic counting network

So far, we have described counting networks as if they were switches in a network. On a shared-memory multiprocessor, however, a balancing network can be implemented as an object in memory. Each balancer is an object whose wires are references from one balancer to another. Each thread repeatedly traverses the object, starting on some input wire and emerging at some output wire, effectively shepherding a token through the network. Here, we show how to implement a BITONIC [2k] network as a shared-memory data structure.

```
1   public class Balancer {
2     boolean toggle = true;
3     public synchronized int traverse() {
4       try {
5         if (toggle) {
6           return 0;
7         } else {
8           return 1;
9         }
10      } finally {
11        toggle = !toggle;
12      }
13    }
14  }
```

FIGURE 12.14

The Balancer class: a **synchronized** implementation.

The Balancer class (Fig. 12.14) has a single Boolean field: toggle. The synchronized traverse() method complements the toggle field and returns an output wire, either 0 or 1. The Balancer class's traverse() method does not need an argument because the wire on which a token exits a balancer does not depend on the wire on which it enters.

The Merger class (Fig. 12.15) has three fields: The width field must be a power of 2, half[] is a two-element array of half-width Merger objects (empty if the network has width 2), and layer[] is an array of width/2 balancers implementing the final network layer. The class provides a traverse(i) method, where i is the wire on which the token enters. (For merger networks, unlike balancers, a token's path depends on its input wire.) If the input wire is one of the first width/2, then the token is sent to half[0] if i is even and to half[1] if i is odd. Otherwise, it is sent to half[0] if i is odd and to half[1] if i is even. No matter which half-width merger network it traverses, a token that emerges on wire i is fed to the balancer at layer[i].

The Bitonic class (Fig. 12.16) also has three fields: width must be a power of 2, half[] is a two-element array of half-width Bitonic objects (uninitialized if the network has width 2), and merger is a full-width Merger object. The class provides a traverse(i) method, where i is the token's input wire. If the input wire is one of the first width/2, then it is sent through half[0], otherwise through half[1]. A token that emerges from the half-merger subnetwork on wire i then traverses the final merger network from input wire i if it passed through half[0], or from input wire i+width/2 if it passed through half[1].

Note that the Bitonic class uses a simple synchronized Balancer implementation, but if the Balancer implementation were lock-free (or wait-free), the network implementation as a whole would be lock-free (or wait-free).

```
1   public class Merger {
2     Merger[] half;  // two half-width merger networks
3     Balancer[] layer; // final layer
4     final int width;
5     public Merger(int myWidth) {
6       width = myWidth;
7       layer = new Balancer[width / 2];
8       for (int i = 0; i < width / 2; i++) {
9         layer[i] = new Balancer();
10      }
11      if (width > 2) {
12        half = new Merger[]{new Merger(width/2), new Merger(width/2)};
13      }
14    }
15    public int traverse(int input) {
16      int output = 0;
17      if (input < width / 2) {
18        output = half[input % 2].traverse(input / 2);
19      } else {
20        output = half[1 - (input % 2)].traverse(input / 2);
21      return (2 * output) + layer[output].traverse();
22    }
23  }
```

FIGURE 12.15

The Merger class.

12.5.2.2 Proof of correctness

We now show that BITONIC $[w]$ is a counting network. The proof proceeds as a progression of arguments about the token sequences passing through the network. Before examining the network itself, here are some simple lemmas about sequences with the step property.

Lemma 12.5.2. If a sequence has the step property, then so do all its subsequences.

Lemma 12.5.3. For even k, if $x_0, \ldots, x_{k-1}$ has the step property, then its even and odd subsequences satisfy

$$\sum_{i=0}^{\frac{k}{2}-1} x_{2i} = \left\lceil \sum_{i=0}^{k-1} \frac{x_i}{2} \right\rceil \quad \text{and} \quad \sum_{i=0}^{\frac{k}{2}-1} x_{2i+1} = \left\lfloor \sum_{i=0}^{k-1} \frac{x_i}{2} \right\rfloor .$$

Proof. Either $x_{2i} = x_{2i+1}$ for $0 \le i < k/2$, or by Lemma 12.5.1, there exists a unique j such that $x_{2j} = x_{2j+1} + 1$ and $x_{2i} = x_{2i+1}$ for all $i \ne j$, $0 \le i < k/2$. In the first case, $\sum x_{2i} = \sum x_{2i+1} = \sum x_i/2$, and in the second case, $\sum x_{2i} = \lceil \sum x_i/2 \rceil$ and $\sum x_{2i+1} = \lfloor \sum x_i/2 \rfloor$. $\square$

```
1   public class Bitonic {
2     Bitonic[] half; // two half-width bitonic networks
3     Merger merger; // final merger layer
4     final int width; // network width
5     public Bitonic(int myWidth) {
6       width = myWidth;
7       merger = new Merger(width);
8       if (width > 2) {
9         half = new Bitonic[]{new Bitonic(width/2), new Bitonic(width/2)};
10      }
11    }
12    public int traverse(int input) {
13      int output = 0;
14      int subnet = input / (width / 2);
15      if (width > 2) {
16        output = half[subnet].traverse(input - subnet * (width / 2));
17      }
18      return merger.traverse(output + subnet * (width / 2));
19    }
20  }
```

FIGURE 12.16

The Bitonic class.

Lemma 12.5.4. Let $x_0, \ldots, x_{k-1}$ and $y_0, \ldots, y_{k-1}$ be arbitrary sequences having the step property. If $\sum x_i = \sum y_i$, then $x_i = y_i$ for all $0 \le i < k$.

Proof. Let $m = \sum x_i = \sum y_i$. By Lemma 12.5.1, $x_i = y_i = \left\lceil \frac{m-i}{k} \right\rceil$.   □

Lemma 12.5.5. Let $x_0, \ldots, x_{k-1}$ and $y_0, \ldots, y_{k-1}$ be arbitrary sequences having the step property. If $\sum x_i = \sum y_i + 1$, then there exists a unique j, $0 \le j < k$, such that $x_j = y_j + 1$ and $x_i = y_i$ for $i \ne j$, $0 \le i < k$.

Proof. Let $m = \sum x_i = \sum y_i + 1$. By Lemma 12.5.1, $x_i = \left\lceil \frac{m-i}{k} \right\rceil$ and $y_i = \left\lceil \frac{m-1-i}{k} \right\rceil$. These two terms agree for all i, $0 \le i < k$, except for the unique i such that $i = m - 1 \pmod{k}$.   □

We now show that the MERGER $[w]$ network preserves the step property.

Lemma 12.5.6. If MERGER $[2k]$ is quiescent (where k is a power of 2) and its inputs $x_0, \ldots, x_{k-1}$ and $x'_0, \ldots, x'_{k-1}$ both have the step property, then its output $y_0, \ldots, y_{2k-1}$ also has the step property.

Proof. We argue by induction on $\log k$. It may be worthwhile to consult Fig. 12.17, which shows an example of the proof structure for a MERGER $[8]$ network.

If $2k = 2$, MERGER $[2k]$ is just a balancer, and its outputs are guaranteed to have the step property by the definition of a balancer.

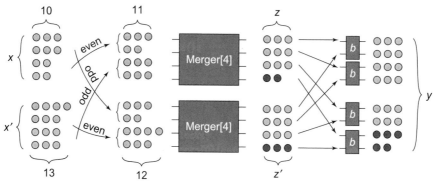

FIGURE 12.17

The inductive proof that a MERGER [8] network correctly merges two width-4 sequences x and x' that have the step property into a single width-8 sequence y that has the step property. The odd and even width-2 subsequences of x and x' all have the step property. Moreover, the difference in the number of tokens between the even sequence from one and the odd sequence from the other is at most 1 (in this example, 11 and 12 tokens, respectively). It follows from the induction hypothesis that the outputs z and z' of the two MERGER [4] networks have the step property, with at most 1 extra token in one of them. This extra token must fall on a specific numbered wire (wire 3 in this case) leading into the same balancer. In this figure, these tokens are darkened. They are passed to the southern-most balancer, and the extra token is pushed north, ensuring the final output has the step property.

If $2k > 2$, let $z_0, \ldots, z_{k-1}$ be the outputs of the first MERGER $[k]$ subnetwork, which merges the even subsequence of x with the odd subsequence of x', and let $z'_0, \ldots, z'_{k-1}$ be the outputs of the second MERGER $[k]$ subnetwork. Since x and x' have the step property by assumption, so do their even and odd subsequences (Lemma 12.5.2), and hence so do z and z' (induction hypothesis). Furthermore, $\sum z_i = \left\lceil \sum x_i/2 \right\rceil + \left\lfloor \sum x'_i/2 \right\rfloor$ and $\sum z'_i = \left\lfloor \sum x_i/2 \right\rfloor + \left\lceil \sum x'_i/2 \right\rceil$ (Lemma 12.5.3). A straightforward case analysis shows that $\sum z_i$ and $\sum z'_i$ can differ by at most 1.

We claim that $0 \le y_i - y_j \le 1$ for any $i < j$. If $\sum z_i = \sum z'_i$, then Lemma 12.5.4 implies that $z_i = z'_i$ for $0 \le i < k/2$. After the final layer of balancers,

$$y_i - y_j = z_{\lfloor i/2 \rfloor} - z_{\lfloor j/2 \rfloor},$$

and the result follows because z has the step property.

Similarly, if $\sum z_i$ and $\sum z'_i$ differ by one, Lemma 12.5.5 implies that $z_i = z'_i$ for $0 \le i < k/2$, except for a unique ℓ such that z_ℓ and z'_ℓ differ by one. Let $x = \min(z_\ell, z'_\ell)$, and thus, $\max(z_\ell, z'_\ell) = x + 1$. From the step property for z and z', we have $z_i = z'_i = x + 1$ for all $i < \ell$, and $z_i = z'_i = x$ for all $i > \ell$. Since z_ℓ and z'_ℓ are joined by a balancer with outputs $y_{2\ell}$ and $y_{2\ell+1}$, it follows that $y_{2\ell} = x + 1$ and $y_{2\ell+1} = x$. Similarly, z_i and z'_i for $i \ne \ell$ are joined by the same balancer. Thus, for any $i < \ell$, $y_{2i} = y_{2i+1} = x + 1$ and for any $i > \ell$, $y_{2i} = y_{2i+1} = x$. The step property follows by choosing $c = 2\ell + 1$ and applying Lemma 12.5.1. $\qquad\square$

The proof of the following theorem is now immediate.

Theorem 12.5.7. In any quiescent state, the outputs of BITONIC $[w]$ have the step property.

12.5.2.3 A periodic counting network

In this section, we show that the Bitonic network is not the only counting network with depth $O(log^2 w)$. We introduce a new counting network with the remarkable property that it is *periodic*, consisting of a sequence of identical subnetworks, as depicted in Fig. 12.18. We define the network BLOCK $[k]$ as follows: When k is equal to 2, the BLOCK $[k]$ network consists of a single balancer. The BLOCK $[2k]$ network for larger k is constructed recursively. We start with two BLOCK $[k]$ networks A and B. Given an input sequence x, the input to A is x^A, and the input to B is x^B. Let y be the output sequence for the two subnetworks, where y^A is the output sequence for A and y^B the output sequence for B. The final stage of the network combines each y_i^A and y_i^B in a single balancer, yielding final outputs z_{2i} and z_{2i+1}.

Fig. 12.19 describes the recursive construction of a BLOCK $[8]$ network. The PERIODIC $[2k]$ network consists of $\log 2k$ BLOCK $[2k]$ networks joined so that the ith

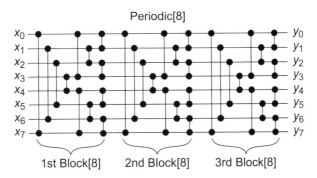

FIGURE 12.18

A PERIODIC $[8]$ counting network constructed from three identical BLOCK $[8]$ networks.

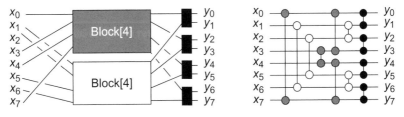

FIGURE 12.19

The left-hand side illustrates a BLOCK $[8]$ network, into which feed two PERIODIC $[4]$ networks. The right-hand illustrates the physical layout of a MERGER $[8]$ network. The balancers are color-coded to match the logical structure in the left-hand figure.

```
1   public class Layer {
2     int width;
3     Balancer[] layer;
4     public Layer(int width) {
5       this.width = width;
6       layer = new Balancer[width];
7       for (int i = 0; i < width / 2; i++) {
8         layer[i] = layer[width-i-1] = new Balancer();
9       }
10    }
11    public int traverse(int input) {
12      int toggle = layer[input].traverse();
13      int hi, lo;
14      if (input < width / 2) {
15        lo = input;
16        hi = width - input - 1;
17      } else {
18        lo = width - input - 1;
19        hi = input;
20      }
21      if (toggle == 0) {
22        return lo;
23      } else {
24        return hi;
25      }
26    }
27  }
```

FIGURE 12.20

The Layer network.

output wire of one is the ith wire of the next. Fig. 12.18 is a PERIODIC [8] counting network.[2]

12.5.2.4 A software periodic counting network

Here is how to implement the periodic network in software. We reuse the Balancer class in Fig. 12.14. A single layer of a BLOCK $[w]$ network is implemented by the LAYER $[w]$ network (Fig. 12.20). A LAYER $[w]$ network joins input wires i and $w - i - 1$ to the same balancer.

In the BLOCK $[w]$ class (Fig. 12.21), after the token emerges from the initial LAYER $[w]$ network, it passes through one of two half-width BLOCK $[w/2]$ networks (called *north* and *south*).

---

[2] While the BLOCK $[2k]$ and MERGER $[2k]$ networks may look the same, they are not: There is no permutation of wires that yields one from the other.

```
1   public class Block {
2     Block north;
3     Block south;
4     Layer layer;
5     int width;
6     public Block(int width) {
7       this.width = width;
8       if (width > 2) {
9         north = new Block(width / 2);
10        south = new Block(width / 2);
11      }
12      layer = new Layer(width);
13    }
14    public int traverse(int input) {
15      int wire = layer.traverse(input);
16      if (width > 2) {
17        if (wire < width / 2) {
18          return north.traverse(wire);
19        } else {
20          return (width / 2) + south.traverse(wire - (width / 2));
21        }
22      } else {
23        return wire;
24      }
25    }
26  }
```

FIGURE 12.21

The Block network.

The PERIODIC $[w]$ network (Fig. 12.22) is implemented as an array of $\log w$ BLOCK $[w]$ networks. Each token traverses each block in sequence, where the output wire taken on each block is the input wire for its successor. (The chapter notes cite the proof that the PERIODIC $[w]$ is a counting network.)

12.5.3 Performance and pipelining

How does counting network throughput vary as a function of the number of threads and the network width? For a fixed network width, throughput rises with the number of threads up to a point, and then the network *saturates*, and throughput remains constant or declines. To understand these results, let us think of a counting network as a pipeline.

- If the number of tokens concurrently traversing the network is less than the number of balancers, then the pipeline is partly empty, and throughput suffers.

```
1   public class Periodic {
2     Block[] block;
3     public Periodic(int width) {
4       int logSize = 0;
5       int myWidth = width;
6       while (myWidth > 1) {
7         logSize++;
8         myWidth = myWidth / 2;
9       }
10      block = new Block[logSize];
11      for (int i = 0; i < logSize; i++) {
12        block[i] = new Block(width);
13      }
14    }
15    public int traverse(int input) {
16      int wire = input;
17      for (Block b : block) {
18        wire = b.traverse(wire);
19      }
20      return wire;
21    }
22  }
```

FIGURE 12.22

The `Periodic` network.

- If the number of concurrent tokens is greater than the number of balancers, then the pipeline becomes clogged because too many tokens arrive at each balancer at the same time, resulting in per-balancer contention.
- Throughput is maximized when the number of tokens is roughly equal to the number of balancers.

If an application needs a counting network, then the best network size to choose is one that ensures that the number of tokens traversing the balancer at any time is roughly equal to the number of balancers.

12.6 Diffracting trees

Counting networks provide a high degree of pipelining, so throughput is largely independent of network depth. Latency, however, does depend on network depth. Of the counting networks we have seen, the most shallow has depth $\Theta(\log^2 w)$. Can we design a logarithmic-depth counting network? The good news is yes, such networks exist, but the bad news is that for all known constructions, the constant factors involved render these constructions impractical.

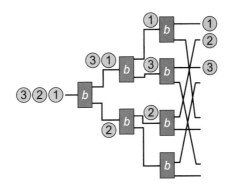

FIGURE 12.23

The TREE [8] class: a tree that counts. Note how the network maintains the step property.

Here is an alternative approach: Consider a set of balancers with a single input wire and two output wires, with the top and bottom labeled 0 and 1, respectively. The TREE [w] network (depicted in Fig. 12.23) is a binary tree structured as follows: Let w be a power of two, and define TREE [$2k$] inductively. When k is equal to 1, TREE [$2k$] consists of a single balancer with output wires y_0 and y_1. For $k > 1$, construct TREE [$2k$] from two TREE [k] trees and one additional balancer. Make the input wire x of the single balancer the root of the tree and connect each of its output wires to the input wire of a tree of width k. Redesignate output wires $y_0, y_1, \ldots, y_{k-1}$ of the TREE [k] subtree extending from the "0" output wire as the even output wires $y_0, y_2, \ldots, y_{2k-2}$ of the final TREE [$2k$] network and the wires $y_0, y_1, \ldots, y_{k-1}$ of the TREE [k] subtree extending from the balancer's "1" output wire as the odd output wires $y_1, y_3, \ldots, y_{2k-1}$ of the final TREE [$2k$] network.

To understand why the TREE [$2k$] network has the step property in a quiescent state, let us assume inductively that a quiescent TREE [k] has the step property. The root balancer passes at most one token more to the TREE [k] subtree on its "0" (top) wire than on its "1" (bottom) wire. The tokens exiting the top TREE [k] subtree have a step property differing from that of the bottom subtree at most one wire j among their k output wires. The TREE [$2k$] outputs are a perfect shuffle of the wires leaving the two subtrees, and it follows that the two step-shaped token sequences of width k form a new step of width $2k$, where the possible single excess token appears at the higher of the two wires j, that is, the one from the top TREE [k] tree.

The TREE [w] network may be a counting network, but is it a *good* counting network? The good news is that it has shallow depth: While a BITONIC [w] network has depth $\log^2 w$, the TREE [w] network depth is just $\log w$. The bad news is contention: Every token that enters the network passes through the same root balancer, causing that balancer to become a bottleneck. In general, the higher the balancer in the tree, the higher the contention.

We can reduce contention by exploiting a simple observation similar to one we made about the EliminationBackoffStack of Chapter 11:

If an even number of tokens pass through a balancer, the outputs are evenly balanced on the top and bottom wires, but the balancer's state remains unchanged.

The basic idea behind *diffracting trees* is to place a "prism" at each balancer, an out-of-band mechanism similar to the EliminationArray, which enables tokens (threads) accessing a stack to exchange items. The prism allows tokens to pair off at random array locations and agree to diffract in different directions, that is, to exit on different wires without traversing the balancer's toggle bit or changing its state. A token traverses the balancer's toggle bit only if it is unable to pair off with another token within a reasonable period of time. If it did not manage to diffract, the token toggles the bit to determine which way to go. It follows that we can avoid excessive contention at balancers if the prism can pair off enough tokens without introducing too much contention.

A Prism is an array of Exchanger<Integer> objects, like the EliminationArray. An Exchanger<T> object permits two threads to exchange T values. If thread *A* calls the object's exchange() method with argument *a*, and *B* calls it with argument *b*, then *A*'s call returns *b* and *B*'s call returns *a*. The first thread to arrive is blocked until the second arrives. The call includes a timeout argument allowing a thread to proceed if it is unable to exchange a value within a reasonable duration.

Before thread *A* visits the balancer's toggle bit, it visits the associated Prism. In the Prism, it picks an array entry at random, and calls that slot's exchange() method, providing its own thread ID as an exchange value. If it succeeds in exchanging IDs with another thread, then the thread with the lower ID exits on wire 0, and the one with the higher ID on wire 1.

Fig. 12.24 shows a Prism implementation. The constructor takes as an argument the capacity of the prism (the maximal number of distinct exchangers). The Prism

```
1  public class Prism {
2    private static final int duration = 100;
3    Exchanger<Integer>[] exchanger;
4    public Prism(int capacity) {
5      exchanger = (Exchanger<Integer>[]) new Exchanger[capacity];
6      for (int i = 0; i < capacity; i++) {
7        exchanger[i] = new Exchanger<Integer>();
8      }
9    }
10   public boolean visit() throws TimeoutException, InterruptedException {
11     int me = ThreadID.get();
12     int slot = ThreadLocalRandom.current().nextInt(exchanger.length);
13     int other = exchanger[slot].exchange(me, duration, TimeUnit.MILLISECONDS);
14     return (me < other);
15   }
16 }
```

FIGURE 12.24

The Prism class.

```
1   public class DiffractingBalancer {
2     Prism prism;
3     Balancer toggle;
4     public DiffractingBalancer(int capacity) {
5       prism = new Prism(capacity);
6       toggle = new Balancer();
7     }
8     public int traverse() {
9       boolean direction = false;
10      try{
11        if (prism.visit())
12          return 0;
13        else
14          return 1;
15      } catch(TimeoutException ex) {
16        return toggle.traverse();
17      }
18    }
19  }
```

FIGURE 12.25

The DiffractingBalancer class: If the caller pairs up with a concurrent caller through the prism, it does not need to traverse the balancer.

class provides a single method, visit(), that chooses the random exchanger entry. The visit() call returns *true* if the caller should exit on the top wire, *false* if the bottom wire, and it throws a TimeoutException if the timeout expires without exchanging a value. The caller acquires its thread ID (line 11), chooses a random entry in the array (line 12), and tries to exchange its own ID with its partner's (line 13). If it succeeds, it returns a Boolean value, and if it times out, it rethrows TimeoutException.

A DiffractingBalancer (Fig. 12.25), like a regular Balancer, provides a traverse() method whose return value alternates between 0 and 1. This class has two fields: prism is a Prism, and toggle is a Balancer. When a thread calls traverse(), it tries to find a partner through the prism. If it succeeds, then the partners return with distinct values, without creating contention at the toggle (line 11). Otherwise, if the thread is unable to find a partner, it traverses (line 16) the toggle (implemented as a balancer).

The DiffractingTree class (Fig. 12.26) has two fields. The child array is a two-element array of child trees. The root field is a DiffractingBalancer that alternates between forwarding calls to the left or right subtree. Each DiffractingBalancer has a capacity, which is actually the capacity of its internal prism. Initially this capacity is the size of the tree, and the capacity shrinks by half at each level.

As with the EliminationBackoffStack, DiffractingTree performance depends on two parameters: prism capacities and timeouts. If the prisms are too big, threads miss one another, causing excessive contention at the balancer. If the prisms are too small, then too many threads concurrently access each exchanger in a prism, resulting in

```
1   public class DiffractingTree {
2     DiffractingBalancer root;
3     DiffractingTree[] child;
4     int size;
5     public DiffractingTree(int mySize) {
6       size = mySize;
7       root = new DiffractingBalancer(size);
8       if (size > 2) {
9         child = new DiffractingTree[]{
10          new DiffractingTree(size/2),
11          new DiffractingTree(size/2)};
12      }
13    }
14    public int traverse() {
15      int half = root.traverse();
16      if (size > 2) {
17        return (2 * (child[half].traverse()) + half);
18      } else {
19        return half;
20      }
21    }
22  }
```

FIGURE 12.26

The DiffractingTree class: fields, constructor, and traverse() method.

excessive contention at the exchangers. If prism timeouts are too short, threads miss one another, and if they are too long, threads may be delayed unnecessarily. There are no hard-and-fast rules for choosing these values, since the optimal values depend on the load and the characteristics of the underlying multiprocessor architecture.

Nevertheless, experimental evidence suggests that it is sometimes possible to choose these values to outperform both the CombiningTree and CountingNetwork classes. Here are some heuristics that work well in practice: Because balancers higher in the tree have more contention, we use larger prisms near the top of the tree, and add the ability to dynamically shrink and grow the random range chosen. The best timeout interval choice depends on the load: If only a few threads are accessing the tree, then time spent waiting is mostly wasted, while if there are many threads, then time spent waiting pays off. Adaptive schemes are promising: lengthen the timeout while threads succeed in pairing off, and shorten it otherwise.

12.7 Parallel sorting

Sorting is one of the most important computational tasks, dating back to Hollerith's tabulating machine in the 19th century, through the first electronic computer systems in the 1940s, and culminating today, when a high fraction of programs use sorting in some form or another. As most computer science undergraduates learn early on, the choice of sorting algorithm depends crucially on the number of items being sorted, the numerical properties of their keys, and whether the items reside in memory or in an external storage device. Parallel sorting algorithms can be classified in the same way.

We present two classes of sorting algorithms: *sorting networks*, which typically work well for small in-memory data sets, and *sample sorting algorithms*, which work well for large data sets in external memory. In our presentation, we sacrifice performance for simplicity. More complex techniques are cited in the chapter notes.

12.8 Sorting networks

In much the same way that a counting network is a network of *balancers*, a sorting network is a network of *comparators*.[3] A comparator is a computing element with two input wires and two output wires, called the *top* and *bottom* wires. It receives two numbers on its input wires, and forwards the larger to its top wire and the smaller to its bottom wire. A comparator, unlike a balancer, is *synchronous*: It outputs values only when both inputs have arrived (see Fig. 12.27).

A *comparison network*, like a balancing network, is an acyclic network of comparators. An input value is placed on each of its w input lines. These values pass through each layer of comparators synchronously, finally leaving together on the network output wires.

A comparison network with input values x_i and output values y_i, $i \in \{0 \ldots w - 1\}$, each on wire i, is a valid *sorting network* if its output values are the input values sorted in descending order, that is, $y_{i-1} \geq y_i$.

The following classic theorem simplifies the process of proving that a given network sorts.

Theorem 12.8.1 (0-1 Principle). If a sorting network sorts every input sequence of 0 s and 1 s, then it sorts any sequence of input values.

FIGURE 12.27

A comparator.

---

[3] Historically sorting networks predate counting networks by several decades.

12.8.1 Designing a sorting network

There is no need to design sorting networks, because we can recycle counting network layouts. A balancing network and a comparison network are *isomorphic* if one can be constructed from the other by replacing balancers with comparators, or vice versa.

Theorem 12.8.2. If a balancing network counts, then its isomorphic comparison network sorts.

Proof. We construct a mapping from steps in the comparison network to steps in the isomorphic balancing network transitions. By Theorem 12.8.1, a comparison network which sorts all sequences of 0 s and 1 s is a sorting network. Take any arbitrary sequence of 0 s and 1 s as inputs to the comparison network, and for the balancing network, place a token on each 1 input wire and no token on each 0 input wire. If we run both networks in lockstep, the balancing network simulates the comparison network.

The proof is by induction on the depth of the network. For level 0 the claim holds by construction. Assuming it holds for wires of a given level k, let us prove it holds for level $k + 1$. On every comparator where two 1 s meet in the comparison network, two tokens meet in the balancing network, so one 1 leaves on each wire in the comparison network on level $k + 1$, and one token leaves on each wire in the balancing network on level $k + 1$. On every comparator where two 0 s meet in the comparison network, no tokens meet in the balancing network, so a 0 leaves on each level $k + 1$ wire in the comparison network, and no tokens leave in the balancing network. On every comparator where a 0 and 1 meet in the comparison network, the 1 leaves on the north (upper) wire and the 1 on the south (lower) wire on level $k + 1$, while in the balancing network the token leaves on the north wire, and no token leaves on the south wire.

If the balancing network is a counting network, that is, it has the step property on its output level wires, then the comparison network must have sorted the input sequence of 0 s and 1 s. □

The converse is false: not all sorting networks are counting networks. We leave it as an exercise to verify that the ODDEVEN network in Fig. 12.28 is a sorting network but not a counting network.

Corollary 12.8.3. Comparison networks isomorphic to BITONIC [] and PERIODIC [] networks are sorting networks.

Sorting a set of size w by comparisons requires $\Omega(w \log w)$ comparisons. A sorting network with w input wires has at most $O(w)$ comparators in each level, so its depth can be no smaller than $\Omega(\log w)$.

Corollary 12.8.4. The depth of any counting network is at least $\Omega(\log w)$.

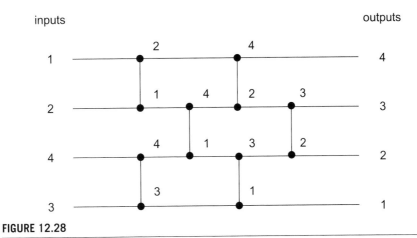

inputs   outputs

FIGURE 12.28

The ODDEVEN sorting network.

12.8.1.1 A bitonic sorting algorithm

We can represent any width-w sorting network, such as BITONIC $[w]$, as a collection of d layers of up to $w/2$ balancers each. We can represent a sorting network layout as a table, where each entry is a pair that describes which two wires meet at that balancer at that layer. (For example, in the BITONIC [4] network of Fig. 12.11, wires 0 and 1 meet at the first balancer in the first layer, and wires 0 and 3 meet at the first balancer of the second layer.) Let us assume, for simplicity, that we are given an unbounded table bitonicTable$[i][d][j]$, where each array entry contains the index of the associated north ($j = 0$) or south ($j = 1$) input wire to balancer i at depth d.

An *in-place* array-based sorting algorithm takes as input an array of items to be sorted (here we assume these items have unique integer keys) and returns the same array with the items sorted by key. Here is how we implement BitonicSort, an in-place array-based sorting algorithm based on a bitonic sorting network. Let us assume that we wish to sort an array of $2 \cdot p \cdot s$ elements, where p is the number of threads (and typically also the maximal number of available processors on which the threads run) and $p \cdot s$ is a power of 2. The network has $p \cdot s$ comparators at every layer.

Each of the p threads emulates the work of s comparators. Unlike counting networks, which act like uncoordinated raves, sorting networks are synchronous: All inputs to a comparator must arrive before it can compute the outputs. The algorithm proceeds in rounds. In each round, a thread performs s comparisons in a layer of the network, switching the array entries of items if necessary, so that they are properly ordered. In each network layer, the comparators join different wires, so no two threads attempt to exchange the items of the same entry, avoiding the need to synchronize operations at any given layer.

To ensure that the comparisons of a given round (layer) are complete before proceeding to the next one, we use a synchronization construct called a Barrier (studied in more detail in Chapter 18). A barrier for p threads provides an await() method,

```
1   public class BitonicSort {
2     static final int[][][] bitonicTable = ...;
3     static final int width = ...; // counting network width
4     static final int depth = ...; // counting network depth
5     static final int p = ...;   // number of threads
6     static final int s = ...;   // a power of 2
7     Barrier barrier;
8     ...
9       public <T> void sort(Item<T>[] items) {
10        int i = ThreadID.get();
11        for (int d = 0; d < depth; d++) {
12          barrier.await();
13          for (int j = 0; j < s; j++) {
14            int north = bitonicTable[(i*s)+j][d][0];
15            int south = bitonicTable[(i*s)+j][d][1];
16            if (items[north].key < items[south].key) {
17              Item<T> temp = items[north];
18              items[north] = items[south];
19              items[south] = temp;
20            }
21          }
22        }
23      }
```

FIGURE 12.29

The BitonicSort class.

whose call does not return until all p threads have called await(). The BitonicSort implementation appears in Fig. 12.29. Each thread proceeds through the layers of the network round by round. In each round, it awaits the arrival of the other threads (line 12), ensuring that the items array contains the prior round's results. It then emulates the behavior of s balancers at that layer by comparing the items at the array positions corresponding to the comparator's wires, and exchanging them if their keys are out of order (lines 14–19).

The BitonicSort takes $O(s \log^2 p)$ time for p threads running on p processors, which, if s is constant, is $O(\log^2 p)$ time.

12.9 Sample sorting

The BitonicSort is appropriate for small data sets that reside in memory. For larger data sets (where n, the number of items, is much larger than p, the number of threads), especially ones that reside on out-of-memory storage devices, we need a different approach. Because accessing a data item is expensive, we must maintain as much locality of reference as possible, so having a single thread sort items sequentially is cost-effective. A parallel sort like `BitonicSort`, where an item is accessed by multiple threads, is simply too expensive.

We attempt to minimize the number of threads that access a given item through randomization. This use of randomness differs from that in the `DiffractingTree`, where it was used to distribute memory accesses. Here we use randomness to guess the distribution of items in the data set to be sorted.

Since the data set to be sorted is large, we split it into buckets, throwing into each bucket the items that have keys within a given range. Each thread then sorts the items in one of the buckets using a sequential sorting algorithm, and the result is a sorted set (when viewed in the appropriate bucket order). This algorithm is a generalization of the well-known *quicksort* algorithm, but instead of having a single *splitter* key to divide the items into two subsets, we have $p - 1$ splitter keys that split the input set into p subsets.

The algorithm for n items and p threads involves three phases:

1. Threads choose $p - 1$ splitter keys to partition the data set into p buckets. The splitters are published so all threads can read them.
2. Each thread sequentially processes n/p items, moving each item to its bucket, where the appropriate bucket is determined by performing a binary search with the item's key among the splitter keys.
3. Each thread sequentially sorts the items in its bucket.

Barriers between the phases ensure that all threads have completed one phase before the next starts.

Before we consider the first phase, we look at the second and third phases.

The second phase's time complexity is $(n/p) \log p$, consisting of reading each item from memory, disk, or tape, followed by a binary search among p splitters cached locally, and finally adding the item into the appropriate bucket. The buckets into which the items are moved could be in memory, on disk, or on tape, so the dominating cost is that of the n/p accesses to the stored data items.

Let b be the number of items in a bucket. The time complexity of the third phase for a given thread is $O(b \log b)$, to sort the items using a sequential version of, say, *quicksort*.[4] This part has the highest cost because it consists of read and write phases that access relatively slow memory, such as disk or tape.

The time complexity of the algorithm is dominated by the thread with the most items in its bucket in the third phase. It is therefore important to choose the splitters to be as evenly distributed as possible, so each bucket receives approximately n/p items in the second phase.

The key to choosing good splitters is to have each thread pick a set of *sample* splitters that represent its own n/p size data set, and choose the final $p - 1$ splitters from among all the sample splitter sets of all threads. Each thread selects uniformly at random s keys from its data set of size n/p. (In practice, it suffices to choose s to

---

[4] If the item's key size is known and fixed, one could use algorithms like *Radixsort*.

be 32 or 64 keys.) Each thread then participates in running the parallel BitonicSort (Fig. 12.29) on the $s \cdot p$ sample keys selected by the p threads. Finally, each thread reads the $p - 1$ splitter keys in positions $s, 2s, \ldots, (p - 1)s$ in the sorted set of splitters, and uses these as the splitters in the second phase. This choice of s samples, and the later choice of the final splitters from the sorted set of all samples, reduces the effects of an uneven key distribution among the n/p size data sets accessed by the threads.

For example, a sample sort algorithm could choose to have each thread pick $p - 1$ splitters for its second phase from within its own n/p size data set, without ever communicating with other threads. The problem with this approach is that if the distribution of the data is uneven, the size of the buckets may differ greatly, and performance would suffer. For example, if the number of items in the largest bucket is doubled, so is the worst-case time complexity of the sorting algorithm.

The first phase's complexity is s (a constant) to perform the random sampling, and $O(\log^2 p)$ for the parallel Bitonic sort. The overall time complexity of sample sort with a good splitter set (where every bucket gets $O(n/p)$ of the items) is

$$O(\log^2 p) + O((n/p)\log p) + O((n/p)\log(n/p)),$$

which overall is $O((n/p)\log(n/p))$.

12.10 Distributed coordination

This chapter covered several distributed coordination patterns. Some, such as combining trees, sorting networks, and sample sorting, have high parallelism and low overhead. All these algorithms contain synchronization bottlenecks, that is, points in the computation where threads must wait to rendezvous with others. In combining trees, threads must synchronize to combine; when sorting, threads synchronize at barriers.

In other schemes, such as counting networks and diffracting trees, threads never wait for one another. (Although we implement balancers using **synchronized** methods, they could be implemented in a lock-free manner using compareAndSet().) Here, the distributed structures pass information from one thread to another, and while a rendezvous could prove advantageous (as in the Prism array), it is not necessary.

Randomization, which is useful in many places, helps to distribute work evenly. For diffracting trees, randomization distributes work over multiple memory locations, reducing the chance that too many threads simultaneously access the same location. For sample sort, randomization helps distribute work evenly among buckets, which threads later sort in parallel.

Finally, we saw that pipelining can ensure that some data structures can have high throughput, even though they have high latency.

Although we focus on shared-memory multiprocessors, it is worth mentioning that the distributed algorithms and structures considered in this chapter also work in message passing architectures. The message passing model might be implemented directly in hardware, as in a network of processors, or it could be provided on top of a shared-memory architecture through a software layer such as MPI.

In shared-memory architectures, switches (such as combining tree nodes or balancers) are naturally implemented as shared-memory counters. In message passing architectures, switches are naturally implemented as processor-local data structures, where wires that link one processor to another also link one switch to another. When a processor receives a message, it atomically updates its local data structure and forwards messages to the processors managing other switches.

12.11 **Chapter notes**

The idea behind combining trees is due to Allan Gottlieb, Ralph Grishman, Clyde Kruskal, Kevin McAuliffe, Larry Rudolph, and Marc Snir [53]. The software CombiningTree presented here is adapted from an algorithm by PenChung Yew, Nian-Feng Tzeng, and Duncan Lawrie [168] with modifications by Maurice Herlihy, Beng-Hong Lim, and Nir Shavit [71], all based on an original proposal by James Goodman, Mary Vernon, and Philip Woest [51].

Counting networks were invented by Jim Aspnes, Maurice Herlihy, and Nir Shavit [14]. Counting networks are related to *sorting networks*, including the groundbreaking Bitonic network of Kenneth Batcher [16], and the periodic network of Martin Dowd, Yehoshua Perl, Larry Rudolph, and Mike Saks [40]. Miklós Ajtai, János Komlós, and Endre Szemerédi discovered the AKS sorting network, an $O(\log w)$ depth sorting network [8]. (This asymptotic expression hides large constants that make networks based on AKS impractical.)

Mike Klugerman and Greg Plaxton [93,94] were the first to provide an AKS-based counting network construction with $O(\log w)$ depth. The 0-1 principle for sorting networks is by Donald Knuth [95]. A similar set of rules for balancing networks is provided by Costas Busch and Marios Mavronicolas [26]. Diffracting trees were invented by Nir Shavit and Asaph Zemach [158].

Sample sorting was suggested by John Reif and Leslie Valiant [148] and by Huang and Chow [80]. The sequential Quicksort algorithm to which all sample sorting algorithms relate is due to Tony Hoare [76]. There are numerous parallel radix sort algorithms in the literature such as the one by Daniel Jiménez-González, Joseph Larriba-Pey, and Juan Navarro [91] or the one by Shin-Jae Lee, Minsoo Jeon, Dongseung Kim, and Andrew Sohn [111].

Monty Python and the Holy Grail was written by Graham Chapman, John Cleese, Terry Gilliam, Eric Idle, Terry Jones, and Michael Palin and codirected by Terry Gilliam and Terry Jones [28].

12.12 Exercises

Exercise 12.1. Prove Lemma 12.5.1.

Exercise 12.2. Implement a *trinary* CombiningTree, that is, one that allows up to three threads coming from three subtrees to combine at a given node. Can you estimate the advantages and disadvantages of such a tree when compared with a *binary* combining tree?

Exercise 12.3. Implement a CombiningTree using Exchanger objects to perform the coordination among threads ascending and descending the tree. What are the possible disadvantages of your construction when compared to the CombiningTree class presented in Section 12.3?

Exercise 12.4. Implement the cyclic array-based shared pool described in Section 12.2 using two simple counters and a ReentrantLock per array entry.

Exercise 12.5. Provide an efficient lock-free implementation of a Balancer.

Exercise 12.6. (Hard) Provide an efficient wait-free implementation of a Balancer (i.e., not by using the universal construction).

Exercise 12.7. Prove that the TREE $[2k]$ balancing network constructed in Section 12.6 is a counting network, that is, that in any quiescent state, the sequences of tokens on its output wires have the step property.

Exercise 12.8. Let B be a width-w balancing network of depth d in a quiescent state s. Let $n = 2^d$. Prove that if n tokens enter the network on the same wire, pass through the network, and exit, then B will have the same state after the tokens exit as it did before they entered.

Exercise 12.9. Let X and Y be k-smooth sequences of length w. A *matching* layer of balancers for X and Y is one where each element of X is joined by a balancer to an element of Y in a one-to-one correspondence.

Prove that if X and Y are each k-smooth and Z is the result of matching X and Y, then Z is $(k+1)$-smooth.

Exercise 12.10. Consider a BLOCK $[k]$ network in which each balancer has been initialized to an arbitrary state (either *up* or *down*). Show that no matter what the input distribution is, the output distribution is $(\log k)$-smooth.

Hint: You may use the claim in Exercise 12.9.

Exercise 12.11. A *smoothing network* is a balancing network that ensures that in any quiescent state, the output sequence is 1-smooth.

Counting networks are smoothing networks, but not vice versa.

A Boolean sorting network is one in which all inputs are guaranteed to be Boolean. Define a *pseudosorting balancing network* to be a balancing network with a layout isomorphic to a Boolean sorting network.

Let $\mathcal{N}$ be the balancing network constructed by taking a smoothing network $\mathcal{S}$ of width w, taking a pseudosorting balancing network $\mathcal{P}$ also of width w, and joining the ith output wire of $\mathcal{S}$ to the ith input wire of $\mathcal{P}$.

Show that $\mathcal{N}$ is a counting network.

Exercise 12.12. A *3-balancer* is a balancer with three input lines and three output lines. Like its 2-line relative, its output sequences have the step property in any quiescent state. Construct a depth-3 counting network with six input and output lines from 2-balancers and 3-balancers. Explain why it works.

Exercise 12.13. Suggest ways to modify the BitonicSort class so that it will sort an input array of width w, where w is not a power of 2.

Exercise 12.14. Consider the following w-thread counting algorithm. Each thread first uses a bitonic counting network of width w to take a counter value v. It then goes through a *waiting filter*, in which each thread waits for threads with lower values to catch up.

The waiting filter is an array filter[] of w Boolean values. Define the phase function

$$\phi(v) = \lfloor (v/w) \rfloor \bmod 2.$$

A thread that exits with value v spins on filter[$(v - 1) \bmod n$] until that value is set to $\phi(v - 1)$. The thread responds by setting filter[$v \bmod w$] to $\phi(v)$, and then returns v.

1. Explain why this counter implementation is linearizable.
2. An exercise here shows that any linearizable counting network has depth at least w. Explain why the filter[] construction does not contradict this claim.
3. On a bus-based multiprocessor, would this filter[] construction have better throughput than a single variable protected by a spin lock? Explain.

Exercise 12.15. If a sequence $X = x_0, \ldots x_{w-1}$ is k-smooth, then the result of passing X through a balancing network is k-smooth.

Exercise 12.16. Prove that the BITONIC $[w]$ network has depth $(\log w)(1 + \log w)/2$ and uses $(w \log w)(1 + \log w)/4$ balancers.

Exercise 12.17. Show that the OddEven network in Fig. 12.28 is a sorting network but not a counting network.

Exercise 12.18. Can counting networks do anything besides increments? Consider a new kind of token, called an *antitoken*, which we use for decrements. Recall that when a token visits a balancer, it executes getAndComplement(): It atomically reads the toggle value and complements it, and then departs on the output wire indicated by the old toggle value. Instead, an antitoken complements the toggle value, and then departs on the output wire indicated by the new toggle value. Informally, an antitoken "cancels" the effect of the most recent token on the balancer's toggle state, and vice versa.

```
1    public synchronized int antiTraverse() {
2      try {
3        if (toggle) {
4          return 1;
5        } else {
6          return 0;
7        }
8      } finally {
9        toggle = !toggle;
10     }
11   }
```

FIGURE 12.30

The antiTraverse() method.

Instead of simply balancing the number of tokens that emerge on each wire, we assign a *weight* of $+1$ to each token and -1 to each antitoken. We generalize the step property to require that the sums of the weights of the tokens and antitokens that emerge on each wire have the step property. We call this property the *weighted step property*.

Fig. 12.30 shows an antiTraverse() method that moves an antitoken though a balancer. (Other networks would need different antiTraverse() methods.)

Let B be a width-w balancing network of depth d in a quiescent state s. Let $n = 2^d$. Show that if n tokens enter the network on the same wire, pass through the network, and exit, then B will have the same state after the tokens exit as it did before they entered.

Exercise 12.19. Let B be a balancing network in a quiescent state s, and suppose a token enters on wire i and passes through the network, leaving the network in state s'. Show that if an antitoken now enters on wire i and passes through the network, then the network goes back to state s.

Exercise 12.20. Show that if balancing network B is a counting network for tokens alone, then it is also a balancing network for tokens and antitokens.

Exercise 12.21. A *switching network* is a directed graph, where edges are called *wires* and nodes are called *switches*. Each thread shepherds a *token* through the network. Switches and tokens are allowed to have internal states. A token arrives at a switch via an input wire. In one atomic step, the switch absorbs the token, changes its state and possibly the token's state, and emits the token on an output wire. Here, for simplicity, switches have two input and output wires. Note that switching networks are more powerful than balancing networks, since switches can have arbitrary state (instead of a single bit) and tokens also have state.

An *adding network* is a switching network that allows threads to add (or subtract) arbitrary values.

We say that a token is *in front of* a switch if it is on one of the switch's input wires. Start with the network in a quiescent state q_0, where the next token to run will take value 0. Imagine we have one token t of weight a and $n-1$ tokens $t_1, \ldots, t_{n-1}$ all of weight b, where $b > a$, each on a distinct input wire. Denote by S the set of switches that t traverses if it traverses the network by starting in q_0.

Prove that if we run the $t_1, \ldots, t_{n-1}$ one at a time though the network, we can halt each t_i in front of a switch of S.

At the end of this construction, $n - 1$ tokens are in front of switches of S. Since switches have two input wires, it follows that t's path through the network encompasses at least $n - 1$ switches, so any adding network must have depth at least $n - 1$, where n is the maximum number of concurrent tokens. This bound is discouraging because it implies that the size of the network depends on the number of threads (also true for CombiningTrees, but not counting networks), and that the network has inherently high latency.

Exercise 12.22. Extend the proof of Exercise 12.21 to show that a *linearizable* counting network has depth at least n.

Concurrent hashing and natural parallelism

13.1 Introduction

In earlier chapters, we studied how to extract parallelism from data structures like queues, stacks, and counters, which seemed to provide few opportunities for parallelism. In this chapter we take the opposite approach. We study *concurrent hashing*, a problem that seems to be "naturally parallelizable" or, using a more technical term, *disjoint-access-parallel*, meaning that concurrent method calls are likely to access disjoint locations, implying that there is little need for synchronization.

We study hashing in the context of Set implementations. Recall that the Set interface provides the following methods:

- add(x) adds x to the set, and returns *true* if x was absent, and *false* otherwise;
- remove(x) removes x from the set, and returns *true* if x was present, and *false* otherwise; and
- contains(x) returns *true* if x is present, and *false* otherwise.

In sequential programming, hashing is often used to implement these methods with constant average time complexity. In this chapter, we aim to do the same for concurrent Set implementations. (By contrast, the Set implementations of Chapter 9 require time linear in the size of the set.) Although hashing seems naturally parallelizable, devising an effective concurrent hash-based Set implementations is far from trivial.

When designing Set implementations, we should keep the following principle in mind: *We can buy more memory, but we cannot buy more time.* Between a fast algorithm that consumes more memory and a slower algorithm that consumes less memory, we tend to prefer the faster algorithm (within reason).

A *hash set* (sometimes called a *hash table*) is an efficient way to implement a set. A hash set is typically implemented as an array, called the *table*. Each table entry is a reference to zero or more *items*. A *hash function* maps items to integers so that distinct items usually map to distinct values. (Java provides each object with a hashCode() method that serves this purpose.) To add, remove, or test an item for membership, apply the hash function to the item (modulo the table size) to identify the table entry associated with that item. (We call this step *hashing* the item.)

Any hash set algorithm must deal with *collisions*: what to do when distinct items hash to the same table entry. *Closed addressing* simply stores a set of items, traditionally called a *bucket*, at each entry. *Open addressing* attempts to find an alternative table entry for the item, for example by applying alternative hash functions.

The Art of Multiprocessor Programming. https://doi.org/10.1016/B978-0-12-415950-1.00023-9

It is sometimes necessary to *resize* the table. In closed-address hash sets, buckets may become too large to search efficiently. In open-address hash sets, the table may become too full to find alternative table entries.

Anecdotal evidence suggests that in most applications, sets are subject to the following distribution of method calls: 90% contains(), 9% add(), and 1% remove() calls. As a practical matter, sets are more likely to grow than to shrink, so we focus here on *extensible hashing*, in which hash sets only grow (shrinking them is a problem for the exercises).

13.2 Closed-address hash sets

We start by defining a *base* hash set implementation common to all the concurrent closed-address hash sets we consider here. Later, we extend the base hash set with different synchronization mechanisms.

The BaseHashSet<T> class is an *abstract class*, that is, it does not implement all its methods. Fig. 13.1 shows its fields, constructor, and abstract methods. The table[] field is an array of buckets, each of which is a set implemented as a list. For convenience, we use ArrayList<T>, which supports the standard sequential add(), remove(), and contains() methods. We sometimes refer to the length of the table[] array, that is, the number of buckets in it, as its *capacity*. The setSize field stores the number of items in the set. The constructor takes the initial capacity of the table as an argument.

PRAGMA 13.2.1

Here and elsewhere, we use the standard Java List<T> interface (from package java.util). A List<T> is an ordered collection of T objects, where T is a type. It specifies many methods, of which we use the following: add(x), which appends x to the end of the list; get(i), which returns (but does not remove) the item at position i; and contains(x), which returns *true* if the list contains x.

The List interface is implemented by many classes. Here, we use the ArrayList class for convenience.

The *abstract methods* of BaseHashSet<T> class, which it does not implement, are: acquire(x), which acquires the locks necessary to manipulate item x; release(x), which releases them; resize(), which doubles the capacity of the table[] array; and policy(), which decides whether to resize. The acquire(x) method must be *reentrant*, meaning that if a thread that has already called acquire(x) makes the same call, then it will proceed without deadlocking with itself.

Fig. 13.2 shows the contains(x) and add(x) methods of the BaseHashSet<T> class. Each method first calls acquire(x) to perform the necessary synchronization and then enters a **try** block whose **finally** block calls release(x). The contains(x) method simply tests whether x is present in the associated bucket (line 21), while add(x) adds x to the list if it is not already present (line 30).

```
 1  public abstract class BaseHashSet<T> {
 2    protected volatile List<T>[] table;
 3    protected AtomicInteger setSize;
 4    public BaseHashSet(int capacity) {
 5      setSize = new AtomicInteger(0);
 6      table = (List<T>[]) new List[capacity];
 7      for (int i = 0; i < capacity; i++) {
 8        table[i] = new ArrayList<T>();
 9      }
10    }
11    ...
12    public abstract void acquire(T x);
13    public abstract void release(T x);
14    public abstract void resize();
15    public abstract boolean policy();
16  }
```

FIGURE 13.1

BaseHashSet<T> class: fields, constructor, and abstract methods.

How big should the bucket array be to ensure that method calls take constant expected time? Consider an add(x) call. The first step, hashing x to determine the bucket, takes constant time. The second step, checking whether x is in the bucket, requires traversing the list. This traversal takes constant expected time only if the lists have constant expected length, so the table capacity should be proportional to the number of items in the set, that is, the size of the set. Because the set may vary in size over time, to ensure that method call times remain (more or less) constant, we must occasionally *resize* the table to ensure that list lengths remain (more or less) constant.

We still need to decide *when* to resize the table, and how resize() synchronizes with other methods. There are many reasonable alternatives. For closed-addressing algorithms, one simple strategy is to resize the table when the average bucket size exceeds a fixed threshold. An alternative policy employs two fixed quantities, the *bucket threshold* and the *global threshold*; we resize the table

- if more than, say, a quarter of the buckets exceed the bucket threshold, or
- if any single bucket exceeds the global threshold.

Either of these strategies work can well in practice. For simplicity, we adopt the first policy in this chapter.[1]

---

[1] This choice introduces a scalability bottleneck, threads adding or removing items all contend on the counter that tracks the size of the set. We use an AtomicInteger, which limits scalability. It can be replaced by other, more scalable, counter implementations, if necessary.

```
17    public boolean contains(T x) {
18      acquire(x);
19      try {
20        int myBucket = x.hashCode() % table.length;
21        return table[myBucket].contains(x);
22      } finally {
23        release(x);
24      }
25    }
26    public boolean add(T x) {
27      boolean result = false;
28      acquire(x);
29      try {
30        int myBucket = x.hashCode() % table.length;
31        if (! table[myBucket].contains(x)) {
32          table[myBucket].add(x);
33          result = true;
34          setSize.getAndIncrement();
35        }
36      } finally {
37        release(x);
38      }
39      if (policy())
40        resize();
41      return result;
42    }
```

FIGURE 13.2

BaseHashSet<T> class: the contains() and add() methods hash the item to choose a bucket.

13.2.1 A coarse-grained hash set

Fig. 13.3 shows the CoarseHashSet<T> class's fields, constructor, and acquire(x) and release(x) methods. The constructor first initializes its superclass (line 4). Synchronization is provided by a single reentrant lock (line 2), acquired by acquire(x) (line 8) and released by release(x) (line 11).

Fig. 13.4 shows the CoarseHashSet<T> class's policy() and resize() methods. We use a simple policy: We resize when the average bucket length exceeds 4 (line 16). The resize() method locks the set (line 19), and checks that no other thread has resized the table in the meantime (line 22). It then allocates and initializes a new table with double the capacity (lines 24–28) and transfers items from the old to the new buckets (lines 29–33). Finally, it unlocks the set (line 35).

Like the coarse-grained list studied in Chapter 9, the coarse-grained hash set is easy to understand and easy to implement. Unfortunately, it is also a sequential bottleneck. Method calls take effect in a one-at-a-time order, even when they access separate buckets (and do not resize).

```
1   public class CoarseHashSet<T> extends BaseHashSet<T>{
2     final Lock lock;
3     CoarseHashSet(int capacity) {
4       super(capacity);
5       lock = new ReentrantLock();
6     }
7     public final void acquire(T x) {
8       lock.lock();
9     }
10    public void release(T x) {
11      lock.unlock();
12    }
13    ...
14  }
```

FIGURE 13.3

CoarseHashSet<T> class: fields, constructor, and acquire() and release() methods.

```
15    public boolean policy() {
16      return setSize.get() / table.length > 4;
17    }
18    public void resize() {
19      lock.lock();
20      try {
21        if (!policy()) {
22          return; // someone beat us to it
23        }
24        int newCapacity = 2 * table.length;
25        List<T>[] oldTable = table;
26        table = (List<T>[]) new List[newCapacity];
27        for (int i = 0; i < newCapacity; i++)
28          table[i] = new ArrayList<T>();
29        for (List<T> bucket : oldTable) {
30          for (T x : bucket) {
31            table[x.hashCode() % table.length].add(x);
32          }
33        }
34      } finally {
35        lock.unlock();
36      }
37    }
```

FIGURE 13.4

CoarseHashSet<T> class: the policy() and resize() methods.

```
1   public class StripedHashSet<T> extends BaseHashSet<T>{
2     final ReentrantLock[] locks;
3     public StripedHashSet(int capacity) {
4       super(capacity);
5       locks = new Lock[capacity];
6       for (int j = 0; j < locks.length; j++) {
7         locks[j] = new ReentrantLock();
8       }
9     }
10    public final void acquire(T x) {
11      locks[x.hashCode() % locks.length].lock();
12    }
13    public void release(T x) {
14      locks[x.hashCode() % locks.length].unlock();
15    }
16    ...
17  }
```

FIGURE 13.5

StripedHashSet<T> class: fields, constructor, and acquire() and release() methods.

13.2.2 A striped hash set

We now present a closed-address hash table with greater parallelism and less lock contention. Instead of using a single lock to synchronize the entire set, we split the set into independently synchronized pieces. We introduce a technique called *lock striping*, which will be useful for other data structures as well. Fig. 13.5 shows the fields and constructor for the StripedHashSet<T> class. The set is initialized with an array locks[] of L locks, and an array table[] of $N = L$ buckets, where each bucket is an unsynchronized List<T>. Although these arrays are initially of the same length, table[] will grow when the hash table is resized, but lock[] will not. When the hash table is resized, we double the table capacity N without changing the lock array size L; lock i protects each table entry j, where $j = i$ (mod L). The acquire(x) and release(x) methods use x's hash code to pick which lock to acquire or release. An example illustrating how a StripedHashSet<T> is resized appears in Fig. 13.6.

There are two reasons not to grow the lock array when we grow the table:

- Associating a lock with every table entry could consume too much space, especially when tables are large and contention is low.
- While resizing the table is straightforward, resizing the lock array (while in use) is more complex, as discussed in Section 13.2.3.

Resizing a StripedHashSet (Fig. 13.7) is almost identical to resizing a CoarseHashSet<>. One difference is that in StripedHashSet, the resize() method acquires all the locks in lock[] in ascending order (lines 19–21). It cannot deadlock with a contains(), add(), or remove() call because these methods acquire only a single lock. A resize() call cannot deadlock with another resize() call because both

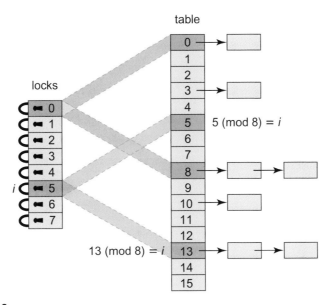

FIGURE 13.6

Resizing a `StripedHashSet` lock-based hash table. As the table grows, the striping is adjusted to ensure that each lock covers $2^{N/L}$ entries. In the figure above, $N=16$ and $L=8$. When N is doubled from 8 to 16, the memory is striped so that lock $i=5$, for example, covers both locations that are equal to 5 modulo L.

calls start without holding any locks, and acquire the locks in the same order. What if two or more threads try to resize at the same time? As in `CoarseHashSet<T>`, after a thread has acquired all the locks, if it discovers that some other thread has changed the table capacity (line 24), then it releases the locks and gives up. (It could just double the table size anyway, since it already holds all the locks.) Otherwise, it creates a new `table[]` array with twice the capacity (line 26), and transfers items from the old table to the new (line 31). Finally, it releases the locks (line 37).

To summarize, striped locking permits more concurrency than a single coarse-grained lock because method calls whose items hash to different locks can proceed in parallel. The `add()`, `contains()`, and `remove()` methods take constant expected time, but `resize()` takes linear time and is a "stop-the-world" operation: It halts all concurrent method calls while it increases the table's capacity.

13.2.3 A refinable hash set

What if we want to refine the granularity of locking as the table size grows, so that the number of locations in a stripe does not continuously grow? Clearly, if we want to resize the lock array, then we need to rely on another form of synchronization. Resizing is rare, so our principal goal is to devise a way to permit the lock array to be resized without substantially increasing the cost of normal method calls.

```
18   public void resize() {
19     for (Lock lock : locks) {
20       lock.lock();
21     }
22     try {
23       if (!policy()) {
24         return; // someone beat us to it
25       }
26       int newCapacity = 2 * table.length;
27       List<T>[] oldTable = table;
28       table = (List<T>[]) new List[newCapacity];
29       for (int i = 0; i < newCapacity; i++)
30         table[i] = new ArrayList<T>();
31       for (List<T> bucket : oldTable) {
32         for (T x : bucket) {
33           table[x.hashCode() % table.length].add(x);
34         }
35       }
36     } finally {
37       for (Lock lock : locks) {
38         lock.unlock();
39       }
40     }
41   }
```

FIGURE 13.7

StripedHashSet<T> class: To resize the set, lock each lock in order, and then check that no other thread has resized the table in the meantime.

Fig. 13.8 shows the fields and constructor for the RefinableHashSet<T> class. To add a higher level of synchronization, we introduce a global owner field that combines a Boolean value with a reference to a thread in an AtomicMarkableReference<Thread> so they can be modified atomically (see Pragma 9.8.1). We use owner as a mutual exclusion flag between the resize() method and any of the add() methods, so that while resizing, there will be no successful updates, and while updating, there will be no successful resizes. Normally, the Boolean value is *false*, meaning that the set is not in the middle of resizing. While a resizing is in progress, however, the Boolean value is *true*, and the associated reference indicates the thread that is in charge of resizing. Every add() call must read the owner field. Because resizing is rare, the value of owner should usually be cached.

Each method locks the bucket for x by calling acquire(x), shown in Fig. 13.9. It spins until no other thread is resizing the set (lines 19–21), and then reads the lock array (line 22). It then acquires the item's lock (line 24), and checks again, this time while holding a lock (line 26), to make sure no other thread is resizing, and that no resizing took place between lines 21 and 26.

If it passes this test, the thread can proceed. Otherwise, the lock it has acquired could be out-of-date because of an ongoing update, so it releases it and starts over.

```
1   public class RefinableHashSet<T> extends BaseHashSet<T>{
2     AtomicMarkableReference<Thread> owner;
3     volatile ReentrantLock[] locks;
4     public RefinableHashSet(int capacity) {
5       super(capacity);
6       locks = new ReentrantLock[capacity];
7       for (int i = 0; i < capacity; i++) {
8         locks[i] = new ReentrantLock();
9       }
10      owner = new AtomicMarkableReference<Thread>(null, false);
11    }
12    ...
13  }
```

FIGURE 13.8

RefinableHashSet<T> class: fields and constructor.

```
14    public void acquire(T x) {
15      boolean[] mark = {true};
16      Thread me = Thread.currentThread();
17      Thread who;
18      while (true) {
19        do {
20          who = owner.get(mark);
21        } while (mark[0] && who != me);
22        ReentrantLock[] oldLocks = locks;
23        ReentrantLock oldLock = oldLocks[x.hashCode() % oldLocks.length];
24        oldLock.lock();
25        who = owner.get(mark);
26        if ((!mark[0] || who == me) && locks == oldLocks) {
27          return;
28        } else {
29          oldLock.unlock();
30        }
31      }
32    }
33    public void release(T x) {
34      locks[x.hashCode() % locks.length].unlock();
35    }
```

FIGURE 13.9

RefinableHashSet<T> class: acquire() and release() methods.

When starting over, it will first spin until the current resize completes (lines 19–21) before attempting to acquire the locks again. The release(x) method releases the lock acquired by acquire(x).

The resize() method (Fig. 13.10) is similar to the resize() method for the StripedHashSet class. However, instead of acquiring all the locks in lock[], the

```
36    public void resize() {
37      boolean[] mark = {false};
38      Thread me = Thread.currentThread();
39      if (owner.compareAndSet(null, me, false, true)) {
40        try {
41          if (!policy()) { // someone else resized first
42            return;
43          }
44          quiesce();
45          int newCapacity = 2 * table.length;
46          List<T>[] oldTable = table;
47          table = (List<T>[]) new List[newCapacity];
48          for (int i = 0; i < newCapacity; i++)
49            table[i] = new ArrayList<T>();
50          locks = new ReentrantLock[newCapacity];
51          for (int j = 0; j < locks.length; j++) {
52            locks[j] = new ReentrantLock();
53          }
54          initializeFrom(oldTable);
55        } finally {
56          owner.set(null, false);
57        }
58      }
59    }
```

FIGURE 13.10

RefinableHashSet<T> class: resize() method.

```
60    protected void quiesce() {
61      for (ReentrantLock lock : locks) {
62        while (lock.isLocked()) {}
63      }
64    }
```

FIGURE 13.11

RefinableHashSet<T> class: quiesce() method.

method attempts to set itself as the owner (line 39) and then calls quiesce() (line 44) to ensure that no other thread is in the middle of an add(), remove(), or contains() call. The quiesce() method (Fig. 13.11) visits each lock and waits until it is unlocked.

The acquire() and the resize() methods guarantee mutually exclusive access via the flag principle using the mark field of the owner flag and the table's locks array: acquire() first acquires its locks and then reads the mark field, while resize() first sets mark and then reads the locks during the quiesce() call. This ordering ensures that any thread that acquires a lock after quiesce() has completed will see that the set is in the process of being resized, and will back off until the resizing is complete.

Similarly, resize() will first set the mark field and then read the locks, and will not proceed while any add(), remove(), or contains() call holds its lock.

To summarize, we have designed a hash table in which both the number of buckets and the number of locks can be continually resized. One limitation of this algorithm is that threads cannot access the items in the table during a resize.

13.3 A lock-free hash set

The next step is to make the hash set implementation lock-free, and to make resizing *incremental*, meaning that each add() method call performs a small fraction of the work associated with resizing. This way, we do not need to "stop the world" to resize the table. Each of the contains(), add(), and remove() methods takes constant expected time.

To make resizable hashing lock-free, it is not enough to make the individual buckets lock-free: Resizing the table requires atomically moving entries from old buckets to new buckets. If the table doubles in capacity, then we must split the items in the old bucket between two new buckets. If this move is not done atomically, entries might be temporarily lost or duplicated. Without locks, we must synchronize using atomic methods such as compareAndSet(). Unfortunately, these methods operate only on a single memory location, which makes it difficult to move a node atomically from one linked list to another.

13.3.1 Recursive split-ordering

We now describe a hash set implementation that works by flipping the conventional hashing structure on its head:

> *Instead of moving the items among the buckets, move the buckets among the items.*

More specifically, keep all items in a single lock-free linked list, similar to the LockFreeList class studied in Chapter 9. A bucket is just a reference into the list. As the list grows, we introduce additional bucket references so that no object is ever too far from the start of a bucket. This algorithm ensures that once an item is placed in the list, it is never moved, but it does require that items be inserted according to a *recursive split-order* algorithm that we describe shortly.

Fig. 13.12 illustrates a lock-free hash set implementation. It shows two components: a lock-free linked list and an expanding array of references into the list. These references are *logical* buckets. Any item in the hash set can be reached by traversing the list from its head, while the bucket references provide shortcuts into the list to minimize the number of list nodes traversed when searching. The principal challenge is ensuring that the bucket references into the list remain well distributed as the number of items in the set grows. Bucket references should be spaced evenly enough to allow constant-time access to any node. It follows that new buckets must be created and assigned to sparsely covered regions in the list.

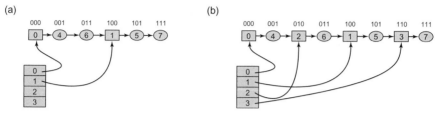

FIGURE 13.12

This figure explains the recursive nature of the split ordering. Part (a) shows a split-ordered list consisting of two buckets. The array of buckets refer into a single linked list. The split-ordered keys (above each node) are the reverse of the bit-wise representation of the items' keys. The active bucket array entries 0 and 1 have special sentinel nodes within the list (square nodes), while other (ordinary) nodes are round. Items 4 (whose reverse bit order is "001") and 6 (whose reverse bit order is "011") are in bucket 0, since the least significant bit (LSB) of the original key is "0." Items 5 and 7 (whose reverse bit orders are "101" and "111," respectively) are in bucket 1, since the LSB of their original key is 1. Part (b) shows how each of the two buckets is split in half once the table capacity grows from two buckets to four. The reverse-bit values of the two added buckets 2 and 3 happen to perfectly split buckets 0 and 1.

As before, the capacity N of the hash set is always a power of two. The bucket array initially has capacity 2 and all bucket references are *null*, except for the bucket at index 0, which refers to an empty list. We use the variable bucketSize to denote this changing capacity of the bucket structure. Each entry in the bucket array is initialized when first accessed, and subsequently refers to a node in the list.

When an item with hash code k is inserted, removed, or searched for, the hash set uses bucket index k (mod N). As with earlier hash set implementations, we decide when to double the table capacity by consulting a policy() method. Here, however, the table is resized incrementally by the methods that modify it, so there is no explicit resize() method. If the table capacity is 2^i, then the bucket index is the integer represented by the key's i LSBs; in other words, each bucket b contains items each of whose hash code k satisfies $k = b$ (mod 2^i).

Because the hash function depends on the table capacity, we must be careful when the table capacity changes. An item inserted before the table was resized must be accessible afterwards from both its previous and current buckets. When the capacity grows to 2^{i+1}, the items in bucket b are split between two buckets: Those for which $k = b$ (mod 2^{i+1}) remain in bucket b, while those for which $k = b + 2^i$ (mod 2^{i+1}) migrate to bucket $b + 2^i$. Here is the key idea behind the algorithm: We ensure that these two groups of items are positioned one after the other in the list, so that splitting bucket b is achieved by simply setting bucket $b + 2^i$ after the first group of items and before the second. This organization keeps each item in the second group accessible from bucket b.

As depicted in Fig. 13.12, items in the two groups are distinguished by their ith binary digits (counting backwards, from least significant to most significant). Those with digit 0 belong to the first group, and those with 1 to the second. The next hash table doubling will cause each group to split again into two groups differentiated by the $(i + 1)$st bit, and so on. For example, the items 4 ("100" binary) and 6 ("110") share the same LSB. When the table capacity is 2^1, they are in the same bucket, but when it grows to 2^2, they will be in distinct buckets because their second bits differ.

This process induces a total order on items, which we call *recursive split-ordering*, as can be seen in Fig. 13.12. Given a key's hash code, its order is defined by its bit-reversed value.

To recapitulate: a *split-ordered hash set* is an array of buckets, where each bucket is a reference into a lock-free list where nodes are sorted by their bit-reversed hash codes. The number of buckets grows dynamically, and each new bucket is initialized when accessed for the first time.

To avoid an awkward "corner case" that arises when deleting a node referenced by a bucket reference, we add a *sentinel* node, which is never deleted, to the start of each bucket. Specifically, suppose the table capacity is 2^{i+1}. The first time that bucket $b + 2^i$ is accessed, a sentinel node is created with key $b + 2^i$. This node is inserted in the list via bucket b, the *parent* bucket of $b + 2^i$. Under split-ordering, $b + 2^i$ precedes all items of bucket $b + 2^i$, since those items must end with $(i + 1)$ bits forming the value $b + 2^i$. This value also comes after all the items of bucket b that do not belong to $b + 2^i$: They have identical LSBs, but their ith bit is 0. Therefore, the new sentinel node is positioned in the exact list location that separates the items of the new bucket from the remaining items of bucket b. To distinguish sentinel items from ordinary items, we set the most significant bit (MSB) of ordinary items to 1, and leave the sentinel items with 0 at the MSB. Fig. 13.17 illustrates two methods: makeOrdinaryKey(), which generates a split-ordered key for an object, and makeSentinelKey(), which generates a split-ordered key for a bucket index.

Fig. 13.13 illustrates how inserting a new key into the set can cause a bucket to be initialized. The split-order key values are written above the nodes using 8-bit words. For instance, the split-order value of 3 is the bit-reverse of its binary representation, which is 11000000. The square nodes are the sentinel nodes corresponding to buckets with original keys that are 0, 1, and 3 modulo 4 with their MSB being 0. The split-order keys of ordinary (round) nodes are exactly the bit-reversed images of the original keys after turning on their MSB. For example, items 9 and 13 are in the "1 (mod 4)" bucket, which can be recursively split in two by inserting a new node between them. The sequence of figures describes an object with hash code 10 being added when the table capacity is 4 and buckets 0, 1, and 3 are already initialized.

The table is grown incrementally; there is no explicit resize operation. Recall that each bucket is a linked list, with nodes ordered based on the split-ordered hash values. As mentioned earlier, the table resizing mechanism is independent of the policy used to decide when to resize. To keep the example concrete, we implement the following policy: We use a shared counter to allow add() calls to track the average bucket load. When the average load crosses a threshold, we double the table capacity.

To avoid technical distractions, we keep the array of buckets in a large, fixed-size array. We start out using only the first array entry, and use progressively more of the array as the capacity grows. When the add() method accesses an uninitialized

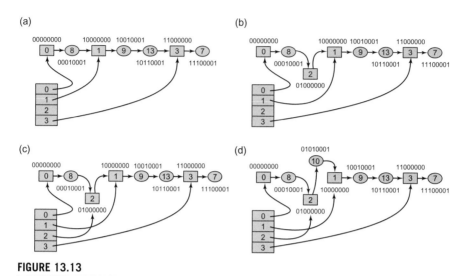

FIGURE 13.13

How the add() method places key 10 to the lock-free table. As in earlier figures, the split-order key values, expressed as 8-bit binary words, appear above the nodes. For example, the split-order value of 1 is the bit-wise reversal of its binary representation. In step (a), buckets 0, 1, and 3 are initialized, but bucket 2 is uninitialized. In step (b), an item with hash value 10 is inserted, causing bucket 2 to be initialized. A new sentinel is inserted with split-order key 2. In step (c), bucket 2 is assigned a new sentinel. Finally, in step (d), the split-order ordinary key 10 is added to bucket 2.

bucket that should have been initialized given the current table capacity, it initializes it. While conceptually simple, this design is far from ideal, since the fixed array size limits the ultimate number of buckets. In practice, it would be better to represent the buckets as a multilevel tree structure, which would cover the machine's full memory size, a task we leave as an exercise.

13.3.2 The BucketList class

Fig. 13.14 shows the fields, the constructor, and some utility methods of the BucketList class that implements the lock-free list used by the split-ordered hash set. Although this class is essentially the same as the LockFreeList class from Chapter 9, there are two important differences. The first is that items are sorted in recursive-split order, not simply by hash code. The makeOrdinaryKey() and makeSentinelKey() methods (lines 10 and 14) show how we compute these split-ordered keys. (To ensure that reversed keys are positive, we use only the lower three bytes of the hash code.) Fig. 13.15 shows how the contains() method is modified to use the split-ordered key. (As in the LockFreeList class, the find(x) method returns a record containing x's node, if it exists, along with the immediately preceding and subsequent nodes.)

The second difference is that while the LockFreeList class uses only two sentinels, one at each end of the list, the BucketList<T> class places a sentinel at the start of each

```
1   public class BucketList<T> implements Set<T> {
2     static final int HI_MASK = 0x80000000;
3     static final int MASK = 0x00FFFFFF;
4     Node head;
5     public BucketList() {
6       head = new Node(0);
7       head.next =
8         new AtomicMarkableReference<Node>(new Node(Integer.MAX_VALUE), false);
9     }
10    public int makeOrdinaryKey(T x) {
11      int code = x.hashCode() & MASK; // take 3 lowest bytes
12      return reverse(code | HI_MASK);
13    }
14    private static int makeSentinelKey(int key) {
15      return reverse(key & MASK);
16    }
17    ...
18  }
```

FIGURE 13.14

BucketList<T> class: fields, constructor, and utilities.

```
19    public boolean contains(T x) {
20      int key = makeOrdinaryKey(x);
21      Window window = find(head, key);
22      Node curr = window.curr;
23      return (curr.key == key);
24    }
```

FIGURE 13.15

BucketList<T> class: the contains() method.

new bucket whenever the table is resized. It requires the ability to insert sentinels at intermediate positions within the list, and to traverse the list starting from such sentinels. The BucketList<T> class provides a getSentinel(x) method (Fig. 13.16) that takes a bucket index, finds the associated sentinel (inserting it if absent), and returns the tail of the BucketList<T> starting from that sentinel.

13.3.3 The LockFreeHashSet<T> class

Fig. 13.17 shows the fields and constructor for the LockFreeHashSet<T> class. The set has the following mutable fields: bucket is an array of BucketList<T> references into the list of items, bucketSize is an atomic integer that tracks how much of the bucket array is currently in use, and setSize is an atomic integer that tracks how many objects are in the set. These fields are used to decide when to resize.

```
25    public BucketList<T> getSentinel(int index) {
26      int key = makeSentinelKey(index);
27      boolean splice;
28      while (true) {
29        Window window = find(head, key);
30        Node pred = window.pred;
31        Node curr = window.curr;
32        if (curr.key == key) {
33          return new BucketList<T>(curr);
34        } else {
35          Node node = new Node(key);
36          node.next.set(pred.next.getReference(), false);
37          splice = pred.next.compareAndSet(curr, node, false, false);
38          if (splice)
39            return new BucketList<T>(node);
40          else
41            continue;
42        }
43      }
44    }
```

FIGURE 13.16

BucketList<T> class: getSentinel() method.

```
1   public class LockFreeHashSet<T> {
2     protected BucketList<T>[] bucket;
3     protected AtomicInteger bucketSize;
4     protected AtomicInteger setSize;
5     public LockFreeHashSet(int capacity) {
6       bucket = (BucketList<T>[]) new BucketList[capacity];
7       bucket[0] = new BucketList<T>();
8       bucketSize = new AtomicInteger(2);
9       setSize = new AtomicInteger(0);
10    }
11    ...
12  }
```

FIGURE 13.17

LockFreeHashSet<T> class: fields and constructor.

Fig. 13.18 shows the LockFreeHashSet<T> class's add() method. If x has hash code k, add(x) retrieves bucket k (mod N), where N is the current table size, initializing it if necessary (line 15). It then calls the BucketList<T>'s add(x) method. If x was not already present (line 18), it increments setSize and checks whether to increase bucketSize, the number of active buckets. The contains(x) and remove(x) methods work in much the same way.

```
13    public boolean add(T x) {
14      int myBucket = BucketList.hashCode(x) % bucketSize.get();
15      BucketList<T> b = getBucketList(myBucket);
16      if (!b.add(x))
17        return false;
18      int setSizeNow = setSize.getAndIncrement();
19      int bucketSizeNow = bucketSize.get();
20      if (setSizeNow / bucketSizeNow > THRESHOLD)
21        bucketSize.compareAndSet(bucketSizeNow, 2 * bucketSizeNow);
22      return true;
23    }
```

FIGURE 13.18

LockFreeHashSet<T> class: add() method.

```
24    private BucketList<T> getBucketList(int myBucket) {
25      if (bucket[myBucket] == null)
26        initializeBucket(myBucket);
27      return bucket[myBucket];
28    }
29    private void initializeBucket(int myBucket) {
30      int parent = getParent(myBucket);
31      if (bucket[parent] == null)
32        initializeBucket(parent);
33      BucketList<T> b = bucket[parent].getSentinel(myBucket);
34      if (b != null)
35        bucket[myBucket] = b;
36    }
37    private int getParent(int myBucket){
38      int parent = bucketSize.get();
39      do {
40        parent = parent >> 1;
41      } while (parent > myBucket);
42      parent = myBucket - parent;
43      return parent;
44    }
```

FIGURE 13.19

LockFreeHashSet<T> class: If a bucket is uninitialized, initialize it by adding a new sentinel. Initializing a bucket may require initializing its parent.

Fig. 13.19 shows the initialBucket() method, whose role is to initialize the bucket array entry at a particular index, setting that entry to refer to a new sentinel node. The sentinel node is first created and added to an existing *parent* bucket, and then the array entry is assigned a reference to the sentinel. If the parent bucket is not

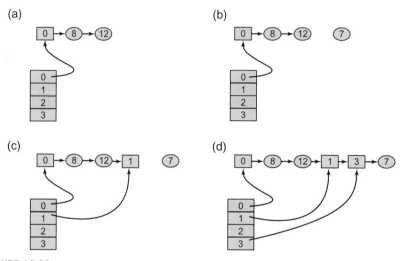

FIGURE 13.20

Recursive initialization of lock-free hash table buckets. (a) The table has four buckets; only bucket 0 is initialized. (b) We wish to insert the item with key 7. Bucket 3 now requires initialization, which in turn requires recursive initialization of bucket 1. (c) Bucket 1 is initialized by first adding the 1 sentinel to the list, then setting the bucket to this sentinel. (d) Then bucket 3 is initialized in a similar fashion, and finally 7 is added to the list. In the worst case, insertion of an item may require recursively initializing a number of buckets logarithmic in the table size, but it can be shown that the expected length of such a recursive sequence is constant.

initialized (line 31), initialBucket() is applied recursively to the parent. To control the recursion, we maintain the invariant that the parent index is less than the new bucket index. It is also prudent to choose the parent index as close as possible to the new bucket index, but still preceding it. We compute this index by unsetting the bucket index's most significant nonzero bit (line 39).

The add(), remove(), and contains() methods require a constant expected number of steps to find a key (or determine that the key is absent). To initialize a bucket in a table of bucketSize N, the initialBucket() method may need to recursively initialize (i.e., split) as many as $O(\log N)$ of its parent buckets to allow the insertion of a new bucket. An example of this recursive initialization is shown in Fig. 13.20. In part (a), the table has four buckets; only bucket 0 is initialized. In part (b), the item with key 7 is inserted. Bucket 3 now requires initialization, further requiring recursive initialization of bucket 1. In part (c), bucket 1 is initialized. Finally, in part (d), bucket 3 is initialized. Although the worst-case complexity in such a case is logarithmic, not constant, it can be shown that the *expected length* of any such recursive sequence of splits is constant, making the overall expected complexity of all the hash set operations constant.

13.4 An open-address hash set

We now turn our attention to a concurrent open-address hashing algorithm. Open-address hashing, in which each table entry holds a single item rather than a set, seems harder to make concurrent than closed-address hashing. We base our concurrent algorithm on a sequential algorithm known as cuckoo hashing.

13.4.1 Cuckoo hashing

Cuckoo hashing is a (sequential) hashing algorithm in which a newly added item displaces any earlier item occupying the same slot.[2] For brevity, a *table* is a k-entry array of items. For a hash set of size $N = 2k$, we use a two-entry array table[] of tables,[3] and two independent hash functions,

$$h_0, h_1 : KeyRange \rightarrow 0, \ldots, k-1$$

(denoted as hash0() and hash1() in the code), mapping the set of possible keys to entries in the array. To test whether a value x is in the set, contains(x) tests whether either table[0][$h_0(x)$] or table[1][$h_1(x)$] is equal to x. Similarly, remove(x) checks whether x is in either table[0][$h_0(x)$] or table[1][$h_1(x)$], and removes it if found.

The add(x) method (Fig. 13.21) is the most interesting. It successively "kicks out" conflicting items until every key has a slot. To add x, the method swaps x with y, the current occupant of table[0][$h_0(x)$] (line 6). If the prior value y was *null*, it is done (line 7). Otherwise, it swaps the newly nestless value y for the current occupant of table[1][$h_1(y)$] in the same way (line 8). As before, if the prior value was *null*, it is done. Otherwise, the method continues swapping entries (alternating tables) until it finds an empty slot. An example of such a sequence of displacements appears in Fig. 13.22.

We might not find an empty slot, either because the table is full, or because the sequence of displacements forms a cycle. We therefore need an upper limit on the number of successive displacements we are willing to undertake (line 5). When this limit is exceeded, we resize the hash table, choose new hash functions (line 12), and start over (line 13).

Sequential cuckoo hashing is attractive for its simplicity. It provides constant-time contains() and remove() methods, and it can be shown that over time, the average number of displacements caused by each add() call will be constant. Experimental evidence shows that sequential cuckoo hashing works well in practice.

---

[2] Cuckoos are a family of birds (not clocks) found in North America and Europe. Most species are nest parasites: they lay their eggs in other birds' nests. Cuckoo chicks hatch early, and quickly push the other eggs out of the nest.

[3] This division of the table into two arrays helps in presenting the concurrent algorithm. There are sequential cuckoo hashing algorithms that use, for the same number of hashed items, only a single array of size $2k$.

```
1   public boolean add(T x) {
2     if (contains(x)) {
3       return false;
4     }
5     for (int i = 0; i < LIMIT; i++) {
6       if ((x = swap(0, hash0(x), x)) == null) {
7         return true;
8       } else if ((x = swap(1, hash1(x), x)) == null) {
9         return true;
10      }
11    }
12    resize();
13    add(x);
14  }
```

FIGURE 13.21

Sequential cuckoo hashing: the add() method.

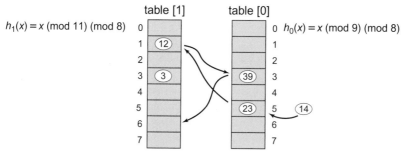

$h_1(x) = x \pmod{11} \pmod{8}$ table [1]   table [0] $h_0(x) = x \pmod{9} \pmod{8}$

FIGURE 13.22

A sequence of displacements starts when an item with key 14 finds both locations Table[0][$h_0(14)$] and Table[1][$h_1(14)$] taken by the values 3 and 23, and ends when the item with key 39 is successfully placed in Table[1][$h_1(39)$].

13.4.2 Concurrent cuckoo hashing

The principal obstacle to making the sequential cuckoo hashing algorithm concurrent is the add() method's need to perform a long sequence of swaps. To address this problem, we now define an alternative cuckoo hashing algorithm, the PhasedCuckooHashSet<T> class. We break up each method call into a sequence of *phases*, where each phase adds, removes, or displaces a single item x.

Rather than organizing the set as a two-dimensional table of items, we use a two-dimensional table of *probe sets*, where a probe set is a constant-sized set of items with the same hash code. Each probe set holds at most PROBE_SIZE items, but the algorithm tries to ensure that when the set is quiescent (i.e., no method calls are in progress), each probe set holds no more than THRESHOLD < PROBE_SIZE items. An example of

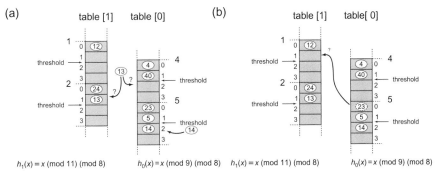

FIGURE 13.23

The PhasedCuckooHashSet<T> class: add() and relocate() methods. The figure shows the array segments consisting of eight probe sets of size 4 each, with a threshold of 2. Shown are probe sets 4 and 5 of Table[0][] and 1 and 2 of Table[1][]. In part (a), an item with key 13 finds Table[0][4] above threshold and Table[1][2] below threshold, so it adds the item to the probe set Table[1][2]. The item with key 14, on the other hand, finds that both of its probe sets are above threshold, so it adds its item to Table[0][5] and signals that the item should be relocated. In part (b), the method tries to relocate the item with key 23, the oldest item in Table[0][5]. Since Table[1][1] is below threshold, the item is successfully relocated. If Table[1][1] were above threshold, the algorithm would attempt to relocate item 12 from Table[1][1], and if Table[1][1] were at the probe set's size limit of four items, it would attempt to relocate the item with key 5, the next oldest item, from Table[0][5].

```
 1   public abstract class PhasedCuckooHashSet<T> {
 2     volatile int capacity;
 3     volatile List<T>[][] table;
 4     public PhasedCuckooHashSet(int size) {
 5       capacity = size;
 6       table = (List<T>[][]) new java.util.ArrayList[2][capacity];
 7       for (int i = 0; i < 2; i++) {
 8         for (int j = 0; j < capacity; j++) {
 9           table[i][j] = new ArrayList<T>(PROBE_SIZE);
10         }
11       }
12     }
13     ...
14   }
```

FIGURE 13.24

PhasedCuckooHashSet<T> class: fields and constructor.

the PhasedCuckooHashSet structure appears in Fig. 13.23, where the PROBE_SIZE is 4 and the THRESHOLD is 2. While method calls are in-flight, a probe set may temporarily hold more than THRESHOLD but never more than PROBE_SIZE items. (In our examples, it is convenient to implement each probe set as a fixed-size List<T>.) Fig. 13.24 shows the PhasedCuckooHashSet<T>'s fields and constructor.

```
15    public boolean remove(T x) {
16      acquire(x);
17      try {
18        List<T> set0 = table[0][hash0(x) % capacity];
19        if (set0.contains(x)) {
20          set0.remove(x);
21          return true;
22        } else {
23          List<T> set1 = table[1][hash1(x) % capacity];
24          if (set1.contains(x)) {
25            set1.remove(x);
26            return true;
27          }
28        }
29        return false;
30      } finally {
31        release(x);
32      }
33    }
```

FIGURE 13.25

PhasedCuckooHashSet<T> class: the remove() method.

To postpone our discussion of synchronization, the PhasedCuckooHashSet<T> class is defined to be *abstract*: it does not implement all its methods. It has the same abstract methods as the BaseHashSet<T> class: The acquire(x) method acquires all the locks necessary to manipulate item x, release(x) releases them, and resize() resizes the set. (As before, we require acquire(x) to be reentrant.)

From a bird's-eye view, the PhasedCuckooHashSet<T> works as follows: It adds and removes items by first locking the associated probe sets in both tables. To remove an item, it proceeds as in the sequential algorithm, checking if it is in one of the probe sets and, if so, removing it. To add an item, it attempts to add it to one of the probe sets. An item's probe sets serve as temporary overflow buffers for long sequences of consecutive displacements that might occur when adding an item to the table. The THRESHOLD value is essentially the size of the probe sets in a sequential algorithm. If a probe set already has this many items, the item is added anyway to one of the PROBE_SIZE–THRESHOLD overflow slots. The algorithm then tries to relocate another item from the probe set. There are various policies one can use to choose which item to relocate. Here, we move the oldest items out first, until the probe set is below threshold. As in the sequential cuckoo hashing algorithm, one relocation may trigger another, and so on.

Fig. 13.25 shows the PhasedCuckooHashSet<T> class's remove(x) method. It calls the abstract acquire(x) method to acquire the necessary locks and then enters a **try** block whose **finally** block calls release(x). In the **try** block, the method simply checks whether x is present in Table[0][$h_0(x)$] or Table[1][$h_1(x)$]. If so, it removes x and returns *true*; otherwise, it returns *false*. The contains(x) method works similarly.

```
34   public boolean add(T x) {
35     T y = null;
36     acquire(x);
37     int h0 = hash0(x) % capacity, h1 = hash1(x) % capacity;
38     int i = -1, h = -1;
39     boolean mustResize = false;
40     try {
41       if (present(x)) return false;
42       List<T> set0 = table[0][h0];
43       List<T> set1 = table[1][h1];
44       if (set0.size() < THRESHOLD) {
45         set0.add(x); return true;
46       } else if (set1.size() < THRESHOLD) {
47         set1.add(x); return true;
48       } else if (set0.size() < PROBE_SIZE) {
49         set0.add(x); i = 0; h = h0;
50       } else if (set1.size() < PROBE_SIZE) {
51         set1.add(x); i = 1; h = h1;
52       } else {
53         mustResize = true;
54       }
55     } finally {
56       release(x);
57     }
58     if (mustResize) {
59       resize(); add(x);
60     } else if (!relocate(i, h)) {
61       resize();
62     }
63     return true; // x must have been present
64   }
```

FIGURE 13.26

PhasedCuckooHashSet<T> class: the add() method.

Fig. 13.26 illustrates the add(x) method. Like remove(), it calls acquire(x) to acquire the necessary locks and then enters a **try** block whose **finally** block calls release(x). It returns *false* if the item is already present (line 41). If either of the item's probe sets is below threshold (lines 44 and 46), it adds the item and returns. Otherwise, if either of the item's probe sets is above threshold but not full (lines 48 and 50), it adds the item and makes a note to rebalance the probe set later. Finally, if both sets are full, it makes a note to resize the entire set (line 53). It then releases the lock on x (line 56).

If the method was unable to add x because both its probe sets were full, it resizes the hash set and tries again (line 58). If the probe set at row r and column c was above threshold, it calls relocate(r, c) (described later) to rebalance probe set sizes.

```
65    protected boolean relocate(int i, int hi) {
66      int hj = 0;
67      int j = 1 - i;
68      for (int round = 0; round < LIMIT; round++) {
69        List<T> iSet = table[i][hi];
70        T y = iSet.get(0);
71        switch (i) {
72        case 0: hj = hash1(y) % capacity; break;
73        case 1: hj = hash0(y) % capacity; break;
74        }
75        acquire(y);
76        List<T> jSet = table[j][hj];
77        try {
78          if (iSet.remove(y)) {
79            if (jSet.size() < THRESHOLD) {
80              jSet.add(y);
81              return true;
82            } else if (jSet.size() < PROBE_SIZE) {
83              jSet.add(y);
84              i = 1 - i;
85              hi = hj;
86              j = 1 - j;
87            } else {
88              iSet.add(y);
89              return false;
90            }
91          } else if (iSet.size() >= THRESHOLD) {
92            continue;
93          } else {
94            return true;
95          }
96        } finally {
97          release(y);
98        }
99      }
100     return false;
101   }
```

FIGURE 13.27

PhasedCuckooHashSet<T> class: the relocate() method.

If the call returns *false*, indicating that it failed to rebalance the probe sets, then add()
resizes the table.

The relocate() method appears in Fig. 13.27. It takes the row and column coordi-
nates of a probe set observed to have more than THRESHOLD items, and tries to reduce
its size below threshold by moving items from this probe set to alternative probe sets.

This method makes a fixed number (LIMIT) of attempts before giving up. Each time around the loop, the following invariants hold: iSet is the probe set we are trying to shrink, y is the oldest item in iSet, and jSet is the other probe set where y could be. The loop identifies y (line 70), locks both probe sets to which y could belong (line 75), and tries to remove y from the probe set (line 78). If it succeeds (another thread could have removed y between lines 70 and 78), then it prepares to add y to jSet. If jSet is below threshold (line 79), then the method adds y to jSet and returns *true* (no need to resize). If jSet is above threshold but not full (line 82), then it tries to shrink jSet by swapping iSet and jSet (lines 82–86) and resuming the loop. If jSet is full (line 87), the method puts y back in iSet and returns *false* (triggering a resize). Otherwise it tries to shrink jSet by swapping iSet and jSet (lines 82–86). If the method does not succeed in removing y at line 78, then it rechecks the size of iSet. If it is still above threshold (line 91), then the method resumes the loop and tries again to remove an item. Otherwise, iSet is below threshold, and the method returns *true* (no resize needed). Fig. 13.23 shows an example execution of the PhasedCuckooHashSet<T>, where the item with key 14 causes a relocation of the oldest item 23 from the probe set table[0][5].

13.4.3 Striped concurrent cuckoo hashing

We first consider a concurrent cuckoo hash set implementation using lock striping (Section 13.2.2). The StripedCuckooHashSet class extends PhasedCuckooHashSet, providing a fixed 2-by-L array of reentrant locks. As usual, lock[i][j] protects table[i][k], where k (mod L) $= j$. Fig. 13.28 shows the StripedCuckooHashSet class's fields and constructor. The constructor calls the PhasedCuckooHashSet<T> constructor (line 4) and then initializes the lock array.

The StripedCuckooHashSet class's acquire(x) and release(x) methods (Fig. 13.29) lock and unlock lock[0][$h_0(x)$] and lock[1][$h_1(x)$] (in that order, to avoid deadlock).

```
1  public class StripedCuckooHashSet<T> extends PhasedCuckooHashSet<T>{
2    final ReentrantLock[][] lock;
3    public StripedCuckooHashSet(int capacity) {
4      super(capacity);
5      lock = new ReentrantLock[2][capacity];
6      for (int i = 0; i < 2; i++) {
7        for (int j = 0; j < capacity; j++) {
8          lock[i][j] = new ReentrantLock();
9        }
10     }
11   }
12   ...
13 }
```

FIGURE 13.28

StripedCuckooHashSet class: fields and constructor.

```
14   public final void acquire(T x) {
15     lock[0][hash0(x) % lock[0].length].lock();
16     lock[1][hash1(x) % lock[1].length].lock();
17   }
18   public final void release(T x) {
19     lock[0][hash0(x) % lock[0].length].unlock();
20     lock[1][hash1(x) % lock[1].length].unlock();
21   }
```

FIGURE 13.29

StripedCuckooHashSet class: acquire() and release().

```
22   public void resize() {
23     int oldCapacity = capacity;
24     for (Lock aLock : lock[0]) {
25       aLock.lock();
26     }
27     try {
28       if (capacity != oldCapacity) {
29         return;
30       }
31       List<T>[][] oldTable = table;
32       capacity = 2 * capacity;
33       table = (List<T>[][]) new List[2][capacity];
34       for (List<T>[] row : table) {
35         for (int i = 0; i < row.length; i++) {
36           row[i] = new ArrayList<T>(PROBE_SIZE);
37         }
38       }
39       for (List<T>[] row : oldTable) {
40         for (List<T> set : row) {
41           for (T z : set) {
42             add(z);
43           }
44         }
45       }
46     } finally {
47       for (Lock aLock : lock[0]) {
48         aLock.unlock();
49       }
50     }
51   }
```

FIGURE 13.30

StripedCuckooHashSet class: the resize() method.

The only difference between the resize() methods of StripedCuckooHashSet (Fig. 13.30) and StripedHashSet is that the latter acquires the locks in lock[0] in ascending order (line 24). Acquiring these locks in this order ensures that no other thread is in the middle of an add(), remove(), or contains() call, and avoids deadlocks with other concurrent resize() calls.

13.4.4 A refinable concurrent cuckoo hash set

This section introduces the RefinableCuckooHashSet class (Fig. 13.31), using the methods of Section 13.2.3 to resize the lock arrays. Just as for the RefinableHashSet class, we introduce an owner field of type AtomicMarkableReference<Thread> that combines a Boolean value with a reference to a thread. If the Boolean value is *true*, the set is resizing, and the reference indicates which thread is in charge of resizing.

Each phase locks the buckets for x by calling acquire(x), shown in Fig. 13.32. It reads the lock array (line 24), and then spins until no other thread is resizing the set (lines 21–23). It then acquires the item's two locks (lines 27 and 28), and checks if the lock array is unchanged (line 30). If the lock array has not changed between lines 24 and 30, then the thread has acquired the locks it needs to proceed. Otherwise, the locks it has acquired are out of date, so it releases them and starts over. The release(x) method, also shown in Fig. 13.32, releases the locks acquired by acquire(x).

The resize() method (Fig. 13.33) is almost identical to the resize() method for StripedCuckooHashSet. One difference is that the locks[] array has two dimensions.

The quiesce() method (Fig. 13.34), like its counterpart in the RefinableHashSet class, visits each lock and waits until it is unlocked. The only difference is that it visits only the locks in locks[0].

```
1   public class RefinableCuckooHashSet<T> extends PhasedCuckooHashSet<T>{
2     AtomicMarkableReference<Thread> owner;
3     volatile ReentrantLock[][] locks;
4     public RefinableCuckooHashSet(int capacity) {
5       super(capacity);
6       locks = new ReentrantLock[2][capacity];
7       for (int i = 0; i < 2; i++) {
8         for (int j = 0; j < capacity; j++) {
9           locks[i][j] = new ReentrantLock();
10        }
11      }
12      owner = new AtomicMarkableReference<Thread>(null, false);
13    }
14    ...
15  }
```

FIGURE 13.31

RefinableCuckooHashSet<T>: fields and constructor.

```
16    public void acquire(T x) {
17      boolean[] mark = {true};
18      Thread me = Thread.currentThread();
19      Thread who;
20      while (true) {
21        do { // wait until not resizing
22          who = owner.get(mark);
23        } while (mark[0] && who != me);
24        ReentrantLock[][] oldLocks = locks;
25        ReentrantLock oldLock0 = oldLocks[0][hash0(x) % oldLocks[0].length];
26        ReentrantLock oldLock1 = oldLocks[1][hash1(x) % oldLocks[1].length];
27        oldLock0.lock();
28        oldLock1.lock();
29        who = owner.get(mark);
30        if ((!mark[0] || who == me) && locks == oldLocks) {
31          return;
32        } else {
33          oldLock0.unlock();
34          oldLock1.unlock();
35        }
36      }
37    }
38    public void release(T x) {
39      locks[0][hash0(x)].unlock();
40      locks[1][hash1(x)].unlock();
41    }
```

FIGURE 13.32

RefinableCuckooHashSet<T>: acquire() and release() methods.

13.5 Chapter notes

The term *disjoint-access-parallelism* was coined by Amos Israeli and Lihu Rappoport [84]. Maged Michael [126] has shown that simple algorithms using a reader–writer lock [124] per bucket have reasonable performance without resizing. The lock-free hash set based on split-ordering described in Section 13.3.1 is by Ori Shalev and Nir Shavit [156]. The optimistic and fine-grained hash sets are adapted from a hash set implementation by Doug Lea [108], used in java.util.concurrent.

Other concurrent closed-addressing schemes include ones by Meichun Hsu and Wei-Pang Yang [79], Vijay Kumar [97], Carla Schlatter Ellis [43], and Michael Greenwald [54]. Hui Gao, Jan Friso Groote, and Wim Hesselink [50] proposed an almost wait-free extensible open-addressing hashing algorithm, and Chris Purcell and Tim Harris [143] proposed a concurrent nonblocking hash table with open addressing. Cuckoo hashing is credited to Rasmus Pagh and Flemming Rodler [136], and the concurrent version is by Maurice Herlihy, Nir Shavit, and Moran Tzafrir [73].

```
42    public void resize() {
43      int oldCapacity = capacity;
44      Thread me = Thread.currentThread();
45      if (owner.compareAndSet(null, me, false, true)) {
46        try {
47          if (capacity != oldCapacity) { // someone else resized first
48            return;
49          }
50          quiesce();
51          capacity = 2 * capacity;
52          List<T>[][] oldTable = table;
53          table = (List<T>[][]) new List[2][capacity];
54          locks = new ReentrantLock[2][capacity];
55          for (int i = 0; i < 2; i++) {
56            for (int j = 0; j < capacity; j++) {
57              locks[i][j] = new ReentrantLock();
58            }
59          }
60          for (List<T>[] row : table) {
61            for (int i = 0; i < row.length; i++) {
62              row[i] = new ArrayList<T>(PROBE_SIZE);
63            }
64          }
65          for (List<T>[] row : oldTable) {
66            for (List<T> set : row) {
67              for (T z : set) {
68                add(z);
69              }
70            }
71          }
72        } finally {
73          owner.set(null, false);
74        }
75      }
76    }
```

FIGURE 13.33

RefinableCuckooHashSet<T>: the resize() method.

```
77    protected void quiesce() {
78      for (ReentrantLock lock : locks[0]) {
79        while (lock.isLocked()) {}
80      }
81    }
```

FIGURE 13.34

RefinableCuckooHashSet<T>: the quiesce() method.

```
1  public class UnboundedResizeLockFreeHashSet<T> {
2      public UnboundedResizeLockFreeHashSet(int initialMinimumNumBuckets) { ... }
3      private BucketList<T> getBucketList(int hashCode) { ... }
4      private void resize() { ... }
5      public boolean add(T x) { ... }
6      public boolean remove(T x) { ... }
7      public boolean contains(T x) { ... }
8  }
```

FIGURE 13.35

The UnboundedResizeLockFreeHashSet class.

13.6 Exercises

Exercise 13.1. Modify the StripedHashSet to allow resizing of the range lock array using read–write locks.

Exercise 13.2. For the LockFreeHashSet, show an example of the problem that arises when deleting an entry pointed to by a bucket reference, if we do not add a *sentinel* entry, which is never deleted, to the start of each bucket.

Exercise 13.3. For the LockFreeHashSet, when an uninitialized bucket is accessed in a table of size N, it might be necessary to recursively initialize (i.e., split) as many as $O(\log N)$ of its parent buckets to allow the insertion of a new bucket. Show an example of such a scenario. Explain why the expected length of any such recursive sequence of splits is constant.

Exercise 13.4. For the LockFreeHashSet, design a lock-free data structure to replace the fixed-size bucket array. Your data structure should allow an arbitrary number of buckets.

Exercise 13.5. For the LockFreeHashSet, design a lock-free data structure to replace the fixed-size bucket array. Your data structure should allow for unbounded doubling of the number of buckets in order to keep the average bucket length below THRESHOLD. Describe how you would implement the methods in Fig. 13.35 and how your implementation preserves lock-freedom, correctness, and expected or amortized $O(1)$ work.

Exercise 13.6. Outline correctness arguments for LockFreeHashSet's add(), remove(), and contains() methods.

Hint: You may assume the LockFreeList algorithm's methods are correct.

Skiplists and balanced search

14

14.1 Introduction

We have seen several concurrent implementations of sets based on linked lists and on hash tables. We now turn our attention to concurrent search structures with logarithmic depth. There are many concurrent logarithmic search structures in the literature. Here, we are interested in search structures intended for in-memory data, as opposed to data residing on outside storage such as disks.

Many popular sequential search structures, such as red-black trees or AVL trees, require periodic *rebalancing* to maintain the structure's logarithmic depth. Rebalancing works well for sequential tree-based search structures, but for concurrent structures, rebalancing may cause bottlenecks and contention. Instead, we focus here on concurrent implementations of a proved data structure that provides expected logarithmic-time search without the need to rebalance: the SkipList. In the following sections, we present two SkipList implementations. The LazySkipList class is a lock-based implementation, while the LockFreeSkipList class is not. In both algorithms, the typically most frequent method, contains(), which searches for an item, is wait-free. These constructions follow the design patterns outlined earlier in Chapter 9.

14.2 Sequential skiplists

For simplicity, we treat the list as a set, meaning that keys are unique. A SkipList is a collection of sorted linked lists, which mimics, in a subtle way, a balanced search tree. Nodes in a SkipList are ordered by key. Each node is linked into a subset of the lists. Each list has a *level*, ranging from 0 to a maximum. The bottom-level list contains all the nodes, and each higher-level list is a sublist of the lower-level lists. Fig. 14.1 shows a SkipList with integer keys. The higher-level lists are *shortcuts* into the lower-level lists, because, roughly speaking, each link at level i skips over about 2^i nodes in the lowest-level list, (e.g., in the SkipList shown in Fig. 14.1, each reference at level 3 skips over 2^3 nodes). Between any two nodes at a given level, the number of nodes in the level immediately below it is effectively constant, so the total height of the SkipList is roughly logarithmic in the number of nodes. One can find a node with a given key by searching first through the lists in higher levels, skipping

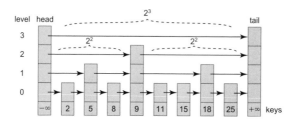

FIGURE 14.1

The SkipList class: This example has four levels of lists. Each node has a key, and the head and tail sentinels have $\pm\infty$ keys. The list at level i is a shortcut where each reference skips over 2^i nodes of the next lower level list. For example, at level 3, references skip 2^3 nodes; at level 2, 2^2 nodes, and so on.

over large numbers of lower nodes, and progressively descending until a node with the target key is found (or not) at the bottom level.

The SkipList is a *probabilistic* data structure. (No one knows how to provide this kind of performance without randomization.) Each node is created with a random top level (topLevel) and belongs to all lists up to that level. Top levels are chosen so that the expected number of nodes in each level's list decreases exponentially. Let $0 < p < 1$ be the conditional probability that a node at level i also appears at level $i + 1$. All nodes appear at level 0. The probability that a node at level 0 also appears at level $i > 0$ is p^i. For example, with $p = 1/2$, $1/2$ of the nodes are expected to appear at level 1, $1/4$ at level 2, and so on, providing a *balancing* property like the classical sequential tree-based search structures, but without the need for complex global restructuring.

We put head and tail sentinel nodes at the beginning and end of the lists with the maximum allowed height. Initially, when the SkipList is empty, the head (left sentinel) is the predecessor of the tail (right sentinel) at every level. The head's key is less than any key that may be added to the set, and the tail's key is greater.

Each SkipList node's next field is an array of references, one for each list to which it belongs, and so finding a node means finding its predecessors and successors. Searching the SkipList always begins at the head. The find() method proceeds down the levels one after the other, and traverses each level as in the LazyList using references to a predecessor node pred and a current node curr. Whenever it finds a node with a greater or matching key, it records the pred and curr as the predecessor and successor of a node in arrays called preds[] and succs[], and continues to the next lower level. The traversal ends at the bottom level. Fig. 14.2(a) shows a sequential find() call.

To add a node to a skiplist, a find() call fills in the preds[] and succs[] arrays. The new node is created and linked between its predecessors and successors. Fig. 14.2(b) shows an add(12) call.

To remove a victim node from the skiplist, the find() method initializes the victim's preds[] and succs[] arrays. The victim is then removed from the list at all levels by redirecting each predecessor's next reference to the victim's successor.

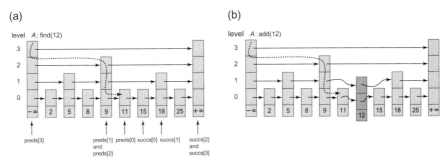

FIGURE 14.2

The SkipList class: add() and find() methods. In part (a), find() traverses at each level, starting at the highest level, for as long as curr is less than or equal to the target key 12. Otherwise, it stores pred and curr in the preds[] and succs[] arrays at each level and descends to the next level. For example, the node with key 9 is preds[2] and preds[1], while tail is succs[2] and the node with key 18 is succs[1]. Here, find() returns *false* since the node with key 12 was not found in the lowest-level list, and so an add(12) call in part (b) can proceed. In part (b), a new node is created with a random topLevel = 2. The new node's next references are redirected to the corresponding succs[] nodes, and each predecessor node's next reference is redirected to the new node.

14.3 A lock-based concurrent skiplist

We now describe the first concurrent skiplist design, the LazySkipList class. This class builds on the LazyList algorithm of Chapter 9: Each level of the SkipList structure is a LazyList, and as in the LazyList algorithm, the add() and remove() methods use optimistic fine-grained locking, while the contains() method is wait-free.

14.3.1 A bird's-eye view

Here is a bird's-eye view of the LazySkipList class. Start with Fig. 14.3. As in the LazyList class, each node has its own lock and a marked field indicating whether it is in the abstract set, or has been logically removed. All along, the algorithm maintains the *skiplist property*: Higher-level lists are always contained in lower-level lists.

The skiplist property is maintained using locks to prevent structural changes in the vicinity of a node while it is being added or removed, and by delaying any access to a node until it has been inserted into all levels of the list.

To add a node, it must be linked into the list at several levels. Every add() call calls find(), which traverses the skiplist and returns the node's predecessors and successors at all levels. To prevent changes to the node's predecessors while the node is being added, add() locks the predecessors, validates that the locked predecessors still refer to their successors, and then adds the node in a manner similar to the sequential add() shown in Fig. 14.2. To maintain the skiplist property, a node is not considered to be logically in the set until all references to it at all levels have been properly set. Each node has an additional flag, fullyLinked, set to *true* once it has been linked in

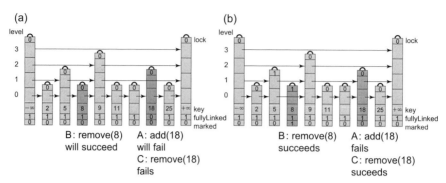

FIGURE 14.3

The LazySkipList class: failed and successful add() and remove() calls. In part (a), the add(18) call finds the node with key 18 unmarked but not yet fullyLinked. It spins waiting for the node to become fullyLinked in part (b), at which point it returns *false*. In part (a), the remove(8) call finds the node with key 8 unmarked and fully linked, which means that it can acquire the node's lock in part (b). It then sets the mark bit, and proceeds to lock the node's predecessors, in this case, the node with key 5. Once the predecessor is locked, it physically removes the node from the list by redirecting the bottom-level reference of the node with key 5, completing the successful remove(). In part (a), a remove(18) fails, because it found the node not fully linked. The same remove(18) call succeeds in part (b) because it found that the node is fully linked.

all its levels. We do not allow access to a node until it is fully linked, so for example, the add() method, when trying to determine whether the node it wishes to add is already in the list, must spin waiting for it to become fully linked. Fig. 14.3 shows a call to add(18) that spins waiting until the node with key 18 becomes fully linked.

To remove a node from the list, remove() uses find() to check whether a victim node with the target key is already in the list. If so, it checks whether the victim is ready to be deleted, that is, is fully linked and unmarked. In part (a) of Fig. 14.3, remove(8) finds the node with key 8 unmarked and fully linked, which means that it can remove it. The remove(18) call fails, because it found that the victim is not fully linked. The same remove(18) call succeeds in part (b) because it found that the victim is fully linked.

If the victim can be removed, remove() logically removes it by setting its mark bit. It completes the physical deletion of the victim by locking its predecessors at all levels and then the victim node itself, validating that the predecessors are unmarked and still refer to the victim, and then splicing out the victim node one level at a time. To maintain the skiplist property, the victim is spliced out from top to bottom.

For example, in part (b) of Fig. 14.3, remove(8) locks the predecessor node with key 5. Once this predecessor is locked, remove() physically removes the node from the list by redirecting the bottom-level reference of the node with key 5 to refer to the node with key 9.

In both the add() and remove() methods, if validation fails, find() is called again to find the newly changed set of predecessors, and the attempt to complete the method resumes.

The wait-free contains() method calls find() to locate the node containing the target key. If it finds a node, it determines whether the node is in the set by checking whether it is unmarked and fully linked. This method, like the LazyList class's contains(), is wait-free because it ignores any locks or concurrent changes in the SkipList structure.

To summarize, the LazySkipList class uses a technique familiar from earlier algorithms: It holds locks on all locations to be modified, validates that nothing important has changed, completes the modifications, and releases the locks (in this context, the fullyLinked flag acts like a lock).

14.3.2 **The algorithm**

Fig. 14.4 shows the LazySkipList's Node class. A key is in the set if and only if the list contains an unmarked, fully linked node with that key. Key 8 in part (a) of Fig. 14.3 is an example of such a key.

Fig. 14.5 shows the skiplist find() method. (The same method works in both the sequential and concurrent algorithms.) The find() method returns −1 if the item is not found. It traverses the SkipList using pred and curr references starting at the head and at the highest level.[1] This highest level can be maintained dynamically to reflect the highest level actually in the SkipList, but for brevity, we do not do so here. The find() method goes down the levels one after the other. At each level, it sets curr to be the pred node's successor. If it finds a node with a matching key, it records the level (line 48). If it does not find a node with a matching key, then find() records the pred and curr as the predecessor and successor at that level in the preds[] and succs[] arrays (lines 51–52), continuing to the next lower level starting from the current pred node. Part (a) of Fig. 14.2 shows how find() traverses a SkipList. Part (b) shows how find() results would be used to add() a new item to a SkipList.

Because we start with pred at the head sentinel node and always advance the window only if curr is less than the target key, pred is always a predecessor of the target key, and never refers to the node with the key itself. The find() method returns the preds[] and succs[] arrays as well as the level at which the node with a matching key was found.

The add(k) method, shown in Fig. 14.6, uses find() (Fig. 14.5) to determine whether a node with the target key k is already in the list (line 43). If an unmarked node with the key is found (lines 62–67), then add(k) returns *false*, indicating that the key k is already in the set. However, if that node is not yet fully linked (indicated by the fullyLinked field), then the thread waits until it is linked (because the key k is not in the abstract set until the node is fully linked). If the node found is marked,

---

[1] In Fig. 14.5, we make the curr field volatile to prevent compiler optimizations of the loop on line 44. Recall that making the node array volatile does not make the array entries volatile.

```
1    public final class LazySkipList<T> {
2      static final int MAX_LEVEL = ...;
3      final Node<T> head = new Node<T>(Integer.MIN_VALUE);
4      final Node<T> tail = new Node<T>(Integer.MAX_VALUE);
5      public LazySkipList() {
6        for (int i = 0; i < head.next.length; i++) {
7          head.next[i] = tail;
8        }
9      }
10     ...
11     private static final class Node<T> {
12       final Lock lock = new ReentrantLock();
13       final T item;
14       final int key;
15       final Node<T>[] next;
16       volatile boolean marked = false;
17       volatile boolean fullyLinked = false;
18       private int topLevel;
19       public Node(int key) { // sentinel node constructor
20         this.item = null;
21         this.key = key;
22         next = new Node[MAX_LEVEL + 1];
23         topLevel = MAX_LEVEL;
24       }
25       public Node(T x, int height) {
26         item = x;
27         key = x.hashCode();
28         next = new Node[height + 1];
29         topLevel = height;
30       }
31       public void lock() {
32         lock.lock();
33       }
34       public void unlock() {
35         lock.unlock();
36       }
37     }
38   }
```

FIGURE 14.4

The LazySkipList class: constructor, fields, and Node class.

then some other thread is in the process of deleting it, so the add() call simply retries. Otherwise, it checks whether the node is unmarked and fully linked, indicating that the add() call should return *false*. It is safe to check if the node is unmarked before the node is fully linked, because remove() methods do not mark nodes unless they

```
39    int find(T x, Node<T>[] preds, Node<T>[] succs) {
40      int key = x.hashCode();
41      int lFound = -1;
42      Node<T> pred = head;
43      for (int level = MAX_LEVEL; level >= 0; level--) {
44        volatile Node<T> curr = pred.next[level];
45        while (key > curr.key) {
46          pred = curr; curr = pred.next[level];
47        }
48        if (lFound == -1 && key == curr.key) {
49          lFound = level;
50        }
51        preds[level] = pred;
52        succs[level] = curr;
53      }
54      return lFound;
55    }
```

FIGURE 14.5

The LazySkipList class: the wait-free find() method. This algorithm is the same as in the sequential SkipList implementation. The preds[] and succs[] arrays are filled from the maximum level to level 0 with the predecessor and successor references for the given key.

are fully linked. If a node is unmarked and not yet fully linked, it must become unmarked and fully linked before it can become marked (see Fig. 14.7). This step is the linearization point (line 66) of an unsuccessful add() method call.

The add() method calls find() to initialize the preds[] and succs[] arrays to hold the ostensible predecessor and successor nodes of the node to be added. These references are unreliable, because they may no longer be accurate by the time the nodes are accessed. If no unmarked fully linked node was found with key k, then the thread proceeds to lock and validate each of the predecessors returned by find() from level 0 up to the topLevel of the new node (lines 74–80). To avoid deadlocks, both add() and remove() acquire locks in ascending order. The topLevel value is determined at the very beginning of the add() method using the randomLevel() method.[2] The validation (line 79) at each level checks that the predecessor is still adjacent to the successor and that neither is marked. If validation fails, the thread must have encountered the effects of a conflicting method, so it releases (in the **finally** block on line 87) the locks it acquired and retries.

If the thread successfully locks and validates the results of find() up to the topLevel of the new node, then the add() call will succeed because the thread holds

---

[2] The randomLevel() method is designed based on empirical measurements to maintain the skiplist property. For example, in the java.util.concurrent package, for a maximal SkipList level of 31, randomLevel() returns 0 with probability $\frac{3}{4}$, i with probability $2^{-(i+2)}$ for $i \in [1, 30]$, and 31 with probability 2^{-32}.

```
56    boolean add(T x) {
57      int topLevel = randomLevel();
58      Node<T>[] preds = (Node<T>[]) new Node[MAX_LEVEL + 1];
59      Node<T>[] succs = (Node<T>[]) new Node[MAX_LEVEL + 1];
60      while (true) {
61        int lFound = find(x, preds, succs);
62        if (lFound != -1) {
63          Node<T> nodeFound = succs[lFound];
64          if (!nodeFound.marked) {
65            while (!nodeFound.fullyLinked) {}
66            return false;
67          }
68          continue;
69        }
70        int highestLocked = -1;
71        try {
72          Node<T> pred, succ;
73          boolean valid = true;
74          for (int level = 0; valid && (level <= topLevel); level++) {
75            pred = preds[level];
76            succ = succs[level];
77            pred.lock.lock();
78            highestLocked = level;
79            valid = !pred.marked && !succ.marked && pred.next[level]==succ;
80          }
81          if (!valid) continue;
82          Node<T> newNode = new Node(x, topLevel);
83          for (int level = 0; level <= topLevel; level++)
84            newNode.next[level] = succs[level];
85          for (int level = 0; level <= topLevel; level++)
86            preds[level].next[level] = newNode;
87          newNode.fullyLinked = true; // successful add linearization point
88          return true;
89        } finally {
90          for (int level = 0; level <= highestLocked; level++)
91            preds[level].unlock();
92        }
93      }
94    }
```

FIGURE 14.6

The LazySkipList class: the add() method.

all the locks it needs. The thread then allocates a new node with the appropriate key and randomly chosen topLevel, links it in, and sets the new node's fullyLinked flag. Setting this flag is the linearization point of a successful add() method (line 87). It then releases all its locks and returns *true* (line 89). The only time a thread modifies an unlocked node's next field is when it initializes the new node's next references (line 83). This initialization is safe because it occurs before the new node is accessible.

The remove() method appears in Fig. 14.7. It calls find() to determine whether a node with the appropriate key is in the list. If so, the thread checks whether the node is ready to be deleted (line 104), meaning it is fully linked, unmarked, and at its top level. A node found below its top level was either not yet fully linked (see the node with key 18 in part (a) of Fig. 14.3) or marked and already partially unlinked by a concurrent remove() method call (the remove() method could continue, but the subsequent validation would fail).

If the node is ready to be deleted, the thread locks the node (line 109) and verifies that it is still not marked. If it is still not marked, the thread marks the node, logically deleting that item. This step (line 114) is the linearization point of a successful remove() call. If the node was marked, then the thread returns *false* since the node was already deleted. This step is one linearization point of an unsuccessful remove(). Another occurs when find() does not find a node with a matching key, or when the node with the matching key was marked, or not fully linked, or not found at its top level (line 104).

The rest of the method completes the physical deletion of the victim node. To remove the victim from the list, the remove() method first locks (in ascending order, to avoid deadlock) the victim's predecessors at all levels up to the victim's topLevel (lines 120–124). After locking each predecessor, it validates that the predecessor is still unmarked and still refers to the victim. It then splices out the victim one level at a time (line 128). To maintain the skiplist property, that any node reachable at a given level is reachable at lower levels, the victim is spliced out from top to bottom. If the validation fails at any level, then the thread releases the locks for the predecessors (but not the victim) and calls find() to acquire the new set of predecessors. Because it has already set the victim's isMarked field, it does not try to mark the node again. After successfully removing the victim node from the list, the thread releases all its locks and returns *true*.

Finally, we recall that if no node was found, or the node found was marked, or not fully linked, or not found at its top level, then the method simply returns *false*. It is easy to see that it is correct to return *false* if the node is not marked, because for any key, there can at any time be at most one node with this key in the SkipList (i.e., reachable from the head). Moreover, once a node is entered into the list (which must have occurred before it is found by find()), it cannot be removed until it is marked. It follows that if the node is not marked, and not all its links are in place, it must be in the process of being added into the SkipList, but the adding method has not reached the linearization point (see the node with key 18 in part (a) of Fig. 14.3).

If the node is marked at the time it is found, it might not be in the list, and some unmarked node with the same key may be in the list. However, in that case, just like for the LazyList remove() method, there must have been some point during the remove() call when the key was not in the abstract set.

```
95    boolean remove(T x) {
96      Node<T> victim = null; boolean isMarked = false; int topLevel = -1;
97      Node<T>[] preds = (Node<T>[]) new Node[MAX_LEVEL + 1];
98      Node<T>[] succs = (Node<T>[]) new Node[MAX_LEVEL + 1];
99      while (true) {
100       int lFound = find(x, preds, succs);
101       if (lFound != -1) victim = succs[lFound];
102       if (isMarked ||
103           (lFound != -1 &&
104           (victim.fullyLinked
105           && victim.topLevel == lFound
106           && !victim.marked))) {
107         if (!isMarked) {
108           topLevel = victim.topLevel;
109           victim.lock.lock();
110           if (victim.marked) {
111             victim.lock.unlock();
112             return false;
113           }
114           victim.marked = true;
115           isMarked = true;
116         }
117         int highestLocked = -1;
118         try {
119           Node<T> pred, succ; boolean valid = true;
120           for (int level = 0; valid && (level <= topLevel); level++) {
121             pred = preds[level];
122             pred.lock.lock();
123             highestLocked = level;
124             valid = !pred.marked && pred.next[level]==victim;
125           }
126           if (!valid) continue;
127           for (int level = topLevel; level >= 0; level--) {
128             preds[level].next[level] = victim.next[level];
129           }
130           victim.lock.unlock();
131           return true;
132         } finally {
133           for (int i = 0; i <= highestLocked; i++) {
134             preds[i].unlock();
135           }
136         }
137       } else return false;
138     }
139   }
```

FIGURE 14.7

The LazySkipList class: the remove() method.

```
140  boolean contains(T x) {
141      Node<T>[] preds = (Node<T>[]) new Node[MAX_LEVEL + 1];
142      Node<T>[] succs = (Node<T>[]) new Node[MAX_LEVEL + 1];
143      int lFound = find(x, preds, succs);
144      return (lFound != -1
145          && succs[lFound].fullyLinked
146          && !succs[lFound].marked);
147  }
```

FIGURE 14.8

The LazySkipList class: the wait-free contains() method.

The wait-free contains() method (Fig. 14.8) calls find() to locate the node containing the target key. If it finds a node it checks whether it is unmarked and fully linked. This method, like that of the LazyList class of Chapter 9, is wait-free, ignoring any locks or concurrent changes in the SkipList list structure. A successful contains() call's linearization point occurs when the predecessor's next reference is traversed, having been observed to be unmarked and fully linked. An unsuccessful contains() call, like the remove() call, occurs if the method finds a node that is marked. Care is needed, because at the time the node is found, it might not be in the list, while an unmarked node with the same key may be in the list. As with remove(), however, there must have been some point during the contains() call when the key was not in the abstract set.

14.4 A lock-free concurrent skiplist

The basis of our LockFreeSkipList implementation is the LockFreeList algorithm of Chapter 9: Each level of the SkipList structure is a LockFreeList, each next reference in a node is an AtomicMarkableReference<Node>, and list manipulations are performed using compareAndSet().

14.4.1 A bird's-eye view

Here is a bird's-eye view of the of the LockFreeSkipList class.

Because we cannot use locks to manipulate references at all levels at the same time, the LockFreeSkipList cannot maintain the skiplist property that each list is a sublist of the list at levels below it.

Since we cannot maintain the skiplist property, we take the approach that the abstract set is defined by the bottom-level list: A key is in the set if there is a node with that key whose next reference is unmarked in the bottom-level list. Nodes in higher-level lists in the skiplist serve only as shortcuts to the bottom level. There is no need for a fullyLinked flag as in the LazySkipList.

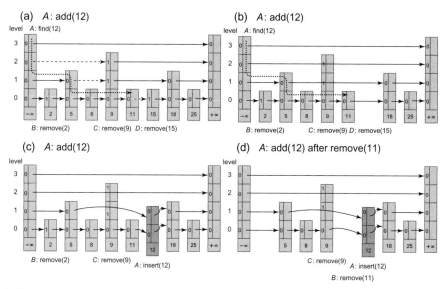

FIGURE 14.9

The LockFreeSkipList class: an add() call. Each node consists of links that are unmarked (a 0) or marked (a 1). In part (a), add(12) calls find(12) while there are three ongoing remove() calls. The find() method "cleans" the marked links (denoted by 1s) as it traverses the skiplist. The traversal is not the same as a sequential find(12), because marked nodes are unlinked whenever they are encountered. The path in the figure shows the nodes traversed by the pred reference, which always refers to unmarked nodes with keys less than the target key. Part (b) shows the result of redirecting the dashed links. We denote bypassing a node by placing the link in front of it. Node 15, whose bottom-level next reference was marked, is removed from the skiplist. Part (c) shows the subsequent addition of the new node with key 12. Part (d) shows an alternate addition scenario that would occur if the node with key 11 were removed before the addition of the node with key 12. The bottom-level next reference of the node with key 9 is not yet marked, and so the bottom-level predecessor node, whose next reference is marked, is redirected by the add() method to the new node. Once thread C completes marking this reference, the node with key 9 is removed and the node with key 5 becomes the immediate predecessor of the newly added node.

How do we add or remove a node? We treat each level of the list as a LockFreeList. We use compareAndSet() to insert a node at a given level, and we mark the next references of a node to remove it.

As in the LockFreeList, the find() method cleans up marked nodes. The method traverses the skiplist, proceeding down each list at each level. As in the LockFreeList class's find() method, it repeatedly snips out marked nodes as they are encountered, so that it never looks at a marked node's key. Unfortunately, this means that a node may be physically removed while it is in the process of being linked at the higher levels. A find() call that passes through a node's middle-level references may remove these references, so, as noted earlier, the skiplist property is not maintained.

The add() method calls find() to determine whether a node is already in the list and to find its set of predecessors and successors. A new node is prepared with a randomly chosen topLevel, and its next references are directed to the potential successors returned by the find() call. The next step is to try to logically add the new node to the abstract set by linking it into the bottom-level list, using the same approach as in the LockFreeList. If the addition succeeds, the item is logically in the set. The add() call then links the node in at higher levels (up to its top level).

Fig. 14.9 shows the LockFreeSkipList class. In part (a), add(12) calls find(12) while there are three ongoing remove() calls. Part (b) shows the results of redirecting the dashed links. Part (c) shows the subsequent addition of the new node with key 12. Part (d) shows an alternate addition scenario that would occur if the node with key 11 were removed before the addition of the node with key 12.

The remove() method calls find() to determine whether an unmarked node with the target key is in the bottom-level list. If an unmarked node is found, it is marked starting from the topLevel. All next references up to but not including the bottom-level reference are logically removed from their appropriate level list by marking them. Once all levels but the bottom one have been marked, the method marks the bottom-level's next reference. This marking, if successful, removes the item from the abstract set. The physical removal of the node is the result of its physical removal from the lists at all levels by the remove() method itself and the find() methods of other threads that access it while traversing the skiplist. In both add() and remove(), if at any point a compareAndSet() fails, the set of predecessors and successors might have changed, and so find() must be called again.

The key to the interaction between the add(), remove(), and find() methods is the order in which list manipulations take place. The add() method sets its next references to the successors before it links the node into the bottom-level list, meaning that a node is ready to be removed from the moment it is logically added to the list. Similarly, the remove() method marks the next references top-down, so that once a node is logically removed, it is not traversed by a find() method call.

As noted, in most applications, calls to contains() usually outnumber calls to other methods. As a result contains() should not call find(). While it may be effective to have individual find() calls physically remove logically deleted nodes, contention results if too many concurrent find() calls try to clean up the same nodes at the same time. This kind of contention is much more likely with frequent contains() calls than with calls to the other methods.

However, contains() cannot use the approach taken by the LockFreeList's wait-free contains(): Look at the keys of all reachable nodes independently of whether they are marked or not. The problem is that add() and remove() may violate the skiplist property. It is possible for a marked node to be reachable in a higher-level list after being physically deleted from the lowest-level list. Ignoring the mark could lead to skipping over nodes reachable in the lowest level.

Note, however, that the find() method of the LockFreeSkipList is not subject to this problem because it never looks at keys of marked nodes, removing them instead. We will have the contains() method mimic this behavior, but without cleaning up marked nodes. Instead, contains() traverses the skiplist, ignoring the keys of marked nodes, and skipping over them instead of physically removing them. Avoiding the physical removal allows the method to be wait-free.

14.4.2 The algorithm in detail

As we present the algorithmic details, the reader should keep in mind that the abstract set is defined only by the bottom-level list. Nodes in the higher-level lists are used only as shortcuts into the bottom-level list. Fig. 14.10 shows the structure of the list's nodes.

The add() method, shown in Fig. 14.11, uses find(), shown in Fig. 14.13, to determine whether a node with key k is already in the list (line 61). As in the LazySkipList, add() calls find() to initialize the preds[] and succs[] arrays to hold the new node's ostensible predecessors and successors.

If an unmarked node with the target key is found in the bottom-level list, find() returns *true* and the add() method returns *false*, indicating that the key is already in the set. The unsuccessful add()'s linearization point is the same as the successful find()'s (line 43). If no node is found, then the next step is to try to add a new node with the key into the structure.

A new node is created with a randomly chosen topLevel. The node's next references are unmarked and set to the successors returned by the find() method (lines 47–50).

The next step is to try to add the new node by linking it into the bottom-level list between the preds[0] and succs[0] nodes returned by find(). As in the LockFreeList, we use compareAndSet() to set the reference while validating that these nodes still refer one to the other and have not been removed from the list (line 55). If the compareAndSet() fails, something has changed and the call restarts. If the compareAndSet() succeeds, the item is added, and line 55 is the call's linearization point.

The add() then links the node in at higher levels (line 58). For each level, it attempts to splice the node in by setting the predecessor, if it refers to the valid successor, to the new node (line 62). If successful, it breaks and moves on to the next level. If unsuccessful, the node referenced by the predecessor must have changed, and find() is called again to find a new valid set of predecessors and successors. We discard the result of calling find() (line 64) because we care only about recomputing the ostensible predecessors and successors on the remaining unlinked levels. Once all levels are linked, the method returns *true* (line 67).

The remove() method, shown in Fig. 14.12, calls find() to determine whether an unmarked node with a matching key is in the bottom-level list. If no node is found in the bottom-level list, or the node with a matching key is marked, the method returns *false*. The linearization point of the unsuccessful remove() is that of the find() method called on line 77. If an unmarked node is found, then the method logically removes the associated key from the abstract set, and prepares it for physical removal. This step uses the set of ostensible predecessors (stored by find() in preds[]) and

```
1   public final class LockFreeSkipList<T> {
2     static final int MAX_LEVEL = ...;
3     final Node<T> head = new Node<T>(Integer.MIN_VALUE);
4     final Node<T> tail = new Node<T>(Integer.MAX_VALUE);
5     public LockFreeSkipList() {
6       for (int i = 0; i < head.next.length; i++) {
7         head.next[i]
8             = new AtomicMarkableReference<LockFreeSkipList.Node<T>>(tail, false);
9       }
10    }
11    public static final class Node<T> {
12      final T value; final int key;
13      final AtomicMarkableReference<Node<T>>[] next;
14      private int topLevel;
15      // constructor for sentinel nodes
16      public Node(int key) {
17        value = null; key = key;
18        next = (AtomicMarkableReference<Node<T>>[])
19               new AtomicMarkableReference[MAX_LEVEL + 1];
20        for (int i = 0; i < next.length; i++) {
21          next[i] = new AtomicMarkableReference<Node<T>>(null,false);
22        }
23        topLevel = MAX_LEVEL;
24      }
25      // constructor for ordinary nodes
26      public Node(T x, int height) {
27        value = x;
28        key = x.hashCode();
29        next = (AtomicMarkableReference<Node<T>>[])
30               new AtomicMarkableReference[height + 1];
31        for (int i = 0; i < next.length; i++) {
32          next[i] = new AtomicMarkableReference<Node<T>>(null,false);
33        }
34        topLevel = height;
35      }
36    }
```

FIGURE 14.10

The LockFreeSkipList class: fields and constructor.

the nodeToRemove (returned from find() in succs[]). First, starting from the topLevel, all links up to and not including the bottom-level link are marked (lines 83–89) by repeatedly reading next and its mark and applying a compareAndSet(). If the link is found to be marked (either because it was already marked or because the attempt succeeded), the method moves on to the next-level link. Otherwise, the current level's link is reread since it must have been changed by another concurrent thread, so the marking attempt must be repeated. Once all levels but the bottom one have been marked, the method marks the bottom-level's next reference. This marking (line 96), if successful, is the linearization point of a successful remove(). The remove() method

```
37    boolean add(T x) {
38      int topLevel = randomLevel();
39      int bottomLevel = 0;
40      Node<T>[] preds = (Node<T>[]) new Node[MAX_LEVEL + 1];
41      Node<T>[] succs = (Node<T>[]) new Node[MAX_LEVEL + 1];
42      while (true) {
43        boolean found = find(x, preds, succs);
44        if (found) {
45          return false;
46        } else {
47          Node<T> newNode = new Node(x, topLevel);
48          for (int level = bottomLevel; level <= topLevel; level++) {
49            Node<T> succ = succs[level];
50            newNode.next[level].set(succ, false);
51          }
52          Node<T> pred = preds[bottomLevel];
53          Node<T> succ = succs[bottomLevel];
54          if (!pred.next[bottomLevel].compareAndSet(succ, newNode,
55                                          false, false)) {
56            continue;
57          }
58          for (int level = bottomLevel+1; level <= topLevel; level++) {
59            while (true) {
60              pred = preds[level];
61              succ = succs[level];
62              if (pred.next[level].compareAndSet(succ, newNode, false, false))
63                break;
64              find(x, preds, succs);
65            }
66          }
67          return true;
68        }
69      }
70    }
```

FIGURE 14.11

The LockFreeSkipList class: the add() method.

tries to mark the next field using compareAndSet(). If successful, it can determine that it was the thread that changed the mark from *false* to *true*. Before returning *true*, the find() method is called again. This call is an optimization: As a side effect, find() physically removes all links to the node it is searching for if that node is already logically removed.

On the other hand, if the compareAndSet() call failed, but the next reference is marked, then another thread must have concurrently removed it, so remove() returns *false*. The linearization point of this unsuccessful remove() is the linearization point

```
71    boolean remove(T x) {
72      int bottomLevel = 0;
73      Node<T>[] preds = (Node<T>[]) new Node[MAX_LEVEL + 1];
74      Node<T>[] succs = (Node<T>[]) new Node[MAX_LEVEL + 1];
75      Node<T> succ;
76      while (true) {
77        boolean found = find(x, preds, succs);
78        if (!found) {
79          return false;
80        } else {
81          Node<T> nodeToRemove = succs[bottomLevel];
82          for (int level = nodeToRemove.topLevel;
83               level >= bottomLevel+1; level--) {
84            boolean[] marked = {false};
85            succ = nodeToRemove.next[level].get(marked);
86            while (!marked[0]) {
87              nodeToRemove.next[level].compareAndSet(succ, succ, false, true);
88              succ = nodeToRemove.next[level].get(marked);
89            }
90          }
91          boolean[] marked = {false};
92          succ = nodeToRemove.next[bottomLevel].get(marked);
93          while (true) {
94            boolean iMarkedIt =
95              nodeToRemove.next[bottomLevel].compareAndSet(succ, succ,
96                                                    false, true);
97            succ = succs[bottomLevel].next[bottomLevel].get(marked);
98            if (iMarkedIt) {
99              find(x, preds, succs);
100             return true;
101           }
102           else if (marked[0]) return false;
103         }
104       }
105     }
106   }
```

FIGURE 14.12

The LockFreeSkipList class: the remove() method.

of the remove() method by the thread that successfully marked the next field. Note that this linearization point must occur during the remove() call because the find() call found the node unmarked before it found it marked.

Finally, if the compareAndSet() fails and the node is unmarked, then the next node must have changed concurrently. Since the nodeToRemove is known, there is no need to call find() again, and remove() simply uses the new value read from next to retry the marking.

```
107   boolean find(T x, Node<T>[] preds, Node<T>[] succs) {
108     int bottomLevel = 0;
109     int key = x.hashCode();
110     boolean[] marked = {false};
111     boolean snip;
112     Node<T> pred = null, curr = null, succ = null;
113     retry:
114       while (true) {
115         pred = head;
116         for (int level = MAX_LEVEL; level >= bottomLevel; level--) {
117           curr = pred.next[level].getReference();
118           while (true) {
119             succ = curr.next[level].get(marked);
120             while (marked[0]) {
121               snip = pred.next[level].compareAndSet(curr, succ,
122                                                     false, false);
123               if (!snip) continue retry;
124               curr = pred.next[level].getReference();
125               succ = curr.next[level].get(marked);
126             }
127             if (curr.key < key){
128               pred = curr; curr = succ;
129             } else {
130               break;
131             }
132           }
133           preds[level] = pred;
134           succs[level] = curr;
135         }
136         return (curr.key == key);
137       }
138   }
```

FIGURE 14.13

The LockFreeSkipList class: a more complex find() than in LazySkipList.

As noted, both the add() and remove() methods rely on find(). This method searches the LockFreeSkipList, returning *true* if and only if a node with the target key is in the set. It fills in the preds[] and succs[] arrays with the target node's ostensible predecessors and successors at each level. It maintains the following two properties:

- It never traverses a marked link. Instead, it removes the node referred to by a marked link from the list at that level.
- Every preds[] reference is to a node with a key strictly less than the target.

The find() method in Fig. 14.13 proceeds as follows: It starts traversing the SkipList from the topLevel of the head sentinel, which has the maximal allowed node

```
139   boolean contains(T x) {
140     int bottomLevel = 0;
141     int v = x.hashCode();
142     boolean[] marked = {false};
143     Node<T> pred = head, curr = null, succ = null;
144     for (int level = MAX_LEVEL; level >= bottomLevel; level--) {
145       curr = curr.next[level].getReference();
146       while (true) {
147         succ = curr.next[level].get(marked);
148         while (marked[0]) {
149           curr = pred.next[level].getReference();
150           succ = curr.next[level].get(marked);
151         }
152         if (curr.key < v){
153           pred = curr;
154           curr = succ;
155         } else {
156           break;
157         }
158       }
159     }
160     return (curr.key == v);
161   }
```

FIGURE 14.14

The LockFreeSkipList class: the wait-free contains() method.

level. It then proceeds in each level down the list, filling in preds and succs nodes that are repeatedly advanced until pred refers to a node with the largest value on that level that is strictly less than the target key (lines 118–132). As in the LockFreeList, it repeatedly snips out marked nodes from the given level as they are encountered (lines 120–126) using a compareAndSet(). Note that the compareAndSet() validates that the next field of the predecessor references the current node. Once an unmarked curr is found (line 127), it is tested to see if its key is less than the target key. If so, pred is advanced to curr. Otherwise, curr's key is greater than or equal to the target's, so the current value of pred is the target node's immediate predecessor. The find() method breaks out of the current level search loop, saving the current values of pred and curr (line 133).

The find() method proceeds this way until it reaches the bottom level. Here is an important point: The traversal at each level maintains the two properties described earlier. In particular, if a node with the target key is in the list, it will be found at the bottom level even if traversed nodes are removed at higher levels. When the traversal stops, pred refers to a predecessor of the target node. The method descends to each next lower level without skipping over the target node. If the node is in the list, it will be found at the bottom level. Moreover, if the node is found, it cannot be marked be-

A: contains(18) returns true

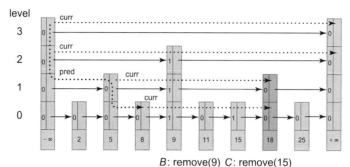

B: remove(9) C: remove(15)

FIGURE 14.15

Thread *A* calls contains(18), which traverses the list starting from the top level of the head node. The dotted line marks the traversal by the pred field, and the sparse dotted line marks the path of the curr field. The curr field is advanced to tail on level 3. Since its key is greater than 18, pred descends to level 2. The curr field advances past the marked reference in the node with key 9, again reaching tail, which is greater than 18, so pred descends to level 1. Here pred is advanced to the unmarked node with key 5, and curr advances past the marked node with key 9 to reach the unmarked node with key 18, at which point curr is no longer advanced. Though 18 is the target key, the method continues to descend with pred to the bottom level, advancing pred to the node with key 8. From this point, curr traverses past marked Nodes 9 and 15 and Node 11 whose key is smaller than 18. Eventually curr reaches the unmarked node with key 18, returning *true*.

cause if it were marked, it would have been snipped out on lines 120–126. Therefore, the test on line 136 need only check if the key of curr is equal to the target key to determine if the target is in the set.

The linearization points of both successful and unsuccessful calls to the find() methods occur when the curr reference at the bottom-level list is set, at either line 117 or 124, for the last time before the find() call's success or failure is determined on line 136. Fig. 14.9 shows how a node is successfully added to the LockFreeSkipList.

The wait-free contains() method appears in Fig. 14.14. It traverses the SkipList in the same way as the find() method, descending level-by-level from the head. Like find(), contains() ignores keys of marked nodes. Unlike find(), it does not try to remove marked nodes. Instead, it simply jumps over them (lines 148–151). For an example execution, see Fig. 14.15.

The method is correct because contains() preserves the same properties as find(), among them, that pred, in any level, never refers to an unmarked node whose key is greater than or equal to the target key. The pred variable arrives at the bottom-level list at a node before, and never after, the target node. If the node is added before the contains() method call starts, then it will be found. Moreover, recall that add() calls find(), which unlinks marked nodes from the bottom-level list before adding the new node. It follows that if contains() does not find the desired node, or finds the desired node at the bottom level but marked, then any concurrently added node that was not

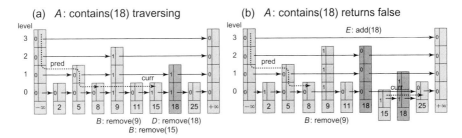

FIGURE 14.16

The LockFreeSkipList class: a contains() call. In part (a), contains(18) traverses the list starting from the top level of the head node. The dotted line marks the traversal by the pred field. The pred field eventually reaches Node 8 at the bottom level and we show the path of curr from that point on using a sparser dotted line. The curr traverses past Node 9 and reaches the marked Node 15. In part (b), a new node with key 18 is added to the list by a thread E. Thread E, as part of its find(18) call, physically removes the old nodes with keys 9, 15, and 18. Now thread A continues its traversal with the curr field from the removed node with key 15 (the nodes with keys 15 and 18 are not recycled since they are reachable by thread A). Thread A reaches the node with key 25, which is greater than 18, returning *false*. Even though at this point there is an unmarked node with key 18 in the LockFreeSkipList, this node was inserted by E concurrently with A's traversal and is linearized after A's add(18).

found must have been added to the bottom level after the start of the contains() call, so it is correct to return *false* on line 160.

Fig. 14.16 shows an execution of the contains() method. In part (a), a contains(18) call traverses the list starting from the top level of the head node. In part (b), the contains(18) call traverses the list after the node with key 18 has been logically removed.

14.5 Concurrent skiplists

We have seen two highly concurrent SkipList implementations, each providing logarithmic search without the need to rebalance. In the LazySkipList class, the add() and remove() methods use optimistic fine-grained locking, meaning that the method searches for its target node without locking, and acquires locks and validates only when it discovers the target. The contains() method, usually the most common, is wait-free. In the LockFreeSkipList class, the add() and remove() methods are lock-free, building on the LockFreeList class of Chapter 9. In this class too, the contains() method is wait-free.

In Chapter 15, we see how one can build highly concurrent priority queues based on the concurrent SkipList we presented here.

14.6 Chapter notes

Bill Pugh invented skiplists, both sequential [142] and concurrent [141]. The LazySkipList is by Maurice Herlihy, Yossi Lev, Victor Luchangco, and Nir Shavit [66]. The LockFreeSkipList presented here is credited to Maurice Herlihy, Yossi Lev, and Nir Shavit [70]. It is partly based on an earlier lock-free skiplist algorithm developed by to Kier Fraser [48], a variant of which was incorporated into the java.util.concurrent package by Doug Lea [109].

14.7 Exercises

Exercise 14.1. Recall that a skiplist is a *probabilistic* data structure. Although the expected performance of a contains() call is $O(\log n)$, where n is the number of items in the list, the worst-case performance could be $O(n)$. Draw a picture of an eight-element skiplist with worst-case performance, and explain how it got that way.

Exercise 14.2. You are given a skiplist with probability p and MAX_LEVEL M. If the list contains N nodes, what is the expected number of nodes at each level from 0 to $M - 1$?

Exercise 14.3. Modify the LazySkipList class so find() starts at the level of the highest node currently in the structure, instead of the highest level possible (MAX_LEVEL).

Exercise 14.4. Modify the LazySkipList to support multiple items with the same key.

Exercise 14.5. Suppose we modify the LockFreeSkipList class so that on line 102 of Fig. 14.12, remove() restarts the main loop instead of returning *false*.

Is the algorithm still correct? Address both safety and liveness issues. That is, what is an unsuccessful remove() call's new linearization point, and is the class still lock-free?

Exercise 14.6. Explain how in the LockFreeSkipList class a node might end up in the list at levels 0 and 2, but not at level 1. Draw pictures.

Exercise 14.7. Modify the LockFreeSkipList so that the find() method snips out a sequence of marked nodes with a single compareAndSet(). Explain why your implementation cannot remove a concurrently inserted unmarked node.

Exercise 14.8. Will the add() method of the LockFreeSkipList work even if the bottom level is linked and then all other levels are linked in some arbitrary order? Is the same true for the marking of the next references in the remove() method; the bottom level next reference is marked last, but references at all other levels are marked in an arbitrary order?

Exercise 14.9. (Hard) Modify the LazySkipList so that the list at each level is bidirectional, and allows threads to add and remove items in parallel by traversing from either the head or the tail.

```
1    boolean contains(T x) {
2      int bottomLevel = 0;
3      int key = x.hashCode();
4      Node<T> pred = head;
5      Node<T> curr = null;
6      for (int level = MAX_LEVEL; level >= bottomLevel; level--) {
7        curr = pred.next[level].getReference();
8        while (curr.key < key ) {
9          pred = curr;
10         curr = pred.next[level].getReference();
11       }
12     }
13     return curr.key == key;
14   }
```

FIGURE 14.17

The LockFreeSkipList class: an *incorrect* contains().

Exercise 14.10. Fig. 14.17 shows a buggy contains() method for the LockFreeSkipList class. Give a scenario where this method returns a wrong answer. Hint: The reason this method is wrong is that it takes into account keys of nodes that have been removed.

Priority queues

15

15.1 Introduction

A *priority queue* is a multiset of *items*, where each item has an associated *priority*, a score that indicates its importance (by convention, smaller scores are more important, indicating a higher priority). A priority queue typically provides an add() method to add an item to the set, and a removeMin() method to remove and return the item of minimal score (highest priority). Priority queues appear everywhere, from high-level applications to low-level operating system kernels.

A *bounded-range* priority queue is one where each item's score is taken from a discrete set of items, while an *unbounded-range* priority queue is one where scores are taken from a very large set, say, 32-bit integers, or floating-point values. Not surprisingly, bounded-range priority queues are generally more efficient, but many applications require unbounded ranges. Fig. 15.1 shows the priority queue interface.

15.1.1 Concurrent priority queues

In a concurrent setting, where add() and removeMin() method calls can overlap, what does it mean for an item to be in the set?

We consider two alternative consistency conditions, both introduced in Chapter 3. First, *linearizability*, requires that each method call appear to take effect at some instant between its invocation and its response. Second, *quiescent consistency*, is a weaker condition that requires that in any execution, at any point, if no additional method calls are introduced, then when all pending method calls complete, the values they return are consistent with some valid sequential execution of the object. If an application does not require its priority queues to be linearizable, then it is usually more efficient to require them to be quiescently consistent. Careful thought is usually required to decide which approach is correct for a particular application.

```
public interface PQueue<T> {
  void add(T item, int score);
  T removeMin();
}
```

FIGURE 15.1

Priority queue interface.

The Art of Multiprocessor Programming. https://doi.org/10.1016/B978-0-12-415950-1.00025-2
Copyright © 2021 Elsevier Inc. All rights reserved.

15.2 An array-based bounded priority queue

A bounded-range priority queue has *range m* if its priorities are taken from the range $0, \ldots, m - 1$. For now, we consider bounded priority queue algorithms that use two component data structures: Counter and Bin. A Counter (see Chapter 12) holds an integer value, and supports getAndIncrement() and getAndDecrement() methods that atomically increment and decrement the counter value and return the counter's prior value. These methods may optionally be *bounded*, meaning they do not advance the counter value beyond some specified bound.

A Bin is a pool that holds arbitrary items, and supports a put(x) method for inserting an item x and a get() method for removing and returning an arbitrary item, returning *null* if the bin is empty. Bins can be implemented using locks or in a lock-free manner using the stack algorithms of Chapter 11.

Fig. 15.2 shows the SimpleLinear class, which maintains an array of bins. To add an item with score i, a thread simply places the item in the ith bin. The removeMin() method scans the bins in decreasing priority and returns the first item it successfully removes. If no item is found it returns *null*. If the bins are quiescently consistent, so is SimpleLinear. The add() and removeMin() methods are lock-free if the Bin methods are lock-free.

```
1   public class SimpleLinear<T> implements PQueue<T> {
2     int range;
3     Bin<T>[] pqueue;
4     public SimpleLinear(int myRange) {
5       range = myRange;
6       pqueue = (Bin<T>[])new Bin[range];
7       for (int i = 0; i < pqueue.length; i++){
8         pqueue[i] = new Bin();
9       }
10    }
11    public void add(T item, int key) {
12      pqueue[key].put(item);
13    }
14    public T removeMin() {
15      for (int i = 0; i < range; i++) {
16        T item = pqueue[i].get();
17        if (item != null) {
18          return item;
19        }
20      }
21      return null;
22    }
23  }
```

FIGURE 15.2

The SimpleLinear class: add() and removeMin() methods.

15.3 **A tree-based bounded priority queue**

The SimpleTree (Fig. 15.3) is a lock-free quiescently consistent bounded-range priority queue. It is a binary tree of TreeNode objects (Fig. 15.4). As depicted in Fig. 15.5, the tree has m leaves where the ith leaf node has a bin holding items of score i. There are $m - 1$ shared bounded counters in the tree's internal nodes that keep track of the number of items in the leaves of the subtree rooted in each node's left (lower score/higher priority) child.

An add(x, k) call adds x to the bin at the kth leaf, and increments node counters in leaf-to-root order. The removeMin() method traverses the tree in root-to-leaf order.

```
1   public class SimpleTree<T> implements PQueue<T> {
2     int range;
3     List<TreeNode> leaves;
4     TreeNode root;
5     public SimpleTree(int logRange) {
6       range = (1 << logRange);
7       leaves = new ArrayList<TreeNode>(range);
8       root = buildTree(logRange, 0);
9     }
10    public void add(T item, int score) {
11      TreeNode node = leaves.get(score);
12      node.bin.put(item);
13      while(node != root) {
14        TreeNode parent = node.parent;
15        if (node == parent.left) {
16          parent.counter.getAndIncrement();
17        }
18        node = parent;
19      }
20    }
21    public T removeMin() {
22      TreeNode node = root;
23      while(!node.isLeaf()) {
24        if (node.counter.boundedGetAndDecrement() > 0 ) {
25          node = node.left;
26        } else {
27          node = node.right;
28        }
29      }
30      return node.bin.get();
31    }
32  }
```

FIGURE 15.3

The SimpleTree bounded-range priority queue.

```
33    public class TreeNode {
34      Counter counter;
35      TreeNode parent, right, left;
36      Bin<T> bin;
37      public boolean isLeaf() {
38        return right == null;
39      }
40    }
```

FIGURE 15.4

The SimpleTree class: the inner TreeNode class.

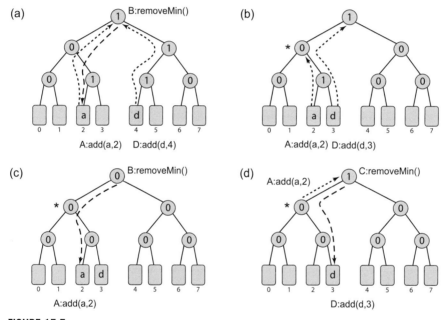

FIGURE 15.5

The SimpleTree priority queue is a tree of bounded counters. Items reside in bins at the leaves. Internal nodes hold the number of items in the subtree rooted at the node's left child. In part (a), threads A and D add items by traversing up the tree, incrementing the counters in the nodes when they ascend from the left. Thread B follows the counters down the tree, descending left if the counter had a nonzero value (we do not show the effect of B's decrements). Parts (b)–(d) show a sequence in which concurrent threads A and B meet at the node marked by a star. In part (b), thread D adds d, and then A adds a and ascends to the starred node, incrementing a counter along the way. In part (c), B traverses down the tree, decrementing counters to zero and popping a. In part (d), A continues its ascent, incrementing the counter at the root even though B already removed any trace of a from the starred node down. Nevertheless, all is well, because the nonzero root counter correctly leads C to item d, the item with the highest priority.

Starting from the root, it finds the leaf with highest priority whose bin is nonempty. It examines each node's counter, going right if the counter is zero and decrementing it and going left otherwise (line 24).

An add() traversal by a thread A moving up may meet a removeMin() traversal by a thread B moving down. As in the story of Hansel and Gretel, the descending thread B follows the trail of nonzero counters left by the ascending add() to locate and remove A's item from its bin. Part (a) of Fig. 15.5 shows an execution of the SimpleTree.

One may be concerned about the following "Grimm" scenario, shown in Fig. 15.5. Thread A, moving up, meets thread B, moving down, at a tree node marked by a star. Thread B moves down from the starred node to collect A's item at the leaf, while A continues up the tree, incrementing counters until it reaches the root. What if another thread, C, starts to follow A's path of nonzero counters from the root down to the starred node where B encountered A? When C reaches the starred node, it may be stranded there in the middle of the tree, and seeing no marks it would follow the right child branches to an empty Bin, even though there might be other items in the queue.

Fortunately, this scenario cannot happen. As depicted in parts (b)–(d) of Fig. 15.5, the only way the descending thread B could meet the ascending thread A at the starred node is if another add() call by an earlier thread D incremented the same set of counters from the starred node to the root, allowing the descending thread B to reach the starred node in the first place. The ascending thread A, when incrementing counters from the starred node to the root, is simply completing the increment sequence leading to the item inserted by some other thread D. To summarize, if the item returned by some thread on line 24 is *null*, then the priority queue is indeed empty.

The SimpleTree algorithm is not linearizable, since threads may overtake each other, but it is quiescently consistent. The add() and removeMin() methods are lock-free if the bins and counters are lock-free (the number of steps needed by add() is bounded by the tree depth and removeMin() can fail to complete only if items are continually being added and removed from the tree). A typical insertion or deletion takes a number of steps logarithmic in the lowest priority (maximal score) in the range.

15.4 An unbounded heap-based priority queue

This section presents a linearizable priority queue that supports priorities from an unbounded range. It uses fine-grained locking for synchronization.

A *heap* is a tree where each tree node contains an item and a score. If b is a child node of a, then b's priority is no greater than a's priority (i.e., items higher in the tree have lower scores and are more important). The removeMin() method removes and returns the root of the tree, and then rebalances the root's subtrees. Here, we consider binary trees, where there are only two subtrees to rebalance.

15.4.1 A sequential heap

Figs. 15.6 and 15.7 show a *sequential* heap implementation. An efficient way to represent a binary heap is as an array of nodes, where the tree's root is array entry 1, and

```
1   public class SequentialHeap<T> implements PQueue<T> {
2     private static final int ROOT = 1;
3     int next;
4     HeapNode<T>[] heap;
5     public SequentialHeap(int capacity) {
6       next = ROOT;
7       heap = (HeapNode<T>[]) new HeapNode[capacity + 1];
8       for (int i = 0; i < capacity + 1; i++) {
9         heap[i] = new HeapNode<T>();
10      }
11    }
12    public void add(T item, int score) {
13      int child = next++;
14      heap[child].init(item, score);
15      while (child > ROOT) {
16        int parent = child / 2;
17        int oldChild = child;
18        if (heap[child].score < heap[parent].score) {
19          swap(child, parent);
20          child = parent;
21        } else {
22          return;
23        }
24      }
25    }
26    ...
27  }
```

FIGURE 15.6

The SequentialHeap class: inner node class and add() method.

the right and left children of array entry i are entries $2 \cdot i$ and $(2 \cdot i) + 1$, respectively. The next field is the index of the first unused node.

Each node has an item and a score field. To add an item, the add() method sets child to the index of the first empty array slot (line 13). (For brevity, we omit code to resize a full array.) The method then initializes that node to hold the new item and score (line 14). At this point, the heap property may be violated, because the new node, which is a leaf of the tree, may have higher priority (lower score) than an ancestor. To restore the heap property, the new node "percolates up" the tree. We repeatedly compare the new node's priority with its parent's, swapping them if the parent's priority is lower (it has a higher score). When we encounter a parent with a higher priority, or we reach the root, the new node is correctly positioned, and the method returns.

To remove and return the highest-priority item, the removeMin() method records the root's item, which is the highest-priority item in the tree. (For brevity, we omit the code to deal with an empty heap.) It then moves a leaf entry up to replace the root

```
28    public T removeMin() {
29      int bottom = --next;
30      T item = heap[ROOT].item;
31      heap[ROOT] = heap[bottom];
32      if (bottom == ROOT) {
33        return item;
34      }
35      int child = 0;
36      int parent = ROOT;
37      while (parent < heap.length / 2) {
38        int left = parent * 2; int right = (parent * 2) + 1;
39        if (left >= next) {
40          return item;
41        } else if (right >= next || heap[left].score < heap[right].score) {
42          child = left;
43        } else {
44          child = right;
45        }
46        if (heap[child].score < heap[parent].score) {
47          swap(parent, child);
48          parent = child;
49        } else {
50          return item;
51        }
52      }
53      return item;
54    }
```

FIGURE 15.7

The SequentialHeap class: the removeMin() method.

(lines 29–31). If the tree is empty, the method returns the recorded item (line 32). Otherwise, the heap property may be violated, because the leaf node recently promoted to the root may have lower priority than some of its descendants. To restore the heap property, the new root "percolates down" the tree. If both children are empty, we are done (line 39). If the right child is empty, or if the right child has lower priority than the left, then we examine the left child (line 41). Otherwise, we examine the right child (line 43). If the child has higher priority than the parent, then we swap the child and parent, and continue moving down the tree (line 46). When both children have lower priorities, or we reach a leaf, the displaced node is correctly positioned, and the method returns.

15.4.2 A concurrent heap

The FineGrainedHeap class is mostly just a concurrent version of the SequentialHeap class. As in the sequential heap, add() creates a new leaf node, and percolates it

```
1   public class FineGrainedHeap<T> implements PQueue<T> {
2     private static int ROOT = 1;
3     private static int NO_ONE = -1;
4     private Lock heapLock;
5     int next;
6     HeapNode<T>[] heap;
7     public FineGrainedHeap(int capacity) {
8       heapLock = new ReentrantLock();
9       next = ROOT;
10      heap = (HeapNode<T>[]) new HeapNode[capacity + 1];
11      for (int i = 0; i < capacity + 1; i++) {
12        heap[i] = new HeapNode<T>();
13      }
14    }
15    ...
16  }
```

FIGURE 15.8

The FineGrainedHeap class: fields.

up the tree until the heap property is restored. To allow concurrent calls to proceed in parallel, the FineGrainedHeap class percolates items up the tree as a sequence of discrete atomic steps that can be interleaved with other such steps. In the same way, removeMin() deletes the root node, moves a leaf node to the root, and percolates that node down the tree until the heap property is restored. The FineGrainedHeap class percolates items down the tree as a sequence of discrete atomic steps that can be interleaved with other such steps.

Warning: The code presented here does *not* deal with heap overflow (adding an item when the heap is full) or underflow (removing an item when the heap is empty). Dealing with these cases makes the code longer, without adding much of interest.

The class uses a heapLock field to make short, atomic modifications to two or more fields (Fig. 15.8).

The HeapNode class (Fig. 15.9) provides the following fields: The lock field is a lock (line 23) held for short-lived modifications, and also while the node is being percolated *down* the tree. For brevity, the class exports lock() and unlock() methods to lock and unlock the node directly. The tag field has one of the following states: EMPTY means the node is not in use, AVAILABLE means the node holds an item and a score, and BUSY means that the node is being percolated *up* the tree, and is not yet in its proper position. While the node is BUSY, the owner field holds the ID of the thread responsible for moving it. For brevity, the class provides an amOwner method that returns *true* if and only if the node's tag is BUSY and the owner is the current thread.

The asymmetry in synchronization between the removeMin() method, which percolates down the tree holding the lock, and the add() method, which percolates up the tree with the tag field set to BUSY, ensures that a removeMin() call is not delayed if it encounters a node that is in the middle of being shepherded up the tree by an add()

```
17    private static enum Status {EMPTY, AVAILABLE, BUSY};
18    private static class HeapNode<S> {
19      Status tag;
20      int score;
21      S item;
22      int owner;
23      Lock lock;
24      public void init(S myItem, int myScore) {
25        item = myItem;
26        score = myScore;
27        tag = Status.BUSY;
28        owner = ThreadID.get();
29      }
30      public HeapNode() {
31        tag = Status.EMPTY;
32        lock = new ReentrantLock();
33      }
34      public void lock() {lock.lock();}
35      ... // other methods omitted
36    }
```

FIGURE 15.9

The FineGrainedHeap class: inner HeapNode class.

call. As a result, an add() call must be prepared to have its node swapped out from underneath it. If the node vanishes, the add() call simply moves up the tree. It is sure to encounter that node somewhere between its present position and the root.

The removeMin() method (Fig. 15.10) acquires the global heapLock, decrements the next field, returning the index of a leaf node, locks the first unused slot in the array, and releases heapLock (lines 38–42). It then stores the root's item in a local variable to be returned later as the result of the call (line 43). It marks the node as EMPTY and unowned, swaps it with the leaf node, and unlocks the (now empty) leaf (lines 44–46).

At this point, the method has recorded its eventual result in a local variable, moved the leaf to the root, and marked the leaf's former position as EMPTY. It retains the lock on the root. If the heap had only one item, then the leaf and the root are the same, so the method checks whether the root has just been marked as EMPTY. If so, it unlocks the root and returns the item (lines 47–51).

The new root node is now percolated down the tree until it reaches its proper position, following much the same logic as the sequential implementation. The node being percolated down is locked until it reaches its proper position. When we swap two nodes, we lock them both and swap their fields. At each step, the method locks the node's right and left children (line 58). If the left child is empty, we unlock both children and return (line 60). If the right child is empty or the left child has higher priority, then we unlock the right child and examine the left (line 64). Otherwise, we unlock the left child and examine the right (line 67).

```
37    public T removeMin() {
38      heapLock.lock();
39      int bottom = --next;
40      heap[ROOT].lock();
41      heap[bottom].lock();
42      heapLock.unlock();
43      T item = heap[ROOT].item;
44      heap[ROOT].tag = Status.EMPTY;
45      heap[ROOT].owner = NO_ONE;
46      swap(bottom, ROOT);
47      heap[bottom].unlock();
48      if (heap[ROOT].tag == Status.EMPTY) {
49        heap[ROOT].unlock();
50        return item;
51      }
52      heap[ROOT].tag = Status.AVAILABLE;
53      int child = 0;
54      int parent = ROOT;
55      while (parent < heap.length / 2) {
56        int left = parent * 2;
57        int right = (parent * 2) + 1;
58        heap[left].lock();
59        heap[right].lock();
60        if (heap[left].tag == Status.EMPTY) {
61          heap[right].unlock();
62          heap[left].unlock();
63          break;
64        } else if (heap[right].tag == Status.EMPTY || heap[left].score < heap[right].score) {
65          heap[right].unlock();
66          child = left;
67        } else {
68          heap[left].unlock();
69          child = right;
70        }
71        if (heap[child].score < heap[parent].score && heap[child].tag != Status.EMPTY) {
72          swap(parent, child);
73          heap[parent].unlock();
74          parent = child;
75        } else {
76          heap[child].unlock();
77          break;
78        }
79      }
80      heap[parent].unlock();
81      return item;
82    }
```

FIGURE 15.10

The `FineGrainedHeap` class: the `removeMin()` method.

```
83   public void add(T item, int score) {
84     heapLock.lock();
85     int child = next++;
86     heap[child].lock();
87     heap[child].init(item, score);
88     heapLock.unlock();
89     heap[child].unlock();
90
91     while (child > ROOT) {
92       int parent = child / 2;
93       heap[parent].lock();
94       heap[child].lock();
95       int oldChild = child;
96       try {
97         if (heap[parent].tag == Status.AVAILABLE && heap[child].amOwner()) {
98           if (heap[child].score < heap[parent].score) {
99             swap(child, parent);
100            child = parent;
101          } else {
102            heap[child].tag = Status.AVAILABLE;
103            heap[child].owner = NO_ONE;
104            return;
105          }
106        } else if (!heap[child].amOwner()) {
107          child = parent;
108        }
109      } finally {
110        heap[oldChild].unlock();
111        heap[parent].unlock();
112      }
113    }
114    if (child == ROOT) {
115      heap[ROOT].lock();
116      if (heap[ROOT].amOwner()) {
117        heap[ROOT].tag = Status.AVAILABLE;
118        heap[child].owner = NO_ONE;
119      }
120      heap[ROOT].unlock();
121    }
122  }
```

FIGURE 15.11

The FineGrainedHeap class: the add() method.

If the child has higher priority than the parent, then we swap the parent and child, and unlock the (former) parent (line 71). Otherwise, we unlock the child and the parent and return.

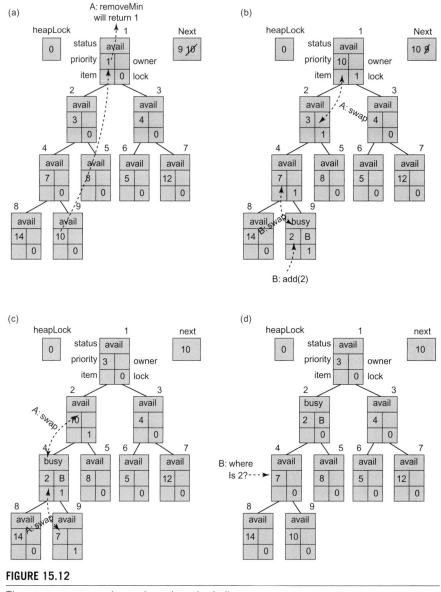

FIGURE 15.12

The FineGrainedHeap class: a heap-based priority queue.

The concurrent add() method (Fig. 15.11) acquires the heapLock, allocates, locks, initializes, and unlocks an empty leaf node (lines 84–89). This leaf node has tag BUSY, and the owner is the calling thread. It then unlocks the leaf node, proceeds to percolate that node up the tree, using the child variable to keep track of the node. It locks the parent and then the child (all locks are acquired in ascending order). If the parent is AVAILABLE and the child is owned by the caller, then it compares their priorities. If the child has higher priority, then the method swaps their fields, and moves up (line 98). Otherwise the node is where it belongs, and it is marked AVAILABLE and unowned (line 101). If the child is not owned by the caller, then the node must have been moved up by a concurrent removeMin() call so the method simply moves up the tree to search for its node (line 106).

Fig. 15.12 shows an execution of the FineGrainedHeap class. In part (a), the heap tree structure is depicted, with the priorities written in the nodes and the respective array entries above the nodes. The next field is set to 10, the next array entry into which a new item can be added. As can be seen, thread A starts a removeMin() method call, collecting the value 1 from the root as the one to be returned, moving the leaf node with score 10 to the root, and setting next back to 9. The removeMin() method checks whether 10 needs to be percolated down the heap. In part (b), thread A percolates 10 down the heap, while thread B adds a new item with score 2 to the heap in the recently emptied array entry 9. The owner of the new node is B, and B starts to percolate 2 up the heap, swapping it with its parent node of score 7. After this swap, it releases the locks on the nodes. At the same time, A swaps the node with scores 10 and 3. In part (c), A, ignoring the busy state of 2, swaps 10 and 2, and then 10 and 7, using hand-over-hand locking. It has thus swapped 2, which was not locked, from under thread B. In part (d), when B moves to the parent node in array entry 4, it finds that the busy node with score 2 it was percolating up has disappeared. However, it continues up the heap and locates the node with 2 as it ascends, moving it to its correct position in the heap.

15.5 A skiplist-based unbounded priority queue

One drawback of the FineGrainedHeap priority queue algorithm is that the underlying heap structure requires complex, coordinated rebalancing. In this section, we examine an alternative that requires no rebalancing.

Recall from Chapter 14 that a skiplist is a collection of ordered lists. Each list is a sequence of *nodes*, and each node contains an *item*. Each node belongs to a subset of the lists, and nodes in each list are sorted by their hash values. Each list has a *level*, ranging from 0 to a maximum. The bottom-level list contains all the nodes, and each higher-level list is a sublist of the lower-level lists. Each list contains about half the nodes of the next lower-level list. As a result, inserting or removing a node from a skiplist containing k items takes expected time $O(\log k)$.

In Chapter 14, we used skiplists to implement sets of items. Here, we adapt skiplists to implement a priority queue of items tagged with priorities. We describe a PrioritySkipList class that provides the basic functionality needed to implement an efficient priority queue. We base the PrioritySkipList class (Fig. 15.13) on the LockFreeSkipList class of Chapter 14, though we could just as easily have based it on the LazySkipList class. Later, we describe a SkipQueue wrapper (Fig. 15.14) to cover some of the PrioritySkipList<T> class's rough edges.

```
1   public final class PrioritySkipList<T> {
2     public static final class Node<T> {
3       final T item;
4       final int score;
5       AtomicBoolean marked;
6       final AtomicMarkableReference<Node<T>>[] next;
7       // sentinel node constructor
8       public Node(int myPriority) { ... }
9       // ordinary node constructor
10      public Node(T x, int myPriority) { ... }
11    }
12    boolean add(Node node) { ... }
13    boolean remove(Node<T> node) { ... }
14    public Node<T> findAndMarkMin() {
15      Node<T> curr = null;
16      curr = head.next[0].getReference();
17      while (curr != tail) {
18        if (!curr.marked.get()) {
19          if (curr.marked.compareAndSet(false, true))
20            return curr;
21        } else {
22          curr = curr.next[0].getReference();
23        }
24      }
25    }
26    return null; // no unmarked nodes
27  }
28  ...
29 }
```

FIGURE 15.13

The PrioritySkipList<T> class: inner Node<T> class.

Here is a bird's-eye view of the algorithm. The PrioritySkipList class sorts items by priority instead of by hash value, ensuring that high-priority items (the ones we want to remove first) appear at the front of the list. Fig. 15.15 shows such a PrioritySkipList structure. Removing the item with highest priority is done *lazily* (see Chapter 9). A node is *logically removed* by marking it as removed, and is later *physically removed* by unlinking it from the list. The removeMin() method works in two steps: First, it scans through the bottom-level list for the first unmarked node. When it finds one, it tries to mark it. If it fails, it continues scanning down the list, but if it succeeds, then removeMin() calls the PrioritySkipList class's logarithmic-time remove() method to physically remove the marked node.

We now turn our attention to the algorithm details. Fig. 15.13 shows an outline of the PrioritySkipList class, a modified version of the LockFreeSkipList class of

```
1   public class SkipQueue<T> {
2     PrioritySkipList<T> skiplist;
3     public SkipQueue() {
4       skiplist = new PrioritySkipList<T>();
5     }
6     public boolean add(T item, int score) {
7       Node<T> node = (Node<T>)new Node(item, score);
8       return skiplist.add(node);
9     }
10    public T removeMin() {
11      Node<T> node = skiplist.findAndMarkMin();
12      if (node != null) {
13        skiplist.remove(node);
14        return node.item;
15      } else{
16        return null;
17      }
18    }
19  }
```

FIGURE 15.14

The SkipQueue<T> class.

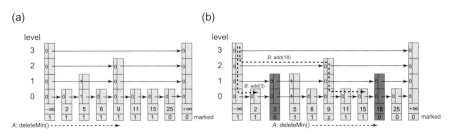

FIGURE 15.15

The SkipQueue priority queue: an execution that is quiescently consistent but not linearizable. In part (a), thread A starts a removeMin() method call. It traverses the lowest-level list in the PrioritySkipList to find and logically remove the first unmarked node. It traverses over all marked nodes, even ones like the node with score 5, which is in the process of being physically removed from the SkipList. In part (b), while A is visiting the node with score 9, thread B adds a node with score 3, and then adds a node with score 18. Thread A marks and returns the node with score 18. A linearizable execution could not return an item with score 18 before the item with score 3 is returned.

Chapter 14. It is convenient to have the add() and remove() calls take skiplist nodes instead of items as arguments and results. These methods are straightforward adaptations of the corresponding LockFreeSkipList methods, and are left as exercises. This class's nodes differ from LockFreeSkipList nodes in two fields: An integer score field (line 4) and an AtomicBoolean marked field used for logical deletion from the priority queue (not from the skiplist) (line 5). The findAndMarkMin() method scans the lowest-level list until it finds a node whose marked field is *false*, and then atomically tries to set that field to *true* (line 19). If it fails, it tries again. When it succeeds, it returns the newly marked node to the caller (line 20).

Fig. 15.14 shows the SkipQueue<T> class. This class is just a wrapper for a PrioritySkipList<T>. The add(x, p) method adds item x with score p by creating a node to hold both values, and passing that node to the PrioritySkipList class's add() method. The removeMin() method calls the PrioritySkipList class's findAndMarkMin() method to mark a node as logically deleted, and then calls remove() to physically remove that node.

The SkipQueue class is quiescently consistent: If an item x was present before the start of a removeMin() call, then the item returned will have a score less than or equal to that of x. This class is not linearizable: A thread might add a higher-priority (lower score) item and then a lower-priority item, and the traversing thread might find and return the later inserted lower-priority item, violating linearizability. This behavior is quiescently consistent, however, because one can reorder add() calls concurrent with any removeMin() to be consistent with a sequential priority queue.

The SkipQueue class is lock-free. A thread traversing the lowest level of the SkipList might always be beaten to the next logically undeleted node by another call, but it can fail repeatedly only if other threads repeatedly succeed.

In general, the quiescently consistent SkipQueue tends to outperform the linearizable heap-based queue. If there are n threads, then the first logically undeleted node is always among the first n nodes in the bottom-level list. Once a node has been logically deleted, then it will be physically deleted in the worst case in $O(\log k)$ steps, where k is the size of the list. In practice, a node will probably be deleted much more quickly, since that node is likely to be close to the start of the list.

There are, however, several sources of contention in the algorithm that affect its performance and require the use of back-off and tuning. Contention could occur if several threads concurrently try to mark a node, where the losers proceed together to try to mark the next node, and so on. Contention can also arise when physically removing an item from the skiplist. All nodes to be removed are likely to be neighbors at the start of the skiplist, so chances are high that they share predecessors, which could cause repeated compareAndSet() failures when attempting to snip out references to the nodes.

15.6 Chapter notes

The FineGrainedHeap priority queue is by Galen Hunt, Maged Michael, Srinivasan Parthasarathy, and Michael Scott [82]. The SimpleLinear and SimpleTree priority queues are credited to Nir Shavit and Asaph Zemach [158]. The SkipQueue is by Itai Lotan and Nir Shavit [115], who also present a linearizable version of the algorithm.

15.7 Exercises

Exercise 15.1. Give an example of a quiescently consistent priority queue execution that is not linearizable.

Exercise 15.2. Implement a quiescently consistent Counter with a lock-free implementation of the boundedGetAndIncrement() and boundedGetAndDecrement() methods using a counting network or diffracting tree.

Exercise 15.3. In the SimpleTree algorithm, what would happen if we replace the boundedGetAndDecrement() method with a regular getAndDecrement()?

Exercise 15.4. Use boundedGetAndIncrement() methods in treeNode counters to devise a SimpleTree algorithm with bounded capacity.

Exercise 15.5. In the SimpleTree class, what would happen if add(), after placing an item in the appropriate Bin, incremented counters in the same *top-down* manner as in the removeMin() method? Give a detailed example.

Exercise 15.6. Prove that the SimpleTree is a quiescently consistent priority queue implementation.

Exercise 15.7. Modify FineGrainedHeap to allocate new heap nodes dynamically. What are the performance limitations of this approach?

Exercise 15.8. Fig. 15.16 shows a *bit-reversed* counter. We could use the bit-reversed counter to manage the next field of the FineGrainedHeap class. Prove the following: For any two consecutive insertions, the two paths from the leaves to the root have no common nodes other than the root. Why is this a useful property for the FineGrainedHeap?

Exercise 15.9. Provide code for PrioritySkipList's add() and remove() methods.

Exercise 15.10. The PrioritySkipList class used in this chapter is based on the LockFreeSkipList class. Write a PrioritySkipList class based on the LazySkipList class.

Exercise 15.11. Describe a scenario in the SkipQueue implementation in which contention would arise from multiple concurrent removeMin() method calls.

Exercise 15.12. The SkipQueue class is quiescently consistent but not linearizable. Here is one way to make this class linearizable by adding a simple timestamping mechanism. After a node is completely inserted into the SkipQueue, it acquires a timestamp. A thread performing a removeMin() notes the time at which it starts its traversal of the lower level of the SkipQueue, and only considers nodes whose timestamp is earlier than the time at which it started its traversal, effectively ignoring nodes inserted during its traversal. Implement this class and justify why it works.

```
1   public class BitReversedCounter {
2     int counter, reverse, highBit;
3     BitReversedCounter(int initialValue) {
4       counter = initialValue;
5       reverse = 0;
6       highBit = -1;
7     }
8     public int reverseIncrement() {
9       if (counter++ == 0) {
10        reverse = highBit = 1;
11        return reverse;
12      }
13      int bit = highBit >> 1;
14      while (bit != 0) {
15        reverse ^= bit;
16        if ((reverse & bit) != 0) break;
17        bit >>= 1;
18      }
19      if (bit == 0)
20        reverse = highBit <<= 1;
21      return reverse;
22    }
23    public int reverseDecrement() {
24      counter--;
25      int bit = highBit >> 1;
26      while (bit != 0) {
27        reverse ^= bit;
28        if ((reverse & bit) == 0) {
29          break;
30        }
31        bit >>= 1;
32      }
33      if (bit == 0) {
34        reverse = counter;
35        highBit >>= 1;
36      }
37      return reverse;
38    }
39  }
```

FIGURE 15.16

A bit-reversed counter.

Scheduling and work distribution

16.1 Introduction

In this chapter, we show how to decompose certain kinds of tasks into subtasks that can be executed in parallel. Some applications break down naturally into parallel tasks. For example, when a request arrives at a web server, the server can just create a thread (or assign an existing thread) to handle the request. Applications that can be structured as producers and consumers also tend to be easily parallelizable. In this chapter, however, we look at applications that have inherent parallelism, but where it may not be obvious how to take advantage of it.

Let us start by thinking about how to multiply two matrices in parallel. Recall that if a_{ij} is the value at position (i, j) of matrix A, then the product C of two $n \times n$ matrices A and B is given by

$$c_{ij} = \sum_{k=0}^{n-1} a_{ik} \cdot b_{kj}.$$

As a first step, we could put one thread in charge of computing each c_{ij}. Fig. 16.1 shows a matrix multiplication program that creates an $n \times n$ array of Worker threads (line 14), where the worker thread in position (i, j) computes c_{ij}. The program starts each task (line 19) and then waits for each one to finish (line 25).[1] Each worker computes one entry in the product matrix (Fig. 16.2).

At first glance, this design seems ideal: The program is highly parallel, and the threads do not even have to synchronize. In practice, this design would perform poorly for all but very small matrices. Here is why: Threads require memory for stacks and other bookkeeping information. Creating, scheduling, and destroying threads takes a substantial amount of computation. Creating lots of short-lived threads is an inefficient way to organize a multithreaded computation, like manufacturing a new car whenever you need to run an errand, and scrapping it when you are done.

A more effective way to organize such a program is to create a *pool* of long-lived threads. Each thread in the pool repeatedly waits until it is assigned a *task*, a short-lived unit of computation. The thread executes its assigned task, and when the task is complete, the thread rejoins the pool to await its next assignment. Thread pools can

---

[1] Real code should check that all the dimensions agree. Here we omit most safety checks for brevity.

The Art of Multiprocessor Programming. https://doi.org/10.1016/B978-0-12-415950-1.00026-4

```
1   class MMThread {
2     double[][] lhs, rhs, prod;
3     int n;
4     public MMThread(double[][] lhs, double[][] rhs) {
5       n = lhs.length;
6       this.lhs = lhs;
7       this.rhs = rhs;
8       this.prod = new double[n][n];
9     }
10    void multiply() {
11      Worker[][] worker = new Worker[n][n];
12      for (int row = 0; row < n; row++) {
13        for (int col = 0; col < n; col++) {
14          worker[row][col] = new Worker(row,col);
15        }
16      }
17      for (int row = 0; row < n; row++) {
18        for (int col = 0; col < n; col++) {
19          worker[row][col].start();
20        }
21      }
22      for (int row = 0; row < n; row++) {
23        for (int col = 0; col < n; col++) {
24          try {
25            worker[row][col].join();
26          } catch (InterruptedException ex) {
27          }
28        }
29      }
30    }
```

FIGURE 16.1

The MMThread task: matrix multiplication using threads.

be platform-dependent: For example, large-scale multiprocessors may provide large pools, and small multiprocessors may provide small pools. Thread pools avoid the cost of creating and destroying threads in response to short-term fluctuations in demand. Using a thread pool is like calling a taxi or ride sharing service whenever you need to run an errand.

In addition to performance benefits, thread pools have a less obvious but equally important advantage: they insulate application programmers from platform-specific details such as the number of concurrent threads that can be scheduled efficiently. Thread pools make it possible to write a single program that runs equally well on a uniprocessor, a small-scale multiprocessor, and a large-scale multiprocessor. They provide a simple interface that hides complex, platform-dependent engineering tradeoffs.

```
31   class Worker extends Thread {
32       int row, col;
33       Worker(int row, int col) {
34         this.row = row; this.col = col;
35       }
36       @Override
37       public void run() {
38         double dotProduct = 0.0;
39         for (int i = 0; i < n; i++) {
40           dotProduct += lhs[row][i] * rhs[i][col];
41         }
42         prod[row][col] = dotProduct;
43       }
44     }
```

FIGURE 16.2

The MMThread task: inner Worker thread class.

In Java, thread pools are given a uniform structure through the *executor service* interface (java.util.ExecutorService). This interface provides methods to submit a task, to wait for a set of submitted tasks to complete, and to cancel uncompleted tasks. There are many different kinds of thread pools, adapted to many different kinds of tasks and scheduling strategies. Here, we restrict our attention to one particular executor service, called ForkJoinPool, intended for tasks that can split their work into smaller parallel tasks.

Fork-join tasks that return a value of type T inherit from RecursiveTask<T>, while those that produce only side effects inherit from RecursiveAction. A task's fork() method allocates a thread from the pool to execute that task, and the task's join() method allows the caller to wait for that task to complete. A task's work is done by its compute() method. Fork-join tasks work best when tasks do not acquire locks, and all tasks are of roughly equal size.

Here is the simplest way to create a fork-join pool:

```
ForkJoinPool forkJoinPool = new ForkJoinPool();
```

This call creates a pool where the number of threads is determined by the available resources. It is also possible to request a specific number of threads, and to set a number of other, more advanced parameters.

It is important to understand that assigning a task to a thread ("forking" that task) does not guarantee that any computation actually happens in parallel. Instead, forking a task is *advisory*: It tells the underlying thread pool that it may execute that task in parallel, if it has the resources to do so.

We now consider how to implement parallel matrix operations using fork-join tasks. Fig. 16.3 shows a Matrix class that provides get() and set() methods to access matrix elements (lines 16–21), along with a constant-time split() method that splits

```
1   class Matrix {
2     int dim;
3     double[][] data;
4     int rowDisplace, colDisplace;
5     Matrix(int d) {
6       dim = d;
7       rowDisplace = colDisplace = 0;
8       data = new double[d][d];
9     }
10    Matrix(double[][] matrix, int x, int y, int d) {
11      data = matrix;
12      rowDisplace = x;
13      colDisplace = y;
14      dim = d;
15    }
16    double get(int row, int col) {
17      return data[row + rowDisplace][col + colDisplace];
18    }
19    void set(int row, int col, double value) {
20      data[row + rowDisplace][col + colDisplace] = value;
21    }
22    int getDim() {
23      return dim;
24    }
25    Matrix split(int i, int j) {
26      int newDim = dim / 2;
27      return new Matrix(data,
28                        rowDisplace + (i * newDim),
29                        colDisplace + (j * newDim),
30                        newDim);
31    }
32    ...
33  }
```

FIGURE 16.3

The Matrix class.

an n-by-n matrix into four $(n/2)$-by-$(n/2)$ submatrices (lines 25–31). These submatrices are *backed* by the original matrix, meaning that changes to the submatrices are reflected in the original, and vice versa. This class also provides methods (not shown) to add and multiply matrices in the usual sequential way.

For simplicity, we consider only matrices whose dimension n is a power of 2. Any such matrix can be decomposed into four submatrices:

$$A = \begin{pmatrix} A_{00} & A_{01} \\ A_{10} & A_{11} \end{pmatrix}.$$

Matrix addition $C = A + B$ can be decomposed as follows:

$$\begin{pmatrix} C_{00} & C_{01} \\ C_{10} & C_{11} \end{pmatrix} = \begin{pmatrix} A_{00} & A_{01} \\ A_{10} & A_{11} \end{pmatrix} + \begin{pmatrix} B_{00} & B_{01} \\ B_{10} & B_{11} \end{pmatrix}$$

$$= \begin{pmatrix} A_{00} + B_{00} & A_{01} + B_{01} \\ A_{10} + B_{10} & A_{11} + B_{11} \end{pmatrix}.$$

These four sums can be done in parallel.

Fig. 16.4 shows the `MatrixAddTask` class, a parallel matrix addition class based on the fork-join framework. Because the `MatrixAddTask` does not return a result, it extends `RecursiveAction`. It has three fields (lines 5–8), initialized by the constructor: `lhs` ("left-hand side") and `rhs` ("right-hand side") are the matrices to be summed, and `sum` is the result, which is updated in place. Each task does the following: If the matrix size falls below a certain platform-dependent threshold, the sum is computed sequentially (lines 12–13). Otherwise, it creates new recursive tasks for each of its arguments' four submatrices and places them in a list (lines 16–25). It then forks each of those tasks (lines 27–28), and then joins them[2] (lines 30–31). Note that the order of the forks and joins is important: to maximize the opportunity for parallelism, we must complete all `fork()` calls before making any `join()` calls.

Fig. 16.5 shows how to set up a simple matrix addition using a fork-join pool. The top-level code initializes the three matrices (lines 1–3) and creates a top-level task (line 4) and a fork-join pool (line 5). The pool's `invoke()` method (line 6) schedules the top-level task, which splits itself into smaller parallel tasks, and returns when the entire computation is complete.

Matrix multiplication $C = A \cdot B$ can be decomposed as follows:

$$\begin{pmatrix} C_{00} & C_{01} \\ C_{10} & C_{11} \end{pmatrix} = \begin{pmatrix} A_{00} & A_{01} \\ A_{10} & A_{11} \end{pmatrix} \cdot \begin{pmatrix} B_{00} & B_{01} \\ B_{10} & B_{11} \end{pmatrix}$$

$$= \begin{pmatrix} A_{00} \cdot B_{00} + A_{01} \cdot B_{10} & A_{00} \cdot B_{01} + A_{01} \cdot B_{11} \\ A_{10} \cdot B_{00} + A_{11} \cdot B_{10} & A_{10} \cdot B_{01} + A_{11} \cdot B_{11} \end{pmatrix}$$

$$= \begin{pmatrix} A_{00} \cdot B_{00} & A_{00} \cdot B_{01} \\ A_{10} \cdot B_{00} & A_{10} \cdot B_{01} \end{pmatrix} + \begin{pmatrix} A_{01} \cdot B_{10} & A_{01} \cdot B_{11} \\ A_{11} \cdot B_{10} & A_{11} \cdot B_{11} \end{pmatrix}.$$

The eight product terms can be computed in parallel, and when those computations are done, the sum can be computed. (We have seen that the matrix summation program itself has internal parallelism.)

Fig. 16.6 shows the parallel matrix multiplication task. Matrix multiplication is structured in a similar way to addition. Because the `MatrixMulTask` does not return a result, it extends `RecursiveAction`. It has three fields (lines 4–7) initialized by the constructor: `lhs` and `rhs` are the matrices to be multiplied, and `product` is the result, updated in place. Each task does the following: If the matrix size falls below a certain

---

[2] This code uses the functional notation introduced in Chapter 17.

```
1   public class MatrixAddTask extends RecursiveAction {
2     static final int N = ...;
3     static final int THRESHOLD = ...;
4     Matrix lhs, rhs, sum;
5     public MatrixAddTask(Matrix lhs, Matrix rhs, Matrix sum) {
6       this.lhs = lhs;
7       this.rhs = rhs;
8       this.sum = sum;
9     }
10    public void compute() {
11      int n = lhs.getDim();
12      if (n <= THRESHOLD) {
13        Matrix.add(lhs, rhs, sum);
14      } else {
15        List<MatrixAddTask> tasks = new ArrayList<>(4);
16        for (int i = 0; i < 2; i++) {
17          for (int j = 0; j < 2; j++) {
18            tasks.add(
19                    new MatrixAddTask(
20                            lhs.split(i, j),
21                            rhs.split(i, j),
22                            sum.split(i, j)
23                    )
24            );
25          }
26        }
27        tasks.stream().forEach((task) -> {
28          task.fork();
29        });
30        tasks.stream().forEach((task) -> {
31          task.join();
32        });
33      }
34  }
```

FIGURE 16.4

The MatrixAddTask class: fork-join parallel matrix addition.

```
1   Matrix lhs = ...; // initialize matrix
2   Matrix rhs = ...; // initialize matrix
3   Matrix sum = new Matrix(N);
4   MatrixAddTask matrixAddTask = new MatrixAddTask(lhs, rhs, sum);
5   ForkJoinPool forkJoinPool = new ForkJoinPool();
6   forkJoinPool.invoke(matrixAddTask);
```

FIGURE 16.5

Top-level code for matrix addition.

```
1   public class MatrixMulTask extends RecursiveAction {
2     static final int THRESHOLD = ...;
3     Matrix lhs, rhs, product;
4     public MatrixMulTask(Matrix lhs, Matrix rhs, Matrix product) {
5       this.lhs = lhs;
6       this.rhs = rhs;
7       this.product = product;
8     }
9     public void compute() {
10      int n = lhs.getDim();
11      if (n <= THRESHOLD) {
12        Matrix.multiply(lhs, rhs, product);
13      } else {
14        List<MatrixMulTask> tasks = new ArrayList<>(8);
15        Matrix[] term = new Matrix[]{new Matrix(n), new Matrix(n)};
16        for (int i = 0; i < 2; i++) {
17          for (int j = 0; j < 2; j++) {
18            for (int k = 0; k < 2; k++) {
19              tasks.add(
20                    new MatrixMulTask(
21                          lhs.split(j, i),
22                          rhs.split(i, k),
23                          term[i].split(j, k)
24                    )
25              );
26            }
27          }
28        }
29        tasks.stream().forEach((task) -> {
30          task.fork();
31        });
32        tasks.stream().forEach((task) -> {
33          task.join();
34        });
35        (new MatrixAddTask(term[0], term[1], product)).compute();
36      }
37    }
38  }
```

FIGURE 16.6

The MatrixMulTask class: fork-join parallel matrix addition.

platform-dependent threshold, the product is computed sequentially (lines 11–12). Otherwise, it allocates two temporary matrices to hold intermediate terms (line 15). It then creates new, recursive tasks for each of the eight submatrix products, and places them in a list (lines 16–28). It then forks each of those tasks (lines 29–30),

```
1   class FibTask extends RecursiveTask<Integer> {
2     int arg;
3     public FibTask(int n) {
4       arg = n;
5     }
6     protected Integer compute() {
7       if (arg > 1) {
8         FibTask rightTask = new FibTask(arg - 1);
9         rightTask.fork();
10        FibTask leftTask = new FibTask(arg - 2);
11        return rightTask.join() + leftTask.compute();
12      } else {
13        return arg;
14      }
15    }
16  }
```

FIGURE 16.7

The FibTask class: Fibonacci using fork-join tasks.

and then joins them (lines 32–33). Finally, it creates a new MatrixAddTask to sum the temporary matrices, and calls its compute() method directly (line 35).

The matrix examples use fork-join tasks only for their side effects. Fork-join tasks can also be used to pass values from completed tasks. For example, here is how to decompose the well-known Fibonacci function into a multithreaded program. Recall that the Fibonacci sequence is defined as follows:

$$
F(n) = \begin{cases} 0 & \text{if } n = 0, \\ 1 & \text{if } n = 1, \\ F(n-1) + F(n-2) & \text{if } n > 1. \end{cases}
$$

Fig. 16.7 shows one way to use fork-join tasks to compute Fibonacci numbers. (This particular implementation is very inefficient, but we use it here to illustrate multithreaded dependencies.) The compute() method creates and forks a *right* subtask to compute $F(n-1)$. It then creates a *left* subtask to compute $F(n-2)$, and calls that task's compute() method directly. It then joins the right task, and sums the subtasks' results. (Think about why this structure is more efficient than forking both subtasks.)

16.2 Analyzing parallelism

Think of a multithreaded computation as a *directed acyclic graph*, or *dag* for short, where each node represents a task, and each directed edge links a *predecessor* task to a *successor* task, where the successor depends on the predecessor's result. For example, a conventional thread is just a chain of nodes where each node depends on

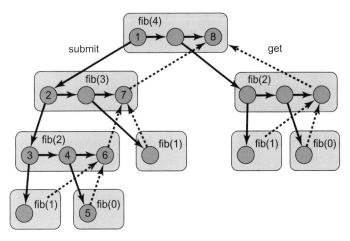

FIGURE 16.8

The dag created by a multithreaded Fibonacci execution. The caller creates a FibTask(4) task, which in turn creates FibTask(3) and FibTask(2) tasks. The round nodes represent computation steps and the arrows between the nodes represent dependencies. For example, there are arrows pointing from the first two nodes in FibTask(4) to the first nodes in FibTask(3) and FibTask(2), respectively, representing fork() calls, and arrows from the last nodes in FibTask(3) and FibTask(2) to the last node in FibTask(4), representing join() calls. The computation's span has length 8 and is marked by numbered nodes.

its predecessor. By contrast, a node that forks a task has two successors: One node is its successor in the same thread, and the other is the first node in the forked task's computation. There is also an edge in the other direction, from child to parent, that occurs when a thread that has forked a task calls that task's join() method, waiting for the child computation to complete. Fig. 16.8 shows the dag corresponding to a short Fibonacci execution.

Some computations are inherently more parallel than others. Let us make this notion precise. Assume that all individual computation steps take the same amount of time, which constitutes our basic measuring unit. Let T_P be the minimum time (measured in computation steps) needed to execute a multithreaded program on a system of P dedicated processors. T_P is thus the program's *latency*, the time it would take it to run from start to finish, as measured by an outside observer. We emphasize that T_P is an idealized measure: It may not always be possible for every processor to find steps to execute, and actual computation time may be limited by other concerns, such as memory usage. Nevertheless, T_P is clearly a lower bound on how much parallelism one can extract from a multithreaded computation.

Some instances of T_P are important enough to have special names. T_1, the number of steps needed to execute the program on a single processor, is called the computation's *work*. Work is also the total number of steps in the entire computation. In one time step (of the outside observer), P processors can execute at most P computation steps, yielding the following *work law*:

$$T_P \geq T_1/P. \tag{16.2.1}$$

The other extreme is also of special importance: T_∞, the number of steps to execute the program on an unlimited number of processors, is called the *span*.[3] Because finite resources cannot do better than infinite resources, we have the following *span law*:

$$T_P \geq T_\infty. \tag{16.2.2}$$

The *speedup* on P processors is the ratio

$$T_1/T_P.$$

We say a computation has *linear speedup* if $T_1/T_P = \Theta(P)$. Finally, a computation's *parallelism* is the maximum possible speedup: T_1/T_∞. A computation's parallelism is also the *average* amount of work available at each step along its longest path, and so provides a good estimate of the number of processors one should devote to a computation. In particular, it makes little sense to use substantially more processors than dictated by the problem's parallelism.

To illustrate these concepts, we now revisit the concurrent matrix add and multiply implementations introduced in Section 16.1.

Let $A_P(n)$ be the number of steps needed to add two $n \times n$ matrices on P processors. The matrix addition requires four half-size matrix additions, plus a constant amount of work to split the matrices. The work $A_1(n)$ is given by the recurrence

$$
\begin{aligned}
A_1(n) &= 4A_1(n/2) + \Theta(1) \\
&= \Theta(n^2).
\end{aligned}
$$

This work is the same as the conventional doubly nested loop implementation.

Because the half-size additions can be done in parallel, the span is

$$
\begin{aligned}
A_\infty(n) &= A_\infty(n/2) + \Theta(1) \\
&= \Theta(\log n).
\end{aligned}
$$

Let $M_P(n)$ be the number of steps needed to multiply two $n \times n$ matrices on P processors. The matrix multiplication requires eight half-size matrix multiplications and one full-size matrix addition. The work $M_1(n)$ is given by the recurrence

$$
\begin{aligned}
M_1(n) &= 8M_1(n/2) + A_1(n) \\
&= 8M_1(n/2) + \Theta(n^2) \\
&= \Theta(n^3).
\end{aligned}
$$

---

[3] Span is sometimes called the *critical path length*.

This work is also the same as the conventional triply nested loop implementation. The half-size multiplications can be done in parallel, but the addition cannot start until the multiplications are complete, so the span is

$$
\begin{aligned}
M_\infty(n) &= M_\infty(n/2) + A_\infty(n) \\
&= M_\infty(n/2) + \Theta(\log n) \\
&= \Theta(log^2 n).
\end{aligned}
$$

The parallelism for matrix multiplication is given by

$$
M_1(n)/M_\infty(n) = \Theta(n^3/\log^2 n),
$$

which is pretty high. For example, suppose we want to multiply two 1000-by-1000 matrices. Here, $n^3 = 10^9$, and $\log n = \log 1000 \approx 10$ (logs are base 2), so the parallelism is approximately $10^9/10^2 = 10^7$. Roughly speaking, this instance of matrix multiplication could, in principle, keep roughly ten million processors busy, a number well beyond the powers of any multiprocessor we are likely to see in the near future.

You should understand that a computation's parallelism is a highly idealized upper bound on the performance of any multithreaded matrix multiplication program. For example, when there are idle threads, it may not be easy to assign those threads to idle processors. Moreover, a program that displays less parallelism but consumes less memory may perform better because it encounters fewer page faults. The actual performance of a multithreaded computation remains a complex engineering problem, but the kind of analysis presented in this chapter is an indispensable first step in understanding the degree to which a problem can be solved in parallel.

16.3 Realistic multiprocessor scheduling

Our analysis so far has been based on the assumption that each multithreaded program has P dedicated processors. This assumption, unfortunately, is not realistic. Multiprocessors typically run a mix of jobs, where jobs come and go dynamically. One might start, say, a matrix multiplication application on P processors. At some point, the operating system may decide to download a new software upgrade, preempting one processor, and the application then runs on $P - 1$ processors. The upgrade program pauses waiting for a disk read or write to complete, and in the interim the matrix application has P processors again.

Modern operating systems provide user-level *threads* that encompass a program counter and a stack. (A thread that includes its own address space is often called a *process*.) The operating system kernel includes a *scheduler* that runs threads on physical processors. The application, however, typically has no control over the mapping between threads and processors, and so cannot control when threads are scheduled.

As we have seen, one way to bridge the gap between user-level threads and operating system-level processors is to provide the software developer with a three-level model. At the top level, multithreaded programs (such as matrix multiplication) decompose an application into a dynamically varying number of short-lived *tasks*. At the middle level, a user-level *scheduler* maps these tasks to a fixed number of *threads*. At the bottom level, the *kernel* maps these threads onto hardware *processors*, whose availability may vary dynamically. This last level of mapping is not under the application's control: Applications cannot tell the kernel how to schedule threads (indeed, commercially available operating systems kernels are hidden from users).

Assume for simplicity that the kernel works in discrete steps: At step i, the kernel chooses an arbitrary subset of user-level threads to run for one step. A node is *ready* at a step if its associated computational step in the program dag is ready to execute. A schedule is *greedy* if it executes as many of the ready nodes as possible.

Theorem 16.3.1. For a multithreaded program with work T_1, span T_∞, and P user-level threads, any greedy execution has length T, which is at most

$$T \le \frac{T_1}{P} + T_\infty.$$

Proof. Let P be the number of available processors. A *complete step* is one where at least P nodes are ready, so a greedy schedule runs some choice of P nodes. By contrast, an *incomplete step* is one where fewer than P nodes are ready, so a greedy schedule runs them all. Every step in the execution is either complete or incomplete. The number of complete steps cannot exceed T_1/P, because each such step executes P nodes. The number of incomplete steps cannot exceed T_∞, because each incomplete step shortens the span of the unexecuted dag by 1. □

It turns out that this bound is within a factor of 2 of optimal. Achieving an optimal schedule is NP-complete, so greedy schedules are a simple and practical way to achieve performance that is reasonably close to optimal.

Theorem 16.3.2. Any greedy scheduler is within a factor of 2 of optimal.

Proof. Recall that T_P is a program's optimal execution time on a platform with P processors. Let T_P^* be its execution time under a greedy schedule. From the work law (Eq. (16.2.1)) and the span law (Eq. (16.2.2)),

$$T_P \ge \max(\frac{T_1}{P}, T_\infty).$$

From Theorem 16.3.1,

$$T_P^* \le \frac{T_1}{P} + T_\infty$$
$$\le 2\max(\frac{T_1}{P}, T_\infty).$$

It follows that

$$T_P^* \le 2T_P.$$ □

Theorem 16.3.3. Any greedy scheduler achieves near-perfect linear speedup whenever $T_1/T_\infty \gg P$.

Proof. From

$$
\begin{aligned}
T_P^* &\leq T_1/P + T_\infty \\
&\approx T_1/P,
\end{aligned}
$$

implying the speedup $T_1/T_P \approx P$.   □

16.4 **Work distribution**

We now understand that the key to achieving a good speedup is to keep user-level threads supplied with tasks, so that the resulting schedule is as greedy as possible. Multithreaded computations, however, create and destroy tasks dynamically, sometimes in unpredictable ways. A *work distribution* algorithm is needed to assign ready tasks to idle threads as efficiently as possible.

One simple approach to work distribution is *work dealing*: an overloaded task tries to offload tasks to other, less heavily loaded threads. This approach may seem sensible, but it has a basic flaw: If most threads are overloaded, then they waste effort in a futile attempt to exchange tasks. Instead, we first consider *work stealing*, in which a thread that runs out of work tries to "steal" work from others. An advantage of work stealing is that if all threads are already busy, then they do not waste time trying to offload work on one another.

16.4.1 **Work stealing**

Each thread keeps a pool of tasks waiting to be executed in the form of a *double-ended queue*, or *deque* (DEQue), providing pushBottom(), popBottom(), and popTop() methods (a pushTop() method is not needed). When a thread creates a new task, it calls pushBottom() to push that task onto its deque. When a thread needs a task to work on, it calls popBottom() to remove a task from its own deque. If the thread discovers its deque is empty, then it becomes a *thief*: it chooses a *victim* thread, and calls the popTop() method of that thread's deque to "steal" a task for itself.

In Section 16.5, we present an efficient linearizable implementation of a deque. Fig. 16.9 shows one possible way to implement a thread used by a work-stealing thread pool. The threads share an array of deques (line 2), one for each thread. Each thread repeatedly removes a task from its own deque and executes it (lines 10–13). If it runs out, then it repeatedly chooses a victim thread at random and tries to steal a task from the top of the victim's deque (lines 14–20). To avoid code clutter, we ignore the possibility that stealing may trigger an exception.

This simple thread pool may keep trying to steal forever, long after all work in all queues has been completed. To prevent threads from endlessly searching for nonexistent work, we can use a termination detecting barrier as described in Section 18.6.

```
1   public class WorkStealingThread {
2     DEQue[] queue;
3     public WorkStealingThread(DEQue[] queue) {
4       this.queue = queue;
5     }
6     public void run() {
7       int me = ThreadID.get();
8       RecursiveAction task = queue[me].popBottom();
9       while (true) {
10        while (task != null) {
11          task.compute();
12          task = queue[me].popBottom();
13        }
14        while (task == null) {
15          Thread.yield();
16          int victim = ThreadLocalRandom.current().nextInt(queue.length);
17          if (!queue[victim].isEmpty()) {
18            task = queue[victim].popTop();
19          }
20        }
21      }
22    }
23  }
```

FIGURE 16.9

The WorkStealingThread class: a simplified work-stealing thread pool.

16.4.2 Yielding and multiprogramming

As noted earlier, multiprocessors provide a three-level model of computation: Short-lived *tasks* are executed by system-level *threads*, which are scheduled by the operating system on a fixed number of *processors*. A *multiprogrammed environment* is one in which there are more threads than processors, implying that not all threads can run at the same time, and that any thread can be preemptively suspended at any time. To guarantee progress, we must ensure that threads that have work to do are not unreasonably delayed by (*thief*) threads that are idle except for task stealing. To prevent this situation, we have each thief call Thread.yield() immediately before trying to steal a task (line 15 in Fig. 16.9). This call yields the thief's processor to another thread, allowing descheduled threads to regain a processor and make progress. (Calling yield() has no effect if there are no descheduled threads capable of running.)

16.5 Work-stealing deques

Here is how to implement a work-stealing deque: Ideally, a work-stealing algorithm should provide a linearizable implementation whose pop methods always return a task if one is available. In practice, however, we can settle for something weaker, allowing a popTop() call to return *null* if it conflicts with a concurrent popTop() call. Though we could have the unsuccessful thief simply try again, it makes more sense in this context to have a thread retry the popTop() operation on a different, randomly chosen deque each time. To support such a retry, a popTop() call may return *null* if it conflicts with a concurrent popTop() call.

We now describe two implementations of the work-stealing deque. The first is simpler, because it has bounded capacity. The second is somewhat more complex, but virtually unbounded in its capacity; that is, it does not suffer from the possibility of overflow.

16.5.1 A bounded work-stealing deque

For the thread pool deque, the common case is for a thread to push and pop a task from its own queue, calling pushBottom() and popBottom(). The uncommon case is to steal a task from another thread's deque by calling popTop(). Naturally, it makes sense to optimize the common case. The key idea behind the BoundedDEQue in Figs. 16.10 and 16.11 is to allow the pushBottom() and popBottom() methods to use only reads and writes in the common case. The BoundedDEQue consists of an array of tasks indexed by bottom and top fields that reference the top and bottom of the deque, as depicted in Fig. 16.12. The pushBottom() and popBottom() methods use reads and writes to manipulate the bottom reference. However, once the top and bottom fields are close (there might be only a single item in the array), popBottom() switches to compareAndSet() calls to coordinate with potential popTop() calls.

Let us describe the algorithm in more detail. The BoundedDEQue algorithm is clever in the way it avoids the use of costly compareAndSet() calls. This elegance comes at a cost: It is delicate and the order among instructions is crucial. We suggest the reader take time to understand how interactions among methods are determined by the order in which reads, writes, and compareAndSet() calls occur.

The BoundedDEQue class has three fields: tasks, bottom, and top (Fig. 16.10, lines 2–4). The tasks field is an array that holds the RecursiveAction tasks in the queue, bottom is the index of the first empty slot in tasks, and top is an AtomicStampedReference<Integer> (see Pragma 10.6.1). The top field encompasses two logical fields; the *reference* is the index of the first task in the queue, and the *stamp* is a counter incremented each time the reference is reset to 0. The stamp is needed to avoid an "ABA problem" of the type that often arises when using compareAndSet(). Suppose thread *A* calls popTop() to steal a task using only compareAndSet() on the task (without the stamp). *A* records the task whose index is given by top, but then is delayed before it can steal the task by calling compareAndSet() to increment top. While *A* is suspended, the owner thread *B* removes all tasks from the deque and replaces them with new tasks, eventually restoring top to its prior value. When *A* resumes, its compareAndSet() call will succeed, but *A* will have stolen the wrong task. The stamp, incremented each time the deque becomes empty, ensures that *A*'s compareAndSet() call will fail because the stamps no longer match.

```
1   public class BoundedDEQue {
2     RecursiveAction[] tasks;
3     volatile int bottom;
4     AtomicStampedReference<Integer> top;
5     public BoundedDEQue(int capacity) {
6       tasks = new RecursiveAction[capacity];
7       top = new AtomicStampedReference<Integer>(0, 0);
8       bottom = 0;
9     }
10    public void pushBottom(RecursiveAction r){
11      tasks[bottom] = r;
12      bottom++;
13    }
14    // called by thieves to determine whether to try to steal
15    boolean isEmpty() {
16      return (top.getReference() < bottom);
17    }
18  }
19  }
```

FIGURE 16.10

The `BoundedDEQue` class: fields, constructor, `pushBottom()`, and `isEmpty()` methods.

The `popTop()` method (Fig. 16.11) checks whether the `BoundedDEQue` is empty, and if not, tries to steal the top element by calling `compareAndSet()` to increment `top`. If the `compareAndSet()` succeeds, the theft is successful, and otherwise the method simply returns *null*. This method is nondeterministic: Returning *null* does not necessarily mean that the queue is empty.

As we noted earlier, we optimize for the common case, where each thread pushes and pops from its own local `BoundedDEQue`. Most of the time, a thread can push and pop tasks on and off its own `BoundedDEQue` by simply loading and storing the `bottom` index. If there is only one task in the queue, then the caller might encounter interference from a thief trying to steal that task. So if `bottom` is close to `top`, the calling thread switches to using `compareAndSet()` to pop tasks.

The `pushBottom()` method (Fig. 16.10, line 10) simply stores the new task at the `bottom` queue location and increments `bottom`.

The `popBottom()` method (Fig. 16.11) is more complex. If `bottom` is 0, then the queue is empty, and the method returns immediately (line 15). Otherwise, it decrements `bottom`, claiming a task (line 17). Here is a subtle but important point. If the claimed task was the last in the queue, then it is important that thieves notice that the `BoundedDEQue` is empty (line 6). But, because `popBottom()`'s decrement is neither atomic nor synchronized, the Java memory model does not guarantee that the decrement will be observed right away by concurrent thieves. To ensure that thieves

```
1   public RecursiveAction popTop() {
2     int[] stamp = new int[1];
3     int oldTop = top.get(stamp);
4     int newTop = oldTop + 1;
5     int oldStamp = stamp[0];
6     if (bottom <= oldTop)
7       return null;
8     RecursiveAction r = tasks[oldTop];
9     if (top.compareAndSet(oldTop, newTop, oldStamp, oldStamp))
10      return r;
11    else
12      return null;
13  }
14  public RecursiveAction popBottom() {
15    if (bottom == 0)
16      return null;
17    int newBottom = --bottom;
18    RecursiveAction r = tasks[newBottom];
19    int[] stamp = new int[1];
20    int oldTop = top.get(stamp);
21    int newTop = 0;
22    int oldStamp = stamp[0];
23    int newStamp = oldStamp + 1;
24    if (newBottom > oldTop)
25      return r;
26    if (newBottom == oldTop) {
27      bottom = 0;
28      if (top.compareAndSet(oldTop, newTop, oldStamp, newStamp))
29        return r;
30    }
31    top.set(newTop, newStamp);
32    return null;
33  }
```

FIGURE 16.11

The BoundedDEQue class: popTop() and popBottom() methods.

can recognize an empty BoundedDEQue, the bottom field must be declared **volatile**.[4]
Repeatedly rereading **volatile** variables can be expensive, so the code uses a local
copy (newBottom) of bottom, which is safe because that field is not written by any
other thread.

After the decrement, the caller reads the task at the new bottom index (line 18),
and tests whether the current top field refers to a smaller index. If so, the caller can-

---

[4] In a C or C++ implementation, you would need to introduce a *write barrier*, as described in Appendix B.

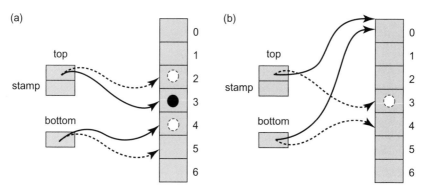

FIGURE 16.12

The BoundedDEQue implementation. In part (a), popTop() and popBottom() are called concurrently while there is more than one task in the BoundedDEQue. The popTop() method reads the element in entry 2 and calls compareAndSet() to redirect the top reference to entry 3. The popBottom() method redirects the bottom reference from 5 to 4 using a simple store and then, after checking that bottom is greater than top, it removes the task in entry 4. In part (b), there is only a single task. When popBottom() detects that, after redirecting from 4 to 3, top and bottom are equal, it attempts to redirect top with a compareAndSet(). Before doing so, it redirects bottom to 0 because this last task will be removed by one of the two popping methods. If popTop() detects that top and bottom are equal, it gives up; otherwise, it tries to advance top using compareAndSet(). If both methods apply compareAndSet() to the top, one wins and removes the task. In any case, win or lose, popBottom() resets top to 0 since the BoundedDEQue is now empty.

not conflict with a thief, and the method returns (line 24). Otherwise, if the top and bottom fields are equal, then there is only one task left in the BoundedDEQue, and there is a danger that the caller conflicts with a thief. The caller resets bottom to 0 (line 27). (Either the caller will succeed in claiming the task, or a thief will steal it.) The caller resolves the potential conflict by calling compareAndSet() to reset top to 0 (incrementing the stamp as it does so), matching bottom (line 26). If this compareAndSet() succeeds, the top has been reset to 0, and the task has been claimed, so the method returns. Otherwise, the queue must be empty because a thief succeeded, but this means that top points to some entry greater than bottom, which was set to 0 earlier. So before the caller returns *null*, it resets top to 0 (line 31).

As noted, an attractive aspect of this design is that an expensive compareAndSet() call is needed rarely, only when the BoundedDEQue is almost empty.

We linearize each unsuccessful popTop() call at the point where it detects that the BoundedDEQue is empty, or at a failed compareAndSet(). Successful popTop() calls are linearized at the point when a successful compareAndSet() took place. We linearize pushBottom() calls when bottom is incremented, and popBottom() calls when bottom is decremented or set to 0, though the outcome of popBottom() in the latter case is determined by the success or failure of the compareAndSet() that follows.

The isEmpty() method of UnboundedDEQue (Fig. 16.14) first reads top and then bottom, checking whether bottom is less than or equal to top (line 33). The order is important for linearizability because top never decreases unless bottom is first reset to 0, so if a thread reads bottom after top and sees it is not greater, the queue is indeed empty because a concurrent modification of top could only have increased top. On the other hand, if top is greater than bottom, then even if top is increased after it was read and before bottom is read (and the queue becomes empty), it is still true that the BoundedDEQue must not have been empty when top was read. The only alternative is that bottom is reset to 0 and then top is reset to 0, so reading top and then bottom will correctly return empty. It follows that the isEmpty() method is linearizable.

For simplicity, the bounded deque algorithm assumes the deque never becomes full.

16.5.2 An unbounded work-stealing deque

A limitation of the BoundedDEQue class is that the queue has a fixed size. For some applications, it may be difficult to predict this size, especially if some threads create significantly more tasks than others. Assigning each thread its own BoundedDEQue of maximal capacity wastes space.

To address these limitations, we now consider the UnboundedDEQue class, an *unbounded double-ended queue* that dynamically resizes itself as needed.

We implement the UnboundedDEQue as a cyclic array, with top and bottom fields as in the BoundedDEQue (except indexed modulo the array's capacity). As before, if bottom is less than or equal to top, the UnboundedDEQue is empty. Using a cyclic array eliminates the need to reset bottom and top to 0. Moreover, it permits top to be incremented but never decremented, eliminating the need for top to be an AtomicStampedReference. Moreover, in the UnboundedDEQue, if pushBottom() discovers that the current circular array is full, it can resize (enlarge) it, copying the tasks into a bigger array, and pushing the new task into the new (larger) array. Because the array is indexed modulo its capacity, there is no need to update the top or bottom fields when moving the elements into a bigger array (although the actual array indices where the elements are stored might change).

The CircularArray class is depicted in Fig. 16.13. It provides get() and put() methods that add and remove tasks and a resize() method that allocates a new circular array and copies the old array's contents into the new array. The use of modular arithmetic ensures that even though the array has changed size and the tasks may have shifted positions, thieves can still use the top field to find the next task to steal.

The UnboundedDEQue class has three fields: tasks, bottom, and top (Fig. 16.14, lines 3–5). The popBottom() and popTop() methods (Fig. 16.15) are almost the same as those of the BoundedDEQue, with one key difference: The use of modular arithmetic to compute indices means the top index need never be decremented. As noted, there is no need for a stamp to prevent ABA problems. Both methods, when competing for the last task, steal it by incrementing top. To reset the UnboundedDEQue to empty, simply increment the bottom field to equal top. In the code, popBottom(), immediately after the compareAndSet() on line 55, sets bottom to equal top +1 whether or not the compareAndSet() succeeds: If it failed, a concurrent thief must have stolen the last

```
1    class CircularArray {
2        private int logCapacity;
3        private RecursiveAction[] currentTasks;
4        CircularArray(int logCapacity) {
5          this.logCapacity = logCapacity;
6          currentTasks = new RecursiveAction[1 << logCapacity];
7        }
8        int capacity() {
9          return 1 << logCapacity;
10       }
11       RecursiveAction get(int i) {
12         return currentTasks[i % capacity()];
13       }
14       void put(int i, RecursiveAction task) {
15         currentTasks[i % capacity()] = task;
16       }
17       CircularArray resize(int bottom, int top) {
18         CircularArray newTasks =
19             new CircularArray(logCapacity+1);
20         for (int i = top; i < bottom; i++) {
21           newTasks.put(i, get(i));
22         }
23         return newTasks;
24       }
25     }
```

FIGURE 16.13

The UnboundedDEQue class: the circular task array.

task and incremented top. Storing top +1 into bottom makes top and bottom equal, resetting the UnboundedDEQue object to an empty state.

The isEmpty() method (Fig. 16.14) first reads top and then bottom, checking whether bottom is less than or equal to top (line 33). The order is important because top never decreases, and so if a thread reads bottom after top and sees it is no greater, the queue is indeed empty because a concurrent modification of top could only have increased the top value. The same principle applies in the popTop() method call. Fig. 16.16 shows an example execution.

The pushBottom() method (Fig. 16.14) is almost the same as that of the BoundedDEQue. One difference is that the method must enlarge the circular array if the current push is about to cause it to exceed its capacity. Another is that top does not need to be a AtomicStampedReference<>. The ability to resize carries a price: Every call to pushBottom() must read top (line 21) to determine if a resize is necessary, possibly causing more cache misses because top is modified by all threads. We can reduce this overhead by having the owner thread save a local value of top, which can be used to compute an upper bound on the UnboundedDEQue size, since the other

```
1   public class UnboundedDEQue {
2     private final static int LOG_CAPACITY = 4;
3     private volatile CircularArray tasks;
4     volatile int bottom;
5     AtomicReference<Integer> top;
6     public UnboundedDEQue(int logCapacity) {
7       tasks = new CircularArray(logCapacity);
8       top = new AtomicReference<Integer>(0);
9       bottom = 0;
10    }
11    boolean isEmpty() {
12      int localTop = top.get();
13      int localBottom = bottom;
14      return (localBottom <= localTop);
15    }
16
17    public void pushBottom(RecursiveAction r) {
18      int oldBottom = bottom;
19      int oldTop = top.get();
20      CircularArray currentTasks = tasks;
21      int size = oldBottom - oldTop;
22      if (size >= currentTasks.capacity()-1) {
23        currentTasks = currentTasks.resize(oldBottom, oldTop);
24        tasks = currentTasks;
25      }
26      currentTasks.put(oldBottom, r);
27      bottom = oldBottom + 1;
28    }
```

FIGURE 16.14

The `UnboundedDEQue` class: fields, constructor, `pushBottom()`, and `isEmpty()` methods.

methods can only make the `UnboundedDEQue` smaller. The owner thread rereads `top` only when this bound on size approaches the threshold where a `resize()` may be necessary.

In summary, we have seen two ways to design a nonblocking linearizable DEQue class. We can get away with using only loads and stores in the most common manipulations of the deque, but at the price of having more complex algorithms. Such algorithms are justifiable for an application such as a thread pool whose performance may be critical to a concurrent multithreaded system.

16.5.3 Work dealing

We have seen that in work-stealing algorithms, idle threads steal tasks from others. An alternative approach is to have each thread periodically *balance* its workloads

```
30    public RecursiveAction popTop() {
31      int oldTop = top.get();
32      int newTop = oldTop + 1;
33      int oldBottom = bottom;
34      CircularArray currentTasks = tasks;
35      int size = oldBottom - oldTop;
36      if (size <= 0) return null;
37      RecursiveAction r = tasks.get(oldTop);
38      if (top.compareAndSet(oldTop, newTop))
39        return r;
40      return null;
41    }
42
43    public RecursiveAction popBottom() {
44      int newBottom = --bottom;
45      int oldTop = top.get();
46      int newTop = oldTop + 1;
47      int size = newBottom - oldTop;
48      if (size < 0) {
49        bottom = oldTop;
50        return null;
51      }
52      RecursiveAction r = tasks.get(newBottom);
53      if (size > 0)
54        return r;
55      if (!top.compareAndSet(oldTop, newTop))
56        r = null;
57      bottom = newTop;
58      return r;
59    }
```

FIGURE 16.15

The `UnboundedDEQue` class: `popTop()` and `popBottom()` methods.

with a randomly chosen partner. To ensure that heavily loaded threads do not waste effort trying to rebalance, we make lightly loaded threads more likely to initiate rebalancing. More precisely, each thread periodically flips a biased coin to decide whether to balance with another. The thread's probability of balancing is inversely proportional to the number of tasks in the thread's queue. In other words, threads with few tasks are likely to rebalance, and threads with nothing to do are certain to rebalance. A thread rebalances by selecting a victim uniformly at random, and, if the difference between its workload and the victim's exceeds a predefined threshold, they transfer tasks until their queues contain the same number of tasks. It can be shown that this algorithm provides strong fairness guarantees: The expected length of each thread's task queue is pretty close to the average. One advantage of this approach is

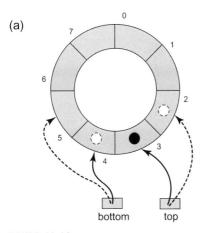 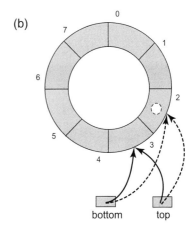

FIGURE 16.16

The UnboundedDEQue class implementation. In part (a), popTop() and popBottom() are executed concurrently while there is more than one task in the UnboundedDEQue object. In part (b), there is only a single task, and initially bottom refers to entry 3 and top to 2. The popBottom() method first decrements bottom from 3 to 2 (we denote this change by a dashed line pointing to entry 2 since it will change again soon). Then, when popBottom() detects that the gap between the newly set bottom and top is 0, it attempts to increment top by 1 (rather than reset it to 0 as in the BoundedDEQue). The popTop() method attempts to do the same. The top field is incremented by one of them, and the winner takes the last task. Finally, the popBottom() method sets bottom back to entry 3, which is equal to top.

that the balancing operation moves multiple tasks at each exchange. A second advantage occurs if one thread has much more work than the others, especially if tasks require approximately equal computation. In the work-stealing algorithm presented here, contention could occur if many threads try to steal individual tasks from the overloaded thread. In such a case, in the work-stealing thread pool, if some thread has a lot of work, chances are that other threads will have to repeatedly compete on the same local task queue in an attempt to steal at most a single task each time. On the other hand, in the work-sharing thread pool, balancing multiple tasks at a time means that work will quickly be spread out among tasks, and there will not be a synchronization overhead per individual task.

Fig. 16.17 illustrates a work-sharing thread pool. Each thread has its own queue of tasks, kept in an array shared by all threads (line 2). Each thread repeatedly deques the next task from its queue (line 10). If the queue was empty, the deq() call returns *null*; otherwise, the thread executes the task (line 11). At this point, the thread decides whether to rebalance. If the thread's task queue has size s, then the thread decides to rebalance with probability $1/(s+1)$ (line 13). To rebalance, the thread chooses a *victim* thread uniformly at random. The thread locks both queues (lines 15–18), in thread ID order (to avoid deadlock). If the difference in queue size exceeds a threshold, it evens out the queue sizes (Fig. 16.17, lines 25–33).

```
1   public class WorkSharingThread {
2     Queue[] queue;
3     private static final int THRESHOLD = ...;
4     public WorkSharingThread(Queue[] queue) {
5       this.queue = queue;
6     }
7     public void run() {
8       int me = ThreadID.get();
9       while (true) {
10        RecursiveAction task = queue[me].deq();
11        if (task != null) task.compute();
12        int size = queue[me].size();
13        if (ThreadLocalRandom.current().nextInt(size+1) == size) {
14          int victim = ThreadLocalRandom.current().nextInt(queue.length);
15          int min = (victim <= me) ? victim : me;
16          int max = (victim <= me) ? me : victim;
17          synchronized (queue[min]) {
18            synchronized (queue[max]) {
19              balance(queue[min], queue[max]);
20            }
21          }
22        }
23      }
24    }
25    private void balance(Queue q0, Queue q1) {
26      Queue qMin = (q0.size() < q1.size()) ? q0 : q1;
27      Queue qMax = (q0.size() < q1.size()) ? q1 : q0;
28      int diff = qMax.size() - qMin.size();
29      if (diff > THRESHOLD)
30        while (qMax.size() > qMin.size())
31          qMin.enq(qMax.deq());
32    }
33  }
```

FIGURE 16.17

The WorkSharingThread class: a simplified work-sharing thread pool.

16.6 **Chapter notes**

The dag-based model for analysis of multithreaded computation was introduced by Robert Blumofe and Charles Leiserson [18]. They also gave the first deque-based implementation of work stealing. Some of the examples in this chapter were adapted from a tutorial by Charles Leiserson and Harald Prokop [112]. The bounded lock-free deque algorithm is credited to Anish Arora, Robert Blumofe, and Greg Plaxton [13]. The unbounded timestamps used in this algorithm can be made bounded using a technique due to Mark Moir [129]. The unbounded deque algorithm is credited to

David Chase and Yossi Lev [29]. The original proof of Theorem 16.3.1 is due to Anish Arora, Robert Blumofe, and Greg Plaxton [13]. The work-sharing algorithm is by Larry Rudolph, Tali Slivkin-Allaluf, and Eli Upfal [151]. The algorithm of Anish Arora, Robert Blumofe, and Greg Plaxton [13] was later improved by Danny Hendler and Nir Shavit [61] to include the ability to steal half of the items in a deque.

Some illustrations were adapted from class notes prepared by Charles Leiserson.

16.7 Exercises

Exercise 16.1. Rewrite `MatrixAddTask` and `MatrixMulTask` to use an executor service.

Exercise 16.2. Consider the following code for an in-place merge-sort:

```
void mergeSort(int[] A, int lo, int hi) {
  if (hi > lo) {
    int mid = (hi - lo)/2;
    executor.submit(new mergeSort(A, lo, mid));
    executor.submit(new mergeSort(A, mid+1, hi));
    awaitTermination();
    merge(A, lo, mid, hi);
}
```

(Here, `submit()` starts the task and immediately returns, and `awaitTermination()` waits until all submitted tasks have finished.)

Assuming that the merge method has no internal parallelism, give the work, span, and parallelism of this algorithm. Give your answers both as recurrences and as $\Theta(f(n))$, for some function f.

Exercise 16.3. Assume that the actual running time of a parallel program on a dedicated P-processor machine is

$$T_P = T_1/P + T_\infty.$$

Your research group has produced two chess programs, a simple one and an optimized one. The simple one has $T_1 = 2048$ seconds and $T_\infty = 1$ second. When you run it on your 32-processor machine, sure enough, the running time is 65 steps. Your students then produce an "optimized" version with $T_1' = 1024$ seconds and $T_\infty = 8$ seconds. When you run it on your 32-processor machine, the running time is 40 steps, as predicted by our formula.

Which program will scale better to a 512-processor machine?

Exercise 16.4. Write an `ArraySum` class that provides a method

```
static public int sum(int[] a)
```

that uses divide-and-conquer to sum the elements of the array argument in parallel.

Exercise 16.5. Professor Jones takes some measurements of his (deterministic) multithreaded program, which is scheduled using a greedy scheduler, and finds that $T_4 = 80$ seconds and $T_{64} = 10$ seconds. What is the fastest that the professor's computation could possibly run on 10 processors? Use the following inequalities and the bounds implied by them to derive your answer (P is the number of processors):

$$T_P \geq \frac{T_1}{P}, \tag{16.7.1}$$

$$T_P \geq T_\infty, \tag{16.7.2}$$

$$T_P \leq \frac{(T_1 - T_\infty)}{P} + T_\infty, \tag{16.7.3}$$

where the last inequality holds on a greedy scheduler.

Exercise 16.6. Give an implementation of the Matrix class used in this chapter. Make sure your split() method takes constant time.

Exercise 16.7. Let $P(x) = \sum_{i=0}^{d} p_i x^i$ and $Q(x) = \sum_{i=0}^{d} q_i x^i$ be polynomials of degree d, where d is a power of 2. We can write

$$P(x) = P_0(x) + (P_1(x) \cdot x^{d/2}),$$
$$Q(x) = Q_0(x) + (Q_1(x) \cdot x^{d/2}),$$

where $P_0(x)$, $P_1(x)$, $Q_0(x)$, and $Q_1(x)$ are polynomials of degree $d/2$.

The Polynomial class shown in Fig. 16.18 provides put() and get() methods to access coefficients and it provides a constant-time split() method that splits a d-degree polynomial $P(x)$ into the two $(d/2)$-degree polynomials $P_0(x)$ and $P_1(x)$ defined above, where changes to the split polynomials are reflected in the original, and vice versa. Your task is to devise parallel addition and multiplication algorithms for this Polynomial class.

- The *sum* of $P(x)$ and $Q(x)$ can be decomposed as follows:

$$P(x) + Q(x) = (P_0(x) + Q_0(x)) + (P_1(x) + Q_1(x)) \cdot x^{d/2}.$$

  • Use this decomposition to construct a task-based concurrent polynomial addition algorithm in the manner of Fig. 16.14.
  • Compute the work and span of this algorithm.
- The *product* of $P(x)$ and $Q(x)$ can be decomposed as follows:

$$P(x) \cdot Q(x) = (P_0(x) \cdot Q_0(x)) + (P_0(x) \cdot Q_1(x) + P_1(x) \cdot Q_0(x)) \cdot x^{d/2} + (P_1(x) \cdot Q_1(x)x^d)$$

  • Use this decomposition to construct a task-based concurrent polynomial multiplication algorithm in the manner of Fig. 16.4.
  • Compute the work and span of this algorithm.

```
1   public class Polynomial {
2     int[] coefficients; // possibly shared by several polynomials
3     int first;   // index of my constant coefficient
4     int degree;  // number of coefficients that are mine
5     public Polynomial(int d) {
6       coefficients = new int[d];
7       degree = d;
8       first = 0;
9     }
10    private Polynomial(int[] myCoefficients, int myFirst, int myDegree) {
11      coefficients = myCoefficients;
12      first = myFirst;
13      degree = myDegree;
14    }
15    public int get(int index) {
16      return coefficients[first + index];
17    }
18    public void set(int index, int value) {
19      coefficients[first + index] = value;
20    }
21    public int getDegree() {
22      return degree;
23    }
24    public Polynomial[] split() {
25      Polynomial[] result = new Polynomial[2];
26      int newDegree = degree / 2;
27      result[0] = new Polynomial(coefficients, first, newDegree);
28      result[1] = new Polynomial(coefficients, first + newDegree, newDegree);
29      return result;
30    }
31  }
```

FIGURE 16.18

The Polynomial class.

Exercise 16.8. Give an efficient and highly parallel multithreaded algorithm for multiplying an $n \times n$ matrix by a length-n vector that achieves $\Theta(n^2)$ work and $\Theta(\log n)$ span. Analyze the work and span of your implementation, and give the parallelism.

Exercise 16.9. Consider the bounded deque implementation in Figs. 16.10 and 16.11.

- The bottom field is volatile to ensure that in popBottom(), the decrement on line 17 is immediately visible. Describe a scenario that explains what could go wrong if bottom were not declared as volatile.
- Why should we attempt to reset the bottom field to 0 as early as possible in the popBottom() method? Which line is the earliest in which this reset can be done safely? Can our BoundedDEQue overflow anyway? Describe how.

```
1     Queue qMin = (q0.size() < q1.size()) ? q0 : q1;
2     Queue qMax = (q0.size() < q1.size()) ? q1 : q0;
3     synchronized (qMin) {
4       synchronized (qMax) {
5         int diff = qMax.size() - qMin.size();
6         if (diff > THRESHOLD) {
7           while (qMax.size() > qMin.size())
8             qMin.enq(qMax.deq());
9         }
10      }
11    }
```

FIGURE 16.19

Alternate rebalancing code.

Exercise 16.10. Modify the popTop() method of the linearizable BoundedDEQue implementation so it will return null only if there are no tasks in the queue. Note that you may need to make its implementation blocking.

Exercise 16.11. Do you expect that the isEmpty() method call of a BoundedDEQue in the executor pool code will actually improve its performance?

Exercise 16.12. Consider the popTop() method of UnboundedDEQue (Fig. 16.15).

- If the compareAndSet() on line 38 succeeds, it returns the element it read right before the successful compareAndSet() operation. Why is it important to read the element from the array before we do the compareAndSet()?
- Can we use isEmpty() on line 36?

Exercise 16.13. What are the linearization points of the UnboundedDEQue methods? Justify your answers.

Exercise 16.14. Fig. 16.19 shows an alternate way of rebalancing two work queues: first, lock the larger queue, then lock the smaller queue, and rebalance if their difference exceeds a threshold. What is wrong with this code?

Data parallelism

Today, in casual conversation, people often refer to multiprocessors as "multicores," although technically, not every multiprocessor is a multicore. When did this usage become common? Fig. 17.1 shows the frequency with which the word "multicore" appears in books since 1900, as reported by Google Ngram, a service that keeps track of words found in scanned books. We can see that this word has been in use since the start of the 20th century, but its frequency has almost tripled since the year 2000. (Earlier uses of "multicore" mostly seem to refer to multicore cable or multicore fiber. But we digress.)

To produce this graph, it was necessary to count the number of times each word appears in a set of documents. How would you write a parallel WordCount program for a multiprocessor? One natural approach is to divide the document into fragments, assign each fragment to a task, and have a set of worker threads execute those tasks (as described in Chapter 16). Working in parallel, each worker thread executes a series of tasks, each counting the words in its own fragment, and reporting the results to a master thread, which merges their results. This kind of algorithm is said to be *data-parallel*, because the key element of the design is distributing data items across multiple worker threads.

The WordCount program is simple, much simpler than programs you are likely to encounter in practice. Nevertheless, it provides an example for understanding how to structure parallel programs that operate on large data sets.

FIGURE 17.1

"Multicore" usage from Google NGram.

The Art of Multiprocessor Programming. https://doi.org/10.1016/B978-0-12-415950-1.00027-6

Let us build on WordCount to do some simple literary detective work. Suppose we are given a collection of documents. Although the documents are all attributed to a single author, we suspect they were actually written by k distinct authors.[1] How can we tell which of these documents were (most likely) written by the same author?

We can adapt WordCount to partition the documents into k *clusters* of similar writings, where (we hope) each cluster consists of the documents written by a distinct author.

Assume we are given a set of N characteristic words whose use frequencies are likely to vary from author to author. We can modify WordCount to construct, for each document, an N-element vector whose ith entry is the number of occurrences of the ith characteristic word, normalized so the sum of the entries is 1. Each document's vector is thus a *point* in an $(N-1)$-dimensional Euclidean space. The *distance* between two documents is just the distance between their vectors as points in space, defined in the usual way. Our goal is to partition these points into k clusters, where the points in each cluster are closer to one another than to points in the other clusters.

Perfect clustering is computationally difficult, but there are widely used data-parallel algorithms that provide good approximations. One of the most popular is the KMeans clustering algorithm. As in WordCount, the points are distributed across a set of worker threads. Unlike WordCount, KMeans is iterative. A master thread chooses k candidate cluster centers at random, and divides the points among a set of worker threads. Working in parallel, the worker threads assign each of their points p to the cluster whose center is closest to p, and report that assignment back to the master thread. The master thread merges these assignments and computes new cluster centers. If the old and new centers are too far apart, then the clustering is considered to be of poor quality, and the master thread does another iteration, this time using the newly computed cluster centers in place of the old. The program halts when the clusters become stable, meaning that the old and new centers have become sufficiently close. Fig. 17.2 shows how KMeans clusters converge across iterations.

In this chapter, we examine two approaches to shared-memory data-parallel programming. The first approach is based on the MapReduce programming pattern, in which *mapper* threads operate in parallel on the data, and the results from these mapper threads are merged by *reducer* threads. This structure has been very successful in distributed systems, where processing nodes communicate over a network, but it can also be effective on shared-memory multiprocessors, albeit at a smaller scale.

The second approach is based on *stream programming*, a programming pattern supported by a number of languages (see the chapter notes). We use the interface provided by Java 8. A stream[2] is just a logical sequence of data items. (We say "logical" because these items may not all exist at the same time.) Programmers can create new streams by applying operations to elements of an existing stream, sequentially

---

[1] Modern scholarship asks these questions of many documents, including the Federalist Papers (http://en.wikipedia.org/wiki/Federalist_papers), the Nancy Drew Mystery fiction series (http://en.wikipedia.org/wiki/Nancy_Drew), and various sacred texts (readers are invited to provide their own examples).

[2] These streams should not be confused with the streams Java uses for I/O.

FIGURE 17.2

The k-means task: initial, intermediate, and final clusters.

or in parallel. For example, we can *filter* a stream to select only those elements that satisfy a predicate, *map* a function onto a stream to transforms stream elements from one type to another, or *reduce* a stream to a scalar value, for example, by summing the elements of a stream or taking their average.

Stream programs operate at a higher level than MapReduce programs. Whether the simplicity of stream programming outweighs the fine-grained control of MapReduce programming depends entirely on the application.

17.1 MapReduce

First, we give a high-level description of how to structure a MapReduce application. Once we have understood the requirements of such algorithms, we describe a general (but simplified) MapReduce framework. Finally, we explain how to apply that framework to specific problems such as WordCount and KMeans.

A MapReduce program first divides the data into fragments that can be analyzed independently, and assigns each fragment to one of n *mapper* tasks. In its simplest form, a mapper task scans its fragment, and produces a list of *key–value* pairs $(k_0, v_0), \ldots, (k_m, v_m)$, where the key and value types depend on the application.

The framework collects these key–value pairs, and for each key k, it merges the values paired with k into a list. Each such key–list pair is assigned to a *reducer* task, which produces an application-specific *output* value for that key. The output of the MapReduce program is a map matching each key to its output value.

There are many possible variations of this structure. Sometimes the inputs to mapper tasks are given as key–value pairs, sometimes the reducers produce key–value pairs, or multiple key–output pairs, and sometimes there are distinct input, intermediate, and final key types. For simplicity, we choose not to use any of these variations, but it would be straightforward to incorporate them in our examples.

17.1.1 The MapReduce framework

The *MapReduce framework* is in charge of creating and scheduling worker threads, calling the user-provided mapper and reducer tasks, and communicating and managing their arguments and results. We describe a simple MapReduce framework parameterized by an *input type* IN, a *key type* K, a *value type* V, and an *output type* OUT. In practice, MapReduce frameworks are more complicated, with configuration settings and optimizations omitted here for simplicity.

A Mapper task (Fig. 17.3) extends the RecursiveTask<> class from Java's fork-join framework, described in Chapter 16. Its setInput() method provides the task with an input of type IN, which it stores in the object's input field. The compute() method, inherited from RecursiveTask<>, pairs keys of type K with values of type V, accumulating them in a Map<K,V> result.

A Reducer task (Fig. 17.4) also extends RecursiveTask<>. Its setInput() method provides the task with a key and a list of values, and its compute() method produces a single result of type OUT.

```
1  public abstract class Mapper<IN, K, V> extends RecursiveTask<Map<K, V>> {
2    protected IN input;
3    public void setInput(IN anInput) {
4      input = anInput;
5    }
6  }
```

FIGURE 17.3

The Mapper class.

```
1  public abstract class Reducer<K, V, OUT> extends RecursiveTask<OUT> {
2    protected K key;
3    protected List<V> valueList;
4    public void setInput(K aKey, List<V> aList) {
5      key = aKey;
6      valueList = aList;
7    }
8  }
```

FIGURE 17.4

The Reducer class.

```
1  class MapReduce<IN, K, V, OUT> implements Callable<Map<K, OUT>> {
2    MapReduce()
3    Map<K,OUT> call()
4    void setMapperSupplier(Supplier<Mapper<IN,K,V>> aMapperSupplier)
5    void setReducerSupplier(Supplier<Reducer<K,V,OUT>> aReducerSupplier)
6    void setInput(List<IN> anInput)
7  }
```

FIGURE 17.5

The MapReduce framework: methods.

Fig. 17.5 shows the methods of the MapReduce framework. (We discuss its implementation in Section 17.1.4.) Even in the simplified form described here, the MapReduce framework has several kinds of settings, too many to provide gracefully as arguments to the constructor. Instead, it provides individual methods to control each setting. The setMapperSupplier() and setReducerSupplier() methods are used to tell the MapReduce framework how to create new mapper and reducer tasks. The setInput() method takes a list of IN objects, and one mapper task is created for each such input. Finally, the call() method does the work: It returns a Map<K,OUT> pairing each key with an output value.

PRAGMA 17.1.1

The parameter type Supplier<> of the setMapperSupplier() and setReducerSupplier() methods is a Java functional interface, implemented by an object with a single get() method. To tell the MapReduce framework how to create mapper and reducer tasks, we use Java's *lambda* construct for anonymous method definition. For example, here is how to tell the MapReduce framework to use the WordCount class's implementation of mappers:

```
mapReduce.setMapperSupplier(() -> new WordCount.Mapper());
```

The argument to setMapperSupplier() is a lambda: a parameter list and an expression separated by an arrow. The empty parentheses on the left indicate that the method takes no arguments, and the expression on the right states that the method creates and returns a new WordCount.Mapper object. This pattern, where a lambda takes no arguments and simply calls another method or operator, is so common it has a shorthand syntax:

```
mapReduce.setMapperSupplier(WordCount.Mapper::new);
```

Lambdas in Java have many other features, and the reader is encouraged to consult Java documentation for a more complete picture. As discussed in the chapter notes, other languages such as C#, C++, Scala, and Clojure support similar constructs.

```
1   public class WordCount {
2     static List<String> text;
3     static int numThreads = ...;
4     ...
5     public static void main(String[] args) {
6       text = readFile("document.tex");
7       List<List<String>> inputs = splitInputs(text, numThreads);
8       MapReduce<List<String>, String, Long, Long> mapReduce = new MapReduce<>();
9       mapReduce.setMapperSupplier(WordCount.Mapper::new);
10      mapReduce.setReducerSupplier(WordCount.Reducer::new);
11      mapReduce.setInput(inputs);
12      Map<String, Long> map = mapReduce.call();
13      displayOutput(map);
14    }
15    ...
16    static class Mapper extends Mapper<List<String>, String, Long> {
17      public Map<String, Long> compute() {
18        Map<String, Long> map = new HashMap<>();
19        for (String word : input) {
20          map.merge(word, 1L, (x, y) -> x + y);
21        }
22        return map;
23      }
24    }
25    static class Reducer extends Reducer<String, Long, Long> {
26      public Long compute() {
27        long count = 0;
28        for (long c : valueList) {
29          count += c;
30        }
31        return count;
32      }
33    }
34  }
```

FIGURE 17.6

A MapReduce-based WordCount application.

17.1.2 A MapReduce-based WordCount application

Fig. 17.6 shows one way to implement the WordCount application using the MapReduce framework. This application is structured as a class with static fields, methods, and inner classes. The application's main() method (lines 5–14) first reads the document, storing in its static text field a reference to a list of lower-case strings stripped of punctuation and numerals (line 6). It partitions that list into approximately equal sub-lists, one for each mapper (line 7). It creates a MapReduce instance using List<String>

and the input type, String as the key type, and Long as the value and output types. In lines 9–11 the main() method initializes the framework, using lambdas to specify how to create mapper and reducer tasks, and provides the framework with a list containing each mapper's input. The computation is triggered by calling MapReduce.call, which returns a Map<String,Long>, pairing each string found in the document with the number of times it occurs (line 12).

The mapper and reducer tasks for this application are defined by static nested classes (lines 16–25). The WordCount.Mapper task (line 16) does most of the work. As noted, its input is the List<String> it scans. Its key type is String, and its value type is Integer. It creates a HashMap<String,Integer> to hold its results (line 18). For each word in its sublist, the map's merge() method binds that word to 1 if the word is not already in the map, and otherwise increments the value bound to that word (line 20). It then returns the map.

When all the mapper tasks have completed, the MapReduce framework merges each word's counts into a list, and passes each key–list pair to a WordCount.Reducer task. It takes as input a word and its list of counts, and simply sums and returns them (line 28).

17.1.3 A MapReduce-based KMeans application

Fig. 17.7 shows a KMeans application using the MapReduce framework. Like WordCount, this application is structured as a class with static fields, methods, and inner classes. The application's main() method reads the data points from a file as a List<Point> (line 8). It chooses distinct random points as starting cluster centers (line 9). It creates a MapReduce instance (line 11), using List<Point> as the input type IN, Integer as the key type K, List<Point> as the value type V, and Point as the output type OUT. In lines 12–14 the main() method uses lambdas to specify how to create mapper and reducer tasks, and provides the framework with a list of input lists of approximately equal size, one for each mapper. The computation is triggered by calling MapReduce.call, which returns a Map<Integer,Point> pairing each of k cluster IDs to the central point of each cluster. (It would be easy to have mappers also return the clusters themselves, but we omit this step for brevity.)

The EPSILON constant determines when the process is deemed to have converged (line 3), and the convergence variable keeps track of the distance between successive rounds' centers (line 15). The application repeatedly iterates calls to the MapReduce framework (line 16), starting with randomly chosen cluster centers, and using the cluster centers generated by each iteration as the cluster centers for the next (line 19). The iteration halts when the distance between successive centers converges to less than EPSILON. (Of course, in a real implementation, it would be prudent to stop if the process does not appear to be converging.)

17.1.4 The MapReduce implementation

We now describe the implementation of the simple MapReduce framework that appears in Fig. 17.8. As noted earlier, a production-quality MapReduce framework

```
1   public class KMeans {
2     static final int numClusters = ...;
3     static final double EPSILON = 0.01;
4     static List<Point> points;
5     static Map<Integer, Point> centers;
6
7     public static void main(String[] args) {
8       points = readFile("cluster.dat");
9       centers = Point.randomDistinctCenters(points);
10      MapReduce<List<Point>, Integer, List<Point>, Point> mapReduce
11            = new MapReduce<>();
12      mapReduce.setMapperSupplier(KMeans.Mapper::new);
13      mapReduce.setReducerSupplier(KMeans.Reducer::new);
14      mapReduce.setInput(splitInput(points, numWorkerThreads));
15      double convergence = 1.0;
16      while (convergence > EPSILON) {
17        Map<Integer, Point> newCenters = mapReduce.call();
18        convergence = distance(centers, newCenters);
19        centers = newCenters;
20      }
21      displayOutput(centers);
22    }
23    static class Mapper extends Mapper<List<Point>, Integer, List<Point>> {
24      public Map<Integer, List<Point>> compute() {
25        Map<Integer, List<Point>> map = new HashMap<>();
26        for (Point point : input) {
27          int myCenter = closestCenter(centers, point);
28          map.putIfAbsent(myCenter, new LinkedList<>());
29          map.get(myCenter).add(point);
30        }
31        return map;
32      }
33    }
34    static class Reducer extends Reducer<Integer, List<Point>, Point> {
35      public Point compute() {
36        List<Point> cluster = new LinkedList<>();
37        for (List<Point> list : valueList) {
38          cluster.addAll(list);
39        }
40        return Point.barycenter(cluster);
41      }
42    }
43  }
```

FIGURE 17.7

A MapReduce-based KMeans application.

```
1  public class MapReduce<IN, K, V, OUT> implements Callable<Map<K, OUT>> {
2    private List<IN> inputList;
3    private Supplier<Mapper<IN, K, V>> mapperSupplier;
4    private Supplier<Reducer<K, V, OUT>> reducerSupplier;
5    private static ForkJoinPool pool;
6    public MapReduce() {
7      pool = new ForkJoinPool();
8      mapperSupplier = () -> {throw new UnsupportedOperationException("No mapper supplier");}
9      reducerSupplier = () -> {throw new UnsupportedOperationException("No reducer supplier");}
10   }
11   public Map<K, OUT> call() {
12     Set<Mapper<IN, K, V>> mappers = new HashSet<>();
13     for (IN input : inputList) {
14       Mapper<IN, K, V> mapper = mapperSupplier.get();
15       mapper.setInput(input);
16       pool.execute(mapper);
17       mappers.add(mapper);
18     }
19     Map<K, List<V>> mapResults = new HashMap<>();
20     for (Mapper<IN, K, V> mapper : mappers) {
21       Map<K, V> map = mapper.join();
22       for (K key : map.keySet()) {
23         mapResults.putIfAbsent(key, new LinkedList<>());
24         mapResults.get(key).add(map.get(key));
25       }
26     }
27     Map<K, Reducer<K, V, OUT>> reducers = new HashMap<>();
28     mapResults.forEach(
29         (k, v) -> {
30           Reducer< K, V, OUT> reducer = reducerSupplier.get();
31           reducer.setInput(k, v);
32           pool.execute(reducer);
33           reducers.put(k, reducer);
34         }
35     );
36     Map<K, OUT> result = new HashMap<>();;
37     reducers.forEach(
38         (key, reducer) -> {
39           result.put(key, reducer.join());
40         }
41     );
42     return result;
43   }
44   ...
45 }
```

FIGURE 17.8

The MapReduce implementation.

would have many more configuration settings and options. Note also that MapReduce frameworks designed for distributed systems are likely to look quite different, because communication is more expensive, and fault tolerance is a concern.

The framework's constructor initializes the object's fields. The framework uses a work-stealing ForkJoinPool to execute mapper and reducer tasks (line 7). The constructor sets the default mapper and reducer creation methods (lines 8 and 9) to throw exceptions if the user forgets to initialize them. The class is designed for reuse.

The call() method does all the work in four phases. In the first phase, for each input in its list of inputs (line 13), it creates a mapper task using the user-provided supplier (line 14), initializes that task's input (line 15), starts the asynchronous task (line 16), and stores the task in a Set<Mapper> (line 17).

In the second phase, the call() method creates a Map<K,List<V>> to hold the results of the mapper tasks (line 19). It then revisits each mapper task (line 20), joins it (line 21) to get its result, and adds that result to that key's list to merge the accumulators associated with each key (lines 22–24).

The third phase is similar to the first, except that reducer tasks are created (line 30), one per output key, initialized (line 31), and started (line 32).

In the final phase, the results of the reducer tasks are collected and returned (lines 36–42).

17.2 Stream computing

Java (starting from Java 8) provides explicit support for data-parallel computation through the Stream<> class[3] (java.util.Stream) . Streams are not data structures: Instead, they should be thought of as pipelines that carry values from a source (often a container such as a List<>), through a series of transformations (perhaps applied in parallel), to a destination (also often a container).

Java streams are an example of *functional programming*, a discipline in which programs are treated like mathematical functions, producing new values and data structures, but never modifying existing ones. Functional programming has a long history, but it is only relatively recently that it has entered the repertoire of techniques that every serious programmer should understand.

Functional programming is attractive because it avoids many of the complex side effects and interactions that form the focus of most of this book. For a long time, however, functional programming was widely viewed as an unnatural programming style that produced elegant but inefficient programs. Nevertheless, Jim Morris once remarked:

> *Functional languages are unnatural to use; but so are knives and forks, diplomatic protocols, double-entry bookkeeping, and a host of other things modern civilization has found useful.*

---

[3] These streams should not be confused with I/O streams, which are unrelated.

As for efficiency, Morris goes on to compare functional programming to two Japanese arts: Haiku, a form of poetry, and Karate, a form of martial arts. Your mastery of Haiku will be appreciated only by those who already appreciate Haiku, but in a bar fight, your mastery of Karate will be appreciated even by those who do not know Karate.

Is functional programming more like Haiku or more like Karate? For a long time, most computer scientists dismissed functional programming as Haiku. Today, however, improvements in hardware, compiler, and run-time technology have rendered such sweeping dismissals obsolete. Nevertheless, even today, the functional programming style should not be applied without careful thought. Here, we focus on the use of a functional programming style, in which *aggregate* operations are applied to the values in Java streams.

A stream's transformations and reductions are applied *lazily*: No computation occurs until it becomes absolutely necessary. Instead, *intermediate operations* set the stage for the desired transformations without performing them. Laziness ensures that by the time the work must be done, the compiler and run-time systems have accumulated as much information as possible about the programmer's intended transformations, enabling optimizations that would not be possible if operations were applied in an eager, one-at-a-time manner. For example, multiple intermediate operations can be accumulated lazily and then fused into a single traversal when the results are needed. Laziness also allows streams to be *unbounded:* One can construct, for example, an unbounded stream of prime numbers, or an unbounded stream of random points.

Once the desired (lazy) transformations have been set in place, a *terminal* operation applies those transformations and returns the result in the form of a container object, such as a `List<>` or `Set<>`, or perhaps as a scalar, such as a `Long` or `Double`. Once a terminal operation has been applied to a stream, that stream is deemed to be consumed, and cannot be reused.

One of the most common terminal operations is `collect()`, which folds the stream elements into a cumulative result called a `Collection`. Such transformations can be done either sequentially or in parallel. The `java.util.Collectors` class provides a useful set of predefined `Collection` instances.

In the next sections, we will use the `WordCount` and `KMeans` applications to introduce many of the basic concepts associated with aggregate data. Before discussing how to design and implement parallel stream-based versions of these applications, we look at sequential stream-based versions, to help readers become accustomed to this style of programming. A word of warning: This book is not a language reference manual. There are some restrictions and corner cases to consider when using streams, either in Java or in other languages that provide similar functionality (see the chapter notes). Before you use these constructs in a real application, consult the language documentation.

```
1    static List<String> readFile(String fileName) {
2       try {
3         Pattern pattern = Pattern.compile("\\W|\\d|_");
4         BufferedReader reader = new BufferedReader(new FileReader("document.tex"));
5         return reader
6                 .lines()
7                 .map(String::toLowerCase)
8                 .flatMap(s -> pattern.splitAsStream(s))
9                 .collect(Collectors.toList());
10      } catch (FileNotFoundException ex) {
11         ...
12      }
13   }
```

FIGURE 17.9

Stream-based `WordCount` application: the `readFile()` method.

17.2.1 A stream-based `WordCount` application

The `WordCount` application's first step is to read the target file, line-by-line, splitting each line into individual words, and converting each word to lower case. Fig. 17.9 shows one way to solve this task using aggregate operations. (Most applications that use streams are written in this kind of "chained" style.) The method first prepares a regular expression to be used to split lines into words (line 3). It then creates a `BufferedReader` to read from the document file (line 4). The `lines()` method returns a `Stream<String>` whose elements are lines read from the `BufferedReader`. Here are the next steps:

Line 7 The `map()` method takes as argument a lambda expression and creates a new stream by applying that lambda to each stream element, replacing each element with another. Here, we transform each line to lower case.

Line 8 The `flatMap()` method takes as an argument a lambda expression and creates a new stream by applying that lambda to each stream element, replacing each element with a *stream* of other elements, and then "flattening" these streams into a single stream. Here, we transform each line to a stream of individual words: by calling the `Pattern` class's `splitAsStream()` method to replace each line with a stream of individual words.

Line 9 At last, it is time to produce a result. As noted earlier, the `collect()` method is a common way of storing the stream elements in a kind of "accumulator" object, in this case a `List<String>`.

The `readLines()` method shown here is sequential.

Using aggregate operations (Fig. 17.10), `WordCount` is quite succinct. It calls `readFile()`, which returns a list of lower-case strings (line 16). It turns the list into a stream (line 18) and then collects the stream contents into a `Map<String,Long>` (line 19). Here, the `groupingBy()` collector takes two arguments (line 20). The first argument is a lambda that states how to compute each stream element's key. The call to

```
14   public class WordCount {
15     public static void main(String[] args) {
16       List<String> text = readFile("document.tex");
17       Map<String,Long> map = text
18               .stream()
19               .collect(
20                     Collectors.groupingBy(
21                             Function.identity(),
22                             Collectors.counting()))
23             );
24       displayOutput(map);
25     }
26   }
```

FIGURE 17.10

Stream-based WordCount application: aggregate data.

Function.identity() returns the *identity* function, which returns its own input, meaning that each string is its own key (line 21). The second argument is a *downstream* reducer that operates on the stream of strings that map to the same key (line 22). Of course, the stream of strings that map to x is a stream of k copies of x, where k is the number of times that string appears in the document. The Collectors.counting() container simply counts the number of elements in the stream.

17.2.2 A stream-based KMeans application

Recall that each iteration of KMeans algorithm has k tentative central points around which it clusters points. Once the clusters are complete, if the new centers are too far from the old centers, it computes a new tentative center for each cluster. The *barycenter* of a set of points $p_0, \ldots, p_{n-1}$ is given by

$$b = \frac{1}{n} \sum_{i=0}^{n-1} p_i.$$

Fig. 17.11 shows a stream-based barycenter() function. It first turns the List<Point> into a stream (line 4) and then applies reduce() to the stream to produce a single value. The argument to reduce() is a lambda defining a binary operator that combines two points into a third. Reduction repeatedly applies this operator to the stream elements until there is only one Point left. In this case, the binary operation is the Point class's plus() method, and reduce() simply sums the points in the stream (line 5). The result of this summation is not, however, a Point. Because reduction must be defined even for empty streams, the result is an object of type Optional<Point>, which may contain a Point or be empty. The method calls the result's get() operation to extract the Point, and multiplies the point by $\frac{1}{n}$, where n is the number of points in the cluster (line 6).

```
1    static public Point barycenter(List<Point> cluster) {
2      double numPoints = (double) cluster.size();
3      Optional<Point> sum = cluster
4            .stream()
5            .reduce(Point::plus);
6      return sum.get().scale(1 / numPoints);
7    }
```

FIGURE 17.11

The barycenter() method.

```
1    static public Stream<Point> randomPointStream() {
2      return Stream.generate(
3            () -> new Point(ThreadLocalRandom.current().nextDouble(),
4                            ThreadLocalRandom.current().nextDouble())
5      );
6    }
```

FIGURE 17.12

A stream of randomly generated points.

Suppose we have two methods that compute barycenters, one sequential and one parallel, and suppose we want to design an experiment to compare how they perform. Because the effectiveness of parallelism often depends on scale, a natural way to compare these methods is to generate a sequence of increasingly large sets of random points, take the barycenter of each set using both methods, and compare their performance as a function of the set size. This application illustrates a powerful aspect of streams: the ability to define *unbounded* streams that lazily produce an arbitrary number of values. Fig. 17.12 shows how to define a stream that produces an arbitrary number of randomly generated points. The call

```
Stream<Point> limited = unbounded.limit(k);
```

constructs a new stream of length k from an unbounded stream.

The stream-based KMeans application starts out like its MapReduce-based counterpart: It reads the data points from a file as a List<Point> (line 12), chooses distinct random points as starting cluster centers (line 13), and iterates the algorithm until it converges (line 15) (Fig. 17.13).

In the first step, the application clusters the data points around the centers by creating a Map<Integer,List<Point>> that maps each center point's index to the set of points closest to that center (line 16).

In the second step, it constructs a stream from the first step's map, and turns it back into a map, except replacing each cluster with its barycenter (line 21). The first argument to op() is a lambda expression that maps the stream element to a key, and the second maps the stream element to a value. Here, the key is the center index, and the value is the cluster's barycenter.

```
7   public class KMeans {
8     static final double EPSILON = 0.01;
9     static List<Point> points;
10    static Map<Integer, Point> centers;
11    public static void main(String[] args) {
12      points = KMeans.readFile("cluster.dat");
13      centers = randomDistinctCenters(points);
14      double convergence = 1.0;
15      while (convergence > EPSILON) {
16        Map<Integer, List<Point>> clusters = points
17              .stream()
18              .collect(
19                  Collectors.groupingBy(p -> KMeans.closestCenter(centers, p))
20              );
21        Map<Integer, Point> newCenters = clusters
22              .entrySet()
23              .stream()
24              .collect(
25                  Collectors.toMap(
26                        e -> e.getKey(),
27                        e -> Point.barycenter(e.getValue())
28                  )
29              );
30        convergence = distance(centers, newCenters);
31        centers = newCenters;
32      }
33      displayResults(clusters, centers);
34    }
```

FIGURE 17.13

Stream-based KMeans application: aggregate data.

17.2.3 Making aggregate operations parallel

We have seen that the contents of a container such as a List<T> or Map<K,V> can be fed into a Stream<>, and its contents can be manipulated by aggregate operations such as map(), filter(), reduce(), or collect(). These aggregate operations are carried out sequentially, operating in a one-at-a-time order on the values in the stream.

Instead of constructing a sequential Stream<> from a container, one can construct a ParallelStream<>. The Java runtime partitions a parallel stream into multiple substreams, applies aggregate operations to the substreams in parallel, and then combines the results. For example, this code will print this list of Boston street names in alphabetical order:

```
Arrays.asList("Arlington", "Berkeley", "Clarendon", "Dartmouth", "Exeter")
        .stream()
        .forEach(s -> System.out.printf("%s\n", s));
```

while this code will print the list of streets in a nondeterministic order:

```
Arrays.asList("Arlington", "Berkeley", "Clarendon", "Dartmouth", "Exeter")
        .parallelStream()
        .forEach(s -> System.out.printf("%s\n", s));
```

One can also transform a sequential stream into a parallel stream by calling the parallel() method:

```
Stream<T> seqStream = ...;                  // sequential stream
Stream<T> parStream = seqStream.parallel(); // parallel stream
```

Recall that *reduction* operations transform a stream into a container or a scalar value. Here, for convenient reference, is the key reduction in the stream-based WordCount application of Fig. 17.10:

```
Map<String,Long> map = text
        .stream()
        .collect(
                Collectors.groupingBy(
                        Function.identity(),
                        Collectors.counting())
        );
```

Here is a parallel version:

```
ConcurrentMap<String,Long> map = text
        .parallelStream()
        .collect(
                Collectors.groupingByConcurrent(
                        Function.identity(),
                        Collectors.counting())
        );
```

We made three changes: we replaced the call to stream() with a call to parallelStream(), and the call to groupingBy() with a call to groupingByConcurrent(), which returns a ConcurrentMap<String,Long>.

There are some pitfalls to avoid when combining lambda expressions with concurrent streams. First, a lambda expression operating on a stream, sequential or parallel, is said to be *interfering* if it alters the stream's source. Interfering lambda expressions will usually cause run-time exceptions. For example, if list is a List<Integer>, the following code will throw ConcurrentModificationException because the list is being modified at the same time the stream is navigating through each of its values.

```
list.stream().forEach(s -> list.add(0));
```

A lambda expression is *stateful* if its effect depends on aspects of its environment that could change from one call to another. Stateful lambda expressions, while not illegal, should be used with care. The following two lines of code use the same stateful lambda expression. The first line simply copies values, in order, from a source list to a target list. In the second line, however, the target list's add() method may be called

```
1   public static void main(String[] args) {
2     List<String> text = readFile("document.tex");
3     Spliterator<String> spliterator = text
4           .stream()
5           .spliterator();
6     Map<String, Long> result = (new RecursiveWordCountTask(spliterator)).compute();
7     displayOutput(result);
8   }
```

FIGURE 17.14

The RecursiveWordCount application: main() method.

concurrently, possibly resulting in an exception if the target list is not thread-safe. Even if the target is properly synchronized, the order in which elements are copied may be different each time the code is run.

```
source.stream().forEach(s -> target.add(s));
source.parallelStream().forEach(s -> target.add(s));
```

For many applications, parallelStream() is likely to be an effective way of executing aggregate operations in parallel. But what about applications that want more explicit control over how aggregate operations are parallelized?

A Spliterator<T> provides the ability to split a stream into parts, providing the opportunity to operate on the parts in parallel. In a typical spliterator use, the stream is recursively split until it falls below a threshold size, at which point it can be processed sequentially. Fig. 17.14 shows the main method of RecursiveWordCount. It turns the document into a Stream<String> and then into a spliterator. The actual work is done by the RecursiveWordCountTask class shown in Fig. 17.15.

This class inherits from RecursiveTask<Map<String, Long>>, so its compute() method does all the work. The task constructor takes a single argument, a Spliterator<String>. The compute() method first initializes a Map<String,Long> to hold the result (line 17). If the spliterator is larger than the THRESHOLD value (line 19), and if the spliterator is successfully split (line 19), then the method creates two subtasks: left and right (lines 21–22). (As its name suggests, the trySplit() method might not split the stream, returning *null* for any reason.)

The task then calls its children recursively. It forks the left child, allowing it to run in parallel with its caller (line 23), and it executes the right child directly, without forking (line 24). It merges the map returned by the right child with the result map (line 25), then it joins the left child, and does the same (line 28).

Otherwise, if the stream is below threshold, or it cannot be split, then the task uses the forEachRemaining() operator to add the words in the stream directly to its result map.

```
9    static class RecursiveWordCountTask extends RecursiveTask<Map<String, Long>> {
10       final int THRESHOLD = ...;
11       Spliterator<String> rightSplit;
12
13       RecursiveWordCountTask(Spliterator<String> aSpliterator) {
14          rightSplit = aSpliterator;
15       }
16       protected Map<String, Long> compute() {
17          Map<String, Long> result = new HashMap<>();
18          Spliterator<String> leftSplit;
19          if (rightSplit.estimateSize() > THRESHOLD
20                  && (leftSplit = rightSplit.trySplit()) != null) {
21             RecursiveWordCountTask left = new RecursiveWordCountTask(leftSplit);
22             RecursiveWordCountTask right = new RecursiveWordCountTask(rightSplit);
23             left.fork();
24             right.compute().forEach(
25                     (k, v) -> result.merge(k, v, (x, y) -> x + y)
26             );
27             left.join().forEach(
28                     (k, v) -> result.merge(k, v, (x, y) -> x + y)
29             );
30          } else {
31             rightSplit.forEachRemaining(
32                     word -> result.merge(word, 1L, (x, y) -> x + y)
33             );
34          }
35          return result;
36       }
37    }
```

FIGURE 17.15

The `RecursiveWordCountTask` class.

17.3 Chapter notes

The notion of MapReduce as a programming pattern for distributed systems is due to Dean and Ghemawat [34]. MapReduce frameworks for shared-memory multiprocessors include the Phoenix++ framework [161] and Metis [120].

Microsoft's C# and Visual Basic support *Language-Integrated query* (LINQ), which provides functionality comparable to that of Java streams, although expressed in the syntax of a query language.

The Jim Morris quotes are taken from a Xerox PARC technical report [132].

17.4 Exercises

Exercise 17.1. Java's LongStream<> class is a specialized kind of stream whose elements are **long** values. (For computations involving lots of arithmetic, a LongStream<> may be more efficient than a Stream<Long>.) This class provides a static range(i,j) method that returns a stream containing **long** values i ... j−1 and a static rangeClosed(i,j) method that returns a stream containing i ... j.

Using only the LongStream<> class (no loops), define a class Primes with the following methods:

```
private static boolean isPrime(long n)
```

tests whether a number is prime, and

```
private static long countPrimes(int max)
```

counts the number of primes less than a maximum.

Exercise 17.2. A *comparator* is a lambda expression that takes two arguments. It returns a negative integer if its first argument is "less" than its second, a positive integer if it is "greater," and 0 if the arguments are equivalent. Fill in the missing comparators in the following program.

```
public static void main(String[] args) {
   String[] strings = {"alfa", "bravo", "charlie", "delta", "echo"};

   // sort strings by length, shortest first
   Arrays.sort(strings, ...);
   System.out.println(Arrays.asList(strings));

   // sort strings by their second letter
   Arrays.sort(strings, ...);
   System.out.println(Arrays.asList(strings));

   // order strings that start with 'c' first, then sort normally
   Arrays.sort(strings, ...);
   System.out.println(Arrays.asList(strings));
 }
```

Your output should look like:

```
[alfa, echo, bravo, delta, charlie]
[echo, delta, charlie, alfa, bravo]
[charlie, alfa, bravo, delta, echo]
```

Exercise 17.3. Fig. 17.16 shows part of a MatrixVector class that uses MapReduce to multiply an $N \times N$ matrix by an N-element vector. For simplicity, it creates one mapper task for each matrix entry (in practice, it would be more efficient to have each mapper correspond to a larger submatrix).

The input matrix and vector are stored in static vector and matrix fields of the MatrixVector class (lines 3–4). Because Java does not permit arrays to be stored

```
1   public class MatrixVector {
2     static final int N = ...;
3     static double[] vector;
4     static double[][] matrix;
5     static class RowColumn {
6       int row;
7       int col;
8       RowColumn(int aRow, int aCol) {
9         row = aRow;
10        col = aCol;
11      }
12      public boolean equals(Object anObject) {
13        RowColumn other = (RowColumn) anObject;
14        return (this.row == other.row && this.col == other.col);
15      }
16    }
17    public static void main(String[] args) {
18      vector = readVector("vector.dat");
19      matrix = readMatrix("matrix.dat");
20      MapReduce<RowColumn, Integer, Double, Double> mapReduce = new MapReduce<>();
21      List<RowColumn> inputList = new ArrayList<>(N * N);
22      for (int r = 0; r < N; r++) {
23        for (int c = 0; c < N; c++) {
24          inputList.add(new RowColumn(r, c));
25        }
26      }
27      mapReduce.setInput(inputList);
28      mapReduce.setMapperSupplier(MatrixVector.Mapper::new);
29      mapReduce.setReducerSupplier(MatrixVector.Reducer::new);
30      Map<Integer, Double> output = mapReduce.call();
31      displayOutput(output);
32    }
33    // Exercise: missing mapper and reducer classes?
34    ...
35  }
```

FIGURE 17.16

The MatrixVector class used in Exercise 17.3.

directly in maps or lists, the Mapper and Reducer classes, as static inner classes of
MatrixVector, access the vector and matrix fields directly. A matrix position is identified by a RowColumn object that holds a row and column number (line 5). (As a
technical aside, RowColumn objects can be used as keys in maps because they provide an equals() operation that compares row and column numbers.) Each mapper
is initialized with its own RowColumn object, identifying its position in the matrix
(lines 21–26).

Your task is to fill in the missing Mapper and Reducer classes. They should be static
inner classes that access the static matrix and vector fields.

```
 1  public class MatrixMultiply {
 2    static final int N = ...;
 3    static double[][] matrixA;
 4    static double[][] matrixB;
 5    static class RowColumn {
 6      int row;
 7      int col;
 8      RowColumn(int aRow, int aCol) {
 9        row = aRow;
10        col = aCol;
11      }
12      public boolean equals(Object anObject) {
13        RowColumn other = (RowColumn) anObject;
14        return (this.row == other.row && this.col == other.col);
15      }
16    }
17    public static void main(String[] args) {
18      vector = readMatrix("matrixA.dat");
19      matrix = readMatrix("matrixB.dat");
20      MapReduce<RowColumn, RowColumn, Double, Double> mapReduce = new MapReduce<>();
21      List<RowColumn> inputList = new ArrayList<>(N * N);
22      for (int i = 0; i < N; i++) {
23        for (int j = 0; j < N; j++) {
24          inputList.add(new RowColumn(i, j));
25        }
26      }
27      mapReduce.setInput(inputList);
28      mapReduce.setMapperSupplier(MatrixMultiply.Mapper::new);
29      mapReduce.setReducerSupplier(MatrixMultiply.Reducer::new);
30      Map<RowColumn, Double> output = mapReduce.call();
31      displayOutput(output);
32    }
33    // Exercise: missing mapper and reducer classes?
34    ...
35  }
```

FIGURE 17.17

The MatrixMultiply class used in Exercise 17.4.

Exercise 17.4. Fig. 17.17 shows part of the code for a MatrixMultiply class that multiplies one $N \times N$ matrix (matrixA) by another (matrixB). For simplicity, it creates one mapper task for each entry of matrixA.

The two matrices are stored in static matrixA and matrixB fields of the MatrixMultiply class (lines 3–4). Because Java does not permit arrays to be stored directly in maps or lists, the Mapper and Reducer classes, as static inner classes of MatrixVector, access the matrixA and matrixB fields directly. A matrix position is identified by a RowColumn object that holds a row and column number (line 5). (As a technical aside, RowColumn objects can be used as keys in maps because they provide an equals() operation that compares row and column numbers.) Each mapper is initialized with its own RowColumn object, identifying its position in the matrix (lines 21–26).

Your task is to fill in the missing Mapper and Reducer classes. They should be static inner classes that access the static matrixA and matrixB fields.

Exercise 17.5. In the *single-source shortest-path* (SSSP) problem, we are given a directed graph G and a source node s in G, and we must compute, for each node n in G, the length of the shortest directed path from s to n in G. For simplicity, we assume in this example that each edge has length 1.0, but it should be easy to assign different edge weights.

Fig. 17.18 shows part of an iterated MapReduce SSSP implementation. Here, each node is represented as an Integer, and each distance as a Double. The graph is a Map<Integer,List<Integer>> carrying each node to a list of its neighbors (line 2). Node 0 is the source. The best-known distances from the source are tracked in a

```
1   public class SSSP {
2     static Map<Integer, List<Integer>> graph;
3     static Map<Integer, Double> distances;
4     static final Integer N = ...;
5     static final Double EPSILON = ...;
6     public static void main(String[] args) {
7       graph = makeGraph(N);
8       distances = new TreeMap();
9       Map<Integer, Double> newDistances = new TreeMap<>();
10      newDistances.put(0, 0.0);
11      for (int i = 1; i < N; i++) {
12        newDistances.put(i, Double.MAX_VALUE);
13      }
14      MapReduce<Integer, Integer, Double, Double> mapReduce
15            = new MapReduce<>();
16      mapReduce.setMapperSupplier(SSSP.Mapper::new);
17      mapReduce.setReducerSupplier(SSSP.Reducer::new);
18      boolean done = false;
19      while (!done) {
20        distances.putAll(newDistances);
21        mapReduce.setInput(
22              listOfFiniteDistanceNodes(distances)
23        );
24        newDistances.putAll(mapReduce.call());
25        done = withinEpsilon(distances, newDistances);
26      }
27      displayOutput(distances);
28    }
29  }
```

FIGURE 17.18

The SSSP class used in Exercise 17.5.

Map<Integer,Double> (line 8), initially 0.0 for node 0, and essentially infinite for the rest (line 10).

Like KMeans, SSSP is iterative. Unlike KMeans, the number of mappers varies at each iteration. We do a breadth-first traversal of the graph: Initially the source has distance 0, and in the first iteration, we assign its neighbors distance 1.0, in the next iteration we assign their neighbors the minimum of their current distance and 2.0, and so on. The method call at line 20 returns the list of nodes that have been discovered to be reachable from the source, and we feed these nodes to the next iteration's mapper tasks. The algorithm terminates when there is an iteration where no node's distance improves by more than a predefined EPSILON (line 25).

Your job is to fill in the missing Mapper and Reducer classes. They should be static inner classes that access the static graph and distances fields.

Exercise 17.6. In Fig. 17.18, Exercise 17.5, the listOfFiniteDistanceNodes() method takes a Map<Integer,Double> and returns a list of the Integer keys bound to values less than Double.MAX_VALUE. Implement this method using stream operators.

Exercise 17.7. In Fig. 17.18, Exercise 17.5, the withinEpsilon() method takes two Map<Integer,Double> arguments, which are assumed to have the same set of keys. It returns *true* if and only if the values bound to each key differ by less than a predefined constant EPSILON. Implement this method using stream operators.

Exercise 17.8. Let m0 and m1 be two Map<<,I>nteger, Double> objects. Using data-parallel streams, write a single-statement distance() method that returns the sum of the absolute values of the differences between each key's bindings, for keys that appear in both maps. Your method should be equivalent to this:

```
double distance(Map<Integer, Double> m0, Map<Integer, Double> m1) {
  Double sum = 0.0;
  for (int key : m0.keySet()) {
    if (m1.containsKey(key)) {
      sum += Math.abs(m0.get(key) - m1.get(key));
    }
  }
  return sum;
}
```

Exercise 17.9. Start with a list of strings, similar to this:

```
List<String> strings = Arrays.asList("alfa", "bravo", "charlie",
    "delta", "echo");
```

Using stream operations,

1. Print each string on a separate line.
2. Print each string on a separate line, followed by three exclamation points!!!
3. Discard each string of four characters or less, then discard the strings that do not contain the letter "l," and print each remaining string on a separate line.

Exercise 17.10. The following code fragment creates a small database mapping cities to their zip codes.

```
Map<String, String> map = new HashMap<>();
    map.put("Cambridge", "03219");
    map.put("Providence", "02912");
    map.put("Palo Alto", "94305");
    map.put("Pittsburgh", "15213");
```

Use a stream and stream operators to invert this map, constructing a new map that carries zip codes to cities.

Exercise 17.11. Write a FibStream class that provides a single get() method that returns an unbounded Stream<Long> of the Fibonacci numbers.

Exercise 17.12. Suppose you are given a Stream<Point> containing a sequence of points of unknown, but nonzero size. Write a method

```
Point streamBary(Stream<Point> stream)
```

that computes their barycenter.

Hint: The counting() method that counts the number of stream elements is terminal, so you cannot continue to use the stream if you count its elements directly. Instead, you must find out how to use a single reduction to sum the points and count them simultaneously.

```
1    public static void main(String[] args) {
2      points = readFile("cluster.dat");
3      centers = randomDistinctCenters(points);
4      pool = new ForkJoinPool();
5      double convergence = 1.0;
6      while (convergence > EPSILON) {
7        Spliterator<Point> pointSplit = points
8              .stream()
9              .spliterator();
10       RecursiveClusterTask clusterTask = new RecursiveClusterTask(pointSplit);
11       Map<Integer, Set<Point>> clusters = pool.invoke(clusterTask);
12       Spliterator<Map.Entry<Integer, Set<Point>>> centerSplit = clusters
13             .entrySet()
14             .stream()
15             .spliterator();
16       RecursiveCenterTask centerTask = new RecursiveCenterTask(centerSplit);
17       Map<Integer, Point> newCenters = pool.invoke(centerTask);
18       convergence = distance(centers, newCenters);
19       centers = newCenters;
20     }
21     displayOutput(centers);
22   }
```

FIGURE 17.19

Code for Exercise 17.13.

Exercise 17.13. Fig. 17.19 shows the main() method for a recursive spliterator of the KMeans application. The RecursiveClusterTask class is a recursive fork-join task that computes the clusters, and the RecursiveCenterTask class is a recursive fork-join task that computes the centers from the clusters. Write the code for the RecursiveClusterTask and RecursiveClusterTask classes in the style of Fig. 17.15.

Barriers

18

18.1 Introduction

Imagine you are writing the graphical display for a computer game. Your program prepares a sequence of *frames* to be displayed by a graphics package (perhaps a hardware coprocessor). This kind of program is sometimes called a *soft real-time* application: real-time because it must display at least 35 frames per second to be effective, and soft because occasional failure is not catastrophic. On a single-thread machine, you might write a loop like this:

```
while (true) {
  frame.prepare();
  frame.display();
}
```

If, instead, you have *n* parallel threads available, then it makes sense to split the frame into *n* disjoint parts, and have each thread prepare its part in parallel with the others.

```
int me = ThreadID.get();
while (true) {
  frame[me].prepare();
  frame[me].display();
}
```

The problem with this approach is that different threads require different amounts of time to prepare and display their portions of the frame. Some threads might start displaying the ith frame before others have finished the $(i-1)$st.

To avoid such synchronization problems, we can organize computations such as this as a sequence of *phases*, where no thread should start the ith phase until the others have finished the $(i-1)$st. We have seen this phased computation pattern before: In Chapter 12, the sorting network algorithms required each comparison phase to be separate from the others. Similarly, in the sample sorting algorithm, each phase had to make sure that prior phases had completed before proceeding.

The mechanism for enforcing this kind of synchronization is called a *barrier*; its interface is shown in Fig. 18.1. A barrier is a way of forcing asynchronous threads to act almost as if they were synchronous. When a thread finishing phase i calls the barrier's await() method, it is blocked until all n threads have also finished that phase. Fig. 18.2 shows how one could use a barrier to make the parallel rendering program work correctly. After preparing frame i, all threads synchronize at a barrier before

The Art of Multiprocessor Programming. https://doi.org/10.1016/B978-0-12-415950-1.00028-8

```
1  public interface Barrier {
2    public void await();
3  }
```

FIGURE 18.1

The Barrier interface.

```
1  private Barrier b;
2    ...
3    while (true) {
4      frame[my].prepare();
5      b.await();
6      frame[my].display();
7    }
```

FIGURE 18.2

Using a barrier to synchronize concurrent displays.

starting to display that frame. This structure ensures that all threads concurrently displaying a frame display the same frame.

Barrier implementations raise many of the same performance issues as spin locks in Chapter 7, as well as some new issues. Clearly, barriers should be fast, in the sense that we want to minimize the duration between when the last thread reaches the barrier and when the last thread leaves the barrier. It is also important that threads leave the barrier at roughly the same time. A thread's *notification time* is the interval between when some thread has detected that all threads have reached the barrier, and when that specific thread leaves the barrier. Having uniform notification times is important for many soft real-time applications. For example, picture quality is enhanced if all portions of the frame are updated at more-or-less the same time.

18.2 Barrier implementations

Fig. 18.3 shows the SimpleBarrier class, which creates an AtomicInteger counter initialized to n, the barrier size. Each thread applies getAndDecrement() to lower the counter. If the call returns 1 (line 10), then that thread is the last to reach the barrier, so it resets the counter for the next use (line 11). Otherwise, the thread spins on the counter, waiting for the value to fall to zero (line 13). This barrier class may look like it works, but it does not.

Unfortunately, the attempt to make the barrier reusable breaks it. Suppose there are only two threads. Thread A applies getAndDecrement() to the counter, discovers it is not the last thread to reach the barrier, and spins waiting for the counter value to reach 0. When B arrives, it discovers it is the last thread to arrive, so it resets the counter to n, in this case 2. It finishes the next phase and calls await(). Meanwhile, A

```
1  public class SimpleBarrier implements Barrier { // incorrect
2    AtomicInteger count;
3    int size;
4    public SimpleBarrier(int n){
5      count = new AtomicInteger(n);
6      size = n;
7    }
8    public void await() {
9      int position = count.getAndDecrement();
10     if (position == 1) {
11       count.set(size);
12     } else {
13       while (count.get() != 0){};
14     }
15   }
16 }
```

FIGURE 18.3

An incorrect implementation of the SimpleBarrier class.

continues to spin; it never saw the counter reach 0. Eventually, *A* is waiting for phase 0 to finish, while *B* is waiting for phase 1 to finish, and the two threads starve.

Perhaps the simplest way to fix this problem is to alternate between two barriers, using one for even-numbered phases and another for odd-numbered ones. However, such an approach wastes space, and requires too much bookkeeping from applications.

18.3 Sense reversing barrier

A *sense reversing* barrier is an elegant and practical solution to the problem of reusing barriers. As shown in Fig. 18.4, a phase's *sense* is a Boolean value: *true* for even-numbered phases and *false* otherwise. Each SenseBarrier object has a Boolean sense field indicating the sense of the currently executing phase. Each thread keeps its current sense as a thread-local object (Pragma 18.3.1). Initially the barrier's sense is the complement of the local sense of all the threads. When a thread calls await(), it checks whether it is the last thread to decrement the counter. If so, it reverses the barrier's sense and continues. Otherwise, it spins waiting for the barrier's sense field to change to match its own local sense.

Decrementing the shared counter may cause memory contention, since all the threads are trying to access the counter at about the same time. Once the counter has been decremented, each thread spins on the sense field. This implementation is well suited for cache-coherent architectures, since threads spin on locally cached copies of the field, and the field is modified only when threads are ready to leave the barrier.

```
1   public SenseBarrier(int n) {
2     count = new AtomicInteger(n);
3     size = n;
4     sense = false;
5     threadSense = new ThreadLocal<Boolean>() {
6       protected Boolean initialValue() { return !sense; };
7     };
8   }
9   public void await() {
10    boolean mySense = threadSense.get();
11    int position = count.getAndDecrement();
12    if (position == 1) {
13      count.set(size);
14      sense = mySense;
15    } else {
16      while (sense != mySense) {}
17    }
18    threadSense.set(!mySense);
19  }
```

FIGURE 18.4

The SenseBarrier class: a sense reversing barrier.

The sense field is an excellent way of maintaining a uniform notification time on symmetric cache-coherent multiprocessors.

PRAGMA 18.3.1

The constructor code for the sense reversing barrier, shown in Fig. 18.4, is mostly straightforward. The one exception occurs on lines 5 and 6, where we initialize the thread-local threadSense field. This somewhat complicated syntax defines a thread-local Boolean value whose initial value is the complement of the sense field's initial value. See Appendix A.2.4 for a more complete explanation of thread-local objects in Java.

18.4 Combining tree barrier

One way to reduce memory contention (at the cost of increased latency) is to use the combining paradigm of Chapter 12. Split a large barrier into a tree of smaller barriers, and have threads combine requests going up the tree and distribute notifications going down the tree. A *tree barrier* (Fig. 18.5) is characterized by a *size n*, the total number of threads, and a *radix r*, the number of children of each node For convenience, we assume there are exactly $n = r^{d+1}$ threads, where d is the depth of the tree.

```
1   public class TreeBarrier implements Barrier {
2     int radix;
3     Node[] leaf;
4     ThreadLocal<Boolean> threadSense;
5     ...
6     public void await() {
7       int me = ThreadID.get();
8       Node myLeaf = leaf[me / radix];
9       myLeaf.await();
10    }
11    ...
12  }
```

FIGURE 18.5

The TreeBarrier class: Each thread indexes into an array of leaf nodes and calls that leaf's await() method.

Specifically, the combining tree barrier is a tree of *nodes*, where each node has a counter and a sense, just as in the sense reversing barrier. A node's implementation is shown in Fig. 18.6. Thread i starts at leaf node $\lfloor i/r \rfloor$. The node's await() method is similar to the sense reversing barrier's await(), the principal difference being that the last thread to arrive, the one that completes the barrier, visits the parent barrier before waking up the other threads. When r threads have arrived at the root, the barrier is complete, and the sense is reversed. As before, thread-local Boolean sense values allow the barrier to be reused without reinitialization.

The tree-structured barrier reduces memory contention by spreading memory accesses across multiple barriers. It may or may not reduce latency, depending on whether it is faster to decrement a single location or to visit a logarithmic number of barriers.

The root node, once its barrier is complete, lets notifications percolate down the tree. This approach may be good for a NUMA architecture, but it may cause nonuniform notification times. Because threads visit an unpredictable sequence of locations as they move up the tree, this approach may not work well on cacheless NUMA architectures.

PRAGMA 18.4.1

Tree nodes are declared as an *inner class* of the tree barrier class, so nodes are not accessible outside the class. As shown in Fig. 18.7, the tree is initialized by a recursive build() method. The method takes a parent node and a depth. If the depth is nonzero, it creates *radix* children, and recursively creates the children's children. If the depth is 0, it places each node in a leaf[] array. When a thread enters the barrier, it uses this array to choose a leaf to start from. See Appendix A.2.1 for a more complete discussion of inner classes in Java.

```
13    private class Node {
14      AtomicInteger count;
15      Node parent;
16      volatile boolean sense;
17
18      public Node() {
19        sense = false;
20        parent = null;
21        count = new AtomicInteger(radix);
22      }
23      public Node(Node myParent) {
24        this();
25        parent = myParent;
26      }
27      public void await() {
28        boolean mySense = threadSense.get();
29        int position = count.getAndDecrement();
30        if (position == 1) { // I'm last
31          if (parent != null) { // Am I root?
32            parent.await();
33          }
34          count.set(radix);
35          sense = mySense;
36        } else {
37          while (sense != mySense) {};
38        }
39        threadSense.set(!mySense);
40      }
41    }
42  }
```

FIGURE 18.6

The TreeBarrier class: internal tree node.

18.5 Static tree barrier

The barriers seen so far either suffer from contention (the simple and sense reversing barriers) or have excessive communication (the combining tree barrier). In the latter barrier, which threads traverse up the tree is varying and unpredictable, which makes it difficult to lay out the barriers on cacheless NUMA architectures. Surprisingly, there is a simple barrier that allows a static layout and yet has low contention.

The *static tree barrier* of Fig. 18.8 works as follows: Each thread is assigned to a node in a tree (Fig. 18.9). The thread at a node waits until all nodes below it in the tree have finished, and then informs its parent. It then spins waiting for the global sense bit to change. Once the root learns that its children are done, it toggles the global sense bit to notify the waiting threads that all threads are done. On a cache-coherent mul-

```
43   public class TreeBarrier implements Barrier {
44     int radix;
45     Node[] leaf;
46     int leaves;
47     ThreadLocal<Boolean> threadSense;
48
49     public TreeBarrier(int n, int r) {
50       radix = r;
51       leaves = 0;
52       leaf = new Node[n / r];
53       int depth = 0;
54       threadSense = new ThreadLocal<Boolean>() {
55         protected Boolean initialValue() { return true; };
56       };
57       // compute tree depth
58       while (n > 1) {
59         depth++;
60         n = n / r;
61       }
62       Node root = new Node();
63       build(root, depth - 1);
64     }
65     // recursive tree constructor
66     void build(Node parent, int depth) {
67       if (depth == 0) {
68         leaf[leaves++] = parent;
69       } else {
70         for (int i = 0; i < radix; i++) {
71           Node child = new Node(parent);
72           build(child, depth - 1);
73         }
74       }
75     }
76     ...
77   }
```

FIGURE 18.7

The `TreeBarrier` class: initializing a combining tree barrier. The `build()` method creates *r* children for each node, and then recursively creates the children's children. At the bottom, it places leaves in an array.

tiprocessor, completing the barrier requires log(*n*) steps moving up the tree, while notification simply requires changing the global sense, which is propagated by the cache-coherence mechanism. On machines without coherent caches, threads propagate notification down the tree as in the combining barrier we saw earlier.

```
1   public class StaticTreeBarrier implements Barrier {
2     int radix;
3     boolean sense;
4     Node[] node;
5     ThreadLocal<Boolean> threadSense;
6     int nodes;
7
8     public StaticTreeBarrier(int size, int myRadix) {
9       radix = myRadix;
10      nodes = 0;
11      node = new Node[size];
12      int depth = 0;
13      while (size > 1) {
14        depth++;
15        size = size / radix;
16      }
17      build(null, depth);
18      sense = false;
19      threadSense = new ThreadLocal<Boolean>() {
20        protected Boolean initialValue() { return !sense; };
21      };
22    }
23    // recursive tree constructor
24    void build(Node parent, int depth) {
25      if (depth == 0) {
26        node[nodes++] = new Node(parent, 0);
27      } else {
28        Node myNode = new Node(parent, radix);
29        node[nodes++] = myNode;
30        for (int i = 0; i < radix; i++) {
31          build(myNode, depth - 1);
32        }
33      }
34    }
35    public void await() {
36      node[ThreadID.get()].await();
37    }
38  }
```

FIGURE 18.8

The StaticTreeBarrier class: Each thread indexes into a statically assigned tree node and calls that node's await() method.

18.6 Termination detection barriers

All the barriers considered so far were directed at computations organized in phases, where each thread finishes the work for a phase, reaches the barrier, and then starts a new phase.

```
39      public Node(Node myParent, int count) {
40        children = count;
41        childCount = new AtomicInteger(count);
42        parent = myParent;
43      }
44      public void await() {
45        boolean mySense = threadSense.get();
46        while (childCount.get() > 0) {};
47        childCount.set(children);
48        if (parent != null) {
49          parent.childDone();
50          while (sense != mySense) {};
51        } else {
52          sense = !sense;
53        }
54        threadSense.set(!mySense);
55      }
56      public void childDone() {
57        childCount.getAndDecrement();
58      }
```

FIGURE 18.9

The `StaticTreeBarrier` class: internal `Node` class.

There is another interesting class of programs, in which each thread finishes its own part of the computation, only to be put to work again when another thread generates new work. An example of such a program is the simplified work stealing executor pool from Chapter 16 (Fig. 18.10). Once a thread exhausts the tasks in its local queue, it tries to steal work from other threads' queues. The execute() method itself may push new tasks onto the calling thread's local queue. Once all threads have exhausted all tasks in their queues, the threads will run forever while repeatedly attempting to steal items. Instead, we would like to devise a *termination detection* barrier so that these threads can all terminate once they have finished all their tasks.

Each thread is either *active* (it has a task to execute) or *inactive* (it has none). Note that any inactive thread may become active as long as some other thread is active, since an inactive thread may steal a task from an active one. Once all threads have become inactive, then no thread will ever become active again. Detecting that the computation as a whole has terminated is the problem of determining that at some instant in time, there are no longer any active threads.

None of the barrier algorithms studied so far can solve this problem. Termination cannot be detected by having each thread announce that it has become inactive, and simply count how many have done so, because threads may repeatedly change from inactive to active and back. For example, we have suppose work stealing threads A, B, and C. We would like the threads to be able to exit from the loop on line 9. An incorrect strategy would assign each thread a Boolean value indicating whether it

```
1   public class WorkStealingThread {
2     DEQue[] queue;
3     public WorkStealingThread(DEQue[] queue) {
4       this.queue = queue;
5     }
6     public void run() {
7       int me = ThreadID.get();
8       RecursiveAction task = queue[me].popBottom();
9       while (true) {
10        while (task != null) {
11          task.compute();
12          task = queue[me].popBottom();
13        }
14        while (task == null) {
15          int victim = ThreadLocalRandom.current().nextInt(queue.length);
16          if (!queue[victim].isEmpty()) {
17            task = queue[victim].popTop();
18          }
19        }
20      }
21    }
22  }
```

FIGURE 18.10

Work stealing executor pool revisited.

```
1   public interface TDBarrier {
2     void setActive(boolean state);
3     boolean isTerminated();
4   }
```

FIGURE 18.11

Termination detection barrier interface.

is active or inactive. When A becomes inactive, it may then observe that B is also inactive, and then observe that C is inactive. Nevertheless, A cannot conclude that the overall computation has completed, as B might have stolen work from C after A checked B, but before it checked C.

A *termination detection* barrier (Fig. 18.11) provides methods setActive(v) and isTerminated(). Each thread calls setActive(*true*) to notify the barrier when it becomes active, and setActive(*false*) to notify the barrier when it becomes inactive. The isTerminated() method returns *true* if and only if all threads had become inactive at some earlier instant. Fig. 18.12 shows a simple implementation of a termination detection barrier.

```
1   public class SimpleTDBarrier implements TDBarrier {
2     AtomicInteger count;
3     public SimpleTDBarrier(int n){
4       count = new AtomicInteger(n);
5     }
6     public void setActive(boolean active) {
7       if (active) {
8         count.getAndIncrement();
9       } else {
10        count.getAndDecrement();
11      }
12    }
13    public boolean isTerminated() {
14      return count.get() == 0;
15    }
16  }
```

FIGURE 18.12

A simple termination detection barrier.

The barrier encompasses an AtomicInteger initialized to 0. Each thread that becomes active increments the counter (line 8) and each thread that becomes inactive decrements it (line 10). The computation is deemed to have terminated when the counter reaches 0 (line 14).

The termination detection barrier works only if used correctly. Fig. 18.13 shows how to modify the work stealing thread's run() method to return when the computation has terminated. Initially, every thread registers as active (line 3). Once a thread has exhausted its local queue, it registers as inactive (line 10). Before it tries to steal a new task, however, it must register as active (line 14). If the theft fails, it registers as inactive again (line 17).

Note that a thread sets its state to active before stealing a task. Otherwise, if a thread were to steal a task while inactive, then the thread whose task was stolen might also declare itself inactive, resulting in a computation where all threads declare themselves inactive while the computation continues.

Here is a subtle point: A thread tests whether the queue is empty (line 13) before it attempts to steal a task. This way, it avoids declaring itself active if there is no chance the theft will succeed. Without this precaution, it is possible that the threads will not detect termination because each one repeatedly switches to an active state before a steal attempt that is doomed to fail.

Correct use of the termination detection barrier must satisfy both a safety and a liveness property. The safety property is that if isTerminated() returns *true*, then the computation really has terminated. Safety requires that no active thread ever declare itself inactive, because it could trigger an incorrect termination detection. For example, the work stealing thread of Fig. 18.13 would be incorrect if the thread declared itself to be active only after successfully stealing a task. By contrast, it is safe for an

```
1    public void run() {
2      int me = ThreadID.get();
3      tdBarrier.setActive(true);
4      RecursiveAction task = queue[me].popBottom();
5      while (true) {
6        while (task != null) {
7          task.compute();
8          task = queue[me].popBottom();
9        }
10       tdBarrier.setActive(false);
11       while (task == null) {
12         int victim = ThreadLocalRandom.current().nextInt(queue.length);
13         if (!queue[victim].isEmpty()) {
14           tdBarrier.setActive(true);
15           task = queue[victim].popTop();
16           if (task == null) {
17             tdBarrier.setActive(false);
18           }
19         }
20         if (tdBarrier.isTerminated()) {
21           return;
22         }
23       }
24     }
25   }
26 }
```

FIGURE 18.13

Work stealing executor pool: the run() method with termination.

inactive thread to declare itself active, which may occur if the thread is unsuccessful in stealing work at line 15.

The liveness property is that if the computation terminates, then isTerminated() eventually returns *true*. (It is not necessary that termination be detected instantly.) While safety is not jeopardized if an inactive thread declares itself active, liveness will be violated if a thread that does not succeed in stealing work fails to declare itself inactive again (line 15), because termination will not be detected when it occurs.

18.7 Chapter notes

John Mellor-Crummey and Michael Scott [124] provide a survey of several barrier algorithms, though the performance numbers they provide should be viewed from a historical perspective. The combining tree barrier is based on code due to John Mellor-Crummey and Michael Scott [124], which is in turn based on the combining tree algorithm of Pen-Chung Yew, Nian-Feng Tzeng, and Duncan Lawrie [168].

The dissemination barrier is credited to Debra Hensgen, Raphael Finkel, and Udi Manber [64]. The tournament tree barrier used in the exercises is credited to John Mellor-Crummey and Michael Scott [124]. The simple barriers and the static tree barrier are most likely folklore. We learned of the static tree barrier from Beng-Hong Lim. The termination detection barrier and its application to an executor pool are based on a variation suggested by Peter Kessler to an algorithm by Dave Detlefs, Christine Flood, Nir Shavit, and Xiolan Zhang [47].

18.8 Exercises

Exercise 18.1. Fig. 18.14 shows how to use barriers to make a parallel prefix computation work on an asynchronous architecture.

A *parallel prefix* computation, given a sequence $a_0, \ldots, a_{m-1}$, of numbers, computes in parallel the partial sums:

$$b_i = \sum_{j=0}^{i} a_j.$$

In a synchronous system, where all threads take steps at the same time, there are simple, well-known algorithms for m threads to compute the partial sums in $\log m$ steps. The computation proceeds in a sequence of rounds, starting at round zero. In round r, if $i \geq 2^r$, thread i reads the value at $a[i - 2^r]$ into a local variable. Next, it

```
1   class Prefix extends java.lang.Thread {
2     private int[] a;
3     private int i;
4     public Prefix(int[] myA, int myI) {
5       a = myA;
6       i = myI;
7     }
8     public void run() {
9       int d = 1, sum = 0;
10      while (d < m) {
11        if (i >= d)
12          sum = a[i-d];
13        if (i >= d)
14          a[i] += sum;
15        d = d * 2;
16      }
17    }
18  }
```

FIGURE 18.14

Parallel prefix computation.

adds that value to $a[i]$. Rounds continue until $2^r \geq m$. It is not hard to see that after $\log_2(m)$ rounds, the array a contains the partial sums.

1. What could go wrong if we executed the parallel prefix on $n > m$ threads?
2. Add one or more barriers to this program to make it work properly in a concurrent setting with n threads. What is the minimum number of barriers that are needed?

Exercise 18.2. Change the sense reversing barrier implementation so that waiting threads call wait() instead of spinning.

- Give an example of a situation where suspending threads is better than spinning.
- Give an example of a situation where the other choice is better.

```
1    private class Node {
2      volatile boolean flag;    // signal when done
3      boolean active;           // active or passive?
4      Node parent;              // parent node
5      Node partner;             // partner node
6      // create passive node
7      Node() {
8        flag    = false;
9        active = false;
10       partner = null;
11       parent = null;
12     }
13     // create active node
14     Node(Node myParent) {
15       this();
16       parent = myParent;
17       active = true;
18     }
19     void await(boolean sense) {
20       if (active) { // I'm active
21         if (parent != null) {
22           while (flag != sense) {}; // wait for partner
23           parent.await(sense);    // wait for parent
24           partner.flag = sense;   // tell partner
25         }
26       } else {                    // I'm passive
27         partner.flag = sense;     // tell partner
28         while (flag != sense) {}; // wait for partner
29       }
30     }
31   }
```

FIGURE 18.15

The TourBarrier class.

Exercise 18.3. Change the tree barrier implementation so that it takes a `Runnable` object whose `run()` method is called once after the last thread arrives at the barrier, but before any thread leaves the barrier.

Exercise 18.4. Modify the combining tree barrier so that nodes can use any barrier implementation, not just the sense reversing barrier.

Exercise 18.5. A *tournament tree barrier* (class `TourBarrier` in Fig. 18.15) is an alternative tree-structured barrier. Assume there are n threads, where n is a power of 2. The tree is a binary tree consisting of $2n - 1$ nodes. Each leaf is owned by a single, statically determined, thread. Each node's two children are linked as *partners*. One partner is statically designated as *active*, and the other as *passive*. Fig. 18.16 illustrates the tree structure.

Each thread keeps track of the current sense in a thread-local variable. When a thread arrives at a passive node, it sets its active partner's sense field to the current sense, and spins on its own sense field until its partner changes that field's value to the current sense. When a thread arrives at an active node, it spins on its sense field until its passive partner sets it to the current sense. When the field changes, that particular barrier is complete, and the active thread follows the parent reference to its parent node. Note that an active thread at one level may become passive at the next level. When the root node barrier is complete, notifications percolate down the tree. Each thread moves back down the tree setting its partner's sense field to the current sense.

- Explain how this barrier slightly improves the combining tree barrier of Fig. 18.5.
- The tournament barrier code uses `parent` and `partner` references to navigate the tree. We could save space by eliminating these fields and keeping all the nodes in a single array with the root at index 0, the root's children at indices 1 and 2, the

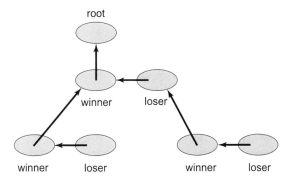

FIGURE 18.16

The `TourBarrier` class: information flow. Nodes are paired statically in active/passive pairs. Threads start at the leaves. Each thread in an active node waits for its passive partner to show up, then it proceeds up the tree. Each passive thread waits for its active partner for notification of completion. Once an active thread reaches the root, all threads have arrived, and notifications flow down the tree in the reverse order.

grandchildren at indices 3–6, and so on. Reimplement the tournament barrier to use indexing arithmetic instead of references to navigate the tree.

Exercise 18.6. The combining tree barrier uses a single thread-local sense field for the entire barrier. Suppose instead we were to associate a thread-local sense with each node as in Fig. 18.17. Either explain why this implementation is equivalent to the other one, except that it consumes more memory, or give a counterexample showing that it is incorrect.

```
1    private class Node {
2       AtomicInteger count;
3       Node parent;
4       volatile boolean sense;
5       int d;
6       // construct root node
7       public Node() {
8         sense = false;
9         parent = null;
10        count = new AtomicInteger(radix);
11        ThreadLocal<Boolean> threadSense;
12        threadSense = new ThreadLocal<Boolean>() {
13          protected Boolean initialValue() { return true; };
14      };
15      }
16      public Node(Node myParent) {
17        this();
18        parent = myParent;
19      }
20      public void await() {
21        boolean mySense = threadSense.get();
22        int position = count.getAndDecrement();
23        if (position == 1) { // I'm last
24          if (parent != null) { // root?
25            parent.await();
26          }
27          count.set(radix);    // reset counter
28          sense = mySense;
29        } else {
30          while (sense != mySense) {};
31        }
32        threadSense.set(!mySense);
33      }
34    }
```

FIGURE 18.17

Thread-local tree barrier.

Exercise 18.7. The tree barrier works "bottom-up," in the sense that barrier completion moves from the leaves up to the root, while wakeup information moves from the root back down to the leaves. Figs. 18.18 and 18.19 show an alternative design, called a *reverse tree barrier*, which works just like a tree barrier except for the fact that barrier completion starts at the root and moves down to the leaves. Either sketch an argument why this is correct, perhaps by reduction to the standard tree barrier, or give a counterexample showing why it is incorrect.

```
1  public class RevBarrier implements Barrier {
2    int radix;
3    ThreadLocal<Boolean> threadSense;
4    int leaves;
5    Node[] leaf;
6    public RevBarrier(int mySize, int myRadix) {
7      radix = myRadix;
8      leaves = 0;
9      leaf = new Node[mySize / myRadix];
10     int depth = 0;
11     threadSense = new ThreadLocal<Boolean>() {
12       protected Boolean initialValue() { return true; };
13     };
14     // compute tree depth
15     while (mySize > 1) {
16       depth++;
17       mySize = mySize / myRadix;
18     }
19     Node root = new Node();
20     root.d = depth;
21     build(root, depth - 1);
22   }
23   // recursive tree constructor
24   void build(Node parent, int depth) {
25     // are we at a leaf node?
26     if (depth == 0) {
27       leaf[leaves++] = parent;
28     } else {
29       for (int i = 0; i < radix; i++) {
30         Node child = new Node(parent);
31         child.d = depth;
32         build(child, depth - 1);
33       }
34     }
35   }
```

FIGURE 18.18

Reverse tree barrier part 1.

```
36    public void await() {
37      int me = ThreadInfo.getIndex();
38      Node myLeaf = leaf[me / radix];
39      myLeaf.await(me);
40    }
41    private class Node {
42      AtomicInteger count;
43      Node parent;
44      volatile boolean sense;
45      int d;
46      // construct root node
47      public Node() {
48        sense = false;
49        parent = null;
50        count = new AtomicInteger(radix);
51      }
52      public Node(Node myParent) {
53        this();
54        parent = myParent;
55      }
56      public void await(int me) {
57        boolean mySense = threadSense.get();
58        // visit parent first
59        if ((me % radix) == 0) {
60          if (parent != null) { // root?
61            parent.await(me / radix);
62          }
63        }
64        int position = count.getAndDecrement();
65        if (position == 1) { // I'm last
66          count.set(radix);    // reset counter
67          sense = mySense;
68        } else {
69          while (sense != mySense) {};
70        }
71        threadSense.set(!mySense);
72      }
73    }
74  }
```

FIGURE 18.19

Reverse tree barrier part 2: correct or not?.

Exercise 18.8. Implement an n-thread reusable barrier from an n-wire counting network and a single Boolean variable. Sketch a proof that the barrier works.

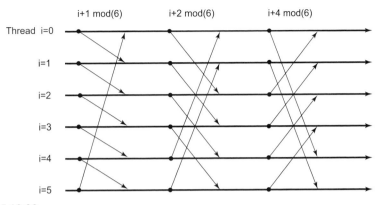

FIGURE 18.20

Communication in the dissemination barrier. In each round r a thread i communicates with thread $i + 2^r$ (mod n).

Exercise 18.9. A *dissemination barrier* is a symmetric barrier implementation in which threads spin on statically assigned locally cached locations using only loads and stores. As illustrated in Fig. 18.20, the algorithm runs in a series of rounds. At round r, thread i notifies thread $i + 2^r$ (mod n) (where n is the number of threads) and waits for notification from thread $i - 2^r$ (mod n).

For how many rounds must this protocol run to implement a barrier? What if n is not a power of 2? Justify your answers.

Exercise 18.10. Give a reusable implementation of a dissemination barrier in Java.
Hint: Consider keeping track of both the parity and the sense of the current phase.

Exercise 18.11. Create a table that summarizes the total number of operations in the static tree, combining tree, and dissemination barriers.

Exercise 18.12. Can you devise a "distributed" termination detection algorithm for the executor pool in which threads do not repeatedly update or test a central location for termination, but rather use only local uncontended variables? Variables may be unbounded, but state changes should take constant time (so you cannot parallelize the shared counter).
Hint: Adapt the atomic snapshot algorithm from Chapter 4.

Exercise 18.13. In the termination detection barrier, the state is set to active before stealing the task; otherwise the stealing thread could be declared inactive; then it would steal a task, and before setting its state back to active, the thread it stole from could become inactive. This would lead to an undesirable situation in which all threads are declared inactive yet the computation continues. Can you devise a terminating executor pool in which the state is set to active only *after* successfully stealing a task?

Optimism and manual memory management

19

For the remaining chapters of this book, we focus on challenges and opportunities that arise when creating concurrent software using the C++ programming language. C++ has rich support for concurrency, with language-level threads, locks, a memory consistency model, and the `atomic<>` template, but it lacks the automatic memory management (i.e., garbage collection) of Java, and its consequent memory safety guarantees. In this chapter, we focus on the challenges that arise for optimistic synchronization when the programmer is responsible for explicitly managing memory.

19.1 Transitioning from Java to C++

C++ and Java have (not coincidentally) very similar syntax. Both allocate memory with the **new** keyword, both use the **class** keyword to declare types, and many of the primitive types (e.g., **int**, **float**, **double**) are the same.

One notable difference is with regard to **volatile** fields. The features provided by the Java **volatile** keyword and the java.util.concurrent.atomic package are provided in C++ through the std::atomic<> template (defined in the <atomic> header). The std::atomic<T> template defines *atomic objects* of type T, so we can easily define objects equivalent to AtomicInteger and AtomicReference, for example. It is also easy to define an array of atomic registers. Because C++ programmers can cast between pointers and integers, we can also use std::atomic<> to achieve the behaviors of an AtomicMarkableReference. Pragma 19.1.1 gives several examples.

The load() and store() methods of atomic objects take an optional parameter, which can be used to relax the memory ordering guarantees when the object is accessed. In this chapter, we never provide such a parameter, and so always get the default, which provides the strongest guarantees (i.e., linearizability).

19.2 Optimism and explicit reclamation

The optimistic techniques we describe in much of this book make the following assumption: If the linearization of an operation O_l causes some other pending operation O_p to restart, no harm will come if it takes some time for O_p to realize that it has become invalid and must retry from the beginning. In languages like Java and C#,

The Art of Multiprocessor Programming. https://doi.org/10.1016/B978-0-12-415950-1.00029-X

PRAGMA 19.1.1

In C++, atomic variables should be declared using the `std::atomic<>` template.

```
1   #include <cstdint> // for the uintptr_t type
2   #include <atomic> // for std::atomic
3
4   // an atomic pointer to an Object
5   std::atomic<Object *> ptr;
6
7   // an array of atomic pointers to Objects
8   std::atomic<Object *> *arr;
9
10  // an atomic pointer to an array of atomic pointers to Objects
11  std::atomic<std::atomic<Object *> *> arr_ptr;
12
13  // read an atomic variable
14  Object *ref = ptr.load();
15
16  // store to an atomic variable
17  ptr.store(ref);
18
19  // mark the low bit of ptr
20  ptr.store((Object *)(1 | (uintptr_t)ptr.load()));
21
22  // unmark the low bit of ptr
23  ptr.store((Object *)((~1) & (uintptr_t)ptr.load()));
24
25  // check the low bit of ptr
26  bool marked = (1 & (uintptr_t)ptr.load());
27
28  // safely dereference ptr when its low bit might be marked
29  *(Object *)((~1) & (uintptr_t)ptr.load());
```

The `uintptr_t` type is an unsigned integer that is guaranteed to be the same number of bits as a pointer: It is helpful when casting between pointers and integers from code that can be run in 32-bit and 64-bit environments. Casting between pointers and integers is, in general, unsafe; we use it only when an algorithm needs a mark bit that is modified atomically with a pointer.

---

which have automatic memory reclamation (garbage collection), this assumption is reasonable. However, in C++, doomed-to-retry operations might not be harmless.

The essence of the problem is that in C++, merely holding a pointer to an object does not ensure that the use of that object will be safe: If another thread reclaims the memory corresponding to that object (using **delete** or free), then all bets are off. Consider the interleaving in Fig. 19.1, where thread T_1 reads the next pointer of

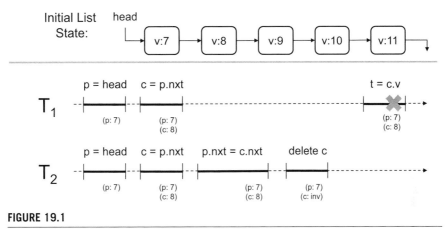

FIGURE 19.1

Concurrent access to a lazy list by two threads.

the node holding the value 7. T_2 deletes the node holding the value 8, and then at some point in the future T_1 attempts to dereference the pointer. The memory of the deleted object could be used by the program in some way that T_1 does not expect, or the memory of the deleted object could be returned to the operating system. Many hard-to-trace bugs could result. A few of the most common are listed below.

First, thread T_2 might call **new** to create a different object of the same type, and the call to **new** may have returned the same memory region that formerly stored 8. T_2 might still be initializing (constructing) the object, in which case accesses to the node by T_1 will produce undefined behavior.

Second, suppose that thread T_2 calls **new** to constructs a new node with the value 25, and inserts it into the list. If T_1 was searching for 9, it might conclude that the node holding 7 points to the node holding 25, and thus that 9 is not in the list.

Third, some other thread T_3 might call **new** to create a completely different type of object. If **new** returns the region that formerly stored 8, then accesses to that object by T_3 will race with invalid attempts to use that same memory as a list node by T_1. These races violate type safety and are completely dependent on low-level decisions by the allocator about when to give the deleted memory to a different thread.

Fourth, the allocator may decide to return the memory region to the operating system. In this case, any subsequent access by T_1 will cause a segmentation fault.

Note that in all cases, T_1 may exhibit incorrect or dangerous behaviors. Using optimistic algorithms in programming languages with manual memory reclamation, like C++, requires us to pay close attention to the pending operations in a program's history, and establish sufficient conditions for avoiding the bad behaviors described above. In this chapter, we derive a sufficient condition for using optimistic algorithms in C and C++, and then we explore two implementations.

19.3 Protecting pending operations

When a region of memory is reclaimed, the programmer cannot know how that region of memory will be reused, or even whether it is reused. The first step in developing a general solution to prevent the sorts of races described in the previous section is to recognize that such races first become possible when the region is reclaimed (via free or **delete**). We define the act of reclaiming a region of memory as racing with any concurrent access to the region. We can prevent these races by delaying reclamation. If we think in terms of pending operations on a concurrent data structure, a sufficient condition is that *memory is only reclaimed when it is impossible for any pending operation to access it in the future*.

In a language with automatic memory management, this property can be ensured by a *garbage collector*, which tracks every reference to every object allocated in the program. These references could be on the heap, in a thread's stack, or in a thread's registers. An object can be reclaimed when no references to it remain, since it can never be accessed again.

The property is also achieved by *reference counting*. In a reference-counted implementation of the list, a counter of type atomic<**int**> is associated with each node. Whenever a reference to node N is created (either in a local variable or by pointing some other node's next pointer to N), the count must first be incremented. Whenever a reference to N is destroyed (for example, by overwriting a local variable), the count is subsequently decremented. When the count reaches zero, there are no outstanding references to the node, and it can be reclaimed.

C++ supports reference counting via the std::atomic_shared_ptr<> template. To use it, threads never create local variables of type Node *; instead, they use local variables of type std::atomic_shared_ptr<Node *>. Similarly, the type of the Node's next pointer must be std::atomic_shared_ptr<Node *>.

Under the hood, std::atomic_shared_ptr<Node *>> introduces two overheads. First, the reference count associated with a std::atomic_shared_ptr<Node *> must be stored on the heap. With one std::atomic_shared_ptr<Node *> per list node, reference counting effectively doubles the number of memory locations accessed during a list traversal. Fortunately, this overhead affects only latency, not scalability. However, the second overhead affects scalability. Every reader of a node must first increment the node's reference count; later, it must decrement the reference count, once the node is not needed anymore. In a linked list, every traversal references the same prefix of list nodes. For each node, each thread will write to the counter twice, and as we know, concurrent writes to the same location cause cache contention.

Before constructing more scalable approaches, it is useful to ask why reference counting works. By incrementing a counter associated with a node *before* accessing the node, an operation can ensure that other threads know of its intention to use the node. In response, those other threads promise not to reclaim the node if the count is nonzero. And in exchange for this guarantee of protection, the operation inherits the responsibility to reclaim a node if it discovers (upon decrementing the counter) that it had inhibited reclamation by some other thread.

Thus we can say that reference counting serves two roles: It allows operations to *protect* a node from concurrent deletion, and it allows threads to *delegate* the reclamation of a node. While delegation means that a node is not reclaimed *immediately*, from the perspective of the deleting thread, it is reclaimed *as soon as possible* without violating safety.

It would be correct to allow operations to protect a node from concurrent deletion, but require the deleting thread to defer reclamation, *without delegating to another thread*. That is, if a region of memory has outstanding references, the deleting operation will not reclaim it immediately. Instead, it will put it into some set, and then periodically query the set for entries that have no remaining references. When such an entry is found, it can be reclaimed immediately and removed from the set.

One can think of this strategy as a sort of fine-granularity garbage collection, where the programmer controls which regions of memory are reclaimed immediately, and which are deferred.

We can vary how we implement the set (for example, by using per-thread sets), the frequency with which threads search for reclaimable memory, and the mechanisms by which operations protect nodes. In doing so, we can trade tight bounds on the amount of unreclaimed memory for low run-time overhead and minimal communication between threads.

19.4 **An object for managing memory**

Fig. 19.2 presents a generic interface for protecting memory during an optimistic operation. There are many different ways to implement the object; we discuss two in this chapter. What matters for now is to understand the specification of the object.

```
1   class MemManager {
2     void register_thread(int num); // called once, before any call to op_begin()
3                                    // num indicates the maximum number of
4                                    // locations the caller can reserve
5     void unregister_thread(); // called once, after the last call to op_end()
6
7     void op_begin(); // indicate the beginning of a concurrent operation
8     void op_end(); // indicate the end of a concurrent operation
9
10    bool try_reserve(void* ptr); // try to protect a pointer from reclamation
11    void unreserve(void* ptr); // stop protecting a pointer
12    void sched_for_reclaim(void* ptr); // try to reclaim a pointer
13  }
```

FIGURE 19.2

An interface for protecting memory during an optimistic operation.

To have a single interface that is suitable for a variety of memory reclamation algorithms, our object has seven methods. The most important part of the interface are the last three functions. They let a thread try to protect some memory from reclamation, stop requesting protection for memory, and schedule memory for reclamation as soon as it has no outstanding protection requests from concurrent threads.

19.5 Traversing a list

Suppose that we wanted to use the MemManager object to protect an optimistic traversal of a nonblocking list-based integer set (Section 9.8). First, of course, we must translate the code to C++. To do this, we make use of std::atomic<> variables instead of the **volatile** keyword in Java. Then we can redesign the find() method of the Window class from Fig. 9.23, so that it protects memory during optimistic accesses.

Fig. 19.3 presents the data type for nodes in our C++ nonblocking list, as well as some helper functions for setting and unsetting the low bit of pointers. Setting and unsetting the low bit of pointers is the C++ equivalent of the AtomicMarkableReference<> class in Java. Note that in C++, we can set the low bit of a pointer directly, but we cannot use a pointer whose low bit is 1: we must copy the pointer and explicitly unset the low bit of the copy before using it.

```
1   class Node<T>{
2     T item;
3     int key;
4     std::atomic<Node<T>*> next;
5   public:
6     Node() : item(), next(nullptr) { }
7     Node(T _item, int _key, Node* n) : item(_item), key(_key), next(n) { }
8   };
9   // return whether the low bit of the pointer is marked or not
10  bool is_marked(Node* ptr) {
11    return ((uintptr_t)ptr)&1;
12  }
13  // clear the mark bit of a pointer
14  Node* unmark(Node* ptr) {
15    return (Node*)(((uintptr_t)ptr) & ~(uintptr_t)1);
16  }
17  // set the mark bit of a pointer
18  Node* mark(Node* ptr) {
19    return (Node*)(((uintptr_t)ptr) | 1);
20  }
```

FIGURE 19.3

C++ nonblocking linked list: node data type and helper functions.

```
21   bool find(int key, Node<T>*&prev, Node<T>*&curr, Node<T>*&next, MemManager* mm) {
22     prev = list;
23     mm->try_reserve(prev);
24     curr = prev->next.load();
25     while (curr != nullptr) {
26       if (mm->try_reserve(curr))  {
27         if (prev->next.load() != curr) {
28           mm->unreserve(prev); mm->unreserve(curr);
29           return find(key, prev, curr, next);
30         }
31       }
32       next = curr->next.load();
33       if (is_marked(next)) { // curr is logically deleted
34         Node<T> *tmp = unmark(next);
35         if (!prev->next.compare_exchange_strong(curr, tmp)) {
36           mm->unreserve(prev); mm->unreserve(curr);
37           return find(key, prev, curr, next);
38         }
39         mm->unreserve(curr);
40         mm->sched_for_reclaim(curr);
41         curr = tmp;
42       }
43       else {
44         int ckey = curr->key;
45         if (prev->next.load() != curr) {
46           mm->unreserve(prev); mm->unreserve(curr);
47           return find(key, prev, curr, next);
48         }
49         if (ckey >= key) {
50           return ckey == key;
51         }
52         mm->unreserve(prev);
53         prev = curr;
54         curr = next;
55       }
56     }
57     return false;
58   }
```

FIGURE 19.4

Traversing a nonblocking linked list with safe reclamation.

With these definitions, a list is defined as a pointer to the head node. We refer to this pointer as list. As in other high-performance optimistic lists, we avoid a corner case by making the first node in the list a "sentinel" node, whose value is never read. In that way, list is never null.

Fig. 19.4 reintroduces the find() function from the nonblocking list-based set from Section 9.8, rewritten in C++. The main difference in our C++ version is that it must explicitly manage memory. We use an explicit MemManager object for this purpose.

Note that find() is an internal function. A public function that calls find() must do so between calls to MemManager's op_begin() and op_end() methods. Also, find() protects up to two locations at a time, so it must be preceded by a call to register_thread(i), with the value of i no less than 2.

Starting with the sentinel node, our traversal follows the same pattern as the non-blocking Java list: We keep track of a window of three consecutive nodes, prev, curr, and next. At all points, the memory representing prev is safe to access, because it has already been reserved (or it is the sentinel). Also, prev always references a node whose key is less than the search key. Note, too, that prev and curr are guaranteed to be unmarked.

Before using the successor of prev, we must protect it via a call to try_reserve() (line 26). If this returns **true**, then MemManager cannot guarantee that curr was not reclaimed between the time when it was read (line 24 or line 32) and the time when try_reserve() was called. In this case, the code double-checks that *after* the call to try_reserve(), curr still succeeds prev. If not, the find() operation retries.

Line 32 finds the successor of the current node, as next. If the pointer to next is not marked, then at line 45, we ensure that prev remains linked to curr. If so, we check the key stored at curr, and use its value to determine whether to continue traversing or to return. If the find() operation should continue, it will no longer use the prev pointer, so it unreserves it.

If find() discovers a marked node at curr, it uses compare_exchange_strong() to unlink curr, and then hands curr to MemManager for reclamation. When find() returns true, prev and curr are reserved and protected from reclamation.

With the find() function, the public operations on our nonblocking C++ linked list are straightforward. They appear in Fig. 19.5.

19.6 Hazard pointers

Our first solution for protecting the in-use nodes of the nonblocking list uses a variant of a technique known as *hazard pointers*. The approach has two main components. The first is a mechanism through which threads can share the locations they have reserved, so that other threads may see those reservations any time they attempt to reclaim memory. The second is a per-thread mechanism for deferring the reclamation of memory.

Fig. 19.6 presents the two main data types of this implementation. Every thread has its own ThreadContext object, which it can access directly via MemManager::self. The entire set of these objects is organized as a linked list, represented by MemManager::head. Within a thread's context, there is a private set of locations that the thread has scheduled for reclamation, and a shared array of locations that the thread does not want other threads to reclaim. For convenience, our code does not allow threads to remove their contexts from the shared set. That is, unregister_thread() does not remove a thread's context from the set rooted at MemManager::head.

```
59   bool add(int key) {
60     mm->op_begin();
61     Node<T> *prev, *curr, *next;
62     while (true) {
63       if (find(key, prev, curr, next, mm)) {
64         mm->op_end();
65         return false;
66       }
67       Node *new_node = new Node(key, curr);
68       if (prev->next.compare_exchange_strong(curr, new_node)) {
69         mm->op_end();
70         return true;
71       }
72       mm->unreserve(prev); mm->unreserve(curr);
73     }
74   }
75   bool contains(int key, MemManager* mm) {
76     mm->op_begin();
77     Node<T> *prev, *curr, *next;
78     bool ans = find(key, prev, curr, next, mm);
79     mm->op_end();
80     return ans;
81   }
82   bool remove(int key, MemManager* mm) {
83     mm->op_begin();
84     Node<T> *prev, *curr, *next;
85     while (true) {
86       if (!find(key, prev, curr, next, mm)) {
87         mm->op_end();
88         return false;
89       }
90       if (!curr->next.compare_exchange_strong(next, mark(next))) {
91         mm->unreserve(prev); mm->unreserve(curr);
92         continue;
93       }
94       if (prev->next.compare_exchange_strong(curr, next)) {
95         mm->sched_for_reclaim(curr);
96       } else {
97         mm->unreserve(prev); mm->unreserve(curr);
98         find(key, prev, curr, next, mm);
99       }
100      mm->op_end();
101      return true;
102    }
103  }
```

FIGURE 19.5

Public methods of the C++ nonblocking list-based set.

```
1   class ThreadContext {
2    public:
3     std::vector<void*> pending_reclaims;
4     std::atomic<void*> *reservations;
5     ThreadContext *next;
6     const int num;
7
8     ThreadContext(int _num, MemManager m): num(_num) {
9       reservations = new std::atomic<void*>[_num];
10      for (int i = 0; i < num; ++i)
11        reservations[i] = nullptr;
12      while (true) {
13        next = m.head;
14        if (m.head.compare_exchange_strong(next, this))
15          break;
16      }
17    }
18  }
19  class MemManager {
20   public:
21    static thread_local ThreadContext *self = nullptr;
22    std::atomic<ThreadContext*> head;
23    ...
24  }
```

FIGURE 19.6

Data types to support hazard pointers with blocking reclamation.

Fig. 19.7 presents the rest of our implementation of hazard pointers. Since our implementation is blocking, and since we never unlink thread contexts, both register_thread() and unregister_thread() are trivial: The former creates a thread context and inserts it at the head of MemManager's list; the latter is a no-op. Similarly, op_begin() is a no-op: Its postcondition is that the calling thread has no reservations and no pending reclamations. Both of these properties are provided by op_end().

During execution, a thread reserves a pointer ptr by finding an empty slot in its reservations array and writing ptr into it. The array positions are all std::atomic<>, so that we can be sure that any such write will be strongly ordered: all previously issued reads and writes will complete before it, and all subsequent reads and writes will not happen until after it.

Note that in our hazard pointer implementation, try_reserve() always returns *true*. This is necessary to prevent races. Consider the moment when thread T_r executes line 24 of the find() method. When the line completes, prev points to curr, but T_r has not yet reserved curr. At that point, another thread T_d could mark and unlink curr. If T_d scanned T_r's reservations array, it would not find curr, and thus it could reclaim curr immediately. A subsequent access to curr by T_r would cause a race. By

```
25   MemManager::register_thread(int num) { self = new ThreadContext(num, this); }
26   MemManager::unregister_thread() { /* no-op */ }
27   MemManager::op_begin() { /* no-op */ }
28   void MemManager::sched_for_reclaim(void* ptr) { self->pending_reclaims.push_back(ptr); }
29   bool MemManager::try_reserve(void* ptr) {
30     for (int i = 0; i < num; ++i) {
31       if (self->reservations[i] == nullptr) {
32         self->reservations[i].store(ptr);
33         return true;
34       }
35     }
36     throw error;
37   }
38   void MemManager::unreserve(void* ptr) {
39     for (int i = 0; i < num; ++i) {
40       if (self->reservations[i] == ptr) {
41         self->reservations[i].store(nullptr);
42         return;
43       }
44     }
45   }
46   void MemManager::op_end() {
47     for (int i = 0; i < self->num; ++i)
48       self->reservations[i].store(nullptr);
49     for (auto i : pending_reclaims) {
50       wait_until_unreserved(p);
51       free(p);
52     }
53     pending_reclaims.clear();
54   }
55   MemManager::wait_until_unreserved(void* ptr) {
56     ThreadContext* curr = head;
57     while (curr) {
58       for (int i = 0; i < curr->num; ++i) {
59         while (curr->reservations[i] == ptr)
60           wait();
61       }
62       curr = curr->next;
63     }
64   }
```

FIGURE 19.7

MemManager methods to support hazard pointers with blocking reclamation.

returning *true*, try_reserve() notifies the find() function that accesses to curr are not yet guaranteed to be safe; find() must double-check that prev still points to curr. Note that try_reserve() stored curr in an atomic<> field, which guarantees that the double-check follows the write of curr to reservations.

In our nonblocking list implementation, as in many other algorithms, a location is not reclaimed by the thread that *marks* a node, but the thread that unlinks it. This is one of many situations in which more than one thread may have a reservation for a memory region that is logically deleted from the data structure. In general, the number of reservations for an unlinked node should rapidly drop to zero, but is most likely to be nonzero immediately after being unlinked. Thus it would be unwise for the unlinking thread to attempt to reclaim memory immediately. Instead, sched_for_reclaim(ptr) places ptr into a thread-private vector, and delays reclamation until op_end().

The postconditions of our implementation of op_end() are the same as the preconditions of op_begin(): The thread has no reservations and no outstanding reclamations. Achieving the former is simple, and is achieved by the loop on line 47. To ensure that there are no outstanding reclamations, the caller of op_end() iterates through the elements in its pending_reclaims set. For each entry, the caller iterates through the MemManager's set of thread contexts, and for each context, the caller checks if the context includes a reservation for the entry. If it does, the caller spin-waits until the reservation changes. Since the entry has already been unlinked, it would seem that the caller of op_begin() can be sure that no subsequent reservation will appear, and hence the location is safe to reclaim. However, there is one troublesome ordering. Suppose that some thread T_i is *about to* reserve location l, and some thread T_r has called op_end() and has seen that T_i does not have l in reservations. We cannot allow T_i to subsequently write l into reservations and use l. Again, this is why try_reserve() must return *true*: to ensure that T_i will double-check, see that l has been unlinked, and restart.

It is possible to make a hazard pointer implementation lock-free if we are willing to allow a bounded amount of memory to remain unclaimed for an unbounded amount of time. Suppose that every time a thread reached line 60, it instead skipped reclamation for the current entry in pending_reclaims, and moved on to the next. With T threads and *num* maximum reserved addresses per thread, up to $T \times num$ locations could be unreclaimable at any time. For higher performance, this bound is typically multiplied by an order of magnitude.

19.7 Epoch-based reclamation

Our hazard pointer implementation is precise, ensuring that reclamation can happen as soon as possible, so that there is no unnecessary backlog of to-be-reclaimed memory. However, that precision comes at a great cost: During the course of every operation, there will be a linear number of calls to try_reserve(), each of which performs an expensive *strongly ordered* write to shared memory. While writes are more expensive than reads, the fact of $O(n)$ writes should not have too significant of an impact on modern CPUs, because they are to a small, fixed number of locations (the thread's reservations array). However, since each of these writes is to a std::atomic<> variable, each entails a memory fence, and every memory fence increases latency significantly.

When the percentage of remove() operations is small, the cost of these fences is hard to justify: They protect find() from unlikely interleavings with the infrequently called remove() operation. If we relax guarantees on the number of unreclaimed locations, we can eliminate many of these fences. To do so, we introduce the concept of *epochs*.

Suppose that every thread had its own shared counter, initialized to zero. Whenever the thread called op_begin(), it would increment that counter. Whenever it called op_end(), it would increment that counter again. If we looked at a thread's counter and found an even number, we could immediately conclude that the thread was not between op_begin() and op_end(). That, in turn, must mean that the thread could not have any references to the nodes of our linked list.

Unfortunately, if one thread is repeatedly executing operations on the list, another thread may never see an even number. Instead, it may see a different odd number each time it looks. However, this information is equally useful: It means that the thread has completed one operation and started another. Any memory that was unlinked concurrently with the former operation cannot be accessed during the current operation attempt, and thus as soon as the counter changed from one odd number to another odd number, the unlinked memory would be unreachable, and safe to reclaim.

Putting these ideas together, we can create a remarkably simple MemManager object. This new version will not be able to put any bounds on the number of unreclaimed objects, because a single thread stalling in the middle of its find() operation will make it impossible for any other thread to reclaim *anything*. When remove() calls are exceptionally rare, or when a program (such as an operating system itself) can guarantee that a call to find() cannot stall indefinitely, the cost of unbounded garbage is more than offset by the performance improvement that comes from the elimination of $O(n)$ memory fences.

In Fig. 19.8, we implement a MemManager based on epochs. As with our implementation of hazard pointers, we have chosen to make the implementation blocking, by having each thread immediately reclaim all the memory it unlinked when it reaches op_end().

As with the hazard pointer implementation, we have a global shared list of thread contexts, and each thread keeps a private vector of the locations it has scheduled for reclamation. However, we no longer need to track the individual pointers accessed by the operation: instead, a thread maintains a std::atomic<> counter, which it increments to odd in op_begin(). The increment has strong memory ordering, which means that *before* an operation touches any of the shared memory that comprises the nodes of the list, that thread has notified all other threads that they may not reclaim anything.

In op_end(), a thread increments its counter to even, indicating that it will no longer access any of the shared memory of the list. As with the increment in op_begin(), this increment is strongly ordered, so that it is guaranteed to happen *after* all of the parent operation's loads and stores to shared memory. If a thread has deferred reclamation of any locations, then it must wait until the execution of every concurrent thread has, at least momentarily, been outside of a data structure oper-

```
1   struct ThreadContext {
2     std::vector<void*> pending_reclaims;
3     std::atomic<uint64_t> counter;
4     ThreadContext *next;
5
6     ThreadContext(MemManager m) {
7       while (true) {
8         next = m.head;
9         if (m.head.compare_exchange_strong(next, this))
10          break;
11      }
12    }
13  }
14  struct MemManager {
15    static thread_local ThreadContext *self = nullptr;
16    std::atomic<ThreadContext*> head;
17    ...
18  }
19  MemManager::register_thread(int num) { self = new ThreadContext(this); }
20  MemManager::unregister_thread() { /* no-op */ }
21  MemManager::op_begin() { self->counter++; }
22  void MemManager::sched_for_reclaim(void* ptr) { self->pending_reclaims.push_back(ptr); }
23  bool MemManager::try_reserve(void* ptr) { return false; }
24  void MemManager::unreserve(void* ptr) { }
25
26  void MemManager::op_end() {
27    self->counter++;
28    if (pending_reclaims.count() == 0)
29      return;
30    wait_until_unreserved()
31    for (auto p : pending_reclaims)
32      free(p);
33  }
34  void MemManager::wait_until_unreserved() {
35    ThreadContext* curr = head;
36    while (curr) {
37      uint64_t val = curr->counter;
38      if (odd(val))
39      do {
40        wait();
41      } while (curr->counter.read() == val)
42      curr = curr->next;
43    }
44  }
```

FIGURE 19.8

Epoch-based reclamation.

ation. It does this by checking each thread's counter: If the counter is even or if it changes from one odd number to a larger odd number, then that thread can no longer find a pointer to the locations awaiting reclamation. Once all threads' progress has been verified, the deferred reclamations can be performed.

Given these implementations of op_begin() and op_end(), try_reserve() can be a single statement: **return false**. To understand why this is correct, consider an interleaving between a call to find() and a call to remove() that marks location *l* for deletion. If find() discovered a node whose next pointer was *l*, then it must have done so *after* it made its counter odd. At the time when it read *l*, the node at *l* had not yet been unlinked, and therefore the corresponding remove() operation could not have reached its op_end(). If, at this point, the find() thread were to delay, and the remove() thread were to reach op_begin(), *l* would not be reclaimed: The remove() thread is guaranteed to see the find() thread's odd counter value, and wait. Therefore, there is no benefit in double-checking the reachability of *l*: Its fields can be accessed without any additional checks to ensure that it has not been reclaimed.

19.8 Chapter notes

Variants of the hazard pointer technique were discovered by Michael [127] and by Herlihy, Luchangoo, & Moir [67]. Subsequently, Petrank et al. proposed improvements to reduce the fence overhead [22,31]. Michael also showed how to eliminate the fence overhead, when reclamation is extremely rare, by leveraging interprocess interrupts [44].

Epoch-based techniques were used by Fraser [48] in the context of nonblocking data structures, and subsequently adapted for use in software transactional memory by Hudson et al. [81]. They were also proposed by McKenney in the context of operating systems [123], where they protected kernel data structures. In that context, movement from user mode to kernel mode would make a processor's counter odd, and returning to user mode would make it even again.

Research into both of these techniques has given much attention to attempting to provide nonblocking progress without an unbounded worst-case space overhead. To achieve nonblocking guarantees, op_end() pushes the contents of pending_reclaims into a per-thread buffer. When the buffer becomes large, hazard pointer implementations use a variant of wait_until_unreserved that skips nodes with outstanding reservations. The number of skipped nodes can be bounded. Nonblocking epoch-based techniques bundle several operations' worth of contents from pending_reclaims into a new buffer, to which is added a snapshot of all threads' counters. Each time one of these bundles is collected, the corresponding counter snapshot is compared with past ones. Bundles whose snapshots have been superseded by the new snapshot can be reclaimed. In the worst case, this technique can lead to out-of-memory errors if a single operation delays arbitrarily during an operation. However, Brown showed that interprocess interrupts can be used to prevent this pathological scenario [23].

19.9 Exercises

Exercise 19.1. If the LockFreeStack (Section 11.2) used hazard pointers to protect memory, would it still be vulnerable to the ABA problem? Why or why not?

Exercise 19.2. Describe how to use hazard pointers to protect the memory in the lock-free unbounded queue from Section 10.5.

Exercise 19.3. The presentation of hazard pointers in Section 19.6 was blocking. The easiest way to make it nonblocking is defer reclamation of reserved objects. Under this strategy, what is the worst-case number of unreclaimed objects for any one thread's `pending_reclaims` vector? What is the worst-case number of unreclaimed objects in a system with T threads?

Exercise 19.4. If a hazard pointer implementation is willing to let some objects go unreclaimed for a longer duration, then its `op_end` method could begin by copying all of the threads' reservations to a private list. It could then intersect that list with its `pending_reclaims` to identify the objects that were ready to reclaim. Under what circumstances would this be advantageous? Under what circumstances would it harm performance?

Exercise 19.5. For each of the following data structures, discuss the number of hazard pointers that would be required in the worst case when implementing the data structure with optimistic concurrency control:

1. lock-free queue,
2. lock-free stack,
3. lazy list,
4. skip list.

Exercise 19.6. The `std::atomic<>` types in C++ support *relaxed* memory ordering. What orderings can be relaxed in the hazard pointer implementation from Section 19.6?

Exercise 19.7. Similar to Exercise 19.3, we could make the epoch-based reclamation in Section 19.7 nonblocking. Rewrite the code in Fig. 19.8 so that threads do not wait at commit time.

Exercise 19.8. In our implementation of epoch-based memory reclamation, we did not require threads to attain an atomic snapshot of all other threads' counters when deciding whether it was safe to reclaim an object. Why was this correct?

Transactional programming

20

Although C++ affords the programmer more control than Java and other high-level languages, the need to explicitly manage memory creates significant challenges, particularly with speculative execution. To ensure that speculative operations do not access reclaimed memory, reclamation is often delayed, which can lead to large amounts of unused memory being allocated for long periods of time.

In addition, some seemingly correct programs are classified as racy according to the C++ memory model, so their behavior is undefined. Eliminating these races while maintaining good performance is nontrivial, and can lead to code that is difficult to extend and maintain. More generally, the complexity of a program's synchronization mechanisms increases greatly with the complexity of the program, requiring more sophisticated, and difficult, techniques to achieve good performance. A data structure with a large set of operations (especially range queries and other multi-item operations) requires more careful concurrency than one with few operations; a program that uses many threads is likely to need a finer granularity for its locks than one with few threads.

Transactional programming addresses this complexity by raising the level of abstraction: a programmer focuses on identifying *which* regions require atomicity, rather than *how* to make code regions appear to be atomic. Determining how to ensure atomicity without sacrificing performance is left to run-time systems and specialized hardware.

20.1 Challenges in concurrent programming

We begin with a review of techniques discussed in this book and challenges in applying them, especially in the context of unmanaged languages such as C++.

20.1.1 Problems with locking

Locking, as a synchronization discipline, has many pitfalls for the inexperienced programmer. *Priority inversion* occurs when a lower-priority thread is preempted while holding a lock needed by higher-priority threads. *Convoying* is a form of congestion that is easiest to understand in the context of the hand-over-hand locking pattern: If threads acquire and release locks in a fixed order, then the order in which threads acquire the first lock in the sequence dictates the order in which threads progress through the data structure; if one thread delays, other threads cannot bypass it. *Deadlock* can occur if threads attempt to lock the same set of objects in different orders. Deadlock avoidance can be awkward if threads must lock many objects, particularly if the set of objects is not known in advance. Furthermore, if the operating system suspends a thread while it holds a lock, then the entire program can grind to a halt.

A major obstacle to writing good lock-based code is that the association between locks and data is established mostly by convention. It exists in the mind of the programmer, and may be documented only in comments. Consider the following typical comment from a Linux header file[1] describing the conventions governing the use of a particular kind of buffer:

```
/*
 * When a locked buffer is visible to the I/O layer BH_Launder
 * is set. This means before unlocking we must clear BH_Launder,
 * mb() on alpha and then clear BH_Lock, so no reader can see
 * BH_Launder set on an unlocked buffer and then risk to deadlock.
 */
```

Over time, interpreting and observing many such conventions spelled out in this way complicates code maintenance.

Another challenge with locking is determining the appropriate lock granularity. Consider a nonresizable hash table implemented as a fixed-size array of linked lists. Should one lock protect the entire table? Or should there be one lock per array entry, or even one for each node in the linked lists? If there are few threads, and each rarely accesses the hash table, then a single lock protecting the entire table should suffice. If many threads frequently access the hash table, then fine-grained locking may be required to prevent the hash table from becoming a scalability bottleneck. Although it improves scalability, finer granularity increases complexity and overhead. If the table is frequently read but rarely written, we might consider readers–writer locks.

A hash table implementation is likely to be written as a generic data structure with a specific contention scenario in mind. If that scenario never manifests during program execution, then the hard-coded strategy may perform poorly. If the number of threads and the way they use the table change over time, then different strategies could be optimal at different points in the program execution. Furthermore, each option could be pessimal in some cases.

20.1.2 Problems with explicit speculation

We have seen that the problems with locking can sometimes be mitigated by optimistic synchronization (see, for example, Section 9.6). For example, executing read-only critical sections speculatively can greatly reduce the impact of the problems described above for data structures that are read often and written infrequently. A useful tool for implementing such data structures is the *sequence lock*.

---

[1] Kernel v2.4.19 /fs/buffer.c.

```
1    std::atomic<int> seqlock;
2    int protected_data;
3
4    int reader() {
5      while (true) {
6        int s1 = seqlock;
7        int ret = protected_data;   // ERROR
8        int s2 = seqlock;
9        if (s1 == s2 && is_even(s1))
10          return ret;
11     }
12   }
13   void writer(int newval) {
14     while (true) {
15       unsigned s = seqlock;
16       if (is_even(s) && seqlock.compare_exchange_strong(s, s+1)  {
17         protected_data = newval;
18         seqlock = s + 2;
19         return;
20       }
21     }
22   }
```

FIGURE 20.1

Incorrect use of a sequence lock: The lock release is not guaranteed to be ordered after the data access.

The core idea behind sequence locks is to use a std::atomic<int> in place of a mutual exclusion lock or spin-lock. The integer starts with value 0, and is incremented whenever the lock is acquired or released. Thus, the lock is free whenever its value is even and held by some thread whenever its value is odd. The value of a sequence lock serves as a kind of version number for the data structure it protects, and while it is even, the data structure does not change.

This observation might lead us to think we can execute a read-only critical section speculatively, without writes or atomic operations, as shown in Fig. 20.1. A reading thread reads the lock, reads the protected data, and then rereads the lock. If the lock value is even, and the same before and after reading the protected data, then no other thread wrote the data in that interval, so the reads of the protected data are valid.

However, this code is incorrect because the program has a data race: A reading thread can execute line 7 at the same time as a writing thread executes line 17. It does not matter that the reader will not *use* the value that it read: The read is still a race, and programs with races have undefined behavior in C++.

There are many ways to fix this code. The simplest is to change the type of protected_data to std::atomic<int>. However, this change would impose signifi-cant overhead because every access to the data would be a synchronization operation.

Furthermore, the default strong ordering on these operations would impose more ordering than necessary among accesses to different variables within a critical section. To avoid this excessive ordering, programmers would need to exploit advanced features of std::atomic<>, especially std::memory_order_relaxed. Lastly, making a variable atomic appears to prevent code reuse. This third challenge can be overcome by using std::atomic_ref<>, a new feature in C++20 that allows a variable to be treated as atomic temporarily.

20.1.3 Problems with nonblocking algorithms

One way to avoid the problems of locking is to devise nonblocking algorithms using atomic primitives such as compare-and-swap (available in C++ as the compare_exchange_strong() method of std::atomic<>). Such nonblocking methods are subtle, and may have high single-thread latency. The principal difficulty is that nearly all synchronization primitives, whether reading, writing, or applying an atomic compare-and-swap, operate only on a single word. This restriction often forces a complex and unnatural structure on algorithms.

Let us review the lock-free queue of Section 10.5 (translated to C++ in Fig. 20.2) with an eye toward the underlying synchronization primitives. On lines 13–14, the

```
1   template <class T>
2   class LockFreeQueue<T> {
3     std::atomic<Node*> head;
4     std::atomic<Node*> tail;
5     ...
6     void enq(T item) {
7       Node* node = new Node(item);
8       while (true) {
9         Node* last = tail;
10        Node* next = last->next;
11        if (last == tail) {
12          if (next == null) {
13            if (last->next.compare_exchange_strong(next, node)) {
14              tail.compare_exchange_strong(last, node);
15              return;
16            }
17          } else {
18            tail.compare_exchange_strong(last, next);
19          }
20        }
21      }
22    }
23  }
```

FIGURE 20.2

The LockFreeQueue class: the enq() method.

```
1   template <class T>
2   bool multiCompareAndSet(std::atomic<T*> *target,
3                          T *expect,
4                          T *update,
5                          int count) {
6     atomic {
7       for (int i = 0; i < count; i++) {
8         if (*target[i] != expected[i])
9           return false;
10      }
11      for (int i = 0; i < count; i++)
12        *target[i] = update[i];
13      return true;
14    }
15  }
```

FIGURE 20.3

Pseudocode for multiCompareAndSet(). This code should execute atomically.

enq() method calls compare_exchange_strong() twice to change both the tail node's next field and the tail field itself to point to the new node. Because these updates occur one-at-a-time, enq() and deq() methods must be prepared to encounter a half-finished enq() (line 13). These methods could be much simpler if we could update both fields together.

For example, suppose we had the multiCompareAndSet() primitive shown in Fig. 20.3, which takes an array of std::atomic<T*> objects, an array of expected T values, and an array of T-values used for updates, and updates all the array elements if they all have the expected values. (No element is updated if any element does not have the expected value.) Unfortunately, there is no easy way to implement multiCompareAndSet() on conventional architectures. If there were, we could replace the complex logic of lines 12–18 in Fig. 20.2 with a single multiCompareAndSet() call (see Fig. 20.4).

20.1.4 Problems with compositionality

One drawback common to all the synchronization mechanisms we have discussed so far is that they cannot easily be *composed*. For example, suppose we want to dequeue an item x from a queue q0 and enqueue it on another queue q1. The transfer must be atomic: Concurrent threads must not observe that x has vanished, nor that it is present in both queues. In Queue implementations based on monitors, each method acquires the lock internally, so we cannot combine two method calls in this way.

There are, of course, *ad hoc* solutions: We could introduce a lock to be acquired by any thread attempting an atomic modification to both q0 and q1 (in addition to the individual locks for q0 and q1). Such a lock requires knowing in advance the identities of the two queues, and it could be a bottleneck (no concurrent transfers).

```
1    void enq(T item) {
2      Node* node = new Node(item);
3      while (true) {
4        Node* last = tail;
5        Node* next = last->next;
6        if (last == tail) {
7          std::atomic<Node*> target[2] = {&last->next, &tail};
8          Node* expect[2] = {next, last};
9          Node* update[2] = {node, node};
10         if (multiCompareAndSet(target, expect, update)) return;
11       }
12     }
13   }
```

FIGURE 20.4

The LockFreeQueue class: simplified enq() method with multiCompareAndSet().

Alternatively, the queues could export their synchronization state (say, via lock() and unlock() methods), and rely on the caller to manage multiobject synchronization. Exposing synchronization state in this way would have a devastating effect on modularity, complicating interfaces and relying on callers to follow complicated conventions. Also, this approach does not work for nonblocking implementations.

20.1.5 Summary

It seems we have a rather dire state of affairs:

- Locks are hard to manage effectively, especially in large systems.
- Atomic primitives, such as compare-and-swap, operate on only one word at a time, resulting in complex algorithms.
- The possibility of races necessitates costly synchronization at all times, even when races are extremely rare.
- It is difficult to compose multiple calls to multiple objects into atomic units.

In the face of these challenges, transactional programming offers an appealing alternative.

20.2 Transactional programming

In transactional programming, a programmer identifies which regions of code cannot interleave with each other, and marks them as transactions. Then, a run-time system, ideally with the assistance of specialized hardware, takes responsibility for finding a way to execute as many transactions concurrently as possible, while ensuring that transactions still appear to execute atomically.

Transactional programming requires programmers to give up some control: the programmer no longer crafts the low-level synchronization protocol, and has limited means to influence how transactions are scheduled and managed. In return, multiple small transactions are automatically composed into larger transactions; transactions appear to atomically modify multiple locations at once; the run-time system can provide optimizations for read-only transactions, where pessimistic locking would incur high costs; and transactions eliminate the need to think about locks, std::atomic<> variables, or other low-level synchronization mechanisms.

A transactional run-time system must ensure that intermediate effects of a transaction are not visible to other transactions: any values a transaction writes must be hidden from other transactions, becoming visible only when the transaction commits. The system must also ensure that a transaction's behavior is consistent with a serial execution, that is, one in which no transactions run concurrently. As an example, suppose that in some program, variables x and y must always be equal. If transaction T_1 reads variable x, and then transaction T_2 increments both x and y and commits, then if T_1 attempts to read y, it should not be allowed to continue executing: It would see a value that does not equal x, which could lead to erroneous behaviors.

Transactional run-time systems often employ speculative execution and fine-grained access tracking. In our example, tracking the individual accesses of T_1 and T_2 makes it possible to detect that T_1 read x before T_2 wrote x, but that T_1 attempted to read y after T_2 wrote it. Speculative execution requires that the run-time system somehow transform the execution of T_1, so that upon detecting a conflict on y, it can roll back T_1 and let it try again.

20.2.1 An example of transactional programming

To see the benefits of transactional programming, consider the code in Fig. 20.5. When a thread calls this function, it iterates through the indices in which and, for each index, checks whether the corresponding position in counters is positive. If so,

```
1   std::mutex counter_lock;
2   int *counters = ...;
3
4   void increment_pos_counters(size_t num, size_t *which) {
5     std::lock_guard<std::mutex> guard(counter_lock);
6     for (size_t i = 0; i < num; ++i) {
7       if (counters[which[i]] > 0)
8         ++counters[which[i]];
9     }
10  }
```

FIGURE 20.5

A lock-based algorithm for conditionally incrementing counters.

it increments that counter. To avoid races, the thread locks the entire array of counters for the duration of the operation.

Suppose two threads call this function simultaneously, with the first thread's which array consisting only of the value 0, the second thread's which array consisting only of the value 1023, and all positions in the counters array set to 1. In that case, acquiring the lock would not be necessary because the threads would not access the same location in the counters array. Consequently, the program missed the opportunity for greater parallelism. On the other hand, if the second thread's which array also held the value 0, then acquiring the lock would be necessary, or the two threads' accesses to counter[0] would race.

We could enable greater parallelism by replacing counter_lock with an array of locks. Threads could then use a two-phase locking strategy, in which they acquire each location's lock before accessing the corresponding position in counters, and release all of the locks at the end of the function. To know which locks to release, and also because an index may appear more than once in which, the thread must track the locks it has acquired. To avoid deadlock, all threads must also acquire the locks in the same predetermined order. (They can do this by sorting which first.) Although this fine-grained strategy is more scalable, it may actually be slower than the coarse-grained strategy because it must acquire more locks.

With transactional programming, we can dispense with thinking about locks at all. We simply execute the entire operation as a single transaction, and rely on the transactional run-time system to avoid races while exploiting parallelism as much as possible. The code might resemble that in Fig. 20.6. The transactional system would watch what other threads were doing. If a thread's speculative execution would race with another thread, the system would stop the thread before the race manifested, undo its operations, and try again.

```
1   int *counters = ...;
2
3   void increment_pos_counters(size_t num, size_t *which) {
4     transaction {
5       for (size_t i = 0; i < num; ++i) {
6         if (counters[which[i]] > 0)
7           ++counters[which[i]];
8       }
9     }
10  }
```

FIGURE 20.6

A transactional version of Fig. 20.5.

20.3 **Hardware support for transactional programming**

Speculation and access tracking have the lowest overhead when implemented in hardware. We now give an overview of how to provide hardware support for transactional programming. Some modern microprocessors already include such support.

20.3.1 **Hardware speculation**

Modern microprocessors execute hundreds of instructions simultaneously, even within a single core. Three features make this level of parallelism possible. First, many microprocessors can fetch multiple instructions in a single cycle, and schedule them on parallel arithmetic/logic units. Second, modern microprocessors are pipelined: different instructions can be in different stages of their execution (using different circuits) at the same time. Finally, to keep their pipelines and execution units busy, a modern microprocessor does not stall when it encounters a branch. Instead, it predicts which direction the branch will take, and executes the corresponding instruction stream speculatively. If the microprocessor subsequently determines that an instruction should not have been executed, it undoes the instruction's effect and the effects of instructions that depended on it. If the instructions would overwrite memory, the processor buffers the writes until it is known that the instruction was supposed to execute (e.g., all branches were predicted correctly); the buffered writes are discarded if the prediction was wrong.

Since processors can already speculate, and undo the effects of any speculative instructions that fail, to support transactions, we only need to allow the programmer to specify a granularity for speculation that extends beyond the pipeline: In addition to aborting any yet-to-complete instructions from a transaction that aborts, the effects of completed instructions by that transaction also need to be undone. To support undoing changes to registers, the instruction that starts a transaction stores their original state, so that the registers can be reset if the transaction aborts. To support undoing changes to memory, the processor must be able to roll back values in the cache that correspond to the writes that the failed transaction made. Invalidation is the simplest mechanism for rolling back a transaction's writes.

20.3.2 **Basic cache coherence**

Hardware-supported transactional programming relies on the cache coherence protocol for fine-grained access tracking and for detecting conflicting memory accesses by concurrent transactions. Before discussing the details, we briefly review cache coherence. Readers unfamiliar with cache coherence protocols may consult Appendix B for more background.

In modern multiprocessors each processor has an attached *cache*, a small high-speed memory used to avoid communicating with large and slow main memory. Each cache entry holds a group of neighboring words called a *line*, and has some way of mapping addresses to lines. Consider a simple architecture in which processors and memory communicate over a shared broadcast medium called a *bus*. Each cache line has a *tag*, which encodes state information. In the standard *MESI* protocol, each cache line is in one of the following states:

- *Modified*: The line in the cache has been modified, and must eventually be written back to memory. No other processor has this line cached.
- *Exclusive*: The line has not been modified, but no other processor has this line cached. (A line is typically loaded in exclusive mode before being modified.)
- *Shared*: The line has not been modified, and other processors may have this line cached.
- *Invalid*: The line does not contain meaningful data.

The *cache coherence* protocol detects synchronization conflicts among individual loads and stores, and ensures that different processors agree on the state of the shared memory. When a processor loads or stores a memory address *a*, it broadcasts the request on the bus, and the other processors and memory listen in (sometimes called *snooping*).

A full description of a cache coherence protocol can be complex, but here are the principal transitions of interest to us.

- When a processor requests to load a line in modified mode, the other processors invalidate any copies of that line. A processor with a modified copy of that line must write the line back to memory before the load can be fulfilled.
- When a processor requests to load a line into its cache in shared mode, any processor with an exclusive or modified copy must change its state to shared. A processor with a modified copy must also write that line back to memory before the load can be fulfilled.
- If the cache becomes full, it may be necessary to *evict* a line. If the line is shared or exclusive, it can simply be discarded, but if it is modified, it must be written back to memory.

Note that modern cache coherence protocols detect and resolve synchronization conflicts between writers and between readers and writers, and they already allow changes to memory to stay in the cache for a while, instead of immediately and directly updating memory.

20.3.3 Transactional cache coherence

Many of the state transitions in the MESI protocol are asynchronous: They occur in one processor on account of a memory operation performed by another processor. While we customarily think of a data race as something that manifests at a much higher level of abstraction, there is a close relationship between the programming language concept of a race and the state transitions in the MESI protocol.

Consider the case of two threads attempting to increment a counter at the same time. The statement counter++ translates to three assembly instructions: one to fetch the value of counter to a register, one to increment the value in that register, and one to update the value of counter by writing the register's value to memory. A race occurs if there is *any* interleaving between the three instructions issued by one thread, and the three instructions issued by the other. If we examined every possible interleaving, and looked at the MESI state transitions that occur, we would find that whenever there is a data race, then at some time while the three instructions are being executed, either some line is invalidated or some line in the Modified state is downgraded to Shared or Exclusive. This observation holds for any section of code that accesses shared memory: If a race occurs with any of its accesses to shared memory, then the line containing the accessed data is either invalidated or downgraded from Modified during the execution of that section of code.

We can use this observation to execute a transaction speculatively, and abort the transaction if a problematic transitions occurs in the cache while the transaction is executing. (If no such transition occurs, then there were no data races with the transaction, so the speculation succeeds.) Assume that each processor has a private L1 cache and executes only one thread at a time. To detect problematic cache line transitions, we add TX_Begin and TX_End instructions that delimit a transaction, a flag that indicates whether a transaction is active, and a bit to each line of the cache that indicates whether the line has been accessed by an active transaction. The TX_Begin instruction saves a private copy of the current values of the processor's registers (a *checkpoint*), raises the flag, and returns *true*, indicating that the transaction is executing speculatively. While the flag is raised, any access to the cache will set the corresponding bit. The TX_End instruction lowers the flag, clears any bits that may have been set, and discards the checkpoint. Thus, if TX_End is executed, the transaction does not abort, and the result is the same as if the code were executed without the transaction (i.e., the speculation succeeded).

With the above mechanics in place, it is straightforward to detect problematic transitions: If a line whose bit is set is about to be evicted or downgraded from Modified, the cache first notifies the processor to abort the speculation.

When a transaction aborts, any cache lines that it modified are invalidated; their values are *not* written back or provided to any other processor. In addition, the flag is lowered, all bits indicating transactional access are cleared, and the checkpoint is used to reset the thread to its state at the beginning of the transaction. Then the TX_Begin instruction returns *false*, indicating that the speculation has failed. Thus, the thread can determine whether it is executing on account of a successful TX_Begin, or in response to an abort.

20.3.4 Limitations of hardware support

Because data in a cache line that has been accessed by a hardware transaction cannot leave the cache without aborting the transaction, the cache size and associativity impose strict limits on the amount of data that a transaction can access. For example, some L1 caches are *direct-mapped*, which means that each address is mapped to a specific line in the cache; its contents must be cached at that line, and must therefore evict any data that were there before. With such a cache, if a transaction accesses two addresses that map to the same cache line, it can never successfully commit.

In addition, on many microprocessors, various events may cause significant delays while a transaction is executing, during which time a cache line accessed by the transaction could be evicted. These events may be induced by the transaction (e.g., by making a system call), or they may be unrelated (e.g., the thread executing the transaction gets swapped out).

Because it is often difficult or impossible to predict when a transaction might not be able to commit, programmers are advised to think of hardware transactional support as being *best effort*, rather than something that can be relied on. Therefore, when using hardware transactions, they should also provide a *fallback* mechanism, in case the transaction cannot be committed.

Requiring programmers to provide a fallback mechanism reduces the burden on computer architects: Transactions are not required to succeed for correctness, only for quality of implementation, so architects are free to exert their best effort.

20.4 Transactional lock elision

The most straightforward way to employ transactional programming in existing lock-based software is through a technique known as *transactional lock elision* (TLE). The core idea in TLE is to modify the critical sections of a program so that they attempt to run as a transactional speculation. If a speculation fails too many times (e.g., due to conflicts with other threads), the execution *falls back* to the original lock.

With hardware support, TLE can be implemented as a special lock, whose `acquire` and `release` methods attempt to use the `TX_Begin` and `TX_End` instructions, respectively. This makes TLE exceptionally easy to use. However, TLE can only *try* to extract more concurrency out of an existing lock-based program, it cannot *guarantee* anything about progress or freedom from pathologies. In particular, the problems we enumerated earlier (e.g., convoying, priority inversion, and deadlock) remain possible: If a speculation fails and falls back to locking, the transactional mechanism is not used, and its benefits on progress and throughput cannot be achieved.

Since it is always correct for a TLE execution to fall back to using the original locks in the program, TLE can be used to accelerate existing critical sections. Typically, critical sections are small: They touch few memory locations, and they do not last for many cycles. If a transaction executing a small critical section fails, it is often worthwhile to retry it a few times before falling back to locking. We could even augment the return value of `TX_Begin` to provide more detail about why a speculation failed, which the code can use to decide whether to retry the critical section speculatively, or to fall back to locking. Fig. 20.7 presents a complete implementation of TLE that uses a spin-lock as the fallback path.

Fig. 20.7 adds a fair bit of complexity around the calls to `TX_Begin` (line 5) and `TX_End` (line 24). Of particular importance, we must remember that line 8 indicates that the critical section will run speculatively, with TLE. If the speculation fails, then control flow will return to line 5. That is, it may appear that `TX_Begin` executes multiple times, with different return values.

```
1   void acquire(spinlock *lock) {
2     int attempts = 0;
3     while (true) {
4       ++attempts;
5       TLE_STATUS status = TX_Begin;
6       if (status == STARTED) {
7         if (!lock.held()) {
8           return;
9         }
10        else {
11          TX_End;
12          attempts--;
13          while (lock.held()) { }
14        }
15      }
16      else if (status != TX_Conflict || attempts >= 4) {
17        lock.acquire();
18        return;
19      }
20    }
21  }
22  void release(spinlock *lock) {
23    if (!lock.held()) {
24      TX_End;
25    }
26    else {
27      lock.release();
28    }
29  }
```

FIGURE 20.7

A complete implementation of TLE, using a spin-lock as the fallback path.

Recall that all modifications to memory that are performed between lines 5 and 24 are undone if the speculation fails. Thus, if we wish to prevent livelock and starvation, it is necessary for us to count the number of attempts *outside* of the transaction. This is accomplished by the attempts variable, which is incremented on each iteration of the loop. Each time the speculation fails, control jumps from line 5 to line 16, where attempts is checked. If the value becomes too large, then the thread stops using TLE, acquires the lock, and then returns. When the thread reaches the end of the critical section, it can observe that the lock is held, conclude that it must be the lock holder, and release the lock to complete the critical section. In a similar fashion, when a speculation fails, and conflict with another thread is not the cause, then line 16 reports a value in status that indicates the critical section must be run while holding the lock.

Note that line 7 follows every successful call to TX_Begin. This code serves two purposes. The first is to identify situations in which one thread attempts to run a critical section via TLE while another thread is actively running a critical section using the lock. By checking the lock after calling TX_Begin, the thread can discover cases where the lock is held. When the lock is held, the thread quietly completes its TLE region without doing any meaningful work. Starting on line 11, the thread makes it look like it never even tried to execute speculatively, by decreasing its attempts and then waiting for the lock to be released.

The second purpose of this call is more subtle. Suppose that a thread reaches line 8, and has begun to execute its critical section. Let another thread subsequently reach line 17. At this point, the second thread is unaware of the first thread, as the first thread is executing speculatively. Since the second thread is not using TLE, its writes are immediately visible in memory. If the first and second threads access the same memory locations, but in different orders, there is a danger that the speculative thread might see inconsistent state. Suppose there is a program invariant that variables x and y are equal, and initially x == y == 0. Let the first thread read x == 0, and let then the second thread execute the first line of the sequence y++; x++. Since the second thread is not using TLE, its write to y immediately is visible in memory. Since the first thread did not access y yet, it has no reason to abort. However, if the second thread were to delay and the first thread were to read y, it would see y == 1, and thus y != x.

The presence of line 7 makes the above situation impossible. Note that the first thread read the lock *while it was using TLE*. Thus the lock must be in the thread's cache, with the *transactional* bit set. Consequently, any subsequent change to the lock by another thread, be it nonspeculative or speculative, will cause the cache line holding the lock to move to that thread's cache, in the Modified state. Coherence ensures that the line must first be evicted from the first thread's cache. This will cause the first thread to abort.

20.4.1 Discussion

TLE is a powerful tool for increasing the concurrency of programs whose critical sections rarely conflict. However, we must be careful about critical sections that try to perform I/O. Note that TLE can be employed in user programs, as well as the operating system kernel. What should happen if a TLE critical section in the kernel attempts to interact with a hardware device? If the critical section subsequently aborted, could the device behave erroneously? For that matter, does it make sense for a TLE critical section in a user program to make system calls?

Additionally, the TLE mechanism we described thus far has no way to guarantee progress. Livelock and starvation are both possible. Even in our simple example with a single shared counter, it is possible that one thread is always executing the first line of code between the times when the other thread is executing the third line and when it calls TX_End.

Given these constraints, TLE is best thought of as an optimization, not as a fundamentally new programming model. When critical sections rarely conflict, but threads still find themselves spending time waiting for locks, then using TLE to run the corresponding critical sections is likely to improve performance. Note that TLE does affect how a programmer constructs synchronization code: In programs where TLE is effective, it is often the case that the programmer can get by with a few coarse-grained instead of many fine-grained locks.

20.5 Transactional memory

We have already seen how TLE can optimize the performance of existing lock-based programs. Can transactional programming also simplify the creation of new concurrent programs? If so, how might *de novo* programs be designed differently, if transactions were part of the concurrency toolbox from the get-go?

Transactional memory (TM) refers, broadly, to the programming model that arises when programmers think in terms of transactions instead of locks. The differences between TM and TLE are subtle, but significant:

- Programmers do not think about *how* to implement concurrency. Instead, they mark the regions of code that need to run in isolation from each other, and they leave it up to a run-time system to find an optimal concurrency mechanism.
- Since programmers think in terms of regions requiring isolation, nesting of transactions is natural, if not encouraged.
- Since there is no guarantee of a lock-based fallback, the programming language may need to ensure that transactions do not attempt operations that cannot be undone (e.g., I/O).
- Since everything inside of a transaction can be undone, it is natural, if not beneficial, to expose speculation to the programmer, in the form of explicit self-abort instructions.
- Since there are no locks in the programming model, traditional problems with locking (deadlock, convoying, priority inversion) are not possible.

To illustrate the difference between TLE and TM, consider the code in Fig. 20.8. We expect both functions to be able to complete using transactional speculation, since they each update only two locations. However, the TLE code is significantly more complex. The convention in the TLE program is that every access to either integer passed to the function must be performed while the corresponding lock is held. Thus the program must acquire both locks. In the common case, the acquisitions will use TLE, and will be elided. However, the worst case requires the programmer to produce a consistent lock order to avoid deadlock (in this case, we order based on the addresses of the integers). In addition, the programmer must check that the two integers are not protected by the same lock. In contrast, the designer of the TM code knows that every access to either integer, in any other place in the program, will also use TM. Consequently, it suffices to begin a TM region, increment the counters, and then end the region. If the region conflicts with other threads' accesses, the run-time system will determine an order in which the threads will execute.

```
1   void tle_increment_two(int *i1, std::mutex *m1, int *i2, std::mutex *m2) {
2     int* ptrs[] = ((uintptr_t)i1) > ((uintptr_t)i2) ? {i2, i1} : {i1, i2};
3     std::mutex* locks[] = ((uintptr_t)i1) > ((uintptr_t)i2) ? {m2, m1} : {m1, m2};
4
5     tle_acquire(locks[0]);
6     if (locks[0] != locks[1])
7       tle_acquire(locks[1]);
8     *ptrs[0]++;
9     *ptrs[1]++;
10    tle_release(locks[0]);
11    if (locks[0] != locks[1])
12      tle_release(locks[1]);
13  }
14  void tm_increment_two(int *i1, int *i2) {
15    tm {
16      *i1++;
17      *i2++;
18    }
19  }
```

FIGURE 20.8

Code to atomically increment two counters with TLE (top) and TM (bottom).

20.5.1 Run-time scheduling

Since TM does not have a lock-based fallback, it requires some other mechanism to ensure progress. Historically, this mechanism has been called "contention management," though it may be more appropriately thought of as a scheduler. In the common case, the contention manager does nothing: Threads begin and end transactions, and the transactions should usually succeed. When a thread finds itself repeatedly failing to commit, due to conflicts with other threads, then it may choose to (1) delay itself before trying again, in the hope that the concurrent transactions with which it is conflicting will commit, or (2) employ some mechanism to reduce the number of transactions that run concurrently with it, to decrease the likelihood of a concurrent transaction causing a conflict.

In the first case, a simple and effective strategy, which we saw in Section 7.4, is to use randomized exponential back-off. That is, after n consecutive aborts, the thread will choose a random number between 2^{n-1} and $2^n - 1$ and wait for that many CPU cycles before retrying. Usually randomized exponential back-off will place a hard limit on n, so that in high-conflict situations, threads will not wait for minutes.

In the second case, decreasing the number of running transactions is a heuristic, not a hard-and-fast rule. A simple solution is to use a global Boolean flag. When a thread tries to start a transaction, it first checks the flag. If the flag is true, the thread waits. Once the flag is false, the thread may continue. If a transaction aborts repeatedly, it tries to change the flag from false to true, via a compare-and-swap. If it succeeds, it attempts its transaction until the transaction commits. Otherwise, it waits. When the distressed transaction commits, it clears the flag. In Exercise 20.8, we explore the performance impact of this approach versus falling back to acquiring the lock in TLE.

20.5.2 Explicit self-abort

Since TM regions always run speculatively, the run-time system is allowed to abort a transaction at any time, and for any reason. Of course, every time a transaction aborts, that transaction's previous work is wasted, so the run-time system should avoid causing unnecessary aborts. But since the potential is there, it is worthwhile to consider letting the programmer request self-abort.

Indeed, self-abort appears to be the cornerstone of creating truly compositional programs based on transactions. Consider a program in which a thread receives a list of tuples, where each tuple consists of a *source account*, a *destination account*, and a *transfer amount*. Since a single account can appear multiple times as a source and as a destination, and since the account balances cannot be read without using some kind of synchronization, it is not trivial to determine if the list of operations is valid. The challenge is especially great if each account is protected by a lock that is private to the account object. However, with TM and explicit self-abort, we can encapsulate each account's synchronization entirely within its implementation, and still write correct code. Inspired by the conventions in the C++ TM Technical Specification, we say that if an integer exception escapes a transaction, it causes the transaction to abort, but the exception is retained. With such a definition, Fig. 20.9 shows how TM and self-abort together elegantly implement a solution.

20.6 Software transactions

Thus far, we have assumed hardware support for transactional programming. While there exist microprocessors with such support, it is also possible to implement transactions entirely in software. In addition to offering a pathway to transactional programming on legacy hardware, software transactions also provide a scalable fallback path when hardware transactions fail. In this section, we describe two software implementations that support transactional programming.

To implement transactions in software, we provide a library satisfying the interface in Fig. 20.10, which provides functions to call when beginning, committing, or aborting a transaction, and when reading and writing memory within a transaction.

It would be tedious and error-prone if programmers had to call these functions directly, so we assume programmers can write structured transactional code, and that a compiler inserts the appropriate library calls: Calls to `beginTx` and `commitTx` would be inserted at the beginning and end, respectively, of every transactional region, and every load and store within a transaction would be replaced by the appropriate function call. (The `abortTx` function is used for explicit self-abort.) For example, **int** x = *y would become **int** x = read(y), and global_i = 7 would become write(&global_i, 7).

```
1   class account {
2     double balance;
3   public:
4     static const int ERR_INSUF_FUNDS = 1;
5     void withdraw(double amount) {
6       tm {
7         if (balance < amount)
8           throw ERR_INSUF_FUNDS;
9         balance -= amount;
10      }
11    }
12    void deposit(double amount) { tm { balance += amount; } }
13  };
14  bool transfer_many(vector<account*> from,
15                     vector<account*> to,
16                     vector<double> amounts) {
17    try {
18      tm {
19        for (int i = 0; i < from.size(); ++i) {
20          from[i].withdraw(amounts[i]);
21          to[i].deposit(amounts[i]);
22        }
23      }
24      return true;
25    } catch (int e) {
26      if (e == account::ERR_INSUF_FUNDS) {
27        return false;
28      }
29    }
30  }
```

FIGURE 20.9

Code to atomically perform multiple transfers between accounts, using exception-based
self-abort.

```
1   void beginTx(jmp_buf *b);
2   void write(uintptr_t *addr, uintptr_t val);
3   int read(uintptr_t *addr);
4   void commitTx();
5   void abortTx();
```

FIGURE 20.10

Interface for software transactions.

As a transaction performs reads, it must track every location it has read, so it can later determine if that location was changed by a concurrent transaction. When it performs writes, it must do so in a manner that can be undone if the transaction ultimately aborts. Thus, a software transaction library would also define a *transaction descriptor*, a per-thread object to keep track of the state of an in-progress transaction, and some global synchronization data through which the threads can coordinate their accesses to shared memory. We must also be able to checkpoint a thread's state when it begins a transaction, so we can reset the thread if its transaction aborts. In C++, the setjmp and longjmp instructions suffice for this purpose. For the sake of simplicity, we omit checkpointing in the following discussion.

20.6.1 Transactions with ownership records

One of the key challenges for software transactions is to detect conflicts between concurrent transactions. The *ownership record*, or orec, is a data structure designed for this purpose. An orec superimposes a lock, a version number, and a thread's unique identifier into a single memory word. In its simplest implementation, the lowest bit of an orec serves two roles: It is a lock bit, and it also indicates the meaning of the remaining bits of the orec.

In more detail, we say that when the orec's low bit is zero, it is unlocked, and the remaining bits can be interpreted as a monotonically increasing integer (the version number). When the low bit is one, the orec is locked, and the remaining bits can be interpreted as the unique ID of the thread that holds the lock. In a sense, orecs enhance sequence locks (Section 20.1.2) by adding information about the lock owner.

If we built our software transactions using a single orec, it would not afford much concurrency. Instead, we will use an array of orecs. Fig. 20.11, line 3 declares the table of orecs as an array of NUM_LOCKS atomic integers. Line 6 implements a many-to-one mapping of memory regions to entries in the table. If we assume that every memory word (uintptr_t) is aligned on an 8-byte boundary, then as long as GRAIN is no less than 3, every memory word will map to exactly one entry in lock_table.

Our implementation will be able to detect conflicts on location L by any pair of transactions by watching how those transactions interact with the entry in lock_table that corresponds to L. False conflicts are possible, since there are many more memory locations than table entries. However, if the table size is large enough, false conflicts should be unlikely.

Before discussing the rest of the implementation, let us consider a strawman implementation of transactions that uses orecs in a manner more reminiscent of traditional locks. Given our lock_table, we could run a transaction as follows: Any time the transaction tries to read a location, we could check the corresponding orec. If the orec is locked by the current transaction, then we could read the location directly; if the orec is unlocked, we could lock the orec and then read the location; and if the orec is locked by another transaction, we could abort the transaction, invoke the run-time transaction scheduler (to help avoid livelock), and then try again. Writes would run almost identically, except that they could not simply update a location; if they subsequently aborted, we would need some mechanism to undo that write. The easiest

```
1     atomic<uint64_t> id_gen(1)
2     atomic<uint64_t> clock(0);
3     atomic<uint64_t> lock_table[NUM_LOCKS];
4
5     atomic<uint64_t> *get_lock(void *addr) {
6       return &lock_table[(((uintptr_t)addr)>>GRAIN) % NUM_LOCKS];
7     }
8     struct Descriptor {
9       jmp_buf *checkpoint;
10      uint64_t my_lock;
11      uint64_t start_time;
12      unordered_map<uintptr_t*, uintptr_t> writes;
13      vector<atomic<uint64_t>*> reads;
14      vector<pair<atomic<uint64_t>*, uint64_t>> locks;
15
16      Descriptor() : my_lock(((id_gen++)<<1)|1) { }
17    };
18    void beginTx(jmp_buf *b) {
19      checkpoint = b;
20      start_time = clock;
21    }
22    void write(uintptr_t *addr, uintptr_t val) {
23      writes.insert_or_assign(addr, val);
24    }
25    int read(uintptr_t *addr) {
26      auto it = writes.find(addr);
27      if (it != writes.end())
28        return *it;
29
30      atomic<uint64_t>* l = get_lock(addr);
31      uint64_t pre = *l;
32      uintptr_t val = std::atomic_ref<uintptr_t>(*addr).load(std::memory_order_acquire);
33      uint64_t post = *l;
34      if ((pre&1) || (pre != post) || (pre > start_time))
35        abortTx();
36      reads.push_back(l);
37      return val;
38    }
```

FIGURE 20.11

Software transactions with ownership records (1/2).

approach would be to maintain an *undo log*, into which the old value could be saved *before* the location was updated. If the transaction aborted, it would need to use the log to restore the original values in memory. At commit time, a thread would release its locks and discard its undo log.

The above strategy would allow nonconflicting transactions to run concurrently, without the programmer needing to think about fine-grained locks. Since memory would only be accessed when the thread held the appropriate lock, there would be no races. However, execution would be pessimistic: Any time any transaction accessed any location, that location would be inaccessible to all concurrent transactions. Especially when reads abound, this approach would sacrifice concurrency.

While we could try to craft a solution based on readers–writer locks, so that multiple threads could have read permission on a location simultaneously, doing so would incur overhead, since nonconflicting threads would conflict when acquiring an orec in read mode. Instead, we will use optimistic reads. That is, when a transaction wishes to read a location L, it will first read the value of the orec that corresponds to L. If the orec is locked, then the code continues or aborts according to the same rules as in the strawman algorithm. However, if the orec is unlocked, we will not lock it. Instead we will record the version number stored in the orec. If that version number never changes before the transaction commits, or if it changes only on account of the same transaction subsequently acquiring the orec as a writer, then the transaction knows that its read remained valid.

The second change we will make to the strawman algorithm is to employ commit-time locking. With commit-time locking, a transaction writing to L does not acquire the orec for L until it is ready to commit. Consequently, it must log its writes in a private *redo log* instead of updating L directly.

The above two changes introduce a subtle but significant question: If a transaction reads L, how frequently must it check the orec that corresponds to L? As we will see in the chapter exercises, the transaction could have an incorrect execution if it subsequently read some other location L' and did not then check L's orec. Unfortunately, if a transaction performs n reads, it would incur $O(n^2)$ overhead to *validate* the consistency of all of its reads.

To reduce the validation overhead in the common case, we introduce a monotonically increasing counter, which we call the global clock. This clock will increment every time a writing transaction attempts to commit, and its value will be used to establish the start and end times of transactions. When a transaction commits, it increments clock, and then uses the new value of the clock as the version of every orec that it releases.

While the clock becomes a potential bottleneck for writing transactions, its impact on read validation is dramatic. Suppose that a transaction sees the value T_s in the clock when it begins. If, before reading a location L, the transaction sees that L's orec has a value $T_o \leq T_s$, and after reading L, the transaction sees that the orec's value is still T_o, then the transaction knows that L could not have been modified after it started. If the same property holds for every orec encountered by the transaction, then it never needs to validate during its execution: It only reads locations that have not been modified since it started, and it conservatively aborts if it attempts to read any location whose orec was modified after it started.

Our implementation in Figs. 20.11 and 20.12 illustrates the algorithm in full, for software transactions that operate on word-sized memory locations. Our implementation uses the C setjmp and longjmp instructions to capture the state of the registers immediately before the transaction attempts, and to jump back to that point any time the transaction aborts. It also addresses the requirements of the C++ memory model

```
41   void commitTx() {
42     if (writes.empty()) {
43       reads.clear();
44       return;
45     }
46     for (auto &l : writes) {
47       atomic<uint64_t>* l = get_lock(l.first);
48       uint64_t prev = *l;
49       if ((prev&1 == 0) && (prev <= start_time)) {
50         if (!l->compare_exchange_strong(prev, my_lock))
51           abortTx();
52         locks.push_back(l, prev);
53       }
54       else if (prev != my_lock) {
55         abortTx();
56       }
57     }
58     uint64_t end_time = ++clock;
59     if (end_time != start_time + 1) {
60       for (auto l : reads) {
61         uint64_t v = *i;
62         if (((v&1) && (v != my_lock)) || ((v&1==0) && (v>start_time)))
63           abortTx();
64       }
65     }
66     for (auto w : writes)
67       std::atomic_ref<uintptr_t>(*w.first).store(w.second, std::memory_order_release);
68     for (auto l : locks)
69       *l.first = end_time;
70     writes.clear();
71     locks.clear();
72     readset.clear();
73   }
74   void abortTx() {
75     for (auto l : locks)
76       *l.first = l.second;
77     reads.clear();
78     writes.clear();
79     locks.clear();
80   }
```

FIGURE 20.12

Software transactions with ownership records (2/2).

by using std::atomic_ref<>, a feature of C++20, so that accesses to program memory by transactions will not form a race. This is a preferable alternative to casting pointers to std::atomic<>.

Every transaction uses a Descriptor object to store its state during execution (line 8). The Descriptor tracks three sets: one with the addresses of the orecs it has read, one with the addresses of the orecs it has locked, and one with pairs representing the locations it intends to update, and the values it intends to write to those locations. It also stores its start time and its setjmp buffer. When a thread creates its Descriptor, it increments the global id_gen counter to get a unique integer, and it uses that to craft a value it can store in the orecs it acquires.

When a transaction begins, it reads the clock (line 20) in order to determine its starting time. To write value V to location L, the transaction stores the pair $\langle V, L \rangle$ into its write set (line 23). To read a location L, the transaction starts by checking if L is in its write set, in which case it must return the value it intends to write (line 26). If L is not found, the transaction computes the address of the orec for L. It then reads the value of the orec (line 31), reads the value at L (line 32), and then rereads the value of the orec (line 33). This pattern is necessary: A concurrent transaction that is committing might be concurrently updating the location, and that transaction may have incremented clock and begun its commit sequence before this transaction begins. For the algorithm we present, checking the orec before and after reading L is necessary. Since we expect conflicts to be rare, we optimize read to be as short as possible. If line 34 detects any discrepancy in the two reads of the orec, the transaction aborts and tries again.

The most complex part of our algorithm is when a transaction tries to commit. If the transaction is read-only, then we know that it has not performed any writes, and as of its last read, it would have determined that all of its reads returned values that were written before the transaction started. Thus a read-only transaction can commit without any more effort (line 42). Otherwise, the transaction must acquire the orecs that protect the locations in its write set. This process extends from line 46 to line 57. For each address in the write set, the algorithm reads the current value of the orec. If the orec is already owned by the transaction, no work is needed. If the orec is locked by another transaction, then this transaction must abort. There is one more consideration: If the orec is unlocked, but its value is greater than the transaction's start time, then the transaction aborts. This is a conservative step. Suppose that the transaction has also read a location protected by this orec: Once the transaction acquires the lock, it will be unable to see the old value of the orec, to recognize that its read was invalidated by another transaction's commit. To simplify the subsequent checks, our transactions abort in this case.

Once the locks are acquired, the transaction gets its commit time by incrementing the clock (line 58). If the clock had not changed since the transaction started, then the transaction knows that all of its reads must be valid, and thus it need not check them individually. Otherwise, it must check each entry in its read set (line 59), to make sure the orec has not changed in such a way as to suggest that the corresponding read became invalid.

Once the transaction has validated its reads, it can replay its writes (line 66) and release its locks (line 68). Then it can clear its lists.

Lastly, if a transaction aborts, then it must clear its lists. Since the transaction may abort during the commit operation, it is possible that it has acquired some locks. If it has, it must release them during the abort operation (line 75). Note that in this case, the lock versions can be reset to the values they had before they were acquired:

A concurrent read that "misses" the locking of the orec will not read invalid values, because the values are only updated after aborting becomes impossible.

Our implementation of transactions with orecs has a number of desirable properties. Even though it uses locks internally, its locks are not visible to the programmer, and deadlock is not possible: The necessary condition of "hold and wait" is broken, since a transaction that cannot acquire a lock releases all of its locks and tries again. Furthermore, the use of commit-time locking decreases the likelihood of livelock: Symmetric conflicts among transactions can only manifest if those transactions reach their commit points simultaneously.

20.6.2 Transactions with value-based validation

The orec approach to transactions is not without its drawbacks. Chief among them is the granularity of the mapping of locations to orecs: A simplistic hash function, like the one in Fig. 20.11, can lead to deterministic collisions (for example, with 4096 orecs, the first element of every array of 2^{16} elements will be protected by the same orec); using a complex hash function introduces too much latency. One alternative is to validate by directly using the values returned from calls to the read function. Figs. 20.13 and 20.14 present such an algorithm.

```
1   atomic<uint64_t> lock(0);
2
3   struct Descriptor {
4     jmp_buf *checkpoint;
5     uint64_t start_time;
6     unordered_map<uintptr_t*, uintptr_t> writes;
7     vector<pair<uintptr_t*, uintptr_t>> reads;
8   };
9   void beginTx(jmp_buf *b) {
10    checkpoint = b;
11    start_time = lock;
12    if (start_time & 1)
13      start_time--;
14  }
15  void abortTx() {
16    writes.clear();
17    reads.clear();
18    longjmp(*checkpoint, 1);
19  }
20  int void write(uintptr_t *ptr, uintptr_t val) {
21    writes.insert_or_assign(addr, val);
22  }
```

FIGURE 20.13

Software transactions with value-based validation (1/2).

```
1   uintprt_t read(uintptr_t *ptr) {
2     auto it = writes.find(addr);
3     if (it != writes.end())
4       return *it;
5     uintptr_t val = std::atomic_ref<uintptr_t>(*ptr).load(std::memory_order_acquire);
6     while (start_time != globals.lock.val) {
7       start_time = validate();
8       val = std::atomic_ref<uintptr_t>(*ptr).load(std::memory_order_acquire);
9     }
10    reads.push_back({addr, val});
11    return val;
12  }
13  void commitTx() {
14    if (writes.empty()) {
15      reads.clear();
16      return;
17    }
18    uint64_t from = start_time;
19    while (!lock.compare_exchange_strong(from, from + 1))
20      from = validate();
21    start_time = from;
22    for (auto w : writes)
23      std::atomic_ref<uintptr_t>(*w.first).store(w.second, std::memory_order_release);
24    lock = 2 + start_time;
25    writes.clear();
26    reads.clear();
27  }
28  uint64_t validate() {
29    while (true) {
30      uint64_t time = lock;
31      if (time & 1)
32        continue;
33      for (auto it = reads.begin(), e = reads.end(); it != e; ++it) {
34        if (std::atomic_ref<uintptr_t>(*it.first).load(std::memory_order_acquire) !=
35            it.second)
36          abortTx();
37      }
38      if (time == lock)
39        return time;
40    }
41  }
```

FIGURE 20.14

Software transactions with value-based validation (2/2).

This algorithm resembles our orec algorithm in that it delays transactional writes until commit time (redo logging). The main differences are that it uses a single sequence lock to coordinate when transactions commit, and it does not use the sequence lock to decide when transactions abort. Instead, changes to the sequence lock cause transactions to validate.

The intuition behind this algorithm is that transactions can log the addresses they read, and the values they observed when they performed those reads. When a transaction commits, it increments the sequence lock to an odd value, writes back its entire write set, and then increments the sequence lock to a new even value. A transaction can trivially determine that it is valid if it sees that the sequence lock has the same even value as the last time at which the transaction was valid.

If the sequence lock has changed since the last check, the transaction must wait until the sequence lock is even (unheld). Then it can reread every location in its read set, to ensure that the value is the same as it was when the transaction read it. The only catch is that the transaction must check its *entire* read set, without any intervening writer transaction commits. This manifests in the while loop of the validate function. Note that after a successful validation, a transaction is equivalent to one that started at the time of the validation, and hence can update its start time.

One question that arises is whether a transaction can *start* while the lock is held. Rather than introduce waiting in the beginTx() function, we subtract one from the start time if it would otherwise be odd. This means that a transaction might validate on its first load, instead of waiting to start.

Like the orec algorithm, this approach to transactions is deadlock-free: It only has one lock, and thus there is no potential for deadlock! In addition, note that a transaction's progress is only impeded when it must validate, and every validation corresponds to the completion of a writer transaction. Hence, the algorithm is livelock-free. Unfortunately, starvation is possible, especially for long-running transactions concurrent with a stream of small writers: The long-running transaction might need to validate once per writer.

20.7 Combining hardware and software transactions

Part of the appeal of value-based validation is that it enables hybrid transactional systems, which use hardware transactional execution when possible, and fall back to software execution when a transaction cannot complete in hardware (e.g., because it is too big). One of the simplest approaches is to introduce a mechanism for dynamically switching between two phases: one in which all transactions use hardware support, and one in which none do.

The phase change from hardware mode to software mode is relatively simple to achieve, using a mechanism similar to the fallback in hardware lock elision: The transaction system includes a global flag to indicate if the current mode is "hardware" or "software." Every hardware-mode transaction begins by checking the flag. If the flag changes during the transaction's execution, it will abort, at which point it can switch to software mode. If a hardware transaction cannot complete because of capacity, then after it aborts, it atomically changes the flag value and then starts in software mode.

The return from software to hardware is potentially more challenging. However, value-based validation provides a clean return: When the transaction that precipitated the switch to software mode is about to complete, its final step before validating is to use a transactional write to set the flag false (this write is performed by an augmented `commitTx()` function). So long as every software-mode transaction begins by reading the flag (i.e., via a call to `read()` from within `beginTx()`), then when the distressed transaction commits and resets the mode, its commit will cause all concurrent transactions to validate, abort, and then resume in hardware mode.

This is but one of many mechanisms for combining hardware and software transactional execution. Other approaches use a global lock or epochs (Section 19.7) to manage the transition between modes. Truly *hybrid* systems allow hardware and software transactions to run and commit concurrently.

20.8 Transactional data structure design

One of the most promising roles for TM is in the creation of high-performance concurrent data structures. As an example, consider the difficulty involved in creating a concurrent red/black tree: a lock-based implementation would have difficulty crafting a cycle-free lock acquisition order, because an operation does not know how much rebalancing is necessary until after it reaches its target node; a nonblocking implementation might need to atomically modify many memory locations in order to rebalance during an insert or removal. With transactions, these complex data structure maintenance operations can be done atomically with the modification operation, without requiring the programmer to craft a complex synchronization protocol.

Another benefit of transactions is that they allow data structures to export rich interfaces. Consider a concurrent hashmap: a programmer may desire more methods than the traditional `insert/remove/contains`. With transactions, a generic `modifyKey(k, λ)` method becomes possible, wherein a programmer can atomically (1) find the entry with matching key, (2) apply the λ function to the value associated with that key, and (3) update the value with the computed result. TM is a pathway to composable, modular, generic concurrent data structures.

While TM can transform an arbitrary sequential operation into a concurrent operation, it does not promise scalability. Programmers must make sure that their data structures do not have obvious scalability bottlenecks. For example, if every insertion and removal in a hashmap must update a count of the total number of items, then transactions cannot prevent concurrent counter updates from conflicting. Furthermore, TM is no different than locking in its requirement that all concurrent accesses to a datum agree on the synchronization mechanism being used. Just as it is not correct to allow one thread to perform an unsynchronized access to an item that is simultaneously locked by another thread, it is not correct to allow nontransactional accesses to an item that is simultaneously being accessed transactionally. Lastly, when using software TM, programs must take great care when transitioning memory from a state in which it is accessed transactionally to a state in which it is not. The most dangerous example is memory reclamation: If a transaction unlinks a node from a data structure, commits, and then tries to free that node, it must be sure that no concurrent (doomed to abort) transaction is still accessing that node. We explore this "privatization" problem in an exercise.

20.9 Chapter notes

The transition from Linux Kernel 2.4 to Linux Kernel 2.6 involved a significant effort to improve performance on multiprocessors. Sequence locks were one of the techniques that became widespread as a result [98]. The challenges faced when using sequence locks in C++ are discussed in detail by Hans Boehm [20]. We thank Hans for explaining the subtleties of sequence locks, and suggesting a solution using C++20's `std::atomic_ref<>`.

TLE in modern microprocessors is based on a more general mechanism called *hardware transactional memory*, first proposed by Maurice Herlihy and Eliot Moss [74] as a general-purpose programming model for multiprocessors. Nir Shavit and Dan Touitou [157] proposed the first TM that did not require specialized hardware, instead using software instrumentation on every load and store.

The "orec" algorithm presented in this chapter is a variant of the TL2 algorithm of Dave Dice, Ori Shalev, and Nir Shavit [35]. The value-based approach is due to Luke Dalessandro, Michael Spear, and Michael Scott [33].

The use of transactional hardware for lock elision was developed by Ravi Rajwar and James Goodman [146,145]. Like TM, there are software-only approaches to lock elision [149].

A comparison of commercially available hardware systems that support TM can be found in [133]. Harris, Larus, and Rajwar [59] provide the authoritative survey of both hardware and software TM.

20.10 Exercises

Exercise 20.1. Let G be a global variable, and let H be a variable allocated on the heap. Both G and H are structs with many fields, and a programmer wishes to protect each with a sequence lock. Why is it necessary to use a safe memory reclamation strategy for H, but not for G?

Exercise 20.2. Consider Exercise 20.1. If the structs were protected by readers–writer locks, and a thread was going to read H, would it need a safe memory reclamation strategy? Why or why not?

Exercise 20.3. In our implementation of TM with orecs, we used a simple vector to store transaction read sets. Suppose there were 2^{16} orecs, with a strong hash function for mapping addresses to orecs. How many randomly chosen accesses would a single transaction need to make before it would read the same orec twice?

Exercise 20.4. In Section 20.6.2, we argued that false conflicts on orecs can limit throughput. As in Exercise 20.3, consider a system with 2^{16} orecs. If every thread issued W writes, then with two threads, at what value of W would the probability of false conflicts exceed 50%?

Exercise 20.5. Continuing the example from Exercise 20.4, if there were eight threads, at what value of W would the probability of false conflicts exceed 50%?

Exercise 20.6. Repeat Exercise 20.5, but with 2^{20} orecs.

Exercise 20.7. Instead of buffering writes in a redo log, an STM implementation could update locations while it was executing, and maintain an undo log for restoring values if the transaction aborted. A subtle complication arises: When the transaction aborts, it cannot restore the old value of orecs when it releases them. Why not? Consider the case where transaction T_1 performs a write to location X and then aborts while reading location Y, and transaction T_2 performs a read to location X that is concurrent with both of T_1's operations.

Exercise 20.8. Let T_A be a transaction that has aborted several times in a row, with T_i total transactions in the system. Suppose that the contention manager gives T_A two options:

- Block new transactions from starting, wait for all current transactions to commit, and then begin.
- Block new transactions from starting, and begin immediately.

Which option would you favor? Why? It might help to consider specific workload characteristics in justifying your answer.

Exercise 20.9. Would the choice of software TM or hardware TM influence your answer to Exercise 20.8?

Exercise 20.10. We claimed that it is necessary for a transaction to ensure the validity of its read set every time it reads a new location. If it does not, a destined-to-abort transaction may produce a visible fault. Create an interleaving between two transactions that could produce a divide-by-zero fault if a transaction does not validate after every read.

Exercise 20.11. A common idiom in lock-based programming is to lock a data structure, unlink part of it, and then unlock the data structure. Doing so makes the unlinked part "private" to the thread who did the unlinking, because that part is no longer reachable to other threads.

A challenge that transactional programming introduces is that speculative threads may not know that they are destined to abort, and their transactional accesses to the unlinked part could conflict with the nontransactional accesses by the unlinking thread.

Create a workload where one thread's transaction privatizes a linked list by splitting it at some point, and another thread's transaction is traversing the list. Describe a fault that could occur in the transactional thread.

Exercise 20.12. Consider your solution to Exercise 20.11. Would the algorithm in Section 20.6.1 be vulnerable to that error? Why or why not?

Exercise 20.13. Consider your solution to Exercise 20.11. Would the algorithm in Section 20.6.2 be vulnerable to that error? Why or why not?

Software basics

A.1 Introduction

This appendix describes the basic programming language constructs needed to understand our examples and to write your own concurrent programs. Mostly, we use Java, but the same ideas could be equally well expressed in other high-level languages and libraries. Here, we review the basic software concepts needed to understand this text in Java, C++, and C#. Our discussion here is necessarily incomplete. If in doubt, consult the current documentation for the language or library of interest.

A.2 Java

The Java programming language uses a concurrency model in which *threads* manipulate *objects*[1] by calling the objects' *methods*. The possibly concurrent calls are coordinated using various language and library constructs. We begin by explaining the basic Java constructs used in this text.

A.2.1 Threads

A *thread* executes a single, sequential program. In Java, a thread is an instance of (a subclass of) java.lang.Thread, which provides methods for creating threads, starting them, suspending them, and waiting for them to finish.

First, create a class that implements the Runnable interface. The class's run() method does all the work. For example, here is a simple thread that prints a string:

```java
public class HelloWorld implements Runnable {
  String message;
  public HelloWorld(String m) {
    message = m;
  }
  public void run() {
    System.out.println(message);
  }
}
```

---

[1] Technically, threads are objects.

A Runnable object can be turned into a thread by calling the Thread class constructor, which takes a Runnable object as its argument, like this:

```
final String m = "Hello world from thread " + i;
Thread thread = new Thread(new HelloWorld(m));
```

Java provides a syntactic shortcut, called an *anonymous inner class*, that allows you to avoid defining an explicit HelloWorld class:

```
final String message = "Hello world from thread " + i;
thread = new Thread(new Runnable() {
  public void run() {
    System.out.println(message);
  }
});
```

This snippet creates an anonymous class implementing the Runnable interface, whose run() method behaves as shown.

After a thread has been created, it must be *started*:

```
thread.start();
```

This method causes thread to run (i.e., to execute the run() method). The thread that calls start() returns immediately. If the caller wants to wait for thread to finish, it must *join* the thread:

```
thread.join();
```

The caller is blocked until the joined thread's run() method returns.

Fig. A.1 shows a method that initializes multiple threads, starts them, waits for them to finish, and then prints out a message. The method creates an array of threads, and initializes them in lines 2–10, using the anonymous inner class syntax. At the end of this loop, it has created an array of dormant threads. In lines 11–13, it starts the threads, and each thread executes its run() method, displaying its message. Finally, in lines 14–16, it waits for each thread to finish.

A.2.2 Monitors

Java provides a number of ways to synchronize access to shared data, both built-in and through packages. Here we describe the built-in model, called the *monitor* model, a simple and commonly used approach. We discuss monitors in Chapter 8.

Imagine you are in charge of software for a call center. During peak hours, calls arrive faster than they can be answered. When a call arrives, your switchboard software places that call in a queue; it plays a recorded announcement assuring the caller that you consider this call to be very important, and that calls will be answered in the order received. An *operator*—an employee in charge of answering calls—dispatches an *operator thread* to dequeue and answer the next call. When an operator finishes with one call, he or she dequeues the next call from the queue and answers it.

```
1   public static void main(String[] args) {
2     Thread[] thread = new Thread[8];
3     for (int i = 0; i < thread.length; i++) {
4       final String message = "Hello world from thread " + i;
5       thread[i] = new Thread(new Runnable() {
6         public void run() {
7           System.out.println(message);
8         }
9       });
10    }
11    for (int i = 0; i < thread.length; i++) {
12      thread[i].start();
13    }
14    for (int i = 0; i < thread.length; i++) {
15      thread[i].join();
16    }
17  }
```

FIGURE A.1

This method initializes a number of Java threads, starts them, and then waits for them to finish.

```
1   class CallQueue {    // this code is incorrect
2     final static int QSIZE = 100;  // arbitrary size
3     int head = 0;                    // next item to dequeue
4     int tail = 0;                    // next empty slot
5     Call[] calls = new Call[QSIZE];
6     public enq(Call x) {             // called by switchboard
7       calls[(tail++) % QSIZE] = x;
8     }
9     public Call deq() {              // called by operators
10      return calls[(head++) % QSIZE]
11    }
12  }
```

FIGURE A.2

An *incorrect* queue class.

Fig. A.2 shows a simple but incorrect queue class. The calls are kept in an array calls, where head is the index of the next call to remove and tail is the index of the next free slot in the array.

This class does not work correctly if two operators try to dequeue a call at the same time. The expression

```
return calls[(head++) % QSIZE]
```

does not happen as an *atomic* (i.e., indivisible) step. Instead, the compiler produces code that looks something like this:

```
int temp0 = head;
head = temp0 + 1;
int temp1 = (temp0 % QSIZE);
return calls[temp1];
```

Two operators might execute these statements together: They execute the first line at the same time, then the second, and so on. In the end, both operators dequeue and answer the same call, possibly annoying the customer.

To make this queue work correctly, we must ensure that only one operator at a time can dequeue the next call, a property called *mutual exclusion*. Java provides a useful built-in mechanism to support mutual exclusion. Each object has an (implicit) *lock*. If a thread *A acquires* the object's lock (or, equivalently, *locks* that object), then no other thread can acquire that lock until *A releases* the lock (or, equivalently, *unlocks* the object). If a class declares a method to be **synchronized**, then that method implicitly acquires the lock when it is called, and releases it when it returns.

Here is one way to ensure mutual exclusion for the enq() and deq() methods:

```
public synchronized T deq() {
  return call[(head++) % QSIZE]
}
public synchronized enq(T x) {
  call[(tail++) % QSIZE] = x;
}
```

Once a call to a synchronized method has acquired the object's lock, any other call to a synchronized method of that object is blocked until the lock is released. (Calls to other objects, subject to other locks, are not blocked.) The body of a synchronized method is often called a *critical section*.

There is more to synchronization than mutual exclusion. What should an operator do if he or she tries to dequeue a call, but there are no calls waiting in the queue? The call might throw an exception or return *null*, but what could the operator do then, other than try again? Instead, it makes sense for the operator to *wait* for a call to appear. Here is a first attempt at a solution:

```
public synchronized T deq() { // this is incorrect
  while (head == tail) {}; // spin while empty
  call[(head++) % QSIZE];
}
```

This attempt is not just wrong, it is disastrously wrong. The dequeuing thread waits inside a synchronized method, locking out every other thread, including the switchboard thread that could be trying to enqueue a call. This is a *deadlock*: The dequeuing thread holds the lock waiting for an enqueuing thread, while the enqueuing thread waits for the dequeuing thread to release the lock. Nothing will ever happen.

From this we learn that if a thread executing a synchronized method needs to wait for something to happen, then it must *unlock* the object while it waits. The waiting thread should periodically reacquire the lock to test whether it can proceed. If so, it proceeds; if not, it releases the lock and goes back to waiting.

In Java, each object provides a `wait()` method, which unlocks the object and suspends the caller. While that thread is waiting, another thread can lock and change the object. Later, when the suspended thread resumes, it locks the object again before it returns from the `wait()` call. Here is a revised, but still incorrect, dequeue method:[2]

```
public synchronized T deq() { // this is still incorrect
  while (head == tail) { wait(); }
  return call[(head++) % QSIZE];
}
```

Each operator thread, seeking a call to answer, repeatedly tests whether the queue is empty. If so, it releases the lock and waits; if not, it removes and returns the item. In a similar way, an enqueuing thread checks whether the buffer is full.

When does a waiting thread wake up? The program must *notify* waiting threads when something significant happens. The `notify()` method eventually wakes up one waiting thread, chosen arbitrarily from the set of waiting threads. When that thread awakens, it competes for the lock like any other thread. When that thread reacquires the lock, it returns from its `wait()` call. You cannot control which waiting thread is chosen. By contrast, the `notifyAll()` method wakes up all waiting threads, eventually. Each time the object is unlocked, one of these newly awakened threads will reacquire the lock and return from its `wait()` call. You cannot control the order in which the threads reacquire the lock.

In the call center example, there are multiple operators and one switchboard. Suppose the switchboard software decides to optimize its use of `notify()` as follows. If it adds a call to an empty queue, then it should notify only one blocked dequeuer, since there is only one call to consume. This optimization, while it may seem reasonable, is flawed. Suppose the operator threads *A* and *B* discover the queue is empty, and block waiting for calls to answer. The switchboard thread *S* puts a call in the queue, and calls `notify()` to wake up one operator thread. Because the notification is asynchronous, however, there is a delay. *S* then returns and places another call in the queue, and because the queue already had a waiting call, it does not notify other threads. The switchboard's `notify()` finally takes effect, waking up *A*, but not *B*, even though there is a call for *B* to answer. This pitfall is called the *lost-wakeup* problem: One or more waiting threads fail to be notified that the condition for which they are waiting has become true. See Section 8.2.2 for a more detailed discussion.

A.2.3 Yielding and sleeping

In addition to the `wait()` method, which allows a thread holding a lock to release the lock and pause, Java provides other ways for a thread that does not hold a lock to

---

[2] This program will not compile because the `wait()` call can throw `InterruptedException`, which must be caught or rethrown. As discussed in Pragma 8.2.1, real code must handle such exceptions, but we often elide such handlers to make the examples easier to read.

pause. A yield() call pauses the thread, asking the scheduler to run something else. The scheduler decides whether to pause the thread, and when to restart it. If there are no other threads to run, the scheduler may ignore the yield() call. Section 16.4.2 describes how yielding can be an effective way to prevent livelock. A call to sleep(t), where t is a time value, instructs the scheduler not to run that thread for that duration. The scheduler is free to restart the thread at any later time.

A.2.4 Thread-local objects

Often it is useful for each thread to have its own private instance of a variable. Java supports such *thread-local* objects through the ThreadLocal<T> class, which manages a collection of objects of type T, one for each thread. Because thread-local variables were not built into Java, they have a somewhat complicated and awkward interface. Nevertheless, they are extremely useful, and we use them often, so we review how to use them here.

The ThreadLocal<T> class provides get() and set() methods that read and update the thread's local value, and an initialValue() method that is called the first time a thread tries to get the value of a thread-local object. To initialize each thread's local value appropriately, we define a *subclass* of ThreadLocal<T> that overrides the parent's initialValue() method.

This mechanism is best illustrated by an example. In many of our algorithms, we assume that each of n concurrent threads has a unique thread-local identifier between 0 and $n - 1$. To provide such an identifier, we show how to define a ThreadID class with a single static method: get() returns the calling thread's identifier. When a thread calls get() for the first time, it is assigned the next unused identifier. Each subsequent call by that thread returns that thread's identifier.

Fig. A.3 shows the simplest way to use a thread-local object to implement this useful class. Line 2 declares an integer nextID field that holds the next identifier to be issued. Lines 3–7 define an *inner class* accessible only within the body of the enclosing ThreadID class. This inner class manages the thread's identifier. It is a subclass of ThreadLocal<Integer> that overrides the initialValue() method to assign the next unused identifier to the current thread.

Here is an example how the ThreadID class might be used:

```
thread = new Thread(new Runnable() {
  public void run() {
    System.out.println("Hello world from thread " + ThreadID.get());
  }
});
```

Because the inner ThreadLocalID class is used exactly once, it makes little sense to give it a name (for the same reason that it makes little sense to name your Thanksgiving turkey). Instead, it is more common to use an anonymous class as described earlier.

```
1   public class ThreadID {
2     private static volatile int nextID = 0;
3     private static class ThreadLocalID extends ThreadLocal<Integer> {
4       protected synchronized Integer initialValue() {
5         return nextID++;
6       }
7     }
8     private static ThreadLocalID threadID = new ThreadLocalID();
9     public static int get() {
10      return threadID.get();
11    }
12    public static void set(int index) {
13      threadID.set(index);
14    }
15  }
```

FIGURE A.3

The ThreadID class: Give each thread a unique identifier.

PRAGMA A.2.1

In the type expression ThreadLocal<Integer>, we use Integer instead of **int** because **int** is a primitive type, and only reference types, such as Integer, are allowed in angle brackets. Since Java 1.5, a feature called *autoboxing* allows you to use **int** and Integer values more-or-less interchangeably, for example:

```
Integer x = 5;
int y = 6;
Integer z = x + y;
```

Consult your Java reference manual for complete details.

A.2.5 Randomization

Randomization is an important tool for algorithm design; several algorithms in this book use randomization to reduce contention, for example. When using randomization, it is important to understand the properties of the random number generator used. For example, the Math.random method uses a single global instance of the java.util.Random class to generate random numbers. Although Random is thread-safe, concurrent calls to the same instance by multiple threads can introduce contention and synchronization.

To avoid this contention, we use the ThreadLocalRandom class from the java.util. concurrent package, which, as its name suggests, maintains a separate random number generator[3] for each thread. The static method current() returns the random number generator associated with the caller; it is recommended to always call this method when using ThreadLocalRandom. For example, to generate a random **int** from 0 to $k - 1$, we call

```
ThreadLocalRandom.current().getInt(k)
```

The random numbers generated by ThreadLocalRandom are *not* cryptographically secure. If such security is required, consider using java.security.SecureRandom instead. However, if you do, then be careful not to introduce contention by having multiple threads concurrently access the same random number generator.

A.3 The Java memory model

The Java programming language does not guarantee linearizability, or even sequential consistency, when reading or writing fields of shared objects. Why not? The principal reason is that strict adherence to sequential consistency would outlaw widely used compiler optimizations, such as register allocation, common subexpression elimination, and redundant read elimination, all of which involve reordering memory reads and writes. In a single-thread computation, such reorderings are invisible to the optimized program, but in a multithreaded computation, one thread can spy on another and observe out-of-order executions.

The Java memory model satisfies the *fundamental property* of relaxed memory models: If a program's sequentially consistent executions follow certain rules, then every execution of that program in the relaxed model will still be sequentially consistent. In this section, we describe rules that guarantee that the Java programs are sequentially consistent. We do not try to cover the complete set of rules, which is rather large and complex. Instead, we focus on a set of straightforward rules that suffices for most purposes.

Fig. A.4 shows *double-checked locking*, a once-common programming idiom that falls victim to Java's lack of sequential consistency. Here, the Singleton class manages a single instance of a Singleton object, accessible through the getInstance() method. This method creates the instance the first time it is called. This method must be synchronized to ensure that only one instance is created, even if several threads observe instance to be *null*. Once the instance has been created, however, no further synchronization should be necessary. As an optimization, the code in Fig. A.4 enters the synchronized block only when it observes an instance to be *null*. Once it has entered, it *double-checks* that instance is still *null* before creating the instance.

This pattern is incorrect: At line 5, the constructor call appears to take place before the instance field is assigned, but the Java memory model allows these steps to occur

---

[3] Technically, this is a *pseudorandom number generator*.

```
1  public static Singleton getInstance() {
2    if (instance == null) {
3      synchronized(Singleton.class) {
4        if (instance == null)
5          instance = new Singleton();
6      }
7    }
8    return instance;
9  }
```

FIGURE A.4

Double-checked locking.

out of order, effectively making a partially initialized Singleton object visible to other threads.

In the Java memory model, objects reside in a shared memory and each thread has a private working memory that contains cached copies of fields it has read or written. In the absence of explicit synchronization (explained later), a thread that writes to a field might not propagate that update to the shared memory right away, and a thread that reads a field might not update its working memory if the field's copy in the shared memory changes value. Naturally, a Java virtual machine is free to keep such cached copies consistent, and in practice they often do, but they are not required to do so. At this point, we can guarantee only that a thread's own reads and writes appear to that thread to happen in order, and that any field value read by a thread was written to that field (i.e., values do not appear out of thin air).

Certain statements are *synchronization events*. The term "synchronization" usually implies some form of atomicity or mutual exclusion. In Java, however, it also implies reconciling a thread's working memory with the shared memory. Some synchronization events cause a thread to write cached changes back to shared memory, making those changes visible to other threads. Other synchronization events cause the thread to invalidate its cached values, forcing it to reread field values from memory, making other threads' changes visible. Synchronization events are linearizable: They are totally ordered, and all threads agree on that ordering. We now look at different kinds of synchronization events.

A.3.1 Locks and synchronized blocks

A thread can achieve mutual exclusion either by entering a **synchronized** block or method, which acquires an implicit lock, or by acquiring an explicit lock (such as the ReentrantLock from the java.util.concurrent.locks package). These approaches have the same implications for memory behavior.

If all accesses to a particular field are protected by the same lock, then reads and writes to that field are linearizable. Specifically, when a thread releases a lock, modified fields in working memory are written back to shared memory, performing modifications while holding the lock accessible to other threads. When a thread acquires the lock, it invalidates its working memory to ensure fields are reread from shared memory. Together, these conditions ensure that reads and writes to the fields of any object protected by a single lock are linearizable.

A.3.2 Volatile fields

Volatile fields are linearizable. Reading a volatile field is like acquiring a lock: The working memory is invalidated and the volatile field's current value is reread from memory. Writing a volatile field is like releasing a lock: The volatile field is immediately written back to memory.

Although reading and writing a volatile field has the same effect on memory consistency as acquiring and releasing a lock, multiple reads and writes are not atomic. For example, if x is a volatile variable, the expression x++ will not necessarily increment x if concurrent threads can modify x. Some form of mutual exclusion is needed as well. One common usage pattern for volatile variables occurs when a field is read by multiple threads but written by only one.

Also, the compiler does not remove accesses to **volatile** fields, nor the shared-memory accesses of synchronization methods.

PRAGMA A.3.1

Arrays require special attention: If a field or variable containing an array is declared **volatile**, only accesses to the field or variable must be synchronized; accesses to the *elements* of the array need not be synchronized. Therefore, when access to the elements of an array must be synchronized, we must use a special array type that provides such synchronized access.

The java.util.concurrent.atomic package includes classes that provide linearizable memory such as AtomicReference<T> or AtomicInteger. The compareAndSet() and set() methods act like volatile writes, and get() acts like a volatile read.

A.3.3 Final fields

Recall that a field declared to be **final** cannot be modified once it has been initialized. An object's final fields are initialized in its constructor. If the constructor follows certain simple rules, described in the following paragraphs, then the correct value of any final fields will be visible to other threads without synchronization. For example, in the code shown in Fig. A.5, a thread that calls reader() is guaranteed to see x equal to 3, because x is a final field. There is no guarantee that y will be equal to 4, because y is not final.

```
1   class FinalFieldExample {
2     final int x; int y;
3     static FinalFieldExample f;
4     public FinalFieldExample() {
5       x = 3;
6       y = 4;
7     }
8     static void writer() {
9       f = new FinalFieldExample();
10    }
11    static void reader() {
12      if (f != null) {
13        int i = f.x; int j = f.y;
14      }
15    }
16  }
```

FIGURE A.5

Constructor with final field.

```
1   public class EventListener { // this is incorrect
2     final int x;
3     public EventListener(EventSource eventSource) {
4       eventSource.registerListener(this); // register with event source ...
5     }
6     public onEvent(Event e) {
7       ... // handle the event
8     }
9   }
```

FIGURE A.6

Incorrect EventListener class.

If a constructor is synchronized incorrectly, however, final fields may be observed to change value. The rule is simple: The **this** reference must not be released from the constructor before the constructor returns.

Fig. A.6 shows an example of an incorrect constructor in an event-driven system. Here, an EventListener class registers itself with an EventSource class, making a reference to the listener object accessible to other threads. This code may appear safe, since registration is the last step in the constructor, but it is incorrect because if another thread calls the event listener's onEvent() method before the constructor finishes, then the onEvent() method is not guaranteed to see a correct value for x.

In summary, reads and writes to fields are linearizable if the field is either volatile or protected by a unique lock that is acquired by all readers and writers.

A.4 C++

Prior to the 2011 C++ standard (C++11), C++ did not have native support for threads. Instead, like C, it relied on operating system-specific mechanisms for threading. This reliance came at a steep cost: Code was not portable across operating systems, and programmers could not reason formally about the correctness of their code.

Since 2011, C++ has used a concurrency model that includes threads, locks, condition variables, and std::atomic<> variables. To use these features, a programmer must include the appropriate header files:

```
#include <thread> // thread objects; since C++11
#include <mutex> // mutual exclusion locks; since C++11
#include <atomic> // atomic variables; Since C++11
#include <shared_mutex> // readers/writer locks; since C++14
#include <condition_variable> // condition variables; Since C++14
```

It may also be necessary to provide a flag at compile time to enable these features (e.g., -std=c++11 or -std=c++14). The C++ standard is updated every 3 years, and each update since C++11 has added additional features for concurrency.

A.4.1 Threads in C++

The std::thread object represents a thread. The constructor to this object can take either a function or a lambda expression. Arguments to that function or lambda can also be provided, as shown in the example in Fig. A.7. (On certain operating systems, such as some flavors of Linux, the linker may need to be given pthread-related flags (e.g., -lpthread) in order to compile the program.)

On lines 10 and 12, the threads are created by providing the name of the function that the thread should run. In the former case, the function takes no parameters. In the latter, it takes two integer arguments, which are also passed to the thread constructor.

In addition, a thread can be created by providing it with a lambda to execute. The examples on lines 17–32 illustrate some of the ways that a thread can be given a lambda expression to run.

In C++, unlike Java, a single call creates the thread and also starts executing it. A program must call join on all of its threads before terminating.[4] A common idiom is to store created threads in a std::vector, so that they are easily found and joined. An example appears below:

```
std::vector<std::thread> threads;
for (int i = 0; i < 16; ++i)
  threads.push_back(std::thread(f, i));
for (int i = 0; i < 16; ++i)
  threads[i].join();
```

---

[4] This requirement can be avoided by using a thread's detach() method.

```
1   #include <iostream>
2   #include <thread>
3
4   void f1() { std::cout << "Hello from f1" << std::endl; }
5   void f2(int a, int b) {
6     std::cout << "f2 invoked with " << a << ", " << b << std::endl;
7   }
8
9   int main() {
10    std::thread t1(f1);
11    t1.join();
12    std::thread t2(f2, 1, 2);
13    t2.join();
14    std::thread t3(f2, 5, 7);
15    t3.join();
16    int i = 7;
17    std::thread t4([&]() {
18      std::cout << "lambda invoked with captured i == " << i << std::endl;
19    });
20    t4.join();
21    std::thread t5(
22        [&](int a) {
23          std::cout << "lambda invoked with captured i == " << i
24                    << " and a == " << a << std::endl;
25        },
26        1024);
27    t5.join();
28    auto f = [&](int k) {
29      f1();
30      f2(i, i * k);
31    };
32    std::thread t6(f, 99);
33    t6.join();
34  }
```

FIGURE A.7

Examples of creating and joining threads in C++.

A.4.2 Locks in C++

The most commonly used locks in C++ are std::mutex, std::recursive_mutex, and std::shared_mutex. Programmers acquire and release a std::mutex by using its lock() and unlock() methods. There is also a try_lock() method, which prevents a thread from blocking when it attempts to acquire a lock that is held by another thread:

```
std::mutex m;
```

```
...
m.lock();
f();
m.unlock();
...
if (m.try_lock()) {
  f();
  m.unlock();
} else {
  std::cout << "couldn't acquire lock" << std::endl;
}
```

A std::recursive_mutex maintains an internal counter and ID field, so that a thread that attempts to lock() a mutex that it already holds does not block but instead increments the counter. A thread must unlock() a recursive_mutex as many times as it has locked it. The std::shared_mutex supports all the operations of std::mutex, and also has methods lock_shared(), unlock_shared(), and try_lock_shared(), which allow threads to use it as a readers–writers lock.

Although C++ does not have finally blocks, the *resource-acquisition-is-initialization* (RAII) idiom can be used to achieve the same effect: If an object is constructed on the stack, its destructor runs when the object goes out of scope. The std::lock_guard wrapper object manages lock acquisition and release:

```
std::mutex m;
...
{
  std::lock_guard<std::mutex> g(m);
  // mutex m is locked
  if (i == 9)
    return; // releases m because g destructs
  f();
  // releases m because g destructs
}
```

A.4.3 Condition variables

C++14 added condition variables as a language feature. Condition variables can be used to create objects that behave like Java monitors. However, programmers must explicitly manage the association between mutexes and condition variables.

One complication that arises is that std::lock_guard does not allow a programmer to unlock and relock the mutex: for as long as the lock_guard is in scope, the mutex must be acquired. When a condition variable is used to make a thread wait, the critical section must break atomicity. To do so, it must release the lock. It would be unfortunate if programmers had to give up the convenience of lock_guard when using condition variables. Fortunately, the std::unique_lock wrapper is like lock_guard, but also allows threads to unlock and relock the underlying mutex. See Fig. A.8 for an example.

```
1   #include <condition_variable>
2   #include <iostream>
3   #include <mutex>
4   #include <string>
5   #include <thread>
6
7   std::mutex m;
8   std::condition_variable cv_full, cv_empty;
9   int data;
10  bool data_ready;
11
12  void consumer_thread(int items) {
13    for (int i = 0; i < items; ++i) {
14      std::unique_lock<std::mutex> g(m);
15      cv_full.wait(g, []() { return data_ready; });
16      std::cout << "consumed " << data << std::endl;
17      data_ready = false;
18      cv_empty.notify_one();
19    }
20  }
21  void producer_thread(int count, int *items) {
22    for (int i = 0; i < count; ++i) {
23      std::unique_lock<std::mutex> g(m);
24      cv_empty.wait(g, []() { return !data_ready; });
25      data = items[i];
26      std::cout << "produced " << data << std::endl;
27      data_ready = true;
28      cv_full.notify_one();
29    }
30  }
31  int main() {
32    int items[] = {1, 1, 2, 3, 5, 8, 13, 21, 34, 55};
33    std::thread producer(producer_thread, 10, items);
34    std::thread consumer(consumer_thread, 10);
35    producer.join();
36    consumer.join();
37  }
```

FIGURE A.8

Example of using condition variables in C++.

The std::condition_variable object requires that its associated mutex is accessed through a unique_lock. The std::condition_variable object provides two different wait() methods. We use the more advanced version, which takes a predicate as a second parameter and uses it to decide when to stop waiting. Consider the call to wait() on line 24. It could be written as:

```
while (data_ready)
  cv_empty.wait(g);
```

While this code is equivalent, most programmers prefer to use a predicate, which avoids having to remember that condition variables, like Java monitors, are subject to spurious wakeups.

Condition variables also have methods that let the programmer control how a thread waits (e.g., by incorporating timeouts). There is also a notify_all() to wake all threads that are waiting on a condition variable. C++ allows the programmer to call notify_one or notify_all while holding the lock, and also while not holding the lock. Although notifying without the lock may be faster in some cases, it is easier to assert the correctness of code when it holds the lock while calling a notify function.

A.4.4 Atomic variables

The C++ memory model allows programmers to reason about the correctness of programs. It defines a happens-before order between thread lifecycle events (e.g., via thread constructors and calls to join()), and ensures that programmers can reason about the orders that are created among threads that use a common mutex. For fine-grained ordering, C++ defines the std::atomic<> type, which is similar to **volatile** in Java: By default, these variables are never cached in registers by the compiler, and their use implies fences and ordering (both during compilation and during execution) with respect to both regular data accesses and other std::atomic<> accesses.

Similar to **volatile** in Java, std::atomic<> can represent atomic scalar values, atomic floating-point values, and atomic pointers. It is also possible to have pointers to std::atomic<>, an improvement over **volatile** in Java. Through operator overloading, std::atomic<> integers support fetch-and-modify operations for arithmetic and logic. For example, in the following code, increments of x will be achieved via a hardware read–modify–write operation, and will not be vulnerable to races:

```
std::atomic<int> counter;
...
{
  counter++;
  --counter;
  counter *= 16;
  counter ^= 0xFACE;
}
```

The std::atomic<> type also provides compare_exchange_strong() for performing compare-and-set operations.

When accessing a std::atomic<> variable, a programmer can treat it as if it were of a nonatomic type. For example, the following are valid:

```
std::atomic<int> my_int;
my_int = 7;
int local = my_int;
```

When a program uses this syntax, the compiler will enforce the strictest ordering that it can. That is, an atomic load will prevent subsequent accesses from happening before it, a store will prevent preceding accesses from happening after it, and any read–modify–write operation will prevent any reorderings across it. A programmer can relax these orderings by using explicit load and store methods:

```
std::atomic<int> my_int;
my_int.store(7);
int local = my_int.load();
```

By default, the load and store methods ensure strict ordering, but the guarantees can be relaxed by specifying an additional parameter (e.g., std::memory_order_relaxed). In some programs, such relaxation can significantly improve performance. This idea is explored, briefly, in Chapter 20.

A.4.5 Thread-local storage

In C++, variable may have the thread_local storage class specifier, which indicates that each thread reads and writes a different logical instance of the variable. For example, in the code in Fig. A.9, many threads increment a shared counter, and also thread-local counters.

```
thread_local int local_counter = 0;
std::atomic<int> global_counter(0);
std::mutex m;

void increment(int howmany) {
  for (int i = 0; i < howmany; ++i) {
    local_counter++;
    global_counter++;
  }
  std::lock_guard<std::mutex> g(m);
  std::cout << "Thread exiting with local = " << local_counter
            << " and global = " << global_counter << std::endl;
}
int run_threads(int thread_count, int increments_per_thread) {
  std::vector<std::thread> threads;
  for (int i = 0; i < thread_count; ++i)
    threads.push_back(std::thread(increment, increments_per_thread));
  for (int i = 0; i < thread_count; ++i)
    threads[i].join();
}
```

FIGURE A.9

A C++ program that uses thread-local variables.

If we call `run_threads` with multiple threads (e.g., `run_threads(4, 1048576);`), the final value of the global counter will be equal to the sum of the `increments_per_thread` values passed to each of the threads. The threads increment the counter concurrently. As they do so, they also increment `local_counter`. However, each thread's increments are to a per-thread copy. Thus there are no races on `local_counter`, and its value does not equal `global_counter` when the program completes.

A.5 C#

C# is a Java-like language that runs on Microsoft's .Net platform.

A.5.1 Threads

C# provides a threading model similar to Java's. C# threads are implemented by the `System.Threading.Thread` class. When you create a thread, you tell it what to do by passing it a `ThreadStart` *delegate*, a kind of pointer to the method you want to call. For example, here is a method that prints a simple message:

```
void HelloWorld()
{
    Console.WriteLine("Hello World");
}
```

We then turn this method into a `ThreadStart` delegate, and pass that delegate to the thread constructor:

```
ThreadStart hello = new ThreadStart(HelloWorld);
Thread thread = new Thread(hello);
```

C# provides a syntactic shortcut, called an *anonymous method*, that allows you to define a delegate directly, for example, by combining the previous steps into a single expression:

```
Thread thread = new Thread(delegate()
{
    Console.WriteLine("Hello World");
});
```

As in Java, after a thread has been created, it must be *started*:

```
thread.Start();
```

This call causes the thread to run, while the caller returns immediately. If the caller wants to wait for the thread to finish, it must *join* the thread:

```
thread.Join();
```

The caller is blocked until the thread's method returns.

Fig. A.10 shows a method that initializes a number of threads, starts them, waits for them to finish, and then prints out a message. The method creates an array of

```
1   static void Main(string[] args)
2   {
3       Thread[] thread = new Thread[8];
4       // create threads
5       for (int i = 0; i < thread.Length; i++)
6       {
7           String message = "Hello world from thread" + i;
8           ThreadStart hello = delegate()
9           {
10              Console.WriteLine(message);
11          };
12          thread[i] = new Thread(hello);
13      }
14      // start threads
15      for (int i = 0; i < thread.Length; i++)
16      {
17          thread[i].Start();
18      }
19      // wait for them to finish
20      for (int i = 0; i < thread.Length; i++)
21      {
22          thread[i].Join();
23      }
24      Console.WriteLine("done!");
25  }
```

FIGURE A.10

This method initializes a number of C# threads, starts them, waits for them to finish, and then prints out a message.

threads, initializing each thread with its own ThreadStart delegate. We then start the threads, and each thread executes its delegate, displaying its message. Finally, we wait for each thread to finish, and display a message when they are all done. Except for minor syntactic differences, this code is similar to what you would write in Java.

A.5.2 Monitors

For simple mutual exclusion, C# provides the ability to *lock* an object much like the synchronized modifier in Java:

```
int GetAndIncrement()
{
    lock (this)
    {
        return value++;
    }
}
```

```
1    class Queue<T>
2    {
3        int head, tail;
4        T[] call;
5        public Queue(int capacity)
6        {
7            call = new T[capacity];
8            head = tail = 0;
9        }
10       public void Enq(T x)
11       {
12           Monitor.Enter(this);
13           try
14           {
15               while (tail - head == call.Length)
16               {
17                   Monitor.Wait(this); // queue is full
18               }
19               calls[(tail++) % call.Length] = x;
20               Monitor.Pulse(this);  // notify waiting dequeuers
21           }
22           finally
23           {
24               Monitor.Exit(this);
25           }
26       }
27       public T Deq()
28       {
29           Monitor.Enter(this);
30           try
31           {
32               while (tail == head)
33               {
34                   Monitor.Wait(this); // queue is empty
35               }
36               T y = calls[(head++) % call.Length];
37               Monitor.Pulse(this);  // notify waiting enqueuers
38               return y;
39           }
40           finally
41           {
42               Monitor.Exit(this);
43           }
44       }
45   }
```

FIGURE A.11

A bounded Queue class.

Unlike Java, C# does not allow you to use a lock statement to modify a method directly. Instead, the lock statement is used to enclose the method body.

Concurrent data structures require more than mutual exclusion: They also require the ability to wait and signal conditions. Unlike in Java, where every object is an implicit monitor, in C# you must explicitly create the monitor associated with an object. To acquire a monitor lock, call Monitor.Enter(this), and to release the lock, call Monitor.Exit(this). Each monitor has a single implicit condition, which is waited upon by Monitor.Wait(this), and signaled by Monitor.Pulse(this) or Monitor.PulseAll(this), which respectively wake up one or all sleeping threads. Fig. A.11 shows how to implement a bounded queue using C# monitors.

A.5.3 Thread-local objects

C# provides a very simple way to make a static field thread-local: Simply prefix the field declaration with the attribute [ThreadStatic]:

```
[ThreadStatic]
static int value;
```

Do not provide an initial value for a [ThreadStatic] field, because the initialization happens once, not once per thread. Instead, each thread will find the field initially has that type's default value: zero for integers, *null* for references, and so on.

Fig. A.12 shows how to implement the ThreadID class (Java version in Fig. A.3). There is one point about this program that may require a comment. The first time a thread inspects its [ThreadStatic] identifier, that field will be zero, the default value for integers. To distinguish between an uninitialized zero and a thread ID zero, this field holds the thread ID displaced by one: Thread 0 has field value 1, and so on.

```
1   class ThreadID
2   {
3       [ThreadStatic] static int myID;
4       static int counter;
5       public static int get()
6       {
7           if (myID == 0)
8           {
9               myID = Interlocked.Increment(ref counter);
10          }
11          return myID - 1;
12      }
13  }
```

FIGURE A.12

The ThreadID class provides each thread a unique identifier implemented using [ThreadStatic].

A.6 Appendix notes

The Java programming language was created by James Gosling [52]. Dennis Ritchie is credited with creating C. The basic monitor model is credited to Tony Hoare [77] and Per Brinch Hansen [57], although they used different mechanisms for waiting and notification. The mechanisms used by Java (and later by C#) were originally proposed by Butler Lampson and David Redell [107].

Hardware basics

B

A novice was trying to fix a broken Lisp machine by turning the power off and on. Knight, seeing what the student was doing spoke sternly: "You cannot fix a machine just by power-cycling it with no understanding of what is going wrong." Knight turned the machine off and on. The machine worked.

(From "AI Koans," a collection of jokes popular at MIT in the 1980s.)

B.1 Introduction (and a puzzle)

You can do a pretty good job of programming a uniprocessor without understanding much about computer architecture, but the same is not true of multiprocessors. You cannot program a multiprocessor effectively unless you know what a multiprocessor *is*. We illustrate this point by a puzzle. We consider two programs that are logically equivalent, but one is much less efficient than the other. Ominously, the simpler program is the inefficient one. This discrepancy cannot be explained, nor the danger avoided, without a basic understanding of modern multiprocessor architectures.

Here is the background to the puzzle. Suppose two threads share a resource that can be used by only one thread at a time. To prevent concurrent use, each thread must *lock* the resource before using it, and *unlock* it afterward. We study many ways to implement locks in Chapter 7. For the puzzle, we consider two simple implementations in which the lock is a single Boolean field. If the field is *false*, the lock is free, and otherwise it is in use. We manipulate the lock with the getAndSet(v) method, which atomically swaps its argument v with the field value. To acquire the lock, a thread calls getAndSet(*true*). If the call returns *false*, then the lock was free, and the caller succeeded in locking the object. Otherwise, the object was already locked, and the thread must try again later. A thread releases a lock simply by storing *false* into the Boolean field.

In Fig. B.1, the *test-and-set* (TASLock) lock repeatedly calls getAndSet(*true*) (line 4) until it returns *false*. By contrast, in Fig. B.2, the *test-and-test-and-set* lock (TTASLock) repeatedly reads the lock field (by calling state.get() at line 5) until it returns *false*, and only then calls getAndSet() (line 6). It is important to understand that reading the lock value is atomic, and applying getAndSet() to the lock value is atomic, but the combination is not atomic: Between the time a thread reads the lock value and the time it calls getAndSet(), the lock value may have changed.

```
1  public class TASLock implements Lock {
2    ...
3    public void lock() {
4      while (state.getAndSet(true)) {} // spin
5    }
6    ...
7  }
```

FIGURE B.1

The TASLock class.

```
1   public class TTASLock implements Lock {
2     ...
3     public void lock() {
4       while (true) {
5         while (state.get()) {}; // spin
6         if (!state.getAndSet(true))
7           return;
8       }
9     }
10    ...
11  }
```

FIGURE B.2

The TTASLock class.

Before you proceed, you should convince yourself that the TASLock and TTASLock algorithms are logically the same. The reason is simple: In the TTASLock algorithm, reading that the lock is free does not guarantee that the next call to getAndSet() will succeed, because some other thread may have acquired the lock in the interval between reading the lock and trying to acquire it. So why bother reading the lock before trying to acquire it?

Here is the puzzle: While the two lock implementations may be logically equivalent, they perform very differently. In a classic 1989 experiment, Anderson measured the time needed to execute a simple test program on several contemporary multiprocessors. He measured the elapsed time for n threads to execute a short critical section one million times. Fig. B.3 shows how long each lock takes, plotted as a function of the number of threads. In a perfect world, both the TASLock and TTASLock curves would be as flat as the ideal curve on the bottom, since each run does the same number of increments. Instead, we see that both curves slope up, indicating that lock-induced delay increases with the number of threads. Curiously, however, the TASLock is much slower than the TTASLock lock, especially as the number of threads increases. Why?

This appendix covers much of what you need to know about multiprocessor architecture to write efficient concurrent algorithms and data structures. Along the way, we will explain the divergent curves in Fig. B.3.

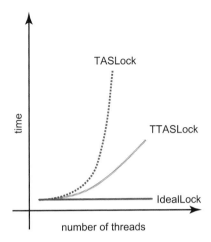

FIGURE B.3

Schematic performance of a TASLock, a TTASLock, and an ideal lock.

We are concerned with the following components:

- The *processors* are hardware devices that execute software *threads*. There are typically more threads than processors, and each processor runs a thread for a while, sets it aside, and turns its attention to another thread.
- The *interconnect* is a communication medium that links processors to processors and processors to memory.
- The *memory* is actually a hierarchy of components that store data, ranging from one or more levels of small, fast *caches* to a large and relatively slow *main memory*. Understanding how these levels interact is essential to understanding the actual performance of many concurrent algorithms.

From our point of view, one architectural principle drives everything else: *Processors and main memory are far apart*. It takes a long time for a processor to read a value from memory. It also takes a long time for a processor to write a value to memory, and longer still for the processor to be sure that value has actually been installed in memory. Accessing memory is more like mailing a letter than making a phone call. Almost everything we examine in this appendix is the result of trying to alleviate the long time it takes ("high latency") to access memory.

Processor and memory speed change over time, but their *relative* performance changes slowly. Consider the following analogy. Imagine that it is 1980, and you are in charge of a messenger service in mid-town Manhattan. While cars outperform bicycles on the open road, bicycles outperform cars in heavy traffic, so you choose to use bicycles. Even though the technology behind both bicycles and cars has advanced, the *architectural* comparison remains the same. Then, as now, if you are designing an urban messenger service, you should use bicycles, not cars.

B.2 Processors and threads

A multiprocessor consists of multiple hardware *processors*, each of which executes a sequential program. When discussing multiprocessor architectures, the basic unit of time is the *cycle*: the time it takes a processor to fetch and execute a single instruction. In absolute terms, cycle times change as technology advances (from about 10 million cycles per second in 1980 to about 3000 million in 2005), and they vary from one platform to another (processors that control toasters have longer cycles than processors that control web servers). Nevertheless, the relative cost of instructions such as memory access changes slowly when expressed in terms of cycles.

A *thread* is a sequential program. While a processor is a hardware device, a thread is a software construct. A processor can run a thread for a while and then set it aside and run another thread, an event known as a *context switch*. A processor may set aside a thread, or *deschedule* it, for a variety of reasons. Perhaps the thread has issued a memory request that will take some time to satisfy, or perhaps that thread has simply run long enough, and it is time for another thread to make progress. When a thread is descheduled, it may resume execution on another processor.

B.3 Interconnect

The *interconnect* is the medium by which processors communicate with the memory and with other processors. There are essentially two kinds of interconnect architectures in use: *symmetric multiprocessing* (SMP) and *nonuniform memory access* (NUMA). See Fig. B.4.

In an SMP architecture, processors and memory are linked by a *bus* interconnect, a broadcast medium that acts like a tiny ethernet. Both processors and the main memory have *bus controller* units in charge of sending and listening for messages broadcast on the bus. (Listening is sometimes called *snooping*.) SMP architectures are easier to build, but they are not scalable to large numbers of processors because eventually the bus becomes overloaded.

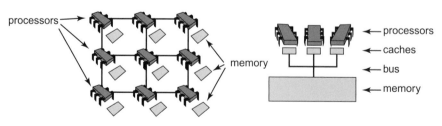

FIGURE B.4

An SMP architecture with caches on the right and a cacheless NUMA architecture on the left.

In a NUMA architecture, a collection of *nodes* are linked by a point-to-point network, like a tiny local area network. Each node contains one or more processors and a local memory. One node's local memory is accessible to the other nodes, and together, the nodes' memories form a global memory shared by all processors. The NUMA name reflects the fact that a processor can access memory residing on its own node faster than it can access memory residing on other nodes. Networks are more complex than buses, and require more elaborate protocols, but they scale better than buses to large numbers of processors.

The division between SMP and NUMA architectures is a simplification: For example, some systems have hybrid architectures, where processors within a cluster communicate over a bus, but processors in different clusters communicate over a network.

From the programmer's point of view, it may not seem important whether the underlying platform is based on a bus, a network, or a hybrid interconnect. It is important, however, to realize that the interconnect is a finite resource shared among the processors. If one processor uses too much of the interconnect's bandwidth, then the others may be delayed.

B.4 Memory

Processors share a *main memory*, which is a large array of *words*, indexed by *address*. The size of a word or an address is platform-dependent, but typically it is either 32 or 64 bits. Simplifying somewhat, a processor reads a value from memory by sending a message containing the desired address to memory. The response message contains the associated *data*, that is, the contents of memory at that address. A processor writes a value by sending the address and the new data to memory, and the memory sends back an acknowledgment when the new data have been installed.

B.5 Caches

On modern architectures, a main memory access may take hundreds of cycles, so there is a real danger that a processor may spend much of its time just waiting for the memory to respond to requests. Modern systems alleviate this problem by introducing one or more *caches*: small memories that are situated closer to the processors and are therefore much faster than main memory. These caches are logically situated "between" the processor and the memory: When a processor attempts to read a value from a given memory address, it first looks to see if the value is already in the cache, and if so, it does not need to perform the slower access to memory. If the desired address's value was found, we say the processor *hits* in the cache, and otherwise it *misses*. In a similar way, if a processor attempts to write an address that is in the cache, it does not need to perform the slower access to memory. The proportion of requests satisfied in the cache is called the cache *hit ratio* (or *hit rate*).

Caches are effective because most programs display a high degree of *locality*: If a processor reads or writes a memory address (also called a memory location), then it is likely to read or write the same location again soon. Moreover, if a processor reads or writes a memory location, then it is also likely to read or write *nearby* locations soon. To exploit this second observation, caches typically operate at a *granularity* larger than a single word: A cache holds a group of neighboring words called *cache lines* (sometimes called *cache blocks*).

In practice, most processors have two or three levels of caches, called $L1$, $L2$, and $L3$ caches. All but the last (and largest) cache typically reside on the same chip as the processor. An L1 cache typically takes one or two cycles to access. An on-chip L2 may take about 10 cycles to access. The last level cache, whether L2 or L3, typically takes tens of cycles to access. These caches are significantly faster than the hundreds of cycles required to access the memory. Of course, these times vary from platform to platform, and many multiprocessors have even more elaborate cache structures.

The original proposals for NUMA architectures did not include caches because it was felt that local memory was enough. Later, however, commercial NUMA architectures did include caches. Sometimes the term *cache-coherent NUMA* (cc-NUMA) is used to mean NUMA architectures with caches. Here, to avoid ambiguity, we use NUMA to include cache-coherence unless we explicitly state otherwise.

Caches are expensive to build and therefore significantly smaller than the memory: Only a fraction of the memory locations will fit in a cache at the same time. We would therefore like the cache to maintain values of the most highly used locations. This implies that when a location needs to be cached and the cache is full, it is necessary to *evict* a line, discarding it if it has not been modified, and writing it back to main memory if it has. A *replacement policy* determines which cache line to replace to make room for a given new location. If the replacement policy is free to replace any line, then we say the cache is *fully associative*. If, on the other hand, there is only one line that can be replaced, then we say the cache is *direct-mapped*. If we split the difference, allowing any line from a *set* of size k to be replaced to make room for a given line, then we say the cache is *k-way set associative*.

B.5.1 Coherence

Sharing (or, less politely, *memory contention*) occurs when one processor reads or writes a memory address that is cached by another. If both processors are reading the data without modifying it, then the data can be cached at both processors. If, however, one processor tries to update the shared cache line, then the other's copy must be *invalidated* to ensure that it does not read an out-of-date value. In its most general form, this problem is called *cache-coherence*. The literature contains a variety of very complex and clever cache coherence protocols. Here we review one of the most commonly used, called the *MESI* protocol (pronounced "messy") after the names of possible cache line states. (Modern processors tend to use more complex protocols with additional states.) Here are the cache line states:

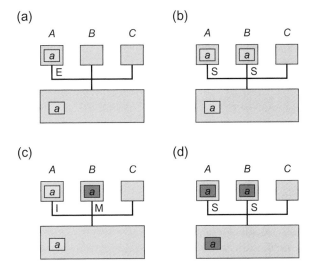

FIGURE B.5

Example of the MESI cache-coherence protocol's state transitions. (a) Processor A reads data from address a, and stores the data in its cache in the *exclusive* state. (b) When processor B attempts to read from the same address, A detects the address conflict, and responds with the associated data. Now a is cached at both A and B in the *shared* state. (c) If B writes to the shared address a, it changes its state to *modified*, and broadcasts a message warning A (and any other processor that might have those data cached) to set its cache line state to *invalid*. (d) If A then reads from a, it broadcasts a request, and B responds by sending the modified data both to A and to the main memory, leaving both copies in the *shared* state.

- *Modified*: The line has been modified in the cache, and it must eventually be written back to main memory. No other processor has this line cached.
- *Exclusive*: The line has not been modified, and no other processor has this line cached.
- *Shared*: The line has not been modified, and other processors may have this line cached.
- *Invalid*: The line does not contain meaningful data.

We illustrate this protocol by a short example depicted in Fig. B.5. For simplicity, we assume processors and memory are linked by a bus.

Processor A reads data from address a, and stores the data in its cache in the *exclusive* state. When processor B attempts to read from the same address, A detects the address conflict, and responds with the associated data. Now a is cached at both A and B in the *shared* state. If B writes to the shared address a, it changes its state to *modified*, and broadcasts a message warning A (and any other processor that might have those data cached) to set its cache line state to *invalid*. If A then reads from a, it broadcasts a request, and B responds by sending the modified data both to A and to the main memory, leaving both copies in the *shared* state.

False sharing occurs when processors that are accessing logically distinct data nevertheless conflict because the locations they are accessing lie on the same cache line. This observation illustrates a difficult trade-off: Large cache lines are good for locality, but they increase the likelihood of false sharing. The likelihood of false sharing can be reduced by ensuring that data objects that might be accessed concurrently by independent threads lie far enough apart in memory. For example, having multiple threads share a byte array invites false sharing, but having them share an array of double-precision integers is less dangerous.

B.5.2 Spinning

A processor is *spinning* if it is repeatedly testing some word in memory, waiting for another processor to change it. Depending on the architecture, spinning can have a dramatic effect on overall system performance.

On an SMP architecture without caches, spinning is a very bad idea. Each time the processor reads the memory, it consumes bus bandwidth without accomplishing any useful work. Because the bus is a broadcast medium, these requests directed to memory may prevent other processors from making progress.

On a NUMA architecture without caches, spinning may be acceptable if the address in question resides in the processor's local memory. Even though multiprocessor architectures without caches are rare, we will still ask, when we consider a synchronization protocol that involves spinning, whether it permits each processor to spin on its own local memory.

On an SMP or NUMA architecture with caches, spinning consumes significantly fewer resources. The first time the processor reads the address, it takes a cache miss, and loads the contents of that address into a cache line. Thereafter, as long as those data remain unchanged, the processor simply rereads from its own cache, consuming no interconnect bandwidth, a process known as *local spinning*. When the cache state changes, the processor takes a single cache miss, observes that the data have changed, and stops spinning.

B.6 Cache-conscious programming, or the puzzle solved

We now know enough to explain why the TTASLock examined in Appendix B.1 outperforms the TASLock. Each time the TASLock applies getAndSet(*true*) to the lock, it sends a message on the interconnect causing a substantial amount of traffic. In an SMP architecture, the resulting traffic may be enough to saturate the interconnect, delaying all threads, including a thread trying to release the lock, or even threads not contending for the lock. By contrast, while the lock is busy, the TTASLock spins, reading a locally cached copy of the lock, and producing no interconnect traffic, explaining its improved performance.

The TTASLock is still far from ideal. When the lock is released, all its cached copies are invalidated, and all waiting threads call getAndSet(*true*), resulting in a burst of traffic, smaller than that of the TASLock, but nevertheless significant.

We further discuss the interactions of caches with locking in Chapter 7. Here we consider some simple ways to structure data to avoid false sharing.

- Objects or fields that are accessed independently should be aligned and padded so that they end up on different cache lines.
- Keep read-only data separate from data that are modified frequently. For example, consider a list whose structure is constant, but whose elements' value fields change frequently. To ensure that modifications do not slow down list traversals, one could align and pad the value fields so that each one fills up a cache line.
- When possible, split an object into thread-local pieces. For example, a counter used for statistics could be split into an array of counters, one per thread, each one residing on a different cache line. Splitting the counter allows each thread to update its own replica, avoiding the invalidation traffic that would be incurred by having a single shared counter.
- If a lock protects data that is frequently modified, then keep the lock and the data on distinct cache lines, so that threads trying to acquire the lock do not interfere with the lock-holder's access to the data.
- If a lock protects data that are frequently uncontended, then try to keep the lock and the data on the same cache lines, so that acquiring the lock will also load some of the data into the cache.

B.7 Multicore and multithreaded architectures

In a *multicore* architecture, as in Fig. B.6, multiple processors are placed on the same chip. Each processor on that chip typically has its own L1 cache, but they share a

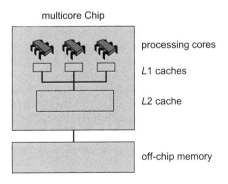

FIGURE B.6

A multicore SMP architecture. The *L2* cache is on chip and shared by all processors while the memory is off-chip.

common L2 cache. Processors can communicate efficiently through the shared L2 cache, avoiding the need to go through memory, and to invoke the cumbersome cache-coherence protocol.

In a *multithreaded* architecture, a single processor may execute two or more threads at once. Many modern processors have substantial internal parallelism. They can execute instructions out of order, or in parallel (e.g., keeping both fixed and floating-point units busy), or even execute instructions speculatively before branches or data have been computed. To keep hardware units busy, multithreaded processors can mix instructions from multiple streams.

Modern processor architectures combine multicore with multithreading, where multiple individually multithreaded cores may reside on the same chip. The context switches on some multicore chips are inexpensive and are performed at a very fine granularity, essentially context switching on every instruction. Thus, multithreading serves to hide the high latency of accessing memory: Whenever a thread accesses memory, the processor allows another thread to execute.

B.7.1 Relaxed memory consistency

When a processor writes a value to memory, that value is kept in the cache and marked as *dirty*, meaning that it must eventually be written back to main memory. On most modern processors, write requests are not applied to memory when they are issued. Rather, they are collected in a hardware queue called a *write buffer* (or *store buffer*), and applied to memory together at a later time. A write buffer provides two benefits. First, it is often more efficient to issue several requests together, a phenomenon called *batching*. Second, if a thread writes to an address more than once, earlier requests can be discarded, saving a trip to memory, a phenomenon called *write absorption*.

The use of write buffers has a very important consequence: The order in which reads and writes are issued to memory is not necessarily the order in which they occur in the program. For example, recall the flag principle of Chapter 1, which was crucial to the correctness of mutual exclusion: If two processors each first write their own flag and then read the other's flag location, then one of them will see the other's newly written flag value. With write buffers, this is no longer true: both threads may write, each in its respective write buffer, but these writes might not be applied to the shared memory until after each processor reads the other's flag location in memory. Thus, neither reads the other's flag.

Compilers make matters even worse. They are good at optimizing performance on single-processor architectures. Often, this optimization involves *reordering* a thread's reads and writes to memory. Such reordering is invisible for single-threaded programs, but it can have unexpected consequences for multithreaded programs in which threads may observe the order in which writes occur. For example, if one thread fills a buffer with data and then sets an indicator to mark the buffer as full, then concurrent threads may see the indicator set before they see the new data, causing them to read stale values. The erroneous *double-checked locking* pattern described in Appendix A.3 is an example of a pitfall produced by unintuitive aspects of the Java memory model.

Different architectures provide different guarantees about the extent to which memory reads and writes can be reordered. As a rule, it is better not to rely on such guarantees, and instead to use more expensive techniques, described in the following paragraph, to prevent such reordering.

Every architecture provides a *memory barrier* instruction (sometimes called a *fence*), which forces writes to take place in the order they are issued, but at a price. A memory barrier flushes the write buffer, ensuring that all writes issued before the barrier become visible to the processor that issued the barrier. Memory barriers are often inserted automatically by atomic read–modify–write operations such as `getAndSet()`, or by standard concurrency libraries. Thus, explicit use of memory barriers is needed only when processors perform read–write instructions on shared variables outside of critical sections.

On one hand, memory barriers are expensive (hundreds of cycles, maybe more), and should be used only when necessary. On the other hand, synchronization bugs can be very difficult to track down, so memory barriers should be used liberally, rather than relying on complex platform-specific guarantees about limits to memory instruction reordering.

The Java language itself allows reads and writes to object fields to be reordered if they occur outside `synchronized` methods or blocks. Java provides a `volatile` keyword that ensures that reads and writes to a `volatile` object field that occur outside `synchronized` blocks or methods are not reordered. (The `atomic` template provides similar guarantees for C++.) Using this keyword can be expensive, so it should be used only when necessary. We note that in principle, one could use volatile fields to make double-checked locking work correctly, but there would not be much point, since accessing volatile variables requires synchronization anyway.

Here ends our primer on multiprocessor hardware. We now continue to discuss these architectural concepts in the context of specific data structures and algorithms. A pattern will emerge: The performance of multiprocessor programs is highly dependent on synergy with the underlying hardware.

B.8 Hardware synchronization instructions

As discussed in Chapter 5, any modern multiprocessor architecture must support powerful synchronization primitives to be universal, that is, to provide concurrent computation's equivalent of a universal Turing machine. It is therefore not surprising that implementations of Java and C++ rely on such specialized hardware instructions (also called hardware primitives) in implementing synchronization, from spin locks and monitors to the most complex lock-free data structures.

Modern architectures typically provide one of two kinds of universal synchronization primitives. The *compare-and-swap* (CAS) instruction is supported in architectures by AMD, Intel, and Oracle. It takes three arguments: an address a in memory, an *expected* value e, and an *update* value v, and returns a Boolean. It *atomically* executes the following: If the memory at address a contains the expected value e, write the update value v to that address and return *true*, otherwise leave the memory unchanged and return *false*.

On Intel and AMD architectures, CAS is called CMPXCHG; on Oracle SPARC systems, it is called CAS.[1] Java's java.util.concurrent.atomic library provides atomic Boolean, integer, and reference classes that implement CAS by a compareAndSet() method. (Because most of our examples are in Java, we often refer to compareAndSet() instead of CAS.) The atomic template of C++ provides the same functionality.

The CAS instruction has one pitfall. Perhaps the most common use of CAS is the following. An application reads value a from a given memory address, and computes a new value c for that location. It intends to store c, but only if the value a at the address has not changed since it was read. One might think that applying a CAS with expected value a and update value c would accomplish this goal. There is a problem: A thread could have overwritten the value a with another value b, and later written a again to the address. The CAS will replace a with c, but the application may not have done what it was intended to do (for example, if the address stores a pointer, the new value a may be the address of a recycled object). This problem is known as the *ABA problem*, and discussed in detail in Chapter 10.

The other hardware synchronization primitive is a pair of instructions: *load-linked* and *store-conditional* (LL/SC). The LL instruction reads from an address a, and a later SC instruction attempts to store a new value at that address. The SC instruction succeeds if the contents of a have not changed since that thread issued the earlier LL instruction. It fails if the contents of a have changed in the interval.

LL/SC instructions are supported by a number of architectures: Alpha AXP (ldl_l/stl_c), IBM PowerPC (lwarx/stwcx) MIPS ll/sc, and ARM (ldrex/strex). LL/SC does not suffer from the ABA problem, but in practice there are often severe restrictions on what a thread can do between an LL and the matching SC. A context switch, another LL, or another load or store instruction may cause the SC to fail.

It is a good idea to use atomic fields and their associated methods sparingly because they are often based on CAS or LL/SC. A CAS or LL/SC instruction takes significantly more cycles to complete than a load or store: It includes a memory barrier and prevents out-of-order execution and various compiler optimizations. The precise cost depends on many factors, and varies not only from one architecture to the next, but also from one application of the instruction to the next within the same architecture. It suffices to say that CAS or LL/SC can be an order of magnitude slower than a simple load or store.

B.9 Appendix notes

Tom Anderson [12] did the classic experiments on spin locks. John Hennessy and David Patterson [63] give a comprehensive treatment of computer architecture. The

---

[1] Instead of a Boolean, CAS on SPARC returns the location's prior value, which can be used to retry an unsuccessful CAS. CMPXCHG on Intel's Pentium effectively returns both a Boolean and the prior value.

MESI protocol is used by Intel's Pentium processor [83]. The tips on cache-conscious programming are adapted from Benjamin Gamsa, Orran Krieger, Eric Parsons, and Michael Stumm [49]. Sarita Adve and Karosh Gharachorloo [1] give an excellent survey of memory consistency models.

B.10 Exercises

Exercise B.1. Thread A must wait for a thread on another processor to change a flag bit in memory. The scheduler can either allow A to spin, repeatedly retesting the flag, or it can deschedule A, allowing some other thread to run. Suppose it takes a total of 10 milliseconds for the operating system to switch a processor from one thread to another. If the operating system deschedules thread A and immediately reschedules it, then it wastes 20 milliseconds. If, instead, A starts spinning at time t_0, and the flag changes at t_1, then the operating system will have wasted $t_1 - t_0$ time doing unproductive work.

A *prescient* scheduler is one that can predict the future. If it foresees that the flag will change in less than 20 milliseconds, it makes sense to have A spin, wasting less than 20 milliseconds, because descheduling and rescheduling A wastes 20 milliseconds. If, on the other hand, it takes more than 20 milliseconds for the flag to change, it makes sense to replace A with another thread, wasting no more than 20 milliseconds.

Your assignment is to implement a scheduler that never wastes more than *twice* the time a prescient scheduler would have wasted under the same circumstances.

Exercise B.2. Imagine you are a lawyer, paid to make the best case you can for a particular point of view. How would you argue the following claim: "If context switches took negligible time, then processors would not need caches, at least for applications that encompass large numbers of threads"?

Extra credit: Critique your argument.

Exercise B.3. Consider a direct-mapped cache with 16 cache lines, indexed 0 to 15, where each cache line encompasses 32 words.

- Explain how to map an address a to a cache line in terms of bit shifting and masking operations. Assume for this question that addresses refer to words, not bytes: address 7 refers to the eighth word in memory.
- Compute the best and worst possible hit ratios for a program that loops four times through an array of 64 words.
- Compute the best and worst possible hit ratios for a program that loops four times through an array of 512 words.

Exercise B.4. Consider a direct-mapped cache with 16 cache lines, indexed 0 to 15, where each cache line encompasses 32 words.

Consider a two-dimensional 32×32 array a of words. This array is laid out in memory so that $a[0,0]$ is next to $a[0,1]$, and so on. Assume the cache is initially empty, but that $a[0,0]$ maps to the first word of cache line 0.

Consider the following *column-first* traversal:

```
int sum = 0;
for (int i = 0; i < 32; i++) {
  for (int j = 0; j < 32; j++) {
    sum += a[i,j];  // 2nd dim changes fastest
  }
}
```

and the following *row-first* traversal:

```
int sum = 0;
for (int i = 0; i < 32; i++) {
  for (int j = 0; j < 32; j++) {
    sum += a[j,i];  // 1st dim changes fastest
  }
}
```

Compare the number of cache misses produced by the two traversals, assuming the oldest cache line is evicted first.

Exercise B.5. In the MESI cache-coherence protocol, what is the advantage of distinguishing between exclusive and modified modes?

What is the advantage of distinguishing between exclusive and shared modes?

Exercise B.6. Implement the test-and-set and test-and-test-and-set locks shown in Figs. B.1 and B.2, test their relative performance on a multiprocessor, and analyze the results.

Bibliography

[1] Sarita Adve, Kourosh Gharachorloo, Shared memory consistency models: a tutorial, Computer 29 (12) (1996) 66–76.

[2] Yehuda Afek, Hagit Attiya, Danny Dolev, Eli Gafni, Michael Merritt, Nir Shavit, Atomic snapshots of shared memory, Journal of the ACM 40 (4) (1993) 873–890.

[3] Yehuda Afek, Dalia Dauber, Dan Touitou, Wait-free made fast, in: STOC '95: Proceedings of the Twenty-Seventh Annual ACM Symposium on Theory of Computing, ACM Press, New York, NY, USA, 1995, pp. 538–547.

[4] Yehuda Afek, Gideon Stupp, Dan Touitou, Long-lived and adaptive atomic snapshot and immediate snapshot (extended abstract), in: Symposium on Principles of Distributed Computing, 2000, pp. 71–80.

[5] Yehuda Afek, Eytan Weisberger, Hanan Weisman, A completeness theorem for a class of synchronization objects, in: PODC '93: Proceedings of the Twelfth Annual ACM Symposium on Principles of Distributed Computing, ACM Press, New York, NY, USA, 1993, pp. 159–170.

[6] A. Agarwal, M. Cherian, Adaptive backoff synchronization techniques, in: Proceedings of the 16th International Symposium on Computer Architecture, May 1989, pp. 396–406.

[7] Ole Agesen, David Detlefs, Alex Garthwaite, Ross Knippel, Y.S. Ramakrishna, Derek White, An efficient meta-lock for implementing ubiquitous synchronization, ACM SIGPLAN Notices 34 (10) (1999) 207–222.

[8] M. Ajtai, J. Komlós, E. Szemerédi, An $O(n \log n)$ sorting network, in: Proc. of the 15th Annual ACM Symposium on Theory of Computing, 1983, pp. 1–9.

[9] G.M. Amdahl, Validity of the single-processor approach to achieving large scale computing capabilities, in: AFIPS Conference Proceedings, Atlantic City, NJ, AFIPS Press, Reston, VA, April 1967, pp. 483–485.

[10] James H. Anderson, Composite registers, Distributed Computing 6 (3) (1993) 141–154.

[11] James H. Anderson, Mark Moir, Universal constructions for multi-object operations, in: PODC '95: Proceedings of the Fourteenth Annual ACM Symposium on Principles of Distributed Computing, ACM Press, New York, NY, USA, 1995, pp. 184–193.

[12] Thomas E. Anderson, The performance of spin lock alternatives for shared-memory multiprocessors, IEEE Transactions on Parallel and Distributed Systems 1 (1) (1990) 6–16.

[13] Nimar S. Arora, Robert D. Blumofe, C. Greg Plaxton, Thread scheduling for multiprogrammed multiprocessors, in: Proceedings of the Tenth Annual ACM Symposium on Parallel Algorithms and Architectures, ACM Press, 1998, pp. 119–129.

[14] James Aspnes, Maurice Herlihy, Nir Shavit, Counting networks, Journal of the ACM 41 (5) (1994) 1020–1048.

[15] David F. Bacon, Ravi B. Konuru, Chet Murthy, Mauricio J. Serrano, Thin locks: featherweight synchronization for Java, in: SIGPLAN Conference on Programming Language Design and Implementation, 1998, pp. 258–268.

[16] K. Batcher, Sorting networks and their applications, in: Proceedings of AFIPS Joint Computer Conference, 1968, pp. 307–314.

[17] R. Bayer, M. Schkolnick, Concurrency of operations on B-trees, Acta Informatica 9 (1977) 1–21.

[18] Robert D. Blumofe, Charles E. Leiserson, Scheduling multithreaded computations by work stealing, Journal of the ACM 46 (5) (1999) 720–748.

[19] Hans-J. Boehm, Threads cannot be implemented as a library, in: Proceedings of the 2005 ACM SIGPLAN Conference on Programming Language Design and Implementation, PLDI '05, ACM, New York, NY, USA, 2005, pp. 261–268.

[20] Hans-J. Boehm, Can seqlocks get along with programming language memory models?, in: Proceedings of the 2012 ACM SIGPLAN Workshop on Memory Systems Performance and Correctness, Beijing, China, June 2012, pp. 12–20.

[21] Elizabeth Borowsky, Eli Gafni, Immediate atomic snapshots and fast renaming, in: PODC '93: Proceedings of the Twelfth Annual ACM Symposium on Principles of Distributed Computing, ACM Press, New York, NY, USA, 1993, pp. 41–51.

[22] Anastasia Braginsky, Alex Kogan, Erez Petrank, Drop the anchor: lightweight memory management for non-blocking data structures, in: Proceedings of the 25th ACM Symposium on Parallelism in Algorithms and Architectures, Montreal, Quebec, Canada, July 2013.

[23] Trevor Brown, Reclaiming memory for lock-free data structures: there has to be a better way, in: Proceedings of the 34th ACM Symposium on Principles of Distributed Computing, Portland, OR, June 2015.

[24] James E. Burns, Nancy A. Lynch, Bounds on shared memory for mutual exclusion, Information and Computation 107 (2) (December 1993) 171–184.

[25] James E. Burns, Gary L. Peterson, Constructing multi-reader atomic values from non-atomic values, in: PODC '87: Proceedings of the Sixth Annual ACM Symposium on Principles of Distributed Computing, ACM Press, New York, NY, USA, 1987, pp. 222–231.

[26] Costas Busch, Marios Mavronicolas, A combinatorial treatment of balancing networks, Journal of the ACM 43 (5) (1996) 794–839.

[27] Tushar Deepak Chandra, Prasad Jayanti, King Tan, A polylog time wait-free construction for closed objects, in: PODC '98: Proceedings of the Seventeenth Annual ACM Symposium on Principles of Distributed Computing, ACM Press, New York, NY, USA, 1998, pp. 287–296.

[28] Graham Chapman, John Cleese, Terry Gilliam, Eric Idle, Terry Jones, Michael Palin, Monty Phyton and the Holy Grail, 1975.

[29] David Chase, Yossi Lev, Dynamic circular work-stealing deque, in: SPAA '05: Proceedings of the Seventeenth Annual ACM Symposium on Parallelism in Algorithms and Architectures, ACM Press, New York, NY, USA, 2005, pp. 21–28.

[30] Alonzo Church, A note on the entscheidungsproblem, The Journal of Symbolic Logic (1936).

[31] Nachshon Cohen, Erez Petrank, Efficient memory management for lock-free data structures with optimistic access, in: Proceedings of the 27th ACM Symposium on Parallelism in Algorithms and Architectures, Portland, OR, June 2015.

[32] T. Craig, Building FIFO and priority-queueing spin locks from atomic swap, Technical Report TR 93-02-02, University of Washington, Department of Computer Science, February 1993.

[33] Luke Dalessandro, Michael Spear, Michael L. Scott, NOrec: streamlining STM by abolishing ownership records, in: Proceedings of the 15th ACM Symposium on Principles and Practice of Parallel Programming, Bangalore, India, January 2010.

[34] Jeffrey Dean, Sanjay Ghemawat, MapReduce: simplified data processing on large clusters, in: Proceedings of the 6th Conference on Symposium on Operating Systems Design & Implementation - Volume 6, OSDI'04, USENIX Association, Berkeley, CA, USA, 2004, p. 10.

[35] Dave Dice, Ori Shalev, Nir Shavit, Transactional locking II, in: Proceedings of the 20th International Symposium on Distributed Computing, Stockholm, Sweden, September 2006.

[36] David Dice, Implementing fast Java monitors with relaxed-locks, in: Java Virtual Machine Research and Technology Symposium, 2001, pp. 79–90.

[37] David Dice, Virendra J. Marathe, Nir Shavit, Lock cohorting: a general technique for designing NUMA locks, ACM Transactions on Parallel Computing 1 (2) (2015) 13.

[38] E.W. Dijkstra, The structure of the THE multiprogramming system, Communications of the ACM 11 (5) (1968) 341–346.

[39] Danny Dolev, Nir Shavit, Bounded concurrent time-stamping, SIAM Journal on Computing 26 (2) (1997) 418–455.

[40] Martin Dowd, Yehoshua Perl, Larry Rudolph, Michael Saks, The periodic balanced sorting network, Journal of the ACM 36 (4) (1989) 738–757.

[41] Arthur Conan Doyle, A Study in Scarlet and the Sign of Four, Berkley Publishing Group, ISBN 0425102408, 1994.

[42] Cynthia Dwork, Orli Waarts, Simple and efficient bounded concurrent timestamping and the traceable use abstraction, Journal of the ACM 46 (5) (1999) 633–666.

[43] C. Ellis, Concurrency in linear hashing, ACM Transactions on Database Systems 12 (2) (1987) 195–217.

[44] Facebook, Folly: Facebook Open-source Library, https://github.com/facebook/folly/, 2017.

[45] F.E. Fich, D. Hendler, N. Shavit, Linear lower bounds on real-world implementations of concurrent objects, in: Proc. of the 46th Annual Symposium on Foundations of Computer Science, FOCS 2005, 2005, pp. 165–173.

[46] Michael J. Fischer, Nancy A. Lynch, Michael S. Paterson, Impossibility of distributed consensus with one faulty process, Journal of the ACM 32 (2) (1985) 374–382.

[47] C. Flood, D. Detlefs, N. Shavit, C. Zhang, Parallel garbage collection for shared memory multiprocessors, in: Proc. of the Java TM Virtual Machine Research and Technology Symposium, 2001.

[48] K. Fraser, Practical Lock-Freedom, Ph.D. dissertation, Kings College, University of Cambridge, Cambridge, England, September 2003.

[49] B. Gamsa, O. Kreiger, E.W. Parsons, M. Stumm, Performance issues for multiprocessor operating systems, Technical report, Computer Systems Research Institute, University of Toronto, 1995.

[50] H. Gao, J.F. Groote, W.H. Hesselink, Lock-free dynamic hash tables with open addressing, Distributed Computing 18 (1) (2005) 21–42.

[51] James R. Goodman, Mary K. Vernon, Philip J. Woest, Efficient synchronization primitives for large-scale cache-coherent multiprocessors, in: Proceedings of the Third International Conference on Architectural Support for Programming Languages and Operating Systems, ACM Press, 1989, pp. 64–75.

[52] James Gosling, Bill Joy, Guy Steele, Gilad Bracha, The Java Language Specification, third edition, Prentice Hall PTR, ISBN 0321246780, 2005.

[53] A. Gottlieb, R. Grishman, C.P. Kruskal, K.P. McAuliffe, L. Rudolph, M. Snir, The NYU ultracomputer - designing an MIMD parallel computer, IEEE Transactions on Computers C-32 (2) (February 1984) 175–189.

[54] M. Greenwald, Two-handed emulation: how to build non-blocking implementations of complex data structures using DCAS, in: Proceedings of the 21st Annual Symposium on Principles of Distributed Computing, ACM Press, 2002, pp. 260–269.

[55] S. Haldar, K. Vidyasankar, Constructing 1-writer multireader multivalued atomic variables from regular variables, Journal of the ACM 42 (1) (1995) 186–203.

[56] Sibsankar Haldar, Paul Vitányi, Bounded concurrent timestamp systems using vector clocks, Journal of the ACM 49 (1) (2002) 101–126.

[57] Per Brinch Hansen, Structured multi-programming, Communications of the ACM 15 (7) (1972) 574–578.

[58] Tim Harris, A pragmatic implementation of non-blocking linked-lists, in: Proceedings of 15th International Symposium on Distributed Computing, DISC 2001, Lisbon, Portugal, in: Lecture Notes in Computer Science, vol. 2180, Springer Verlag, October 2001, pp. 300–314.

[59] Tim Harris, James R. Larus, Ravi Rajwar, Transactional Memory, 2nd edition, Synthesis Lectures on Computer Architecture, Morgan and Claypool, 2010.

[60] S. Heller, M. Herlihy, V. Luchangco, M. Moir, W.N. Scherer III, N. Shavit, A lazy concurrent list-based set algorithm, in: Proc. of the Ninth International Conference on Principles of Distributed Systems, OPODIS 2005, 2005, pp. 3–16.

[61] Danny Hendler, Nir Shavit, Non-blocking steal-half work queues, in: Proceedings of the Twenty-First Annual Symposium on Principles of Distributed Computing, ACM Press, 2002, pp. 280–289.

[62] Danny Hendler, Nir Shavit, Lena Yerushalmi, A scalable lock-free stack algorithm, in: SPAA '04: Proceedings of the Sixteenth Annual ACM Symposium on Parallelism in Algorithms and Architectures, ACM Press, New York, NY, USA, 2004, pp. 206–215.

[63] J.L. Hennessy, D.A. Patterson, Computer Architecture: A Quantitative Approach, Morgan Kaufmann Publishers, 1995.

[64] D. Hensgen, R. Finkel, U. Manber, Two algorithms for barrier synchronization, International Journal of Parallel Programming (ISSN 0885-7458) 17 (1) (1988) 1–17.

[65] M. Herlihy, A methodology for implementing highly concurrent data objects, ACM Transactions on Programming Languages and Systems 15 (5) (November 1993) 745–770.

[66] M. Herlihy, Y. Lev, V. Luchangco, N. Shavit, A provably correct scalable skiplist (brief announcement), in: Proc. of the 10th International Conference on Principles of Distributed Systems, OPODIS 2006, 2006.

[67] M. Herlihy, V. Luchangco, M. Moir, The repeat offender problem: a mechanism for supporting lock-free dynamic-sized data structures, in: Proceedings of the 16th International Symposium on DIStributed Computing, vol. 2508, Springer-Verlag Heidelberg, January 2002, pp. 339–353.

[68] M. Herlihy, V. Luchangco, M. Moir, Obstruction-free synchronization: double-ended queues as an example, in: Proceedings of the 23rd International Conference on Distributed Computing Systems, IEEE, 2003, pp. 522–529.

[69] Maurice Herlihy, Wait-free synchronization, ACM Transactions on Programming Languages and Systems 13 (1) (1991) 124–149.

[70] Maurice Herlihy, Yossi Lev, Nir Shavit, A lock-free concurrent skiplist with wait-free search, 2007.

[71] Maurice Herlihy, Beng-Hong Lim, Nir Shavit, Scalable concurrent counting, ACM Transactions on Computer Systems 13 (4) (1995) 343–364.

[72] Maurice Herlihy, Nir Shavit, On the nature of progress, in: Proceedings of the 15th International Conference on Principles of Distributed Systems, OPODIS'11, Springer-Verlag, Berlin, Heidelberg, 2011, pp. 313–328.

[73] Maurice Herlihy, Nir Shavit, Moran Tzafrir, Concurrent cuckoo hashing, Technical report, Brown University, 2007.

[74] Maurice P. Herlihy, J. Eliot B. Moss, Transactional memory: architectural support for lock-free data structures, in: Proceedings of the 20th International Symposium on Computer Architecture, San Diego, CA, May 1993.

[75] Maurice P. Herlihy, Jeannette M. Wing, Linearizability: a correctness condition for concurrent objects, ACM Transactions on Programming Languages and Systems 12 (3) (1990) 463–492.

[76] C.A.R. Hoare, "Algorithm 63: partition," "Algorithm 64: quicksort," and "Algorithm 65: find", Communications of the ACM 4 (7) (1961) 321–322.

[77] C.A.R. Hoare, Monitors: an operating system structuring concept, Communications of the ACM 17 (10) (1974) 549–557.

[78] Richard Horsey, The Art of Chicken Sexing, Cogprints, 2002.

[79] M. Hsu, W.P. Yang, Concurrent operations in extendible hashing, in: Symposium on Very Large Data Bases, 1986, pp. 241–247.

[80] J.S. Huang, Y.C. Chow, Parallel sorting and data partitioning by sampling, in: Proceedings of the IEEE Computer Society's Seventh International Computer Software and Applications Conference, 1983, pp. 627–631.

[81] Richard L. Hudson, Bratin Saha, Ali-Reza Adl-Tabatabai, Benjamin Hertzberg, A scalable transactional memory allocator, in: Proceedings of the International Symposium on Memory Management, Ottawa, ON, Canada, June 2006.

[82] Galen C. Hunt, Maged M. Michael, Srinivasan Parthasarathy, Michael L. Scott, An efficient algorithm for concurrent priority queue heaps, Information Processing Letters 60 (3) (1996) 151–157.

[83] Intel Corporation, Pentium Processor User's Manual, Intel Books, 1993.

[84] A. Israeli, L. Rappaport, Disjoint-access-parallel implementations of strong shared memory primitives, in: Proceedings of the 13th Annual ACM Symposium on Principles of Distributed Computing, Los Angeles, CA, August 14–17, 1994, pp. 151–160.

[85] Amos Israeli, Ming Li, Bounded time stamps, Distributed Computing 6 (5) (1993) 205–209.

[86] Amos Israeli, Amnon Shaham, Optimal multi-writer multi-reader atomic register, in: Symposium on Principles of Distributed Computing, 1992, pp. 71–82.

[87] Mohammed Gouda, James Anderson, Ambuj Singh, The elusive atomic register, Technical Report TR 86.29, University of Texas at Austin, 1986.

[88] Prasad Jayanti, Robust wait-free hierarchies, Journal of the ACM 44 (4) (1997) 592–614.

[89] Prasad Jayanti, A lower bound on the local time complexity of universal constructions, in: PODC '98: Proceedings of the Seventeenth Annual ACM Symposium on Principles of Distributed Computing, ACM Press, New York, NY, USA, 1998, pp. 183–192.

[90] Prasad Jayanti, Sam Toueg, Some results on the impossibility, universality, and decidability of consensus, in: WDAG '92: Proceedings of the 6th International Workshop on Distributed Algorithms, Springer-Verlag, London, UK, 1992, pp. 69–84.

[91] D. Jimenez-Gonzalez, J.J. Navarro, J.-L. Lirriba-Pey, Cc-radix: a cache conscious sorting based on radix sort, in: Proc. of the 11th Euromicro Conference on Parallel, Distributed and Network-Based Processing, 2003, pp. 101–108.

[92] Lefteris M. Kirousis, Evangelos Kranakis, Paul M.B. Vitányi, Atomic multireader register, in: Proceedings of the 2nd International Workshop on Distributed Algorithms, Springer-Verlag, London, UK, 1988, pp. 278–296.

[93] M.R. Klugerman, Small-depth counting networks and related topics, Technical Report MIT/LCS/TR-643, MIT Laboratory for Computer Science, 1994.

[94] Michael Klugerman, C. Greg Plaxton, Small-depth counting networks, in: STOC '92: Proceedings of the Twenty-Fourth Annual ACM Symposium on Theory of Computing, ACM Press, New York, NY, USA, 1992, pp. 417–428.

[95] D. Knuth, The Art of Computer Programming: Fundamental Algorithms, vol. 3, Addison-Wesley, 1973.

[96] Clyde P. Kruskal, Larry Rudolph, Marc Snir, Efficient synchronization of multiprocessors with shared memory, ACM Transactions on Programming Languages and Systems 10 (4) (1988) 579–601.

[97] V. Kumar, Concurrent operations on extendible hashing and its performance, Communications of the ACM 33 (6) (1990) 681–694.

[98] Christoph Lameter, Effective synchronization on Linux/NUMA systems, in: Proceedings of the May 2005 Gelato Federation Meeting, San Jose, CA, May 2005.

[99] L. Lamport, On interprocess communication, Distributed Computing 1 (1986) 77–101.

[100] Leslie Lamport, A new solution of Dijkstra's concurrent programming problem, Communications of the ACM 17 (5) (1974) 543–545.

[101] Leslie Lamport, Time, clocks, and the ordering of events, Communications of the ACM 21 (7) (July 1978) 558–565.

[102] Leslie Lamport, How to make a multiprocessor computer that correctly executes multiprocess programs, IEEE Transactions on Computers C-28 (9) (September 1979) 690.

[103] Leslie Lamport, Specifying concurrent program modules, ACM Transactions on Programming Languages and Systems 5 (2) (1983) 190–222.

[104] Leslie Lamport, Invited address: solved problems, unsolved problems and non-problems in concurrency, in: Proceedings of the Third Annual ACM Symposium on Principles of Distributed Computing, 1984, pp. 1–11.

[105] Leslie Lamport, On interprocess communication (part II), Distributed Computing 1 (1) (January 1986) 203–213.

[106] Leslie Lamport, A fast mutual exclusion algorithm, ACM Transactions on Computer Systems 5 (1) (January 1987) 1–11.

[107] B. Lampson, D. Redell, Experience with processes and monitors in Mesa, Communications of the ACM 2 (23) (1980) 105–117.

[108] Doug Lea, http://docs.oracle.com/javase/6/docs/api/java/util/concurrent/ConcurrentHashMap.html, 2007.

[109] Doug Lea, http://docs.oracle.com/javase/6/docs/api/java/util/concurrent/ConcurrentSkipListMap.html, 2007.

[110] Doug Lea, Java community process, JSR 166, concurrency utilities, http://www.jcp.org/en/jsr/detail?id=166, 2003.

[111] Shin-Jae Lee, Minsoo Jeon, Dongseung Kim, Andrew Sohn, Partitioned parallel radix sort, Journal of Parallel and Distributed Computing 62 (4) (2002) 656–668.

[112] C. Leiserson, H. Prokop, A minicourse on multithreaded programming, http://supertech.csail.mit.edu/papers/minicourse.pdf, 1998.

[113] Li Ming, John Tromp, Paul M.B. Vitányi, How to share concurrent wait-free variables, Journal of the ACM 43 (4) (1996) 723–746.

[114] Wai-Kau Lo, Vassos Hadzilacos, All of us are smarter than any of us: wait-free hierarchies are not robust, in: STOC '97: Proceedings of the Twenty-Ninth Annual ACM Symposium on Theory of Computing, ACM Press, New York, NY, USA, 1997, pp. 579–588.

[115] I. Lotan, N. Shavit, Skiplist-based concurrent priority queues, in: Proc. of the 14th International Parallel and Distributed Processing Symposium, IPDPS, 2000, pp. 263–268.

[116] M. Loui, H. Abu-Amara, Memory requirements for agreement among unreliable asynchronous processes, in: F.P. Preparata (Ed.), Advances in Computing Research, vol. 4, JAI Press, Greenwich, CT, 1987, pp. 163–183.

[117] Victor Luchangco, Daniel Nussbaum, Nir Shavit, A hierarchical CLH queue lock, in: Euro-Par, 2006, pp. 801–810.

[118] P. Magnussen, A. Landin, E. Hagersten, Queue locks on cache coherent multiprocessors, in: Proceedings of the 8th International Symposium on Parallel Processing, IPPS, IEEE Computer Society, April 1994, pp. 165–171.

[119] Jeremy Manson, William Pugh, Sarita V. Adve, The Java memory model, in: Proceedings of the 32nd ACM SIGPLAN-SIGACT Symposium on Principles of Programming Languages, POPL '05, ACM, New York, NY, USA, 2005, pp. 378–391.

[120] Yandong Mao, Robert Morris, Frans Kaashoek, Optimizing MapReduce for multicore architectures, Technical Report MIT-CSAIL-TR-2010-020, MIT-CSAIL, 2010.

[121] Virendra J. Marathe, Mark Moir, Nir Shavit, Composite abortable locks, in: Proceedings of the 20th International Conference on Parallel and Distributed Processing, IPDPS'06, IEEE Computer Society, Washington, DC, USA, 2006, p. 132.

[122] Paul E. McKenney, Selecting locking primitives for parallel programming, Communications of the ACM 39 (10) (1996) 75–82.

[123] Paul E. McKenney, Exploiting Deferred Destruction: an Analysis of Read-Copy-Update Techniques in Operating System Kernels, PhD thesis, OGI School of Science and Engineering at Oregon Health and Sciences University, 2004.

[124] John Mellor-Crummey, Michael Scott, Algorithms for scalable synchronization on shared-memory multiprocessors, ACM Transactions on Computer Systems 9 (1) (1991) 21–65.

[125] M.M. Michael, M.L. Scott, Simple, fast and practical non-blocking and blocking concurrent queue algorithms, in: Proc. of the Fifteenth Annual ACM Symposium on Principles of Distributed Computing, ACM Press, 1996, pp. 267–275.

[126] Maged M. Michael, High performance dynamic lock-free hash tables and list-based sets, in: Proceedings of the Fourteenth Annual ACM Symposium on Parallel Algorithms and Architectures, ACM Press, 2002, pp. 73–82.

[127] Maged M. Michael, Hazard pointers: safe memory reclamation for lock-free objects, IEEE Transactions on Parallel and Distributed Systems 15 (6) (June 2004) 491–504.

[128] Jaydev Misra, Axioms for memory access in asynchronous hardware systems, ACM Transactions on Programming Languages and Systems 8 (1) (1986) 142–153.

[129] Mark Moir, Practical implementations of non-blocking synchronization primitives, in: PODC '97: Proceedings of the Sixteenth Annual ACM Symposium on Principles of Distributed Computing, ACM Press, New York, NY, USA, 1997, pp. 219–228.

[130] Mark Moir, Laziness pays! Using lazy synchronization mechanisms to improve non-blocking constructions, in: PODC '00: Proceedings of the Nineteenth Annual ACM Symposium on Principles of Distributed Computing, ACM Press, New York, NY, USA, 2000, pp. 61–70.

[131] Mark Moir, Daniel Nussbaum, Ori Shalev, Nir Shavit, Using elimination to implement scalable and lock-free fifo queues, in: SPAA '05: Proceedings of the Seventeenth Annual ACM Symposium on Parallelism in Algorithms and Architectures, ACM Press, New York, NY, USA, 2005, pp. 253–262.

[132] James H. Morris, Real programming in functional languages, Technical Report 81-11, Xerox Palo Alto Research Center, 1981.

[133] Takuya Nakaike, Rei Odaira, Matthew Gaudet, Maged M. Michael, Hisanobu Tomari, Quantitative comparison of hardware transactional memory for Blue Gene/Q, zEnterprise EC12, Intel Core, and POWER8, in: Proceedings of the 42nd Annual International Symposium on Computer Architecture, Portland, OR, June 2015.

[134] Richard Newman-Wolfe, A protocol for wait-free, atomic, multi-reader shared variables, in: PODC '87: Proceedings of the Sixth Annual ACM Symposium on Principles of Distributed Computing, ACM Press, New York, NY, USA, 1987, pp. 232–248.

[135] Isaac Newton, I. Bernard Cohen (Translator), Anne Whitman (Translator), The Principia: Mathematical Principles of Natural Philosophy, University of California Press, 1999.

[136] R. Pagh, F.F. Rodler, Cuckoo hashing, Journal of Algorithms 51 (2) (2004) 122–144.

[137] Christos H. Papadimitriou, The serializability of concurrent database updates, Journal of the ACM 26 (4) (1979) 631–653.

[138] Gary Peterson, Myths about the mutual exclusion problem, Information Processing Letters 12 (3) (June 1981) 115–116.

[139] Gary L. Peterson, Concurrent reading while writing, ACM Transactions on Programming Languages and Systems 5 (1) (1983) 46–55.

[140] S.A. Plotkin, Sticky bits and universality of consensus, in: PODC '89: Proceedings of the Eighth Annual ACM Symposium on Principles of Distributed Computing, ACM Press, New York, NY, USA, 1989, pp. 159–175.

[141] W. Pugh, Concurrent maintenance of skip lists, Technical Report CS-TR-2222.1, Institute for Advanced Computer Studies, Department of Computer Science, University of Maryland, 1989.

[142] W. Pugh, Skip lists: a probabilistic alternative to balanced trees, ACM Transactions on Database Systems 33 (6) (1990) 668–676.

[143] C. Purcell, T. Harris, Non-blocking hashtables with open addressing, in: Proceedings of International Symposium on Distributed Computing, 2005, pp. 108–121.

[144] Zoran Radović, Erik Hagersten, Hierarchical backoff locks for nonuniform communication architectures, in: Ninth International Symposium on High Performance Computer Architecture, Anaheim, California, USA, February 2003, pp. 241–252.

[145] Ravi Rajwar, James R. Goodman, Speculative lock elision: enabling highly concurrent multithreaded execution, in: Proceedings of the 34th IEEE/ACM International Symposium on Microarchitecture, Austin, TX, December 2001.

[146] Ravi Rajwar, James R. Goodman, Transactional lock-free execution of lock-based programs, in: Proceedings of the 10th International Conference on Architectural Support for Programming Languages and Operating Systems, ASPLOS-X, ACM Press, 2002, pp. 5–17.

[147] M. Raynal, Algorithms for Mutual Exclusion, The MIT Press, Cambridge, MA, 1986.

[148] John H. Reif, Leslie G. Valiant, A logarithmic time sort for linear size networks, Journal of the ACM 34 (1) (1987) 60–76.

[149] Amitabha Roy, Steven Hand, Tim Harris, A runtime system for software lock elision, in: Proceedings of the EuroSys2009 Conference, Nuremberg, Germany, March 2009.

[150] L. Rudolph, Z. Segall, Dynamic decentralized cache schemes for MIMD parallel processors, in: Proceedings of the 11th Annual International Symposium on Computer Architecture, ACM Press, 1984, pp. 340–347.

[151] L. Rudolph, M. Slivkin-Allalouf, E. Upfal, A simple load balancing scheme for task allocation in parallel machines, in: Proceedings of the 3rd Annual ACM Symposium on Parallel Algorithms and Architectures, ACM Press, July 1991, pp. 237–245.

[152] Michael Saks, Nir Shavit, Heather Woll, Optimal time randomized consensus — making resilient algorithms fast in practice, in: SODA '91: Proceedings of the Second Annual ACM-SIAM Symposium on Discrete Algorithms, Society for Industrial and Applied Mathematics, Philadelphia, PA, USA, 1991, pp. 351–362.

[153] Michael L. Scott, Non-blocking timeout in scalable queue-based spin locks, in: PODC '02: Proceedings of the Twenty-First Annual Symposium on Principles of Distributed Computing, ACM Press, New York, NY, USA, 2002, pp. 31–40.

[154] Michael L. Scott, William N. Scherer, Scalable queue-based spin locks with timeout, ACM SIGPLAN Notices 36 (7) (2001) 44–52.

[155] Maurice Sendak, Where the Wild Things Are, HarperCollins, ISBN 0060254920, 1988.

[156] O. Shalev, N. Shavit, Split-ordered lists: lock-free extensible hash tables, Journal of the ACM 53 (3) (2006) 379–405.

[157] N. Shavit, D. Touitou, Software transactional memory, Distributed Computing 10 (2) (February 1997) 99–116.

[158] Nir Shavit, Asaph Zemach, Diffracting trees, ACM Transactions on Computer Systems 14 (4) (1996) 385–428.

[159] Eric Shenk, The consensus hierarchy is not robust, in: PODC '97: Proceedings of the Sixteenth Annual ACM Symposium on Principles of Distributed Computing, ACM Press, New York, NY, USA, 1997, p. 279.

[160] Ambuj K. Singh, James H. Anderson, Mohamed G. Gouda, The elusive atomic register, Journal of the ACM 41 (2) (1994) 311–339.

[161] Justin Talbot, Richard M. Yoo, Christos Kozyrakis, Phoenix++: modular MapReduce for shared-memory systems, in: Proceedings of the Second International Workshop on MapReduce and Its Applications, MapReduce '11, ACM, New York, NY, USA, 2011, pp. 9–16.

[162] R.K. Treiber, Systems programming: coping with parallelism, Technical Report RJ 5118, IBM Almaden Research Center, April 1986.

[163] Alan Turing, On computable numbers, with an application to the entscheidungsproblem, Proceedings of the London Mathematical Society (1937).

[164] John D. Valois, Lock-free linked lists using compare-and-swap, in: Proceedings of the Fourteenth Annual ACM Symposium on Principles of Distributed Computing, ACM Press, 1995, pp. 214–222.

[165] Paul Vitányi, Baruch Awerbuch, Atomic shared register access by asynchronous hardware, in: 27th Annual Symposium on Foundations of Computer Science, IEEE Computer Society Press, Los Angeles, Ca., USA, October 1986, pp. 233–243.

[166] W.E. Weihl, Local atomicity properties: modular concurrency control for abstract data types, ACM Transactions on Programming Languages and Systems 11 (2) (1989) 249–282.

[167] William N. Scherer III, Doug Lea, Michael L. Scott, Scalable synchronous queues, in: PPoPP '06: Proceedings of the Eleventh ACM SIGPLAN Symposium on Principles and Practice of Parallel Programming, ACM Press, New York, NY, USA, 2006, pp. 147–156.

[168] P. Yew, N. Tzeng, D. Lawrie, Distributing hot-spot addressing in large-scale multiprocessors, IEEE Transactions on Computers C-36 (4) (April 1987) 388–395.

Index